Interdisciplinary Perspectives on Contemporary Conflict Resolution

Paulo Novais
University of Minho, Portugal

Davide Carneiro
University of Minho, Portugal

A volume in the Advances in Linguistics and
Communication Studies (ALCS) Book Series

Information Science
REFERENCE
An Imprint of IGI Global

Published in the United States of America by
    Information Science Reference (an imprint of IGI Global)
    701 E. Chocolate Avenue
    Hershey PA, USA 17033
    Tel: 717-533-8845
    Fax: 717-533-8661
    E-mail: cust@igi-global.com
    Web site: http://www.igi-global.com

                    Library of Congress Cataloging-in-Publication Data

Names: Novais, Paulo, 1967- editor. | Carneiro, Davide, editor.
Title: Interdisciplinary perspectives on contemporary conflict resolution /
    Paulo Novais and Davide Carneiro, editors.
Description: Hershey : Information Science Reference, 2016. | Includes
    bibliographical references and index.
Identifiers: LCCN 2016001047| ISBN 9781522502456 (hardcover) | ISBN
    9781522502463 (ebook)
Subjects: LCSH: Conflict management.
Classification: LCC HD42 .I5668 2016 | DDC 303.6/9--dc23 LC record available at http://lccn.loc.gov/2016001047

This book is published in the IGI Global book series Advances in Linguistics and Communication Studies (ALCS) (ISSN: Pending; eISSN: Pending)

British Cataloguing in Publication Data
A Cataloguing in Publication record for this book is available from the British Library.

For electronic access to this publication, please contact: eresources@igi-global.com.

Advances in Linguistics and Communication Studies (ALCS) Book Series

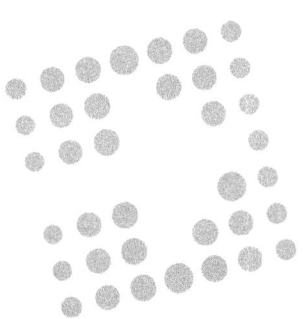

Abigail G. Scheg
Western Governors University, USA

ISSN: Pending
EISSN: Pending

MISSION

The scope of language and communication is constantly changing as society evolves, new modes of communication are developed through technological advancement, and novel words enter our lexicon as the result of cultural change. Understanding how we communicate and use language is crucial in all industries and updated research is necessary in order to promote further knowledge in this field.

The **Advances in Linguistics and Communication Studies (ALCS)** book series presents the latest research in diverse topics relating to language and communication. Interdisciplinary in its coverage, ALCS presents comprehensive research on the use of language and communication in various industries including business, education, government, and healthcare.

COVERAGE

- Non-Verbal Communication
- Media and Public Communications
- Language acquisition
- Computer-Mediated Communication
- Language and Identity
- Forensic Linguistics
- Cross-Cultural Communication
- Computational Linguistics
- Youth Language
- Dialectology

IGI Global is currently accepting manuscripts for publication within this series. To submit a proposal for a volume in this series, please contact our Acquisition Editors at Acquisitions@igi-global.com or visit: http://www.igi-global.com/publish/.

Titles in this Series

For a list of additional titles in this series, please visit: www.igi-global.com

Handbook of Research on Effective Communication, Leadership, and Conflict Resolution
Anthony H. Normore (California State University Dominguez Hills, USA & International Academy of Public safety, USA) Larry W. Long (Illinois State University, USA & International Academy of Public Safety, USA) and Mitch Javidi (North Carolina State University, USA & International Academy of Public Safety, USA)
Information Science Reference • copyright 2016 • 733pp • H/C (ISBN: 9781466699700) • US $315.00 (our price)

Handbook of Research on Cross-Cultural Approaches to Language and Literacy Development
Patriann Smith (University of Illinois at Urbana-Champaign, USA) and Alex Kumi-Yeboah (University at Albany–State University of New York, USA)
Information Science Reference • copyright 2015 • 567pp • H/C (ISBN: 9781466686687) • US $305.00 (our price)

Communication and Language Analysis in the Corporate World
Roderick P. Hart (University of Texas - Austin, USA)
Information Science Reference • copyright 2014 • 435pp • H/C (ISBN: 9781466649996) • US $215.00 (our price)

Communication and Language Analysis in the Public Sphere
Roderick P. Hart (University of Texas - Austin, USA)
Information Science Reference • copyright 2014 • 580pp • H/C (ISBN: 9781466650039) • US $190.00 (our price)

Digital Rhetoric and Global Literacies Communication Modes and Digital Practices in the Networked World
Gustav Verhulsdonck (University of Texas at El Paso, USA) and Marohang Limbu (Michigan State University, USA)
Information Science Reference • copyright 2014 • 398pp • H/C (ISBN: 9781466649163) • US $205.00 (our price)

www.igi-global.com

701 E. Chocolate Ave., Hershey, PA 17033
Order online at www.igi-global.com or call 717-533-8845 x100
To place a standing order for titles released in this series, contact: cust@igi-global.com
Mon-Fri 8:00 am - 5:00 pm (est) or fax 24 hours a day 717-533-8661

Table of Contents

Section 1
About Conflicts

Section 2
Conflict and Its Resolution

Section 3
Applications for Conflict Resolution

Detailed Table of Contents

Section 1
About Conflicts

Conflicts occur naturally in virtually every domain of our existence and every reader for sure had, by this time, their fair share of conflicts. The first section of this book will analyze fundamental issues about conflicts, their diversity, their emergence and their resolution.

Marco Vieira Gomes, University of Minho, Portugal
Paulo Novais, University of Minho, Portugal

The purpose of this chapter is to explore the nature of conflict from a computer science perspective, throwing to light an up to date review of the evolution and state-of-the-art of the intersection of conflict with technology-assisted systems and tools. The objective is to design a document to organize existing literature, provide a baseline understanding in place of an agreed definition of conflict, depict relevant conflict aspects (dimensions), and made overall evaluation of a range of methods and techniques of conflict resolution. It was also explored the challenges that individuals face in using online technology for collaboration and conflict resolution and management purposes. Finally, is presented some preliminary work regarding the most suitable technologies to implement a technological framework for handling conflict in a digital environment.

Francisco Pacheco Andrade, Universidade do Minho, Portugal
Teresa Coelho Moreira, Universidade do Minho, Portugal

The special nature of the characteristics used in biometric systems can present privacy challenges that might not arise with traditional identification methods, such as paper documents, because these data are derived from an individual's physical or behavioural features on the basis of a specific procedure, which is partly automated and yields a (reference) template. On account of their nature, these data require special precautions and the respect of the principles related with privacy and data protection.

Saleem Gul, Institute of Management Sciences, Pakistan
Michael Klausner, University of Pittsburgh – Bradford, USA

This chapter concerns itself with defining conflict and discusses the value it provides to organizations engaging in conflicts. The chapter is structured so that first we will provide a brief on the need to study conflict and negotiations in organizations. Then the discussion will move to the different drivers of organizational conflicts and will conclude with a typology of the different conflicts that exist within organizations. The third section will focus on the models (life-cycles) of conflicts that are available in conflict literature. The final section will focus on the different conflict handling techniques that are available. This section will include a discussion on the different conflict handling styles and negotiation tactics, and a brief on the process of alternate dispute resolution in conflict management.

Cristian Ioja, University of Bucharest, Romania
Mihai R. Nita, University of Bucharest, Romania
Constantina Alina Hossu, University of Bucharest, Romania

Environmental conflicts have become a topical issue in the international research because of their complexity where social, economic, political and cultural factors operate. Their assessment is essential for understanding these factors and thus contributing to the formulation of effective resolution strategies. In this chapter the authors discuss the defining characteristics of the environmental conflicts as well as methods and approaches for their assessment and resolution. European environmental policies are used as examples of environmental conflicts drivers in order to highlight the large number of involved factors that undermine their successful implementation. This chapter ends the discussion with the presentation of the resolution efforts in multi-issue conflicts where a neutral party adds values to the process, advancing it towards an efficient ending.

Pedro Miguel Freitas, Universidade do Minho, Portugal
Pablo Galain Palermo, Max Planck Institute for Foreign and International Criminal Law,
    Germany

In civil law countries, criminal justice is beginning to experience a shift from retributive justice towards restorative justice. Amongst other goals, restorative justice aims to give the victim a pivotal role in the administration of justice, which until now, with the traditional criminal justice, has not happened at a desirable level. It covers very different processes, but victim-offender mediation is certainly the most established one. Although an online version of the victim-offender mediation model is yet to be implemented, we believe that it could be a relevant alternative to an offline setting. It is nevertheless clear that further studies are necessary to fully comprehend the extent of the structure and implications of a ODR system for criminal conflicts.

Section 2
Conflict and Its Resolution

As technology and society progress, new types of conflict emerge and their complexity increases. Fortunately, this evolution also results in new approaches for solving conflicts, and new supporting technologies, both for judicial and extra-judicial conflict resolution processes. This section deals with classic and novel methods and technologies for conflict resolution.

Chapter 6

José Neves, Universidade do Minho, Portugal
John Zeleznikow, Victoria University, Australia
Henrique Vicente, Universidade de Évora, Portugal

The intersection of Artificial Intelligence and The Law stands for a multifaceted matter, and its effects set the advances on culture, organization, as well as the social matters, when the emergent information technologies are taken into consideration. From this point of view, the weight of formal and informal Conflict Resolution settings should be highlighted, and the use of defective data, information or knowledge must be emphasized. Indeed, it is hard to do it with traditional problem solving methodologies. Therefore, in this work the focus is on the development of decision support systems, in terms of its knowledge representation and reasoning procedures, under a formal framework based on Logic Programming, complemented with an approach to computing centered on Artificial Neural Networks. It is intended to evaluate the Quality-of-Judgments and the respective Degree-of-Confidence that one has on such happenings.

Chapter 7

Marco Carvalho Gonçalves, University of Minho, Portugal

This chapter seeks to analyze the implementation and integration of alternative means of dispute resolution in the European Union. Thus, from an initial approach to the various alternative means of dispute resolution, with particular emphasis on negotiation, conciliation, mediation and arbitration, will be held a comparative law analysis of the different legislative solutions adopted by the major EU Member States, allowing to determinate the degree of implementation and development of alternative means of dispute resolution in those Member States. Finally, there will be an analysis of the main legislative instruments adopted by the European institutions with a view to creating and developing alternative means of dispute resolution in Europe, indicating, in the end, some solutions and recommendations that are adequate having a view to effective implementation of alternative justice in the European Union.

Chapter 8

Fernando Viana, CIAB – Centro de Informação, Mediação e Arbitragem de Conflitos de
Consumo (Tribunal Arbitral), Portugal
Francisco Pacheco Andrade, Universidade do Minho, Portugal

Administration of Justice became complex in Consumers and Information Society. It is necessary to look for new solutions for the increasing situations of consumer's litigation. Traditional State Courts are not a solution due to their slow, heavy and costly ways of functioning. The way is clearly open for Arbitration Centers based in friendly mechanisms such as mediation, concilitation and arbitration. Regulation EU nr. 524/2013 of European Parliament and Council of the 21st of May on online consumer's conflict resolution has as aim the creation of a conflict resolution platform at european level. We propose to analyze the Regulation and its implications and to show the functioning of the platform that is being developped and that should be available for both for consumers and corporations from 9th January 2016 on. It will be analyzed the new requirements of access to Justice in the field of Consumer's conflicts, the new ADR Directive and the regulation on ODR in order to meet the challenges brought along by the introduction of the new platform for conflict resolution.

Chapter 9

Vicente Julian, Universidad Politécnica de Valencia, Spain
Victor Sanchez-Anguix, Coventry University, UK
Stella Heras, Universidad Politécnica de Valencia, Spain
Carlos Carrascosa, Universidad Politécnica de Valencia, Spain

Recently, artificial intelligence, has emerged as a new source of scientific works in conflict resolution. The interest in conflict resolution lies in diverse reasons. One of the main reasons is that computational systems have gradually shifted towards a distributed paradigm where heterogeneous entities should include computational conflict resolution mechanisms, such as proposed by agreement technologies. This chapter gives an overview of these technologies, which are needed in order to ensure the accomplishment of the global system goal and to solve conflicts. Among agreement technologies, automated negotiation is proposed as one key mechanism in conflict resolution due to its analogous use in human conflict resolution. Automated negotiation consists of an automated exchange of proposals carried out by software agents on behalf of their users. Another key technology is argumentation, which provides a fruitful means of dealing with conflicts and knowledge inconsistencies. Agents can reach agreements by engaging in argumentation dialogues with their opponents in a discussion.

Chapter 10

P. B. de Moura Oliveira, Universidade de Trás-os-Montes e Alto Douro, Portugal
E. J. Solteiro Pires, Universidade de Trás-os-Montes e Alto Douro, Portugal

This chapter addresses nature and bio-inspired metaheuristics in the context of conflict detection and resolution problems. An approach is presented for a generalization of a population-based bio-inspired search and optimization algorithm, which is depicted for three of the most well-known and firmly established methods: the genetic algorithm, the particle swarm optimization algorithm and the differential evolution algorithm. This integrated approach to a basic general population-based bio-inspired algorithm is presented for single-objective optimization, multi-objective optimization and many-objective optimization. A revision of these three main bio-inspired algorithms is presented for conflict resolution problems in diverse application areas. A bridge between feedback controller design, genetic algorithm, particle swarm optimization and differential evolution is established using a conflict resolution approach. Finally, some perspectives concerning future trends of more recent bio-inspired meta-heuristics is presented.

Chapter 11

    Carlos Ivan Chesnevar, Universidad Nacional del Sur, Argentina
    Ana Gabriela Maguitman, Universidad Nacional del Sur, Argentina
    María Paula González, Universidad Nacional del Sur, Argentina
    Elsa Estevez, United Nations University, Japan

This chapter presents an account of recent advances in the development of a novel e-participation framework which integrates social networks, intelligent information retrieval and argumentation techniques. We discuss a novel conceptualization for Electronic Empowerment Participation (E2P), a radically new perspective on e-Participation, where collective thinking patterns can be identified under the generic form of "arguments", being contrasted automatically and enhancing thus the abilities of the different stakeholders to engage in creative participatory processes. The underlying machinery that makes E2P possible is given by agreement technologies, a new metaphor that integrates several aspects from database theory, artificial intelligence, multi-agent systems and social infrastructures. A core component in this conceptualization is an underlying argument-based approach, which allows to mine opinions from text-based information items based on incrementally generated topics.

Section 3
Applications for Conflict Resolution

As shown in Sections 1 and 2, conflicts are virtually everywhere. This undoubtedly calls for interdisciplinary approaches for not only perceiving and modeling conflicts as already addressed but most of all for solving these conflicts. This section describes new processes for solving new forms of conflict that emerged in the recent years as a result of an unprecedented technological and social evolution.

Chapter 12

    Manuel Fernando Rodrigues, Polytechnic Institute of Porto, Portugal
    Sérgio Manuel Gonçalves, University of Vigo, Spain
    Ricardo Santos, Polytechnic Institute of Porto, Portugal
    Florentino Fdez-Riverola, University of Vigo, Spain
    Davide Carneiro, University of Minho, Portugal

Society has been changing dynamically over the years and technology has been boosting that change. Teaching, as a social activity has not been changing at the same speed. Technology enhanced learning, arises as a way to cope with that challenge, opening new paths for learning. However, sometimes it becomes difficult to cope with student´s challenges: interest, motivation, attention, are difficult to achieve with the so called net-generation. With an amazing new world at the touch of their fingers, the focus is on new, challenging and interesting things, leaving very little room to other activities. Keeping students in the right track, interested and motivated is in fact an enormous challenge. Fatigue and stress play an important role in this equation: they can dramatically decrease students' performance. Controlling these factors, in such a way that´s unaware by students, is the best way to achieve better results, as the data gathering process does not interfere with the parameters being monitored. The aim is to forecast negative situations taking some actions to mitigate them.

    Juan Serrano Cuerda, Universidad de Castilla – La Mancha, Spain
    José Carlos Castillo, Universidad Carlos III de Madrid, Spain
    María T. López, Universidad de Castilla – La Mancha, Spain
    Antonio Fernández-Caballero, Universidad de Castilla – La Mancha, Spain

Real-time pedestrian detection is a key technology for video surveillance. A widespread approach for detecting pedestrians is the use of color information. In recent times, the use of thermal infrared cameras has revealed to be an excellent alternative that offers good results in people segmentation. Nonetheless, thermal infrared cameras are very sensitive to the overall heat detected at each image. Moreover, a great amount of infrared images has low spatial resolution and lower sensitivity than visible spectrum images due to the technological limitations of infrared cameras. This chapter introduces a comparison of three different algorithms for real-time and robust pedestrian detection in the infrared spectrum. The aim of the paper is to look for the best algorithms prepared to resolve the conflicts that arise in the detection process in image sequences. We propose to use simple rules as conflict resolution mechanism when the outputs of the three algorithms do not coincide.

    Pablo Chamoso, University of Salamanca, Spain
    Fernando De la Prieta, University of Salamanca, Spain
    Javier Bajo Pérez, Polytechnic University of Madrid, Spain
    Juan Manuel Corchado Rodríguez, University of Salamanca, Spain

Today, there is a common trend to use tools and methodologies that allow the development of Multi-Agent Systems (MAS) with capabilities of reorganization and adaptation to determine changes in their environments. This work presents an architecture based on different levels and whose key level is the one corresponding to the semi-open type of MAS, structured in such a way that it is able to solve conflicts. In addition, a case study is introduced with the objective of showing the possibilities on conflict resolution basis, where a specifically designed architecture is utilized for that purpose. In particular, the system is applied to the resolution of the conflict raised by the decision of the technology to be used in order to obtain or to measure information in smart cities.

    Ester Martinez-Martin, Jaume-I University, Spain
    Angel P. del Pobil, Jaume-I University, Spain

A long-term goal in Robotics is developing autonomous systems able to assist and support human beings, especially in hazardous and/or repetitive tasks. So, these robotic systems will share their workspace with other robots, people or both of them, possibly having different goals and needs. This fact may result in a conflict that should be solved for properly achieving the intended goals. However, there is no a universal way to do it since different scenarios and behaviours lead to different kinds of conflicts. In addition, execution time is a critical issue in the Robotics field and has to be taken into account when a conflict resolution technique is developed. In this chapter we will discuss the state-of-the-art algorithms applied to several robotic tasks from assembly and disassembly in industrial settings to multi-robot cooperation through collision avoidance in unstructured, crowded environments. So, a deep analysis will highlight approach's applications and utilities, as well as their limitations.

After almost one decade of active research into human computation and crowdsourcing, several approaches and business models based on crowdsourcing have emerged, managing and distributing work to the crowd. Dispute resolution approaches may incorporate crowdsourcing as a step to retrieve relevant data. The reverse relationship has also become a tendency, where crowdsourcing approaches are close to incorporate dispute resolution techniques to perform quality control and data aggregation or filtering. This chapter provides an introduction to crowdsourcing and its relationship with dispute resolution. A discussion regarding the apparent symbiotic relationship between these two research domains is also presented, along with an overview of several approaches and use cases of particular interest.

The development and technological revolution has contributed to a remarkable increase in the supply of training processes in e-learning educational institutions. The interaction and participation in educational activities under this paradigm involves a series of implications from the point of view of safety and privacy. This chapter presents the main vulnerabilities of e-learning systems and their involvement in the emergence of conflicts for the participants from online training activities and for the educational institutions. The study develops from three types of conflicts: the availability and system integrity, the privacy of the information that is exchanged in virtual environment and the process of authentication of the participants. The authors emphasize the main conflicts that can occur and the actions to take into account in e-learning environments to avoid or mitigate the effect of these vulnerabilities, to ensuring design and topology of systems, application code, and communications that are exchanged in training processes.

Preface

There are, in every vocabulary of all our different cultures, words that, for many different reasons, are very challenging to define. Nonetheless, this does not prevent one from using them on a daily basis, without doubt or ambiguity, without the constant need for a precise definition. The term *Conflict* is, undoubtedly, part of this puzzling group of words.

In an etymological sense, its origin can be traced back to the early 15th century. It derives from the Latin term *conflictus*, past participle of *confligere*, meaning something close to "to strike together", formed by *com-*"together"+*fligere* "to strike". This first definition is, without doubt, war-related.

There is no certainty about how this word came to be part of the English vocabulary. On the one hand, and although English is a Germanic language with a grammar and core vocabulary inherited from Proto-Germanic, there is a significant portion of this vocabulary that comes from Romance and Latinate sources. Thus, the term may have been directly borrowed from the Latin. On the other hand, it may also have come from other sources. Namely, there is the French term *conflit*, which was used in Old French and derives directly from the Latin original term, used to define a struggle or a quarrel. Interestingly, this term was also used early on in a psychological sense, to define "incompatible urges in one person".

This points out one first and very important aspect of conflict, which also contributes to the challenges of defining it: there may be different forms of conflict. From these original uses of the term, one can conclude that at least two types of conflict were acknowledged centuries ago: conflicts between at least two parts (the parts that would clash together) and conflicts between parts of one person (inner conflicts). These are nowadays known, respectively, as intra-group conflicts and interpersonal conflicts. Chapters 1 and 3 of this book will shed more light on this issue and provide up-to-date definitions of conflict and its different forms.

There are, nonetheless, other aspects contributing to this mentioned difficulty in precisely defining conflict. Namely, conflict can exist in very different dimensions of our lives. One could even risk to state that conflicts exist in virtually every dimension of our lives. Indeed, there are conflicts in the workplace (as Chapter 3 points out), conflicts in learning environments (as detailed in Chapters 12 and 17), environmental conflicts (addressed Chapter 4) or conflicts between states (with the Arab-Israeli conflict being one of the most well-known examples nowadays), just to name a few. Each of these types of conflict, if we can address them as such, has its own domain, its own characteristics, often its own ontology. The use of a single word for addressing them all may thus result in ambiguity.

From the aforementioned aspects, which constitute by no means an exhaustive characterization or attempt to define the term conflict, it can be concluded that it is a complex term. Nonetheless, up to this point we have been focusing solely on conflicts involving Humans, while conflicts exist outside our species and existed certainly before our first steps as a civilization (Davies, 2012; Falger, 2012).

If we consider, for instance, conflict in the animal world, examples are endless and we grew watching them on Discovery channel. If we were to categorize these conflicts, we would create two main groups (Huntingford, 2013): conflicts over resources (e.g. food, shelter, mates) and conflicts over outcomes (e.g. killing or survival of prey, occurrence of mating, occurrence of parental care, distribution of care between parents). In fact, conflicts exist involving the largest animals or the smallest creatures (Duggal & Emerman, 2012) (e.g. evolutionary conflicts between viruses). In fact, conflicts exist even in plants (Grace, 2012) as each species' strive for resources (e.g. area of land, water, nutrients) shapes the morphology and life history of plants, as well as the structure and dynamics of plant communities.

This book does not aim, as it could not realistically do so, to address all these forms of conflict. We do, however, enunciate them with a clear purpose. Leaving aside conflicts between plants (which take place at a different rhythm and are not easy to witness at a first glance or without an historic contextualization), all other types of conflicts (i.e. between animals) are generally easy to identify. This is so because they generally involve violence. And especially violent are the conflict resolution mechanisms in the animal kingdom. Indeed, animals will often injure or even kill other animals of the same species or of another species, in order to get food, shelter or a sense of security.

There were times in which this was the only approach humans (or our ancestor species) had to solve a conflict. Unfortunately, still today, violence is used often to solve conflicts. Violent approaches are, nonetheless, regarded as very negative and backward. Humans have, throughout the years, developed more refined ways of dealing with conflict that are more advantageous than fighting.

In fact, our refined ways of resolving conflicts are one fundamental part of our notable evolution as a species and of our notion of modern or advanced civilization. The second part of the book is precisely dedicated to this topic: methods for solving conflicts. As will be seen, many different methods exist, some more traditional and others more recent, including litigation in court, mediation, arbitration or negotiation.

There are also, as addressed before, many different domains of the Human existence where conflicts may happen. For this reason, the third section of the book is dedicated to the analysis of very different forms of conflict (e.g. in e-learning, in robotics, in smart cities), focusing especially on those that emerged recently due to technological evolution which are, precisely due to their novelty, the ones that call for work towards the definition of appropriate methods for their analysis and resolution.

This last section is also very important in doing justice to the book's name. In fact, conflicts are now, more than ever, interdisciplinary. Their identification, their understanding and their resolution may involve people from backgrounds as diverse as psychology, computer science, law, mathematics, among others. The purpose of this book is to establish a bridge between these and other fields that are often regarded as not interrelated, in an attempt to foster interest and research in an area that, despite its long and rich history, is still thriving and in need of new tools, new approaches and new methods.

THE CHALLENGES

Given what has been put forward about conflict, not only concerning the traditional characteristics of conflicts but also about the changes induced by evolution at different levels in the past decades, carrying out research or work in the field of conflict, and especially in conflict resolution, is nowadays extremely challenging.

Indeed, even in well-established areas such as states' legal systems, there are still numerous challenges to overcome. First of all, courtrooms – the place where conflicts are usually resolved – are a very competitive environment. Parties involved in a conflict are predisposed to be uncooperative, look at each other as the enemy. This constitutes a negative view on conflict, which could instead be seen as a potentially positive process for both parties instead of a necessarily negative for at least one of the parties. Chapters 1 and 5 look precisely at the positive potential of conflicts.

Another challenge that legal systems nowadays face derives from the increasing rights of citizens. In fact, with the evolution of societies, people gain rights (e.g. new laws to protect citizens, right to more appeals), which is undoubtedly positive. However, it also means an increase in the complexity of legal systems and in the time it takes to solve cases. There are also many new types of conflicts that are either made possible by these laws, or are a consequence of technological evolution. Take for instance complaints and conflicts related to telecommunication operators (Heikkilä, 2002) which, despite their relative small value, make up for a significant portion of nowadays conflicts. These conflicts, as many other new types of conflict, were inexistent two decades ago.

Due to all these factors, conflicts become increasingly complex, with new aspects to consider, new challenges to overcome, specialist terms and specialized language, the appearance of new concepts or the increasing amount of information contained in each case. Consequently, legal systems also increase in complexity in an attempt to provide an answer to all these new cases and their new characteristics, generally by continuously adding new rules or new procedures. Evidently, this has a cost in terms of legal practitioners and in terms of time, a cost that often constitutes a barrier for people seeking justice.

In order to address these current challenges of legal systems, the so-called Alternative Dispute Resolution (Sourdin, 2008) methods emerged, aiming to provide a more positive and cooperative milieu than the courtroom. As addressed by several chapters in Section 2, methods such as mediation, negotiation or arbitration can be used outside of the legal system, generally with smaller costs. Moreover, these methods can nowadays be supported by ICT, in an approach known as Online Dispute Resolution (Wahab & Katsh, 2012). Nonetheless, even these new approaches have disadvantages of their own.

First of all, when conflict resolution starts to take place through telematics, they become subject to telematics' drawbacks. Namely, and especially, to the poor richness of communication (Novais, 2014) when compared to face-to-face approaches (Santos, 2013). It is a fact that we share much (or most) of our meaning in a conversation from aspects such as our body language, our tone of voice, our speech or our gestures, all of which are absent in the majority of online forms of communication. This significantly hampers communication as well as the parties' decision making processes, which even in an unconscious way, are partly based on this contextual information (Carneiro et al., 2013).

There are, however, more drawbacks associated to these alternative methods. Info-exclusion is one of them: if one of the parties is not trained in using a computer or a similar tool, they will certainly be in a disadvantageous situation. There are also the very important issues of security, privacy, data protection and identity, which are one of the most significant challenges in today's information society, in more aspects than those related to conflict resolution. Some of these rather interesting aspects are addressed in Chapter 2. Finally, some of these alternative methods may face a drawback on one of the aspects that they are precisely trying to avoid: the lack of a formal structure. In fact, a courtroom has well-known and established procedures. Such may not happen in an alternative approach, which may be too dependent on human factors and on the parties' decisions and judgement.

Finally there is another aspect worth mentioning, which is more closely related to the guiding line of this book: interdisciplinarity. In fact, and as already mentioned, the field of conflict resolution involves people from increasingly different backgrounds. These people often have different knowledge, different vocabularies, different views on the problems, different paths to achieve solutions and potentially different objectives. This represents a significant challenge, ever more important as technology and all its players assume more important roles. This book aims to bring these different fields of knowledge and their practitioners closer together, in an attempt to address the mentioned challenges. For this purpose, the following section presents a group of potential solutions, some of which are addressed in the remaining chapters.

SEARCHING FOR A SOLUTION

There are certain paths that can be followed towards solutions for the challenges pointed out, some of which already explored in this book. One of the fundamental ones is the carrying out of foundational work, namely in the definition and formalization of conflict (in all its different forms and domains), in the formalization of valid conflict resolution methods and in the identification of new types of conflict, especially those caused by technological and social evolution. Section 1 of the book has significant contributions in these areas in all its different chapters.

Then, there is also the need for the development of autonomous solutions that can, at least to some extent, lighten the burden of legal practitioners, automatizing tasks in which human intervention is no longer fundamental. This can relieve human experts to perform more important tasks an increase the throughput of organizations working towards the resolution of conflicts. When considering conflict resolution processes undertaken online, the improvement of online communication environments should also be sought. Here the focus should lay on the acquisition of contextual information that may be significant for the efficiency of the communication process, such as our body language, our intonation or others. Such an idea is explored in Chapter 12. The implications of such approaches, that do exist, are analyzed previously in Chapter 2.

Conflict resolution processes could also benefit from tools that can compile and provide useful and valuable information for the parties, under the conviction that informed parties will take more realistic decisions, that take into consideration the rights and the obligations of both parties rather than focusing on self-interest. Such information may include, among others, the concepts addressed in Chapter 6. Additionally, tools to automatically generate possible solutions, especially solutions that maximize mutual gain, could also be interesting to increase the probability of achieving mutually satisfactory solutions.

When considering the challenges that affect legal systems, especially in what concerns their current low throughput, one of the potential solutions would be to foster pre-claim conciliation, especially for small-value claims which nowadays make up most of the pending cases. Moreover, other approaches such as the one described in Chapter 5 should also be considered.

Finally, the potential advantages of specific fields of Computer Science, especially those under the umbrella of Artificial Intelligence, should also not be disregarded. In fact, fields such as Decision Support Systems, Case-based Reasoning, Rule-based Systems, Neural Networks, Biologically-inspired methods and many others hold the potential to significantly improve decision-making processes, not necessarily automatizing them but, at least, making them faster, clearer or simpler. Chapters 9 – 11 address some of these issues.

ORGANIZATION OF THE BOOK

The book is organized into seventeen chapters, grouped in three different sections. A brief description of each of the chapters follows:

Chapter 1 analyzes, in a systematic way, conflicts and conflict resolution methods, comparing different approaches in terms of their main characteristics. It attempts to achieve a consensual and broad definition of the term conflict, one in which conflict is not necessarily negative, and looks at conflict handling styles and their importance in the conflict resolution process. Finally, it puts forward a framework to support conflict.

Chapter 2 addresses Biometrics, their current use, and the issues that this use raises, especially in what concerns privacy and data protection. The chapter acknowledges the advantages of the use of biometrics (e.g. low margin of error) for the purpose of identification, especially in given domains. However, it also thoroughly analyzes the requirements that should be met in order to do so in a way that does not threat individual rights.

Chapter 3 starts by looking at different definitions for the term conflict and continues with the identification of triggers for conflicts. It also takes a positive view on conflict and addresses its potential value. It tackles the sometimes challenging task of differentiating between conflicts, disputes and disagreements and does all this while focusing on organizational conflict, undoubtedly one of the largest fields in this domain.

Chapter 4 looks at a very different form of conflict, yet by no means of lesser importance: Environmental Conflicts. Indeed, as pointed out in the chapter, environmental conflicts are very complex and involve social, economic, political and cultural factors. The chapter discusses the defining characteristics of these conflicts and the methods for their assessment and resolution.

In Chapter 5, the interesting concept of Restorative Justice is explored: an approach to criminal conflicts that focuses its efforts on restoring the harm done by criminal activities. Very simplistically, it can be stated that the main aim is to compensate the victim of a criminal activity so that there is no seek for revenge. The authors end their contribution by bridging restorative justice with Online Dispute Resolution, to propose Online Restorative Justice.

Chapter 6 opens Section 2 with a formal approach to knowledge representation and reasoning in the legal domain. One of its significant contributions is the definition of a method for quantifying the quality of judgments in scenarios of incomplete information. The chapter is supported by a realistic case-study that validates the proposed approach.

Chapter 7 starts with a brief overview of alternative means of dispute resolution (e.g. negotiation, conciliation, mediation, arbitration). The author then moves on to analyze the implementation of these alternative means in the member states of the European union to conclude, among other aspects, that European institutions have demonstrated a growing concern in ensuring the implementation and the development of the single European market of alternative means of dispute resolution.

Chapter 8 carries on this analysis at an European level, but focuses on Online Dispute Resolution for consume. It starts by addressing the advent of the society of consume and of information, moving on to the appearance of extrajudicial conflict resolution, especially in the European Union.

Chapter 9, written entirely from a Computer Science perspective, looks at Artificial Intelligence, and in particular at Multi-Agent Systems, as a concrete and very innovative field of application of conflict resolution methodologies. Here, Agreement Technologies are analyzed as a means to achieve agreements between autonomous synthetic entities.

Chapter 10 starts with a very interesting analysis on the diversity of fields in which conflicts happen. It then addresses the use of search and optimization techniques, which can be classified as nature- or bio-inspired, within conflict resolution problem solving, focusing especially on three major techniques: genetic algorithms, differential evolution and particle swarm optimization. Equally interesting is the analysis of specific applications of these techniques in conflict resolution problem solving.

Chapter 11, which closes a section devoted to conflict resolution, presents an account of recent advances in the development of a novel e-participation framework which integrates social networks (particularly Twitter), intelligent information retrieval and argumentation techniques. One of its key contributions is the idea of applying argumentation systems for mining citizens' opinions on a given topic, obtaining an "opinion analysis tree", rooted in the first original topic that allows to analyze all the arguments and their relationships.

Chapter 12 opens section 3, dedicated to practical applications in the field of conflict resolution. This specific chapter looks at conflicts in e-learning environments and how technological tools and the acquisition of contextual information can help to mitigate them.

Chapter 13 addresses video-cameras and their use, specifically for real-time detection of pedestrians. Several segmentation algorithms and the implications of their use are compared throughout the chapter.

Chapter 14 introduces the concept of smart cities, linking their emergence to the rapid growth of the Internet of Things, that makes all resources in a city available at the distance of a service invocation. The authors address conflicts in the context of smart cities, focusing on those cases in which autonomous agents, with potentially conflicting objectives, need to make decisions about which service or technology to use to solve a given problem. The concept of Multi-agent Systems is thus addressed as well.

Chapter 15 presents us with yet another novel field of application of conflict resolution, unthinkable a few decades or years ago: robotics. While the chapter begins rather classically – by addressing conflict handling styles – it quickly advances to assess multi-robot cooperation and, specifically, the emergence of conflicts and how they can be solved in this domain. Several classical problems of robotics are addressed, including path finding and object manipulation. Finally, conflict resolution involving humans and robots are also addressed.

In Chapter 16 the apparent symbiotic relationship between conflict resolution and crowdsourcing is explored, along with an overview of both crowdsourcing and dispute resolution approaches, and use cases that are of particular interest. A systematization of the discussed approaches is also provided, that captures the main challenges and directions for mixed dispute resolution and crowdsourcing approaches.

Finally, Chapter 17 is also dedicated to conflicts in e-Learning but, more specifically, it addresses the main vulnerabilities of e-learning systems and their involvement in the emergence of conflicts for the participants from online training activities and for the educational institutions. The study develops from three types of conflicts: the availability and system integrity, the privacy of the information that is exchanged in virtual environment and the process of authentication of the participants.

Paulo Novais
University of Minho, Portugal

Davide Carneiro
University of Minho, Portugal

REFERENCES

Carneiro, D., Gomes, M., Costa, Â., Novais, P., & Neves, J. (2013). Enriching conflict resolution environments with the provision of context information. *Expert Systems: International Journal of Knowledge Engineering and Neural Networks*, n/a. doi:10.1111/exsy.12049

Davies, N. B., Krebs, J. R., & West, S. A. (2012). *An introduction to behavioural ecology*. John Wiley & Sons.

Duggal, N. K., & Emerman, M. (2012). Evolutionary conflicts between viruses and restriction factors shape immunity. *Nature Reviews. Immunology*, *12*(10), 687–695. doi:10.1038/nri3295 PMID:22976433

Falger, V. (2012). *Sociobiology and conflict: Evolutionary perspectives on competition, cooperation, violence and warfare*. Springer Science & Business Media.

Grace, J. (Ed.). (2012). *Perspectives on plant competition*. Elsevier.

Heikkilä, J. (2002). From supply to demand chain management: Efficiency and customer satisfaction. *Journal of Operations Management*, *20*(6), 747–767. doi:10.1016/S0272-6963(02)00038-4

Huntingford, F. A. (2013). *Animal conflict*. Springer Science & Business Media.

Novais, P., Carneiro, D., Andrade, F., & Neves, J. (2014). Harnessing content and context for enhanced decision making. In *AI approaches to the complexity of legal systems* (pp. 232–246). Springer Berlin Heidelberg. doi:10.1007/978-3-662-45960-7_17

Santos, C. (2013). Increasing media richness in online dispute resolution and the need for personal data protection. *Regulation*, *136*, 3.

Sourdin, T. (2008). *Alternative dispute resolution*. Thomson Lawbook Company.

Wahab, M. S. A., & Katsh, M. E. (2012). *Online dispute resolution: Theory and practice: A treatise on technology and dispute resolution*. Eleven International Pub.

Acknowledgment

We would like to acknowledge the help of all the people involved in this project and, more specifically, to the authors and reviewers that took part in the review process. Without their support, this book would not have become a reality.

First, we would like to thank each one of the authors for their contributions. Our sincere gratitude goes to the chapter's authors who contributed their time and expertise to this book.

Second, we wish to acknowledge the valuable contributions of the reviewers regarding the improvement of quality, coherence, and content of chapters. Some of the authors also served as referees; we highly appreciate their double task.

Finally, to the ones we never forget.

Paulo Novais
University of Minho, Portugal

Davide Carneiro
University of Minho, Portugal

Section 1
About Conflicts

Conflicts occur naturally in virtually every domain of our existence and every reader for sure had, by this time, their fair share of conflicts. The first section of this book will analyze fundamental issues about conflicts, their diversity, their emergence and their resolution.

Chapter 1
Conflict and Its Different Dimensions

Marco Vieira Gomes
University of Minho, Portugal

Paulo Novais
University of Minho, Portugal

ABSTRACT

The purpose of this chapter is to explore the nature of conflict from a computer science perspective, throwing to light an up to date review of the evolution and state-of-the-art of the intersection of conflict with technology-assisted systems and tools. The objective is to design a document to organize existing literature, provide a baseline understanding in place of an agreed definition of conflict, depict relevant conflict aspects (dimensions), and made overall evaluation of a range of methods and techniques of conflict resolution. It was also explored the challenges that individuals face in using online technology for collaboration and conflict resolution and management purposes. Finally, is presented some preliminary work regarding the most suitable technologies to implement a technological framework for handling conflict in a digital environment.

INTRODUCTION

Despite the common notion, conflict is an inherent part of human evolution that allow us to learn, progress, grow, and will continue to remain so (Burton, 1998). Although this positive view on the phenomenon, there is a consensus in the literature: only a well-managed conflict will bring functional outcomes and will prevent or reduce dysfunctional ones. Thus, the first logical step in facing conflict is to characterize the problem and then determine which styles (strategies) must be used. In this regard, to understand what lies behind a conflict and which alternatives exist for dealing with it is essential to obtain an in-deep analysis of conflict. When speaking of analysis, we mean the identification of a set of key concepts and issues that can be framed within a pre-specified framework, which should provide the adequate instruments to assess conflict dynamics. In an attempt to develop such analysis, various approaches may be adopted. Especially when, nowadays, conflict arise and is brought to the digital environment.

DOI: 10.4018/978-1-5225-0245-6.ch001

In that sense, this work aims to outline a complementary approach to conceptualization and management of conflict in virtual environments. In our opinion, this approach must preview the identification, application and further development of methodologies (being able of measuring conflict dimensions/ characteristics applying appropriated metrics) conveniently exploiting the new technologies of communication and information. Recent studies findings indicate that some work has been done in this direction (Lodder & Zeleznikow, 2005). Even though, it should be kept in mind there is a widespread agreement that exists a lack of proper management to conflicts, which are incurring a substantial cost to society as a whole. Therefore, the importance of developing new approaches to improving conflict resolution effectiveness, based on an intersection of conflict handling theories with technology-assisted systems, is obvious (Carneiro, Gomes, Novais, & Neves, 2011).

In summary, the purpose of this chapter is to explore the nature of conflict from a computer science perspective, throwing to light an up to date review of the evolution and state-of-the-art of the field. It is intentioned to open up discussions around the concept of conflict, prompting a deeper consideration of what is included under the term, and stimulating further thinking about the impact and potential future role of conflict resolution in digital environments. The aim is to design a document to organize existing literature, provide a baseline understanding in place of an agreed definition of conflict, depict relevant conflict aspects (dimensions) by analyzing key features of conflict situation, and made overall evaluation of a range of methods and techniques of conflict resolution. Furthermore, a review of conflict literature is presented, aiming to communicate the findings of a wide variety of studies but is by no means definitive. It was also explored the challenges that individuals face in using online technology for collaboration and conflict resolution and management purposes. Consequently, it can be concluded that developments in technology-assisted systems and tools can play a critical role in exacerbating and/or resolving conflicts. Finally, is also presented how recent Artificial Intelligence innovations can facilitate knowledge acquisition, analysis and presentation of conflict-related data. Some online-specific techniques have been reviewed and also is given some preliminary work regarding the most suitable technologies to implement a technological framework for handling conflict in a digital environment.

AN OVERVIEW OF CONFLICT CONCEPT

One of the major difficulties in articulating a clear definition of conflict is determining whether it should be based on subjective or objective criteria. Subjectively, approaches to define conflict involve attempts to explain it analyzing the ways in which parties understand and behave towards each other. On the other hand, the objective aspects used to define are, roughly, those that are widely independent of the parties' perceptions (e.g. power, scarce resources). An approach to overcome the difficulty mentioned earlier is to provide a baseline understanding in place of an agreed definition (using one criterion or another).

Having a working definition to manage conflict, and to understand its components, is a continual process. Undoubtedly this is significant not only from a theoretical viewpoint but mostly from a practical one. For doing so, one must handle with the different nuances that underlie the same words that scholars use to characterize conflict, differentiating it from related concepts, stressing its components and placing them in perspective. Therefore, the ambition of this section is to understand by looking at theoretical and technical approaches that could potentially be useful for the exploration of conflict. Firstly, the goal is to dissect concepts underpinning conflict, starting by emphasizing its key features and showing its state-of-the-art appraisal. Subsequently, this work wants to move forward by presenting a theoretical common ground in which a basic structure used to identify, frame and understand constituents of conflict can be solidly constructed. Despite the authors recognizing that the following terms may be associated with different scales of impacts and intensities, the terms "conflict", "dispute", "conflict resolution", and "conflict management", in this section and throughout this study, are used interchangeably.

A Myriad of Definitions

The definition of conflict has been taught or transmitted to us as a commonly-used notion that serves to label various human experiences, ranging from indecision to disagreement (Buss, 2009). This abundance of meanings leads to a degree of uncertainty about what is meant by conflict, creating conceptual and terminological confusion. Consequently, the concept of conflict has acquired divergent and multiple meanings (it has different semantic associations) turning up very difficult to define. Nonetheless, many scholars have been seeking to generate a suitable definition, yet remains unclear. Despite the fact that there has been no shortage of definitions of conflict, requiring a vast amount of research to generate a very simple understanding of conflict, an accepted definition of 'conflict' is lacking. And it will continue to lack because it is a widely held view that there cannot exist a single universally accepted definition of conflict.

The literature on conflict spans multiple disciplines, such as sociology, game theory, and international relations. Each with their view of what conflict is, varying both across disciplines and by the author. An interesting chronological approach to defining conflict can be found in (Watkin, 2012). In this work, is stated that the concept of conflict has evolved over time. It is emphasized that conflict is a breakdown in the mechanisms of decision-making (March & Simon, 1958). This early view shifted to consider conflict as an incompatibility of goals. A further contribution is given by (Karen A Jehn, 1997) who classify contradictory views on the means to achieve those objectives as important. Meanwhile, others have proposed that conflict exists when views are perceived to be incompatible (Kolb & Putnam, 1992). Furthermore, (Nair, 2008) highlighted that the definition and meaning of what constitutes conflict have not only changed over time, but remains vague and contextual.

Achieving conceptual clarity is a challenge, due the overabundance of approaches to define the meaning of conflict and the number of disciplines involved. Taking into account the work of (Infante, 1998), in a review to define the interpersonal conflict and its nature, it was gathered and analyzed 78 different published definitions from different sources between 1933 and 1996. And it was a study that was not intended to be exhaustive and focused in one type of conflict. This disparity reveals an absence of conceptual clarity. Even though several common aspects underlie most definitions and can be listed as follows: conflict as a "process" rather than an event (Barki & Hartwick, 2004; Dreu, 2008); as the experience or perception of "incompatibilities" (Boulding, 1963; Coleman, 2003; M Deutsch, 1973) as a "struggle" over tangible resources as well as intangible values; status and power (Coser, 1956);and as disagreements involving "task and relationship" issues (K A Jehn, 1995).

According to Tjosvold, many current definitions of conflict were confounded as they assume conflicts involve opposing interests and divergent goals (Tjosvold, 2006). Defining a conflict in this way results in an implicit view of conflict as negative and fails to account for the fact that individuals can have similar interests and goals and yet still have conflict. In this study, conflict is presumed to be associated with both potential destructive and constructive outcomes. Therefore, a definition with less confounding is required. In (Tjosvold, 2006) is suggested that Deutsch's definition (M Deutsch, 1973) into such a category and which is defined as "incompatible activities; one person's actions interfere, obstruct or in some way get in the way of another's action" (p. 90). Deutsch (Morton Deutsch, 2008) further states that "conflict can occur in a cooperative or competitive context, and the processes of conflict resolution that are likely to be displayed will be strongly influenced by the context within which the conflict occurs". One limitation of Deutsch's definition is that it fails to explicitly mention conflict as a process occurring over time. This is an important feature of current definitions, such as those by (Barki & Hartwick, 2004) and (Dreu, 2008).Hence, in this work, conflict is understood using the following definition by (M Deutsch, 1973) which maintained that "conflict exists whenever incompatible activities occur . . . an action that prevents, obstructs, interferes with, injures, or in some way makes it less likely or less effective". Similarly, a conflict can be seen as a conflict of interests that somehow disrupts or blocks an action or process of decision making (Robbins & Judge, 2007). A conflict may be seen thus as a process that begins when one party feels that the other has or is about to negatively affected something that the first party cares about. This definition is flexible enough to cover the full range of aspects regarding conflict and is, in our opinion, the closest to the objectivity required in order to conflict be dealt in a digital environment.

Views of Conflict

Among the different perspectives about conflict, three dominant and distinct views can be listed as follows: the traditional, the behavioral or contemporary, and the interactionist view. These three general schools of thought relating to conflict evolved over time and gradually changed. Verma (Verma, 1998) outlines the three viewpoints:

The early approach to conflict presumed that conflict is a negative thing and, therefore, it had to be suppressed or avoided.

The traditional view (dominant from the late nineteenth century until the mid-1940s) adopts that conflict is harmful, always has a negative impact, and leads to declines in performance as the level of conflict increases. Conflict must, therefore, always be avoided. In this view, conflict is closely associated with such terms as violence, destruction, and irrationality. The response to conflict in the traditional view is to reduce, suppress, or eliminate it. The manager was responsible for freeing the project of any conflict, often using an authoritarian approach. Although that approach sometimes worked, it was not effective; when they are suppressed, the root causes cannot be identified, and the potentially positive aspects of conflict cannot emerge. This traditional view of conflict is still widely held because industrial and business institutions that have a strong influence on our society concur with it. This negative view of conflict played a role in the development of labor unions. Violent or disruptive confrontations between workers and management led people to conclude that conflict was always detrimental and should, therefore, be avoided.

However, with continuous studies and researches regarding the perception of conflict as something harmful and evitable started to fade from the conventional view of conflict. It was argued that conflict is a natural and inevitable phenomenon either with a negative or positive effect, depending how the conflict is handled.

The behavioral or contemporary view, also known as the human relations view, emerged in the late 1940s and held sway through the 1970s. It argues that conflict is natural and inevitable in all organizations and that it may have either a positive or negative effect, depending on how the conflict is handled. Performance may increase with conflict, but only up to a certain level, and then decline if conflict is allowed to grow further or is left unresolved. This approach advocates acceptance of conflict and rationalizes its existence.

More recently, a new perspective emerged focusing the relevant role of conflict in performance and creativity. This viewpoint advocates not only accepting conflict, but also encouraging it.

The newest perspective, the interactionist view assumes that conflict is necessary to increase performance. While the behavioral approach accepts conflict, the interactionist view encourages conflict based on the belief that a harmonious, peaceful, tranquil, too-cooperative project organization is likely to become static, apathetic, stagnant, and unable to respond to change and innovation. This approach helps managers to maintain an appropriate level of conflict -enough to keep projects self-critical, viable, creative, and innovative.

From an operational point of view, these three views of conflict can be synthesized by comparing the actual level of conflict (a) and desired levels of conflict (d). Having the perception of conflict has something undesirable, naturally, the desired level of conflict is always zero. In that sense, if a = 0 does nothing, and if the actual level of conflict rises above zero, it should be resolved. While in the newer perspectives, which advocates that conflict can have positive effects, differ only in terms of the desired level of conflict. In the contemporary view, the desired level of conflict could be equal to or above zero. Meanwhile, in the interactionist view is always above zero.

Table 1. A comparison of conflict views (adapted from Verma, 1998)

	Traditional View	**Behavioral View**	**Interactionist View**
Main Points	Caused by troublemakers Bad Should be avoided Should be suppressed	Inevitable between humans Not always bad Natural result of change Can be managed	Results from commitment to goals Often beneficial Should be stimulated Should aim to foster creativity
Effect on Performance	Performance declines as the level of conflict increases	Performance mainly depends on how effectively the conflict is handled. Generally performance increases to a certain level as conflict level increases, then declines if conflict is allowed to increase further or left unresolved	Certain level of conflict is necessary to increase performance. Performance increases with conflict up to a certain level, then declines if conflict increases further or remains unresolved
Recommend Actions	Do nothing if a = d Resolve conflict if a > d (Where d = 0)	Do nothing if a = d Resolve conflict if a > d (Where d ~ 0)	Do nothing if a = d Resolve conflict if a> d Stimulate conflict if a < d (Where d> 0)

Dimensions and Types of Conflict

Let start by making a distinction between typologies of conflict and dimensions of conflict. A typology classifies conflicts into types. A dimension is variably applied to all types of conflicts. Moreover, they can be conceived of dynamically: a conflict can move along these dimensions; that is what makes them different from a taxonomic, static scheme. These aspects (types and dimensions) are of paramount importance for conflict diagnosis to facilitate resolution. An efficient conflict resolution platform must provide to the users a tool to enhance an accurate analysis of the conflict situation, given to them the ability to outline the nature, aspects and causes of conflict. A framework organizing the literature and provide a baseline understanding of the parameters of conflict is then required to allow practitioners to assess conflict more accurately and consequently diagnose complications.

Furthermore, a framework for diagnosing the components of the conflict can be seen as a process-directing tool for facilitating the resolution of the conflict. However, the demand to get it is a difficult task due to each author in the field will have his own bundle to present. Once again, a universally accepted description is virtually unachievable. Nonetheless, a working definition of the components of the conflict is significant and useful to explore the nature of conflict, how it start and how is carry on. It is even necessary to increase the practical function of conflict resolution mechanism. When it comes to design a framework with these aims, some principles must be followed, such as clarity and functionality. Given these assumptions, and after a review of the literature, three (overlapping) models stand out as being the most frequently used in the field, having the characteristics mentioned earlier. Using a chronological approach, Table 2 summarizes the variations of the Circle of Conflict that classifies the causes of conflict in categories, offers a framework for diagnosis, and (in some versions) even strategic directions to move forwards in resolution. In the table, the variations of The Circle of Conflict, associated drivers and their descriptions are depicted by a)(Moore, 1986, 1996)b)(Mayer, 2000);c)(Furlong, 2006).The circle provides a framework for conflict diagnosis by providing drivers for consideration, each model is slightly different in design. Model a highlights five drivers and divides them into genuine and unnecessary conflict components (indicated by dotted line and arrows). Model b introduces a sixth driver of history, and places needs at the fundamental center of all conflict, it does not classify components. Model c introduces a further driver of external factors, the author suggest concentrating on reducing drivers bellow the central line (indicated by arrows) and managing those above. (Table 2).

According to a definition provided by Watkin (Watkin, 2012), two additional themes of power and timing are included in the circle, alongside the seven categories present in the circles of conflict (depicted in the table 2). Based on the analogy of DNA, Watkin defines the elements as "base pairs" within the conceptual conflict helix, but all the categories presented are interlinked and interactions are not limited to within these couples. In short, this approach highlights nine categories (needs/interests, structures, power, information, communication, emotions, values, timing and history) which can then be used to frame an interdisciplinary review of conflict literature to outline the potential dimensions to be considered in each category. Moreover, it is understood that the characterization presented represents an oversimplification of a very complex process and could be argued by some to be deficient, with some parameters of conflict (e.g. handling modes) absent.

Regarding the task of organize or arrange conflict according to a category or type the foremost objective to be sought is to convert into particular groups or patterns. Meanwhile, there are a lot of ways do to it due to the interdisciplinary nature of the conflict. This implies that conflict can occur at many

Table 2. Variations of The Circle of Conflict (adapted from Watkin, 2012)

Moore (1986; 1996)		Mayer (2000)		Furlong (2008)	
Drivers	Relationship conflicts; Value conflicts; Interest conflicts; Structural conflicts; Data conflicts	Drivers	Emotions; Values; Communication; History; Structures; Needs	Drivers	Relationships; Values; Data; Interests; Structures; External
Relationship	Negative behavior, Misperceptions/ stereotypes, Poor communication, Strong emotions	Emotions	Frustration, Anger, Shame, Guilt	Relationships	Stereotypes, Poor communication, negative behavior
Value	Day to day values, Self-defining values	Values	Beliefs, Core values	Values	Beliefs
Data	Lack of information, Misinformation, Different interpretations	Communication	Lack of information, Perceptions, Misinformation, Stereotypes	Data	Lack or excess of information, misinformation, Data collection problems
Interest	Substantive (physical resources), Procedural Psychological (e.g. trust, fairness, respect)	Needs	Goals that must be met	Interests	Parties wants, needs, desires, concerns
Structural	How a situation is set up, Geographical/Physical relationships, Unequal power distributions, Unequal control of resources, Time constraints, Role definition	Structures	Distribution of resources, Established procedures, Access, Legal parameters, Political structures	Structures	Limitation on resources, geographical constraints, organizational structures
		History	Antecedent conflict conditions, Past interactions	External	Facts unrelated with conflict but affect it e.g. Moods

different levels. An ample documentation concerning this task is available in both theory and practice perspectives. Despite the existence of various conflict types, one commonly accepted classification was identified which classify into four levels as following (Types of Conflict – Four Classifications, 2015):

- **Interpersonal Conflict:** Refers to a conflict between two individuals. This occurs typically due to how people are different from one another. We have varied personalities which usually results to incompatible choices and opinions. Apparently, it is a natural occurrence which can eventually help in personal growth or developing your relationships with others. In addition, coming up with adjustments is necessary for managing this type of conflict. However, when interpersonal conflict gets too destructive, calling in a mediator would help so as to have it resolved.

- **Intrapersonal Conflict:** Occurs within an individual. The experience takes place in the person's mind. Hence, it is a type of conflict that is psychological involving the individual's thoughts, values, principles and emotions. Interpersonal conflict may come in different scales, from the simpler mundane ones like deciding whether or not to go organic for lunch to ones that can affect major decisions such as choosing a career path. Furthermore, this type of conflict can be quite difficult to handle if you find it hard to decipher your inner struggles. It leads to restlessness and uneasiness, or can even cause depression. In such occasions, it would be best to seek a way to let go of the anxiety through communicating with other people. Eventually, when you find yourself out of the situation, you can become more empowered as a person. Thus, the experience evoked a positive change which will help you in your own personal growth.

- **Intragroup Conflict:** Is a type of conflict that happens among individuals within a team. The incompatibilities and misunderstandings among these individuals lead to an intragroup conflict. It is arises from interpersonal disagreements (e.g. team members have different personalities which may lead to tension) or differences in views and ideas (e.g. in a presentation, members of the team might find the notions presented by the one presiding to be erroneous due to their differences in opinion). Within a team, conflict can be helpful in coming up with decisions which will eventually allow them to reach their objectives as a team. However, if the degree of conflict disrupts harmony among the members, then some serious guidance from a different party will be needed for it to be settled.
- **Intergroup Conflict:** Takes place when a misunderstanding arises among different teams within an organization. For instance, the sales department of an organization can come in conflict with the customer support department. This is due to the varied sets of goals and interests of these different groups. In addition, competition also contributes for intergroup conflict to arise. There are other factors which fuel this type of conflict. Some of these factors may include a rivalry in resources or the boundaries set by a group to others which establishes their own identity as a team.

Moreover, from an interactionist view, a performance-oriented approach to classifying conflict is proposed. It is suggested that are two types of conflict as functional and dysfunctional.

Having the notion that some conflicts support the goals of the group and improve its performance, it is argued that conflict can be valuable for the group. When this happens, a functional and constructive outcome can result from a conflicting situation, having positive benefits to individuals, a group, or the organization. This type of healthy conflict is classified as a functional conflict. On the other hand, dysfunctional conflict can damage group cohesion, promote hostilities among those involved, and create an overall negative environment. This is clearly a form of destructive conflict. Of course, the demarcation between functional and dysfunctional is neither clear nor precise. It is assumed that no one level of conflict can be adopted as acceptable or unacceptable under all conditions. The type and level of conflict that creates healthy and positive involvement toward one individual or group's goals today may be regarded as highly dysfunctional. The criterion that differentiates functional from dysfunctional conflict is individual or group performance.

The Process and the Handling Style

There are many approaches in the literature to describe the nature of the conflict phenomena. Though definitions vary, conflict is consistently viewed as a sequential, dynamic process. In other words, it is accepted that conflicts do not just erupt; rather they develop through various stages and tend to follow a pattern, despite the fact that, at the beginning, conflict may be perceived as a state or situation. By recognizing and delineating the different dynamics occurring at each stage of a conflict, can be useful to a better understanding and addressing the dynamics of conflict. Consequently, determining how conflict develops and change over time might permit us to understand better which strategies and tactics for participants and interveners should be applicable to particular stages in the process.

For many years, researchers tried to determine how conflict develops and change. Lois Pondy (Pondy, 1967) proposed one of the earlier process models including multiple stages of conflict, which reflected its sequential and dynamic nature. Indeed, according to his model conflict goes through five stage process that he calls "conflict episodes". These stages are helpful in diagnosing task conflicts (one of two types of conflicts that can happen within a group or team). If one can locate where the group is in the process, he/she can predict where it will go next and thus may try to find ways to manage conflict. Consistent with the Pondy's (Pondy, 1967) view, Thomas (1976) definite conflict as being a multiple stages dynamic process. Meanwhile, Thomas also included perceptions, emotions, behaviors, and outcomes in his definition. Following this convergence in the characterization and definition of conflict, the contemporary approaches to the process model view of conflict have evolved, more focus has been placed on perception as the central core process. One of the most widely-used versions is that of (Robbins & Judge, 2007) and represents a synthesis of prior definitions. It is clear that this approach emphasizes intra-individual and interpersonal processes that are linked to manifestations of conflict. Depicting the process, Robbins' model also comprises five stages: potential opposition or incompatibility, cognition and personalization, intentions, behavior, and outcomes.

Conflicts can develop in stages and consequently may involve many different responses as the conflict proceeds. People involved develop various strategies, solutions or behaviors, to deal with the conflict. In fact, the style of dealing with a conflict that each part has must be seen as having a preponderant role in the outcome of a conflict resolution process, especially in those where parties interact directly (e.g. negotiation, mediation). Moreover, there are several styles of behavior by which conflict can be handled and, depending upon the situation, one style may be more suitable that other. Ultimately, it is acceptable to state that the outcome will largely depend on the conflict resolution style of each party and the interaction of the styles of the parties. Different approaches can be followed to formalize how the conflict is handled strategically or contingently. An earlier conceptual scheme (M Deutsch, 1973) for classifying handling style argues that styles can be arranged on a single dimension ranging from competition or selfishness. It is based on a mere cooperation-competition dichotomy. Meanwhile, this type of schemes were doubted over the capability to reflect the complexity of an individual's perceptions of conflict behavior. It was criticized that this model fails to represent styles having involving high (low) concern for both self and others, which were not included in the dichotomy. Building on earlier work, subsequent researchers then drew on a new two-dimensional grid for classifying the styles. Introduced by Blake and Mouton (Blake & Mouton, 1964), the dual concern model was depicted into two basic dimensions, concern for production and concern for people. They also have specified the similarities and differences among five behavioral styles or modes of handling conflict. Assuming the basic assumptions proposed by Blake and Mouton, other authors have labeled the two dimensions differently having reinterpreted and extended many revisions of this framework. This still happens today, in which numerous researchers continue proposing changes on the model of conceptualizing the way how conflict is handled. Meanwhile, these work helped to consolidate the identification of the five conflict-handling styles by combining the two-dimensional approach. One of the most famous classification of people behavior into five two-dimensional locations in the grid they psychologically occupy was presented by Kenneth Thomas and Ralph Kilmann (Kilmann & Thomas, 1977). In their work, was presented a method to encode the way that we react to a conflict into five different modes. To define these modes, they take into consideration the individual's assertiveness (attempting to satisfy one's own concerns) and cooperativeness (trying to meet other's concerns). The five different conflict resolution styles defined are: competing (assertive and uncooperative), collaborating (assertive and cooperative), compromising (moderate in both assertiveness and cooperativeness), avoiding (unassertive and uncooperative) and accommodating (unassertive and cooperative).

Methods and Techniques for Dealing with Conflict

The process of conflict resolution does not begin with the identification of a particular conflict. It is a continuous process in which actors are always working to create the conditions that discourage dysfunctional conflict and encourage the processes of conflict resolution results that facilitate "win-win" solutions. In a more technical sense, conflict management refers to a broad range of tools used to predict, prevent and respond to conflict. A conflict resolution strategy involves a combination of these types of tools.

These tools are used to encourage the parties to open up, identify the real issues behind the positions uttered publicly and find solutions "win-win" that leave both parties better off with the result. However, it is not possible to achieve results "win-win" all the time. To succeed outside of trade and compromise would be necessary. Even so, in some cases, if a party believes that collaborative efforts will not produce anything better than what he can earn through unilateral action, will not go to any collaborative activity. In this work, a theoretical framework will take into account the methods and techniques used to deal will conflict. The approach of conflict management also uses methods involving negotiation, mediation, arbitration, conciliation, consensus-building (Alternative Dispute Resolution ADR techniques), and litigation (legal process). A range tools of conflict management, and their main characteristics, is resumed in Table 3.

Table 3. A comparison of conflict management tools

	Litigation	Negotiation	Mediation	Arbitration
Result Sought	Court judgement	Mutually acceptable agreement	Mutual acceptable agreement	Arbitration award
Voluntary or Involuntary	Involuntary	Voluntary	Voluntary	Voluntary
Binding or Non-Binding	Binding	Agreement enforceable as contract	Agreement enforceable as contract	Binding
Private or Public	Public	Private	Private	Private
Participants	Judge and parties	Parties only	Mediator and parties	Arbitrator and parties
Third Party Involvement	None	Parties communicate directly	Mediator selected by parties	Arbitrator
First Steps	One party initiates court proceedings	Flexible	Parties agree on mediation and appoint mediator	Parties agree on arbitrator and appoint him

ENVIRONMENT AND CONTEXT TO DEAL WITH CONFLICT

Conflict management is also about creating conflict in the right environment. It can be seen as an ongoing process in which stakeholders continuously work to create the conditions that discourage dysfunctional conflict and encourage conflict resolution processes that facilitate beneficial outcomes. In a practical view, it can be resume to a vast array of tools used to anticipate, prevent and react to conflicts. A successful strategy to lead with conflict must involve a combination of these types of tools with the capability of generally to access contextual factors and social clues. Previous works suggested a notion that having this sort of information can improve the effectiveness of selecting the most situationally appropriate conflict handling response. Taking into account the relevance of the environment and context in which conflict it is being managed, this section tries to analyze the relationship between conflict issues and how it can be addressed in and by digital means. Furthermore, attempts to uncover the most suitable technologies that can response to the challenge of gathering, analyzing and transforming into meaningful content the raw contextual and behavioral data, abundant in conflict situations.

In summary, the primary objective is to identify the baseline artifacts and to outline the prominent issues involved in the development of such technological framework. In other words, the intent is to design a practical framework capable of acquire and provide context and behavioral information about the participants of a conflict situation and about the situation itself. To do it, this kind of framework must encompass the determination of the existence or not of a conflict, its characterization and nature, the generation of possible arguments/proposals and the closure of the process. In order to implement a framework able to comprise this kind of information, this work will follow an approach in line with the concept of Intelligent Environment, in which an intelligent environment supports the conflict management platform with context information. In the following sections, the literature review is presented, establishing the current state of the art and identifying its main drawbacks.

Conflict Handling in a Digital Environment

Taking the advantage of the resources made available by the newest Information and Communications Technologies (ICT), new generations of platforms to support the conflict handling have highlighted the utilization of a more autonomous and efficient use of technical tools. Throughout the years, these systems have been significantly empowered by a range of technologies and methodologies that intersect different fields of knowledge such as Artificial Intelligence, Mathematics or Philosophy. Thus, the paradigm in which reactive communication tools are used by parties to share information have changed to an immersive, intelligent environment (Aarts & Grotenhuis, 2011) which proactively supports the lifecycle of the conflict resolution mechanism with relevant knowledge. This is evidently the most challenging approach to follow as computational systems that implement the cognitive capabilities of a Human expert are not easy to accomplish, especially if we include the ability to perceive the emotions and desires of the parties involved. Indeed, many works have focused on the support of managing activities to resolve conflicts (Cooper & Taleb-Bendiab, 1998). Two general ways have been employed to express and manage conflict issues:

- **Mathematical Model-Based Systems:** Which are generally based on game theory and economic behavior, where a vast majority of developed systems have utilized quantitative models, such as multi-criteria decision making, conflict analysis, group decision theory, multi-objective linear programming and fuzzy arithmetic to search for an efficient solution based upon the negotiation criteria and preferences provided by the users;
- **Heuristics Model-Based Systems**: Which are developed using Artificial Intelligence techniques to model the strategic behavior of the negotiating parties. For instance, systems using knowledge-based systems to model the impact of decisions on competitive negotiations, and model and simulate possible negotiating positions. Moreover, some researchers use case-based reasoning techniques in conjunction with multi-attribute utility theory to assess the negotiation problem and compares it to stored similar past cases, from which a solution to the considered conflict can be adapted. In (Cooper & Taleb-Bendiab, 1998) is presented some works attempting to abstract out strategic knowledge negotiation from domain knowledge, has identified generic classes of negotiation strategies, which are considered as a fundamental concept for the development of a multi-agent negotiation framework. Lander and Lesser, cited by (Cooper & Taleb-Bendiab, 1998), have been among the few who recognize and address the need for a computational distributed control model, which is the essence of multi-agent negotiation. Their developed `negotiated search' algorithm provides a generic search method that explicitly recognizes and exploits search activity between agents, where conflicts are used as a source of control information for the search, but ultimately the control is provided through democratic decisions made by the agents themselves.

Given the wide variety of possibilities, it should be clear that there is no universally best approach or technique. Following these models, a review of the literature is presented with the aim of identifying the models, technologies and failures that a conflict support system can accommodate in a digital environment. When analyzing the current literature, it is concluded that projects targeting the aforementioned particular issues are nearly inexistent. In fact, regardless of the extensive research in social and organizational sciences that address these issues, remarkable advances in computer sciences are still scarce. However, some approaches can be found that address parts of these topics. In (Nandalal et al., 2003) a conflict support system for water resources planning is detailed. However, this work presents a rather static perception of the conflict. No conflict style inventory is used despite the method proposed to resolve the conflict being based in two styles of handling it. In (Ludwig, 2008a), the authors developed an agent-based assistant for electronic negotiations, using the Thomas-Kilmann Conflict Model (Kilmann & Thomas, 1977) and negotiation data from an experiment conducted by human negotiators. In this approach, the process of capturing the participant's behavior uses assumptions based on preferences, obtained through questionnaires. In (Yiu & Construction, 2005)the author applied the Rahim Organizational Conflict Inventory (Rahim, 1983) to classify five negotiation/conflict styles, but the approach has a similar problem to the one of (Ludwig, 2008b) both rely on self-report instruments to measure the personal conflict handling styles. In (Jain & Solomon, 2000) is highlighted the unaddressed issue of the participants' predisposition to conflict on negotiation outcomes and concludes that future research may focus on the effects of realistic elements of negotiations, such as task complexity and participants' predisposition to conflict. Moreover, the work of (Holt & DeVore, 2005) points out the need for a rigorous conflict resolution instrument that measures conflict behavior rather than the self-report instruments used in the past decades. Also, Holt underlines that the participants' interpretations of the conflict style versus the perception by others of their conflict style is critical but still an unexplored topic. The fundamental idea is that these issues should be addressed with dynamic and automated conflict style classification methods incorporated in a conflict support framework that also provides perception/cognition tests.

Intersection of Conflict Resolution and ICT

The relationship between conflict and ICTs was analyzed. It was also explored the challenges that individuals face in using online technology for collaboration and conflict mediation purposes. Therefore, it can be concluded that developments in ICTs have played a critical role in exacerbating and/or resolving conflicts. Was also shown how recent Artificial Intelligence innovations can facilitate knowledge acquisition, network building, and the analysis and presentation of conflict-related data. Indeed, a number of online-specific techniques have been developed to take advantage of the new technology; these include automated negotiation (without human intervention) and negotiation support systems. Meanwhile, regarding the review of literature in previous sections, the main drawbacks of current approaches can thus be summarized:

- The need for a rigorous conflict resolution instrument that measures conflict behavior rather than the self-report instruments;
- Acquisition of information is performed in rudimentary ways, without support;
- Current trend continues to focus mainly on the development of technological tools, leaving aside important issues that are present in traditional dispute resolution processes;

Current conflict handling systems have no autonomy and still rely largely on the human.

In this context, must be pointed out that the use of ICT and Ambient Intelligence applications are not entirely risk-free. In any online medium, communications and data may be intercepted, monitored, altered, accessed, downloaded or even destroyed. However, can be mitigated and minimized through encryption technologies, firewalls, and passwords, as well as privacy enhancing technologies to ensure that information about parties remains confidential and secure.

Intelligent Support of Conflict Resolution

To achieve the goals exposed previously, should be regard several sub-fields of Artificial Intelligence as particularly interesting. The use of Artificial Intelligence and more particularly Ambient Intelligence techniques can help to suppress these gaps. In this work, it is suggested that an intelligent environment for conflict handling should be envisioned as a virtual space in which disputants have a variety of conflict resolution tools at their disposal. Participants or managers should select any tool they consider appropriate for the resolution of their conflict and use the tools in any order or manner they desire, or they can be guided through the process. It is also planned that the process of decision-making should be enriched with valuable knowledge (contextual and behavioral information). Below is presented a scratch of an intelligent system that tries to unveil a way to overcome the main drawbacks elicited from the literature research. Once again, the underlying intent is to outline a system capable of assisting parties to overcome the challenges of conventional conflict handling techniques, in which a user just interacts with the system.

A way to achieve it is to extend the traditional technology-based conflict resolution/management systems, in which a user just interacts with the system, with a new component. A new component that allows for the dynamic adaptation to the interaction context so that users (parties and the conflict manager) can naturally take advantage of interacting with an intelligent system. In other words, an AmI system that surround the user pervasively in his environment, and are invisible to him, providing information ubiquitously gathered. This information, which is transparently provided to a conflict resolution platform, potentially without the interference of the user, will allow the development of shapeable and more flexible conflict resolution approaches.

Taking these premises into account, is presented as follows a general characterization of a system that, in our opinion, will provide some guidelines in how to upgrade the conventional conflict handling to a context-aware framework. The general system working is to sense conflict context, acquire it and then make reasoning on the acquired context and hence acting in on the parties' behalf. Therefore, the system should build up a profile of each party and should be able to link that profile subsequently with the individual performance. While the user conscientiously interacts with the system and materialize his/her decisions and actions, a parallel and transparent process should take place. The aim is to sensory data be conveyed through synchronized and invisible (to the user) means to the conflict support platform. Afterward, a transformation of the sensory data into useful information should be taken. Consequently, after the appropriate sequence of data transformations, the platform must allow the conflict manager to make a contextualized analysis of the user's data. However, the contextualized analysis of user's data is more critical when the data is from heterogeneous sources of diverse nature like sensors, user profile, and social media and also at different timestamps. To overcome this, the features that are extracted from multiple sensor observations should be combined into a single concatenated feature vector and then should feed different classification modules (conflict styles, stress recognition, etc.). To integrate all the multimodal evidence is planned to use a decision level integration strategy. Examples of decision level fusion methods utilized in this work include weighted decision methods and machine-learning techniques and are detailed in previous work (Gomes, Oliveira, Carneiro, Novais, & Neves, 2014). Finally, having access to the context and behavioral information of the parties, the conflict manager must have the possibility to decide what to do. For this, the platform should provide a systematic way of supporting this process of decision-making. Some insight into this issue can be provided in previous work. Namely, in (Gomes, Oliveira, Silva, Carneiro, & Novais, 2014) work is presented a novel approach in which an experiment has been designed to address the estimation of relevant aspects of human-computer interactions in sensory rich environments. In particular, findings presented herein may help to identify the degree of relationship between one's personality characteristics and his current stress state. These results can maximize the benefits of the communication within virtual environment applications in fields such conflict resolution. At the same time, another study that identifying and cataloguing the behavior of parties during a negotiation may help to clarify the role stress plays in the process. To do it the research team focused on gathering behavioral and contextual information about participants and identifying (based on mathematical models) the conflict styles used by each party (Gomes, Oliveira, Carneiro, et al., 2014).

A FRAMEWORK TO HANDLE CONFLICT RESOLUTION

For clarity, the definitions of framework are varied and can refer to software libraries, software applications, structural components of a building, and everything in between. A general definition of framework is "a basic structure underlying a system, concept, or text". In this discussion, framework will refer to a conceptual application that is the basic structure utilized to identify, frame, and understand constituents of conflict. Defining the parameters of conflict is significant not only from a theoretical viewpoint but from a practical one, it is important to consider the conceptual consequences and to find a working definition to aid resolution. Taking this premise into consideration, in this section will be carried out an analysis about how a framework can cover all the phases (as proposed by (Robbins & Judge, 2007)) in a conflict process and how it can be developed.

Modeling Oppositions and Incompatibilities

When conflict is still latent, certain factors like communication, structure and personal variables, can trigger it. It is important to highlight that it is not necessary to have the simultaneous occurrence of all three factors. In this phase, a generic model to identify oppositions or incompatibilities of the mentioned types of an organization/group of people must be selected. Another critical factor is interpersonal or group relationships. Interpersonal situations of conflict are dependent on relationships with the people, on the differences in position/power between individuals/groups and the different tasks/roles of each person/group. Understanding the dynamics of power gives us an understanding of the structure. In this point, an appropriate approach may be the development of a generic model to identify oppositions or incompatibilities that erupt from the situation. Specifically, should deal with disagreements at two levels: objective or subjective. To address objective incompatibilities, the approach should follow an economic point of view, underpinned by game theory (in which each issue in dispute is assigned to a utility value). On the other hand, to deal with subjective disagreements (usually related to personal values and harder to deal with), an ad hoc model should be defined.

Identification and Characterization of the Conflict

Before attempting to manage a conflict, it is necessary to identify the cognitive resources of each party that is experiencing the conflict. Several issues must be addressed in this phase and they are summarized as follows:

- Definition of a model for testing the participants' perception of an actual conflict. Through an analysis of the early background information provided by the participant, the system should highlight if he is or is not aware of the conflict and its nature;
- Definition of a model of the influence of emotions on the escalation of the conflict. Emotions have a significant role in human relationships. In conflict resolution, emotions can be used as a measure of the convictions of the individual and as a measure of the level of escalation;
- Definition of a complete model for characterizing a conflict (e.g. sources, objects of conflict, background information on parties involved). This model should address all the main topics involved in the conflict and its management. Moreover, should support the development of the technological framework to be developed, giving it a strong theoretical background.

Development of a Conflict Support Framework

The central phase of conflict consists in dealing with the actual conflict. Simply speaking, it is the phase in which disputants attempt to cope and manage conflict. From a technological point of view, the pretended framework (a first draft was previously presented) should support the decision-making of the conflict manager. A support characterized by, among other things, facilitating access to information such as the handling style of the parties or their levels of stress. To do it, several main functionalities must be considered and developed:

- **Select the Stakeholders:** The first logic step is to define the stakeholders. These may include human specialists (e.g. mediators, arbitrators, and law experts), the parties and system agents with specific tasks. This first step, therefore, depends on the specific details of each implementation scenario. In other words, the selection will depend on the nature of human experts as also on factors like the part of the law addressed or the conflict methodology (e.g. mediation, negotiation, arbitration);

- **Development of a Service-Oriented Architecture:** The framework for the support the negotiation process should focus on workflows, enhancing the communication between the parties. And for the collection and the providing of information for the manager. The most suitable way of guarantee this requirements is, in our opinion, to underpin the architecture under a service-oriented approach;

- **Generation of Arguments/Solutions:** The focus should be on the development of algorithms for automatic generation of arguments or solutions. The main objective is to provide the platform the capability of intelligently generating arguments that the parties (or the manager) can use to influence the behavior of the participants. Build on previous work, it is suggested the use of evolutionary algorithms for the generation of solutions and their utility, supporting the manager in one of the hardest tasks in negotiation;

- **Incorporation of Machine Learning:** The main objective is to research and apply machine-learning algorithms that can contribute to an automated or semi-automated improvement of some aspects of the framework. Moreover, the framework should also collect statistical information on the success or failure of the strategies followed. This will improve the system's overall performance since successful strategies for similar cases will be preferred over the other;

- **Predicting and Classifying Human Behavior:** Suggested by (Galitsky & de la Rosa, 2011) the following sequence of problems needs to be solved for predicting and classifying human behavior using a conflict management system:
  - Discover how to reconstruct behavior patterns from the intelligent environment sensory/interaction data. (Galitsky & de la Rosa, 2011) stands that it turns out that communicative actions and their subjects are essential elements of behavior discourse.
  - Construct a formal language to represent communicative actions. Find attributes of communicative actions so that similarity between them can be defined. Analyze how the mental space is "covered" by communicative actions, and form a substitution matrix for them to measure similarity, can be a way of doing it.
  - Build a way to extract information from the natural language for communicative actions and their subjects and parameters (which is significantly harder due to implicit references to these subjects in natural language).

- ◦ Observe that the sequence of behavior patterns can be packaged as a scenario. Defining a scenario as a graph including communicative actions and interaction between their subjects, based on causal links and relations for argumentation seems a plausible method of dealing with this.
- ◦ Define relationships between scenarios via subgraphs, with respective operations on vertices and arcs. Define similarity between scenarios based on graphs and similarities between individual communicative actions.
- ◦ Build a machine learning framework and select a particular learning approach well suited to operate with scenario graphs. Evaluate whether concept learning is an adequate approach.

The development of such a framework should result in a set of services or functionalities that will support the work of the manager and improve parties' commitment to the resolution process. The underlying idea is to release the participants from processual issues so that they can dedicate more time to more complex issues.

CONCLUSION

One of the principal aims of this chapter is not only to describe a comprehensive understanding of the concept and the constituents of conflict, but also to identify the potential inputs for the development of a conceptual and technological framework to manage conflict. The achieved outcomes were presented in each section and resulted in a thorough knowledge about the main domains addressed. In this specific point, the underlying intent was to determine the main techniques and paradigms used in this field as well as the anatomy of a conflict process. In our opinion, this will challenge individual assumptions as to the nature of a conflict, providing a broad guide as to what the dimensions of a given conflict may be. Moreover, it was also aimed to evaluate the relationship between conflict and ICTs. The chapter seeks to explain how technological advances and innovation can facilitate the delivery of a more informed and practical approach to deal with complex conflict-related issues. In that sense, this work moves forward exposing an approach based on the idea that an AmI system has the capability to create scenarios that enhance the possibilities of finding the path to achieving functional outcomes, using accessible and perceivable information. In other words, the primary concern was to provide the building blocks of an environment where a group of devices could cohabit and share information towards a common goal: sensing and acting in a non-intrusive way to influence the conflict process. The primary concern was to design an environment where a group of devices could cohabit and share information towards a common goal: sensing and acting in a non-intrusive way to influence the conflict process.

REFERENCES

Aarts, E., & Grotenhuis, F. (2011). Ambient Intelligence 2. 0. *Towards Synergetic Prosperity*, *3*, 3–11. doi:10.3233/AIS-2011-0090

Barki, H., & Hartwick, J. (2004). Conceptualizing the construct of interpersonal conflict. *The International Journal of Conflict Management*, *15*(3), 216–244. doi:10.1108/eb022913

Blake, R., & Mouton, J. (1964). *The Managerial Grid*. Houston, TX: Gulf Publishing.

Boulding, K. E. (1963). *Conflict and defense*. New York, NY: Harper & Row.

Burton, J. W. (1998). Conflict Resolution: The Human Dimension. *The International Journal for Peace Studies*. Retrieved from http://www.gmu.edu/programs/icar/ijps/vol3_1/burton.htm

Buss, H. (2009). *Measuring and Reducing the Cost of Conflict at Work in UNHCR: The Business Case of Conflict Management*. Institut universitaire Kurt Bösch.

Carneiro, D., Gomes, M., Novais, P., & Neves, J. (2011). Developing Dynamic Conflict Resolution Models Based on the Interpretation of Personal Conflict Styles. In L. Antunes & H. S. Pinto (Eds.), *EPIA* (Vol. 7026, pp. 44–58). Springer. doi:10.1007/978-3-642-24769-9_4

Coleman, P. T. (2003). Characteristics of Protracted, Intractable Conflict: Toward the Development of a Metaframework-I. *Peace and Conflict*, *9*(1), 1–37. doi:10.1207/S15327949PAC0901_01

Cooper, S., & Taleb-Bendiab, A. (1998). CONCENSUS: Multi-party negotiation support for conflict resolution in concurrent engineering design. *Journal of Intelligent Manufacturing*, *9*(2), 155–159. doi:10.1023/A:1008820029707

Coser, L. A. (1956). *The Functions of Social Conflict*. Academic Press.

de Dreu, C. K. W. (2008). The virtue and vice of workplace conflict : Food for (pessimistic) thought. *Journal of Organizational Behavior*, *29*(1), 5–18. doi:10.1002/job.474

Deutsch, M. (1973). *The resolution of conflict: Constructive and destructive processes*. New Haven, CT: Yale University Press.

Deutsch, M. (2008). Cooperation and Conflict: A Personal Perspective on the History of the Social Psychological Study of Conflict Resolution. In International Handbook of Organizational Teamwork and Cooperative Working (pp. 9–43). John Wiley & Sons Ltd. http://doi.org/ doi:<ALIGNMENT.qj></ALIGNMENT>10.1002/9780470696712.ch2

Furlong, G. T. (2006). The conflict resolution toolbox: models and maps for analyzing diagnosing and resolving conflict. New Delhi: Wiley India (P) Ltd.

Galitsky, B., & de la Rosa, J. L. (2011). Concept-based learning of human behavior for customer relationship management. *Information Sciences*, *181*(10), 2016–2035. doi:10.1016/j.ins.2010.08.027

Gomes, M., Oliveira, T., Carneiro, D., Novais, P., & Neves, J. (2014). Studying the Effects of Stress on Negotiation Behavior. *Cybernetics and Systems*, *45*(3), 279–291. doi:10.1080/01969722.2014.894858

Gomes, M., Oliveira, T., Silva, F., Carneiro, D., & Novais, P. (2014). Establishing the Relationship between Personality Traits and Stress in an Intelligent Environment. In *Modern Advances in Applied Intelligence* (pp. 378–387). Springer International Publishing. doi:10.1007/978-3-319-07467-2_40

Holt, J. L., & DeVore, C. J. (2005). Culture, gender, organizational role, and styles of conflict resolution: A meta-analysis. *International Journal of Intercultural Relations*, *29*(2), 165–196. doi:10.1016/j.ijintrel.2005.06.002

Infante, E. (1998). On the interpersonal conflict definition: Cluster analysis application to the semantic study. *Revista de Psicología Social*, *13*(3), 485–493. doi:10.1174/021347498760349733

Jain, B. A., & Solomon, J. S. (2000). The effect of task complexity and conflict handling styles on computer-supported negotiations. *Information & Management*, *37*(4), 161–168. doi:10.1016/S0378-7206(99)00049-X

Jehn, K. A. (1995). A Multimethod Examination of the Benefits and Detriments of Intragroup Conflict. *Administrative Science Quarterly*, *40*(2), 256–282. doi:10.2307/2393638

Jehn, K. A. (1997). A qualitative analysis of conflict types and dimensions in organizational groups. *Administrative Science Quarterly*, *42*(3), 530–557. doi:10.2307/2393737

Kilmann, R. H., & Thomas, K. W. (1977). Developing a Forced-Choice Measure of Conflict-Handling Behavior: The MODE Instrument. *Educational and Psychological Measurement*, *37*(2), 309–325. doi:10.1177/001316447703700204

Kolb, D. M., & Putnam, L. L. (1992). The multiple faces of conflict in organizations. *Journal of Organizational Behavior*, *13*(3), 311–324. doi:10.1002/job.4030130313

Lodder, A. R., & Zeleznikow, J. (2005). Preface. *Artificial Intelligence and Law*, *13*(2), 189–192. doi:10.1007/s10506-006-9010-4

Ludwig, S. A. (2008a). Agent-Based Assistant for e-Negotiations. *Work (Reading, Mass.)*, 514–524.

Ludwig, S. A. (2008b). Agent-based assistant for e-negotiations. In *Proceedings of the 17th international conference on Foundations of intelligent systems* (pp. 514–524). Berlin: Springer-Verlag. doi:10.1007/978-3-540-68123-6_56

March, J. G., & Simon, H. A. (1958). *Organizations*. New York: Wiley.

Mayer, B. (2000). *The dynamics of conflict resolution: A practitioners guide*. Wiley.

Moore, C. W. (1986). *The Mediation Process: Practical Strategies for Resolving Conflict*. Wiley.

Moore, C. W. (1996). *The Mediation Process: Practical Strategies for Resolving Conflict* (2nd ed.). Wiley.

Nair, N. (2008). Towards understanding the role of emotions in conflict: A review and future directions. *The International Journal of Conflict Management*, *19*(4), 359–381. doi:10.1108/10444060810909301

Nandalal, K. D. W., & Simonovic, S. P. (2003). Conflict Resolution Support System: A Software for the Resolution of Conflicts in Water Resource Management. University of Western Ontario.

Pondy, L. R. (1967). *Organizational Conflict: Concepts and Models* (Vol. 2). Sage Publications, Inc.

Rahim, M. A. (1983). A Measure of Styles of Handling Interpersonal Conflict. *Academy of Management Journal*, *26*(2), 368–376. doi:10.2307/255985 PMID:10263067

Robbins, S. P., & Judge, T. (2007). *Organizational Behavior*. Pearson/Prentice Hall.

Tjosvold, D. (2006). Defining conflict and making choices about its management. *The International Journal of Conflict Management*, *17*(2), 87–95. doi:10.1108/10444060610736585

Verma, V. K. (1998). Conflict Management. In *The Project Management Institute Project Management Handbook*. Jeffery Pinto.

Watkin, L. (2012). *Environmental conflict and decision-making: the case of hydroelectric power*. Academic Press.

Yiu, T. W., & Construction, C. U. (2005). *A behavioral analysis of construction dispute negotiation*. City University of Hong Kong. Retrieved from http://books.google.pt/books?id=pm7VNwAACAAJ

KEY TERMS AND DEFINITIONS

Ambient Intelligence (AmI): Is the vision that people will be surrounded by intelligent objects that can sense the context and respond according to the desires of the people, assisting people in their day-to-day tasks, making their lives easier. AmI is a multidisciplinary topic, since it combines the features of many of the areas in Computer Science.

Conflict: Is an opposition of interests or values which, in a certain way, disturbs or blocks an action or a decision making-process. In other words, is a long-term, deep-rooted problem that involve seemingly non-negotiable issues and is resistant to resolution.

Conflict Management: Involves the control, but not resolution, of a conflict. The goal of conflict management is to intervene in ways that make the ongoing conflict more beneficial and less damaging to all sides.

Conflict Resolution: Is a process of resolving dispute or disagreement. It mainly aims at reconciling opposing arguments in a manner that going beyond negotiating interests to meet all sides' basic needs, while simultaneously finding a way to identify the causal factors behind the conflict, and find ways to deal with them.

Dispute: Are short-term disagreements that are relatively easy to resolve.

Information and Communications Technology - or Technologies (ICT): Is an umbrella term that includes any communication device or application, as well as the various services and applications associated with them.

Intelligent Environments (IEs): Are spaces with embedded systems and information and communication technologies creating interactive spaces that bring computation into the physical world and enhance occupant's experiences.

Negotiation: Is a collaborative and informal process by means of which parties communicate and, without external influence, try to achieve an outcome that can satisfy both.

Chapter 2
Biometrics and Data Protection:
These Data Are Derived from an Individual

Francisco Pacheco Andrade
Universidade do Minho, Portugal

Teresa Coelho Moreira
Universidade do Minho, Portugal

ABSTRACT

The special nature of the characteristics used in biometric systems can present privacy challenges that might not arise with traditional identification methods, such as paper documents, because these data are derived from an individual's physical or behavioural features on the basis of a specific procedure, which is partly automated and yields a (reference) template. On account of their nature, these data require special precautions and the respect of the principles related with privacy and data protection.

INTRODUCTION

Ten years ago the world was adjusting to the fact that people could access information in the privacy of their own home from the World Wide Web. Today, technology has taken society to another plateau; people can be tracked wherever they go and whatever they do.

Originally, the word "biometrics" (Alterman, 2003)[1] meant applying mathematical measurements to biology. Nowadays, the term refers to a range of techniques, devices and systems that enable machines to recognize individuals, or confirm or authenticate their identities. Such systems measure and analyze people's physical and behavioral attributes, such as facial features, voice patterns, fingerprints, palm prints, finger and palm vein patterns, structures of the eye, iris or retina, or gait[2].

Biometrics involves techniques used to identify[3] individuals based on a particular trait or physical characteristic unique to that individual or on a behavioral characteristic of an individual[4]. Any human physiological and/or behavioral characteristic can be used as a biometric characteristic as long as it satisfies some requirements like universality, distinctiveness, permanence and collectability.

DOI: 10.4018/978-1-5225-0245-6.ch002

Biometric data are digitized, that is, the data which are recorded are held in digital form and can therefore be subject to detailed computer analysis. Biometrics potentially raises profound privacy implications and a wide and uncontrolled utilization of biometrics raises concerns with regard to the protection of fundamental rights (Alterman, 2003)[5] and freedoms of individuals[6].

Biometric systems record personal information about identifiable individuals[7]. That means their use falls under the provisions of the *Portuguese Data Protection Law, law 67/98, 26 of October and, in the employment relationship under the remit of article 18 from the Portuguese Labor Code.*

Article 2 a) of Directive 95/46/EC defines "personal data" as "any information relating to an identified or identifiable natural person (…) ; an identifiable person is one who can be identified, directly or indirectly, in particular by reference to an identification number or to one or more factors specific to his physical, physiological, mental (…) identity". Also Recital 26 adds the following explanation "to determine whether a person is identifiable, account should be taken of all the means likely reasonably to be used either by the controller or by any other person to identify the said person".

In accordance with this definition, measures of biometric identification or their digital translation in a template form in most cases are personal data. And, one must not forget that some biometric data could be considered sensitive in the meaning of Article 8 of Directive 95/46/EC and in particular, data revealing racial or ethnic origin or data concerning health[8].

The special nature of the characteristics used in biometric systems can present privacy challenges that might not arise with traditional identification methods, such as paper documents, because these data are derived from an individual's physical or behavioral features on the basis of a specific procedure, which is partly automated and yields a (reference) template. So, the blanket, unrestricted use of biometric data is not permitted. On account of their nature, these data require special precautions and the respect of the principles related with privacy and data protection, especially the principles of legitimacy, proportionality and transparency, because according to Article 6 of Directive 95/46/EC, personal data must be collected for specified, explicit and legitimate purposes and not further processed in a way incompatible with those purposes. In addition, personal data must be adequate, relevant and not excessive in relation to the purposes for which they are collected and further processed.

It is also of core importance to pay attention to some privacy-friendly principles when using these data and a previous study of Privacy Impact Assessment and security should also be a primary concern because biometric data are irrevocable.

Biometric data is collected at a starting point, referred to as the time of enrolment. Identities can subsequently be established or authenticated when new data is collected and compared with the stored records.

Using biometric data may only be justified in specific cases by taking account of the relevant purposes and the context in which the data are to be processed[9]. According to the new regulation on electronic identification and trust services for electronic transactions (Regulation EU Nr 910/2014) electronic identification must comply with the principles relating to the protection of personal data provided for in Directive 95/46/EC and authentication for online service should concern processing of only those identification data that are adequate, relevant and not excessive to grant access to that service online. These principles must be applied considering the distinction between physical and behavioral biometrics, and the latter are not necessarily innocuous, since the way someone taps on the laptop, associated with sensoring, may be enough to disclose the identity and build a profile of the user of online services. Furthermore, it must be ensured the compatibility between norms and principles concerning Data Protection and the norms and principles concerning the identification of users in electronic environments.

In this regard, the new possibility opened by the Regulation EU Nr 910/2014 on website authentication services should be considered as a tool for enhancing Data Protection and thus enhance trust on online services. But this will only be true if security and liability obligations for service providers are considered.

BIOMETRICS

Identification may be obtained through the use of the so called biometric (Mordini & Petrini, 2007)[10] techniques based on the recognition of characteristics of an individual through an equipment fit for that purpose (Alterman, 2003)[11]. Biometrics may be broadly understood as a technology capable of converting physical characteristics of an individual into digital data[12]. This kind of technology may adopt two quite different approaches: on one side, the capture, measure and digitization of determined physiological characteristics, which we usually call physiological biometrics, including among others the capture and processing of fingerprints, face recognition, geometrics of the hand, iris recognition and so on. On the other side, the possibility of capturing, measuring and digitizing behavioral characteristics, such as the way an individual speaks (voice recognition), the way an individual writes or signs or even the way an individual taps the keys of a computer. We call this group of biometric techniques behavioral biometrics. Yet, the idea of biometrics identification and authentication is not consensual. Some authors do not consider the possibility of biometric signatures or face photographies. Others do not include voice recognition as behavioral biometrics (Mordini & Ashton, 2012)[13]. Some even think that psychological based techniques should be considered[14].

Biometric identification may be voluntary or non-voluntary, mandatory or optional. An obvious advantage of biometrics is that it ensures a very high level of confidence concerning the identification of a person (Chinchilla, 2011)[15]. By the use of these techniques it can be stated, with a very high probability (or low margin of error) that the person behind an electronic terminal really is the one who says it is (O'Connor, 1998)[16]. And yet, of course these techniques are not infallible[17]. Although the error margins are estimated in less than 5% - which is a quite low margin of error for these techniques to be considered quite reliable – the truth is that, with the only exception of the reading and digitization of fingerprints, the biometric characteristics are not necessarily unique for each individual (O'Connor, 1998)[18]. And yet, we tend to consider the margins of error as negligible. Thus being, it is not because of the error possibility that biometric methods will not be used as a way of identifying someone. Furthermore, it is obvious that biometrics deal a lot with statistics (Alterman, 2003)[19] and for that reason most of its techniques may not be considered 100% sure (Chinchilla, 2011)[20]. Furthermore, physical biometrics are faced with the unequivocal fact that people get older and the body changes over time (Alterman, 2003). The ageing process poses thus difficult problems for the use of biometrics (Rebera & Mordini, 2013). Furthermore, the use of biometrics require and is highly dependent on the capability of dealing with complex technologies (Chinchilla, 2011)[21].

But we must also be aware that capturing physical biometrical data may raise delicate issues concerning the rights and freedom of citizens (Mordini & Petrini, 2007)[22] and its use may even be confronted with legal (eventually constitutional) constraints (O'Connor, 1998). And the arguments that have been used in order to sustain that biometric technologies do not raise significant privacy concerns certainly are rebuttable (Alterman, 2003).

Less intrusive appears to be the use of the above referred techniques of behavioral biometrics, namely the one based on the digital processing of the handwritten signature of an individual, the "biometric or dynamics" signature, which digitally translates the geometry and dynamics of handwritten signing, availing in the digital environment the elements that make an handwritten signature as a unique feature of an individual, thus allowing the identification of the signer. The point in "biometrical signature" is that it doesn't just capture the forms of the signature but it also captures, measures and digitize the biometric data, such as speed, acceleration, and sequence of forms [23], making the whole a truly unique sequence for each individual .

BIOMETRICS AND DATA PROTECTION

Many people are increasingly concerned about adequate protection of their biometric data. The EU Data Protection Regulation establishes the definition of biometric data in Article 4, number 11, considering that "'biometric data' means any *personal* data *resulting from specific technical processing* relating to the physical, physiological or behavioral characteristics of an individual which allow*s or confirms the* unique identification *of that individual*, such as facial images, or dactyloscopic data" but it is interesting to notice that, despite this definition, the latest version approved by the Council of European Union, excluded biometric data from article 9, in a different position of the one taken by the European Parliament. When comparing the two versions, the version of the European Parliament in article 9, establishing the "processing of special categories of personal data" included in number 1 biometric data. But this reference was deleted in the version approved by the Council of the European Union, despite the critics of some countries. And, in fact, we consider that some biometric data should be considered sensitive data[24] like the data relating to private life as fingerprints, traditionally associated with illiteracy and crime and face recognition systems can reveal health data or the race and some biometric data is obtained without the owner being aware. So, we consider that these data could be protected by art. 7 of Law No 67/98. And the Regulation of the European Union establishes in Recital 41 that "Personal data which are, by their nature, particularly sensitive in relation to fundamental rights *and freedoms*, deserve specific protection *as the context of their processing may create important risks* (Chinchilla, Rigoberto 2011)[25] *for the fundamental rights and freedoms. These data should also include personal data revealing racial or ethnic origin*".

This type of data is associated with unique characteristics of the person and has specific requirements, in particular the universality of these data, in the sense that they are present in all people, its uniqueness, since it must be distinctive for each person ; permanence, because each person's biometric data remains the same with time (Rebera and Mordini, 2013)[26]; and measurability and accessibility that can exist depending on their nature: some are based on the morphological, physical or physiological nature, and evaluate the physiological characteristics of a person such as fingerprinting, the analysis of the finger image, iris recognition, retinal examination, the face recognition, hand size, recognizing the shape of the ear, the detection of body odor, voice recognition, the analysis of DNA structure; others are based on behavioral analysis, evaluating people's behavior, such as checking the handwritten signature, analysis of typing, analysis of the floor.

The use of these biometric techniques and biometrics presents many philosophical, sociological, political and ethical issues [27] that become even more relevant if these data are stored in centralized databases or in the cloud. This results in two divergent interests: on the one hand the desire to ensure safety in any location and, on the other hand, the need to protect the privacy of individuals (Alterman, 2003)[28].

JURISPRUDENCE FROM THE ECJ

There are some cases of the ECJ that concern biometric data.

The *Willems* judgment concerns biometric data collected for passports, as provided for in an EU Regulation of 2004, as amended in 2009. In fact, the CJEU has ruled on this Regulation several times before, like in the *UK v Council*, Case C-137/05, of 18 December 2007, it ruled that the UK could not participate in the Regulation, since it was closely linked to the parts of Schengen rules (the abolition of internal border controls) in which the UK didn't participate and in *Schwarz*, Case C-291/12, of 17 October 2013 the ECJ ruled that the Regulation was valid from two different angles, as it was correctly adopted using the 'legal base' allowing the EU to adopt measures on external border control, and the interference which it entailed with the right to privacy was justified by the interest in ensuring the identity of passport holders and the validity of the passport, deciding that "Examination of the question referred has revealed nothing capable of affecting the validity of Article 1(2) of Council Regulation (EC) No 2252/2004 of 13 December 2004 on standards for security features and biometrics in passports and travel documents issued by Member States, as amended by Regulation (EC) No 444/2009 of the European Parliament and of the Council of 6 May 2009.".

In Willems the national court had two questions. First of all, did the Regulation apply to some types of identity cards, given that they can in effect be used as passports for travel within the EU? Secondly, the national court asked the CJEU to interpret the data protection rules applicable to the further use of biometric data after it was collected for the purposes of passports. The latter question stemmed from the concern of the litigants in this case that their biometric data would be stored on a centralized database with inadequate security, which would be used for other purposes without a clear identification of who would have access to it[29].

The national court's second question was whether "Article 4(3) of [the passport Regulation, read] in light of Articles 7 and 8 of the Charter of Fundamental Rights of the [EU], Article 8(2) of the [ECHR] and Article 7(f) of [the current data protection Directive], read in conjunction with Article 6(1)(b) of that Directive", required a guarantee that when collecting biometric data under the Regulation, Member States had to apply a 'purpose limitation' rule that such data could only be used for the original purpose for which the passport was issued.

In this case the ECJ decided that "1. Article 1(3) of Council Regulation (EC) No 2252/2004 of 13 December 2004 on standards for security features and biometrics in passports and travel documents is-sued by Member States, as amended by Regulation (EC) No 444/2009 of the European Parliament and of the Council of 6 May 2009, must be interpreted as meaning that that regulation is not applicable to identity cards issued by a Member States to its nationals, such as Netherlands identity cards, regardless of the period of validity and the possibility of using them for the purposes of travel outside that State " and that "2. Article 4(3) of Regulation No 2252/2004, as amended by Regulation No 444/2009, must be interpreted as meaning that it does not require the Member States to guarantee, in their legislation, that biometric data collected and stored in accordance with that regulation will not be collected, processed and used for purposes other than the issue of the passport or travel document, since that is not a matter which falls within the scope of that regulation".

BIOMETRIC DATA IN THE EMPLOYMENT RELATIONSHIP: ARTICLE 18 OF THE PORTUGUESE LABOUR CODE

In Portuguese legal framework the Labour Code establishes some rules regarding the use of biometric data in the employment relationship.

It should nevertheless be clear when analyzing employee data protection and specifically biometric data in the employment relationship, that specific attention must be drawn to the particularities of the employment environment. Indeed, an employment relationship implies, as a general rule, a subordinate relationship. This means that the employer is contractually allowed to exercise authority over the employee and to treat some personal data and, in some cases, even sensitive data. Still, the individual is only subject to the authority of the employer and to this treatment in so far as this is embodied in the specific employment relationship, in other words, in so far as this is relevant for the employment contract. Furthermore, the existence of an employment relationship does not take away the respect of the right to privacy and human dignity. More in particular, monitoring issues will need to take the employee's right to privacy and the protection of his/her personal data into account.

The purpose intended by employers in using this type of data[30] must be based on the need to expedite the achievement of a target that the law recognizes integrate within their power of control. But still, it seems that only in exceptional situations, notably security, is possible to install such systems. We always have to bear in mind the principle of proportionality[31] and verify that the intended purpose could not be obtained by a less intrusive way[32].

The particularity of the use of these data results from the need that the employees has to accept that elements of his physical or morphological identity are captured and stored in a database and presented before a "recognition system" at the beginning and at the end of the daily working period.

We consider it important to carry out a weighting of interests involved to assess the lawfulness of the use of these data types, being preferable to adopt a careful and realistic attitude to use because some biometric technologies are not conveniently tested, presenting thus some risk to the employees privacy.

Thus, it seems that some principles that have to be met at the time of using this type of data are:

It is necessary to occur in the first place, a weighting of suitability and necessity of the environment and the compliance of the reasons given to the principle of proportionality; Compliance with these principles implies, first, a clear definition of the purpose for which the biometric information is collected and processed. It is also necessary to evaluate in terms of proportionality[33] and legitimacy and to see the risks relating to the protection of fundamental rights and freedoms of individuals and, in particular, to examine whether the intended purpose could not be achieved in a less intrusive way.

The employer, before the adoption of any form of this type of control of the biometric data of the employees has to respect the legitimate purpose. This principle is in article 6.°, n.° 1, paragraph b) of the Directive 95/46/EC, and in the art. 5.°, n.° 1, paragraph b), of the Portuguese Data Protection Act, and means that the purposes for which data are collected shall be specified, that these purposes must be explicit, i.e. fully and clearly expressed and that the purposes must be legitimate. One can imagine that for reasons related with the access of employees to same parts of the company it is possible to use this type of control.

It also means that workers' personal data can only be treated if it respect these principles, being essential the explicit definition of these purposes.

However, there is another principle that is essential, mainly when we are dealing with biometric data, which is the proportionality principle[34].

This principle specifies that the only personal data that may be collected is the one which is necessary to achieve the purposes of the data collection operation. In so far as doing so, the employer or the person or organization in charge of the operation should choose for secondary rather than primary data collection, anonymous rather than nominal monitoring, sampling rather than full-scale control, and for voluntary rather than compulsory surveillance and forms of control.

This principle tends to accomplish the search of the balance among the worker's obligations, that radiate of their labor contract, and the extent of constitutional freedom of their privacy, guaranteeing that the modulation of this fundamental right will be accomplished in the measure strictly indispensable to the respect of this principle, that is, with restrictions in the amount and in the quality.

This proportionality principle, when applied to the labor contract, presupposes a previous judgment on the need or indispensability of the measure and on the proportionality of the sacrifices that holds for the workers' fundamental rights.

This principle is in article 6.°, n.° 1, paragraph c) of Directive 95/46/EC, and in the art. 5.°, n.° 1, paragraph c), of the Portuguese Data Protection Act, and it means that the treatment of personal data should respect this principle and must be adequate, relevant and not excessive in relation to the purposes for which they are collected and/or further processed.

This proportionality principle is associated to the quality[35] of the personal data, constituting a fundamental factor for the legality of all data treatment.

In this way, it imposes, the exclusive treatment of the pertinent data in relation to the purpose for which they are collected, being the *ratio* of the norm the one that the treatment of personal data can only take place when it is indispensable for the initial purpose. It is always necessary to accomplish a previous judgment on the need or in the indispensability of the measure and a subsequent judgment on the proportionality of the sacrifices that it leads.

For the purposes of control and access, that is, authentication and verification, biometric systems based on physical characteristics which do not leave traces, such as hand shape, but not the fingerprints, or biometric systems that relate to physical characteristics, but whose data is not registered in a central computer but on a personal card that the employee should bring, or even a mobile phone or ATM card present less risks for the protection of fundamental rights and freedoms of individuals;

Another question that is very important is that the proof by biometric data has been increasingly called into question because of the systems are not 100% reliable. One example is that a person's fingerprint can change after an accident or even be difficult to read in some situations. Therefore, the employer cannot face the introduction of such systems as infallible instruments of recognition and should always accept the employees' opposition to their effectiveness (Guerra, 2004), (Castro, 2005) and (Lane III, 2003).

It is important also the principle of transparency[36] that consists of the knowledge of the surveillance[37] and of the control made by the employer. This principle is essential for the correct treatment of personal data, in general, and of the workers, in special. The employees have to be informed of how, where, when the control is made.

In Portugal, this type of control needs to be notified to the Portuguese National Commission on Protection of Personal Data and also to the Workers' Council who have ten days to give an opinion although it is not binding for the employer (Moreira, 2010), (CNPD – Portuguese National Data Protection Authority, 2004)[38].

CONCLUSION

1. Biometrics involves techniques used to identify individuals based on a particular trait or physical characteristic unique to that individual or on a behavioral characteristic of an individual. Any human physiological and/or behavioral characteristic can be used as a biometric characteristic as long as it satisfies some requirements like universality, distinctiveness, permanence and collectability.

2. Biometric systems record personal information about identifiable individuals. That means their use falls under the provisions of the Portuguese Data Protection Law, law 67/98, 26 of October and, in the employment relationship under the remit of article 18 from the Portuguese Labor Code.

3. This type of data is associated with unique characteristics of the person and has specific requirements, in particular the universality of these data, in the sense that they are present in all people, its uniqueness, since it must be distinctive for each person, permanence, because each person's biometric data remains the same with time and measurability and accessibility

4. The use of these biometric techniques and biometrics presents many philosophical, sociological, political and ethical issues that become even more relevant if these data are stored in centralized databases or in the cloud. This results in two divergent interests because on the one hand the desire to ensure safety in any location and, on the other hand, the need to protect the privacy of individuals.

5. Using biometric data may only be justified in specific cases by taking account of the relevant purposes and the context in which the data are to be processed.

6. One of these cases is in the employment relationship. However, to be possible to use biometric data there are requirements that have to be met.

It is necessary a weighting of suitability and necessity of the environment and the compliance of the reasons given to the principle of proportionality and the legitimacy principle. Compliance with these principles implies, first, a clear definition of the purpose for which the biometric information is collected and processed. It is also necessary to evaluate in terms of proportionality and legitimacy and to see the risks relating to the protection of fundamental rights and freedoms of individuals and, in particular, to examine whether the intended purpose could not be achieved in a less intrusive way.

It is also of core importance to comply with the principle of transparency that means that consists of the knowledge of the surveillance and of the control made by the employer.

REFERENCES

Alterman, A. (2003). A piece of yourself: Ethical issues in biometric identification. *Ethics and Information Technology, 5*(3), 139–150. doi:10.1023/B:ETIN.0000006918.22060.1f

Castro, C. S. (2005). *Direito da Informática, Privacidade e Dados Pessoais*. Coimbra: Almedina. (in Portuguese)

Chinchilla, R. (2011). Ethical and Social consequences of Biometric Technologies. *Journal of Industrial Technology, 27*(1).

Guerra, A. (2004). A privacidade no local de trabalho – as novas tecnologias e o controlo dos trabalhadores através de sistemas automatizados; uma abordagem ao Código do Trabalho. Almedina, Coimbra. (in Portuguese)

Hert, P., Gutwirth, S., Moscibroda, A., Wright, D., & Gonzale-Fuster, G. (2009). Legal Safeguards for Privacy and Data Protection in Ambient Intelligence. *Personal and Ubiquitous Computing, 13*(6), 435–444. doi:10.1007/s00779-008-0211-6

Lane, F. S. III. (2003). *The naked employee – how technology is compromising workplace privacy.* AMACOM.

Mordini, E., & Ashton, H. (2012). *The Transparent Body: Medical Information, Physical Privacy and Respect for Body Integrity. In Second Generation Biometrics: The Ethical, Legal and Social Context* (Vol. 11). The International Library of Ethics, Law and Technology. doi:10.1007/978-94-007-3892-8

Mordini, E., & Petrini, C. (2007). Ethical and Social implications of biometric identification technology. *Annali dell'Istituto Superiore di Sanita, 43*(1), 5–11. PMID:17536148

Moreira, T. C. (2010). *A Privacidade dos Trabalhadores e as Novas Tecnologias de Informação e Comunicação: contributo para um estudo dos limites do poder de controlo electrónico do empregador.* Coimbra: Almedina. (in Portuguese)

O'Connor, S. (1998). Collected, Tagged, & Archived: The Burgeoning Use of Biometrics in Personal Identification. *Bender's Immigr. Bull. 1245.*

Rebera, A. P., & Mordini, E. (2013). Age Factors in Biometric Processing. In The Institution of Engineering and Technology. Stevenage.

KEY TERMS AND DEFINITIONS

Behavioral Biometrics: The possibility of capturing, measuring and digitizing behavioral characteristics, such as the way an individual speaks (voice recognition), the way an individual writes or signs or even the way an individual taps the keys of a computer.

Biometrics: Techniques used to identify individuals based on a particular trait or physical characteristic unique to that individual or on a behavioral characteristic of an individual.

Electronic Control of the Employer: With the use of ICT technologies in the workplace there is a new power of the employer that is the electronic control related with the huge possibilities of control using ICT.

Employment Contract: The employment contract is in article 11 of Portuguese Labor Code and establishes that it is essential the existence of 3 elements: activity by the worker, the payment by the employer; and legal subordination.

Physiological Biometrics: The capture, measure and digitization of determined physiological characteristics.

Powers of the Employer: According to articles 97, 98 and 99 of Portuguese Labor Code the employer has the directive power, the disciplinary power and the regulatory power.

Sensitive Data: Personal data which are, by their nature, particularly sensitive in relation to fundamental rights and freedoms.

ENDNOTES

[1] "The term "biometric", and the concept of biometric identification, originated before the digital era. But today, and presumably for the future, every form of biometric identification is based on the comparison of an image with information stored in a computer database".

[2] See Office of the Privacy Commissioner of Canada, *Data at your fingerprints*.

[3] "Biometric systems "applications that use biometric technologies, which allow the automatic identification, and/or authentication/verification of a person. Authentication/verification applications are often used for various tasks in completely different areas, for different purposes and under the responsibility of a wide range of different entities.", Article 29 Data Protection Working Party "Opinion 3/2012 on developments in biometric technologies", adopted on 27th April 2013.

[4] "Biometric systems are tightly linked to a person because they can use a certain unique property of an individual for identification and or / authentication. While a person's biometric data can be deleted or altered the source from which they have been extracted can in general neither be altered nor deleted", Article 29 Data Protection Working Party "Opinion 3/2012 on developments in biometric technologies", adopted on 27th April 2013.

[5] "we should be wary when an author writes that "increasingly, the way to keep information secure id to offer up a piece of yourself... to be recorded and used to verify your identity".

[6] Article 29 Data Protection Working Party, *Working Documents on Biometrics*, 2003, p. 5.

[7] "While other new technologies that target large populations and have recently raised data protection concerns do not necessarily focus on establishing a direct link to a specific individual – or creating this link requires considerable efforts – biometric data, by their very nature, are directly linked to an individual", Article 29 Data Protection Working Party "Opinion 3/2012 on developments in biometric technologies" adopted on 27th April 2012.

[8] "it is now also possible to use biometric systems for categorization /segregation purposes." Article 29 Data Protection Working Party "Opinion 3/2012 on developments in biometric technologies", referred.

[9] "According to Article 7 of Directive 95/46/EC, the processing of biometric personal data can also be justified if it is "necessary for the purposes of the legitimate interests pursued by the controller or by the third party or parties to whom the data are disclosed, except where such interests are overridden by the interests for fundamental rights and freedoms of the data subject.", Article 29 Data Protection Working Party "Opinion 3/2012 on developments in biometric technologies", referred.

[10] "Biometrics can be used in two ways. The first is identification ("who is this person?"), in which a subject's identity is determined by comparing a measured biometric against a database of stored records: a one-to-many comparison. The second is verification ("is this person who he claims to be?"), which involves a one-to-one comparison between a measured biometric and one known to come from a particular person.".

[11] ""Biometric identification" is a general term for technologies that permit matches between a "live" digital image of a part of the body and a previously recorded image of the same part, usually indexed to personal or financial information".

[12] "...biological properties, behavioral aspects, physiological characteristics, living traits or repeatable actions where those features and/or actions are both unique to that individual and measurable, even if the patterns used in practice to technically measure them involve a certain degree of probability.", Article 29 Working Party "Opinion 3/2012 on developments in biometric technologies" referred.

13   "'voice' does not constitute a specific behavior (when considered as 'speech' in general and combined with face dynamics it fits the definition more closely). Here we consider 'voice' in terms of the numerical model of the sound, rhythm and pattern of an individual's voice. Such sounds and patterns are unique as the physical components and vibrations of vocal chords involved in producing them are different in each person. ".

14   ""An emerging field of psychological-based techniques should also be taken into account. It includes measuring of response to concrete situations or specific tests to conform to a psychological profile.", Article 29 Data Protection Working Party "Opinion 3/2012 on developments in biometric technologies", referred.

15   "Typically, the level of security provided by most biometric systems far exceeds the level of security provided by passwords, PINs or Tokens".

16   "biometrics generate a greater degree of confidence that the person at the terminal is who they say they are".

17   "When biometric systems are used it is difficult to produce 100% error-free results. This may be due to differences in the environment at data acquisition (lighting, temperature, etc.) and differences in the equipment used (cameras, scanning devices, etc.)", Article 29 Data Protection Working Party "Opinion 3/2012 on developments in biometric technologies", referred.

18   O'Connor (1998) refers DNA as a characteristic identifying individuals but emphasizing that, for identical twins, DNA is not unique of one only individual.

19   "Biometric scanning systems typically do not record the entire imprint of a physical feature but only that portion, or "template", that should be time-invariant within some statistical limit ".

20   "Biometric systems are not 100% accurate. Biometric systems accuracy during the template comparison process of authentication depends on external variables, namely, temperature, training level of the enrollment process technicians, physical condition of the individual to be authenticated, etc. Biometric systems accuracy is also dependent on internal variables such as quality of the equipment and the proprietary algorithms being used.".

21   "Building massive biometric applications in society requires a critical mass of technicians capable of managing the applications properly. Typical activities of these technicians are to collect samples for enrollment using complex sensors, to authenticate identity documents (i.e. passports or birth certificates) of individuals before enrolling them, maintain the biometric facility under proper conditions, follow maintenance protocols properly and judge the quality of the samples collected" And "What happens when a biometric file is stolen? A password or a credit card can be relatively easy replaced and the stolen information… with a biometric it is very difficult, if not impossible, for any individual to disassociate oneself from one's biometric somehow invalidated…. " … "If biometric databases are not protected properly and information is stolen, the consequences can be permanently devastating".

22   "Many of the problems are related to individual rights such as the protection of personal data, confidentiality, personal liberty, the relationship between individual and collective rights.".

23   Cfr. http://www.penop.com, (last seen in September 2015).

24   "Some biometric data could be considered sensitive in the meaning of Article 8 of Directive 95/46/EC and in particular, data revealing racial or ethnic origin or data concerning health. For example DNA data of a person often include health data or can reveal the racial or ethnic origin. In this case DNA data are sensitive data and the special safeguards provided by article 8 must apply in addition to the general data protection principles of the Directive. In order to assess the sensitivity

of data processed by a biometric system the context of the processing should also be taken into account", Article 29 Data Protection Working Party "Opinion 3/2012 on developments in biometric technologies", referred.

25 "How will population with disabilities (or lacking physical traits) be enrolled or authenticated in biometric databases? People with just one hand, no iris or retina, no fingers, and in general people lacking physicals characteristics in need of using a biometric facility, may suffer discrimination and unnecessary delays in biometric systems. A well-developed, well-designed biometric system should allow these persons alternative ways to enroll and authenticate, yet delays and processes of bypassing the biometric systems may give them hardships each time they want to access a resource or use a facility which may be an ethical violation of their rights.".

26 Although this may not be entirely true. (Rebera & Mordini 2013): " That the ageing process poses a problem for biometrics is well-understood. No biometric is 100%permanent: people's biometrics change over time. Hence the technical challenge is to develop techniques whereby an individual may be identifiable by his or her biometrics, throughout his or her lifetime, despite this mutability".

27 "Many of the ethical and social questions raised by biometrics can be summarized under a main heading: biometrics and human dignity. Ever since the Magna Charta to the Charter of Fundamental rights of the EU, the respect for the body and for dignity have been basic components of the human being and have been fundamental conditions for freedom and equality.", Working Paper on Data Protection Working Party of European Commission (2003).

28 "we have a fundamental privacy interest in controlling identifying representations of ourselves, including biometric images.".

29 "The first such ground of legitimacy given in Article 7(a) is where the data subject has given consent to the processing. According to the data protection directive, Article 2(h), consent must be freely given, specific and informed indication of the data subject's wishes. It must be clear that such consent cannot be obtained freely through mandatory acceptance of general terms and conditions, or through opt-out possibilities. Furthermore, consent must be revocable. " "Consent is only valid when sufficient information on the use of biometric data is given. Since biometric data may be used as a unique and universal identifier providing clear and easily accessible information on how the specific data are used is to be regarded as absolutely necessary to guarantee fair processing. Therefore this is a crucial requirement for a valid consent in the use of biometric data.", Article 29 Data Protection Working Party "Opinion 3/2012 on developments in biometric technologies", referred.

30 "A prerequisite to using biometrics is a clear definition of the purpose for which the biometric data are collected and processed, taking into account the risks for the protection of fundamental rights and freedoms of individuals.", Article 29 Data Protection Working Party "Opinion 3/2012 on developments in biometric technologies", referred.

31 "The principle of purpose limitation has to be respected together with the other data protection principles; especially the proportionality, necessity and data minimization principles have to be kept in mind when the different purposes of an application are defined.", Article 29 Data Protection Working Party "Opinion 3/2012 on developments in biometric technologies", referred.

32 "In analyzing the proportionality of a proposed biometric system a prior consideration is whether the system is necessary to meet the identified need, i.e. is essential for satisfying that need rather than being the most convenient or cost effective.", Article 29 Data Protection Working Party "Opinion 3/2012 on developments in biometric technologies", referred.

33   "The use of biometrics raises the issue of proportionality of each category of processed data in the light of the purpose for which the data are processed. As biometric data may only be used if adequate, relevant and not excessive, it implies a strict assessment of the necessity and proportionality of the processed data and if the intended purpose could be achieved in a less intrusive way.", Article 29 Data Protection Working Party "Opinion 3/2012 on developments in biometric technologies", referred.

34   "Biometric data processed must be accurate and relevant in proportion to the purpose for which there they were collected. The data must be accurate at enrolment and when establishing the link between the person and the biometric data.", Article 29 Data Protection Working Party "Opinion 3/2012 on developments in biometric technologies", referred.

35   "Biometric data processed must be accurate and relevant in proportion to the purpose for which there they were collected. The data must be accurate at enrolment and when establishing the link between the person and the biometric data.", Article 29 Data Protection Working Party "Opinion 3/2012 on developments in biometric technologies", referred.

36   Transparency and "fair processing, data subjects must be aware of the collection and/or use of their biometric data (Art. 6 of Directive 95/46/EC). Any system that would collect such data without the data subjects' knowledge must be avoided.", Article 29 Data Protection Working Party "Opinion 3/2012 on developments in biometric technologies", referred.

37   "The data controller must make sure that data subjects are adequately informed", Article 29 Data Protection Working Party "Opinion 3/2012 on developments in biometric technologies", referred.

38   For more developments about this issue see CNPD, Princípios sobre a utilização de dados biométricos no âmbito do controlo de acessos e de assiduidade, 2004.

Chapter 3
Organisational Conflict and Its Management

Saleem Gul
Institute of Management Sciences, Pakistan

Michael Klausner
University of Pittsburgh – Bradford, USA

ABSTRACT

This chapter concerns itself with defining conflict and discusses the value it provides to organizations engaging in conflicts. The chapter is structured so that first we will provide a brief on the need to study conflict and negotiations in organizations. Then the discussion will move to the different drivers of organizational conflicts and will conclude with a typology of the different conflicts that exist within organizations. The third section will focus on the models (life-cycles) of conflicts that are available in conflict literature. The final section will focus on the different conflict handling techniques that are available. This section will include a discussion on the different conflict handling styles and negotiation tactics, and a brief on the process of alternate dispute resolution in conflict management.

INTRODUCTION

Conflict and negotiation pervade all sorts of organizations. It is therefore important to understand the nature and types of conflicts so that they may be adequately resolved using appropriate negotiation strategies. To achieve this goal, this chapter first engages with the concepts of conflict and negotiations at a theoretical level and then empirically. The chapter is structured so that first we develop a case for the study of organizational conflicts and negotiations. We first provide a discussion on the different triggers of conflict. This setup's the ground for a discussion on the value of conflict; here we discuss both the positives and negatives of conflicts. We then position our discussion towards the resolution of conflicts. Then the discussion turns to the different ways of measuring conflict and the conflict management styles. Then, we provide a discussion based on empirical evidence pertaining to the causes of organizational conflicts and strategies of conflict prevention and handling. Finally, the last section concludes the chapter.

DOI: 10.4018/978-1-5225-0245-6.ch003

BACKGROUND

Conflicts are common to all types of organizations because we perceive or value things differently. The concept of a conflict denotes some type of disagreement, incompatibility or opposition among groups (Perrow, 1986). Conflicts may arise from disagreements and oppositions in cognitions, emotions, behaviors, and goals and the means to achieve them (Klausner & Groves, 1994). A collection of key definitions of conflict and their underlying theme is provided in Table 1.

Table 1. Conflict definitions

Definition	Source	Underlying Theme	Perceives Conflict
An antagonistic struggle	(Coser, 1956)	Hostility	Negatively
A breakdown in standard mechanisms of decision-making	(March & Simon, 1958)	Lack of consensus	Negatively
A struggle over values and claims to scarce status, power, and resources	(Boulding, 1962)	Scarcity	Negatively
A struggle over values and claims to scarce status, power and resources in which the aims of the opponents are to neutralize, injure, or eliminate the rivals	(Coser, 1967)	Scarcity/hostility	Negatively
A breach in normally expected behavior	(Beals & Siegel, 1966)	Poor Behavior	Negatively
A threat to cooperation	(Marek, 1966)	Lack of cooperation	Negatively
Opposing processes in any of several forms – competition, status, rivalry, bargaining, sabotage, verbal abuse, etc.	(Walton, 1966)	Opposition (may not be hostile)	Negatively
Any social situation or process in which two or more social entities are linked by at least one form of antagonistic interaction	(Fink, 1968)	Hostility	Negatively
As existing whenever incompatible activities occur in an action which prevents, obstructs, interferes with, injures, or in some way makes it less likely or less effective	(Deutsch, 1973)	Interference	Negatively
Arising when a difference between two (or more) people necessitates change in at least one person in order for their engagement to continue and develop – the differences cannot coexist without some adjustment	(Jordan, 1990)	Difference	Negatively
A situation in which interdependent people express (manifest or latent) differences in satisfying their individual needs and interests, and they experience interference from each other in accomplishing these goals	(Donohue & Colt, 1992)	Interference	Negatively
As a process that begins when one party or individual perceives that one or more others have frustrated or are about to frustrate a major concern of theirs	(Thomas, 1992)	Hindrance	Negatively
An expressed struggle between at least two interdependent parties who perceive incompatible goals, scarce resources, and interference from others in achieving their goals	(Hocker & Wilmot, 1995)	Struggle	Negatively
A way of confronting reality and creating new solutions	(Socklingam & Doswell, 1999)	Solution	Positively
The perceived incompatibility between values/goals	(Deutsch & Coleman, 2000; Reichers, 1986)	Clash	Negatively

Organizational conflict (OC) can arise at different levels. That is, it may be *interpersonal, intergroup,* or *inter-organizational*. Organizations experience conflict differently, either in its intensity or in the way it is expressed. It has been argued that such variations are due to the power relationships within organizations (Klausner & Groves, 1994). Kolb and Bartunek (1992) propose that conflicts within organizations often are hidden or suppressed. This may be attributed to employees' disengaging from or avoiding those they disagree with, or because they may be exhibiting a 'passive aggressive' stance. Alternatively, conflict can be hidden or suppressed through the exercise of manipulative strategies by management.

The term 'conflict' conjures up several conceptions. Initial formulations categorizes a conflict as being either functional or dysfunctional (Pondy, 1967), thereby bringing to the fore the idea that certain types of conflict may actually be good for an organization (Deutsch, 1973). E.g., Socklingam and Doswell (1999) are of the view that conflicts can be positive in that they are a way to confront reality and to creating new solutions. Therefore, it could be argued that those associating a negative feel with conflict would call for its eradication, while those seeing some sort of a positive outcome of conflict will argue for its management.

TRIGGERS OF CONFLICT AND THEIR CLASSIFICATION

Conflicts may be viewed as emanating from either of four states (Pondy, 1964), these are: (1) antecedent conditions (such as scarcity of resources, policy differences etc.), (2) affective states (such as stress, tension, hostility, anxiety etc.), (3) cognitive states of individuals (such as perceptions of awareness), and (4) 'conflictful behavior' (such as passive resistance, or over oppression). These can be contracted into two main factors, that is, the psychological or interpersonal and the social interactional. Psychological factors are based on personality traits and behavioral temperaments that irritate others. Extremes of which manifest as psychopathic behaviors or personality disorders. In this chapter we will only focus on the social interactional factors of conflict. These include misattributed motives and behaviors stemming from errors in explaining and interpreting behavior (L. Ross, 1977) or conspiracy theories (Klausner & Groves, 1994), lapses in communication, prejudice and discrimination, caustic experiences in the past resulting in grudges, misread causal connections or behaviors, dissimilarity between groups, destructive criticism, and perceived inequity or fairness (Baron, 1990; Bies, Shapiro, & Cummings, 1988).

Teleologically conflict may be either naturalistic or Aristotelian. That is, either conflicting situations give rise to conflict; or because there is conflict, there are conflicting situations, respectively. Regardless of the accepted perspective, when parties engaged in conflict work towards a conclusion they might be extrinsically or intrinsically driven. Those working towards an extrinsic finality may be considered as having pro-social motivation and those following an intrinsic finality as having selfish motivation (Carnevale & Pruitt, 1992).

According to Thomas (1976) conflict episodes stem from 'disagreement, denial of a request, violation in agreement, insult, active interference with performance, vying for scare resources, breaking a norm, diminishing one's status, ignoring one's feelings, etc.' Others believe that conflicts arise because of the mismatch between rigidly drafted contracts and the dynamic reality they are designed to control (Clegg, 1990). Other drivers of conflict include promotion and compensation, management style, personal life, and individual performance (Morrill, 1995). Conflict may also be caused by personality mismatches (Hill, 1977) and the roles assigned to individuals (Getzels & Guba, 1954; Parsons, 1951). Conflicts arising based on assignment are known as role conflicts and there are said to occur when an actor is required to fill two or more roles whose expectations are inconsistent.

Conflicts may arise from the hierarchical authority structures deployed within an organization. For example, the two boss problem inherent in the matrix organizational structure. Within organizations, conflicts may be triggered by the managers' future orientation (Gibson, Ivancevish, & Donnelly Jr., 1991). While, conflicts between organizational employees may stem from an excess of competition (Baron, 1990). Interestingly, competition and conflict over scares resources have a tendency to aggravate power differences (Jones & Deckro, 1993), leading to latent conflicts becoming overt.

Also, conflicts are more likely from certain types of reward structures and incentives e.g. when the reward structure focuses on the group rather than the organization (Gibson et al., 1991). Research shows that conflict is most likely when there is a perception of goal incompatibility between interdepended work units (Kochan, Cummings, & Huber, 1976). Additionally, it has been argued that the degree and type of interdependence can encourage conflict (Baron, 1990). (Thompson, 1967) identified three types of task interdependencies: pooled, sequential, and reciprocal. Where, the reciprocal interdependencies contribute the most to any conflict.

Other factors driving conflicts include: strength of the organizational ties – where high-conflict organizations were found to have weak ties (Nelson & Quick, 1996), negative responses to innovations in organizational processes (Klausner & Groves, 1994), lack of clear responsibilities, lines of authority, and performance expectations (Greenberg & Baron, 1993), specialization of roles that may lead to different conclusions about an issue (Hague, 1974), and lastly conflicts may arise when 'memberships and identification with social groupings that transcend organizational boundaries are carried into organizational life' (Trice & Beyer, 1993).

Conflict is processual. Different models have been suggested to capture this process. One such conflict lifecycle suggests that a conflict has an initiating event, an influencing event, and a concluding event (Goldman, 1966). Pondy (1967) presents five stages of a conflict episode, these are: latency, perception, feeling, manifestation, and aftermath. While, Thomas' (1976) model includes: frustration, conceptualization, behavior, and outcome. A discussion on the different stages of conflict is presented later in this chapter.

Please note that conflict does not necessarily occur simply because of the presence of incompatibilities, disagreements, or difference within social interactions. Rather, for conflict to occur, some threshold level of intensity must be experienced before parties become aware of the conflict (Rahim, 2001). Therefore, depending on the varied threshold tolerances of the individuals involved in an interaction, conflicts may arise at different times during similar situations.

The different types of conflicts discussed so far are classifiable into categories based on the sources of the conflict, see Table 2.

The Value of Conflict

The process of conflict is not entirely evil and detrimental to organizational productivity. Rather, it is an inevitable aspect of human nature (Wilson & Jerrell, 1981). Literature argues that conflict within an organization produces positive, negative, or neutral outcomes. However, an important question to ask is, from whose perspective? Conflicts can be positive for some members of an organization, but not for others. The positivity of a conflict can be temporal e.g. a conflict may be productive in the short-term but destructive in the long run. Additionally, a conflict may be troubling for an organizational unit, but good for the organization as a whole.

Table 2. Conflict types and their description

Conflict Type	Other Names	Description
Affective Conflict	Psychological conflict; Relationship conflict Emotional conflict; Interpersonal conflict; and Individual conflict	Interpersonal clashes characterized by anger, frustration, and other negative feelings
Substantive Conflict	Task conflict; Cognitive conflict; Issue conflict; Organizational/viewpoint conflict	Disagree over tasks or content
Conflict of Interest		Parties sharing the same understanding of the situation, prefers a different and somewhat incompatible solution to a problem
Conflict of Values	Ideological conflict	Two social entities differ in their values or ideologies
Goal Conflict		Preferred outcome or an end-state of two social entities is inconsistent and may involve divergent preferences over all of the decision outcomes (zero-sum)
Realistic / Nonrealistic Conflict	Intrinsic/Extrinsic conflict	Realistic conflict refers to incompatibilities that have rational context (i.e. tasks, goals, values, and means and ends). Associated with 'mostly rational or goal-oriented' disagreements Nonrealistic conflict occurs as a result of a party's needs for releasing tension and expressing hostility, ignorance, or error. It 'is an end in itself having little to do with group or organizational goals'
Institutionalized / Non-Institutionalized Conflict		Institutionalized conflict is characterized by situations where actors follow explicit rules, display predictable behavior, and their relationships have continuity. Racial conflicts are non-institutionalized and the above three conditions are nonexistent
Retributive Conflict		Entities feel the need for a drawn-out conflict to punish the opponent
Misattributed Conflict		Incorrect assignment of causes to a conflict
Displaced Conflict		Conflicting parties either direct their frustrations or hostilities to social entities that are not involved in a conflict or argue over secondary (minor) issues

Klausner and Groves (1994) point out several consequences of organizational conflicts, these include: creation of organizational change, problem solving, fostering creativity, and innovation, reinforcing organizational norms and culture, and increased stereotyping among organizational members. Additionally, the existence of conflict has been shown to affect organizational commitment and intent to stay.

Initial formulations propose a categorization of conflict as being either functional or dysfunctional (Pondy, 1967) or alternatively as normative or dynamic. The normative or functional view regards conflict as problematic and argues for its elimination, whereas the dynamic view considers conflict as natural and beneficial in the changing dynamics of a relationship. In addition, conflict is laden with cultural baggage e.g. Chua and Gundykunst (1987) have differentiated between the conflict perception of high-context cultures and low-context cultures. The high-context cultures view conflicts normatively; as opposed to the dynamic view held by low-context cultures.

Jehn (1994, 1995) reformulated conflicts as 'task conflicts' and 'relationship conflicts'. Task conflicts refer to cognitive disagreements arising from differences in perspectives, ideas, and opinions (Chen, 2006; Jehn & Mannix, 2001). Whereas relationship conflicts are 'affective disagreements' arising from personal dislikes and disaffections – these tends to include annoyance and animosity among individuals (Amason & Sapienza, 1997). Task conflicts are considered as positive, arguably because they are positively related to the quality of ideas and innovation (West & Anderson, 1996), increase constructive debate (Jehn, Northcraft, & Neale, 1999), lead to affective group decision making (Amason, 1996), prevent group think (Turner & Pratkanis, 1994) and should therefore be encouraged (Amason, 1996; Jehn, 1994, 1995). Whereas, relational or value-goal (Leung, Liu, & Ng, 2005) conflicts are considered negative because of the consequences they generate. For example, relational conflicts are thought to affect 'group climates' i.e. the sense of camaraderie within a group, and reducing team effectiveness (Jehn, 1997). Therefore, such conflicts are discouraged (De Dreu & Van de Vliert, 1997; Simons & Peterson, 2000).

Although, task and relationship conflicts are different in nature they are not mutually exclusive. For example, Jehn (1997) explains that task conflicts may transform into relationship conflicts. A possible explanation is that task related criticism may be misconstrued as a personal insult (Amason, 1996) evoking prevaricated responses from the parties involved. However, it has been observed that this only happens when there is excessive task conflict (Jehn, 1997). Conversely, a relationship conflict may affect task performance however, research has not yet been able to establish a conclusive relationship (De Dreu, 2006; De Dreu & Weingart, 2003).

In discussing the functional and dysfunctional outcomes of conflicts, Rahim (2001) argues that for a social system to benefit from conflict it must strive to reduce the negative effects of conflict and enhance its positive effects. A summary of the positive and negative outcomes of conflicts is presented in table 3.

The consequences of a conflict, whether positive or negative, are determined by the characteristics of the conflict, desired outcomes of the parties involved, and an awareness of the conflict management strategies. Certainly, there is no singular level of conflict within an organization, i.e. the intensity of conflict can vary and is contingent upon whether the managers of conflict can harness its productive functions (Coser, 1956; March & Simon, 1958). An excess of conflict can reduce organizational commitment and is an impediment to trust and empowerment (Jensen & Scacchi, 2004). Simply suppressing the conflict is not an option, as it has been shown to lower trust and is therefore dysfunctional to an organization.

The underlying belief that task conflicts have some positive aspects has fostered debates aimed at finding the optimal level of conflict. High levels of task conflict are thought to reduce team satisfaction and commitment (Amason & Sapienza, 1997), causes stress, opposition, and discontent between group members, and creates an indisposition to working together in the future (Jehn, 1995). While low levels of task conflicts results in 'group-think' and complacency in decision making (ibid). A moderate amount of task conflict is therefore considered ideal (Brown & Gaertner, 2003) as it promotes innovation and a higher level of intra-group trust (Lovelace, Shapiro, & Weingart, 2001). An alternative perspective

Table 3. Positive and negative outcomes of conflict, adapted from Rahim (2001)

Positive (Functional) Outcomes	Negative (Dysfunctional) Outcomes
Innovation, creativity, and growth	Job stress, burnout, and dissatisfaction
Improves organizational decision making	Reduces communication between individuals and groups
Alternative solutions to a problem being found	Result in giving rise to a climate of distrust and suspicion
Synergistic solutions to common problems	Damages relationships
Individual and group performance improvement	Job performance may be reduced
Individuals and groups may be forced to search for new approaches	Leads to an increase in resistance to change
Individuals and groups may be required to articulate and clarify their positions	Affects organizational commitment and loyalty

emerged in De Dreu and Weingart's (2003) paper, which in reporting the results of a content analysis study found both task and relationship conflicts to be disruptive. In a later article, De Dreu and Gelfand (2008) takes the position that traditional views regarding the benefits of workplace conflict are unsound and methodologically flawed, and that conditions where such conflicts are actually positive and beneficial are few.

The ongoing debate between the scholars of conflict pertaining to whether conflict ought to be considered beneficial or detrimental to the outcome of a given situation can be viewed as a continuum. On the one end of which are researchers harboring the belief that task conflict contributes positively to idea generation and innovation and should therefore be welcomed and stimulated in the workplace. On the other end are those that offer an utter rejection of conflict having any positive aspects what-so-ever, a position that has already been criticized by Follett (1925), who considered conflict a normal process whereby socially valuable differences registered themselves for the enrichment of all concerned. In the middle of the continuum are those who are ambivalent but tend to refer more to the positive consequences of task conflict (e.g. Amason, 1996; Jehn, 1994, 1995). Caution needs to be exercised however, as too much task conflict or unmanaged task conflict may lead to an increase in relationship conflict and decrease in participant satisfaction (cf. Leung et al., 2005; Medina, Munduate, Dorado, & Guerra, 2005).

Conflict can be managed or resolved but not eradicated, for managing people's perceptions, preconceived ideas, and learned behavior in the face of conflict is not a simple task. Any attempts to eradicate conflict should be denounced as these are nothing more than, in the words of Popper (1966), 'utopian engineering'. One possible solution is proposed by Burton (1998), who asserts that if conflicts are accepted as stemming from social problems then their resolution and prevention (management) is a reality, made possible by removing the conflict source and thereby adjusting institutional and social norms to the needs of individuals. The concepts of conflict resolution and conflict management are considered as means to achieving the optimum levels of conflict within an organizational setting.

Robbins (1974) summarizes the various perspectives on conflict in the form of three philosophies of conflict. The first philosophy, termed the classicists or traditionalists, is based on the assumption that conflict is detrimental to an organization and must be reduced or eliminated. The second philosophy, is of the behaviorists, believes that conflict as inevitable. They at times advocate the enhancement of conflict, however they do no actively create conditions that generate conflict. The final philosophy, of the interactionists, differs from the former two and is characterized by an absolute necessity of conflicts and explicit encouragement of opposition.

The aim of the parties in conflict may extend from simply attempting to gain acceptance of a preference, or securing a resource advantage, to the extremes of injuring or eliminating opponents (Bisno, 1988). Organizational conflicts may be classified as occurring intra-organizationally (i.e. within the organization) or inter-organizationally (i.e. between two or more organizations). Intra-organizational conflict may be classified on the basis of the level at which it occurs. Thus, intra-organizational conflict comprises intra-personal (or intra-individual or intra-psychic) conflict, interpersonal (or dyadic) conflict, intragroup (or intradepartmental) conflict, and intergroup (or interdepartmental) conflict (Rahim, 2001).

Measuring and Handling Conflict

The various conflict handling techniques presented in the literature could be classified based on the number of factors they take into consideration. Four such categories are proposed by Rahim (2001), termed the 2-5 styles, these are discussed in more detail next.

The 2-style model of conflict handling originates from the earlier work of Deutsch (1949) who suggested a simple cooperative-competitive model of social conflict. Unfortunately, due to the overly simplistic view of conflict adopted by this model it does not situate itself well in the resolution of actual conflicts that are more complex and seldom follow a purely cooperative or competitive stance. Evidence of this is available in Game Theory literature, which acknowledges the existence of 'nonzero-sum games' and 'mixed-motive' conflicts (Rahim, 2001).

There are several 3-style models. Putnam and Wilson (1982) identified three style of handling conflict: Non-confronting (obliging), solution-orientation (integrating), and control (dominating). Hocker and Wilmot (1991) argue that 'conflict styles cluster similarly to conflict tactics', into three types: Avoidance, competitive (distributive), and collaborative (integrative). Further work by Lawrence and Lorsch (1967; 1967) in measuring five modes of conflict resolution found that only three are sued i.e. forcing, smoothing, and confrontation. Additionally, studies of conflicts involving high levels of emotions, such as those found in marital conflict, identify two different 3-style models depending on desired outcome of the conflict. For example, Billingham and Sack (1987) model includes: Reasoning, verbal aggression, and violence; whereas, Rands, Levinger, and Mellinger (1981) model includes: Attack, avoid, and compromise.

Pruitt (1983) identifies four styles of handling conflict. These include: Yielding, problem-solving, inaction, and contending. Latter work by Pruitt and Carnevale (1993) suggests that the problem-solving style is the most effective conflict management style. Another 4-style model is suggested by Kurdek (1994) that includes problem-solving, conflict engagement, withdrawal, and compliance. The 5-style models of conflict handling are based on the work of Follett (1925), who conceptualized three main conflict handling techniques – dominating, compromise, and integration – and other, secondary techniques: Avoidance and suppression. Latter work by Blake and Mouton (1964) presents a classification scheme of the modes (styles) of handling conflict into five types, based on the attitudes of the manager's concern for production and people, these are: Forcing, withdrawing, smoothing, compromising, and problem solving. This scheme is later reinterpreted by Thomas (1976) who considers a parties intentions in formulating his classification i.e. cooperativeness (attempting to satisfy the others concerns) and assertiveness (attempting to satisfy one's own concerns). Follow up work by Rahim (1983) and Rahim and Bonoma (1979) differentiates the conflict handling styles on the basis of two fundamental dimensions: Concern for self and concern for others, is essence portraying the motivational orientation of an individual engaged in conflict. Their five style of conflict handling are: Integrating, obliging, dominating, avoiding, and compromising.

Amongst the models discussed, Blake and Mouton's (1964) managerial grid was regarded as the leading thesis on handling conflict (Kabanoff, 1987; Pruitt & Rubin, 1986; Rahim, 1986; Shockley-Zalabak, 1988; Van de Vliert & Prein, 1989) for a longtime and formed the underlying criteria on which various conflict measurement instruments are based, these are listed in table 4. MODE has been criticized for its poor discrimination between the theoretically and practically important styles of competing and collaborating, an area where the ROCI performs much better (Van de Vliert & Kabanoff, 1990). On the other hand, KCSI professes to be more culturally sensitive and easier to implement than MODE. However, out literature survey did not reveal any research papers corroborating this claim.

Table 4. Conflict measurement instruments

Instrument	Developed by
Conflict Management Survey	Hall (1969)
Management of Difference Exercise (MODE) survey	Thomas and Kilmann (1974)
Organizational Communication Conflict Instrument	Putnam and Wilson (1982)
Conflict Management Message Style Instrument	R. Ross and DeWine (1982)
Rahim Organizational Conflict Inventory (ROCI)	Rahim (1983)
Kraybill Conflict Style Inventory (KCSI)	Kraybill (2011)

Causes of Organizational Conflict: An Empirically Founded View

Fundamentally, organizational conflict (OC) is rooted in peoples' perceptions of themselves, others, the situation and the organization as a whole. When their perceptions differ significantly from those of other organizational members OC is likely to occur. Peoples' perception "is subject to many factors that can lead to important differences in the way any two people perceive the same person or message" (Tolbert & Hall, 2009).

There are a plethora of reasons why two or more individuals may perceive and interpret the same stimulus (each other, situations, environments, messages, etc.) in different and at times sometimes contradictory ways. "Perceivers may respond to cues they are not even aware of, be influenced by emotional factors, use irrelevant cues, weigh evidence in an unbalanced way or fail to identify all of the factors on which their judgments are based." (Tolbert & Hall, 2009). There are myriad factors that cause people to interpret and assess the same stimuli differently, among them are: relevant prior experiences with the stimuli, stereotypes, personality, socialization, values and socio-demographic variables such as race, religion, ethnicity, area of residence, sex, sexual orientation, to name just a few. Thus it should not be surprising when people perceive the same stimuli differently. Contradictory assessments of books, products, restaurants, remedies and other items are common in reviews of such on websites such as Amazon.

Additionally, people hold deeply rooted assumptions about their roles, and the roles of others, which may be unstated and not brought to the surface until the respective role violations occur. For example, an executive may assume that it is okay to ask his administrative assistant to do personal errands for him such as buying a birthday gift for his wife or picking up his clothes from the dry cleaners. The administrative assistant, however, may hold an equally strong assumption that such requests are illegitimate. Conflict will occur when the assistant complains about such requests. Both parties will experience psychic stress as their deeply held premises about what is or is no expected of each other is breached (Garfinkel, 1967).

While OC conflict can emerge as a consequence of "personality differences" among people in the majority of instances OC results from a variety of structural sources. This was not always believed to be the case, in part, because most people, many social scientists included, tended to view OC as a function organizational members' personality clashes. As, R. Nevitt Sanford (1964: 95), put it: Twenty years ago it seemed easy to account for organizational conflict by blaming the problem behavior of individuals. But the simple formula, "trouble is due to trouble-makers' unfortunately is inadequate in the light of our present knowledge of the social process.

Even today people, especially those in supervisory capacities, have a tendency to blame a "few bad apples" if some organizational members engage in unethical or even criminal behavior. It is not uncommon, for instance, for police commissioners to blame a "few bad apples" when cases of police brutality occur. Similarly, CEO's of major banks tended to deny the existence of any systemic problems when some banks had to be bailed out by the government due to the large number of subprime loans that were made. While the aforementioned examples involve deviant or criminal behavior, the same tendency to "individualize" or "psychologize" blame occurs in cases of OC.

Many times conflict that may seem to be based on personality differences are, in fact, caused by incompatible role requirements among people holding different positions within the organization. For example, a salesperson, who is compensated by commissions earned when a sale is made may often find herself in conflict with the credit manager whose job is to make certain that potential customers are good credit risks. The root cause of the conflict here is not in personality differences between the salesperson and the credit manager but in the incompatible demands of the positions they occupy within the organization.

A former president/CEO of several corporations put it well when she noted that the "inner ring" of a corporation consisting of the president/CEO, executive and mid-level management, division heads, marketing, manufacturing, purchasing, sales, etc. has its "own agenda which can sometimes be aligned with the corporation's or completely antithetical to it." (Anonymous, 2015, anon via response to questionnaire).

Seemingly incompatible goals among different organizational units are also a common source of OC. A university's chemistry department may want funds to be used for new laboratory equipment while the history department may want funds to hire another faculty person. Since the university's resources are limited conflict between the two departments may occur. Organizational resources in the form of money, people, equipment, etc. are always limited. Each unit of an organization will endeavor to obtain as many resources from the organization as possible. This can produce a major source of OC. A zero-sum type of situation arises since the more resources that unit "A" obtains, the less will be available for unit "B." OC conflict due to scarce resources is especially apt to occur when organizations engage in cost cutting measures. Fewer resources means that there will be increased competition for them among different organizational units. In addition, conflict may arise when employees are asked to take on additional work that was previously done by those who were let go.

Another structurally based source of OC is role ambiguity. When organizational members do not have clear-cut notions of what their role requirements are; uncertainty, stress and conflict are likely to develop. It is important for people not only to know what their role obligations are but also what those of other organizational members are. If there is no congruence among peoples' perceptions of the duties and obligations associated with their positions and those of others, all kinds of OCs are likely to emerge. In addition, it is essential that people know the jurisdictional boundaries associated with both their positions and the positions of other organizational members. For example, a faculty member who is in charge of a particular program may feel that a jurisdictional boundary" has been violated if the college's dean vetoes a personnel or other kind of change that the director of the program wants. Codification of the rights, obligations and jurisdictional boundaries associated with each organizational position outlined in a "handbook "given to new organizational members would be helpful in precluding or reducing OC caused by role and jurisdictional ambiguity.

The nature of an organization's reward and incentive system is often a source of OC. If members of an organization believe that they are not being compensated commensurate with their contributions to the organization OC is probable. Feelings of inequity whether valid or not are likely to have a negative impact on employees morale, and satisfaction. If rewards are based on work teams or department performance, rather than on each member's contributions conflict may arise if people feel that they contributed more than other team members.

Some corporations have a policy of eliminating employees who rank on the lowest rung of a set of performance criteria. This approach exacerbates competition among employees as they try to avoid low rankings and may lead to conflict even to the point of sabotaging each other's work.

Reward and incentive structures that clearly specify the criteria for reward allocation will be helpful in reducing OC due to perceived compensation inequalities. People, in general desire clear cut criteria for promotion and salary increases. For example, junior faculty wants to know what criteria they must meet in order to be granted tenure. How many articles, in which type of academic journals, as well as kinds and degree of university service and teaching evaluation scores would be needed for tenure.

Another source of OC are differences in employees based on such factors as sex, sexual orientation, race, religion, ethnicity, nationality and age. As the work force has become increasingly diverse OC based on these differences are more likely to occur. Organizations may lessen the likelihood of OC emerging because of these differences by incorporating some form of 'sensitivity" training into the initial socialization of new members. In addition, organizational values that emphasize non-discrimination, teamwork, respect and appreciation of diversity and which are demonstrated in both tangible and symbolic ways by upper-level management will also be helpful.

OC may occur when a company acquires another company whose internal culture is quite different, even contradictory, from that of the acquiring company. For example, a company that has a rather traditional, formal, strait-laced culture may acquire a relatively young company that has an informal, looser type of culture. Manifestations of the different organizational cultures may manifest themselves in a variety of ways including: dress, hierarchy of authority, management philosophy, reward system expectations, customer interactions, values, etc.

Companies contemplating acquiring other companies should determine whether there would be a good "cultural fit" between it and the company being considered for acquisition. All too often the acquiring company focuses on quantitative factors such as decreased costs, increasing market share, utilization of a new technology acquired, etc. After "crunching" the numbers it may conclude that they should make a proposal for the a company only to find out after the acquisition is completed that differences in each company's organizational cultures pose a serious threat to the success of the acquisition.

Strategies to Prevent and Deal with Organizational Conflicts

There are a variety of ways to preclude and, if it occurs, resolve OC. These approaches represent a multi-pronged and multi-level approach ranging from the micro, middle range and macro level.

Clear Goals

Goal clarity is an important factor in preventing OC. In a study of high performance work teams (HPWTs) Klausner (2007) found that clear cut organizational goals that were effectively conveyed to members was one of the key ingredients of those teams. Such would also be the case for the organization as a whole. Indeed, the manager of a forest products company mentioned it as the "most" important ingredient (Disney, 1998). Richard Feynman, one of the physicists who worked on the Manhattan project, said that his team worked differently when members became aware of the purpose of their work. The pace, quality and quantity of their work improved after they understood the positive impact accomplishment of their goal would have (Goleman, 1997). Similarly, Katzenback and Smith (1994) observe that the majority of high performance team members they interviewed described their teams as "special" and their experiences as having participated in something" bigger and better than myself". What is true of teams would also be true for the organization as a whole. Having members understand the positive implications for organizational goal attainment both for themselves and for their organization can do much to prevent OC. It is important that members view organizational goals as superordinate to their own personal goals; doing so will enhance cooperation among members resulting in less chance of OC (Sherif, 1966). Strong commitment to an organization's goals serves to neutralize personality clashes by having people orient their efforts and energy towards organizational goal achievement (Klausner, 2007). This point is nicely illustrated by a member of the Knight-Ridder newspaper team, "We all became focused on the customer. We didn't let other things like personality get in the way (Katzenback & Smith, 1994). Goal clarity also aids in increasing cohesion among organizational members (B. Fisher & Thomas, 1996).

Clear Roles

As we noted, lack of role clarity leads to uncertainty, frustration, anxiety and conflict. "Knowledge of who does what which is shared among members helps create the magic of synergy, of everyone working together" (B. Fisher & Thomas, 1996). Shared perceptions of roles also contribute to feelings of identification with the organization (Klausner, 2007).

Participative Rather Than Autocratic Decision-Making

Conflict over organizational policies, procedures and goals is less likely to arise if members are actively involved in creating them. Edicts that are handed down from the top are more likely to meet with resistance than if those who it will affect are given the opportunity to convey their ideas. Getting members to "buy into" decisions and have a sense of ownership of them helps to alleviate the status-power differences inherent within organizations.

A former President and Chief Executive Officer of several corporations indicated that: "more organizational conflict occurs when management comes across as dictators rather than leaders. She goes on to say that, OC is most apt to occur when management "presents themselves 'above' the ranks immune from the same rules as everyone else...." (Anonymous, 2015).

Organizational Culture

As previously, mentioned, organizational cultures that have values which stress cooperation, camaraderie, mutual trust, respect and tolerance for differences provide a climate that will tend to reduce incidences of OC. Values, by definition, are abstract and intangible, thus people need to be reminded of them. This can be done via posters, slogans, rewards and recognition for those that manifest them and ongoing socialization practices. In addition, semi-structured activities that foster a friendly, mellow and cooperative social climate (parties, outings, birthday celebrations, rituals) will help to reinforce the corporate culture and values. Most important, upper management must "walk the corporate culture talk" by behaving towards each other and towards their employees in ways that reflect the organization's values.

An organizational culture that fosters a positive social climate characterized by mutual respect, trust and cooperation among all levels within the organization will be especially helpful when conflicts arise. If a foundation of good will and camaraderie has been developed over time, each side will not view each other merely as "adversaries" but as individuals just like themselves who have their own interests, problems, and issues to deal with. Roger Fisher, William Ury and Bruce Patton in their well-known book: Getting to Yes, note that, "A working relationship where trust, understanding, respect And friendship are built up over time can make each new negotiation smoother and more efficient" (R. Fisher, Ury, & Patton, 1991). They also note that the parties should attempt to find common ground, areas where each other's interests overlap, doing so will help to modulate points of contention and disagreement. For example, company unions when negotiating with employers could emphasize that they want the company to prosper and be successful just as management does. Conversely, management could underscore how important it is to them for employees to feel content with their compensation. Once commonalities of interest are shown a foundation is built upon which differences can be amicably discussed.

Use of Cross-Functional Teams

The creation of cross-functional teams where a work team is comprised of people from different units having different areas of expertise can be effective in avoiding or resolving OC. Such teams provide a context whereby perspective-taking and empathy is facilitated. All too often organizational members interact primarily with others who have the same specialization and view things from the same perspective. This tends to promote insularity and produces stronger subunit boundaries.

Another advantage of the creation and use of cross-functional teams is that members of the organization get to know one another as "individuals" having similar interests, concerns, and aspirations. This is especially important when there is much diversity among organizational members. Which is very prevalent and is becoming more and more so.

Open and Non-Defensive Communication

Open, clear and regular communication within organizations is another ingredient that can prevent or reduce dysfunctional OC. Thomas and Fisher (1996) found that, "lack of shared information and easy access to relevant information was the number one roadblock to effective teamwork". The same would equally apply to organizations. In addition, communication patterns that are "non-defensive" are most likely to work best. Non-defensive communications are honest, assertive, confident, balanced and open-minded. They are characterized by both self-control and self-possession without rejecting the listener" (Nelson & Quick, 1996).

Defensive communications, in contrast, are characterized by hostility, attacks, put downs, labeling, power plays, deception and sarcasm. Such types of communication will tend to produce conflict and exacerbate conflicts already existing (Nelson & Quick, 1996; Wells, 1980). Moreover, they engender misunderstandings, resentment, hurt feelings, frustration, alienation and retaliatory behaviors. Defensive communication patterns tend to be self-perpetuating. The target of such communications will to respond defensively; thus, a vicious cycle is created.

Direct and open communication is especially important when there are rumors about such things as possible plant closings, personnel transfers, acquisition of the company by another company, etc. A former President and CEO of several corporations said that, "direct communication with the staff is always a good route to take because when there is an 'unknown', employees will fill in the blanks with their own thoughts, spread rumors and create a vacuum of fear and establish a precedence of distrust (what is management hiding from us?)" (Anonymous, 2015). While many schools offer courses in public speaking, few, if any, offer courses in "listening" which is an equally important skill for effective communication. To improve listening skills, organizations could give workshops on the topic that would include various kinds of experiential exercises such as role-playing.

Codification of Conflict Resolution Procedures

If organizations have a predetermined set of procedures for members to follow when conflicts arise, chances of resolution will be enhanced. These procedures could be written in a handbook or document that members receive upon joining the organization. Most colleges, for example, issue student "handbooks" to new students, which among other things, indicates what procedures they are to follow if they have any kind of grievances. Companies, especially large ones, are apt to have a set of procedures indicating the steps employees are to take if they have some gripe. If employees belong to a union then the union will also specify the kinds of options available to employees if they have a disagreement with management. When such procedures are institutionalized within an organization, it provides individuals with a sense of structure and guidelines to follow when conflict arises.

Also a position of ombudsmen may be created which would provide members with another alternative if they were not satisfied with an outcome to a dispute. The person designated, as ombudsmen could be an "outsider" who is not formally employed by the company but used as a "consultant" to help adjudicate certain conflicts when in-house conflict resolution procedures have not been successful.

Negotiation

Negotiation is one of the most common responses to OC. It is the process by which parties that are engaging in conflict agree to communicate with each other for the purpose of resolving the conflict in a way that will be mutually satisfying. In order for the negotiation to be successful it is crucial that the parties negotiate in "good faith" and avoid certain tendencies that would preclude success (Lewicki, 1983). These are: selective disclosure. This involves withholding or deemphasizing information that would be unfavorable to one's position and emphasizing information that would be favorable. Negotiations are hindered by:

Misrepresentation

This refers to a "mild" form of deception.

Deception and Lying

This is when a party engages in outright, blatant and intentional falsehoods. For example, the president of a company may contend that the company is earning significantly less than it actually is in order to get a workers and their union to reduce their demands for increased wages.

False Threats and False Promises

One or both parties make promises or threats that they have no intention of carrying out. For instance, a company's president may say that the company will relocate to another city if the salary demands of the union are not lowered. Conversely, the union negotiator may threaten the company with a strike, when, in fact, neither party has any intention in carrying out the aforementioned.

Inflict Direct or Indirect Harm

Since, by definition, the parties involved in negotiations already have an adversarial mind-set, it will be very tempting for them to use all or some of these tactics in order to achieve the outcome they wish. If one of the parties believes that the other party is using one of these tactics there can be an escalation of the conflict to the degree that precludes a successful outcome.

Escalation of the conflict during the negotiation process can manifest itself in several ways according to Thomas (1984) "…it might involve increasing the number or size of the issues disputed, increasing hostility between parties, increasing competitiveness, pursuing increasingly extreme demands or objectives, using increasingly coercive tactics and decreasing trust". A vicious cycle tends to emerge since the aggrieved party is apt to respond in kind when it believes the other party has not negotiated in good faith. Despite the obstacles to successful negotiation outcomes, mutually acceptable outcomes do occur. Since both parties are averse to "losing face" most successful outcomes are the result, in large part, of one or both sides "reframing" their notions of the issues and the potential consequences (ibid). During the process of negotiation one side may realize that its position may entail some undesirable consequences (ibid). For instance, if threatened by a strike a company may decide to increase their benefit or wage proposal since it may feel that a strike may result in worse undesirable consequences (loss of revenue, loss of customers, harm to its reputation) than would meeting the demands of the workers.

Another impediment to successful negotiations occurs when one or both sides have a "zero-sum" conceptualization of the negotiation process. They may believe that for them to "win" the other side must "lose." "Either or" and "all or none" types of mind-sets are especially likely to develop during times of stress and when the stakes are high. Thus it is important that both parties don't think in terms of a zero-sum outcome but instead reframe their thinking in terms of a "win-win" outcome where each side will get some of what they want but not all.

GRIT is an acronym for graduated reciprocation in tension reduction. It is an approach to conflict resolution that was developed by Professor Charles Osgood at the University of Illinois in 1959. He initially developed the approach to be applied to macro political conflicts and hostilities especially between the U.S. and Russia. The nature of the strategy is such however, that it can also be applied to interpersonal, intra-organizational and inter organizational conflicts as well. Application of GRIT involves one side indicating that it will make a concession to the other side with the idea that that the other side will reciprocate. If indeed the other side reciprocates the other party makes another concession, usually one that is more significant than the first one. This process persists until the issue that caused the conflict is completely resolved to the satisfaction of both parties. This approach works best when the both the size and importance of the concessions made by each side are perceived to be about equal.

For example, if a conflict between the employees' union and management, is at a standstill, management, after refusing the union's demand that workers have 10 days of sick leave rather than the 5 that they currently have, may propose 7. If accepted by the union, in reciprocation, it may propose that a 5%

increase in wages annually would be acceptable to them compared to the 8% that they initially demanded. As important as the substantive modifications are, equally important is the climate of mutual trust and respect that is engendered between the two sides. Once the process of reciprocal concessions begins it creates a virtuous cycle that can lead to the elimination of the conflict.

CONCLUSION

This chapter has covered a lot of groundwork and provides a quick and through introduction to the concepts and underlying discussions on organizational conflicts and their resolution. The chapter provided a detailed discussion based on extant literature and followed up with an empirically grounded discussion on the theoretical constructs. The reader will appreciate that this chapter only begins to scratch the surface; it remains a burden on the readers to explore the topics in detail themselves.

REFERENCES

Amason, A. C. (1996). Distinguishing the Effects of Functional and Dysfunctional Conflict on Strategic Decision Making: Resolving a Paradox for Top Management Groups. *Academy of Management Journal*, *39*(1), 123–148. doi:10.2307/256633

Amason, A. C., & Sapienza, H. J. (1997). The Effects of Top Management Team Size and Interaction Norms on Cognitive and Affective Conflict. *Journal of Management*, *23*(4), 495–516. doi:10.1177/014920639702300401

Baron, R. A. (1990). Conflict in Organizations. In K. R. Murphy & F. E. Saal (Eds.), *Psychology in Organizations: Integrating Science and Practice*. Hillsdale, NJ: Lawrence Erlbaum and Associates.

Beals, A. R., & Siegel, B. J. (1966). *Divisiveness and social conflict: an athropological approach*. Stanford, CA: Stanford University Press.

Bies, R. J., Shapiro, D. L., & Cummings, L. L. (1988). Casual Accounts and Managing Organizational Conflict. *Communication Research*, *15*(4), 381–399. doi:10.1177/009365088015004003

Billingham, R. E., & Sack, A. R. (1987). Conflict Tactics and The Level of Emotional Commitment Among Unmarried. *Human Relations*, *40*(1), 59–74. doi:10.1177/001872678704000105

Bisno, H. (1988). *Managing Conflict*. Newbury Park, CA: Sage.

Blake, R. R., & Mouton, J. S. (1964). *The Managerial Grid*. Houston, TX: Gulf Publishing Company.

Boulding, E. (1962). *Conflict and Defense*. New York: Harper and Row.

Brown, R., & Gaertner, S. (Eds.). (2003). *Blackwell Handbook of Social Psychology: Intergroup Processes*. Oxford, UK: Blackwell publishing. doi:10.1002/9780470693421

Burton, J. W. (1998). Conflict Resolution: The Human Dimension. *International Journal of Peace Studies*, *3*(1), 4.

Carnevale, P. J., & Pruitt, D. G. (1992). Negotiation and Mediation. *Annual Review of Psychology*, *43*(1), 531–582. doi:10.1146/annurev.ps.43.020192.002531

Chen, M. (2006). Understanding the Benefits and Detriments of Conflict on Team Creativity Process. *Creativity and Innovation Management*, *15*(1), 105–116. doi:10.1111/j.1467-8691.2006.00373.x

Chua, E. G., & Gundykunst, W. B. (1987). Conflict Resolution Styles in Low and High-Context Cultures. *Communication Research Reports*, *4*(1), 32–37.

Clegg, S. (1990). *Modern Organizations: Organization Studies in the Postmodern World*. London: Sage Publications Ltd.

Coser, L. A. (1956). *The Functions of Social Conflict*. New York: Macmillan.

Coser, L. A. (1967). *Continuities in the study of Social Conflict*. New York: Free Press.

De Dreu, C. K. W. (2006). When Too Much and Too Llittle Hurts: Evidence For a Curvilinear Relationship Between Task Conflict and Innovation in Teams. *Journal of Management*, *32*(1), 83–107. doi:10.1177/0149206305277795

De Dreu, C. K. W., & Gelfand, M. J. (2008). *The Psychology of Conflict and Conflict Management in Organizations*. Oxford, UK: Taylor & Francis.

De Dreu, C. K. W., & Van de Vliert, E. (Eds.). (1997). *Using Conflict in Organizations*. London: Sage.

De Dreu, C. K. W., & Weingart, L. R. (2003). Task Versus Relationship Conflict, Team Member Satisfaction, and Team Effectiveness: A Meta-Analysis. *The Journal of Applied Psychology*, *88*, 741–749. doi:10.1037/0021-9010.88.4.741 PMID:12940412

Deutsch, M. (1949). A Theory of Cooperation and Competition. *Human Relations*, *2*(2), 129–152. doi:10.1177/001872674900200204

Deutsch, M. (1973). Conflicts: Productive and Destructuve. In F. E. Jandt (Ed.), *Conflict Resolution Through Communication* (p. 156). New York: Harper & Row.

Deutsch, M., & Coleman, P. (Eds.). (2000). *The Handbook of Conflict Resolution: Theory and practice*. San Francisco, CA: Jossey Bass.

Donohue, W., & Colt, R. (1992). *Managing Interpersonal Conflict*. Newbury Park, CA: Sage. doi:10.4135/9781483325873

Fink, C. F. (1968). Some Conceptual Difficulties in the Theory of Social Conflict. *The Journal of Conflict Resolution*, *12*(4), 412–460. doi:10.1177/002200276801200402

Fisher, B., & Thomas, B. (1996). *Real Dream Teams*. Delray Beach, FL: St. Louis Press.

Fisher, R., Ury, W. L., & Patton, B. (1991). *Getting to Yes: Negotiating Agreement without Giving In*. New York, NY: Penguin Books.

Follett, M. P. (1925). Constructive Conflict. In H. C. Metcalf (Ed.), *Scientific Foundations of Business Administration*. Baltimore, MD: Williams and Wilkins.

Garfinkel, H. (1967). *Studies in Ethnomethodology*. Englewood Cliffs, NJ: Prentice Hall.

Getzels, J. W., & Guba, E. (1954). Role, Role Confict, and Effectiveness: An Empirical Study. *American Sociological Review*, *19*(2), 164–175. doi:10.2307/2088398

Gibson, J. L., Ivancevish, J. M., & Donnelly, J. H. Jr. (1991). *Organizations: Behavior Structure Processes*. Homewood, Illinois: Irwin.

Goldman, R. M. (1966). A Theory of Conflict Processes and Organizational Offices. *The Journal of Conflict Resolution*, *10*(3), 328–343. doi:10.1177/002200276601000305

Goleman, D. (1997). *Working with Emotional Intelligence*. New York, NY: Bantam.

Greenberg, J., & Baron, R. A. (1993). *Behavior in Organizations: Understanding and Managing the Human Side of Work* (4th ed.). Boston, MA: Allyn and Bacon.

Hague, J. (1974). *Communication and Organizational Control*. New York: Wiley.

Hall, J. (1969). *Conflict Management Survey*. Conroe, TX: Teleometrics.

Hocker, J. L., & Wilmot, W. W. (1991). *Interpersonal Conflict* (3rd ed.). Dubuque, IA: Brown.

Hocker, J. L., & Wilmot, W. W. (1995). *Interpersonal Conflict* (4th ed.). Dubuque, IA: Brown & Benchmark.

Jehn, K. A. (1994). Enhancing effectivenes: An investigation of advantages and disadvantages of value-based intragroup conflict. *The International Journal of Conflict Management*, *5*(3), 223–238. doi:10.1108/eb022744

Jehn, K. A. (1995). A Multi-Method Examination of the Benefits and Detriments of Intragroup Conflict. *Administrative Science Quarterly*, *40*(2), 256–282. doi:10.2307/2393638

Jehn, K. A. (1997). A Qualitative Analysis of Conflict Types and Dimensions in Organizational Groups. *Administrative Science Quarterly*, *42*(5), 530–557. doi:10.2307/2393737

Jehn, K. A., & Mannix, E. A. (2001). The dynamic nature of conflict: A longitudinal study of intragroup conflict and group performance. *Academy of Management Journal*, *44*(2), 238–251. doi:10.2307/3069453

Jehn, K. A., Northcraft, G., & Neale, M. A. (1999). Why difference makes a difference: A field study of diversity, conflict and performance in work group. *Administrative Science Quarterly*, *44*(4), 741–763. doi:10.2307/2667054

Jensen, C., & Scacchi, W. (2004). *Collaboration, Leadership, Control, and Conflict Negotiation in the Netbeans.org Community*. Paper presented at the 4th workshop on Open Source Software Engineering, Edinburgh, UK. doi:10.1049/ic:20040264

Jones, R. E., & Deckro, R. F. (1993). The Social Psychology of Project Management Conflict. *European Journal of Operational Research*, *64*(2), 216–228. doi:10.1016/0377-2217(93)90178-P

Jordan, J. V. (1990). *Courage in Connection: Conflict, Compassion, and Creativity*. Retrieved from Kabanoff, B. (1987). Predictive Validity of the MODE Conflict Instrument. *The Journal of Applied Psychology*, *72*, 160–163.

Katzenback, J. R., & Smith, D. K. (1994, March-April). The Discipline of Teams. *Harvard Business Review*.

Klausner, M. (2007). High Performance Work Teams. In A. Farazmand (Ed.), *Strategic Public Personnel Administration* (Vol. 2, pp. 301–318). Westport, CT: Proeger.

Klausner, M., & Groves, M. A. (1994). Organizational Conflict. In A. Farazmand (Ed.), *Handbook of Bureaucracy* (pp. 355–372). New York, NY: CRC Press.

Kochan, T., Cummings, L. C., & Huber, G. (1976). Operationalizin the Concepts of Goals and Goal Incompatibility in Organizational Behavior Research. *Human Relations*, *29*(6), 527–544. doi:10.1177/001872677602900603

Kolb, D., & Bartunek, J. M. (Eds.). (1992). *Hidden Conflict in Organizations: Uncovering Behind-the-Scenes Disputes*. Newbury Park, CA: Sage. doi:10.4135/9781483325897

Kraybill, R. (2011). *Style Matters*. Academic Press.

Kurdek, L. A. (1994). Conflict Resolution Styles in Gay, Lesbian, Heterosexual Nonparent, and Heterosexual Parent Couples. *Journal of Marriage and the Family*, *56*(3), 705–722. doi:10.2307/352880

Lawrence, P. R., & Lorsch, J. W. (1967). Differentiation and Integration in Complex Organizations. *Administrative Science Quarterly*, *12*(1), 1–47. doi:10.2307/2391211

Lawrence, P. R., & Lorsch, J. W. (1967). New Management job: The Integrator. *Harvard Business Review*, (November - December), 142–151.

Leung, M., Liu, A. M. M., & Ng, S. T. (2005). Is There a Relationship Between Construction Conflicts and Participants' Satisfaction? *Engineering, Construction, and Architectural Management*, *12*(2), 149–167. doi:10.1108/09699980510584494

Lewicki, R. J. (1983). Lying and Deception: A Behavioral Model. In M. H. Bazerman & R. J. Lewicki (Eds.), *Negotiating in Organizations*. Beverly Hills, CA: Sage.

Lovelace, K., Shapiro, D. L., & Weingart, L. R. (2001). Maximizing Crossfunctional New Product Teams' Innovativeness and Constraint Ahderence: A Conflict Information Exchanges Perspective. *Academy of Management Journal*, *44*, 779–783. doi:10.2307/3069415

March, J., & Simon, H. A. (1958). *Organizations*. New York, NY: Wiley.

Marek, J. (1966). Conflict, a battle of strategies. In J. Lawrence (Ed.), *Organizational research and the social science* (p. 64). London: Tavistock.

Medina, F. J., Munduate, L., Dorado, M., & Guerra, J. M. (2005). Types of Intragroup Conflict and Affective Reactions. *Journal of Managerial Psychology*, *20*(3/4), 219–230. doi:10.1108/02683940510589019

Morrill, C. (1995). *The Executive Way: Conflict Management in Corporations*. Chicago: The University of Chicago Press.

Nelson, D., & Quick, J. (1996). *Organizational Behavior*. Minneapolis, MN: West.

Parsons, T. (1951). *The Social System*. Glencoe, IL: The Free Press.

Perrow, C. (1986). *Complex Organizations*. New York, NY: Random House.

Pondy, L. (1964). Organizational Conflict: Concepts and Models. In H. J. Leavitt, L. Pondy, & M. Boje (Eds.), *Readings in Managerial Psychology* (p. 513). Chicago: Chicago University Press.

Pondy, L. (1967). Reflections on Organizational Conflict. *Journal of Organizational Behavior, 13*(3), 257–261. doi:10.1002/job.4030130305

Popper, K. R. (1966). The Open Society and Its Enemies: The Spell of Plato (vol. 1; 5th ed.). London: Routledge & Kegan Paul.

Pruitt, D. G. (1983). Strategic Choice in Negotiation. *The American Behavioral Scientist, 27*(2), 167–194. doi:10.1177/000276483027002005

Pruitt, D. G., & Carnevale, P. J. (1993). *Negotiation and Social Conflict*. Buckingham, UK: Open University Press.

Pruitt, D. G., & Rubin, J. Z. (1986). *Social Conflict: Escalation, Stalemate, Settlement*. New York, NY: Random House.

Putnam, L. L., & Wilson, C. E. (1982). Communicative Strategies in Organizational Conflicts: Reliability and Validity of a Measurement Scale. In M. Burgoon (Ed.), *Communication Yearbook 6* (pp. 629–652). Beverly Hills, CA: Sage.

Rahim, M. A. (1983). *Rahim Organizational Conflict Inventories*. Palo Alto, Calif.: Consulting Psychologists Press.

Rahim, M. A. (1986). *Managing Conflict in Organizations*. New York, NY: Praeger.

Rahim, M. A. (2001). *Managing Conflict in Organizations* (3rd ed.). Westport, CT: Quorum Books.

Rahim, M. A., & Bonoma, T. V. (1979). Managing Organizational Conflict: A Model for Diagnosis and Intervention. *Psychological Reports, 44*(3c), 1323–1344. doi:10.2466/pr0.1979.44.3c.1323

Rands, M., Levinger, G., & Mellinger, G. D. (1981). Patterns of Conflict Resolution and Marital Satisfaction. *Journal of Family Issues, 2*, 297–321.

Reichers, A. E. (1986). Conflict and Organizational Commitments. *The Journal of Applied Psychology, 71*(3), 7. doi:10.1037/0021-9010.71.3.508

Robbins, S. P. (1974). *Managing Organizational Conflict: A Nontraditional Approach*. Englewood Cliffs, NJ: Prentice-Hall.

Ross, L. (1977). The Intuitive Psycologist and His Shortcomings: Distortions in the Attribution Process. In L. Berkowitz (Ed.), *Advances in Experimental and Social Psycology*. New York, NY: Academic Press.

Ross, R., & DeWine, S. (1982). Interpersonal Conflict: Measurement and Validation. Louisville, KY: Academic Press.

Sherif, M. (1966). *In Common Predicament: Social Psychology of Intergroup Conflict and Cooperation*. Boston: Houghton Mifflin.

Shockley-Zalabak, P. (1988). Assessing the Hall conflict Management Survey. *Management Communication Quarterly, 1*(3), 302–320. doi:10.1177/0893318988001003003

Simons, T. L., & Peterson, R. S. (2000). Task Conflict and Relationship Conflict in Top Management Teams: The Pivotal Role of Intragroup Trust. *The Journal of Applied Psychology, 85*(1), 102–111. doi:10.1037/0021-9010.85.1.102 PMID:10740960

Socklingam, S., & Doswell, A. (1999). Conflict in BPR. *Knowledge and Process Management, 6*(3), 146–153. doi:10.1002/(SICI)1099-1441(199909)6:3<146::AID-KPM63>3.0.CO;2-3

Thomas, K. W. (1976). Conflict and Conflict Management. In M. D. Dunnette (Ed.), *Handbook of Industrial and Organizational Psychology*. Chicago: Rand-McNally.

Thomas, K. W. (1984). Dynamics of Escalation/De-Escalation. In J. Veiga & J. Yanouzas (Eds.), *The Dynamics of Organization Theory* (pp. 283–300). St. Paul, MN: West.

Thomas, K. W. (1992). Conflict and Negotiation Processes in Organizations. In M. D. Dunnette (Ed.), *Handbook of Industrial and Organizational Psychology* (2nd ed.; pp. 889–935). Palo Alto, CA: Consulting Psychologists Press.

Thomas, K. W., & Kilmann, R. H. (1974). *The Thomas-Kilmann Conflict Mode Instrument*. Tuxedo, NY: Xicom.

Thompson, J. D. (1967). *Organizations in Action*. New York, NY: McGraw-Hill.

Tolbert, P., & Hall, R. (2009). *Organizations: Structures, Processes and Outcomes*. Upper Saddle River, NJ: Pearson.

Trice, H., & Beyer, J. M. (1993). *The Culture of Work Organizations*. Englewood Cliffs, NJ: Prentice Hall.

Turner, M. E., & Pratkanis, A. (1994). Social Identity Maintenance Prescriptions for Preventing Groupthink: Reducing Identity Protection and Enhancing Intellectual Conflict. *The International Journal of Conflict Management, 5*(3), 254–270. doi:10.1108/eb022746

Van de Vliert, E., & Kabanoff, B. (1990). Toward Theory-Based Measures of Conflict Management. *Academy of Management Journal, 33*(1), 199–209. doi:10.2307/256359

Van de Vliert, E., & Prein, H. C. M. (1989). The Difference in the Meaning of Forcing in the Conflict Management of Actors and Observers. In M. A. Rahim (Ed.), *Managing conflict: An interdisciplinary approach* (pp. 51–63). New York, NY: Praeger.

Walton, R. E. (1966). A theory of conflict in lateral organizational relationships. In J. Lawrence (Ed.), *Operational research and the social sciences* (p. 411). London: Tavistock.

Wells, T. (1980). *Keeping Your Cool Under Fire: Communicating Non-defensively*. New York, NY: McGraw-Hill.

West, M. A., & Anderson, N. R. (1996). Innovation in top management teams. *The Journal of Applied Psychology, 81*(6), 680–693. doi:10.1037/0021-9010.81.6.680

Wilson, J. A., & Jerrell, S. L. (1981). Conflict: Malignant, Beneficial, or Benign. *New Directions for Higher Education*, *1981*(3), 105–123. doi:10.1002/he.36919813510

KEY TERMS AND DEFINITIONS

Aristotelian: A belief based on the philosophy of Aristotle where one seeks out a deeper understanding of the good of an action, deed, or speech so that the most value of that good may be achieved.

Conflict: A condition typified by some sort of struggle between two or more parties arising from concerns over the distribution or allocation of resources.

Conflict Episode: A conflict event that will have a beginning and ending, a reason for the conflict, actors participating in the conflict, and parties that will be affected (directly or indirectly).

Conflict Styles: Several styles of handling conflicts have been identified. These are named based on the number of techniques proposed by each style. At present the highest number of tactics in a conflict style is five.

High-Context Culture: A culture that is contextually dense and requires that cultural norms and values be withheld during a conflict-episode.

High Performance Work Team: A team that is highly focused on its goals and seeks to achieve optimum business results.

Utopian Engineering: A belief based on the philosophy of Plato that one could conceive and implement a planned ideal society. Such a belief is criticized because it ignores the multidimensional complexities of human nature and social reality.

Chapter 4
Environmental Conflicts

Cristian Ioja
University of Bucharest, Romania

Mihai R. Nita
University of Bucharest, Romania

Constantina Alina Hossu
University of Bucharest, Romania

ABSTRACT

Environmental conflicts have become a topical issue in the international research because of their complexity where social, economic, political and cultural factors operate. Their assessment is essential for understanding these factors and thus contributing to the formulation of effective resolution strategies. In this chapter the authors discuss the defining characteristics of the environmental conflicts as well as methods and approaches for their assessment and resolution. European environmental policies are used as examples of environmental conflicts drivers in order to highlight the large number of involved factors that undermine their successful implementation. This chapter ends the discussion with the presentation of the resolution efforts in multi-issue conflicts where a neutral party adds values to the process, advancing it towards an efficient ending.

INTRODUCTION

Conflicts are not wanted by societies, although they may stimulate progress (Iojă et al., 2015), though they occur spontaneously or controlled, and establish new balances in the society. Conflicts undermine the socio-economic systems, provide easy access to resources or ecosystem services and withdraw the attention from the real problems that may happen concomitantly. Although conflicts are often caused by the infringement of legislation or by the care for society or environment, the political and economic interests are definitely the *real fuel* of contemporary conflicts.

DOI: 10.4018/978-1-5225-0245-6.ch004

Environmental conflicts are situations where at least one actor opposes (as the result of the infringement of some principles listed in the environmental policies, strategies and legislation), to another actor who promotes a plan, project, or activity that supports or changes the status quo (Iojă et al., 2015; Schmidtz & Willott, 2002; Torre et al., 2014). Most environmental conflicts have a complex history, where feelings of suspicion, mistrust, misunderstanding, lack of sympathy, or desire for power mix together with previous experiences and the diverse interests of actors and become the seeds of conflicts.

Environmental conflicts are often fueled by administrative documents, such as: petitions, complaints and appeals; communication media, such as newspapers, televisions, internet, social networks or other means of communication; verbal confrontations or public debates, protests by blocking access to certain areas or institutions as well as violence. Environmental conflicts are mostly solved by court actions (e.g. litigation) or by consensual approaches (e.g. negotiation) (Susskind & Cruikshank, 1987).

This chapter presents a wide range of approaches used in environmental conflicts assessment and resolution. The environmental conflicts which are targeted are those which result from the unsuccessful implementation of different environmental policies.

In the *Background* section, the defining characteristics of environmental conflicts are presented. These need a deeper understanding in the processes of conflict management and resolution. The following characteristics of environmental conflicts need to be considered: triggering events (such as a change, competitive interests or law enforcement), spatial characteristics (the location and scale of manifestation), temporal characteristics (duration, actuality, and progress over time), socio-economic dimension (involved actors, mass media means, claimed damage, and cultural characteristics) as well as the ecological dimension (environmental, economic, and social impact and law inconsistency).

In the section entitled *European Union's policies – drivers of environmental conflicts*, the authors present the main changes proposed at European level which cause tensions and the different ways in which different European directives and policies cause environmental conflicts. The relevant policies for this purpose are: the nature conservation policies (with a focus on the establishment of the Natura 2000 ecological network), renewable energy policies (required to meet the carbon emissions targets), waste management policies (promoting a circular economy model), water resources management policies (which refer to the qualitative and quantitative improvement of water resources) and the agriculture policies aiming is to improve the efficiency of agricultural activities by complying with the environmental requirements).

In the sections focused on *Main approaches in environmental conflict assessment and resolution*, data sources which can be used to understand them and various methods and tools are presented. For environmental conflict assessment a range of methods, such as interviews, spatial analysis, multi-criteria analysis and tools for environmental conflicts research (GIS, remote sensing, and diverse software) are presented. Regarding environmental conflicts resolution, the traditional legal processes and the consensual and participative processes are discussed.

In the *Conclusion section* the future research directions in environmental conflicts research are addressed.

The objectives of the paper are: (a) highlighting the defining characteristics and assessment methods of environmental conflicts; (b) presenting the role of environmental European policies in triggering environmental conflicts in the EU, and (c) discussing the main approaches in environmental conflict resolution.

BACKGROUND

Conflicts are always present in a changing society (Torre et al., 2014). Society's orientation towards sustainability, global environmental changes, legislative and demographic changes, changes in the consumption and production patterns as well as attempts to mainstream conservation objectives into land-use practices of communities from areas with valuable biotic and abiotic resources are certainly the global drivers of the increasing diverse environmental conflicts (Daniels & Walker, 2001).

At political level, the top-down strategies have reclaimed their role of imposing increasingly tougher environmental regulations in the European Union. At European level, environmental regulations have an increasing impact on the economy and society, favoring antagonistic groups that activate environmental conflicts. The promotion of the sustainable development principles in economy (greening economy, circular economy, and low carbon economy) or in urban development (sustainable cities and eco-cities), the strengthening of the environmental institutions role at administrative level, the improvement of citizens' response capacity against situations which appear to be unacceptable, the requirement of public participation in decision-making process innumerous domains, all represent factors which contribute to environmental conflicts occurrence (Iojă et al., 2015).

Therefore, as the environmental standards promoted by environmental policies and strategies have expanded, environmental conflicts have also become more diverse. Initially, environmental conflicts were related to claims concerning damages produced by the big polluters (e.g. from the chemical or nuclear industry, from the maritime transportation of hazardous materials) (Melé, 2012), the competition for natural resources exploitation (Cogoy & Steininger, 2007) and the violation of rights-of-use for various resources (including land) (Torre et al., 2014).

The ambitious targets of environmental policies have favored new types of environmental conflicts related to (Figure 1): the *damage or destruction of the natural resources* (e.g., depletion or damage of water resources); *generation of negative externalities* (odors, noise, air, water and soil pollution); *impact on the structure and functionality of some neighboring properties* (proximity conflicts); *access restriction to different natural resources or services* (interdiction of using pastures or forests, fishing and hunting restrictions, etc.); *the need to include public input into the decision making process; the requirement of using certain types of products, services and technologies with a reduced environmental impact* (renewable energy, clean fuels, clean vehicles, or ecological electrical equipment); or *the power differences between different organizations* (government institutions, economic agents, non-governmental organizations, researchers, local communities, etc.) (Daniels & Walker, 2001).

The lack of maturity or will in understanding the true stakes of environmental conflicts as well as the ignorance of getting involved in different stages of conflicts development have turned the local authorities and communities in spectators and helpless participants to these *shows* often with public display (Maser & Pollio, 2012). Thus, the poor involvement or passivity regarding the environmental conflicts have considerably lowered trust in environmental institutions, in public involvement and mechanisms of abuses control, and have limited the benefits for a highly restricted group of participants (Diehk & Gleditsch, 2001).

The notable empowerment of NGO's with very categorical views on some environmental problems has triggered many environmental conflicts, but also has increased the chances for reasonable and fair solutions, even for passive groups participants (Sidaway, 2005). In this general framework, the involve-

Figure 1 Types of environmental conflicts (after C. Iojă et al. (2015))

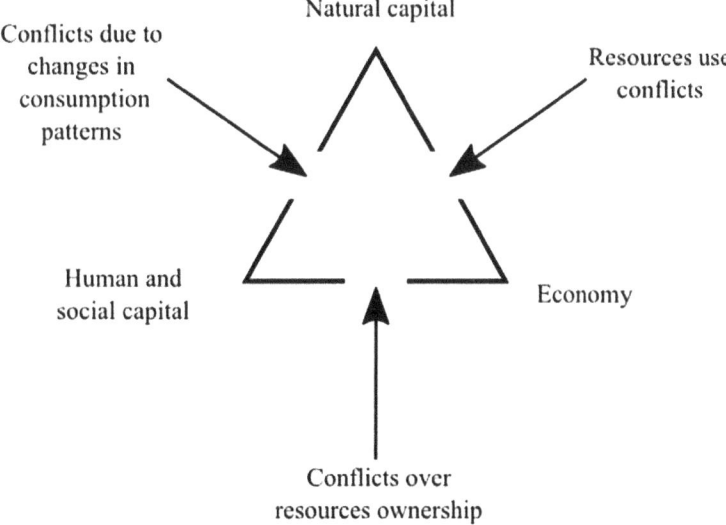

ment of scientists in assessing environmental conflicts is necessary in order to assure both a specialized expertise useful in understanding and constructively managing the conflicts and a certain level of transparency and fairness in their resolution (Owens & Cowell, 2011).

In environmental conflicts management, the understanding of their defining characteristics is very important. The most relevant characteristics are (Figure 2):

Figure 2 Environmental conflicts characteristics (after Iojă et al. (2015))

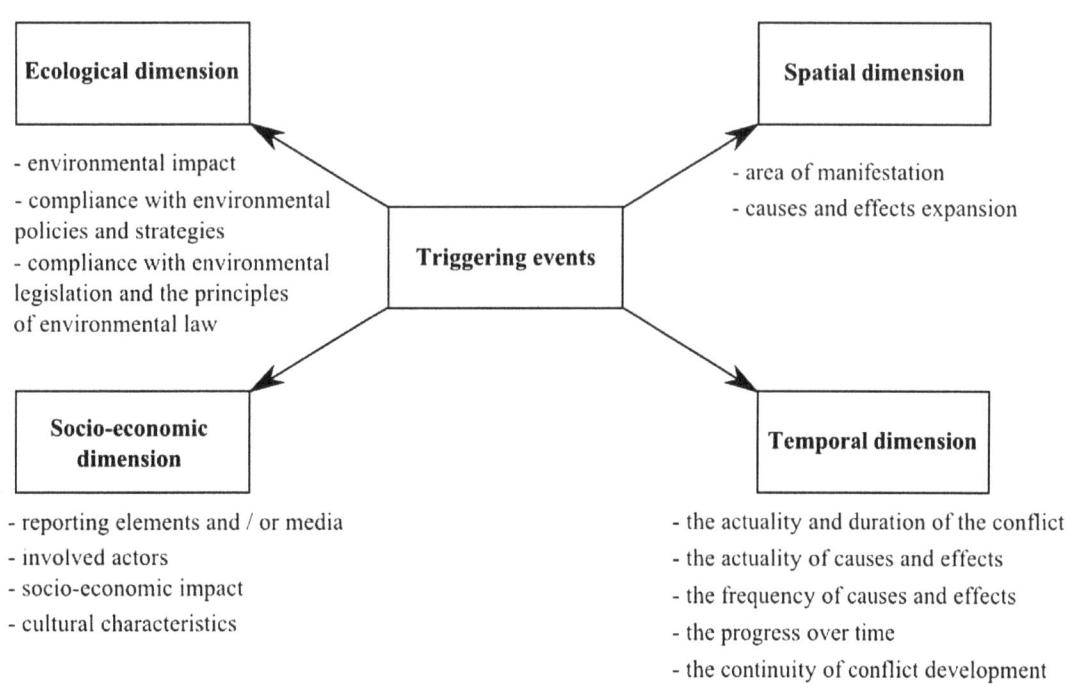

1. *The triggering events* (Table 1). The triggering events of environmental conflicts are those related to: *believes* (of what it is fair or wrong), *interests* (competitions for resources or power), *data* (poor information for understanding the conflict), *relations* (poor means of communication, misunderstandings between parties) and *procedures* (unclear regulations, lack of transparency or poor participation in the decision making process) (Lumerman, Psathakis, & Ortiz, 2011). Zuindeau (2010) considers that the promotion of sustainable development and the change in consumption patterns are among the most important triggering factors of environmental conflicts. Iojă et al. (2015) state that change, competition and legislation are the most important causes of environmental conflicts. In all situations, *the spark* of conflict is ignited by a petition, complaint, appeal or other form of opposition.

2. *The spatial dimension*. Each environmental conflict is triggered by a spatial event which shapes its evolution, the variety of involved actors and the resolution methods. The event can have the shape of a *point* (disputes regarding the construction of an airport), *linear* (oppositions on building a railway) or *diffuse* (protests against pesticides use in agriculture) in manifestation. The scale of environmental conflicts manifestation is an essential spatial characteristic that helps in selecting the most appropriate resolution methods. The complexity of such conflict increases as their area of manifestation is greater. Therefore, most of the environmental conflicts are local. Regional and national environmental conflicts involve oppositions on issues of larger extent, in many cases is about conflicts between large interest groups with different values and identity, but also with much higher power. At continental and global scale, the involved actors go beyond the national bound-

Table 1 Triggering events for environmental conflicts

Triggering Events	Examples
Change	Changes in land use which brought new relations between adjacent uses (including conflicting land uses); Changes in land and other resources ownership; Changes due to the interests of exploiting natural resources (e.g., shale gas); Changes due to a proposed plan and/or project; Changes due to the proposal or extension of some activities with environmental impact; Changes due to the enforcement through legislation of land use restrictions (e.g. the establishment of protected areas); Changes due to the enforcement through legislation of tougher regulations (e.g. changing emissions levels, banning the use of certain substances or products); Changes in people's perception; Changes due to unforeseen events (e.g. natural risks).
Competition	Production vs. Production (e.g. food vs. biofuel); Production vs. Conservation (e.g. mineral resources extraction vs. conservation of large carnivores); Conservation vs. Conservation (e.g. pastures conservation vs. forests conservation); Urbanization vs. Production (e.g. urban expansion vs. built-up increase); Urbanization vs. Conservation (e.g. urban expansion vs. environmental resources conservation); Urbanization vs. Urbanization (e.g. residential areas vs. industrial areas); Competition related to the exploitation of scarce resources (e.g. water resources in arid areas); Competition related to the exploitation of sufficient resources (e.g. inequities in the distribution of the benefits resulted from exploitation).
Legislation	Too ambitious targets which favor certain actors or which produce obvious imbalances at socio-economic level. Public participation in the decision making process; Actors' failure to complain with the environmental law; Inappropriate application of the legislation by the competent institutions; Relations between different institutions.

aries, and the resolution methods are more complex. Relevant at this scale are the environmental conflicts related to the failure to comply with international conventions and treaties, to the negative consequences of some anthropic interventions, to accidental pollution, common resources exploitation or global environmental problems.

3. *The temporal dimension.* Environmental conflicts are defined by duration, actuality, and progress over time. In terms of actuality, environmental conflicts can be: *historical* (inherited), *actual* or *potential*, having a *latent* (passive) or *active, as well as a permanent or temporal* character (Iojă et al., 2015). When conflicts are the consequence of a change, they can occur in different stages of a project: in the pre-construction phase of a site (because of the expropriation), in the construction phase of a site (crossing some properties, the extraction of raw materials), in the exploitation phase (environmental externalities with impact on people's health) or in the post-activity phase (environmental contamination with persistent substances). Another important aspect in the assessment of environmental conflicts is their progress over time. Environmental conflicts can be spontaneous or the result of accumulation of tensions over a longer period (*accumulation phase*). Accumulated tensions tend to shape opposite sides, which have the tendency to force winning as much as possible, based on enemies' weaknesses, or poor communication (*latent phase*). After the accumulation phase and once with the intensification of the actions of the involved parties the escalation of the conflict starts (*escalation phase*). Subsequently, adverse camps seek legitimacy, higher power, trying to support their point of view, aiming to achieve a favorable resolution (*release and active phase*) (Sidaway, 2005). Conflicts progress over time is particularly relevant for chronic conflicts which periodically worsens and evolves towards deep crisis.

4. *The socio-economic dimension.* Environmental conflicts have always developed in interaction with socio-economic and political factors, never being separated from these (Mason & Spillman, 2002). From a socio-economic point of view the environmental conflicts are defined by:

   a. *Reporting elements/media,* such as petitions; complaints; public events through which the affected actors gather together and fight against what disturbs them; media; NGOs and public protests.

   b. *Involved actors.* The actors involved in conflicts have *positions* (attitudes in the negotiation process, attitudes of claim, demand or resolution), *interests* (motivations, needs, and desires), *values* and *divergent beliefs* (visions) (Madden & McQuinn, 2014; Sidaway, 2005), which are often influenced by the local, regional or national characteristics. The actors in environmental conflicts can be: the state, the regional/local government authorities, private companies and investors, citizens (residents, tourists, landowners, etc.), organizations for environmental protection, planning offices, experts with different professional backgrounds, non-governmental organizations, or community groups united by the similarity of issues under debate.

   c. *Interests on conflict resolution or stagnation.* Based on the actors' interests, environmental conflicts can be solved, when all involved actors succeed to meet their objectives (through negotiations and dialogue when they reach a compromise) or can be intractable (when no actor succeeds to achieve his/her objectives, and the conflicts becomes destructive) (Lewicki, Gray, & Elliott, 2003).

   d. *Produced damage.* In each environmental conflict damages exist, which can be material or hedonic, at least for one party. The damage can be anticipated or recorded, being the main argument for the conflict.

e. *Cultural conditions.* Conflicts evolvement is influenced by the cultural characteristics of the involved actors. The previous experiences, the existence of some resolution techniques at local level, beliefs, openness to novelty, education level, predisposition to aggression, social relationships between individuals and structures are only a few of the aspects which define an environmental conflict based on the cultural characteristics.

5. *The ecological dimension.* Each environmental conflict has an ecological component which distinguishes it from other types of conflicts. The impact on the local, regional or national economy, on people's health and well-being, on biotic and abiotic resources, on patrimony goods, or on the functioning of environmental protection institutions, as well as the failure to comply with some principles, objectives or targets imposed by the environmental legislation are the most important reasons that allow the classification of a situation as an environmental conflict (Torre et al., 2014).

POLICIES OF THE EUROPEAN UNION: DRIVERS OF ENVIRONMENTAL CONFLICTS

The protection and wise management of environmental resources has become an important issue at EU level. In order to support a sustainable Europe and increase the awareness towards the real problems many policies have been released. Most of them have become the drivers of several environmental conflicts because of the contradictory preferences which exist in relation to the use of resources. Moreover, such conflicts usually manifest when a misfit exists between EU and national institutions in terms of proposed management objectives or imposed environmental standards.

Previous studies has largely concentrated on the conflicts triggered by EU biodiversity policies such as Birds (79/409/EC) and Habitats (92/43/EC), Waste Framework Directive (2008/98/EC), Water Framework Directive (2000/60/EC), Common Agricultural Policy (CAP), as well as Renewables (2009/28/EC) Directive.

Birds and Habitats Directives

Birds and Habitats Directives are responsible for many environmental conflicts, most of them being triggered by the imposed conservation restrictions over the wild species and natural habitats.

Regarding the *Birds Directive*, conflicts have been reported between different stakeholders who have incompatible interests in relation to rare and vulnerable species listed on the Annex I of the Directive. A good example is the conflict over the conservation of hen harriers (Baxter & Galbraith, 2010). This conflict was triggered by the illegal killing of the hen harriers by those who hunt the red grouse for commercial purposes, because this species reduce the grouse stocks. Other similar examples of conflicts, which involve species listed on the Annex I of the Directive, refer to the conflicts between the conservationists and fishermen because of the damages produced by the continental cormorants to the fishermen (Lindell, Mellin, Musil, Przybysz, & Zimmerman, 1995), as well as the conflicts between those involved in the eagle management and farmers regarding the reintroduction of the sea eagle in Ireland and its threat for sheep farmers (O'Rourke, 2014).

Concerning the *Habitat Directive*, conflicts has been reported both during and after its implementation. The main driver of the conflicts around this directive was the decision to establish an ecological network at European level, namely Natura 2000 network.

Generally, the Habitat Directive faced a slow implementation especially because of the varying and conflicting European and national priorities, unclear consequences of designing sites for Natura 2000 network, negative perceptions over the imposed conservation constraints as well as lack of public consultation and participation (Paavola, 2003). These reasons made the Member States to not devote too much effort in implementing the Directive and attracted strong oppositions in many countries.

For example, in Germany (Stoll-Kleemann, 2001) the oppositions involved even violence because the conservation regulations were seen as unfair restrictions by the landowners of the protected areas which had to be designated as Natura 2000 sites. Landowners considered that the regulations are restricting their personal rights over their land and they cannot benefit anymore from the recreation services offered by the landscapes in the way they did before, they cannot anymore use their land in the way they were used to and they are constrained in their activities by the conservationists. These restrictions were not part of public information and consultation processes and because they are meant to change the use of land and the landscape scenery, they received strong oppositions from some landowners who refused the establishment of Natura 2000 sites.

In Poland, for example, oppositions exist against the Natura 2000 programme, which is considered unnecessary (Grodzinska-Jurczak & Cent, 2011). According to some landowners such a program would trigger conflicts because it would block projects (e.g. infrastructure, housing) or businesses (e.g. agro-tourism, logging) for conservation reasons. A well-known conflict in Poland is triggered by the Natura 2000 network legal protection for the beaver (*Castor fiber*). The conflicts over this species have started between the conservationists and the fish farmers because the beavers destroy the levees as well as the irrigation infrastructure (Kloskowski, 2011). The conflicts have amplified because of the insufficient compensation measures, for the damage caused by the beaver, which have determined the farmers to use lethal as well as non-lethal methods to remove the species. According to the authors, the resolution of these conflicts could be facilitated by sustainable compensation schemes as well as subsidies for implementing non-lethal methods for preventing the damage produced by this species. A collaboration and open dialogue between the stakeholders could contribute to a better management of the nuisance wildlife species. Such human-beaver conflicts are common in areas where the landscape is managed by humans, where beavers build dams and produce damages to the crops (Halley & Rosell, 2002).

Another country where conflicts over the Habitat Directive were prominent is France (Alphandéry & Fortier, 2001). Here the conflicts were related to the first stage in Habitat Directive implementation, namely the identification of Natura 2000 sites. The sites identification faced strong oppositions especially because of the methods used to inventorize the future Natura 2000 sites, methods which were questioned for their scientific quality, being superficial and not fieldwork oriented. Moreover, the surface area for a Natura 2000 site was considered to be too wide and a reduction was desirable. As in the case of Germany most of these conflicts were triggered by the lack of public consultation and participation in the policy planning phase.

The second stage of Habitat Directive, namely, the establishment of the management plan for each designated Natura 2000 site generated problems in terms of measures implementation which failed to achieve ecological benefits due to financial reasons, such as funds scarcity (O'Rourke, 2014).

Renewable Energy Directive

The targets imposed by the *Renewable Energy Directive* (the Directive on the promotion of the use of energy from renewable sources) to the Member States have favored the proposal of many renewable energy projects. Most of the conflicts appear when these projects face opposition because they are proposed to be located in Natura 2000 sites where the species and their habitats which need protection are already designated under the Birds and Habitats Directive. An example of such conflicts is the case of a hydroelectric dam in Portugal and a tidal barrage in the UK (Jackson, 2011). The dam was proposed as an action against climate change and a contribution to Portugal's renewable energy obligations. The conflicts have started because of the legal issues around the project namely its location in Natura 2000 sites and the concerns over the negative impacts of the dam over landscape biodiversity and culture. Although the project rejection was discussed at EU level, because of its negative impact on Natura 2000 network, the law lose in the face of the political power and the energy project was accepted to be implemented. The barrage in the UK faced also legal difficulties in terms of compensation measures for the damage that it would create in the Natura 2000 sites. The negative impacts of the barrage could not be fully compensated as the European Commission requires, because of the large extent of the compensatory habitat and its unusual ecology which make it unique in the UK (Jackson, 2011).

Other example of conflicts around this Directive refers to the conflicts over biomass production for renewable energy in Italy. Conflicts arouse between the stakeholders who want to use the agricultural product for agricultural purposes (e.g. livestock feed) and those who want to use it for biomass production. Moreover, this conflict was a NIMBY conflict, because people believed that they are negatively affected by the sitting of a biomass plant which is unwanted from many reasons (Gissi, Siciliano, & Reho, 2011).

In an early version of the renewables Directive several conflicts involved: (i) the definition of renewables; the inclusion of many different kinds of resources was required and strong debates existed around the inclusion of hydropower (large scale hydropower) and biomass resources (e.g. municipal waste) as renewables, in order to be easier for member states to meet their targets, (ii) the targets flexibility status and (iii) the harmonization over support incentives for renewable electricity (Rowlands, 2005).

Waste Framework Directive

The revised *Waste Framework Directive* (2008/98/EC) aims at keeping away waste disposal in landfills and promote waste prevention, recovery and recycling (Nash, 2009). This shift in waste management hierarchy from traditional landfilling to modern management methods has triggered many environmental conflicts. Wolsink (2010) presents the case of a composting-incinerator facility in the Netherlands which was proposed to be located close to a village. Because Netherlands has insufficient landfill sites, and concerns about the environmental impacts of landfilling have started to appear, most of the investments were directed towards incinerating the waste and therefore the proposal of the facility. The political actors (proponents of waste prevention and sustainable waste management) and the residents opposed to the sitting of this facility, especially to the incinerator, while accepting the composting part. The main concerns were related to the air pollution caused by the incinerator and the risks for people's health and environmental quality.

Another similar case of environmental conflicts was driven by the pressures imposed by the directive to change the waste management practices, from waste disposal to waste recovery and recycling in the U.K. which was a country based on landfilling and less on recycling (Uyarra & Gee, 2013). To accomplish the directive requirements the country has opted for more sustainable waste practices. The proposal of incineration facilities triggered protests and was unwanted by the stakeholders because interferes with other EU directives focused on air pollution reduction. All these have determined the U.K. Greater Manchester conurbation to adopt a sustainable solution for waste management based on waste recycling and composting, keeping away landfill and incinerators.

The landfills negative impacts on people's health and high risk perception have triggered many locational conflicts (Johnson & Scicchitano, 2012). Recent studies have revealed the impact of landfills, highlighting problems such as odor, noise, waste, health risk (Che et al., 2013; Owusu, Oteng-Ababio, & Afutu-Kotey, 2012). Moreover, landfills are considered among the most unwanted public services (Dear, 1992), and occupy the 1st place among the most opposed land-uses in U.S.A. (78%), the 4th place in U.K. (72%) and the 2nd place in Canada (75%) (Saint, Flavell, & Fox, 2009). Decisions regarding the sitting of waste facilities could reach consensus especially if the locals participate in the process, and negotiations and communication are facilitated (Wolsink, 2004).

The focus of the Waste Directive to reduce the environmental impacts of waste landfills has brought fines to several EU countries, including Greece (Botetzagias & Karamichas, 2009), Italy (EC, 2010), and Slovenia (EC, 2014).

Water Framework Directive

The *Water Framework Directive* (WFD) whose aim focuses on achieving a good management of water resources has triggered conflicts in many countries. In Sweden, the planners consider the environmental standards established by the Directive being unclearly formulated. Moreover, the conflicts arise because the Directive impose a top-down control and vertical cooperation while Swedish tradition is characterized by a local control and a horizontal collaboration (Andersson, Petersson, & Jarsjö, 2012; Hedelin & Lindh, 2008).

The way how the countries behave in the policy formulation phase of WFD generates potential conflicts in the practical implementation phase of the Directive (Liefferink, Wiering, & Uitenboogaart, 2011). For example: (i) in Denmark stakeholders' participation is restricted in the policy formulation phase: (ii) in Netherlands there is low sector integration between water management and agriculture, and (iii) in France ambitions to not use the exemptions from deadlines imposed by WFD objectives prevail. All these are weakening the practical implementation of the Directive and inflame potential tensions and conflicts.

The main objective of the water directive, to achieve a good water quality status for all EU waters, has brought many conflicts especially because of the conflicting interests for water use and its protection.

Such a case is the Elbe catchment area, which lies on the territory of Germany and Czech Republic (Nunneri & Hofmann, 2005). The Elbe River catchment is affected by large nutrient emissions from industry (discharges from waste water treatment plants), inhabited areas and agriculture. The need to comply with the WFD targets in terms of water quality improvements has resulted in several conflicts with the farmers as the agriculture has remained the main source for nutrient pollution. The overall goal is to improve water quality and reduce nutrient emissions by convincing farmers to use more ecologically and economic efficient methods for a sustainable agriculture. The conflicts exist because the farmers do not cooperate to the other stakeholders to reach the WFT targets because they were not involved in the early stages of the directive's implementation and, for example, in Czech Republic farmers are not willing to pay higher taxes for the sake of environmental protection (Nunneri & Hofmann, 2005).

Common Agricultural Policy

The *Common Agricultural Policy* (CAP) was introduced in early 1980s. In its first years the policy was focused more on the intensification of agricultural production and less on biodiversity, which resulted in conflicts between agricultural production and biodiversity protection. Consequently, CAP was revised several times since its implementation in order to support biodiversity conservation (Henle, Alard, Clitherow, Cobb, Firbank, Kull, McCracken, Moritz, Niemela, et al., 2008; Young et al., 2005).

Conflicts around Common Agricultural Policy were extended even on species (Tella, Forero, Hiraldo, & Donazar, 1998). One example is the Lesser Kestrel which has become threatened because of the agricultural intensification due to CAP economic incentives. This species do not have any more a good quality foraging habitat because of land use intensification and had to large its habitat for hunting. As a consequence the species starved and its population has started to decrease. Other situation in which the funding incorporated in the CAP affects species concerns the farmland birds. The fact that the agri-environmental schemes (AES) are not allocated represents a risk over farmland birds (Butler, Boccaccio, Gregoryc, Vorisekd, & Norrisa, 2010). According to the authors, the farmland birds are declining because they depend on the implementation of these environmental incentives whose objectives revolve around biodiversity protection. Without these incentives the agricultural landscapes would become too intensified or even abandoned, having negative impact on farmland birds.

The CAP direct payments might also generate conflicts between the corporate farms and the landowners who receive rent for their land from such farms (Latruffe & Davidova, 2007). It is the case of the East European countries, where corporate farms prevail before family farms. These payments arouse landowners' interests to ask for high rents, otherwise they can withdraw their land from the corporate farms.

MAIN APPROACHES IN ENVIRONMENTAL CONFLICTS ASSESSMENT AND RESOLUTION

The assessment of the environmental conflicts characteristics is a topical issue in the international scientific research. This could be useful for the political, administrative and socio-economic targets, those related to circular and green economy, sustainable development, environment protection and conservation or efficient use of natural resources.

The complexity of environmental conflicts sets the diversity of data which can be used for their assessment, while in the meantime considerably hampers the assessment process. Such data can be obtained from the existing databases (Ioja, 2013) or can be generated through various research methods.

Data and Databases Necessary for Environmental Conflicts Assessment

The data related to environmental conflicts that have to be known for their assessment regards:

- Geographical location of the conflict;
- Characteristics of the key events which existed in the development of the environmental conflict;
- Triggering event and causes of the conflict;
- Consequences (including their geographical location);

- The actors involved in the conflict (including their positions and arguments);
- Conflict's reporting means;
- Conflict resolution.

Among the institutions which can offer useful information on environmental conflicts assessment, the most important are those which monitor and control environmental aspects, local governmental institutions, statistics institutes, institutes of natural risks management, environmental research institutes. Also of importance are the non-governmental organizations involved in different conflicts, online databases (http://ejatlas.org/), bibliographic and cartographic materials such as topographic maps, aerial photos, cadastral plans, thematic maps, as well as geospatial databases (Torre et al., 2014).

Conducting *questionnaires* on public perceptions on adjacent land-uses, on the need for setting up new facilities (Ioja, Rozylowicz, Pătroescu, Niţă, & Vânău, 2011; A. C. Tudor, Ioja, Rozylowicz, Patru-Stupariu, & Hersperger, 2015; A. C. Tudor, Iojă, Hersperger, & Patru-Stupariu, 2013), on the activities related to environmental protection and conservation (Dimech, Darmanin, Smith, Kaiser, & Schembri, 2009; Yang, Li, & Chiang, 2011) or on projects development (Morgan-Davis & Waterhouse, 2010) could be an important source of data for assessing the environmental conflicts.

Another method to gather data is *consulting the experts* (A. C. Tudor et al., 2015). This method is useful when: (a) the scientific information is uncertain, the experts' opinion being necessary to clear it up (Canavese, Siquiera Ortega, & Queiros, 2014), (b) not all the necessary information can be expressed in quantifiable terms (Janssen, Krol, Schielen, Hoekstra, & de Kok, 2010), limiting thus the application of the other methods which are based on digital processing (c) it is difficult to obtain some data in an optimal period of time, but there are persons who worked in the field for a long period of time and they might know some useful details (Whitfield, Ruddock, & Bullman, 2008). However, the physical evidence should always prevail over the opinions (Heman & Raybould, 2014).

Mass-media is one of nowadays important actors, due to the ease with which it transfers the information to the public, having an increasing influence in the everyday life. Mass-media is „the main system of events interpretation" used by the modern society (Schmidt, Ivanova, & Schafer, 2013), with an important role in increasing people's awareness and disseminating information. Regarding the environmental problems, a high percentage of population informs only from the press, relying on it in the research and information dissemination (Rubin, 1978). Media is one the ways that science reaches politicians and the general public (Lidskog & Olausson, 2013), but sometimes the environmental problems are re-framed in the journalistic process. Special consideration should be given to social media platforms that are gaining more followers and represent for certain categories of the population (especially the youths) the main source of information and debate on specific topics.

Regarding environmental conflicts, media in general is the space for confrontations between stakeholders (Wodak, de Cillia, Reisigl, & Liebhart, 1999) and, partially, is a social actor that can determine the course of events. In the same time media is an independent actor, with a particular point of view (Lidskog & Olausson, 2013). It can ensure the communication and the transparency of the views on a problem. In the same time it offers a space for discussion and represents an important element in opinions formation, because the environmental organizations, economic agents and representatives of the local and central authorities can participate in the debates (Steffek, 2009).

Methods and Tools for Environmental Conflicts Assessment

The conventional methods to solve environmental conflicts such as court litigation are not any more efficient, because they are expensive, time-consuming, and far from reaching a win-win agreement (Sidaway, 2005). Moreover, these methods only interpret the law, leaving the conflicting interests unresolved. As a consequence, they are being replaced by consensual approaches, known as Environmental Alternative Dispute Resolution (EADR) methods (Foley, 2007) where a third party may or not assist the negotiations to help reach a compromise (Susskind & Cruikshank, 1987). Many alternative strategies for conflict resolution exist; the most used being the practice of assisted negotiation, especially mediation and facilitation.

Other participatory methods such as forums, deliberation and consultation mechanisms and interactive web-sites (Lowndes, Pratchett, & Stoker, 2001a, 2001b) as well as technology, such as public participatory GIS (PPGIS) methodologies (Brown & Brabyn, 2012; Brown & Kyttä, 2014) could support the collaboration between the stakeholders and could favor trust and higher odds so that all the actors to contribute together to the decision-making. Tools, such as Land Use Conflict Risk Assessment (LUCRA, 2011) have been developed to identify and assess the potential for conflicts occurrence and the formulation of resolution strategies. Using this tool requires experience in the field of environmental conflicts and needs scientific information in order to investigate which factors are causing conflicts: who causes the problems?, which are the causes?, in what context?, etc.

Spatial analysis refers to investigating the location, characteristics and spatial relationships, based on the topological, geometric or geographical properties. Spatial analysis starts from basic analysis such as selecting some spatial entities which meet certain criteria or based on their location, which may require classification, proximity analysis, interpolation, modeling or geostatistical analysis (Maantay & Ziegler, 2006). GIS techniques are usually used for the spatial analysis. These require georeferenced cartographic materials (M.R. Niță, 2012), based on which thematic layers with the location and the characteristics of certain elements and phenomena can be built.

In the field of environmental conflicts, the spatial analysis can be very useful for: (a) highlighting conflictual or potentially conflictual land uses (Prather, et al., 2008), (b) assessing the compatibility between at least two land uses (one sensitive land use and the other potentially harmful), (c) delineating the surfaces exposed to certain risks (based on the current regulations or an activity's potential impact (D.A. Onose et al., 2013)), (d) identifying homogeneous spaces according to certain criteria (Beeco & Brown, 2013) or (e) calculating regional trends (Gavrilidis, Grădinaru, Iojă, Cârstea, & Pătru-Stupariu, 2015; Grădinaru et al., 2015; Hu et al., 2014; M. R. Niță, Ioja, Rozylowicz, Onose, & Tudor, 2014).

Cluster analysis is a technique whose aim is to partition individuals/objects/cases based on how similar they are to each other or how different they are from other individuals/objects/cases (Barr & Prillwitz, 2012). In the field of environmental conflicts, the cluster analysis can be used to group conflicts based on their involved issues (von der Dunk, Grêt-Regamey, Dalang, & Hersperger, 2011) and to partition individuals in groups based on their perceptions on environmental conflicts. This method can be also useful also to identify homogenous areas in terms of types and number of environmental conflicts.

Multi-criteria assessment is an useful method in assessing the environmental conflicts because it facilitates discussion between the conflicting parties (European Union, 2005). It can be successfully used to select an optimal location for a project, to establish a conservation strategy when conflicts exist between people and conservation authorities or for ranking some areas based on certain characteristics.

Multi-criteria evaluation can also identify hotspots and cold spots of spatial conflicts as it enables the integration of diverse spatial data (Iojă, Niță, Vânău, Onose, & Gavrilidis, 2014; D. A. Onose et al., 2015; C. A. Tudor, Iojă, Patru-Stupariu, Nita, & Hersperger, 2014).

To increase the efficiency of the previous methods, the decision making support tools are also useful, such as:

- Visual PROMETHEE software for Promethee (Preference Ranking Organization MeTHod for Enrichment Evaluation)
- GAIA (Geometrical Analysis for Interactive Aid) methods (Brans, Vincke, & Mareschal, 1986).
- Super Decisions software for Analytical Network Process (ANP) developed by Thomas Saaty (Saaty, 2001).

Mason and Rychard (2005) identify also:

- *Conflict Wheel* which integrates six dimensions of conflict (dynamic, actors, causes, effects and options).
- *Conflict Tree* which shoes how a conflict develops, in a relational way.
- *Conflict Mapping* which focuses on actors and their relationships.
- *Glasl's Escalation Model* which is a useful tool to establish intervention strategies.
- *INMEDIO's Conflict Perspective Analysis* (CPA) which focuses on complementary approaches of different parties, allowing the analysis of alternatives, a useful step in a mediation process.
- *Needs-Fears Mapping* which focuses on actors and problems, interests, needs, fears, objectives and options.
- *Multi-Causal Role Model* which focuses on causes, on the different quality of reasons, triggers, channels, catalysts, and targets.

Main Approaches in Environmental Conflicts Resolution

A sound approach to avoiding the social, economic and environmental cost of conflicts would be to develop an integrated system ensuring a sustainable mitigation of environmental conflicts. That would require a balanced approach especially on controlling the triggering events of conflicts, process that can prove difficult especially when conflicts are generated by different believes, interests or relations, and their spatial and temporal dimension is a varying element that cannot be controlled by administrative or even research boundaries. Therefore, the resolution is the most common practice in dealing with environmental conflicts.

Neither the less, environmental conflict resolution is a challenging process where each particular conflict situation needs specific resolution methods based on the range of involved stakeholders and the underlying political, socio-economic and institutional conditions.

Environmental conflicts have an important social function which if it is not wisely managed, it can have impacts on the quality of life, can damage the environmental patrimony, can cause tensions and violence as well as economic imbalances and institutional shortcomings. Environmental conflict management refers to the "tangible improvement" of its effects by developing a set of actions aimed at ending the conflict (Sidaway, 2005). The success of conflict management is equivalent to conflict resolution as well as to the benefits resulted from improving the conflict situation. Sometimes, the management of conflicts do not succeed to improve the situation with conventional methods and in this case a third party is called to help the conflicting parties to achieve an agreement. A conflict is ended when there is a signed agreement by all parties and the solutions meet their interests.

The methods used for conflict resolution usually varies based on the complexity of the conflict and its area of occurrence.

For example, at global scale, the United Nations is one of the international institutions which has an important role in increasing the resilience to environmental conflicts, especially of those related to security issues. The increase of resilience is based on improving the management of natural resources which in some areas are considered as a wise way to avoid instability and wars (e.g. areas which have a significant population growth, a high percentage of ecologically fragile ecosystems, natural resources shortage, poor contract terms, non-transparent decision making, negative impacts and corruption, as well as historical tensions).

United Nations promotes four types of services in order to manage environmental conflicts: post-crisis environmental assessment, post-crisis environmental recovery, environmental cooperation for peacebuilding and disaster risk reduction.

One of the most important tools used to assess and transform the conflicts over natural resources into an opportunity for cooperation and a platform for peacebuilding is the Environmental Cooperation for Peacebuilding programme. Its aim is to assist countries, regional organizations and the UN system providing tools for risk assessments, technical advice, targeted training, and a neutral platform for dialogue between stakeholders (UNEP, 2015a).

The main pillars of this programme are *Conflict Prevention, Peacebuilding and Natural Resources* (used to assess and integrate risks and opportunities in conflict prevention), *Greening Peacekeeping Operations* (used to provide expertise for the implementation of some green solutions for energy and water use, waste management, wildlife protection, environmental assessment and management, and natural resource governance), *Environmental Diplomacy and Mediation* (used as a dialogue tool, considering United Nations as neutral part) and *Legal Protection* (used to protect natural resources during the armed conflicts).

The United Nations Environmental Programme has been offered environmental expertise in 40 countries to manage environmental conflicts. The most relevant are the independent assessment of environmental and public health impact of oil contamination in Ogoniland with some proposed solutions (Niger Delta), the post conflict environmental assessment in Afganistan, Democratic Republic of Congo, Sudan and South Sudan for post-conflict recovery, as well as improvement of the society resilience and sustainability (UNEP, 2015b).

At national, regional and local level different public institutions manage environmental conflicts. In some administrative systems neutral parties are called to manage the process.

Many strategies which focus on different key aspects regarding the evolution of the environmental conflicts exist to solve such conflicts.

Daniels and Walker (2001) state that the progress is more important than the success in resolving the environmental conflicts. The authors propose a method (*collaborative learning*) and a three-steps approach for environmental conflicts management: (a) assessing the relationships between the conflicting parties (statute, interests, objectives, concerns, etc.); (b) identifying the procedures for conflict management and decision making; (c) assessing the essence of conflict, which refers to identifying the problems which caused the conflicts and on which negotiations have to take place. Thus, for an efficient conflict resolution process is important to do a stakeholder assessment (starting with the first circle of the stakeholders and continuing until the last cicle), their interests and concerns, conflict intensity and the key issues.

Another method for environmental conflict management is *Conflict Transformation* (Madden & McQuinn, 2014). Conflict transformation conceptualizes the conflicts as an opportunity for a positive change of the causal relationships, of decision-making processes and of conflict effects on long term, and has as motto "*going slow to go fast*". Conflict transformation process considers the social, psychological and intangible causes which have roots in conflicts. Taking these into account in a conflict resolution process increases the chances that the final result to be signed by all affected parties. In this process, the involved actors are encouranged to change their rivalry and distrust attitude and to make efforts to communicate and collaborate.

Another example of conceptual framework for environmental conflict management where conflict assessment is understood as the first approach in leading the conflicts towards resolution is offered by Bean, Fisher, and Eng (2007). The authors recommend the following four steps for the assessment of the environmental conflicts: (a) identifying the key elements of a dispute (e.g. the situation and the context, the roles as well as the desired outcomes) (b) considering the ethics; (c) specifying the products (e.g. written or unwritten reports), and (d) selecting the most appropriate tools and techniques for conflict monitoring and resolution.

To solve the environmental disputes, processes where the stakeholders are assisted by a neutral party which helps them to achieve an agreement have been developed. They are known as alternative dispute resolution processes (EADR, *Environmental Alternative Dispute Resolution*). According to Andrew (2001) and Susskind and Cruikshank (1987) the alternative strategies for conflict resolution differ according to conflict intensity (such as facilitation, consultation, arbitration, etc.) as well as a neutral's assistance (such as unassisted negotiation, assisted negotiation, mediation). EADR techniques are less expensive and bring a higher satisfaction regarding the achieved outcomes. Andrew (2001) shows in his research that the following alternative techniques: negotiation, facilitation and mediation are more efficient in resolving the environmental conflicts that the conventional methods of conflict resolution.

Participatory decision making is based on the principles of negotiation, with the main aim of reaching consensus. They intend to delegitimize the emotions which are part of stakeholders' interests. Achieving a consensus is strongly linked to negotiation and mediation, whose main roles are to move away the misunderstandings between the actors by creating a relaxing and non-conflictual environment. In a process of consensus building, the decisions are taken as a result of collaboration between all parties that are affected by the conflict (Sidaway, 2005). The author highlights the presence of a facilitator whose main role is to moderate the meeting and to ensure that the negotiations are done in an appropriate environment as well as to encourage the participation and the collaboration of all affected parties (e.g. the parties' interests are respected, their legal rights are not prejudiced and confidentiality is maintained) (Susskind & Cruikshank, 1987).

The efficiency of environmental conflicts management is quantified through the success of their resolution. The finality of a conflict resolution can generate different situations (Jurin, Roush, & Danter, 2010):

1. A *win-win* situation, where the involved actors succeed to reach their goals (usually through negotiations and dialogue which further lead to a compromise). This is an ideal situation but it happens very rarely. A win-win situation is desired, because the conflict has no more a negative connotation, as it is able to accomplish the stakeholders' objectives which in many cases refer to the protection of natural resources or the removal of polluting sources.

2. A *win-loss* or *loss-win* situation where only some actors achieve their desired goals, while the other actors lose, considering the resolution process a failure. It is one of the situations in which most often the power (political, financial) is used by the most powerful actors to intimidate the weaker ones.

3. A *loss-loss* situation where no actors achieve their goals. There is no successful outcome and the conflict becomes destructive.

The finality of a conflict does not always improve the relationships between the affected parties. There are situations where the post-conflict strategies are implemented and could help in strengthening relationships and reaching a final agreement. Reconciliation represents one of the post-conflict strategies, which strengthens the relationships between the conflicting parties. For a successful reconciliation is important that the parties interests to be already known and understood (Henle, Alard, Clitherow, Cobb, Firbank, Kull, McCracken, Moritz, Niemelä, et al., 2008).

The complexity of environmental conflicts is inclusively kept in the resolution phase, their finality being constructive or destructive. However, the environmental conflict are a reality of the modern societies whose management should become a priority, at least for the environmental agencies.

FUTURE RESEARCH DIRECTION

The changes, competition, plethora of policies, strategies or environmental plans from the past years as well as the innovative tools used by the involved actors favor increasing complex environmental conflicts whose negative effects are being felt in the society's layers. At the same time, the benefits of the environmental conflicts are limited to organized interests groups which prefer to coordinate the desired developments from the background, using as actors the public institutions, the non-governmental organizations or the individuals.

Institutionalizing public participation in the decision-making process through various European directives (Water framework Directive, Habitats Directive, Environmental Impact Assessment Directive) has increased the role of civil society in managing the ecosystems' resources and services.

The diversification of environmental conflicts related to political, administrative, social or economic aspects tends to become a natural evolution of society. Their constructive resolution is an important goal, in order to avoid crisis or violence.

The conceptual and methodological aspects presented during this chapter are of great practical importance, but it would be of interest to:

*   Develop methods for the multi-criteria assessment of vulnerable areas to the emergence of various types of environmental conflicts.
*   Organizing databases with the quantitative and qualitative characteristics of environmental conflicts, using mass-media, institutions reports or other documentation sources.
*   Testing new analysis methods for quantitative and qualitative data related to environmental conflicts in order to favor their durable and equitable resolution.
*   Conducting interdisciplinary research on the relationships between environmental conflicts and the resilience of natural and human ecosystems.

- Providing detailed evaluation of environmental conflicts characteristics from Natura 2000 ecological network, as part of their management.
- Proposing preliminary analysis instruments of the context in order to avoid the development of environmental conflicts during the public consultation processes conducted under different procedures (environmental impact assessment, spatial planning, management plans, environment action plans, etc.).

Environmental conflicts certify that environmental policies have direct consequences on the social, economic and administrative level. Their wise coordination can favor sustainable communities where benefits are equitable shared, life quality increases and natural resources keep their sustainability.

REFERENCES

Alphandéry, P., & Fortier, A. (2001). Can a Territorial Policy be Based on Science Alone? The System for Creating the Natura 2000 Network in France. *Sociologia Ruralis*, *41*(3), 311–328. doi:10.1111/1467-9523.00185

Andersson, I., Petersson, M., & Jarsjö, J. (2012). Impact of the European Water Framework Directive on local-level water management: Case study Oxunda Catchment, Sweden. *Land Use Policy*, *29*(1), 73–82. doi:10.1016/j.landusepol.2011.05.006

Andrew, J. S. (2001). Examining the Claims of Environmental ADR Evidence from Waste Management Conflicts in Ontario and Massachusetts. *Journal of Planning Education and Research*, *21*(2), 166–183. doi:10.1177/0739456X0102100205

Barr, S., & Prillwitz, J. (2012). Green travelers? Exploring the spatial context of sustainable mobility styles. *Applied Geography (Sevenoaks, England)*, *32*(2), 798–809. doi:10.1016/j.apgeog.2011.08.002

Baxter, J., & Galbraith, C. A. (Eds.). (2010). *People and nature in conflict: can we reconcile hen harrier conservation and game management?* Edinburgh, UK: Academic Press.

Bean, M., Fisher, L., & Eng, M. (2007). Assessment in Environmental and Public Policy Conflict Resolution: Emerging Theory, Patterns of Practice, and a Conceptual Framework. *Conflict Resolution Quarterly*, *24*(4), 447–468. doi:10.1002/crq.184

Beeco, J. A., & Brown, G. (2013). Integrating space, spatial tools and spatial analysis into the human dimensions of parks and outdoor recreation. *Applied Geography (Sevenoaks, England)*, *38*, 76–85. doi:10.1016/j.apgeog.2012.11.013

Botetzagias, I., & Karamichas, J. (2009). Grassroots mobilisations against waste disposal sites in Greece. *Environmental Politics*, *18*(6), 939–959. doi:10.1080/09644010903345702

Brans, J. P., Vincke, P., & Mareschal, B. (1986). How to select and how to rank projects: The PROMETHEE method. *European Journal of Operational Research*, *24*(2), 228–238. doi:10.1016/0377-2217(86)90044-5

Brown, G., & Brabyn, L. (2012). An analysis of the relationships between multiple values and physical landscapes at a regional scale using public participation GIS and landscape character classification. *Landscape and Urban Planning, 107*(3), 317–331. doi:10.1016/j.landurbplan.2012.06.007

Brown, G., & Kyttä, M. (2014). Key issues and research priorities for public participation GIS (PP-GIS): A synthesis based on empirical research. *Applied Geography (Sevenoaks, England), 46*, 122–136. doi:10.1016/j.apgeog.2013.11.004

Butler, S. J., Boccaccio, L., Gregoryc, R. D., Vorisekd, P., & Norrisa, K. (2010). Quantifying the impact of land-use change to European farmland bird populations. *Agriculture, Ecosystems & Environment, 137*(3-4), 348–357. doi:10.1016/j.agee.2010.03.005

Canavese, D., Siquiera Ortega, N. R., & Queiros, M. (2014). The assessment of local sustainability using fuzzy logic: An expert opinion system to evaluate environmental sanitation in the Algarve region, Portugal. *Ecological Indicators, 36*, 711–718. doi:10.1016/j.ecolind.2013.09.030

Che, Y., Yang, K., Jin, Y., Zhang, W., Shang, Z., & Tai, J. (2013). Residents' concerns and attitudes toward a municipal solid waste landfill: Integrating a questionnaire survey and GIS techniques. *Environmental Monitoring and Assessment, 185*(12), 10001–11001. doi:10.1007/s10661-013-3308-y PMID:23793647

Cogoy, M., & Steininger, K. W. (2007). *Transforming Environmental and Natural Resource Use Conflicts. In The Economics of Global Environmental Change: International Cooperation for Sustainability.* Edward Elgar Publishing.

Daniels, S. E., & Walker, G. B. (2001). *Working Through Environmental Conflict: The Collaborative Learning Approach.* Praeger.

Dear, M. (1992). Understanding and Overcoming the NIMBY Syndrome. *Journal of the American Planning Association, 58*(3), 288–300. doi:10.1080/01944369208975808

Diehk, P. F., & Gleditsch, N. P. (Eds.). (2001). *Environmental Conflict.* Oxford, UK: Westview.

Dimech, M., Darmanin, M., Smith, P., Kaiser, M., & Schembri, P. (2009). Fishers' perception of a 35-year old exclusive Fisheries Management Zone. *Biological Conservation, 142*(11), 2691–2702. doi:10.1016/j.biocon.2009.06.019

EC. (2010). *Environment: Italy faces Court for failing to implement EU law on waste.* Author.

EC. (2014). *Environment: European Commission takes Slovenia to Court for pollution problems from waste disposal.* Author.

European Union. (2005). *Multi-criteria analysis.* Retrieved from http://ec.europa.eu/europeaid/evaluation/methodology/tools/too_cri_whe_en.htm#03

Foley, T. (2007). Environmental Conflict Resolution: Relational and Environmental Attentiveness as Measures of Success. *Conflict Resolution Quarterly, 24*(4), 485–504. doi:10.1002/crq.186

Gavrilidis, A. A., Grădinaru, S. R., Iojă, I. C., Cârstea, E. M., & Pătru-Stupariu, I. (2015). Land use and land cover dynamics in the periurban area of an industrialized East-European city. An overview of the last 100 years. *Carpathian Journal of Earth and Environmental Sciences, 10*(4), 29–38.

Gissi, E., Siciliano, G., & Reho, M. (2011). *Biomass production and land use management in the Italian context: regulations, conflicts, and impacts* Paper presented at the 51st Congress of the European Regional Science Association, Barcelona, Spain.

Grădinaru, S. R., Iojă, C. I., Onose, D. A., Gavrilidis, A. A., Pătru-Stupariu, I., Kienast, F., & Hersperger, A. M. (2015). Land abandonment as a precursor of built-up development at the sprawling periphery of former socialist cities. *Ecological Indicators*, *57*, 305–313. doi:10.1016/j.ecolind.2015.05.009

Grodzinska-Jurczak, M., & Cent, J. (2011). Expansion of Nature Conservation Areas: Problems with Natura 2000 Implementation in Poland? *Environmental Management*, *47*(1), 11–27. doi:10.1007/s00267-010-9583-2 PMID:21107836

Halley, D. J., & Rosell, F. (2002). The beaver's reconquest of Eurasia: Status, population development and management of a conservation success. *Mammal Review*, *32*(3), 153–178. doi:10.1046/j.1365-2907.2002.00106.x

Hedelin, B., & Lindh, M. (2008). Implementing the EU Water Framework Directive – Prospects for Sustainable Water Planning in Sweden. *European Environment*, *18*(6), 327–344. doi:10.1002/eet.489

Heman, R., & Raybould, A. (2014). Expert opinion vs. empirical evidence. *GM Crops and Food: Biotechnology in Agriculture and the Food Chain*, *5*(1), 8–10. doi:10.4161/gmcr.28331 PMID:24637724

Henle, K., Alard, D., Clitherow, J., Cobb, P., Firbank, L., Kull, T., & Young, J. et al. (2008). Identifying and managing the conflicts between agriculture and biodiversity conservation in Europe–A review. *Agriculture, Ecosystems & Environment*, *124*(1-2), 60–71. doi:10.1016/j.agee.2007.09.005

Hu, Q., Pan, F., Pan, X., Zhang, D., Li, Q., & Pan, Z. (2014). Spatial analysis of climate change in Inner Mongolia during 1961-2012, China. *Applied Geography (Sevenoaks, England)*.

Ioja, I. C. (2013). Metode de cercetare şi evaluare a stării mediului. Bucureşti: Ed. Etnografică.

Iojă, I. C., Niţă, M., Vânău, G., Onose, D., Gavrilidis, A., & Hossu, C. A. (2015). Environmental Conflicts Management, in Romanian (Managementul conflictelor de mediu). Bucharest: University of Bucharest.

Iojă, I. C., Niţă, M. R., Vânău, G. O., Onose, D. A., & Gavrilidis, A. A. (2014). Using multi-criteria analysis in identifying spatial land-use conflicts in the Bucharest Metropolitan Area. *Ecological Indicators*, *42*, 112–121. doi:10.1016/j.ecolind.2013.09.029

Ioja, I. C., Rozylowicz, L., Pătroescu, M., Niţă, M. R., & Vânau, G. O. (2011). Dog walkers' vs. other visitors' perceptions: The importance of planning sustainable urban parks in Bucharest, romania. *Landscape and Urban Planning*, *103*(1), 74–82. doi:10.1016/j.landurbplan.2011.06.002

Jackson, A. L. R. (2011). Renewable energy vs. biodiversity: Policy conflicts and the future of nature conservation. *Global Environmental Change*, *21*(4), 1195–1208. doi:10.1016/j.gloenvcha.2011.07.001

Janssen, J. A. E. B., Krol, M. S., Schielen, R. M. J., Hoekstra, A. Y., & de Kok, J. L. (2010). Assessment of uncertaintics in expert knowledge, illustrated in fuzzy rule-based models. *Ecological Modelling*, *221*(9), 1245–1251. doi:10.1016/j.ecolmodel.2010.01.011

Johnson, R., & Scicchitano, M. (2012). Don't call me NIMBY: Public attitudes toward solid waste facilities. *Environment and Behavior, 44*(3), 410–426. doi:10.1177/0013916511435354

Jurin, R., Roush, D., & Danter, J. (2010). *Managing Conflicts. In Environmental Communication. Skills and Principles for Natural Resource Managers, Scientists, and Engineers*. New York: Springer - Verlag.

Kloskowski, J. (2011). Human–wildlife conflicts at pond fisheries in eastern Poland: Perceptions and management of wildlife damage. *European Journal of Wildlife Research, 57*(2), 295–304. doi:10.1007/s10344-010-0426-5

Latruffe, L., & Davidova, S. (2007). Common Agricultural Policy direct payments and distributional conflicts over rented land within corporate farms in the New Member States. *Land Use Policy, 24*(2), 451–457. doi:10.1016/j.landusepol.2006.06.003

Lewicki, R., Gray, B., & Elliott, M. (2003). *Making Sense of Intractable Environmental Conflicts. Concepts And Cases* (2nd ed.). Island Press.

Lidskog, R., & Olausson, U. (2013). To spray or not to spray: The discursive construction of contested environmental issues in the news media. *Discourse. Context and Media, 2*(3), 123–130. doi:10.1016/j.dcm.2013.06.001

Liefferink, D., Wiering, M., & Uitenboogaart, Y. (2011). The EU Water Framework Directive: A multi-dimensional analysis of implementation and domestic impact. *Land Use Policy, 28*(4), 712–722. doi:10.1016/j.landusepol.2010.12.006

Lindell, L., Mellin, M., Musil, P., Przybysz, J., & Zimmerman, H. (1995). Status and population development of breeding Cormorants Phalacrocorax carbo sinensis of the central European flyway. *Ardea, 83*(1), 81–92.

Lowndes, V., Pratchett, L., & Stoker, G. (2001a). Trends in public participation: Part 1 - local government perspectives. *Public Administration, 79*(1), 205–222. doi:10.1111/1467-9299.00253

Lowndes, V., Pratchett, L., & Stoker, G. (2001b). Trends in public participation: Part 2 - citizens' perspectives. *Public Administration, 79*(2), 445–455. doi:10.1111/1467-9299.00264

LUCRA. (2011). *Land Use Conflict Risk Assessment*. Australia: New South Wales Government.

Lumerman, P., Psathakis, J., & Ortiz, M. (2011). *Climate Change Impacts on Socio - environmental Conflicts: Diagnosis and Challenges of the Argentinean Situation*. Brussels: Initiative for Peacebuilding.

Maantay, J., & Ziegler, J. (2006). *GIS for the Urban Environment*. Redlands, CA: ESRI Press.

Madden, F., & McQuinn, B. (2014). Conservation's blind spot: The case for conflict transformation in wildlife conservation. *Biological Conservation, 178*, 97–106. doi:10.1016/j.biocon.2014.07.015

Maser, C., & Pollio, C. A. (2012). *Resolving environmental conflicts*. CRC Press.

Mason, S., & Rychard, S. (2005). *Conflict Analysis Tools*. Bern: Academic Press.

Mason, S., & Spillman, K. (2002). *Environmental Conflicts and Regional Conflict Management* (Vol. 2). Welfare Economics and Sustainable Development.

Melé, P. (2012). Pour une géographie des conflits urbains de proximité en Amérique Latine. *Géocarrefour, 87*(1).

Morgan-Davis, C., & Waterhouse, T. (2010). Future of the hills of Scotland: Stakeholders' preferences for policy priorities. *Land Use Policy, 27*(2), 387–398. doi:10.1016/j.landusepol.2009.05.002

Nash, H. A. (2009). The Revised Directive on Waste: Resolving Legislative Tensions in Waste Management? *Journal of Environmental Law, 21*(1), 139–149. doi:10.1093/jel/eqp001

Niță, M. R. (2012). *Dinamica rezidențialului în Zona Metropolitană a Municipiului București și proiecția ei în starea mediului*. București: Ed. Universității din București.

Niță, M. R., Ioja, I. C., Rozylowicz, L., Onose, D. A., & Tudor, A. C. (2014). Land use consequences of the evolution of cemeteries in the Bucharest Metropolitan Area. *Journal of Environmental Planning and Management, 57*(7), 1066-1082. Doi: 10.1080/09640568.2013.815607

Nunneri, C., & Hofmann, J. (2005). A participatory approach for Integrated River Basin Management in the Elbe catchment. *Estuarine, Coastal and Shelf Science, 62*(3), 521–537. doi:10.1016/j.ecss.2004.09.015

O'Rourke, E. (2014). The reintroduction of the white-tailed sea eagle to Ireland: People and wildlife. *Land Use Policy, 38*, 129–137. doi:10.1016/j.landusepol.2013.10.020

Onose, D. A., Niță, M. R., Ciocănea, C. M., Pătroescu, M., Vânău, G. O., & Bodescu, F. (2015). Identifying critical areas of exposure to environmental conflicts using expert opinion and multi-criteria analysis. *Carpathian Journal of Earth and Environmental Sciences, 10*(4), 15–28.

Onose, D. A., Ioja, I. C., Vânău, G. O., Niță, M. R., Ciocănea, C. M., & Mirea, D. A. (2013). Spatial and temporal dynamics of residential areas affected by the industrial function in a post-communist city. Case study Bucharest. *Real Corp 2013 Planning Times*, 821-830.

Owens, S., & Cowell, R. (2011). *Land and Limits: interpreting sustainability in the planning process*. New York: Routledge.

Owusu, G., Oteng-Ababio, M., & Afutu-Kotey, R. L. (2012). Conflicts and governance of landfills in a developing country city, Accra. *Landscape and Urban Planning, 104*(1), 105–113. doi:10.1016/j.landurbplan.2011.10.005

Paavola, J. (2003). *Environmental justice and governnce: theory and lessons from the implementation of the European Union's Habitat Directive*. CSERGE Working Paper EDM, 03-05.

Rowlands, I. H. (2005). The European directive on renewable electricity: Conflicts and compromises. *Energy Policy, 33*(8), 965–974. doi:10.1016/j.enpol.2003.10.019

Rubin, B. D. (Ed.). (1978). *The variable nature of news media influence*. New Brunswick.

Saaty, T. (2001). *Decision Making with Dependence and Feedback: The Analytic Network Process: the Organization and Prioritization of Complexity*. Pittsburgh, PA: RWS Publications.

Saint, P. M., Flavell, R. J., & Fox, P. F. (2009). *NIMBY Wars. The Politics of Land Use*. Hingham, MA: Saint University Press.

Schmidt, A., Ivanova, A., & Schafer, M. (2013). Media attention for climate change around the world: A comparative analysis of newspaper in 27 countries. *Global Environmental Change, 23*(5), 1233–1248. doi:10.1016/j.gloenvcha.2013.07.020

Schmidtz, D., & Willott, E. (Eds.). (2002). *Natural enemies: An anatomy of environmental conflict*. New York: Oxford University Press.

Sidaway, R. (2005). *Resolving environmental disputes: from conflict to consensus*. London: Earthscan.

Steffek, J. (2009). Discursive legitimation in environmental governance: Discourse and Expertise in Forest and Environmental Governance. *Forest Policy and Economics, 11*(5-6), 313–318. doi:10.1016/j.forpol.2009.04.003

Stoll-Kleemann, S. (2001). Opposition to the Designation of Protected Areas in Germany. *Journal of Environmental Planning and Management, 44*(1), 109–128. doi:10.1080/09640560123606

Susskind, L., & Cruikshank, J. (1987). *Breaking the Impasse: Consensual Approaches To Resolving Public*. New York: Basic Books.

Tella, J. L., Forero, M. G., Hiraldo, F., & Donazar, J. A. (1998). Conflicts Between Lesser Kestrel Conservation and European Agricultural Policies as Identified by Habitat Use Analyses. *Conservation Biology, 12*(3), 593–604. doi:10.1046/j.1523-1739.1998.96288.x

Torre, A., Melot, R., Magsi, H., Bossuet, L., Cadoret, A., Caron, A., & Kolokouris, O. et al. (2014). Identifying and measuring land-use and proximity conflicts: Methods and identification. *SpringerPlus, 3*(1), 85. doi:10.1186/2193-1801-3-85 PMID:24600543

Tudor, A. C., Iojă, C. I., Hersperger, A. M., & Patru-Stupariu, I. (2013). Is the residential land use incompatible with cemeteries location? Assessing the attitudes of urban residents. *Carpathian Journal of Earth and Environmental Sciences, 8*(2), 153–162.

Tudor, A. C., Ioja, C. I., Rozylowicz, L., Patru-Stupariu, I., & Hersperger, A. M. (2015). Similarities and differences in the assessment of land-use associationsby local people and experts. *Land Use Policy, 49*, 341–351. doi:10.1016/j.landusepol.2015.07.001

Tudor, C. A., Iojă, C. I., Patru-Stupariu, I., Nita, M. R., & Hersperger, A. M. (2014). How successful is the resolution of land-use conflicts? A comparison of cases from Switzerland and Romania. *Applied Geography (Sevenoaks, England), 47*, 125–136. doi:10.1016/j.apgeog.2013.12.008

UNEP. (2015a). *Environmental Cooperation for Peacebuilding*. UNEP.

UNEP. (2015b). *United Nations Environment Programme*. UNEP.

Uyarra, E., & Gee, S. (2013). Transforming urban waste into sustainable material and energy usage: The case of Greater Manchester (UK). *Journal of Cleaner Production, 50*, 101–110. doi:10.1016/j.jclepro.2012.11.046

von der Dunk, A., Grêt-Regamey, A., Dalang, T., & Hersperger, A. (2011). Defining a typology of peri-urban land-use conflicts –A case study from Switzerland. *Landscape and Urban Planning, 101*(2), 149–156. doi:10.1016/j.landurbplan.2011.02.007

Whitfield, D. P., Ruddock, M., & Bullman, R. (2008). Expert opinion as a tool for quantifying bird tolerance to human disturbance. *Biological Conservation*, *141*(11), 2708–2717. doi:10.1016/j.biocon.2008.08.007

Wodak, R., de Cillia, R., Reisigl, M., & Liebhart, K. (1999). *The discursive construction of national identity*. Edinburgh, UK: Edinburgh University Press.

Wolsink, M. (2004). Policy Beliefs in Spatial Decisions: Contrasting Core Beliefs Concerning Space-making for Waste Infrastructure. *Urban Studies (Edinburgh, Scotland)*, *41*(13), 2669–2690. doi:10.1080/0042098042000294619

Wolsink, M. (2010). Contested environmental policy infrastructure: Socio-political acceptance of renewable energy, water, and waste facilities. *Environmental Impact Assessment Review*, *30*(5), 302–311. doi:10.1016/j.eiar.2010.01.001

Yang, C. M., Li, J. J., & Chiang, H. C. (2011). Stakeholders' perspective on the sustainable utilization of marine protected areas in Green Islanf, Taiwan. *Ocean and Coastal Management*, *54*(10), 771–780. doi:10.1016/j.ocecoaman.2011.08.006

Young, J., Watt, A., Nowicki, P., Alard, D., Clitherow, J., Henle, K., & Richards, C. et al. (2005). Towards sustainable land use: Identifying and managing the conflicts between human activities and biodiversity conservation in Europe. *Biodiversity and Conservation*, *14*(7), 1641–1661. doi:10.1007/s10531-004-0536-z

Zuindeau, B. (Ed.). (2010). *Conflits environnementaux et territoires*. Presses Universitaires du Septentrion.

KEY TERMS AND DEFINITIONS

Agri-Environmental Schemes (AES): Measures funded by the European Union that provide incentives for farmers to manage their land in an environmental friendly manner.

Conflict Resolution: The effort of ending a conflict by using conventional or consensual methods.

Conflict Transformation: The process by which conflicts are transformed into opportunities for improvement.

Environmental Conflicts: Competing demands over the use of natural resources or disagreements about a polluting activity that may affect people's health or environmental quality.

Facilitation: Type of assisted negotiation where a facilitator makes sure that the setting of the meeting is appropriate for the dialogue between the parties and helps the parties to better understand the issues of concern.

Mediation: Type of assisted negotiation where a mediator talks confidentially with the stakeholders in order to knows very well their concerns in order to advance toward a consensus.

Negotiation: Is a process aimed at achieving mutual gains for all parties. It is based on cooperation in order to find solutions that responds to the interests of all stakeholders.

Participatory GIS (PPGIS): The process of using GIS technologies to engage the public in identifying spatial information.

Chapter 5
Restorative Justice and Technology

Pedro Miguel Freitas
Universidade do Minho, Portugal

Pablo Galain Palermo
Max Planck Institute for Foreign and International Criminal Law, Germany

ABSTRACT

In civil law countries, criminal justice is beginning to experience a shift from retributive justice towards restorative justice. Amongst other goals, restorative justice aims to give the victim a pivotal role in the administration of justice, which until now, with the traditional criminal justice, has not happened at a desirable level. It covers very different processes, but victim-offender mediation is certainly the most established one. Although an online version of the victim-offender mediation model is yet to be implemented, we believe that it could be a relevant alternative to an offline setting. It is nevertheless clear that further studies are necessary to fully comprehend the extent of the structure and implications of a ODR system for criminal conflicts.

INTRODUCTION

Conflict resolution is a multidisciplinary and an interactive field of knowledge, where the theory of justice and even criminal law has an important role to play. The conflict between a citizen and law should not be considered solely as a problem between a person and the State[1]. The progress and changes caused by technological advances need to foster a return or approximation to the *interpersonality* nature of conflicts' resolution. After the unthinkable crimes against humanity that have been committed since the second war world, Hegel's thought of human progress based on the necessary sacrifice of some victims is neither valid nor satisfactory (Reyes Mate, 2011; Galain Palermo/Garreaud, 2012). Victims became visible and, according to Walter Benjamin, justice must be done through the compensation of injustice and the reparation of damages committed against them. Habermas advocates for the necessity of "communicative actions" and for the resolution of social conflicts based on dialogue, encounters, and communication. This new philosophical consideration of justice demands new theories of justice.

DOI: 10.4018/978-1-5225-0245-6.ch005

Criminal justice is historically assumed as a State's monopoly. It is a social control method that relies on the imposition of punishments (retribution) with a preventive purpose. Thus, the main purpose of a criminal system is not to punish someone who committed a crime simply because he committed such a crime, but to prevent it from happening again. This is the idea behind current criminal justice systems in most civil law countries, such as Germany, Spain or Portugal.

Even though criminal prevention can be described as promotion of avoidance, by means of punishment, of the (re)occurrence of crimes and of the endangerment or injury to legal goods or values (*Rechtsguts*), its description would be incomplete without mentioning that it encompasses four distinct and intersecting dimensions – general prevention, special prevention, positive prevention and negative prevention. Positive general prevention focuses on the reaffirmation of the value of the legal norm against the unlawfulness of a crime (Hassemer, 1998, 2002; Streng, 1991), while negative general prevention (deterrence) happens when the State acts on the population through intimidation, deterring them from committing crimes, being the punishment of the offender a deterrent example to others. Special prevention can operate in a positive or in a negative fashion. There is a positive special prevention (rehabilitation) when the State aims at the (re)socialization of the offender and negative special prevention (incapacitation) when it regards the offender as a source of danger which needs to be segregated and separated from the community.

This is the abstract and retributive logic that legitimizes the power of the State against citizens who disregard legal criminal norms. This public power to resolve criminal conflicts so far denies any communicative rationality that could support agreements as an alternative path to end any emerging conflicts (Luhmann, 2005). From this punitive logic, that ignores the will and needs of the citizens involved in a crime (either as an offender or as a victim), derives a punishment that puts an end to the legal dispute, but is incapable of fulfilling the underlying goal of law: social pacification. Despite the strong criticism made by scholars, that highlights the serious crisis and failure of the criminal justice system in achieving the purposes stated above, traditional criminal justice systems continue to ignore other methods of resolving serious conflicts (Galain Palermo, 2009). However, a new vision of justice rooted in the will and needs of the people involved, whose place has been expropriated by government officials and lawyers (Christie, 1977; Wright, 1991), promises to bring significant changes to a normative, retributive and traditional legal landscape (Kerner, 1983). Scholars call for a new vision of justice and new questions. Rather than asking "Who has done such act?", one must ask "Who has been harmed?" and then learn what is necessary to do and how can offender, victim and other stakeholders resolve the conflict (Zehr, 2004). The question is whether these new "lenses" with which one should assess the legal conflicts and make the right questions determine a simple correction to the traditional way of seeing justice, in other words, whether they would work as a complement to existing legal techniques, or they imply a major overhaul and reform of the responses to crime.

Now, if restorative justice intends to replace traditional or retributive criminal justice, what would be the paradigm shift? As for the answer, not even the various theories within restorative justice have reached an agreement (Johnstone & Ness, 2007; Luna, 2003, Braithwaite, 2003; Zernova & Wright, 2007). Everything indicates that, more than a paradigm shift, it is a question of determining where and when traditional criminal justice should step in and where and when there should be spaces or realms of interaction between the stakeholders (Galain Palermo, 2009). An additional question should be placed: technology could be a useful instrument for restorative justice?

RESTORATIVE JUSTICE: CONCEPT AND SCOPE

Although the development of modern restorative justice is associated with some English speaking countries, restorative practices have their roots in pre-industrial societies. The ancient Western civilizations (Greece and the Roman Empire), Vedism, Budhism, Taoism and Confucianism, as well as many indigenous cultures in Australia, North America and Europe, implemented restorative practices to prevent acts of revenge between individuals, families and tribes (Huxley, 1939; Braithwaite, 2002; Sherman & Strang, 2010; Gavrielides, 2011).

After giving way to retributive sanctions, further developed with the phenomena of State-Nations, restorative practices were again used during the seventies of the twenty-century in countries such as Canada, New Zealand, Australia, United Kingdom and United States (Sherman & Strang 2010). Evidence from criminology, anthropology, sociology and psychology supporting these restorative practices, alongside successful restorative programs in several countries, broadened the scope of application of restorative justice to solve conflicts of different nature. Meanwhile, criminal science followed a different path, not coincidental with the social reality, in which there was a profound dogmatic and theoretic discussion (Binding, 1913) and attention to legal technicalities and neglect of the victim (Hassemer, 1981). Nevertheless, some scholars demanded more attention to criminal policy as an intersection point between criminal dogmatic and criminology that fostered "GesamteStrafrechtswissenschaft" (Liszt, 1912). Nowadays, a more complete system of the criminal sciences (Roxin, 1973), which includes reparative alternatives among other sanctions (Roxin, 1992; Schöch, 1992), is definitively sought after. In fact, restorative or reparative justice can help displace the focus from the abstract injury of legal goods to the concrete harm done to a victim (Schöch, 1988) and, concomitantly, create a balance between the recomposition of the value of the infringed legal norm and the reconciliation and restoration of social relations. This ultimate goal presents restorative justice as a relevant tool for low level conflicts (administrative offences), medium level conflicts (general criminal offences) and high level conflicts (international crimes, offences against human rights, offences against human life, bodily integrity, etc.).

Restorative justice is an approach to criminal conflicts that focuses its efforts on restoring the harm done by criminal activities. It does not mean however that is part of tort law (Hirsch, 1969, 1990). It is based on the principle that crime affects people, their families and communities (Strang, 2001). The available scientific evidence indicates that restorative justice is an effective strategy for reducing recidivism and post-traumatic stress of victims, and even reduce the costs of the criminal justice. Having a system that allows victims to overcome their fear and even forgive the offender, avoid the traditional criminal justice and have realistic expectations of material and/or symbolic reparation of the harm is of undisputed benefit to the victim. The offender too might benefit from restorative justice, namely when the offender voluntarily assumes responsibility for the crime, not only to explain the reasons for his behavior, but also to avoid social discrimination, stigmatization and the enforcement of a criminal penalty. In a sense, the possibility of an encounter between individuals in a criminal procedure implies, by definition, an intention to reduce the violence inherent to the State's apparatus.

Voluntary adherence to the restorative process is a key-element. But does this willingness or even desire to encounter the victim mean that there is, from a philosophical standpoint, acknowledgement of guilt (Reggio, 2010) that should produce legal consequences (Galain Palermo, 2009)?

It is clear that current criminal justice systems are ineffective, in part because they are unable to reduce criminal recidivism, but also because victims do not have an active voice during criminal procedure. These reasons have led many western cultures to adopt restorative justice as a method of dispute or conflict resolution (Sherman, 1993; Sherman & Strang, 2007).

There isn't a clear and defined meaning of restorative justice. Its concept covers a wide range of practices that lay emphasis on restoring and recovering from the harm produced by violent actions and/ or criminal. Restorative justice's advocates support the idea that criminal justice systems mishandle offenders and victims alike: they are not different nor enemies. In fact, assuming such a perspective can even stimulate desires of vengeance towards the offender while neglecting the fact that many offenders consider themselves victims since childhood (Sherman & Strang, 2007). Restorative justices waives the fundamental principle of traditional criminal justice systems that punishment is more important that restoration. It operates in a completely different manner: it methodologically applies strategies intended to achieve a restoration of harm that takes the form of an agreement between stakeholders that might be considered by a community as a punishment or functional equivalent thereof (Galain Palermo, 2009). Accordingly, imprisonment or other institutional alternatives, dictated by Justice (home detention, probation, etc.), are not necessarily the most efficient path to prevent criminal recidivism and, above all, are not suited to promote restoration after criminal activities. In order to achieve these goals, victims should no longer be outside the criminal procedure and should take a central role. It is clear that such a proposal does not require a process that is distinct from criminal procedure, but a reform of the criminal justice system allowing agreements and "consensual truth" instead of "material truth". At the same time, accepting this duality of procedural objectives affords a dual approach to criminality: traditional mechanisms and solutions to high-level criminality based on punishment (material truth) and also mechanisms and solutions to seek reconciliation, pacification and communal existence (consensual truth). Although this possibility may seem difficult to understand when discussing ordinary offences, it is increasingly accepted in the field of action known as "transitional justice" (Knust, 2013; Galain Palermo, 2015).

But what is the meaning of restorative justice? Although it is a method that has become institutionalized in many countries, there are still debates about what exactly is restorative justice (Vaandering, 2011), which makes it difficult to find a definition covering all perspectives on the term. Marshall (1996), however, has established a broad consensus in the literature: "restorative justice is a process whereby all the parties with a stake in a particular offence come together to resolve collectively how to deal with the aftermath of the offence and its implications for the future". Zehr (2004), one of the promoters of the restorative justice in the West (see also, Albrecht et al, 2006), provides a definition that focus mainly on the purpose of the restorative method: "restorative justice is a process to involve, to the extent possible, those who have a stake in a specific offense to collectively identify and address harms, needs and obligations in order to heal and put things right as possible".

As Umbreit *et al* (2004) point out, restorative justice "is a process rather than a particular program model", which enables its implementation in different ways. This diversity can lead to confusion as to the nature of some programs that are in fact reparative but not restorative. The distinction between these terms is essential to understand which interventions are restorative. Daly and Proietti-Scifoni (2011) say that "restoration" involves restoring after the harm done by the crime, while "reparation" implies actions intended to recreate the *status quo* of the victim, prior to the time the offence occurred. Other programs are restorative, while others point to the latter.

It is important to note the differences between restorative practices and restorative justice. The former involve a set of actions, including criminal sanctions or rehabilitation programs, designed to make offenders aware of the harm they caused, but do not imply necessarily the participation of the victims on deciding how to deal with the future implications of the crime. The latter, meanwhile, has as its fundamental principle the participation of all parties in the process of conflict resolution, and is a sub-category of restorative practices. In this point of view, it is not possible to speak of restorative justice if the victim is not part of the process of conflict resolution. Take the example of the drug addict that assaults another individual, to whom the judge ruled that he must undertake rehabilitation program and, ultimately, become aware of the harm he caused. This case is undoubtedly an example of restorative practice. However, because the victim is not part of the resolution process, it does not qualify as restorative justice. Those cases where there is not a direct and personal victim, for example, in vandalism, do not invalidate the possibility of a process of restorative justice. Here, the involvement of community members (which, in this case, would be the victim) allows the qualification of this restorative practice as restorative justice (Sherman & Newbury-Birch, 2008). In this case, a new question emerges: who and how many community members can assume the place of the victim? The answer is not easy, because these community members should be legitimated to be part of processes leading to reparation agreements. Authors such as McCold (1996) propose a distinction between macro-community (where the offence produces consequences) and micro-community (family members and friends of the parties involved). It is understandable, from a psychological perspective, that the "community of care" of the protagonists of the crime is an important reference to author and victim alike, after a crime has been committed. Much of the success of an agreement depends upon effective emotional and moral support provided by those community members. In legal systems, where the attention rests on the investigation of a crime as a breach of a legal norm and ascertainment of criminal responsibility, and where imprisonment is still one of the most important criminal sanctions currently used, social conflicts are aggravated by a logic of confrontation between perpetrator and victim, which then taints family members and friends. Crime statistics show increasing violence within families (domestic violence, crimes against life, bodily integrity and property) and between neighbors, a reality that requires a substantial change in the way resolution of conflicts is undertaken.

When conflict has a social background, there must be an inclusive answer, not exclusive. The participation of community members in the process of resolution of conflicts might be useful to reduce fear and decrease private vengeances, which indirectly increases a favorable perception of justice. The micro-community can play an important role in a system of restorative justice, especially in countries where public officials (including police officers, prosecutors and judges) are distrusted, therefore promoting social peace.

There are other conceptual problems concerning restorative justice. In order to become a new science (social, legal), there should be more consensus on the ideas and processes driving the restorative process phenomena. Currently, one can find very different philosophical trends in restorative justice proponents: abolitionism, Christian philosophy or even economic neoliberalism applied to the theory of punishment (Reggio, 2010). This topic leads us to this basic question: do we want a State-driven justice that sees judges as guardians of the rule of law, or a community justice that requires neighbors, psychologists or social workers as mediators? Or even computer scientists or artificial intelligences (Andrade, Carneiro and Novais, 2010; Lodder and Zeleznikow, 2010)?

As far as one can see, it is not only a matter of replacing the binominal crime-punishment for a conflict-reparation one. There are fundamental questions that enable this conceptual improvement within a legal framework in which it is guaranteed not only the voluntary participation of the parties but also the protection of constitutional values such as legality and equality. Due process fosters legal validity of the reached agreement while leveling possible asymmetries between parties. This signifies that these agreements should have the same legal value as judgments made by judges. If this not achievable, reason assists to those who say that restorative justice is nothing more than justice between parties and should be surrogate to proper official and traditional conflict resolution in courts (Galain Palermo, 2009).

ONLINE DISPUTE RESOLUTION: AN OVERVIEW

When literature, whether from computer sciences or from legal sciences, devotes its attention to how technology might improve or, at least, change traditional alternative dispute resolution mechanisms (including negotiation, mediation, conciliation), one answer emerges: online dispute resolution (ODR). With ODR traditional alternative dispute resolution mechanisms[2] shift from a physical dimension to a virtual one (Bellucci, Lodder, Zeleznikow, 2004), either completely or partially (Goodman, 2003).

The decision of resolving conflicts using online environments has some advantages that range from greater adaptability and flexibility to convenience, cost saving and lack of jurisdictional quandaries. Goodman (2003) is one of the scholars who associate cost savings and convenience with ODR systems (also, Hang, 2001). The argument goes as follows: if one or both parties have to travel long distances to a pre-determined physical location where mediation or other mechanisms of conflict resolution take place, this signifies that they must afford the costs of travelling[3]. Such costs could be avoided if online technologies were implemented. Further savings could happen depending on the particular nature of the online dispute resolution mechanism. For example, some cyber-mediation websites run in a fully automated fashion without any human intervention apart from both parties in dispute (Hang, 2001; Goodman, 2003), making it unnecessary to even hire an attorney for counseling or other legal services[4].

On the other hand, traditional litigation, or even alternative dispute resolution (ADR) mechanisms, forces parties to be physically present at a certain location at a specific date and time, which sometimes means, namely when the jurisdictionally competent court is far apart from where parties live, that they will face not only a costly process but also a time consuming one. Sometimes this aspect is further aggravated by successive adjournments for reasons parties did not contribute for.

Another beneficial aspect of ODR systems is that they are available day and night, around the clock, irrespective of where parties live and of whether ADR providers' offices' are officially open (Friedman, 1997), allowing parties to engage in the ODR process[5] even when living in completely different countries and time zones (Bellucci, Lodder and Zeleznikow, 2004; Friedman, 1997). An intrinsic characteristic of online communication is that it supports both synchronous and asynchronous interaction, thus enabling disputing parties, and an eventual third party (e.g. mediator), to participate in the resolution process at their own pace, depending on exactly what type of ODR system is chosen. Therefore, asynchronous communication allows parties to write, read and respond to messages at any time (Goodman, 2003). The pace in which the process occurs is defined not by an external entity (e.g. court) but by parties (or third party) themselves, resulting in a feeling of empowerment, ownership of the process and responsibility for its continuous and smooth development. Asynchronous communication has further advantages as it may be argued that "more thoughtful, well-crafted contributions result from the ability of the parties to edit messages prior to sending them" (Goodman, 2003). In traditional litigation and ADR systems parties are faced with the demand of an immediate feedback that occasionally translates into hasty and impulsive responses (Melamed, 2002) capable of undermining an otherwise successful dispute resolution.

ODR systems can be shaped into different models with specific and distinct characteristics. There is a huge flexibility when it comes to designing a platform for conflict resolution. For example, mediators using online tools can emulate some of their mediation techniques but in a digital environment. While discussing the "joy of synchronous communication", James Melamed (2002) depicts exactly this advantage of ODR systems: "Experienced mediators are well aware of the benefits of asynchrony. This is one reason that many mediators «caucus» (meet separately) with participants. Mediators want to slow down the process and assist participants to craft more effective proposals. Surely, the Internet works capably as an extension of individual party caucus and is remarkably convenient and affordable. Internet communications take little time to read and clients do not hear a ticking of the billing meter. When the Internet is utilized for caucus, the non-caucusing participant does not need to sit in the waiting room or library growing resentful at being ignored".

This flexibility of ODR systems is also conveyed by the circumstance that, if it is deemed necessary by the mediator (or other neutral party), parties are not required to meet face-to-face, either physically or virtually[6]. In fact, having parties discussing face-to-face the issues at stake can sometimes result in major and irreversible setbacks in the conflict resolution process, namely in situations where there has been animosity and/or violence among parties (Bellucci, Lodder and Zeleznikow, 2004; Lodder and Zeleznikow, 2010).

Finally, the avoidance of jurisdiction issues is often signaled as an advantage of ODR (Hang, 2001) and ADR systems (Lide, 1996). Especially in commercial disputes, parties can overcome potential disputes over jurisdiction issues with an agreement over what law should be applied in case of a conflict should emerge (Lide, 1996; Hang, 2001).

Detachment, accessibility, confidentiality and security concerns are – to name a few[7] – disadvantages of ODR systems.

A large number of scholars (Eisen, 1998; Hang, 2001; Goodman, 2003) observe that ODR systems do not offer the parties the chance of speaking face-to-face and thus deprive them from the opportunity to confront their emotions and vent their feelings (Hang, 2001; Goodman, 2003). Because online mediation – and ODR systems in general – "imposes an electronic distance on the parties, while mediation is usually an oral form of dispute resolution designed to involve participants in direct interpersonal contact" (Eisen, 1998), effective and meaningful communication between parties is therefore seriously challenged. This is especially true if the chosen mean of communication is e-mail or an analogue written communication method. But technology has met many advances since Eisen and other scholars criticized ODR systems for the (then) lack of human factor. Their critiques were based on the assumption that ODR systems rely heavily, or better still, exclusively, on communication through email. Of course that if we compare a mediation run by e-mail to a traditional face-to-face meeting all the richness and meaningful visual cues provided by a face-to-face meeting vanish altogether. What about variable tones, pitch and volume of the voices, powerful indicators of a personality, feeling or stress? They too are inexistent in a written cybermediation (Goodman, 2003).

Visual and audio cues are of upmost importance. They function as a tool for the mediator to correctly evaluate how the mediation process is evolving and "the substitution of E-mail for dialogue, for example, makes it difficult to give any weight to emotion in mediation" (Eisen, 1998). This leads to a loss in efficacy and higher probability of an unsuccessful outcome of the mediation[8]. Similarly, these visual and audio cues are also instrumental to the parties themselves: if the "parties cannot see each other, they will not be able to read those same emotional messages through body language as they could if they were in the same room together" (Hang, 2001). In fact, "the mediation process is often therapeutic. For many participants, mediation is about «venting» of feelings and emotions that they would be unable to express in a more formal setting such as a courtroom. The opportunity to tell one's version of the case directly to the opposing party and to express accompanying emotions can be cathartic for mediation participants" (Eisen, 1998).

However, with the advent and development of voice and visual communication technologies, now omnipresent in computers, smartphones and tablets, most of these critics are rendered outdated. Virtual face-to-face meetings are now feasible. Still, the literature considers virtual environments "cold" because a large amount of contextual information, e.g. body language and emotions, is not adequately transmitted and acquired by parties (Carneiro, Novais, Andrade, Zeleznikow and Neves, 2012).

A second argument against ODR systems is that its use requires parties to have access to electronic equipment with Internet access (e.g. computer, smartphone, tablet, etc.). Over time, this argument has lost most of its strength. In the beginning of our informational and technological society, smartphones and tablets did not exist, and personal computers were not affordable. If an individual was not wealthy enough to buy a personal computer, he had to use the local library's computer (Hang, 2001), with all constraints that meant: opening hours of the library and need of personal vehicle or public transport to get to the library. Nowadays, however, this is not the case. An additional advantage related to accessibility concerns might be the lack of sufficient knowledge by those who do not use computers in a regular basis (Goodman, 2003).

A third and final disadvantage of ODR systems relates to confidentiality and security.

One major concern with ODR systems is the assurance of confidentiality. A traditional ADR, held in a physical setting provides, is by nature a suitable context for confidentiality protection (Katsh, 1996). Usually, no recordings are made of face-to-face meetings, not only to prevent parties from using them later as court evidence, but mainly because privacy and confidentiality promotes openness and willingness to be part of the ADR process. Additionally, case documents used or produced during ADR sessions can be destroyed after ADR has ended. So, in a physical setting, there is more control over video, audio and written data and, consistently, better chances that the parties will rest assured that, unless they give their permission, no information will spread beyond their and third party neutral's knowledge. Whatever the specific nature of the ADR used, a crucial element is, undoubtedly, confidentiality and ODR presents a difficult challenge. Cybercopying and global and immediate online distribution of information are almost inherent to a proper comprehension on how cyberspace functions. It is one of its great qualities: cyberspace completely revolutionized the perception of society with its ubiquity, flexibility, speed and accessibility. But those same qualities signify that "an online mediator or online ombudsperson needs to be highly sensitive to the confidentiality problem and to understand how copying is inherent in all electronic communications" (Katsh, 1996).

On the other hand, digital environments are all subject to security breaches, even those considered being "almost" full proof[9]. ODR systems are no exception (Hang, 2001). The challenge with the use of ODR systems, namely as a restorative justice tool, is that sensitive information of the cases will be stored and transferred in a digital environment, making it a possible target of cyber attacks. While conscious that there is not absolute perfection when it comes to computer or information security, public or private service providers of ODR systems must adopt state-of-the-art devices, programs and techniques in digital security against illegal accesses, illegal interceptions, data interferences and systems interferences and other actions against the confidentiality, integrity and availability of computer data and systems[10]. Only by assuring a sound degree of security of the ODR systems, parties will trust it and feel confident to use it. "Protecting trust and the discussion process in ADR is very import because parties are more likely to speak freely when they can be sure that their words will not come back to be held against them" (Hang, 2001).

ONLINE RESTORATIVE JUSTICE?

E-commerce has been the main reason behind the development of ODR systems. For a couple of reasons (Bellucci, Lodder and Zeleznikow, 2004): if parties negotiated online – the seller electronically advertised and sold something that has been bought, again electronically, by someone else (buyer) – having access to Internet is an acquired fact; additionally, most of the information relevant to the case is already online, which makes ODR systems seem a natural choice to end a conflict that emerged electronically. The question is whether an online environment could be a suitable context for restorative justice. To provide an answer to this question, we shall focus our attention on one the most accepted e globally used mechanisms of restorative justice: victim-offender mediation (Santana, 2007). Victim-offender mediation programs establish a (direct or indirect) communication channel or process between offender and victim, mediated by a neutral third party (mediator), offering them the opportunity to discuss, in a safe, structured and private environment, the reasons behind the crime, the impact it had on the victim and, whenever possible, a mutually consented restorative plan. Mediation can offer an opportunity for the victims to express their feelings and describe to the offender how the crime affected them – financially, physically or emotionally – and at the same time give the offenders a chance to learn about the outcomes of their behavior and come to terms with their responsibility and part in it. The offender does not have to admit full responsibility for every aspect of the crime (Staiger, 2010), but it is expected from him at least an admission of the crime and that he played a relevant role.

There is no predetermined goal or result of the victim-offender mediation: a financial settlement will not be always the preferred outcome. This particularity is something that sets apart victim-offender mediation and other types of mediation, in domains such as civil or commercial disputes. On the one hand, parties of a victim-offender program are not disputants – the offender voluntarily acknowledges that he victimized, at some extent, another individual –, on the other, victim-offender programs are not primarily about settling for a payment plan as a compensation for the harm done by the offender. The solution to the conflict can simply consist on the offender's expression of remorse and regret. Or he may even agree to compensate for what he has done with his own labor. But a signed restitution agreement can also be part of the solution. It is in the victim and offender's hands to define what constitutes in their minds a suitable solution[11].

Although cyber-mediation in criminal matters is still, as far as we are aware, practically nonexistent[12], it is technically feasible and might be adequate for a specific set of offences. On the one hand, there are no technical obstacles that hamper the development and use of cyber-mediation platforms. These platforms exist since the late 1990s with relative success, e.g., ICANN UDRP, Cybersettle and SquareTrade (Lodder and Zeleznikow, 2010). From a technological point of view, the future of cyber-mediation should involve exploring current mechanisms and models used in ecommerce, labor and other fields, and adapting them for the specific needs of a restorative justice model. In other words, the choice on what type of technology should support cyber-mediation in criminal matters must have into account the strengths and goals of restorative justice. Information technology must therefore match the process (Lodder and Zeleznikow, 2010) and be a positive contribution towards its goals. Conceptually, offline victim-offender mediation might work as a reference model, at least at an early stage of cyber-mediation. According to literature (Staiger, 2010), victim-offender mediation contemplates two means of communication between parties: direct and indirect. Direct victim-offender mediation relies on voluntarily face-to-face meetings between the parties with the presence of a trained mediator, although there can be preparatory individual meetings to prepare the encounter between offender and victim. For situations where offender and victim do not want or are unable to meet directly, indirect victim-offender meditation is a suitable alternative to direct mediation. It is an umbrella term that covers different communication processes in which the mediator acts as an intermediate, e.g., offenders and victims individual conversations with the mediator are videotaped and then shared to one another. Both means of communication are easily implemented on a digital environment.

On the other hand, a specific set of offences emerges as a prime candidate for online victim-offender mediation: cybercrimes. These offences present unique characteristics in relation to conventional crimes, one of them being the intrinsic role of technology in them. Examples of such crimes could be an unauthorized access to an online account (email, social network, cloud storage, etc.) or defamation in a social network. If someone posts a damaging affirmation against someone else's character or reputation in a social network like Facebook would online victim-offender mediation be completely inconceivable? If not, what would be the legal implications of an agreement reached as a result of this restorative practice? Would it replace traditional criminal justice? If at all necessary, who would be responsible for the supervision of the process?

None of above questions has an immediate and definitive answer. It is for us clear that further studies are necessary to fully comprehend the extent of the structure and implications of an ODR system for criminal conflicts.

CONCLUSION

Criminal law is bound to experience progressive changes towards a new theory of justice, especially in civil law countries, that until recently had not come in contact, at least in a structured and sustained manner. It might constitute a "new" paradigm capable of profound transformation on how crimes and responses to them are perceived and fabricated. Central to this paradigm is the idea that the victim should have a more important role in the response to the crime. It is becoming increasingly clear that the individual harmed by the criminal behavior cannot continue to be set aside and ignored, as if the crime did not affect him and all is a matter of the State deciding, as it see fits, to deal with the offender. Technology can help develop new restorative environments and mechanisms, but irrespectively of the actual online platforms or similar mechanisms chosen it should be underlined that the principles of restorative justice must always be protected and followed, from their design stage up to their implementation. Here technology is simply instrumental towards an end: restoration.

REFERENCES

Andrade, F., Carneiro, D., & Novais, P. (2010). A Inteligência Artificial na Resolução de Conflitos em Linha. *Scientia Iuridica, 59*(321), 137–164.

Bellucci, E., Lodder, A., & Zeleznikow, J. (2004). Integrating artificial intelligence, argumentation and game theory to develop an online dispute resolution environment. In *Proceedings of the 16th IEEE International Conference on Tools with Artificial Intelligence*. Washington, DC: IEEE Computer Society. doi:10.1109/ICTAI.2004.75

Binding, K. (1913). *Grundriß des deutschen Strafrechts. Allgemeiner Teil* (8th ed.). Leipzig, Germany: Meiner.

Braithwaite, J. (2002). *Restorative justice and responsive regulation*. Oxford, UK: Oxford University Press.

Braithwaite, J. (2003). Principles of Restorative Justice. In A. Hirsch, J. Roberts, A. Bottoms, K. Roach, & M. Schiff (Eds.), *Restorative Justice and Criminal Justice. Competing or Reconcilable Paradigms?* (pp. 1–20). Oxford, UK: Hart Publishing.

Carneiro, D., Novais, P., Andrade, F., Zeleznikow, J., & Neves, J. (2012). *Context-aware Environments for Online Dispute Resolution*. Paper presented at GDN 2012 - The 12th international annual meeting of the Group Decision and Negotiation Conference, Recife, Brazil.

Christie, N. (1977). Conflicts as property. *The British Journal of Criminology, 17*(1), 1–15.

Daly, K., & Proietti-Scifoni, G. (2010). Reparation and restoration. In M. Tonry (Ed.), *Oxford Handbook of Crime and Criminal Justice* (pp. 207–253). New York: Oxford University Press.

Eisen, J. (1998). Are We Ready for Mediation in Cyberspace? *Brigham Young University Law Review, 1998*, 1305–1358.

Friedman, G. (1996). Alternative Dispute Resolution and Emerging Online Technologies: Challenges and Opportunities. *Hastings Communications and Entertainment Law Journal, 19*, 695–718.

Galain Palermo, P. (2009). *La reparación del daño como equivalente funcional de la pena*. Montevideo: Universidad Católica del Uruguay.

Galain Palermo, P. (2015). *Justicia de Transición? Mecanismos políticos y jurídicos para la elaboración del pasado*. Valencia: Tirant lo Blanch.

Galain Palermo, P., & Garreaud, A. (2012). Truth Commissions and the Reconstruction of the Past in the Post-Dictatorial Southern Cone: Concerning the Limitations for Understanding Evil. In K. Ambos, L. Coutinho, M. Palma, & P. Mendes (Eds.), Eichmann in Jerusalem – 50 Years After: An Interdisciplinary Approach (pp. 181-198). Berlin: Duncker & Humblot.

Gavrielides, T. (2011). Restorative Practices: From the early societies to the 1970s. *Internet Journal of Criminology, 2011*, 1–20.

Goodman, J. (2003). The pros and cons of online dispute resolution: An assessment of cyber-mediation websites. *Duke Law and Technology Review, 2*(1), 1–16.

Hang, L. (2001). Online Dispute Resolution Systems: The Future of Cyberspace Law. *Santa Clara Law Review*, *41*, 837–866.

Hassemer, W. (1981). *Einführung in die Grundlagen des Strafrechts*. Munich, Germany: Beck.

Hassemer, W. (1988). Variationen der positiven Generalprävention. In B. Schünemann et al. (Ed.), *Positive Generalprävention Kritische Analysen im deutsch-englischen Dialog, Upsala Symposium 1996* (pp. 29-50). Heidelberg, Germany: Müller.

Hassemer, W. (2002). Darf der strafende Staat Verurteilte bessern wollen? Resozialisiergun im Rahmen positiver Generalprävention. In C. Prittwitz et al. (Eds.), *Festschrift für Klaus Lürsenn* (pp. 221–240). Baden-Baden: Nomos.

Hirsch, H. (1969). Zur Abrenzung Von Strafrecht und Zivilrecht. In P. Bockelmann, A. Kaufmann, & U. Klug (Eds.), *Festschrift für Karl Engish zum 70. Geburtstag* (pp. 304–327). Frankfurt: Klostermann.

Hirsch, H. (1990). Wiedergutmachung des Schadens im Rahmen des materiellen Strafrechts. *ZStW*, *102*(3), 534–562. doi:10.1515/zstw.1990.102.3.534

Huxley, E. (1939). *Red strangers*. London: Chatto and Windus.

Johnstone, G., & Ness, D. (2007). The meaning of restorative justice. In G. Johnstone & D. Ness (Eds.), *Handbook of Restorative Justice* (pp. 5–23). Devon: Willan Publishing.

Katsch, E. (1996). Dispute Resolution in Cyberspace. *Connecticut Law Review*, *28*, 953–980.

Kerner, H. (1983). *Diversion statt Strafe? Probleme und Gefahren einer neuen Strategie strafrechtlicher Sozialkontrolle*. Heidelberg: Kriminalistik Verlag.

Knust, N. (2013). *Entwicklung eines pluralistischen Rechtsmodells am Beispiel des ruandischen Völkermordes*. Berlin: Duncker & Humblot.

Lide, C. (1996). ADR and Cyberspace: The Role of Alternative Dispute Resolution in Online Commerce, Intellectual Property and Defamation. *Ohio State Journal on Dispute Resolution*, *12*, 192–222.

Liszt, F. (1912). *Lehrbuch des Deutschen Strafrechts*. Berlin: Walter de Gruyter.

Lodder, A., & Zeleznikow, J. (2010). *Enhanced Dispute Resolution through the use of Information Technology*. Cambridge, UK: Cambridge University Press. doi:10.1017/CBO9780511777554

Luhmann, N. (2005). *Soziologische Aufklärung 6. Die Soziologie und der Mensch* (2nd ed.). Wiesbaden: Verlag für Sozialwissenschaften.

Luna, E. (2003). Punishment Theory, Holism, and the Procedural Conception of Restorative Justice. *Utah Law Review*, (1), 205–302.

Marshall, T. (1996). The evolution of restorative justice in Britain. *European Journal on Criminal Policy and Research*, *4*(4), 21–43. doi:10.1007/BF02736712

Mate, M. (2011). *Tratado de la injusticia*. Madrid: Anthropos.

McCold, P. (1996). Restorative justice and the role of community. In B. Galaway & J. Hudson (Eds.), *Restorative Justice: International Perspectives* (pp. 85–101). New York: Criminal Justice Press.

Melamed, J. (2002). *Divorce Mediation and the Internet*. Retrieved May, 30, 2015, from http://www.mediate.com/articles/melamed9.cfm

Reggio, F. (2010). *Giustizia dialogica. Luci e ombre della Restorative Justice*. Milan: Franco Angeli.

Roxin, C. (1973). *Kriminalpolitik und Strafrechtssystem*. Berlin, New York: De Gruyter. doi:10.1515/9783110903577

Roxin, C. (1992). Zur Wiedergutmachung als einer "dritten Spur" im Sanktionensystem. In G. Arzt et al. (Eds.), *Festschrift für Jürgen Baumann zum 70 Geburtstag 22. Juni 1992* (pp. 243–254). Bielefeld: Gieseking Verlag.

Santana, G. (2007). *La justicia restaurativa y la mediación penal*. Madrid: Iustel.

Schöch, H. (1988). Strafrecht im demokratischen Rechtsstat. Yur konkreten Utopie der Wiedergutmachung im Strafverfahren. In A. Kaufmann et al. (Eds.), *Festschrift für Maihofer zum 70. Geburtstag* (pp. 461–479). Frankfurt: Kostermann.

Schöch, H. (1992). Verwarnung statt Strafe. In G. Arzt et al. (Eds.), *Festschrift für Jürgen Baumann zum 70 Geburtstag 22. Juni 1992* (pp. 255–268). Bielefeld: Gieseking Verlag.

Sherman, L. (1993). Defiance, Deterrence and Irrelevance: A Theory of the Criminal Sanction. *Journal of Research in Crime and Delinquency*, *30*(4), 445–473. doi:10.1177/0022427893030004006

Sherman, L., & Strang, H. (2007). *Restorative justice: the evidence*. The Smith Institute.

Sherman, L., & Strang, H. (2010). Restorative Justice as a Psychological Treatment: Healing Victims and Reintegrating Offenders. In G. Towl & D. Crichton (Eds.), *Handbook of Forensic Psychology*. Amsterdam: Elsevier.

Sherman, L., Strang, H., & Newbury-Birch, D. (2008). *Restorative justice*. Youth Justice Board.

Staiger, I. (2010). Restorative Justice and Victims of Terrorism. In R. Letschert, I. Staiger, & A. Pemberton (Eds.), *Assisting Victims of Terrorism: Towards a European Standard of Justice* (pp. 267–337). London: Springer.

Strang, H. (2001). *Restorative Justice Programs in Australia: A report to the Criminology Council*. Retrieved May, 30, 2015, from http://www.criminologyresearchcouncil.gov.au/reports/strang/

Streng, F. (1991). *Strafrechtliche Sanktionen. Grundlagen und Anwendung*. Stuttgart: Kohlhammer.

Umbreit, M., Coates, R., & Vos, B. (2004). Restorative justice versus community justice: Clarifying a muddle or generating confusion? *Contemporary Justice Review*, *7*(1), 81–89. doi:10.1080/1028258042000212030

Vaandering, D. (2011). A faithful compass: Rethinking the term restorative justice to find clarity. *Contemporary Justice Review*, *14*(3), 307–328. doi:10.1080/10282580.2011.589668

Wright, M. (1991). *Justice for Victims and Offenders. A restorative Response to Crime* (2nd ed.). Winchester: Waterside Press.

Wright, M., & Zernova, M. (2007). Alternative visions of restorative justice. In G. Johnstone & D. Ness (Eds.), *Handbook of Restorative Justice* (pp. 91–108). Devon: Willan Publishing.

Zehr, H. (2004). *El Pequeño Libro de la Justicia Restaurativa.* Good Books.

KEY TERMS AND DEFINITIONS

Negative General Prevention: Focus on the intimidation of the population, deterring them from committing crimes, being the punishment of the offender a deterrent example to others.

Negative Special Prevention: To regard the offender as a source of danger which needs to be segregated and separated from the community. Also known as incapacitation.

Positive General Prevention: Focus on the reaffirmation of the value of the legal norm against the unlawfulness of a crime.

Positive Special Prevention: (Re)socialization or rehabilitation of the offender.

Restorative Justice: An approach to criminal conflicts that focuses its efforts on restoring the harm done by criminal activities with the involvement of all stakeholders.

Restorative Practices: Set of actions, including criminal sanctions or rehabilitation programs, to make offenders aware of the harm they caused, but do not imply necessarily the participation of the victims on deciding how to deal with the future implications of the crime.

Victim-Offender Mediation: Process where offender and victim, mediated by a neutral third party (mediator), have the opportunity to discuss, in a safe, structured and private environment, the reasons behind the crime, the impact it had on the victim and, whenever possible, a mutually consented restorative plan.

ENDNOTES

[1]   The State here embodies an abstract normative system harmed by the offence.

[2]   According to Bellucci, Lodder and Zeleznikow (2004), Alternative Dispute Resolution "refers to procedures for settling disputes by means other than litigation", such as arbitration, mediation or negotiation. These authors define arbitration as "a process of dispute resolution in which a neutral third party [the arbitrator] renders a decision after a hearing at which both parties have an opportunity to be heard" (Bellucci, Lodder and Zeleznikow, 2004). Mediation "is a non-binding process and most often voluntary. A third-party neutral, known as the mediator, assists the parties in formulating their own resolution of the dispute" (Lodder and Zeleznikow, 2010). Finally, negotiation "is a process where the parties involved modify their demands to achieve a mutually acceptable compromise. (…) The essence of negotiation is that there is no third party whose role is to act as facilitator or umpire in the communications between the parties as they attempt to resolve their dispute" (Lodder and Zeleznikow, 2010).

[3]   Electronic communication technologies, such as email or instant messaging with attachment transmission capabilities, may, even in situations where offline or physical mechanisms of conflict resolution are used, be relevant to achieve cost saving. It is important to note that in legal systems around the world telephone and fax machines are still used for official communication between parties and courts (Friedman, 1997).

4   Hang (2001) perceives ODR as a low-cost alternative to traditional litigation.

5   For example, by consulting or obtaining case data or giving their input further advancing the process.

6   E.g. using videoconference web applications.

7   For Goodman (2003), ODR systems also have a limited range of disputes, meaning that there isn't an online solution/model that can fit all dispute cases. Fully automated cyber-mediation, for example, is better suited – if not, only suited – for cases where the only disputed matter is the amount of the settlement. More complex cases do not benefit from an ODR system of this typology. Friedman (1997) adds the place of hearing, language, writing requirement for arbitration clauses and ambiguity of statues as to Subject Matter Arbitrability to the list of disadvantages (or challenges, according to the author) of ODR systems: the definition of the place of hearing is, for traditional legal mechanisms, a fundamental step, that, in an online environment, deprived of physical landmarks and frontiers, faces deep conceptual difficulties; the option for a certain language can too present problems, not only because there must be an agreement on the applicable language but there is also the matter of parties being able to communicate fluently in that language; as for writing requirement for arbitration clauses, Friedman draws attention to the legal necessity, imposed by American laws, of having the arbitration agreement in writing, and questions whether online arbitration agreements meet this requirement; lastly, according to US legislation, the use of arbitration is allowed in all subject matters.

8   "The online medium, at least the e-mail environment, makes it difficult for the mediator to manage or temper the tone of the interactions without sounding controlling and judgmental. The mediator, at least in the beginning, is a disembodied voice and cannot use her own physical «personhood» to se the parties at ease and create an environment for sustained problem solving. Similarly, absent the physical presence of the disputants, the mediator has difficulty using the intuitive cues of body language, facial expression, and verbal tonality that are part of face-to-face mediation processes" (Katsh, Rifkin and Gaitenby, 2000).

9   A recent example is the compromising breach of the US Office of Personnel Management's records. This agency is responsible for storing personnel records of over 4 million federal workers, including sensitive date such as mental health history, criminal records, drug and alcohol use and financial data. The source of this cyber attack is yet to be determined but it constituted a serious blow to US national security and showed how vulnerable information systems are.

10   See the leading international legal instrument on cybercrime, the Convention on Cybercrime of the Council of Europe, signed in Budapest in 2001.

11   Nevertheless, legal limitations can diminish the scope of the agreement.

12   Lide (1996) offers an example that can have a criminal nature and possibly be suited for ODR: defamation.

Section 2
Conflict and Its Resolution

As technology and society progress, new types of conflict emerge and their complexity increases. Fortunately, this evolution also results in new approaches for solving conflicts, and new supporting technologies, both for judicial and extra-judicial conflict resolution processes. This section deals with classic and novel methods and technologies for conflict resolution.

Chapter 6
Quality of Judgment Assessment

José Neves
Universidade do Minho, Portugal

John Zeleznikow
Victoria University, Australia

Henrique Vicente
Universidade de Évora, Portugal

ABSTRACT

The intersection of Artificial Intelligence and The Law stands for a multifaceted matter, and its effects set the advances on culture, organization, as well as the social matters, when the emergent information technologies are taken into consideration. From this point of view, the weight of formal and informal Conflict Resolution settings should be highlighted, and the use of defective data, information or knowledge must be emphasized. Indeed, it is hard to do it with traditional problem solving methodologies. Therefore, in this work the focus is on the development of decision support systems, in terms of its knowledge representation and reasoning procedures, under a formal framework based on Logic Programming, complemented with an approach to computing centered on Artificial Neural Networks. It is intended to evaluate the Quality-of-Judgments and the respective Degree-of-Confidence that one has on such happenings.

INTRODUCTION

While identifying the abstract perceptions for a multi-domain Online Dispute Resolution (ODR), there is the need to determine which information would be useful, namely if a party should ask if he/she will reach a better outcome using an alternative dispute resolution process instead of litigation.

The concept can be defined in terms of the BATNA – Best Alternative to a Negotiated Agreement, or the possible best outcome along a particular path if he/she tries to get his/her interests satisfied in a way that does not require negotiation with the counterpart (Klaming, Van Veenen, & Leenes, 2008; Lodder

DOI: 10.4018/978-1-5225-0245-6.ch006

& Zeleznikow, 2010; Notini, 2005). In fact, by knowing their BATNA, parties would, on the one hand, become better protected against agreements that should be rejected and, on the other hand, in a better condition to reach an agreement that better satisfy their interests (De Vries, Leenes, & Zeleznikow, 2005).

On the opposite side one should also consider the notion of a WATNA, or the Worst Alternative to a Negotiated Agreement (Steenbergen, 2005). The WATNA aims to estimate the worst possible outcome along a litigation path. It can be quite relevant in the calculation of the real risks that parties will face in a judicially determined litigation, envisioning the worst possible outcome for a party.

With these two immaterial figures, a party is aware of the best and worst scenario if the dispute is to be solved in a court.

It is also interesting for a party to analyze the space between the BATNA and the WATNA as a useful element to be taken into account for decision making. Of course, the less space there is between BATNA and WATNA, the less dangerous it becomes for a party not to accept the agreement (unless, their BATNA is really disadvantageous). A wider space between BATNA and WATNA would usually mean that it could become rather dangerous for a party not to accept the ODR agreement (except in situations when the WATNA is really not inconvenient at all for a party).

On the one hand, it may be argued that knowledge about the space between the BATNA and the WATNA is quite central, independent of the problem domain. It is close to the Zone of Possible Agreement (ZOPA) proposed by Raiffa (1982). It is the zone where an agreement can be met that is acceptable for both parties.

On the other hand, if the parties are to solve the dispute through litigation, what is the most likely outcome? In fact, sticking only with the BATNA and the WATNA may not be realistic, once these are usually not the most likely outcomes, but merely informative values that establish boundaries. Thus, an informed party should also consider the concept of MLATNA – Most Likely Alternative to a Negotiated Agreement (Steenbergen 2005).

Using the same arguments, it can also be argued that the existence of metrics that measure one´s confidence on each possible outcome could also be extremely useful for any party. Thus, it is also considered the figure of *possible case*, i.e., a conceivable outcome with an associated value of confidence.

Concluding, different conceptions that are significant for any party may be considered in the development of an ODR tool, namely: (1) the *BATNA*; (2) the *WATNA*; (3) the *ZOPA*; (4) the *MLATNA* and (5) the *Possible Cases*. These terms establish what is identified in this work as the minimum set of information that a party should consider prior to getting involved in a litigation or alternative conflict resolution process. Another interesting concept that should be taken into account in this context is the legal precedent one (Landes & Posner, 1976). The concept of legal precedence defines a case that establishes a rule (or principle) that could/should be used by practitioners when deciding on subsequent similar cases. There are legal domains in which precedents are divided into binding and persuasive precedents. The former type is generally the result of a process in a higher court and means that all lower courts must honor it. The persuasive precedent, in turn, arises from cases that are decided in lower courts and does not denote an obligation (Carneiro, Novais, Andrade, Zeleznikow, & Neves, 2009; Carneiro, Novais, & Neves 2014).

Devising a valid, fair and appealing solution for a conflict resolution process may be a challenge, mostly when the concept of fairness may be subjective. In that sense, there is the need not only to generate a solution that is valid, but also to detail why such solution is fair, given the circumstances. For discussions of fairness in ADR and ODR, see Zeleznikow and Bellucci (2012).

In light of the several AI-based approaches analyzed, the choice was on the use of a combination of a Logic Programming (LP) to knowledge representation and reasoning, plus a nature-inspired approach based on *Artificial Neural Networks (ANNs)* to computing, used to structure data and capture complex relationships between inputs and outputs (Vicente, Couto, Machado, Abelha, & Neves, 2012; Vicente et al., 2012; Vicente, Roseiro, Arteiro, Neves, & Caldeira, 2013). ANNs are computational tools which attempt to simulate the architecture and internal operational features of the human brain and nervous system. ANNs can be defined as a connected structure of basic computation units, called artificial neurons or nodes, with learning capabilities. Multilayered feed-forward neural network architecture are one of the most popular ANNs structures, often used for prediction as well as for classification. This architecture is molded on three or more layers of artificial neurons, including an input layer, an output layer and a number of hidden layers with a certain number of active neurons connected with modifiable weights. In addition, there is also a bias, which is only connected to neurons in the hidden and output layers. The number of nodes in the input layer set the number of independent variables, and the number of nodes in the output layer denotes the number of dependent ones (Haykin, 2009).

Indeed, the main aim of this work was to determine if a different approach could be devised that would not rely on questionnaires. In fact the estimation of the conflict handling style was implemented through the analysis of the interactions between parties, during the negotiation process, particularly focusing on the evolution of the utility of the proposal' issues. This results in a dynamic approach, that provides in real-time an estimation of the conflict handling style of each party, thus detecting significant changes. A prototype was successfully implemented that transparently monitors a negotiation process.

In modeling this intermediate domain with *Logic Programming (LP)* we are not taking on a narrow conception of logic as just another language to solve routine computational problems. Undeniably, the significative point is that logic may be used to represent knowledge in countless diverse contexts, and can be animated or mechanized in many different ways. For discussions of using logic in fairness and in particular in Dispute Resolution see Kraus et al. (1998), and Matwin et al. (1989).

KNOWLEDGE REPRESENTATION AND REASONING

Many approaches for knowledge representation and reasoning have been proposed using *Logic Programming (LP)*, namely in the area of Model Theory (Gelfon & Lifschitz, 1988; Kakas, Kowalski, & Toni, 1998; Pereira & Anh, 2009) and Proof Theory (Neves, 1984; Neves et al., 2007). In this work it is followed the proof theoretical approach in terms of an extension to the *LP* language to knowledge representation and reasoning. An *Extended Logic Program (ELP)* is a finite set of clauses in the form:

$$\left\{ \begin{array}{l} p \leftarrow p_1, \ldots, p_n, not\ q_1, \ldots, not\ q_m \\ ?\left(p_1, \ldots, p_n, not\ q_1, \ldots, not\ q_m\right)\ \left(n, m \geq 0\right) \\ exception_{p_1} \quad \cdots \quad exception_{p_j} \quad \left(j \leq m, n\right) \end{array} \right\} :: scoring_{value}$$

where "*?*" is a domain atom denoting falsity, the p_i, q_j, and p are classical ground literals, i.e., either positive atoms or atoms preceded by the classical negation sign ¬ (Neves, 1984). Under this formalism, every program is associated with a set of abducibles (Kakas et al., 1998; Pereira & Anh, 2009) given here in the form of exceptions to the extensions of the predicates that make the program. The term *scoring*$_{value}$ stands for the relative weight of the extension of a specific *predicate* with respect to the extensions of the peers ones that make the overall program.

In order to evaluate the knowledge that stems from a logic program, an evaluation of the *Quality-of-Information* (*QoI*) was set in dynamic environments aiming at decision-making purposes (Lucas, 2004; Machado, Abelha, Novais, & Neves, 2010).

The *QoI* with respect to the extension of a *predicate*$_i$ will be given by a truth-value in the interval [0, 1], i.e., if the information is *known* (*positive*) or *false* (*negative*) the *QoI* for the extension of *predicate*$_i$ is 1. For situations where the information is unknown, the *QoI* is given by:

$$QoI_i = \lim_{N \to \infty} \frac{1}{N} = 0 \ (N \gg 0)$$

where *N* denotes the cardinality of the set of terms or clauses of the extension of *predicate*$_i$ that stand for the incompleteness under consideration. For situations where the extension of *predicate*$_i$ is unknown but can be taken from a set of values, the *QoI* is given by:

$$QoI_i = \frac{1}{Card}$$

where *Card* denotes the cardinality of the *abducibles* set for *i*, if the *abducibles* set is disjoint. If the *abducibles* set is not disjoint, the *QoI* is given by:

$$QoI_i = \frac{1}{C_1^{Card} + \cdots + C_{Card}^{Card}}$$

where C_{Card}^{Card} is a card-combination subset, with *Card* elements.

The next element of the model to be considered is the relative importance that a predicate assigns to each of its attributes under observation, i.e., w_i^k, which stands for the relevance of attribute *k* in the extension of *predicate*$_i$. It is also assumed that the weights of all the attribute predicates are normalized, i.e.:

$$\sum_{1 \leq k \leq n} w_i^k = 1, \ \forall_i$$

where ∀ denotes the universal quantifier. It is now possible to define a predicate's scoring function $V_i(x)$ so that, for a value $x = x_1, \ldots, x_n$, defined in terms of the attributes of *predicate*$_i$, one may have:

$$V_i(x) = \sum_{1 \leq k \leq n} w_i^k * QoI_i(x) / n$$

allowing one to set:

$$predicate_i(x_1,\ldots,x_n) :: V_i(x)$$

that denotes the inclusive quality of *predicate*$_i$ with respect to all the predicates that make the program. It is now possible to set a logic program (here understood as the predicates' extensions that make the program) scoring function, in the form:

$$LP_{Scoring\ Function} = \sum_{i=1}^{n} V_i(x) * p_i$$

where p_i stands for the relevance of the *predicate*$_i$ in relation to the other predicates whose extensions denote the logic program. It is also assumed that the weights of all the predicates' extensions are normalized, i.e.:

$$\sum_{i=1}^{n} p_i = 1, \ \forall_i$$

It is now possible to engender the universe of discourse, according to the information given in the logic programs that endorse the information about the problem under consideration, according to productions of the type:

$$extensions - of - predicate_i = \bigcup_{1 \leq j \leq m} clause_j (x_1,\ldots,x_n) :: QoI :: DoC$$

where $\bigcup$ and *m* stand, respectively, for set union and the cardinality of the extension of *predicate*$_i$. DoC_i stands for an assessment of *attribute*$_i$ with respect to the terms that make the extension of *predicate*$_i$, i.e., it denotes a measure of one's confidence that the attribute value fits into a given interval, whose boundaries are evaluated in a way that takes into consideration its domain (Neves et al., 2015).

Assuming that a clause denotes a happening, a clause has as argument all the attributes that make the event. The argument values may be of the type unknown or members of a set, or may be in the scope of a given interval, or may qualify a particular observation. Let us consider that the case data is given by the extension of predicate f_1, in the form:

$$f_1 : x_1, x_2, x_3 \rightarrow \{0,1\}$$

where "{" and "}" is one´s notation for sets, and "0" and "1" denote, respectively, the truth values *false* and *true*.

Taking into account the following clause where the former argument stands for itself, with a domain that ranges in the interval [0, 5], the value of the second one may fits into the interval [5, 7.5] with a domain that ranges in the interval [2.5, 10], and the value of the last one is unknown, being represented by the symbol $\bot$, with a domain that ranges in the interval [0, 8]. Therefore, one may have:

$$\{$$

$$\neg\, f_1(x_1, x_2, x_3) \leftarrow not\; f_1(x_1, x_2, x_3)$$

$$f_1(\underbrace{2, \qquad [5,\, 7.5], \qquad \perp}_{attribute's\ values\ for\ x_1, x_2, x_3}) :: 1 :: DoC$$

$$\underbrace{[0,\ 5]\ \ [2.5,\ 10]\ \ [0,\ 8]}_{attribute's\ domains\ for\ x_1, x_2, x_3}$$

$$\} :: 1$$

In this program, the first clause denotes the closure of *predicate f_1*. Once the clauses or terms of the extension of the predicate are established, the next step is to set all the arguments, of each clause, into continuous intervals. In this phase, it is essential to consider the domain of the arguments. As the third argument is unknown, its interval will cover all the possibilities of the domain. The first argument speaks for itself. Therefore, one may have:

$$\{$$

$$\neg f_1(x_1, x_2, x_3) \leftarrow not\; f_1(x_1, x_2, x_3)$$

$$f_1(\underbrace{[2,\ 2],\ \ [5,\ 7.5],\ \ [0,\ 8]}_{attribute's\ values\ ranges\ for\ x_1, x_2, x_3}) :: 1 :: DoC$$

$$\underbrace{[0,\ 5]\ \ [2.5,\ 10]\ \ [0,\ 8]}_{attribute's\ domains\ for\ x_1, x_2, x_3}$$

$$\} :: 1$$

It is now achievable to calculate the *Degree of Confidence* (*DoC*) for each attribute that make the term argument (e.g. with respect to the second attribute it denotes one's confidence that the attribute under consideration fits into the interval $[5, 7.5]$). Next, we set the boundaries of the arguments intervals to be fitted in the interval $[0, 1]$ according to a normalization procedure given by $(Y - Y_{min})/(Y_{max} - Y_{min})$, where the Y_s stand for themselves. One may have:

$$\{$$

$$\neg\, f_1(x_1, x_2, x_3) \leftarrow not\; f_1(x_1, x_2, x_3)$$

$$x_1 = \left[\frac{2-0}{5-0},\ \frac{2-0}{5-0}\right],\ x_2 = \left[\frac{5-2.5}{10-2.5},\ \frac{7.5-2.5}{10-2.5}\right],\ x_3 = \left[\frac{0-0}{8-0},\ \frac{8-0}{8-0}\right]$$

$$f_1(\underbrace{[0.4,\ 0.4],\ [0.33,\ 0.67],\ [0,\ 1]}_{attribute's\ values\ ranges\ for\ x_1, x_2, x_3\ once\ normalized}) :: 1 :: DoC$$

$$\underbrace{[0,\ 1]\qquad\quad [0,\ 1]\qquad\quad [0,\ 1]}_{attribute's\ domains\ for\ x_1, x_2, x_3\ once\ normalized}$$

$$\} :: 1$$

Figure 1. Evaluation of the Degree of Confidence

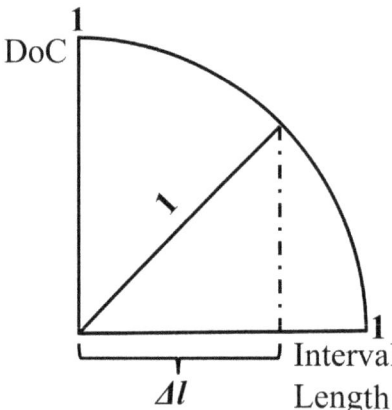

The *Degree of Confidence* (*DoC*) is evaluated using the *Pitagoras* theorem, i.e., $DoC = \sqrt{1 + \Delta l^2}$, as illustrated in Figure 1. Here Δl stands for the length of the arguments intervals, once normalized.

Below, one has the expected representation of the extensions of the predicates that make the universe of discourse, where all the predicates' arguments are real numbers. They speak for one's confidence that the real values of the arguments fit into the attributes' values ranges referred to above. Therefore, one may have:

$$
\begin{aligned}
&\{ \\
&\quad \neg\, f_1(x_1, x_2, x_3) \leftarrow not\ f_1(x_1, x_2, x_3) \\
&\quad f_1(\underbrace{1,\qquad\qquad 0.94,\qquad\qquad 0}_{attribute's\ confidence\ \text{values for}\ x_1, x_2, x_3})\, :: 1 :: 0.65 \\
&\quad \underbrace{[0.4,\ 0.4]\quad [0.33,\ 0.67]\quad [0,\ 1]}_{attribute's\ values\ ranges\ for\ x_1, x_2, x_3\ once\ normalized} \\
&\quad \underbrace{[0,\ 1]\qquad\quad [0,\ 1]\qquad\quad [0,\ 1]}_{attribute's\ domains\ for\ x_1, x_2, x_3\ once\ normalized} \\
&\} :: 1
\end{aligned}
$$

where the *DoC's* for $f_1(1, 0.94, 0)$ is evaluated as $(1+0.94+0)/3 = 0.65$, assuming that all the argument's attributes have the same weight.

According to what was referred to above, it is possible to point out a normalization algorithm, which takes the form:

Begin,

The predicate's extensions that make the Universe-of-Discourse are set ←

$\{$

$\quad \neg f_1(x_1, x_2, x_3) \leftarrow not\ f_1(x_1, x_2, x_3)$

$\quad f_1(\underbrace{2, \quad [5, 7.5], \quad \bot}) :: 1 :: DoC$
$\qquad\quad \text{attribute's values for } x_1, x_2, x_3$

$\quad \underbrace{[0,\ 5]\ [2.5,\ 10]\ [0,\ 8]}$
$\qquad \text{attribute's domains for } x_1, x_2, x_3$

$\}::1$

The attribute's values ranges are rewritten $\leftarrow$

$\{$

$\quad \neg f_1(x_1, x_2, x_3) \leftarrow not\ f_1(x_1, x_2, x_3)$

$\quad f_1(\underbrace{[2,\ 2], \quad [5,\ 7.5], \quad [0,\ 8]}) :: 1 :: DoC$
$\qquad\quad \text{attribute's values ranges for } x_1, x_2, x_3$

$\qquad \underbrace{[0,\ 5] \quad [2.5,\ 10] \quad [0,\ 8]}$
$\qquad\quad \text{attribute's domains for } x_1, x_2, x_3$

$\}::1$

The attribute's boundaries are set to the interval [0, 1] $\leftarrow$

$\{$

$\quad \neg f_1(x_1, x_2, x_3) \leftarrow not\ f_1(x_1, x_2, x_3)$

$\quad f_1(\quad \underbrace{[0.4,\ 0.4],\ [0.33,\ 0.67],\ [0,\ 1]}\quad) :: 1 :: DoC$
$\qquad\quad \text{attribute's values ranges for } x_1, x_2, x_3 \text{ once normalized}$

$\qquad \underbrace{[0,\ 1] \qquad [0,\ 1] \qquad [0,\ 1]}$
$\qquad \text{attribute's domains for } x_1, x_2, x_3 \text{ once normalized}$

$\}::1$

The DoC's values are evaluated $\leftarrow$

$\{$

$\quad \neg f_1(x_1, x_2, x_3) \leftarrow not\ f_1(x_1, x_2, x_3)$

$\quad f_1(\underbrace{1, \qquad\qquad 0.94, \qquad\qquad 0}) :: 1 :: 0.65$
$\qquad\quad \text{attribute's confidence values for } x_1, x_2, x_3$

$\qquad \underbrace{[0.4,\ 0.4]\ [0.33,\ 0.67]\ [0,\ 1]}$
$\qquad \text{attribute's values ranges for } x_1, x_2, x_3 \text{ once normalized}$

$\qquad \underbrace{[0,\ 1] \qquad [0,\ 1] \qquad [0,\ 1]}$
$\qquad \text{attribute's domains for } x_1, x_2, x_3 \text{ once normalized}$

$\}::1$

Figure 2. A knowledge base fragment

Attributes of the Feature Vector:	ODR	Litigation	WATNA	MLATNA	Space Between BATNA and WATNA	Possible Case
Feature Vector Attributes:	[4, 6]	[7, 9]	$\perp$	7	[6, 8]	[0.75, 0.9]
Feature Vector domains:	[0, 10]	[0, 10]	[0, 10]	[0, 10]	[0, 10]	[0, 1]

End.

A CASE STUDY

As a case study, consider a database given in terms of the extensions of the relations (or tables) depicted in Figure 2, which stands for a situation where one has to manage information about the evaluation of judgments' quality. Under this scenario some incomplete and/or unknown data is available. For instance the *WATNA* are unknown, while the *Litigation* ranges in the interval [7, 9].

Applying the rewritten algorithm presented to above to all the fields that make the knowledge base for evaluation of judgments' quality (Figure 2), and looking to the *DoCs* values obtained in this manner, it is possible to set the arguments of the predicate referred to below, that also denotes the objective function with respect to the problem under analyze.

$$quality\_of\_judgment : ODR, \ Lit_{igation}, \ WATNA, \ MLATNA,$$

$$Space_{between \ BATNA/WATNA}, \ P_{ossible}C_{ase} \rightarrow \{0, \ 1\}$$

where 0 (zero) and 1 (one) denote, respectively, the truth values *false* and *true*.

Exemplifying the procedure referred to above to the record that presents the feature vector ($ODR =$ [4, 6], $Lit_{igation} = $ [7, 9], $WATNA = \perp$, $MLATNA = 7$, $Space_{between \ BATNA/WATNA} = $ [6, 8], $P_{ossible} \ C_{ase} = $ [0.75, 0.9]), one may have:

Begin,

The predicate's extensions that make the Universe-of-Discourse are set ←

$\{$

$\quad \neg \ quality\_of\_judgment(ODR, Lit, WATNA, MLATNA, Space, PC)$

$\qquad\qquad \leftarrow not \ quality\_of\_judgment(ODR, Lit, WATNA, MLATNA, Space, PC)$

$\quad quality\_of\_judgment(\underbrace{[4, \ 6], \ [7, \ 9], \ \perp, \quad 7, \quad [6, \ 8], \ [0.75, \ 0.9]}_{attribute's \ values}) :: 1 :: DoC$

$\qquad\qquad \underbrace{[0, \ 10][0, \ 10] \ [0, \ 10] \ [0, \ 10] \ [0, \ 10] \quad [0, \ 1]}_{attribute's \ domains}$

$\} :: 1$

The attribute's values ranges are rewritten ←

{

  ¬ *quality _ of _ judgment*(*ODR, Lit, WATNA, MLATNA, Space, PC*)

  ← *not quality _ of _ judgment*(*ODR, Lit, WATNA, MLATNA, Space, PC*)

  quality _ of _ judgment([4, 6], [7, 9], [1, 10], [7, 7], [6, 8], [0.75, 0.9]) :: 1 :: *DoC*

  $\underbrace{[4,\ 6],\ [7,\ 9],\ [1,\ 10],\ [7,7],\ [6,8],\ [0.75,0.9]}_{attribute's\ values\ ranges}$

  $\underbrace{[0,\ 10]\ [0,\ 10]\ [0,\ 10]\ [0,\ 10]\ [0,\ 10]\quad [0,\ 1]}_{attribute's\ domains}$

} :: 1

The attribute's boundaries are set to the interval [0, 1] ←

{

  ¬ *quality _ of _ judgment*(*ODR, Lit, WATNA, MLATNA, Space, PC*)

  ← *not quality _ of _ judgment*(*ODR, Lit, WATNA, MLATNA, Space, PC*)

  quality _ of _ judgment([0.4, 0.6], [0.7, 0.9], [0, 1], [0.7, 0.7], [0.6, 0.8], [0.75, 0.9]) :: 1 :: *DoC*

  $\underbrace{[0.4,0.6],\ [0.7,0.9],\ [0,\ 1],\ [0.7,0.7],\ [0.6,0.8],\ [0.75,0.9]}_{attribute's\ values\ ranges\ once\ normalized}$

  $\underbrace{[0,\ 1]\qquad [0,\ 1]\qquad [0,\ 1]\qquad [0,\ 1]\qquad [0,\ 1]\qquad [0,\ 1]}_{attribute's\ domains\ once\ normalized}$

} :: 1

The DoC's values are evaluated ←

{

  ¬ *quality _ of _ judgment*(*ODR, Lit, WATNA, MLATNA, Space, PC*)

  ← *not quality _ of _ judgment*(*ODR, Lit, WATNA, MLATNA, Space, PC*)

  quality _ of _ judgment([0.9998, 0.9998, 0, 1, 0.9998, 0.9887]) :: 1 :: 0.831

  $\underbrace{[0.9998,\ 0.9998,\ 0,\ 1,\ 0.9998,\ 0.9887]}_{attribute's\ confidence\ values}$

  $\underbrace{[0.4,\ 0.6]\ [0.7,\ 0.9]\ [0,\ 1]\ [0.7,\ 0.7]\ [0.6,\ 0.8]\ [0.75,\ 0.9]}_{attribute's\ values\ ranges\ once\ normalized}$

  $\underbrace{[0,\ 1]\quad [0,\ 1]\quad [0,\ 1]\quad [0,\ 1]\quad [0,\ 1]\quad [0,\ 1]}_{attribute's\ domains\ once\ normalized}$

} :: 1

End.

ARTIFICIAL NEURAL NETWORKS

The previously presented model of quality of judgment assessment demonstrate how all the information comes together to set an outcome. Indeed, it was set a hybrid computing approach to model the universe of discourse, based on LP and *ANN*s. As an example, let us consider the case given above, where one may have a situation in which the assessment of the quality of judgment is needed. In Figure 3 it is shown how the normalized values of the interval boundaries and their *DoC* and *QoI* values work as inputs to the *ANN*. The output depicts an assessment of the quality of judgment, plus the confidence that one has on such a happening.

The dataset holds information about the factors considered critical in the assessment of the quality of judgment. To ensure statistical significance of the attained results, 30 (thirty) experiments were applied in all tests. In each simulation, the available data was randomly divided into two mutually exclusive partitions, i.e., the training set with 67% of the available data, used during the modeling phase, and the test

Figure 3. The Artificial Neural Network topology

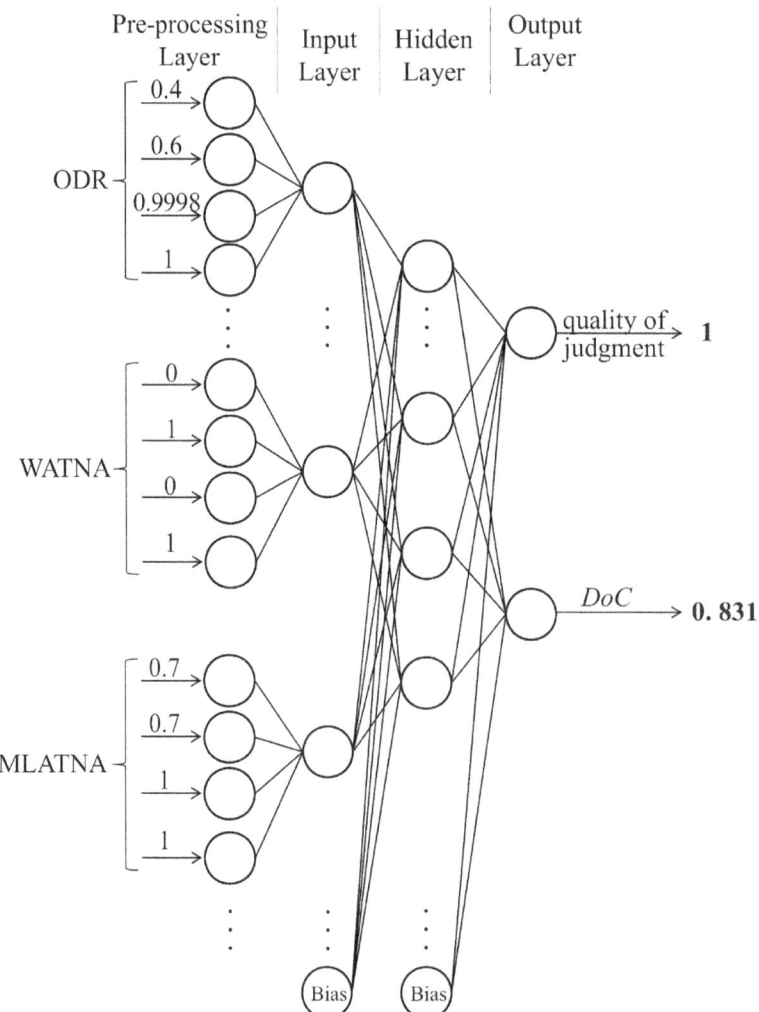

Table 1. The coincidence matrix for ANN model

Target	Predictive			
	Training Set		Test Set	
	False (0)	True (1)	False (0)	True (1)
False (0)	102	16	56	7
True (1)	12	151	9	66

set with the remaining 33% of the cases, used after training in order to evaluate the model performance and to validate it. The back propagation algorithm was used in the learning process of the ANN. As the output function in the pre-processing layer it was used the identity one. In the other layers we used the sigmoid function.

A common tool to evaluate the results presented by the classification models is the coincidence matrix, a matrix of size $L \times L$, where L denotes the number of possible classes. This matrix is created by matching the predicted and target values. L was set to 2 (two) in the present case. Table 1 presents the coincidence matrix (the values denote the average of the 30 experiments). The model accuracy was 90.0% for the training set (253 correctly classified in 281) and 88.4% for test set (122 correctly classified in 138).

CONCLUSION AND FUTURE WORK

The measurement of the quality of judgment would not only be an inestimable process or practice, but something that has its roots or become part of the in-structure of The Law. When the practice is intertwined with its simultaneous evaluation as to its impact on the contenders, then we may have a true discussion about quality, accounting and accountability of the judgments. Indeed, on the one hand, the involvement of all actors, aiming at the improvement of the quality of judgment, are critical factors associated with successful programs, and are an added value to the institutions. On the other hand, once the parameters to assess quality of judgment are not fully represented by objective data (i.e., are of type unknown or not permitted, taken from a set or even from an interval), the problem was put into the area of problems that must be tackled by Artificial Intelligence based methodologies and techniques for problem solving. In fact, the computational framework presented above uses powerful knowledge representation and reasoning methods to set the structure of the information and the associate inference mechanisms. One's approach may revolutionize prediction tools in all its variants, making it more complete than the existing ones. It enables the use of normalized values of the interval boundaries and their respective *QoI* and *DoC* standards, as input to the *ANN*. The output translates the quality of judgment and the confidence that one has on such a happening.

Future work may recommend that the same problem must be approached using others computational formalisms like Genetic Programming (Neves et al., 2007), Case Based Reasoning (Carneiro, Novais, Andrade, Zeleznikow, & Neves, 2013) or Particle Swarm (Mendes, Kennedy, & Neves, 2004), just to name a few.

REFERENCES

Carneiro, D., Novais, P., Andrade, F., Zeleznikow, J., & Neves, J. (2009). The Legal Precedent in Online Dispute Resolution. In G. Governatori (Ed.), Legal Knowledge and Information Systems (pp. 47-52). Amsterdam: IOS Press.

Carneiro, D., Novais, P., Andrade, F., Zeleznikow, J., & Neves, J. (2013). Using case-based reasoning and principled negotiation to provide decision support for dispute resolution. *Knowledge and Information Systems*, *36*(3), 789–826. doi:10.1007/s10115-012-0563-0

Carneiro, D., Novais, P., & Neves, J. (2014). Information Retrieval. In D. Carneiro, P. Novais & J. Neves (Eds.), Conflict Resolution and its Context (pp. 141-162). Cham: Springer.

De Vries, B. R., Leenes, R., & Zeleznikow, J. (2005). Fundamentals of providing negotiation support online: The need for developing BATNAs. In *Proceedings of the Second International ODR Workshop*, (pp.59–67). Tilburg: Wolf Legal Publishers.

Gelfond, M., & Lifschitz, V. (1988). The stable model semantics for logic programming. In R. Kowalski, & K. Bowen (Eds.), *Logic Programming – Proceedings of the Fifth International Conference and Symposium,* (pp. 1070-1080). Academic Press.

Haykin, S. (2009). *Neural Networks and Learning Machines* (3rd ed.). New York: Prentice Hall.

Kakas, A., Kowalski, R., & Toni, F. (1998). The role of abduction in logic programming. In D. Gabbay, C. Hogger, & I. Robinson (Eds.), *Handbook of Logic in Artificial Intelligence and Logic Programming* (Vol. 5, pp. 235–324). Oxford, UK: Oxford University Press.

Klaming, L., Van Veenen, J., & Leenes, R. 2004. I want the opposite of what you want: Summary of a study on the reduction of fixed-pie perceptions in online negotiations. In M. Poblet (Ed.), *Expanding the horizons of ODR – Proceedings of the 5th international workshop on Online Dispute Resolution* (pp. 84-94). Academic Press.

Kraus, S., Sycara, K., & Evenchik, A. (1998). Reaching agreements through argumentation: A logical model and implementation. *Artificial Intelligence Journal*, *104*(1-2), 1–69. doi:10.1016/S0004-3702(98)00078-2

Landes, W. M., & Posner, R. A. (1976). Legal precedent: A theoretical and empirical analysis. *The Journal of Law & Economics*, *19*(2), 249–307. doi:10.1086/466868

Lodder, A., & Zeleznikow, J. (2010). *Enhanced Dispute Resolution through the use of Information Technology*. Cambridge, UK: Cambridge University Press. doi:10.1017/CBO9780511777554

Lucas, P. (2004). Quality checking of medical guidelines through logical abduction. In F. Coenen, A. Preece, & A. Mackintosh (Eds.), *Research and Developments in Intelligent Systems XX* (pp. 309–321). London: Springer. doi:10.1007/978-0-85729-412-8_23

Machado, J., Abelha, A., Novais, P., Neves, J., & Neves, J. (2010). Quality of service in healthcare units. *International Journal of Computer Aided Engineering and Technology*, *2*(4), 436–449. doi:10.1504/IJCAET.2010.035396

Matwin, S., Szpakowicz, S., Koperczak, Z., Kersten, G. E., & Michalowski, G. (1989). NEGOPLAN: An Expert System Shell for Negotiation Support. *IEEE Expert*, 4(4), 50–62. doi:10.1109/64.43285

Mendes, R., Kennedy, J., & Neves, J. (2004). The fully informed particle swarm: Simpler, maybe better. *IEEE Transactions on Evolutionary Computation*, 8(3), 204–210. doi:10.1109/TEVC.2004.826074

Neves, J. (1984). A logic interpreter to handle time and negation in logic databases. In R. L. Muller, & J. J. Pottmyer (Eds.), *Proceedings of the Annual Conference of the ACM on the Fifth Generation Challenge* (pp. 50-54). New York, NY: Association for Computing Machinery.

Neves, J., Guimarães, T., Gomes, S., Vicente, H., Santos, M., Neves, J., . . . Novais, P. (2015). Logic Programming and Artificial Neural Networks in Breast Cancer Detection. In I. Rojas, G. Joya, & A. Catala (Eds.), Advances in Computational Intelligence – Part II (LNCS), (vol. 9095, pp. 211–224). Cham, Switzerland: Springer International Publishing. doi:10.1007/978-3-319-19222-2_18

Neves, J., Machado, J., Analide, C., Abelha, A., & Brito, L. (2007). The halt condition in genetic programming. In J. Neves, M. F. Santos, & J. Machado (Eds.), *Progress in Artificial Intelligence: 13th Portuguese Conference on Artificial Intelligence, EPIA 2007, Workshops: GAIW, AIASTS, ALEA, AMITA, BAOSW, BI, CMBSB, IROBOT, MASTA, STCS, and TEMA, Guimarães, Portugal, December 3-7, 2007, Proceedings* (LNAI), (Vol. 4874, pp. 160-169). Berlin, Germany: Springer. doi:10.1007/978-3-540-77002-2_14

Notini, J. (2005). *Effective alternatives analysis in mediation: "BATNA/WATNA" analysis demystified.* Retrieved March 13, 2015, from http://www.mediate.com/articles/notini1.cfm

Pereira, L. M., & Anh, H. T. (2009). Evolution prospection. In K. Nakamatsu (Ed.), *New Advances in Intelligent Decision Technologies: Results of the First KES International Symposium IDT 2009 (Studies in Computational Intelligence)* (Vol. 199, pp. 51-64). Berlin, Germany: Springer. doi:10.1007/978-3-642-00909-9_6

Raiffa, H. (1982). *The Art and Science of Negotiation: How to Resolve Conflicts and Get the Best Out of Bargaining*. Cambridge, MA: Belknap Press.

Steenbergen, W. (2005). Rationalizing dispute resolution: From best alternative to the most likely one. In *Proceedings of the 5th international workshop on Online Dispute Resolution*. Retrieved April 18, 2015, from http://cli.vu/pubdirectory/250/manuscript.pdf

Vicente, H., Couto, C., Machado, J., Abelha, A., & Neves, J. (2012). Prediction of Water Quality Parameters in a Reservoir using Artificial Neural Networks. *International Journal of Design & Nature and Ecodynamics*, 7(3), 309–318. doi:10.2495/DNE-V7-N3-309-318

Vicente, H., Dias, S., Fernandes, A., Abelha, A., Machado, J., & Neves, J. (2012). Prediction of the Quality of Public Water Supply using Artificial Neural Networks. *Journal of Water Supply: Research & Technology - Aqua*, 61(7), 446–459. doi:10.2166/aqua.2012.014

Vicente, H., Roseiro, J., Arteiro, J., Neves, J., & Caldeira, A. T. (2013). Prediction of bioactive compound activity against wood contaminant fungi using artificial neural networks. *Canadian Journal of Forest Research*, 43(11), 985–992. doi:10.1139/cjfr-2013-0142

Zeleznikow, J., & Bellucci, E. (2012). Legal Fairness in Alternative Dispute Resolution Processes – Implications for Research and Teaching. *Australasian Dispute Resolution Journal*, 23, 265–273.

KEY TERMS AND DEFINITIONS

Artificial Neural Networks: Modeling tools used to structure data and capture complex relationships between inputs and outputs.

Best Alternative to a Negotiated Agreement: The most favorable outcome along a particular path in which one of the parties tries to get their interests satisfied in a way that does not require negotiation with the other party.

Defective Data: Information with some degree of incompleteness, nebulousness, ambiguity and even contradictoriness.

Degree-of-Confidence: A measure of the confidence that the attribute value fits into a given interval, in which boundaries are evaluated taking into consideration its domain.

Most Likely Alternative to a Negotiated Agreement: A metric that gives a value of likeliness to each possible outcome along a litigation path.

Online Dispute Resolution: Refers to the use of innovative techniques and online technologies to facilitate the resolution of disputes between parties, involving negotiation, mediation, arbitration, or a combination of all of them.

Worst Alternative to a Negotiated Agreement: The least favorable outcome along a litigation path, being a relevant factor in the calculation of the real risks that parties will face in a judicially litigation.

Chapter 7

Alternative Dispute Resolution in Civil and Commercial Matters in the EU

Marco Carvalho Gonçalves
University of Minho, Portugal

ABSTRACT

This chapter seeks to analyze the implementation and integration of alternative means of dispute resolution in the European Union. Thus, from an initial approach to the various alternative means of dispute resolution, with particular emphasis on negotiation, conciliation, mediation and arbitration, will be held a comparative law analysis of the different legislative solutions adopted by the major EU Member States, allowing to determinate the degree of implementation and development of alternative means of dispute resolution in those Member States. Finally, there will be an analysis of the main legislative instruments adopted by the European institutions with a view to creating and developing alternative means of dispute resolution in Europe, indicating, in the end, some solutions and recommendations that are adequate having a view to effective implementation of alternative justice in the European Union.

INTRODUCTION

The alternative dispute resolution has assumed a role increasingly important and relevant in the different European legal systems. In fact, courts have proved that are unable to resolve, within a reasonable time, disputes that are brought to their attention. Indeed, the increase in litigation seen over the past few years, particularly in the consumer credit, associated with complex procedural laws, completely blocked the normal functioning of the courts.

Moreover, in certain areas, particularly with regard to consumer relationships, the traditional judicial system proved inadequate to solve practical needs related to such disputes. Sufficient to note that, often the court fee that the parties must support to submit their disputes to the court greatly exceeds the actual value of the dispute at issue.

DOI: 10.4018/978-1-5225-0245-6.ch007

It is also noted that, over the years, legal professionals, including lawyers, have always been very resistant to the possibility of disputes being resolved by other alternative means to judicial proceedings.

It is exactly in this context that the various European legal systems have been seeking to implement simple and low cost dispute resolution mechanisms – particularly arbitration, conciliation, mediation and justice of peace – which are an alternative, rapid and effective way compared to the common justice, looking, at the same time, draw the attention of legal professionals to the advantages of these means.

However, the uncoordinated adoption by European legal systems of different alternative means of dispute resolution eventually led to the creation of inequalities in protection of nationals, which creates imbalances in the normal functioning of the economic and social systems. As a matter of fact, citizens of several European States do not enjoy equal access to alternative means of dispute resolution.

On the other hand, the successive European integration policies implemented over the past years led to the creation of a single European market, characterized by freedom and ease of movement of people, goods and services, which enhanced the appearance of cross-border disputes, particularly in consumer relationships, work, e-commerce and supply of telecommunications services, energy and transport. Paradoxically, the creation of the single European market and the gradual emergence of cross-border disputes has not been accompanied by the development and implementation, in the European context, of alternative means of dispute resolution by comparison to traditional systems of civil and commercial justice.

This situation eventually lead to conflicts and imbalances between different Member States. In fact, in States where there are higher levels of protection and development in the field of alternative dispute resolution, citizens and businesses feel more confident and likely to establish relations with other Member States of the European Union, reality that does not occur in those States where these mechanisms are not yet installed or where such implementation has revealed to be still very low.

Moreover, the economic crisis that has been felt in recent years by most Member States of the European Union, associated with the crisis of traditional justice systems, reinforced the need to implement mechanisms to stimulate the economy, with particular emphasis on creation and development of alternative means of dispute resolution.

Aware of this reality – that affects the normal functioning of the single market and free competition as a central pillar of the European Union – the European institutions have been implementing several instruments, particularly recommendations and directives, which aim to generalize the adoption of alternative means of dispute resolution in the European market and, in parallel, to harmonize the functioning of these mechanisms in the different Member States of the European Union in order to encourage both the on-trade and e-commerce between individuals, or between consumers and businesses, whether commercial relations between different operators of the European economic market.

In this context, it is particularly relevant the adoption of two recommendations (in 1998 and 2001) by the European Commission, which aimed to define common principles for the implementation of efficient authorities for alternative dispute resolution.

In the field of mediation, the Directive 2008/52/EC of the European Parliament and of the Council, of 21 May 2008, defines certain common rules, to be implemented by the different Member States, in order to facilitate access to alternative resolution disputes and promote the amicable settlement of disputes by encouraging the use of mediation and ensuring a balanced relationship between mediation and judicial proceedings.

More recently, the European Commission adopted the Directive 2013/11/EU (ADR Directive), whose main goal, in line with Regulation (EC) n.º 2006/2004 of the European Parliament and of the Council, of 27 October 2004, on cooperation between national authorities responsible for the enforcement of consumer protection laws ("the Regulation on cooperation in consumer protection area"), translates into the creation of a network of specialized agencies in alternative dispute resolution concerning consumption.

However, the steps taken by the European institutions in the field of alternative dispute resolution are clearly insufficient, given the pressing needs of widespread implementation of alternative dispute resolution means in Europe. In fact, the crisis of the justice, while cross phenomenon to most European legal systems, calls for the urgent adoption of simple, timely and cost effective mechanisms, appropriated to satisfy the needs of citizens and businesses in resolving their disputes. At the same time, the implementation of these mechanisms will relieve the pressure currently exerted on the courts under the mass of litigation seen over the last few years, leaving them free to the resolution of disputes that, by their nature or complexity, can not be solved through the alternative ways of conflict resolution.

In this context, the present study will begin by making an approach, based on comparative law, to the different legislative solutions internally adopted by the European Union Member States with regard to alternative dispute resolution in civil and commercial matters. Basically, it will be analyzed how the different States ensure to their citizens and businesses the possibility of using alternative mechanisms of conflict resolution and how these mechanisms are linked with traditional administration of justice systems.

Having made this initial approach, it will be analyzed the legal framework of the various legislative solutions adopted by the European institutions in the field of alternative dispute resolution in civil and commercial matters, with particular emphasis on litigation in purchase and sale of goods and the provision of services and how these different legislative solutions have been implemented and coordinated with the domestic law of the Member States.

Finally, based on an analysis of the current legal situation, the author will try to advance some proposals and solutions to further advance of the European Union with regard to the simple and low cost resolution of domestic and cross-border disputes in civil and commercial matters.

BRIEF OVERVIEW OF ALTERNATIVE MEANS OF DISPUTE RESOLUTION

Traditionally, courts are the common means for resolving disputes (Hartley, 2002). However, in recent years it has been found the emergence of other means which, being an alternative to the courts, can be designated in a generic formulation for alternative means of dispute resolution (Van Gramberg, 2006).

The affirmation of the importance of alternative means of dispute resolution is justified on two important factors: on the one hand, the widespread failure of the judicial system, that is, the inability of the courts to settle disputes in a swift and effective way; on the other hand, the high costs that are required to have access to courts, with particular emphasis on legal fees and other expenses and costs of processes. Indeed, one of the greatest advantages of the alternative means of dispute resolution is reflected in the fact that these means allow the resolution of conflicts that, considering the reduced amount in question or the fear of publicity, would hardly be brought before the courts (Wrbka, 2014).

The main alternative dispute resolution means or, according to some doctrine, extra-judicial means of dispute settlement (Lopes & Boss, 2014), are, fundamentally, the negotiation, conciliation, mediation and arbitration. This enumeration is, however, merely exemplificative, because there are other alternative ways of resolving disputes. This is the case, for example, with the "open door policy", the "peer review" or the "ombudsman" (McDermott & Berkeley in 1996), as well the "opinion binding" (bindend advies), adopted in the Netherlands, or the "recommendations", adopted in Finland and Sweden, particularly in proceedings concerning consumer or insurance.

Let's see in what consists each of these alternative means of dispute resolution.

Negotiation

Negotiation is an alternative means of dispute resolution through which the parties in conflict seek on their own, without the intervention or the help of an impartial third party, to reach an harmonious solution according to their interests (Martí Marmol, 2002). It is, therefore, a private, voluntary and consensual means, which involves the joint operation of the parties so that they are able to obtain a solution to their issue (Frey, 2002). Negotiation can take two distinct forms: competitive and cooperative. In competitive negotiation, each of the negotiating parties want to win the dispute, that is, get the most or the best possible advantage over the opponent. Thus, this model considers the position of each party, taken individually, without regard to the common interest of both. Otherwise, in the cooperative negotiation, the parties are not focused on winning the discussion, but rather to solve their problem. Indeed, what matters is to obtain a consensual and satisfactory solution for both parties, which implies that both work together to obtain the best possible solution (Gouveia, 2014). This means of alternative dispute resolution can not be understood independently or individually. This is because negotiation can be present in other means of alternative dispute resolution, as is the case in mediation, conciliation or arbitration.

Conciliation

Conciliation is an alternative means of dispute resolution through which the entity with authority to settle the dispute (for example, the judge or referee) proposes to the parties equitable solutions that enable them to settle amicably the dispute. Unlike what happens in mediation, the conciliator adopts an active and interventionist position in the process, to the extent that the parties may propose possible solutions to their conflict.

The vast majority of the European civil procedural laws provide the possibility or the obligation of the judge to promote conciliation between the parties, that is, obtain an agreement for resolving the dispute in an equitable, friendly and consensual way.

In any case, conciliation is not exclusive of the courts. In fact, conciliation is also an alternative means of dispute resolution widely used in arbitration. By way of example, the principle 4 (d) of the IBA Guidelines on Conflicts of Interest in International Arbitration stipulates that "An arbitrator may assist the parties in reaching a settlement of the dispute, through conciliation, mediation or otherwise, at any stage of the proceedings. However, before doing so, the arbitrator should receive an express agreement by the parties that acting in such a manner shall not disqualify the arbitrator from continuing to serve the arbitrator".

Mediation

Mediation is one of the most popular means of alternative dispute resolution (Silva, 2010). Through this means, the parties in conflict seek for themselves and voluntarily to achieve a mutual satisfactory solution to their conflict (Arnavas, 2004), through the assistance of a third party (mediator of conflicts).

Compared with other alternative means of dispute resolution, mediation has the great advantage of being cheaper, more sensitive and attentive to the concerns and interests of the parties and better able to find inovative solutions, besides being less formal and intimidating (Arnavas, 2004).

This means of alternative dispute resolution is fundamentally characterized by the principles of voluntariness, confidentiality, equality, impartiality and independence.

Since then, mediation has a voluntary nature, that is, it is only possible to access mediation if the parties give their informed consent accordingly. In particular, parties may enter into a mediation agreement, that is, set out in writing, as part of a contractual relationship, that, in case of dispute, it will be settled by mediation. However, the mediation process may also be suggested or ordered by a court or prescribed by the national law of a particular State.

In addition, parties have full control and availability of mediation. This means that, as well as mediation can only take place if the parties give their consent, in the same way the parties may, at any time, jointly or unilaterally revoke their consent to participate in the mediation process. The availability of mediation by the parties also finds expression in the circumstance to fit them the responsibility for the decisions that are taken in the course of the mediation procedure. Indeed, the mediator can not impose or present proposals according to the parties (Gaio Jûnior, 2008), but should, neutrally and impartially, concentrate its activities in full cooperation with the parties, facilitating communication between them and supporting them in obtaining an agreement that, in a fair and equitable way, put an end to the dispute between both (Van Gramberg, 2006).

Apart from its voluntary nature, mediation features mainly by confidentiality. Indeed, the confidentiality of mediation allows to encourage the parties to adopt a more open and transparent approach, which is essential for the fair resolution of the dispute (Arnavas, 2004).

Being the mediation process confidential, the mediator rests with the obligation to keep secret all the information supplied during that procedure. This duty of confidentiality also extends to confidential information that he receives from a party, being forbiden the possibility of revealing their content to the remaining parts (Van Gramberg, 2006). This does not prevent, however, the mediator to talk to each party separately and in isolation, in particular when that procedure is necessary or appropriate to allow communication or dialogue between the parties. Furthermore, the content of the mediation sessions can not be revealed or valued in court or in arbitration, except where there are reasons of public order, in cases involving the protection of the physical or psychological integrity of any person, or when it's necessary for the application or execution of the agreement reached through mediation.

Mediation is also characterized by equality between the parties, who should be treated fairly throughout the process. In addition, the mediator must ensure a balance between the parties, in particular as regards the possibility to participate in the process in equal conditions.

Finally, the mediator must ensure the fairness of the entire process, as well as its independence. In fact, the mediator must act free of any pressure, not being subject to any subordination.

Arbitration

Arbitration is an alternative means of dispute resolution through which the parties submit the resolution of a dispute to the decision of one or more arbitrators, that is, the decision of the conflict is taken by a third party. It is, therefore, as opposed to state courts, a private means of dispute resolution. It may be mandatory, when the law requires parties to submit the resolution of the conflict to referees, or voluntary, when the parties, by agreement and on his own initiative, agree to use such means.

The greatest advantages of arbitration consists in the possibility to choose an expert arbitrator in the matter subject of litigation, in its speed, informality and low cost, as well as the possibility for the parties to define the substantive and procedural rules which will apply to the resolution of the dispute (Arnavas, 2004).

With regard to its purpose, the arbitration may relate to the settlement of the dispute itself or to resolve any other issues that need to be submitted to an impartial decision-maker.

Concerning to voluntary arbitration, the agreement can relate to a current, existing or a future dispute that results from a contractual or legal relationship. The arbitration agreement should be formalized in writing – here including any means capable of lasting record of that convention as, for example, an exchange of letters, telegrams, fax messages or other means of telecommunication able to provide written proof, including electronic, magnetic or optical media, that offers the same guarantees of reliability, understandability and maintenance – and can be modified or withdrawn by the parties agreement.

Regarding the arbitral tribunal, this may be composed by a single arbitrator or by a panel of arbitrators, in an odd number (usually three), which must be independent, impartial and fully capable. Particularly relevant for comparison to the traditional system of state courts, it is the fact that the parties can appoint the arbitrator or arbitrators who will compose the arbitral tribunal or establish how they will be chosen. Being the arbitral tribunal of three or more arbitrators, each party appoints an equal number of arbitrators, in turn. Then, the arbitrators choose the other remaining arbitrator, who will act as president. The arbitral tribunal, once constituted, has jurisdiction to determine its own competence (*Kompetenz-Kompetenz*), although this is necessary to assess the existence, validity or effectiveness of the arbitration agreement or contract in which it is inserted, or the applicability of the Convention.

The arbitration proceedings shall be ruled by the principles of the disposition, contradictory, equality of arms and confidentiality.

Firstly, with regard to the principle of the disposition, parties have full process availability. In particular, they have the power to define the object of the dispute, the constitution of the tribunal, the place of arbitration, the language to be used and the procedural rules that will guide the activity of the court, namely the initiation of proceedings, the procedural time limits to practice acts, the hearings for presentation of evidence, the admissibility, relevance and value of the evidence to be produced, as well as if the court will decide on the basis of legality or in equity and if the decision will be appealed or not.

On the other hand, the arbitration process is characterized by the adversarial principle, according to which the defendant must be notified to be able to defend and the parties should be able, throughout the process, to rule on the alleged facts and the evidence produced by the opposing party.

The arbitration proceedings shall ensure the full equality of the parties, giving them the option, within a reasonable time, to assert their rights in writing or orally, before being given the final decision.

Finally, the arbitration process is characterized by its confidential nature, according to which the arbitrators and the parties have a duty to maintain the confidentiality of all information they obtain and documents brought to their knowledge through the arbitration process, without prejudice to the right granted to the parties to make public the procedural actions necessary to defend their rights and the duty, imposed by law, to report or disclosure acts to the competent authorities.

IMPLEMENTATION OF ALTERNATIVE MEANS OF DISPUTE RESOLUTION IN THE MEMBER STATES OF THE EUROPEAN UNION

The majority of the Member States of the European Union provide in their domestic law several alternative means of dispute resolution, with particular emphasis on conciliation, mediation and arbitration.

Conciliation

With regard to conciliation, the Portuguese Civil Procedure Code stipulates in its art. 290.°, n.° 4, that the parties may dismiss the dispute by entering into a transaction term, which may result from conciliation reached by the judge. Furthermore, if the right in dispute has available nature, the judge must promote conciliation between the parties to a preliminary hearing [art. 591.°, n.° 1, al. a)] or in any stage of the proceedings, on its own initiative or at the request of the parties, to which they shall appear personally or be represented by a mandatory with special powers.

The Portuguese Civil Procedure Code also provides that the conciliation is headed by the judge, who must work actively to find an equitable solution that proves to be more responsive to the dispute (art. 594.°, n.° 3). Moreover, if the conciliation is unsuccessful, the judge must assign the reasons why the conciliation was frustrated, the concrete solutions that have been suggested by him and the fundaments that, in the opinion of the parties, justify the persistence of the dispute. Even if the conciliation gets frustrated in the previous trial or at any preliminary stage, the judge must promote conciliation of the parties in the beginnig of the judgment (art. 604.°, n.° 2).

This conciliation duty is also planned for some special procedures and processes. This is the case, namely, of the protective measure of temporary aliments (art. 385.°, n.° 3), the special personality guardianship process (art. 879.°, n.° 3) and the special procedure for the allocation of the family residence house (art. 990.°, n.° 2). Similarly, also in cases submitted to the justices of the peace, the law establishes the duty of the justice of the peace, before issuing a decision on the dispute, to try to reconcile the parties (art. 26.° of Law n.° 78/2001, of 13 July).

The conciliation is also of particular focus in work and family litigation. In labor litigation, art. 51.° of the Labor Procedure Code provides for the possibility of a compulsory attempt at conciliation, which is chaired by the judge. This is the case, for example, with compulsory conciliation prior to the trial (art. 70.°). In litigation in family, in addition to the conciliation attempt in special divorce proceedings without the consent of the other spouse (art. 931.° of the Civil Procedure Code), it is extremely important to conciliation under the civil guardianship proceedings (art. 29.° of the Law n.° 141/2016, of 8 September).

In Germany, it is provided for the possibility that the dispute can be settled through conciliation. Thus, under § 278 of the *Zivilprozessordnung*, the court, throughout the process, should take into account the possibility of the dispute, or some aspects of it, be settled amicably. Being the conciliation promoted by the judge, he must inform the parties about the state of the cause and of all the circumstances relevant to their resolution, making them, if necessary, the questions he considers appropriate. In addition to the conciliation promoted by state courts, there are entities with their own competence for dealing with disputes through conciliation (*Schlichtungsstelle*), and, in some cases, prior recourse to these entities is a condition of access to the courts (see, for example, § 15a of *Einführung der Zivilprozessordnung* and § 111 (2) of *Arbeitsgerichtsgesetz*). Equally important are the conciliation authorities in the automotive sector, construction and the liberal professions. Also can be created *ad hoc* conciliation commissions, particularly in labor disputes.

In Italy, conciliation may be contentious or non-contentious. Regarding the contentious conciliation, art. 185.° of the *Codice di Procedura Civile* (CPCIt.) states that the judge, at the request of the parties, may decide to carry out an attempt of conciliation, in which the parties must necessarily be present, notwithstanding the possibility to be assisted by lawyers. Furthermore, pursuant to art. 185.°-bis of CPCIt., the judge shall issue to the parties, at the first hearing or until the end of the statement, a proposal for conciliation where possible depending on the nature of the dispute, the amount involved and the clear simplicity of legal issue to decide. The conciliation is also foreseen by other provisions of the civil procedural law, with particular emphasis on the arts. 420.° of CPCIt. (on the conciliation attempt within work processes), 447.°-bis of CPCIt. (on location) and 708.° of CPCIt. (relating to the separation of spouses). Regarding the non-contentious conciliation, this takes place outside the context of a judicial process and takes usually an informal nature. In particular, with respect to proceedings before the justice of the peace, art. 322.° of the CPCIt. provides that the parties can verbally require the justice of the peace to promote the conciliation between them.

In France, conciliation is regulated in arts. 127.° to 131.° of the *Nouveau Code de Procedure Civile* (NCPC). Thus, in the course of the whole process can be seen the conciliation of the parties, by mutual agreement or at the initiative of the judge, and he has full freedom to try to conciliate the parties at the time he considers more appropriate or suitable for this purpose. In the French legal system are also implemented a great number of conciliation authorities, particularly in the field of leasing and health relationships.

In Belgium, the art. 731.° of the *Code Judiciaire* (CJ) provides that, with regard to a dispute concerning the rights available before proceeding to the instruction and judgment, the parties may, at the initiative of one of them or by mutual agreement, request the judge conducting an attempt at conciliation.

In Finland, the section 26 of the fifth chapter of the Civil Procedure Code provides that if the court deems appropriate, taking into account the will of the parties, the nature of the case and other circumstances, can present them a draft agreement, taking into view to amicable settlement of the dispute.

In Sweden, section 17 of the Chapter 42 of the Civil Procedure Code provides that, if the dispute is likely to be settled by agreement, the court shall, taking into account the nature of the dispute and other particular circumstances of the case, work with the parties to reach an agreement.

In some Member States, prior recourse to extrajudicial conciliation mechanisms constitute a procedural assumption of access to the courts, although this obligation has been identified as a violation of art. 6.° of the European Convention on Human Rights (Blake, S., Browne, J, & Sime, S., 2014).

Thus, in Austria, in some types of disputes, particularly in respect of rents and housing, recourse to conciliation systems is required before access to the courts. In this case, if the attempt at conciliation is frustrated, is assured the parties the possibility to use the judicial means.

In Belgium, with regard to a dispute concerning labour matters, the law stipulates that the judgment of the case must be preceded, under penalty of nullity, by a conciliation attempt (art. 734.° of the CJ).

In the same way, the conciliation is strongly established in Spain, where, in some situations, it is only possible to bring an action to court after being frustrated the attempt at conciliation. In such cases, prior recourse to conciliation is a procedural requirement, under the art. 403.°, n.° 3, of the *Ley de Enjuicia-mento Civil* (LEC). Furthermore, pursuant to art. 415.° of the LEC, the court must promote conciliation between the parties, without prejudice to the possibility of these, by mutual agreement, ask the court to stay the proceedings to be able to submit the dispute to mediation or arbitration.

Similarly, in Greece, the art. 214.º of the Civil Procedure Code establishes a mandatory conciliation procedure for the lawsuits that are within the competence of the lower courts to the extent that the judicial process can proceed only after the realization of this conciliation.

Mediation

With regard to mediation, Law n.º 29/2013, of 19 April, came to establish the general principles of mediation in Portugal, as well as the legal regimes of civil and commercial mediation, the mediators and public mediation. The Portuguese law establishes that mediation can take place in civil and commercial matters - provided that it respects the patrimonial nature of interest or if the parties can enter into transaction on the controversial law - as well as in the family, labor and criminal law. Thus, in the family domain, mediation can take place under the regulation, alteration and failure of the exercise of parental authority regime, divorce and separation of people and goods, conversion of separation of persons and property in divorce, reconciliation of separated spouses, assignment and change of food, provisional or definitive, deprivation of the right to use the surname of the other spouse and authorizing the use of names of former spouse or family home (art. 4.º of Order n.º 18 778/2007, August 22).

In the field of labor law, it is set up a mediation system that aims to promote the speedy and equitable resolution of labor disputes jurisdiction, with particular emphasis on conflicts related to the payment of employment claims, changing the workplace, termination of employment, holiday scheduling and disciplinary procedures. In criminal matters, mediation can take place in the crimes of semi-public nature, in cases involving a crime against persons or property, or particular, unless it is concerned a crime punishable by imprisonment of more than five years, a crime against freedom or sexual self-determination, embezzlement, corruption or influence peddling, if the victim is less than sixteen years old or if applicable summary proceedings. Mediation in criminal cases can take place at the initiative of the prosecutor or by joint request of the the accused and the offended. In this case, it's necessary that the accused and the offended give their voluntary and informed consent, in order to want to participate in mediation. Pursuant to art. 4.º of Law n.º 21/2007, of 12 June, the process of mediation has an informal and flexible nature, being conducted by an impartial third party, the mediator, which should promote closer ties between the defendant and the offended, supporting them in trying to actively find an agreement to allow the repair of damage caused by the wrongful act and contribute to the restoration of social peace. Failing such agreement in mediation, the criminal proceedings shall continue. Otherwise, if the agreement is reached, it implies that the victim gives up the complaint and the accused accepts that withdrawal, without renewal survey possibility should the agreement not be fulfilled. It should also be noted that the Civil Procedure Code provides that the court may determine at any stage of the proceedings and whenever it deems appropriate to refer the case to judicial mediation, suspending the proceedings for that purpose, unless either party opposes this initiative. Similarly, under the principle of the disposition, the parties may agree together to resolve the dispute through mediation, and may appeal, for that purpose, to stay proceedings for a maximum period of three months (art. 273.º).

In Germany, the Law on Voluntary Jurisdiction (*Gesetz über die Freiwillige Gerichtsbarkeit*) establishes several situations in which the court, in case of conflict, should favor the referral of the parties to mediation systems. This is the case in situations of conflict on the exercise of parental responsibilities for minor children (§ 52). It takes also special emphasis mediation in matters of divorce and separation of people and goods.

In French law, mediation may take a judicial or extrajudicial nature, and the court mediation is regulated in arts. 131.°-1 to 131.°-15 NCPC. Thus, pursuant to art. 131.°-1, the judge, after obtaining the consent of the parties, may appoint a mediator, which must hear the parties and compare the different interests in order to allow them to find a solution to all or part of the dispute. With regard to extrajudicial mediation, this means is particularly important in the field of family relations, consumer, banking and insurance.

In Spain, mediation is compulsory for some litigation in labor matters, only being allowed the use of labor courts in the case of frustration of this procedure. Furthermore, pursuant to art. 19.° of the LEC, the parties have full availability of legal proceedings and can, by mutual agreement, stay the proceedings to submit to mediation. According to art. 414.° of the LEC, the judge, once presented the positions of the parties, should call them for a hearing, within which shall inform them of the possibility of recourse to negotiation or mediation with a view to resolution the dispute.

In Austria, mediation is regulated in the federal law on mediation in civil matters (*Bundesgesetz über Mediation in Zivilrechtssachen*). There are also several regional and local level mediation services which are of public nature. In Belgium, the mediation process is regulated in arts. 1724.° to 1737.° of the CJ, foreseeing the law the possibility of being resolved through mediation disputes that deal with available rights. Under the principle of private autonomy, contracts may contain a mediation clause by which the parties agree to use mediation to resolve any disputes arising from the contract. Being proposed legal action in violation of this clause, the court must stay the proceedings unless the clause is null. The Belgian law distinguishes between voluntary mediation (arts. 1730.° to 1733.° of the CJ) and the judicial mediation (arts. 1734.° to 1737.° of the CJ). Thus, with regard to voluntary mediation, the art. 1730.° of the CJ provides that a party may propose to the other, regardless of any judicial proceeding or arbitration, and before, during or after judicial proceedings, recourse to a mediation procedure, being the mediator chosen by the parties or by a third party. With regard to judicial mediation, the art. 1734.° of the CJ establishes that in any stage of the proceedings, the judge, on the joint request of the parties or on its own initiative (in this case, with the agreement of the parties), may order the holding of a mediation, which must not exceed the period of three months. Being reached an agreement in mediation, it shall be approved by the judge, unless it offends public order or, in the case of family mediation, is detrimental to the interests of minors.

In the Netherlands, although mediation is not regulated, it is found that this alternative means of dispute resolution is often used, particularly in cases where the parties enter into a contractual relationship including a mediation agreement. Contrary to what is provided for in most other legal systems, in the Netherlands are no plans to confidentiality of the mediation process, which is why the parties should expressly safeguard the confidentiality of mediation in the agreement that may be concluded between them.

In Sweden, the section 17 of the Chapter 42 of the Civil Procedure Code provides that the court is able to propose to the parties to hold a mediation session before a court-appointed mediator if, given the nature of the dispute, considers that mediation is best suited for their resolution. Apart from the judicial mediation, there are also several organizations which promote mediation, particularly in conflicts in the field of consumer relations, labor, family and renting.

Arbitration

With regard to arbitration, in the legal Portuguese system, Law n.° 63/2011, of 14 December, has approved the Voluntary Arbitration Act. In addition to the voluntary arbitration, there is also the institutionalized arbitration, which is held in arbitration centers, with general or specific, regional or national competence.

In Germany, arbitration is strongly implemented, with emphasis on the existence of arbitration bodies (*Schiedsstelle*) concerning consumer disputes. The arbitration procedure is regulated in §§ 1025 of the ZPO.

In Austria, arbitration is regulated in §§ 577-618 of the ZPO and is essentially dedicated to the resolution of equity litigation.

In Italy, arbitration is regulated in arts. 806.º to 840.º the CPCIt.. There are also arbitration committees, with particular emphasis on chambers of commerce.

In Spain, arbitration is regulated in the Law 60/2003, of 23 December, and assumes essentially an *ad hoc* nature. However, in recent years it has been seen the development of institutionalized arbitration, particularly at the level of Chambers of Commerce.

In Belgium, the arbitration has its legal regime established in arts. 1676.º to 1723.º of the CJ, and it is indicated to disputes which have as their object property rights and available non-property rights.

In the Netherlands, arbitration is regulated in arts. 1020.º to 1076.º of the Civil Procedure Code, foreseeing the law the possibility of the parties agree to arbitration to resolve a particular dispute, present or future, whatever the legal nature of the relationship between the parties. The establishment of an arbitration agreement prevents, pursuant to art. 1022.º of the CJ, recourse to courts, unless it is concerned a particular procedure that is to take place in these courts (for example, order an interim measure in advance or produce a certain proof).

ALTERNATIVE MEANS OF DISPUTE RESOLUTION IN THE EUROPEAN UNION

Under the law of the European Union, institutions have been making efforts in order to ensure the progressive implementation of alternative means of dispute resolution in the legal systems of the various Member States. Indeed, the creation of an european area of free movement of persons, goods and services, as well as freedom, security and justice, demanded the adoption of policies and common action on judicial cooperation in civil and commercial matters. In this context, within the European Councils in Vienna and Tampere, in 1998 and 1999, it was affirmed the need for the various Member States to develop alternative means of dispute resolution, to protect the right of access to justice and courts. In pursuit of this goal, in 2000 the European Council considered that, given the diversity of legal regimes in the different Member States, it became necessary to adopt common principles that would ensure the implementation and the development of alternative means of dispute resolution.

At the same time, aiming to "sensitize a larger number of individuals with regard to alternative means of dispute resolution" and ensure a "better understanding of the achievements and initiatives taken in this area by the Member States and at EU level", the European Commission, by invitation of the Council, presented in 2002 a Green Paper on alternative methods of settling disputes in civil and commercial matters. In this book, the Commission basically highlighted the importance of alternative means of resolving disputes as supplementary means in relation to legal proceedings, emphasizing the prominent role as "instruments in the service of social peace" (Kaufmann-Kohler & Schultz, 2004).

On the other hand, the importance of alternative means of dispute resolution has been affirmed in a context of increasing inability of the courts in settling conflicts within a reasonable time. Indeed, pursuant to arts. 6.º of the European Convention on Human Rights and 47.º of the EU Charter of Fundamental Rights, everyone has the right to have his cause examined, in a fair and public hearing, within a reasonable time by an independent and impartial tribunal established by law. Moreover, by Recommendation n.° R (86) 12 of the Committee of Ministers of the Member States, adopted on 16 September 1986, regarding the adoption of measures to prevent and reduce excessive dependence and activity of the courts, Member States were invited to implement and develop amicable dispute resolution means, under a judicial or extra-judicial process, notably by promoting conciliation procedures, assigning the judge's responsibility to seek amicable ways of resolving disputes, awareness among lawyers importance of these means and easier access to arbitration.

However, the potential of alternative means of dispute resolution is not exhausted in the faster administration of justice. Otherwise, the alternative means of resolving disputes have also been faced by European institutions under a qualitative perspective, in that it allows for greater quality in the administration of justice, providing greater cost savings and efficiency as well as the active participation of the citizens in solving their own conflicts.

On alternative dispute resolution, the European Union's efforts have come to focus on the potential of mediation. In this regard, it assumes particular relevance the Directive 2008/52/EC of the European Parliament and of the Council of 21 May 2008, which sought to harmonize certain legal rules on mediation in the European Union Member States, facilitate the use of mediation in cross-border disputes in civil and commercial matters and ensure a balanced relationship between mediation and judicial proceedings. Indeed, acoording the preamble of the directive, "Mediation can provide a quick and inexpensive extrajudicial solution to disputes in civil and commercial matters through processes tailored to the needs of the parties. It is more likely that the agreements obtained from mediation be enforced voluntarily and preserve an amicable and sustainable relationship between the parties. These benefits become even more pronounced in situations displaying cross-border aspects". This policy applies to cross-border disputes, without prejudice the possibility for Member States to use the provisions of the directive on internal mediation processes. Furthermore, given the geographical distances usually associated with cross-border disputes, this directive encourages the use of information technologies at the service of mediation.

With regard to its object, the directive covers disputes in civil and commercial matters, being, however, excluded from its application disputes which have as their object unavailable rights, taxation, customs, administrative or relating to State liability for acts or omissions in the exercise of his authority (*acta iure imperii*). Furthermore, are also excluded from the object of this Directive the pre-contractual negotiations and processes of an adjudicatory nature, including some judicial conciliation schemes, consumer complaints, arbitration and expert determination.

With regard to its subjective context, the directive can only be applied in cross-border disputes in which the different parties to the dispute agree, on a voluntary basis, to use a mediation process that will enable them to, in a quick and consensual way, get a mutual agreement, in situations where mediation is ordered or encouraged by a court or when the national law of the Member State requires the parties to use mediation. The directive ensures, however, the possibility that the parties have to freely dispose of the procedure, without prejudice of the stipulation of time limits for the duration of the mediation process.

Furthermore, the directive lays down fundamental rules that aim to enhance the use of mediation, particularly with regard to confidentiality, effects of mediation, recognition and enforcement of agreements, flexibility of the process and autonomy of the parties.

In parallel, in order to ensure the efficiency of the mediation process, the European Commission adopted in July 2014 a European Code of Conduct for Mediators, which establishes a set of principles that, having no binding nature, can be adopted by mediators and entities in mediation in civil and commercial matters. Fundamentally, this code of conduct lays down rules on jurisdiction, availability and costs of the mediators, as well as the conduct they must observe during the mediation process, namely the independence, impartiality and confidentiality.

In family law, the European institutions have been aware of cross-border family conflicts and the need to be implemented alternative means of dispute resolution. In fact, given the peculiarity and the nature of the disputes in this area, with particular emphasis on issues related to separation or divorce, shares, regulation of parental responsibilities and the setting of maintenance payments, alternative means of dispute resolution play an important role, even if its application is found limited to available nature of rights. In this context, the Committee of Ministers of the Council of Europe adopted, on 21 January 1998, the Recommendation n.° R (98) 1, under which, recognizing the increase in family disputes - which, by their nature, have very specific characteristics - as well as the undeniable advantages of mediation in this area - particularly by the fact that improves communication between family members, reduces conflicts, allows amicable settlements, ensures the maintenance of relations between parents and children and reduces the costs and time in conflict resolution - called for Member States to establish, promote and strength family mediation, with respect for the principles of voluntariness, impartiality, neutrality, equality, privacy, confidentiality and, when appropriate, the child's best interests.

With regard to consumption, where alternative means of dispute resolution play a key role, particularly in disputes involving small monetary amounts (Bënohr, 2012), the "Green Paper on consumer access to justice and resolution of consumer disputes in the single market" has revealed that the Member States have adopted, in general, simplified court procedures for small claims, with the possibility of conciliation by the court, as well as alternative means of dispute resolution, with special emphasis on mediation and arbitration. However, this document expressed the need to proceed with the creation of common legilslation and with the harmonization of national laws. However, the European Council, in its conclusions of 25 November 1996, came to express its concern in order to "strengthen consumer confidence in the functioning of the internal market and its ability to fully exploit the possibilities that the latter offers them", as well as guarantee the possibility for consumers to settle disputes in an "effective and appropriate means of extrajudicial procedures or other comparable processes". Following this policy, the European Commission adopted, on 30 March 1998, the Recommendation 98/257/EC on the principles applicable to the authorities responsible for the extrajudicial resolution of consumer disputes, recommending that those authorities must respect the principles of independence, transparency, contradiction, effectiveness, legality, freedom and representation. In its Recommendation 2001/310/EC, of 4 April 2001, on the principles applicable to extrajudicial bodies involved in the consensual resolution of consumer disputes, the Commission recommended that such organizations must fulfill the principles of impartiality, transparency, effectiveness and equity.

On the other hand, trying to give consumers an easier access to non-judicial procedures for resolving disputes, the European Commission has set up two networks that allow citizens to settle their disputes over consumer relations in a quickly, simply and efficiently way: the European Extra-Judicial Network "EEC-NET", made up of several national points of contact, which are established in different Member States and allow to bring consumers and companies that are domiciled in different Member States, and the "FIN-NET", which is dedicated to alternative dispute resolution between consumers and financial institutions.

Under the consumer credit, it is worth mentioning the Directive 2008/48/EC of the European Parliament and of the Council of 23 April 2008, on credit agreements for consumers, whose art. 24.°, paragraph 1, states that "Member States shall ensure that adequate and effective out-of-court dispute resolution procedures for the settlement of consumer disputes concerning credit agreements are put in place, using existing bodies where appropriate". In the same way, the art. 14.°, paragraph 2, of the Directive 2008/122/EC of the European Parliament and of the Council, on consumer protection in respect of certain aspects of contracts for timeshare, acquisition of long-term holiday products, resale and exchange contracts, stipulates that "Member States shall encourage the setting up or development of adequate and effective out-of-court complaints and redress procedures for the settlement of consumer disputes under this Directive and shall, where appropriate, encourage traders and their branch organisations to inform consumers of the availability of such procedures".

In the field of e-commerce, assumes particular relevance the Directive 2000/31/EC of the European Parliament and of the Council of 8 June 2000, on certain legal aspects of information society services in the internal market, particularly trade, in which it considered that each Member State should, where necessary, adjust their national legislation when it is likely to hinder the use of alternative resolution of disputes through electronic channels (Cortés, 2010). Thus, pursuant to art. 17.°, paragraph 1, of the Directive, "Member States shall ensure that, in the event of disagreement between an information society service provider and the recipient of the service, their legislation does not hamper the use of out-of-court schemes, available under national law, for dispute settlement, including appropriate electronic means".

More recently, under the arts. 81.°, n.° 2, al. g) and 169.°, n.° 1 and n.° 2, al. a) of the Treaty on the Functioning of the EU - which state that the EU should ensure the development of alternative means of dispute resolution as well as a high level of consumer protection - was adopted the Directive 2013/11/EU, of the European Parliament and of the Council of 21 May 2013, on the alternative resolution of consumer disputes, which must be implemented until July 9, 2015. As remains clear from the preamble to the directive, although alternative dispute resolution "offers a simple, fast and low-cost out-of-court solution to disputes between consumers and traders", the truth is that the alternative dispute resolution means aren't still functioning satisfactorily "in all geographical areas or business sectors in the Union. Consumers and traders are still not aware of the existing out-of-court redress mechanisms, with only a small percentage of citizens knowing how to file a complaint with an ADR entity. Where ADR procedures are available, their quality levels vary considerably in the Member States and crossborder disputes are often not handled effectively by ADR entities". Moreover, the existence of disparities between the different Member States in terms of coverage, quality and dissemination of own alternative means of dispute resolution is responsible for creating imbalances on equality and in competition among consumers and traders, due to the fear that their potential disputes will not be resolved quickly, easily and cheaply. In this context, this Directive, in addition to the Regulation (EU) n.° 534/2013 of the European Parliament and of the Council of 21 May 2013, on resolving online disputes, aims to ensure the proper functioning of the internal market by ensuring consumers the opportunity to submit complaints against traders to entities that ensure, in an independent, impartial, effective, quick and fair process, the extrajudicial resolution of the dispute (art. 1.°). It applies to the resolution of disputes concerning the fulfillment of contractual obligations resulting from the purchase and sale of goods or provision of services between traders established in the Union and consumers residing in the Union through alternative dispute resolution entities (art. 2.°). For this purpose, pursuant to art. 5.°, Member States shall facilitate consumer access to alternative dispute resolution procedures and ensure that disputes will be submitted to a duly qualified alternative dispute resolution entity.

On the other hand, the directive seeks to harmonize the domestic laws of different Member States in relation to alternative dispute resolution procedures. Thus, these procedures must be effective, available and easily accessible, assuming likewise a free and fair nature. Furthermore, the parties must ensure respect for the principles of disposition, contradictory, equality of arms and information, and shall not limit or condition the parties to resort to other dispute resolution routes.

The art. 12.º of the directive stipulates that Member States shall ensure the parties that the use of alternative means of dispute resolution does not produce preclusive effects with respect to limitation periods or lapse.

The directive also takes the concern to ensure free access to information. Thus, besides traders have the obligation to inform consumers about ADR entities that they depend, Member States shall also ensure consumers the assistance as may be necessary to access the ADR entity operating in other Member States of the European Union and the dissemination on the Internet entities and ADR centers in the field of consumer disputes.

SOLUTIONS AND RECOMMENDATIONS

The European institutions have demonstrated a growing concern in ensuring the implementation and the development of alternative means of dispute resolution in the single European market. In fact, the creation of a European area of freedom, security and justice requires not only the possibility for citizens to have their disputes resolved within a reasonable time, but also in an efficient, equitable and economical way.

Thus, if on the one hand the crisis of the justice, cross the large majority of EU Member States, revealed the need for a faster dispute resolution, on the other hand the lack of implementation and development of alternative means of dispute resolution eventually lead to imbalances in competition as well as asymmetries and inequalities between citizens of the different Member States.

That's why it's urgent, in a justice and economic crisis context, that the European institutions create the right conditions for the development of the personal and commercial relations within the European area.

Despite the measures taken in recent years by the European institutions, with particular emphasis on the Directive 2013/11/EU of the European Parliament and of the Council of 21 May 2013, it seems, however, that the adopted measures are still short of what is desirable. Indeed, legislative initiatives have focused primarily on the development of mediation tools in the field of consumer relations. The truth is that these instruments are contained mostly of recommendations and directives, which are not, respectively, binding and directly applicable.

Futhermore, in some legal areas of particular relevance, such as labor law, the measures taken by the European institutions in the field of alternative dispute resolution are still scarce. It reveals indispensable, given the peculiarity of these disputes, the creation of European alternative dispute resolution mechanisms that are especially designed for resolving cross-border disputes, with particular emphasis on conciliation, mediation and arbitration.

CONCLUSION

European policies should focus on the harmonization of alternative means of dispute resolution provided in the different Member States.

First, on conciliation we find that in some Member States the judge is obliged to promote conciliation between the parties, while in others it is not even expected the attempt at conciliation by the court. Now, in the current context of failure of the judicial system, harmonization of European legislation is essential in order for the court to be able to promote conciliation between the parties whenever the nature of the process permits. Besides, it is essential that the European Union promotes, when the simplicity of the cause or the nature of the dispute allows, prior recourse to conciliation as a condition of access to the courts. It should be noted, moreover, that in the judicial system crisis context, where the courts are confronted with a high procedural dispute, the implementation of this normative solution would manifestly have positive effects regarding the decongestion of the activity of the courts.

Another aspect that seems relevant is what concerns the need for the European institutions to promote the development of other alternative means of dispute resolution, particularly in the field of arbitration. In fact, analyzing the legislative policy measures adopted by the European institutions in recent years, we found that this activity was concentrated fundamentally in the promotion of mediation, particularly in the field of consumer and family relations. At the same time, it is essential to expand the alternative means of dispute resolution to other areas, such as in criminal law.

One last note: notwithstanding the many legislative measues adopted by the European institutions in the field of alternative dispute resolution, the efficient use of these means depends greatly of disclosure not only to citizens but also of law students and legal professionals, such as lawyers. In fact, when a citizen or a company seeks the assistance of a legal professional in order to resolve a particular dispute, this is who, in most cases, chooses the legal procedure to adopt. But if the legal professional is not aware of the potential of alternative dispute resolution, he will tend rather to advise the client to propose an action in a court of law.

Similarly, law students must be aware that there are alternative means for resolving disputes. In particular, in the Portuguese case, practice shows that the study of alternative means of dispute resolution still occupies a less important place.

This is a tendency that it is urgent to change. In this context, only with the active dissemination of alternative means of dispute resolution and its potential will be possible, in the near future, the effective integration and development of these means in a European area of freedom, security and justice.

REFERENCES

Arnavas, D. P. (2004). *Alternative Dispute Resolution for Government Contracts*. Riverwoods: CCH Incorporated.

Bënohr, I. (2012). Alternative dispute resolution for consumers in the EU. In C. Christopher Hodges, I. Benöhr, & N. Creutzfeldt-Banda (Eds.), *Consumer ADR in Europe*. Oxford, UK: Bloomsbury Publishing.

Blake, S., Browne, J., & Sime, S. (2014). *A Practical Approach to Alternative Dispute Resolution*. Oxford, UK: Oxford University Press.

Cortés, P. (2010). *Online Dispute Resolution for Consumers in the European Union*. Oxon, UK: Routledge.

Frey, M. (2002). *Alternative Methods of Dispute Resolution*. Cengage Learning.

Gaio Jûnior, A. P. (2008). *Direito Processual Civil*. Belo Horizonte: Del Rey.

Gouveia, M. F. (2014). *Curso de Resolução Alternativa de Litígios*. Coimbra: Almedina.

Hartley, R. E. (2002). *Alternative Dispute Resolution in Civil Justice Systems*. Georgia: LFB Scholarly Publishing LLC.

Kaufmann-Kohler, G., & Schultz, T. (2004). *Online Dispute Resolution: Challenges for Contemporary Justice*. The Hague: Kluwer Law International.

Lopes, D., & Patrão, A. (2014). *Lei da Mediação Comentada*. Coimbra: Almedina.

Martí Màrmol, J. L. (2002). *Perspectivas del Derecho en la Negociación de Conflictos*. UOC.

McDermott, E. P., & Berkeley, A. E. (1996). *Alternative Dispute Resolution in the Workplace: Concepts and Techniques for Human Resource Executives and Their Counsel*. Greenwood Publishing Group.

Silva, S. T. (2010). *Um Novo Direito Administrativo?* Coimbra: Imprensa da Universidade de Coimbra. doi:10.14195/978-989-26-0208-0

Van Gramberg, B. (2006). *Managing Workplace Conflict: Alternative Dispute Resolution in Australia*. Sydney: Federation Press.

Wrbka, S. (2014). *European Consumer Access to Justice Revisited*. Cambridge, UK: Cambridge University Press. doi:10.1017/CBO9781139680431

KEY TERMS AND DEFINITIONS

Alternative Means of Dispute Resolution: Dispute settlement procedures that are alternative to judicial means.

Arbitration: Alternative means of dispute resolution whereby the parties agree to submit the resolution of a dispute, present or future, to a third party.

Conciliation: Alternative means of dispute resolution through which the entity with authority to settle the dispute proposes to the parties equitable solutions that enable them to settle amicably the dispute.

Conflict Mediator: Impartial and independent person that assists the parties in conflict to find, by themselves, a harmonious solution for their dispute.

Equity: Technique that favors consensual and harmonious resolution of disputes, rather than a purely legal solution.

Mediation: Alternative means of dispute resolution through which two or more parties to a dispute seek to reach an agreement with assistance of a mediator of conflicts.

Negotiation: Process through which the parties seek a friendly settlement to resolve a dispute without the intervention of a third party.

Chapter 8

Online Dispute Resolution for Consumers in Portugal and in the European Union:
The Future Platform for Online Dispute Resolution

Fernando Viana
CIAB – Centro de Informação, Mediação e Arbitragem de Conflitos de Consumo (Tribunal Arbitral), Portugal

Francisco Pacheco Andrade
Universidade do Minho, Portugal

ABSTRACT

Administration of Justice became complex in Consumers and Information Society. It is necessary to look for new solutions for the increasing situations of consumer's litigation. Traditional State Courts are not a solution due to their slow, heavy and costly ways of functioning. The way is clearly open for Arbitration Centers based in friendly mechanisms such as mediation, concilitation and arbitration. Regulation EU nr. 524/2013 of European Parliament and Council of the 21st of May on online consumer's conflict resolution has as aim the creation of a conflict resolution platform at european level. We propose to analyze the Regulation and its implications and to show the functioning of the platform that is being developed and that should be available for both for consumers and corporations from 9th January 2016 on. It will be analyzed the new requirements of access to Justice in the field of Consumer's conflicts, the new ADR Directive and the regulation on ODR in order to meet the challenges brought along by the introduction of the new platform for conflict resolution.

DOI: 10.4018/978-1-5225-0245-6.ch008

INTRODUCTION: THE ADVENT OF THE SOCIETY OF CONSUME AND OF INFORMATION

The 20th century saw the advent of automobile as the main mean of transportation in modern industrialized societies, and the banalization of airplanes in passenger's transportation, superseding ships and even trains. Radio, television, personal computers, washing machines, are among hundreds of products that became banalized during the 20th century. And also the creation of new services kept growing during the same period. A quick search in Internet shows us a huge profusion of new services, going from translation services and internet pages creation to all kinds of touristic services (ecological, historical, sporting, radical, religious, sexual). If we think of informatics, we may think of personal computers, tablets, smartphones, an infinity of programs and apps allowing access to an infinity of new services: GPS systems, bar code lecture, localization of persons and objects, elderly support, restaurant or wine choosing, tickets sales for transportation or shows. The possibilities look almost infinite and everyday new services are announced.

Actually, the act of consuming becomes more related to a pleasure than to a need, and producers try to work hard at the level of marketing and publicity inducing the consumer to consume, to feel pleasure, to feel rewarded.

Truly, the problem in modern societies is not so much to produce but rather to sell. Corporations have been feeling a need to find alternative ways to the mere laws of the markets (demand and supply) in order to ensure the sale of the stocks. For this reason, publicity saw its role hugely increased.

But this is not merely a society of consume, it is also an information society. Never had mankind so much access to information. This society arises from a process of accelerated change, economical development and globalization of society and culture. Social economic development depends now on information and knowledge, but mainly of diffusion and sharing of information upon which knowledge is built. Many authors have theorized on the characteristics of information society. Gouveia and Gaio (2004) refer the contribution of several authors to this concept, such as Javier Echeverria to whom information society "is inserted in a process upon which the traditional notion of time and space is transformed by the appearance of a virtual space, trans-territorial and trans-temporal", while for Noam Chomsky information society "is also the fruit of economic globalization in order to promote a huger circulation of capital and information in the hands of big entrepreneurial groups". Thus being, information society is based in the way information is delivered to society through information and communication technologies dealing with information and turning this the central element of all human activities (Castells 2005). And of course, Internet is one of the key elements of Information Society.

Commerce could not be dissociated from the Internet. We can even state that it was the commercial applications of Internet that led to its huge success in such a short time. When Internet was discovered by corporations it had a quick diffusion and huge amounts were invested. Even before Internet and computers, there were already an interesting development of different modalities of distance commerce, such as sales by catalogue, by phone or by TV[1]. Electronic commerce is thus no more than a way of acquiring goods and services using for such purpose electronic equipments that allow to process and to archive data. It must be stated that in our work we will limit ourselves to the electronic commerce between a professional and a consumer (B2C) being consumer understood here in the sense of the Portuguese law[2]. Electronic commerce has been constantly growing, either at world[3] or at national level [4,5]. Internet is thus becoming a gigantic virtual commercial shopping center gathering always more corporations and online consumers, making sales quickly rise and bringing along higher rates of conflituality. Thus being, we must consider new ways of solving disputes arising out of online commerce. This must be done considering also the issues of Justice Administration (Galanter, 1993) already referred on his study on the judicial system, in developed societies such as United States and Canada, that these societies are wealthy, well informed and with great social diversity. And there are:

- More laws, more lawyers, more strategic operators in the legal game – societies spending more money on legal issues, the legal institutions (including Courts and Lawyer's offices) have now a more rational way of working considering cost-efficiency criteria.
- Lawyers, judges, administrators have more initiative and sense of innovation
- Norms are plural and decentralized, and arising out of a multiplicity of sources
- There are more actors applying more norms and patterns to a diverse set of situations, meaning that legal outcomes are contingent and variable. More and more fixed norms are accompanied by variable dialogical patterns
- Law is less autonomous and less tight, and much more open to methods and data coming from other subjects
- Being technically sophisticated, legal work tends to become more expensive, which may push most people to the outskirts of the market, quite often without direct access to law

Law is working more and more through indirect symbolic controls and not so much through physic coaction. Indirect participation through groups and social media increases much faster than direct participation (Galanter, 1993).

If in the 70's of the XX century there was in Portugal an average of 245.000 procedures in judicial courts, in the 90's it out passed 609.000 and in 2012 the number reached 873.438[6].

Recent statistical data of Justice in Portugal shows that this country, with a population around 10 million inhabitants, had in 2004 around 1.600.000 pending processes. And in spite of different reforms undertaken, in the end of 2012[7] there were 1.716.218 pending processes in 1st instance Courts and that the average duration of processes in Civil litigation was of 29 months.

It is well known that Justice arises out of 3 essential dimensions which are fair decisions, costs of justice and time of decision (Zuckerman, 1999). Administration in the area of justice must take in consideration these 3 dimensions, and because we are dealing with a very sensitive field with a huge state intervention, financial resources must be taken in consideration.

In order to confront the crisis of justice several solutions appear as possible (Pedroso, 2006) such as injecting more resources in the system, better managing the existing resources, or making a strong bet in innovation, in technology and in alternative (to conventional justice in court) ways of solving disputes. The new emerging models of ADR (Alternative Dispute Resolution and, more recently, Amicable Dispute Resolution) by the way of decentralized processes and institutions, often informal, allowing to withdraw people from court to other public or private instances (Pedroso, 2006).

From increase in consume (Almeida, 2001)[8] relations resulted an inherent increase in conflictuality. The diversity of consume issues and the impossibility to either predict or regulate them all generates a multiplicity of conflicts that courts are not able to absorb and that will ultimately prevent courts of functioning and focusing on more relevant legal relations.

To this increase in consumer's conflictuality, the State replied with the creation of specialized entities for consume conflict resolution.

EXTRAJUDICIAL CONFLICT RESOLUTION

Alternative Conflict Resolution is not limited in Portugal to Arbitration Centers for Conflicts of Consume[9]. We must not forget that after the launching, in 2001, of a pilot project of "Julgados de Paz" (Judges of Peace, JP)[10] there is now available, all over the country, a network of JPs distributed along the country form north to south[11]. The electronic site of JPs[12] define these as courts with special characteristics, competent to solve processes of reduced value and civil nature, excluding those involving subjects of Family Law, Heritages Law, and Labor Law, in a fast way and at reduced costs.

Also Mediation has been increasing its action among us and it must be referred, besides all the private initiatives of mediation, three institutionalized areas of public (state) mediation: family mediation, labor mediation and criminal mediation.

Public or private, Mediation is regulated by Law 29/2013 from 19th April 2013, which defines Mediation as "a way of alternative resolution of conflicts, carried on by public or private entities in which two or more conflicting parties voluntarily seek for an agreement with the support of a conflict mediator" (art. 2nd a)). Mediation has a characteristic of voluntarity and confidentiality and the parties are helped by a neutral third (the mediator) trying to reach an agreement that might solve the conflict at stake. Contrarily to a judge or arbitrator, the mediator has no power of decision, not being able to impose any deliberation or sentence. As a third neutral, the mediator guides the parties, helps them establish the required communication in order to reach by themselves the basis of a suitable (for both) agreement. The parties are thus responsible for the agreements being built up with the support of the mediator. Mediation sessions are presencial.

Besides mediation and arbitration there are still other ways for solving conflicts, usually hybrid ways between non jurisdictional ways or between theses and jurisdictional ways. One classic example is mediation-arbitration. In this procedure, the mediator-arbitrator plays the role of mediator and if mediation fails, by request of the parties, the mediator is then transformed in an arbitrator capable of making recommendations and of deciding on the conflict. In the United States there is a great variety of CAR being the most often referred: mini-trial, private trial, summary jury trial, court annexed arbitrations, neutral listener, neutral expert fact-finding (Wilde & Gaibrois, 2003).

EXTRAJUDICIAL RESOLUTION OF CONSUMER'S CONFLICTS

In Portugal, consumer's rights have a constitutional dignity (art. 60 Portuguese Republic Constitution). Besides that, there is a Law of Consumer Defense (Law nr. 24/96 from the 31st of July) in whose article 14 a right to legal protection and to an accessible and fast justice is ensured. In this article it is also stated that it is the duty of the organs and departments of Public Administration to promote the creation and supporting Arbitration Centers aimed at solving consumer's conflicts.

Usually, certain advantages are pointed out concerning the use of Arbitration, especially in what voluntary Arbitration is concerned. Actually, with the exception of mandatory Arbitration, this process intends a previous acceptation by the parties of an arbitration convention[13]. Also the confidentiality and flexibility of the process as well as the specialized character of the decision are seen as advantages, along with the simplification of the procedures and ensuring of the necessary rights of defense of the parties, especially in terms of means of proof and defense. An important advantage of Arbitration usually referred is the short delays of the process[14]. Also the fact that Arbitral Decisions have the same executive strength of judicial courts is an unequivocal advantage that, associated with lower costs for the parties marks an important point for this method of conflict resolution.

Arbitration, in terms of organization and functioning is usually developed in two different ways: ad hoc arbitration and institutionalized arbitration. Ad hoc arbitration has the aim of solving disputes according to rules established and agreed upon by the parties themselves. It doesn't require the intervention of any arbitration institution. According to article 1 nr. 1 of the Law of Voluntary Arbitration, if there is no special law making it mandatory to submit it exclusively to state courts or necessary arbitration, any conflict may be submitted by the parties, upon arbitration convention, to the decision of arbitrators. On the other hand, institutional arbitration is conducted within institutions specifically ensuring all support to arbitration and created for that purpose (or at least functioning within institutions promoting an arbitral activity of their won[15]. However, the functioning of these centers depends on governmental authorization[16].

Thus it becomes obvious the need for extrajudicial means of solving conflicts. One of the most used in consume relationships is the reclamation by the consumer himself towards the economic operator, either directly or by the use of the Reclamation's Book[17]. Some corporations of bigger dimension went to the point of creating a special figure "the client Ombudsman" trying to get answers to unsatisfied costumers improving the communicational process and the image of the corporation. However, quite often the costumer gets the impression that this is just a question related to the image of the corporation and that the "client Ombudsman" is not at all independent and neutral.

Yet, the creation of arbitration centers allowed the appearance of organizations that, in an institutionalized[18] and specialized way, make consume conflict resolution widely available, taking out of the court a huge number of processes and ensuring legal security, fast resolution and informality.

As it was already mentioned, the first Arbitration Center to be created among us was the Center for Arbitration of Consumer's Conflicts of Lisbon. This Center has generic competences and territorially limited to the metropolitan area of Lisbon. It has competence for processes whose value is under € 5.000 (five thousand euros) and its functioning is at no cost. In Oporto there is, since 1992 the Center for Information and Arbitration of Oporto, also with generic competences and territorially limited to the metropolitan area of Oporto. It has no limit value and its functioning is also at no cost. The third Center to be created was the Arbitration Center for Conflicts of Consume of the Coimbra District also in 1992 and being available in 16 of the 17 local areas of that District (with the only exception of Pampilhosa da Serra). It has competence limited to the value of € 5.000 (five thousand euros) and its functioning is also at no cost.

Later on, 15th March 1997, appeared the CIAB – Arbitral Court of Consume, also with generic competences and territorially limited, after a period of expansion, to 18 municipalities in 3 Districts (Braga, Viana do Castelo and Vila Real). Its value competence is ilimited and its functioning at no cost. Still in 1997 appeared the Triave – Center of Arbitration for Consume Conflicts in the Ave Valley, also with generic competences and also with ilimited value competence and free of costs for users.

The Center of Information, Mediation and Arbitration for Consume Conflicts of Algarve was created in year 2000. As its name suggests it works in the Algarve Region (district of Faro), it has generic competence, ilimited values and functioning at no cost.

In 2005 it was created a Center for Arbitration for Conflicts of Consume in Madeira Autonomous Region, also with generic competence, a limit value of € 30.000 (thirty thousand euros) and functioning at no cost.

The National Center for Information and Arbitration for Consume Conflicts - CNIACC was the last one to be created and started functioning in 2009. It functions in a subsidiary way all over the country in areas not considered by the other extrajudicial means of solving consume conflicts and its values ilimited and also free of cost.

Besides these Arbitration Centers, having as common characteristic their generic competence for all kinds of conflicts of consume, their geographical competence limited to a defined region and free of costs. There are other arbitration centers but having a specialized competence according to defined subjects, national competence and with determined costs for its activities. Besides that, these other centers deal with other kind of legal relations beyond consume.

There are among us dozens of Arbitration Centers[19], dealing with the most different subjects, but in this work we shall consider only CACC – Centers for Conflicts of Consume Arbitration. These Centers use diverse instruments in order to solve the conflicts, namely mediation, conciliation and arbitration.

Mediation undertaken in Arbitration Centers has some specificities when compared to the mediation offered by the above referred public systems of mediation. The main issue is about the intervention of a third neutral looking at helping the parties to reach an agreement capable of solving the dispute opposing them. There are Centers making a presential mediation available, while other do it indirectly with the support of distance means such as telephone, fax, mail, internet. In all of them mediation is at no cost[20].

If the case is not solved during mediation phase and goes on, an attempt of conciliation agreement must be made before the arbitration session. In conciliation it will be looked for, in a more incisive way[21], an agreement of the parties. If the agreement is reached it will be approved by the arbitrator in a sentence[22].

The Constitution of the Portuguese Republic in article 202 states that "Courts are the sovereign organs competent to administer justice in the name of the people". But art. 209 CPR, dealing with the categories of Courts, expressly admits the existence of Arbitral Courts[23].

As it was already referred, arbitration finds its legal finalities in the Law of Voluntary Arbitration which allows its use in a set of diverse patrimonial (or even non patrimonial) litigation, if the parties may celebrate a transaction on the controverted rights (nr. 2 of article 1 of LVA), if there is an arbitration convention signed by the parties, which must necessarily be in written, due to art. 2nd nr. 1[24]. The arbitral court may be formed by one only arbitrator or by several, necessarily in odd number, although in CACCs the first possibility is the rule, without exceptions. The rules applied to the arbitration procedure may be chosen by the parties, but in CACC situation they result out of the respective regulation (which they all have[25]) on arbitration.

Article 30 of LAV imposes a set of fundamental principles to be respected in the arbitration process:

- The addressee is cited to defend himself
- The principle of the equality of the parties
- The existence of a reasonable opportunity for both parties to make prevail their rights, by written or verbally, before a final sentence is issued
- Respect for the principle of contradiction in all phases of the process

Curiously, contrarily to what happened in the old LVA[26], the current law does not determine a need of a hearing before the final decision. Article 34 nr. 1 allows that, except in case of agreement of the parties stating the contrary, the court will decide if there will be hearings for the production of proof or if the process is only conducted based in documents or other elements of proof.

Although LVA doesn't state it expressly, the parties may designate someone to represent or assist them in the arbitration court[27]. Concerning the means of proof, LVA determines that it is to the Arbitral Court to determine the possibility and value of the proof to be produced (art. 30 nr. 4 of LVA). But arbitration regulation, which is common to the institutionalized arbitration held in CACCs state a wider possibility of using proof means, including testimony of part, documents, expertise and examination. Concerning testimonial proof, it is usual to limit the number of testimonies admitted[28]. The Arbitrators decide according to the law, except if the parties agree to have recourse to solutions of equity[29].

Article 42 nr. 7 of LVA establishes that the "arbitral sentence" is also mandatory between the parties just as a sentence of a state court would be and shall have the same executive force, being used for the execution the state court of 1st instance competent in the terms of the procedural law[30].

As it was already referred, one of the main advantages of Arbitration is higher procedural speed. For instance, LVA states, as general rule, a maximum delay of 12 months for the parties to be notified of the final decision, counted from the date of notification of the last Arbitrator (article 43 nr. 1 of LVA). However, in consume arbitration the issue of procedural speed is even more acute, considering the urgent need of getting a decision in time. For instance, processes concerning essential public services, whenever the consumer is confronted with a threat of suspension of the service, the arbitral court must decide particularly fast. Thus being, quite often arbitral regulations state very short delays (only a few days) for a decision. For instance, article 17 nr. 1 of CIAB – Arbitral Court imposes that once the production of proof ended the arbitral court decides orally and immediately, except if the complexity of the litigation does not allow it, but in that case the final decision must be issued in 10 days[31].

EXTRAJUDICIAL CONFLICT RESOLUTION IN EUROPEAN UNION

The situation is not much different in the other 27 member states of European Union. In this huge space shared by more than 500 million people, it is intended to create a single market arising out of the freedoms stated by the Treaties (free circulation of people, goods, services and capitals). While it has been suggested the creation of procedural forms and even jurisdictions adapted to the small conflicts, within the national institutional frameworks, there has also been promoted new legislation adopting complementary schemes of conflict resolution. It has been proposed faster and lighter procedures, less formal and less costly. Parallel schemes, extrajudicial ways have been promoted based in institutional specificities in the experiences of each one of the countries. In the last years, due to the development of Technologies of Information and Communication (TICs) and to the popularity of the Internet, electronic commerce has been growing exponentially while the security of transactions (technical and legal security), quite often occurring in different legal spaces, is one of the most important aspects to be considered.

Directive 2013/11/UE of the Parliament and Council, of the 21st of May 2013 (ADR "Alternative Conflict Resolution" Directive).

In order to face the challenges of the growing digital dimension of EU inner market, it was adopted, in July 2013, the Directive 2013/11/UE of the European Parliament and Council, from the 21st of May (ADR Directive). This Directive must be transposed to the national law of each state member until the 9th July 2015 and it states that the alternative resolution of conflicts provides a simple, fast and less costly way to solve litigation between consumers and goods and services providers. Yet, ADR is not yet developed enough in the Union territory in a harmonized and coherent way. Sadly enough, although there was the Recommendation 98/257/CE of the Commission, from the 30th of March 2001, on the principles to be applied to the bodies and organisms responsible for extrajudicial resolution of consume conflicts, and also the Recommendation 2001/310/CE of the Commission, from the 4th of April 2001, concerning the principles to be applied to the bodies and organisms responsible for extrajudicial consensual resolution of consumer's conflicts, the truth is that ADR mechanisms were not correctly created are not functioning in a satisfactory way in all geographical areas and in all sectors of activity within the EU. Consumers and Providers of goods and services still do not have a good knowledge on the extrajudicial mechanisms of reparation and only a small percentage of the citizens knows how to submit a claim to an ADR entity. And when they do exist, ADR mechanisms have very different levels of quality from state member to state member, and transborder litigation is not always efficiently dealt with by ADR entities (Consideration 5 of the Directive).

It must also be considered that an ADR entity working efficiently must end up the works for solving the conflict, either online or by conventional means, in a maximum delay of 90 days counting from the date of the reception of the full claim process, including all the documentation concerning the claim, by the ADR entity and with the limit date in the day in which the final result of the ADR procedure is made available. The ADR entity receiving a claim must notify the parties in litigation as soon as it gets all the required documents in order to proceed with the ADR. In exceptional situations due to a high complexity of the cases, particularly when it is not possible for one of the parties, based on justified define a further delay or prorogation of the delay. The parties must be informed of any prorogation and of the time needed for the conclusion of the procedure (Consideration 40 of the Directive). The Directive still establishes that costs will be tendentially free for consumers.

Regulation 524/2013 of the European Parliament and of the Council from the 21st May (ODR Regulation) on Online Conflict Resolution is to be applied in Member States from the 9th January 2016[32] and modifies Regulation (CE) 2006/2004 and Directive 2009/22/CE (Regulation ODR) has as its aim to create a platform of Online Conflict Resolution at the scale of the European Union. This platform must be assumed as an interactive web site, with a unique entry point for the consumers and for goods and service providers aiming at solving their litigation arising out of online transactions by extrajudicial means. General information must also be provided on extrajudicial conflict resolution concerning contracts between consumers and commercial providers arising out of contracts of sales and online services. It must also allow consumers and providers to present their claims using an electronic formulary available in all official languages of EU institutions and with the possibility of annexing the relevant documents. The claims must be transmitted to an ADR entity competent to know the said litigation. The ODR platform shall provide an electronic tool of free management allowing the ODR entities to conduct the online conflict resolution procedure, along with the parties, through the ODR platform. But the ODR entities must not be obliged to use the management tool (Consideration 18 of the Regulation).

The functioning of this consume conflict resolution is based in the provision of an adequate electronic platform, to which the parties may access through the Internet and making possible the contact between consumers and commercial providers in search of a satisfactory (for all) agreement with the intervention of an alternative resolution entity which must also be contacted through the use of the same platform.

It must be noted that there is a distinction to be made between ODR systems. In some of them the human intervention is residual, all the system being prepared to manage the conflict (from the introduction of a claim in the system to an automatic reply given after its analysis by the system and all other procedures are after all pre-defined by the system), being that to any action by the initiator there will be a reply by the system, and quite often the human decider will just validate the final result operated by the machine. In others, on the contrary, there will be a human intervention in every phase, being the informatic systems just instruments of the process making it go through the different phases without errors and finishing in due time. It is this type of ODR which is intended by the Regulation 524/2013 EU in which the ODR at EU level must be based in ADR entities existing in the State Members and respecting the legal traditions of the State Members. The ADR entities to which a claim has been submitted through the ODR platform must, therefore, apply their own procedural rules, namely in terms of costs. However, the Regulation intends to establish some common rules to be applied to the procedures in order to safeguard its efficiency. Such rules must also ensure that the resolution of this kind of disputes must not require the physical presence of the parties or of its legal representatives, with the only exception of cases whenever such procedural rules expressly state that possibility and the parties agree on that (Consideration 25 of the Regulation). Consideration 25 still refers that contact points of ODR must be designed in every member state including at least two ODR Counselors. The ODR contact points must support the parties involved in the litigation but are not obliged to translate the documents concerning the litigation. Member States must have the possibility of delegating the responsibility for their ODR contact points in their respective Centers within the Network of Consumer European Centers. The State Members must make use of it in order to allow the ODR contact points to fully benefit from the experience of the said network in the provision of conflict resolution between consumers and commercial providers. The Commission must create a network of ODR contact points in order to enhance the cooperation and its work must provide, in collaboration with the State Members, adequate training to the ODR contact points.

THE ODR PLATFORM

We are now going to present briefly the functioning of the ODR Platform now being developed by the European Commission and that should be available to European consumers, online operators and Alternative Conflict Resolution entities on the 9th January 2016 (article 22 of the Regulation of Online Dispute Resolution).

According to article 5 nr. 1 of Regulation ODR) the Commission creates a ODR Platform and will be responsible for its functioning including all the required functions of translation, its maintenance, its financing and the security of its data. The ODR platform must be user friendly, that is to say easy to use by common citizens. The creation, functioning and maintenance of the platform must ensure that the privacy of its users is respected from the phase of its conception and that the platform is accessible and usable by all users including, as much as possible, the vulnerable users.

For this work the Sanco DG was involved. In 2012 a group of ODR specialists was invited and in 2014 an ODR Commission was created aiming at having this platform becoming a unique entry point for consumers and providers willing to solve extra judicially litigation concerning the online buy and sell of goods and services (article 5 nr. 2 ODR Regulation).

This work began in 2012 with the definition of the workflow, of the graphism, of the platform's architecture, of interoperability, of confidentiality and security of data in that platform, that is to say of the compatibility of several required legal and technical aspects.

Figure 1. Main interface of the test model of the ODR platform

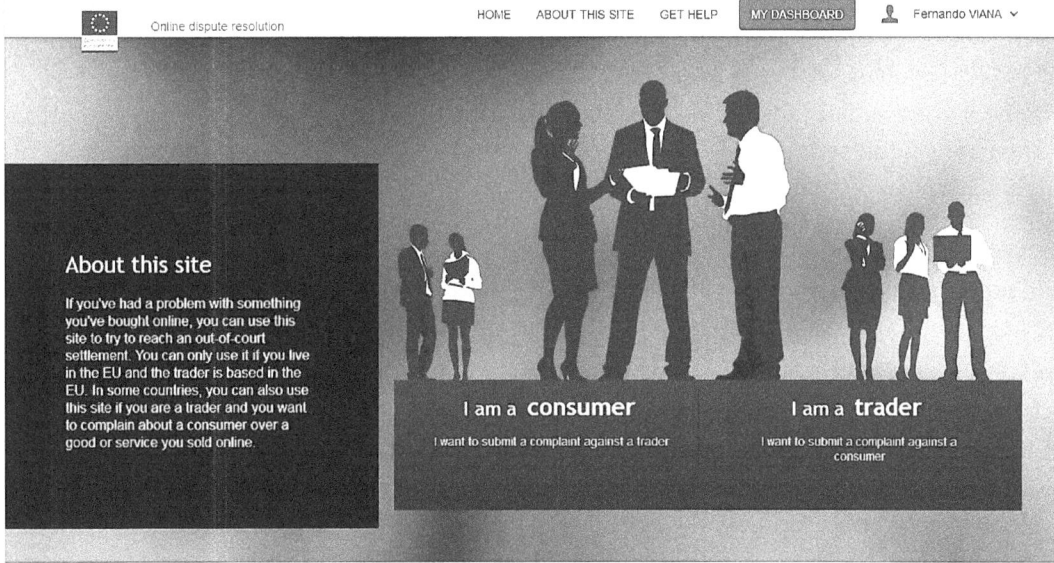

In the end of November 2013 the tests on the platform began, according to article 6 Regulation ODR. Although the period for the tests was temporally limited by the Regulation, the tests went on after the 9th January 2015, due to technical difficulties in the implementation phase of the Platform according to the Regulation requirements[33]. On the other side, according to article 5 nr. 4 of the Regulation it must be available both to the parties and to the ODR entity the translations needed for solving the conflict and shared through the ODR platform.

As referred above, the platform will only be accessible to European consumers and providers from the 9th January 2016[34]. Currently, the test model of the platform has the access page model depicted in Figure 1.

By accessing to the main page, the web users may immediately choose the language in which they want the information to be displayed.

In this page and in the ones linked to this one, developers looked to fully complying to the stated in article 5 nr. 4 h) of the Regulation:

1.   General information on Alternative Dispute Resolution as extrajudicial means of solving disputes;
2.   Information concerning the Alternative Dispute Resolution entities inserted in a list according to Article 20 nr. 2 of the Directive 2013/11/UE with competency to solve litigation in the terms of the Regulation;
3.   An online guide on the ways of submitting claims through the ODR platform;
4.   All relevant information on the ODR contact points designed by the Member States according to article 7 nr. 1 of the Regulation;
5.   Statistical data on the outcomes of the litigation transmitted to the ODR entities through the ODR platform.

According to the quality of the user of the platform (consumer or provider) the user has two options:

- Being a consumer he may submit a claim concerning goods and services acquired online or have access to a previously submitted claim;
- Being a commercial provider he may have access to a claim or submit a claim against another commercial provider[35].

ADVANTAGES AND DISADVANTAGES OF USING ODR[36] IN AN ARBITRATION CENTER

The transition from ADR to ODR has just to do with the introduction of technology as an auxiliary tool in conflict resolution (Katsch & Rifkin, 2001)[37]. But it must be questioned how far we may go in the use of technology. Should technology be the agent of decision in a process? We think that we should not go that far, and that no one must be bound by a decision taken by a machine alone, without human intervention. And yet there are several advantages in the use of Information Technologies as an auxiliary tool to the making of decisions in conflict resolution processes (De Vries, Leenes & Zeleznikow, 2005), (Raiffa, 1982) and (Steenbergen, 2005)[38].

One of the main advantages in the use of ODR is the wide variety of tools that may be used (audio/video conference, mail, chats, forums). On the other side, the explosion of informatics, of telematics, of electronic commerce, of online and distance contracting, necessarily should have an impact in conflict resolution. If almost everything is done online, why shouldn't we solve online the conflicts that arose online? That's is why several well known organizations[39] have created their own ODR systems[40] with synchronous and asynchronous tools associated. Some of the more commonly referred advantages of these systems are the following:

1. Easy access. Access to distance communication instruments and technologies is becoming easier and easier, more commonly used, more intuitive, making it very easy the participation of the consumers;
2. Low cost[41];
3. Possibility of easily interchanging files and applications;
4. The communication between the parties and between these and the third neutral[42] is easy, free, more distanced, the parties may focus more on the issues and less on the persons;
5. The possibility of using Skype[43] allows the visualization of the parties[44].
6. People do not need to leave their own environment, where they feel more comfortable and more protected;
7. Through ODR people leave a more defensive approach and tend to become more open and more available;
8. It is quite useful in situations when a person feels constrained by the presence of the other party or in situations when geographical distance makes it mandatory for the parties the use of such technologies, thus avoiding time and costs needed for deplacements;
9. It allows a much wider choice of mediators or arbitrators, considering the web horizons;

10. It allows the parties to make searches simultaneously with the conflict resolution procedure (for instance, if a price of a good or service is at stake, it is possible with a quick search in Internet to get the required information);

11. Accessibility of Information Technologies[45];

12. Speed of processes. This is one of the most consensual aspects. Usually, ODR processes allow a criterious management of time. In such a way that, sometimes, the consumer may even become suspicious of the quick way in which a decision is reached[46], thinking that if the provider so quickly accepted a decision it could mean that the consumer hasn't done all that could (or should) have been done;

13. These procedures usually ensure many of the most relevant features of judicial procedures, such as independence, contradictory or the equality of the parties;

14. The possibility of registration of all conversations between the parties[47];

15. Confidentiality. Apparently, the use of a computer terminal may (falsely) induce the parties to believe a higher confidentiality is ensured in ODR processes. But this is not at all true;

16. Privacy is also sometimes referred as an advantage, based on the fact that we may manage the procedure from home or in a place where I feel comfortable and not having to go to a public place we may have this feeling of more privacy[48];

17. The existence of tools and systems ensuring the authenticity of the declarations of will, of documents exchange and signature (electronic) thus enhancing integrity, confidentiality and non repudiation of the exchanged information;

Other advantages could be referred, but we must nevertheless state that some of the referred advantages may be highly questionable or even be looked at as (serious) disadvantages:

1. Not being physically present makes it easier for the parties to lie or to omit information, although some authors may reply that, by not being physically present, the parties mat become more collaborative and truly.

2. Distance resolution diminishes communication between the parties and quite often does not provide the third neutral a set of elements (non verbal elements) which are very useful in resolution systems in the physical presence of the parties;

3. The ease of access and use may lead to some irresponsible behavior of the parties, with less reflection, claiming just for claiming and making an abusive use of the rights of participation;

4. The issue of the identity of the parties. OdR systems may sometimes get used by false identities or even persons with (unnoticed) limited capacity or represented by someone with no powers or legitimacy to represent the other;

5. The issue of anonymity. The fact that this procedure is totally online may allow anonymity. But this could also be looked at as an advantage or as a disadvantage;

We must still refer that in Portugal we saw, in 2011, the appearance of CIMACE – Centre for Information, Mediation and Arbitration for Electronic Commerce, then presented by public authorities as an arbitration center to solve conflicts arising out of commercial relations between providers and consumers in an almost totally electronic way. By the time of its creation it was referred that the growth of electronic commerce in Portugal – due to the amelioration of electronic communication networks and corporations investing in commercial interactive platforms - would have as a natural consequence a growth of conflicts arising out of this type of consume relations. CIMACE, being based on the use of information technologies, was thus seen as the first arbitration center entirely virtual and the only one prepared for the use of people with visual incapacities. And it was stressed the advantage of people not needing to deplane themselves. It would be enough to have a computer, an Internet connection and a webcam in order to solve a conflict. In 16th May 2011 the then Minister of Justice, Alberto Martins, was stating that the parties, through CIMACE, might get answers and clarifications to questions arising on the moment of the sale or even after that moment, advancing to mediation if the conflict subsists, and solving it by agreement or else advancing to a specialized arbitration in cases when it was not possible to reach an agreement. And all this online, through the same platform.

CIMACE arose out of an agreement between the Ministry of Justice (represented by the Office for Alternative Dispute Resolution), DECO – the Portuguese Association for the Defense of Consumers, ACEPI – Association for Electronic Commerce and Interactive Publicity, and APED – Portuguese Association for Distribution Companies. However, CIMACE never really started functioning and it soon became another example of waste of public resources that contributed to the difficult situation the country has gone through in the past years.

CONCLUSION

- The Industrial Revolution made available a set of goods and services as never before in the history of mankind. And in the XXth century it made possible the appearance of a society of consume;
- The society paradigm changed. No longer did man consume in order to survive but man itself was transformed in an object of consume, by the combined action of marketing and publicity scientifically working upon human emotions in order to induce consume;
- Internet is a new reality made possible by the increased development of Information and Telecommunication Technologies. The connection of a personal computer to Internet allows many different possibilities, from site consultation to the transfer of files or the access to multimedia contents, interaction with other users through social networks or computer games and online shopping;
- Electronic commerce has been growing both in value and in number of transactions. It may encompass different modalities such as B2B (Business to Business) or B2C (Business to consumer), the latter being more focused on this chapter since more and more commercial providers are proposing to final consumers the acquisition of goods and services online;
- Interpersonal and interinstitutional relationships through Internet generate conflicts that must be solved. Conflict Resolution (Administration of Justice) is essential to a good functioning of society. Otherwise, we shall have denegation of Justice and insecurity;
- Justice must solve an ever growing number of conflicts in all areas of social life. This multiplication of conflicts forced the States to dispend more and more resources in the Justice System, but also to legislate more and more. And in the end, faced with the scarcity of results (the current dysfunctions of the judicial system make it incapable of ensuring the application of fair decisions, taken on due time and at an accessible cost) and force the State to invest in new and different ways of solving conflicts;

- In Portugal as in other different jurisdictions Alternative Dispute Resolution Systems have appeared. Yet ADR as acronym is questionable and among us ADR – Alternative Conflict Resolution includes "Julgados de Paz" (Judges of Peace), public mediation and arbitration centers, including Consume Conflicts Arbitration Centers – CCACs.
- Actually, one of the most common type of conflict is the conflict on consume relations. Interfering deeply with the functioning of the economy and with the satisfaction of the consumer's needs it must be solved fast, efficiently and at a low cost;
- Consume conflict arbitration has been assumed as the best way of solving this kind of conflicts, arising out of the acquisition of goods and service's provision by single or collective person having a professional economic activity aiming at getting benefits;
- In Portugal there is nowadays a network of arbitration centers covering the whole country and making possible the resolution of consume conflicts;
- These Arbitration Centers use the usual ADR systems: mediation, conciliation, arbitration;
- The European Institutions are committed to the creation of an internal market functioning without constraints, being legal security an important pillar for commerce development;
- In this sense and in order to meet the challenges of the construction of a unique internal market functioning safely and with respect for consumer's rights, on 8th July 2013 entered into force Directive 2013/11/EU of the European Parliament and Council from the 21st of May (Directive ADR) on Alternative Dispute Resolution, opening to European consumers the possibility of new, fast, efficient and less costly solutions for solving consumer's conflicts arising in national State Members spaces or in different State Members;
- This Directive and the Regulation 524/2013 of the European Parliament and Council from the 21st of May, (Regulation ODR – Online Conflict Resolution) are two complementary and interconnected instruments;
- ODR Regulation has the aim of creating a ODR Platform that must be available in the whole EU space from the 9th of January 2016. This platform must assume the form of a interactive web site, with one only entry point for consumers and for commercial providers willing to solve extra judicially conflicts arising out of online transactions;
- The ODR platform is now being tested and this work tried to foresee the service that will be available to consumers and commercial providers in the beginning of 2016.

REFERENCES

Almeida, T. (2001). *Lei de defesa do Consumidor Anotada*. Lisboa: Instituto do Consumidor. (In Portuguese)

Castells, M. (2005). A sociedade em rede. In G. Cardoso & C. Conceição (Eds.), *A sociedade em rede em Portugal*. Porto: Campo das Letras.

De Vries, B. R., Leenes, R., & Zeleznikow, J. (2005) Fundamentals of providing negotiation support online: the need for developing BATNAs. In *Proceedings of the Second International ODR Workshop*. Wolf Legal Publishers.

Galanter, M. (1993). *Direito em abundância:a a actividade legislativa no Atlântico Norte. Revista Critica de Ciências Sociais, n.º 36*. Coimbra: Centro de Estudos Sociais. (In Portuguese)

Goodman, J. W. (2003). *The pros and cons of online dispute resolution: an assessment of cyber-mediation websites*. Retrieved from http://scholarship.law.duke.edu/cgi/viewcontent.cgi?article=1073&context=dltr

Gouveia, L. M., & Gaio, S. (Eds.). (2004). Sociedade da Informação: balanço e implicações. Porto: Edições Universidade Fernando Pessoa. (In Portuguese)

Katsch, E., & Rifkin, J. (2001). *Online Dispute Resolution, Resolving Conflicts in Cyberspace*. San Francisco, CA: Jossey-Bass Wiley Company.

Pedroso, J. (2006). A justiça em Portugal entre a(s) crise(s) e a(s) oportunidade(s) – Contributo para a construção de um novo paradigma de política pública de justiça. In Scientia Iuridica, Tomo LV – n.º 306 – abril/junho de 2006. (In Portuguese)

Raiffa, H. (1982). *The art and science of negotiation: how to resolve conflicts and get the best out of bargaining*. Cambridge, MA: The Belknap Press of Harvard University Press.

Steenbergen, W. (2005). Rationalizing Dispute Resolution: from best alternative to the most likely one. In *Proceedings of 3rd ODR Workshop*.

Wilde, Z., & Gaibrois, L. (2003). *O que é a Mediação*. Coimbra Editora. (In Portuguese)

Zuckerman, A. (1999). *Civil Justice in Crisis*. Oxford University Press.

KEY TERMS AND DEFINITIONS

ADR Procedures: Mediation, conciliation and arbitration, in accordance with subparagraph i) of article 3 of Law No. 144/2015 of 8 September, implementing Directive 2013/11 / EU, the European Parliament and of the Council of 21 May 2013 on the alternative resolution of consumer disputes.

Arbitration: Form of extrajudicial resolution of a conflict, where an arbitrator, usually a third party chosen by the parties, decides a question which necessarily involves discussion of available rights.

Conciliation: In conciliation, the third party (mediator) has a kind of more active intervention than the mediator, moving forward with proposals for the parties to choose among them a solution to their dispute.

Consumer Disputes: Those arising from acquisition of goods, provision of services or the transmission of any rights for non-professional use and supplied by a natural or legal person, who performs with professional character an economic activity aimed at obtaining benefits.

Consumer Society: Society developed from the second half of the twentieth century, where supply often exceeds demand, the products are standardized and consumption patterns are commoditized.

Mediation: The European Code of Conduct for Mediators defines it as "the process in which two or more parties agree to appoint a third party (mediator) to help resolve a conflict through an agreement without a sentence, regardless of the procedure the process can be conducted in each Member State. "

ODR Platform: Regulation (EU) No 524/2013 the European Parliament and of the Council of 21 May 2013 on resolving online consumer disputes (ODR Regulation) proposes an ODR platform to be available to companies and consumers from January 9, 2016 that should take the form of an "interactive website, with a single point of entry to consumers and traders seeking to resolve disputes arising from online transactions by extrajudicial means."

ENDNOTES

[1]   The Portuguese Decree 24/2014 (art. 3 f)) A alínea f) do art.º 3.º do Dec-Lei n.º 24/2014, defines distance contracting as " contract celebrated between consumer and the goods or services provider without the simultaneous physical presence of both and integrated in a system of sales or service provision organized for distance commerce through the exclusive use of one or more distance communication techniques, including the contract celebration. Furthermore, article 3 m) considers technique of distance communication any means that, without the simultaneous physical presence of the provider of goods or services and of the consumer, may be used in order to celebrate the contract between the parties.

[2]   Art. 2 nr. 1 of Law 24/96 defines consumer as "the one to whom goods or services are provided, or any rights transmitted, destined to a non professional use, by someone acting as a professional of an economic activity aimed at getting profits.

[3]   According to a Report of ACEPI/IDC (Association of Digital Economy / International Data Corporation) "Digital Economy in Portugal in 2009- 2017, there were in 2012 around 2,5 million internauts in the world, and in the same year there were 850 thousand millions of euros in online sales at world level, generating 350 billion in electronic invoices (being 200 billion in the modality B2C), being 300 thousand millions in Europe. In the same year of 2012 it is estimated that 2 thousand million mobile devices have been sold (PC's, tablets and smartphones).

[4]   According to the referred ACEPI / IDC Report on electronic commerce in Portugal already reaches 49,8 thousand million euros, meaning 32% of the GDP, being estimated that in 2020 it may reach 90 thousand million euros, representing then around 54% of GDP.

[5]   Also the study "One day of our lives in the Internet" promoted by Nova Expressão in partnership with Marktest reveals that currently 79% of the Portuguese assumes to shop on-line. In 2011 it was about only 15%. http://www.marktest.com/wap/a/n/id~1e61.aspx (In Portuguese).

[6]   Actually, due to diverse factors out of the scope of this work, but in which the high costs of legal taxes play an important role, this number decreased to 712.719 in 2013.

[7]   Bulletin of Statistical Information nr. 20 of DGPJ – Direção Geral da Política de Justiça (General Direction of Justice Policy).

[8]   In Portugal, there is a doubt whether or not a consumer may be only a physical person or also a legal person.

[9]   CACC or Arbitration Centers.

[10]   Initially in Lisbon, Seixal, Oliveira do Bairro e Vila Nova de Gaia.

[11]   JPs in Portugal were created by Law 78/2001 of 13th July 2001.

[12]   http://www.conselhodosjulgadosdepaz.com.pt

[13]   After the publication of Law nr. 6/2011 from the 10th of March which modified the Law nr. 23/96, consume conflicts concerning essential public services are now subject to necessary arbitration whenever, by express choice of the users physical persons these conflicts are submitted to the Arbitral Court of legally authorized Arbitration Centers (article 15 nr. 1).

[14]   This is an important advantage since arbitration processes in Arbitration Centers for Consume Conflicts take in average less than 90 days.

[15]   This is what happens to arbitration centers functioning within entrepreneurial associations or chambers of commerce and industry to solve commercial litigation between corporations that require a conflict resolution in short delays of time. As an example, it must be referred the Institute of Arbitration of the Commercial Association of Porto.

[16]   Art. 62 nr. 1 of Law of Voluntary Arbitration states that the creation of institutionalized arbitration centers is subject to authorization of the Ministry of Justice according the corresponding special legislation (Decree of Law 425/86 from the 27th December).

[17]   In Portugal economic operators are generally obliged to have, and make available to costumers, the Reclamation's Book whose models and rules are defined by the Government (Decree of Law 156/2005 from the 15th of September, modified by the Decree of Law 371/2007 from the 6th November and by the Decree of Law 118/2009 from the 19th May).

[18]   The Decree of Law 425/86 from the 27th December defines the procedures to be observed by entities that want to follow voluntary arbitration. As it is stated in its Foreword the diffusion of the mechanisms of voluntary arbitration is one of the ways to unblock the activity of the courts; furthermore, comparative experiences show that this alternative means of conflict solving has the capacity of performing a sure and dignified justice.

[19]   According to information available at DGPJ website http://www.dgpj.mj.pt, acceded in 12th May 2015, there were 32 institutional Arbitration Centers.

[20]   Article 4 of the Regulation of CIAB states in nr. 1 that mediation is a procedure in which a third party tries to get the parties in the conflict closer and providing them the required support for them to solve, by themselves, the conflict. In nr. 2 it is said that mediation must ensure the respect of the principles of independence, impartiality, neutrality, transparency, efficiency, legality, freedom, representation, celerity and confidentiality in accordance with the established in European Conventions.

In nr. 3 it is stated that mediation may be undertaken without the physical presence of the parties, by distance communication means, or by previous scheduling in the presence of the parties.

In nr. 4 it is said that presential mediation depends on the signature of a consent by all the persons present in the session and will occur.

[1.]   If both parties live in the same municipality it will be in the municipalities facilities, except if one or two parties opt for the Center facilities.

[2.]   In case of not occurring common residence, it will be in the Center facilities, except if the parties agree on another location compatible with the logistic capacities of the Center.

Nr. 5: for the purpose of participation in presential mediation sessions, the Center will have resident mediators, duly certified, and it may furthermore be created, on decision of the Administration of the Center, a group of external mediators, included in a list of mediators to whom parties may have access according to rules to be established by the Administration.

Nr. 6 states that parties must, preferently, appear personally in mediation sessions, but they also may be represented by mandator duly credentiated for the purpose, with special powers in order to confess, give up or agree.

Nr. 7 says mediation must be concluded in the maximum delay of 30 days counting from the date of first reply of the addressed party.

Nr. 8 says mediation may have a prorogation for a new 30 days period following fundamented proposal in that sense by the assistant legal officer to the executive director.

Nr. 9 states that mediation may have a prorogation due to an agreement of the parties.

Nr. 10 says that in case the parties agree to require it, the agreement may be in written document signed by both parties and by the mediator .

Nr. 11 says that, in the previous number's case, the original of the agreement will be archived in the process and in the informatics application, and simple copies of it will be delivered to the parties, who may still require the delivery of certified copies.

[21] In conciliation, the conciliator may advance with other possible solutions, contrarily to mediation where the solutions must arise out of the parties.

[22] Nr. 2 of Article 13 of CIAB Regulation refers that the resolution of the conflict by arbitration may only be initiated if previously had occurred the attempt of resolution through conciliation directed by the executive director of the Center or assistant legal officer designed for such purpose.

[23] Nr. 2 of such article states that there may exist maritime courts, arbitral courts and Judges of Peace.

[24] the following numbers of article 2 refer wide possibilities of meeting this requirement of form.

[25] Arbitral regulations of CACCs are not uniform, which is one aspect to be reviewed in its functioning, since it is of utmost convenience an harmonization of the main aspects of its procedural aspects, such as the value of the process, delays, production of proof, among others. A curious remark must be noticed because Decree of Law 425/86 from the 27th December, concerning the procedures of entities willing to go through institutionalized arbitration does not impose the obligation for them to have an arbitral regulation.

[26] Article 16 d) of Law 31/86 from the 29th of August imposed as essential that both parties must be heard, verbally or in written, before a final decision is issued.

[27] Article 13 nr. 4 of CIAB states that in arbitration process it is mandatory to have a constituted lawyer in processes with a value higher than the one of the "Alçada" (reference value) of the Judicial Court in 1st instance. But the parties may designate someone to represent or assist them in the other cases, namely the DECO – Association of Defense of Consumer or an entrepreneurial association in which the party is affiliated. Concerning the representation in mediation sessions in CACCs, see art. 4 nr. 6 of the Regulation of CIAB.

[28] In the Regulation of CIAB – Arbitral Court for Consume it is admitted 3estimonies for each invoked fact and 6 in total (article 15 nr. 1 d)).

[29] Article 39 nr. 1 LAV and art. 17 nr. 3 Regulation of CIAB – Arbitral Court of Consume.

[30] Article 59 nr. 9 LVA.

[31] Yet, the nr. 5 of the same article states that in case of major force or just impeachment of the arbitrator, the referred delay may be widened to 30 days.

[32] Article 22 nr. 2 of the Regulation states that the Regulation is to be applied from the 9th January 2016, with just the following exceptions:

article 2 nr. 3 and article 7 nrs 1 and 5 are to be applied from the 9th July 2015.

article 5 nrs. 1 and 7, article 6, article 7 nr. 7, article 8 nrs. 3 and 4, and articles 11, 16 and 17 are to be applied from the 8th July 2013.

[33] One of such difficulties relates to article 5 nr. 2 of the Regulation which states that "it must be an interactive web site, free of cost and accessible online, in all the official languages of the European Union".

[34] Yet, experimental access is available to those who make part of the specialists group in Alternative Dispute Resolution, appointed by the Portuguese Government in order to participate in the development tests of the platform.

35   Although usually the Portuguese arbitration centers are unidirectional in terms of submission of claims (that is, they only accept claims submitted by consumers in the sense of art. 2 nr. 1 of Law 24/96 of the 31st of July), article 2 nr. 2 of the ODR Regulation allows the access to extrajudicial conflict resolution to commercial providers acting against consumers provided that the legislation of the Member State where consumer has its usual residence allows this litigation to be solved by ADR / ODR. Yet, nr. 4 of the said article does not impose on Member States to assure that ADR entities provide extrajudicial procedures to these conflicts.

36   For advantages and disadvantages of ODR in general cfr. Joseph W. Goodman (2003) "The pros and cons of online dispute resolution: an assessment of cyber-mediation websites" in http://scholarship.law.duke.edu/cgi/viewcontent.cgi?article=1073&context=dltr

37   Katsch & Rifkin (2001) refer technology as the 4th party in Online Dispute Resolution.

38   For instance, applications allowing to easily determine BATNA – Best Alternative to a Negotiated Agreement, WATNA – Worst Alternative to a Negotiated Agreement, MLATNA – Most Likely Alternative to a Negotiated Agreement, EATNA – Estimated Alternative to a Negotiated Agreement or ZOPA – Zone of Possible Agreement in a Conflict.

39   Ebay Resolution Center http://res.ebay.com/ws/eBayISAPI.dll?ResolutionCenter, or Movistar's http://www.movistar.es/particulares/atencion-cliente/reclamaciones for instance.

40   Mediation Arbitration Resolution Services (Mars, USA) in www.resolvemydispute.com, for all kind of litigation, including a web platform with video and conferencing or also ADR Group (United Kingdom) in www.adrgroupe.co.uk, specialized in commercial, civil and family conflicts, providing a platform for discussion and mediation sessions in real time are but a few examples.

41   This is clearly a tendency of ODR systems. Obviously, in certain ODR procedures there are costs and, sometimes, costs that the parties may consider truly high.

42   When it is the case (mediator, conciliator, arbitrator, ombudsman).

43   Software allowing internet communication through voice connections on IP (the VOIP system).

44   That is an interesting possibility, although some might refer that the possibility of not seeing the other party is the really interesting feature of ODR.

45   Of course, quite often advantages may quickly become disadvantages. For instance Accessibility and Info-exclusion (due to economic reasons or digital illiteracy, for instance).

46   For instance, in Telefonica ODR system (Spain).

47   This also may be seen as an advantage or as a disadvantage. In certain mediation procedures secrecy and confidentiality of the meetings are required. But is this confidentiality ensured in an environment such as Internet?

48   However, privacy is very difficult to ensure in environments such as Internet.

Chapter 9
Agreement Technologies for Conflict Resolution

Vicente Julian
Universidad Politécnica de Valencia, Spain

Stella Heras
Universidad Politécnica de Valencia, Spain

Victor Sanchez-Anguix
Coventry University, UK

Carlos Carrascosa
Universidad Politécnica de Valencia, Spain

ABSTRACT

Recently, artificial intelligence, has emerged as a new source of scientific works in conflict resolution. The interest in conflict resolution lies in diverse reasons. One of the main reasons is that computational systems have gradually shifted towards a distributed paradigm where heterogeneous entities should include computational conflict resolution mechanisms, such as proposed by agreement technologies. This chapter gives an overview of these technologies, which are needed in order to ensure the accomplishment of the global system goal and to solve conflicts. Among agreement technologies, automated negotiation is proposed as one key mechanism in conflict resolution due to its analogous use in human conflict resolution. Automated negotiation consists of an automated exchange of proposals carried out by software agents on behalf of their users. Another key technology is argumentation, which provides a fruitful means of dealing with conflicts and knowledge inconsistencies. Agents can reach agreements by engaging in argumentation dialogues with their opponents in a discussion.

INTRODUCTION

Agreement Technologies (AT) is a new discipline, which covers a range of specific techniques for dealing with interactions in dynamic, open environments (Ossowsky, 2013; Sierra, Botti & Ossowski, 2011). They address issues such as finding ways to negotiate, agree and cooperate with other agents, and developing appropriate means of forming and managing coalitions. These aspects are extremely related with the concept of conflict resolution. Conflict is an omnipresent phenomenon in human society, which is related with the necessity to achieve an agreement between entities. Conflict spans from individual decision making trade-offs such as deciding what to do next (sleep, eat, work, play), to complex scenarios including politics and business. Over the last decades, computer science has tried to study conflict from

DOI: 10.4018/978-1-5225-0245-6.ch009

a computational perspective. Conflict is a ubiquitous phenomenon and arises in many areas of our lives. It arises and needs to be dealt with in social settings, such as a group of friends deciding on a vacation or contract negotiation in business and politics (Browder, 2000), as well as in individual settings related to action selection (e.g., how to weigh one's preferences and decide what product to buy). Even if we are not aware of it, we are continuously facing conflict and attempting to solve it.

Different proposals based on agreement technologies have been developed with conflict resolution as their main research goal. For instance, automated negotiation approaches have been proposed as set of algorithms and protocols whose mission is providing effective deals in electronic marketplaces (Jennings et al, 2001; Parsons, Rodriguez-Aguilar & Klein, 2011; Sanchez-Anguix, Julian, Botti, & García-Fornes, 2013). Researchers in argumentation aim to solve conflicts by means of dialogue games, speech particles and information rebuttal (Rahwan et al, 2003). Works in cooperation and coordination try to give a joint solution to a problem, usually with no global information or control (Rebollo, Carrascosa, & Palomares, 2014). Reputation is another way to solve conflicts when an entity must to decide about other entities (Pinyol, Sabater-Mir, 2013). Finally, agent organizations, inspired by the metaphor of human organizations, allow achieving global goals (and solve conflicts) by using norms, plans and structures formally specified (Argente et al 2011; Hübner, Sichman & Boissier).

This chapter explores in detail several works done in the area of agreement technologies, which can be used as a way to engage new conflict resolution approach along with new challenges to face by these technologies. During the chapter we discuss different types of agreement and agreement processes related to conflict resolution, describing and relating the different technologies and application areas involved. First, the different related technologies are briefly introduced. After this, a detailed analysis of negotiation and argumentation technologies is introduced in the following sections.

AGREEMENT TECHNOLOGIES

Open multi-agent systems are distributed systems where heterogeneous agents, with their own goals, can enter and leave the system during the life of the system (Hewitt, 1991). For instance, we can think of an electronic commerce platform as an open system where users, human or even automated software, act according to their own interests: in the case of sellers to maximize their own profits, and in the case of buyers to acquire some goods at relatively good price. Since agents have different goals, act based on their goals, and they can be heterogeneous (i.e., humans and software agents may show different behaviors), it is feasible to find situations where an agent's goals conflict with other agents' goals. If we refer ourselves to the example of electronic commerce, the buyer may want to buy the product at a low price, while the seller may want to maximize its revenue. In these situations, mechanisms that allow agents to coordinate, regulate their behavior, and solve conflicts are needed.

Electronic commerce is not the only application where conflict may make act of presence. For instance, in the last few years, grid computing (Foster, Kesselman & Tuecke, 2001) has emerged as a new paradigm of computation where different entities collaborate to accomplish several tasks. In grid computing, entities share several resources: from hardware resources (e.g., computing nodes) to software resources (e.g., services). How should those resources be distributed among the different tasks or users of the system? Presumably, users want the best response time for their tasks, and resource owners want to take the highest profit of their resources. Resource allocation is a delicate matter, especially when collaboration requires cross-boundary relationships. Software mechanisms that solve conflict in these scenarios are needed.

Even purely cooperative applications like rescue applications (Kitano & Tadokoro, 2001) are not alien to conflict. In multi-robot systems for rescue applications, information is usually distributed among the different robotic agents. Coordination among these entities is a problem itself, which becomes more acute when agents' opinions and information conflict. How should these entities solve conflict and rescue as many persons as possible while making an efficient use of the computational resources? Again, software tools and mechanisms are necessary to tackle with conflicts.

The concept of Agreement Technologies (Luck & McBurney, 2008; Ossowsky, 2013; Sierra et al 2011) has been coined in the last few years as an umbrella term for addressing all of those technologies that are envisioned to collaborate, directly or indirectly, to the resolution of conflicts in software systems, and specifically in MAS systems. Even though which works can be considered agreement technologies are arguable (since the contribution to the resolution of a conflict may be indirect), some authors distinguish between several challenges that need to be solved in the so-called agreement technologies.

In this chapter, we position ourselves with the taxonomy/challenges introduced by Sierra et al (2011). Despite the fact that negotiation and argumentation will be the focus of this chapter, we think that it is important to briefly describe every technology involved in agreement technologies. Next, we briefly describe each of the challenges mentioned by Sierra et al. (see Figure 1): (i) Semantics: The current trend of service-oriented computing (Papazoglou & Georgakopoulos, 2003) has changed the way in which complex systems are built. Nowadays, software is built by using diverse services offered by very different providers. Given the heterogeneity of service providers, it is logic to think that service information is provided in different communication languages, and even using different terms to address the same concept (i.e., different ontologies). Whenever a software system needs to cooperate or solve a conflictive situation with other systems, it requires of mechanisms that allow understanding other software systems by matching and aligning ontologies and semantic concepts (Noy, 2004) (Choi, Song & Han, 2006);

Figure 1. Agreement technologies architecture

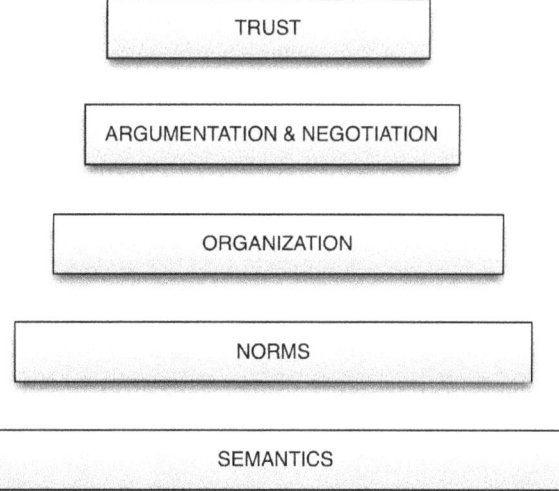

(ii) Norms: Most distributed applications are no longer static but open, and agents can exhibit a varied spectrum of behaviors. One possible way of "solving" conflict is avoiding conflict, establishing mechanisms that preclude agents of reaching a conflictive situation. Normative systems (Boella, Van Der Torre & Verhagen, 2006; Criado, Argente, & Botti, 2013) are envisioned with such purpose (among others). The society of agents is regulated by norms, which define which actions/states are to be punished in the system (e.g., to avoid conflict) and which actions/states are to be rewarded (e.g., promote actions that avoid conflict); (iii) Organizations: Agents usually have limited computational capabilities. Therefore, if a complex problem needs to be solved, agents need to join together as a group and coordinate to reach such complex goal. Agent organizations (Argente et al, 2011; Esparcia & Argente, 2011; Horling & Lesser, 2008) may be seen as large and implicit coordination mechanisms that establish the roles to be played by agents and the interaction protocols to be carried out among organizational members. In this sense, agent organizations may conflict by strictly defining the structure and interactions of the group; (iv) Trust: Trust mechanisms (Sabater & Sierra, 2005; Such, Espinosa, Garcia-Fornes & Botti, 2011), usually used in concordance with reputation models, are devised to help agents to select whom they should interact with. Trust is formed from one's own past experiences with other agents. To put it simply, positive experiences should bias one agent to collaborate and interact with the other party, whereas negative experiences should bias one agent to avoid interactions with the other party. Reputation is built according to the opinion that agent societies have on individuals. Trust and reputation mechanisms may help to reduce conflict by interacting with good partners; and, finally, (v) Negotiation & Argumentation, which can be considered the main components, from the point of view of conflict resolution. For this reason, these two topics will be explained in detail in the following sections.

NEGOTIATION

Negotiation is the main technology of agreement technologies that makes possible for agents to solve conflicts. In this case, imitating how humans solve conflicts, agents negotiate looking for an agreement that is acceptable for all of the involved entities. It would not be possible for agents to solve conflict without this technology, at least not in an efficient way. Despite negotiation being crucial for solving conflicts, it should be highlighted that it requires of other technologies as semantics, norms, organizations, and trust to help in the resolution of conflicts. Semantics may help heterogeneous agents to form a negotiation domain (e.g., negotiation problem) that is understandable by all of the parties involved in the conflict situation. Then, society's norms may be used to formally force agents to respect established agreements. Otherwise, agents would violate agreements whenever it suits them. Organizations establish a framework where roles and possible interaction protocols are formalized, giving room negotiations with clear rules of interaction (e.g., negotiation protocols), and helping agents to identify and search conflicting agents based on the information provided by roles (e.g., sellers and buyers are classical roles in conflict). Trust and reputation may guide agents to select negotiation opponents that are more likely to guarantee a good service. Hence, every technology in agreement technologies collaborates along negotiation in leading conflict situations towards good terms. Despite being part of a new topic like agreement technologies, automated negotiation has been studied by scholars for a few years.

Negotiation can be defined as a process in which two or more parties make a joint decision. The parties first verbalize contradictory demands and then move towards agreement by a process of concession-making or search for new alternatives (Pruitt, 1981). Analogously, automated negotiation consists of an automated search process for an agreement between two or more software parties. Two different research lines can be distinguished in automated negotiation models: game-theoretic models and heuristic models. Since the decade of the 50's, automated negotiation has been studied in game theory. Game theory researchers focus on reaching optimal solutions under assumptions of unbounded computational resources, complete/partial information regarding the strategies and preferences of other parties. Some of the most important theoretical results come from game theory, like the work of Nash (1950), Rubinstein (1982), Binmore et al (1986), and more recent studies like Fatima et al. (2004) and In and Serrano (2003). Although game theory studies are interesting from a theoretical point of view, most of them make strong assumptions that may not hold in real applications. For instance, computational resources are of extreme importance for agents since they may be scarce and shared among different tasks. Thus, negotiation should not always assume un-bounded computational resources. Additionally, since agents are heterogeneous, not all of the agents know the same strategies. Identifying which strategies each agent knows may be a hard task that can only be successful after several negotiations. The same goes for the knowledge regarding the opponents' preferences, reservations values, and so forth. Hence, models that tackle uncertainty and limit the use of computational resources are mandatory for some situations.

Heuristic models tackle the problem mentioned above. They do not calculate the optimum agreement, but they obtain results that aim to be as close as possible to the optimum. Heuristic models assume imperfect knowledge regarding the opponent and the environment, and aim to be computationally tractable while obtaining good results. The reader is assumed to have some working knowledge on heuristic models for automated negotiation. In other case, the reading of several introductory texts and reviews like (Guttman, Moukas & Maes, 1998; Beam, Segev, 1997; Kraus, 1997; Jennings et al, 2001; Lomuscio, Wooldridge & Jennings, 2003; Lopes, Wooldridge & Novais, 2008) is recommended. The amount of literature in automated negotiation is vast and immense, ranging from bilateral negotiations, to multi-party negotiations. An extensive review of all of the problems in automated negotiation would be an almost non-feasible task. Following, we discuss some of the most important works in the area of automated negotiation and bilateral negotiation.

Concession Strategies

The classic view of artificial intelligence with respect to negotiation in incomplete information settings is that agents need to eventually concede in order to reach an agreement (Faratin, Sierra, & Jennings, 1998; Bui, Venkatesh, & Kieronska, 1999; Hindriks & Tykhonov, 2008). However, agents can concede in very different magnitudes and in different rounds of the negotiation. Concession strategies determine how the agents concede and when these concessions are carried out.

The most influential work regarding concession strategies is, perhaps, the work of Faratin et al. (1998). The authors proposed concession strategies that are a mix of different families of concession tactics. The authors divide concession tactics into three different families:

- **Time-Dependent Tactics:** These tactics take into account the remaining time in the negotiation to carry out concessions. In this family, we can distinguish between linear tactics, boulware tactics, and conceder tactics. On the one hand, linear tactics carry out the same amount concession at each negotiation round until the reservation value is reached. On the other hand, conceder tactics concede very rapidly towards the reservation value in the first interactions, whereas boulware tactics concede very slowly during the first negotiation rounds, but it concedes faster as the negotiation process approaches the deadline.

- **Behavior-Dependent Tactics:** In the case of behavior-dependent tactics, the concession carried out by the agent depends on the negotiation movements performed by the opponent in the previous rounds. The classic tactic in this family is tit-for-tat, which mimics the concession carried out by the opponent in the previous round. Other variants of tit-for-tat include random absolute tit-for-tat, which performs the absolute concession carried out by the opponent in the last offer plus/minus a small deviation, and averaged tit-for-tat which takes the window of past opponent offers and carries out the average concession carried out by the opponent.
- **Resource-Dependent Tactics:** This family of tactics computes concession based on the scarceness of a resource in the environment and resource consumption (i.e., time, product quantity, messages, etc.). In general, the scarcer the resource, the more eager should be the agent to maintain/obtain such resource.

Another classic concession based model for bilateral multi-issue negotiations is the Agent Based Market Place (ABMP) framework proposed in (Jonker, Robu & Treur, 2007; Jonker & Treur, 2001). ABMP is a negotiation framework, based on additive utility functions, where proposed bids are concessions to previous bids. The amount of concession is regulated by the concession factor (i.e., reservation utility), the negotiation speed, the acceptable utility gap (the maximal difference between the target utility and the utility of an offer that is acceptable), and the impatience factor, which governs the probability of the agent leaving the negotiation process. Additionally, the framework includes other remarkable characteristics such as the possibility of sharing preference information with the other party, and guessing heuristics that allows agents to determine the ranking of issues and issue values based on the bid history.

Similarity Mechanisms in Negotiation

One of the traditional mechanisms proposed in the literature for solving conflicts is the use of similarity mechanisms. They can be used to solve a current conflict based on solutions given to previous conflicts or as mechanisms that implicitly approximate offers to opponents' preferences. Basically, the two similarity mechanisms more widely used are Case Based Reasoning (Leake, 1994;(Lopez de Mantaras, 2001) and similarity heuristics (Faratin, Sierra & Jennings, 2002; Lai, Sycara & Li, 2008).

Sycara proposed a mediator that uses case based reasoning for solving conflicts in the labor domain (i.e., PERSUADER) (Sycara, 1989, 1990, 1991). PERSUADER takes as input a set of conflicting goals and outputs an agreed plan of actions. The system keeps track of the agreements found in past negotiations and, once a new conflict situation is present, it looks for the most similar past situation. The retrieved agreement is adapted to the present conflict situation, since the rationale behind this heuristic is that similar conflict situations should yield similar solutions.

Another popular use of similarity mechanisms is implicitly approximating one's own proposals to the preferences of the opponent. This is usually carried out by means of similarity heuristics that look for trade-offs. A trade-off consists in decrementing the benefit obtained from some negotiations issues that are not important for us but are important of the other agent, in order to get the decremented benefit as an equivalent increase in the benefit obtained by other issues that are important for us but are not important for the other agent. Faratin et al. (2002) introduced the use of similarity heuristics in bilateral multi-issue negotiations to compute similarity between pairs of others. Given a certain utility u demanded by one of the agents, this agent proposes the offer with utility u that is the most similar to the previous offer proposed by the opponent. The idea behind this heuristic is that the more similar the offer is to the previous opponent offer, the more acceptable it is for the opponent. For computing the similarity between two offers, a fuzzy similarity criterion between issue values. The main drawback of fuzzy similarity heuristics is that they require domain knowledge regarding the similarity between issue values for the opponent.

The use of similarity heuristics was reintroduced again by Lai et al (2008). In this work, a bilateral negotiation protocol for multi-issue negotiations, where agents are capable of sending up to k different offers per round, is presented. The k offers sent by agents are selected from the iso-utility curve, which contains all of the offers with a certain utility. The offer that is selected is the one that is the most similar to the previous opponent offer that reported the most utility. The other k-1 offers are selected randomly from the iso-utility curve. In this case, the similarity heuristic employed is the Euclidean distance. As a similarity measure, Euclidean distance may be less powerful than fuzzy similarity, but it has the advantage of being more general and not requiring domain knowledge.

Bayesian Learning in Negotiation

When reviewing the use of Bayesian learning in negotiation, we cannot forget about the seminal work of Zeng and Sycara (1998). In this article, authors argue about the benefits of using Bayesian models in negotiation. They study a bilateral negotiation case where the buyer attempts to learn the reservation price of a seller by updating its beliefs with Bayesian learning. Despite the fact that it introduces the use of Bayesian learning in negotiation, the applicability of the article is limited since it only focuses on single issue models.

Bayesian classifiers have been used to model the preferences of negotiating agents. In Bui et al. (1999), the authors propose a multi-party cooperative negotiation mechanism for the distributed meeting scheduling domain. Agents start from an initial set of possible agreements and jointly look for good collective agreements by partitioning the set of possible agreements in a tree until a set with only one agreement (leaf node) that is acceptable by all of the agents is found. From the joint set of possible agreements, each agent proposes a partition of such set where the final agreement will be looked for. Agents decide on which set should be explored from all of the partitions that have been proposed. If all of the agents agree on the partition to be selected, the partition becomes the new joint set of possible agreements and the refinement process continues. Otherwise, agents exchange preferences on the proposed partitions and the partition that maximizes the preferences of the group is selected as the next joint set of agreements. In order to save messages exchanged, the agents employ Bayesian classifiers to learn the preferences of other agents according to the information gathered from the cur- rent and past negotiations. Intervals of utility are used as classes and partitions represent attributes of the Bayesian model.

Genetic Algorithms in Negotiation

Genetic Algorithms (GAs) (Goldberg, 1989) have also contributed to the state-of-art in automated negotiation. They are general optimization and learning algorithms based on the evolutionary processes found in the nature. Candidate solutions for a problem form the genetic population of the algorithm, which gradually converges towards high quality solutions by applying genetic operators like mutation and crossover. GAs are general, which means that they do not rely on a specific problem structure. Additionally, they can be used as an implicit learning and adaptation mechanism in environments where dynamics and structure is also uncertain. This is perhaps what makes GA an adequate approach to negotiation problems, since they can be used to learn and adapt both to the opponent and the environment.

The seminal work of GA's in Automated Negotiation is Oliver et al. (1996). They focused on evolving negotiation strategies for bilateral multi-issue negotiations where agents' preferences are represented by means of additive utility functions. In the proposed negotiation framework, a negotiation strategy is a set sequential rules (i.e., rules that are applied in sequential order according to the round), where a rule is a utility threshold that determines if an offer from the opponent is acceptable and a counter-offer to be made to the other party in case that the opponent's offer is not acceptable. Faratin et al. (1998) introduced a negotiation framework for bilateral negotiations where agents' concession strategies can be classified into time-dependent strategies, behavior-dependent strategies and resource-dependent strategies. Matos et al. (1998) proposed a framework where the concession to be carried out in each negotiation issue is a linear combination of the concession of the families of concessions strategies proposed by Faratin. The main research goal of Matos et al. (1998) is determining which the optimal negotiation strategies in different negotiation environments are. For this purpose, an evolutionary process is proposed where the weights given to the concession strategies for each negotiation issue represent a candidate solution in a genetic algorithm. Populations of sellers and buyers with different negotiation strategies negotiate in a round robin way. After each round robin round, negotiation strategies are assigned a fitness value which takes into account the utility obtained in the negotiations and the numbers of messages exchanged. The highest fitness negotiation strategies for sellers and buyers become the parents of the next population of negotiation strategies, which is obtained by the application of genetic operators like mutation and crossover. Eventually, the population of negotiation strategies for sellers and buyers converges towards an optimal set of strategies for the environment under study. The advantage of this proposal with respect to Oliver (1996) is that the evolutionary process does not depend on the number of negotiation rounds but on the number of negotiation issues, which results in a more tractable search space.

Offline Learning in Negotiation

By offline learning we refer to a learning process that is carried out after or before the negotiation process starts. Hence, the model is not updated during the negotiation and it requires of several iterations of the negotiation game to learn an educated model. From the works that we have already reviewed, we can highlight some works like Buffett and Spencer (2007) where the learning of the Bayesian classifiers is carried out before the negotiation starts. However, there are also other approaches that have advocated for the use of learning before or after the negotiation process.

For instance, Coehoorn and Jennings (2004) propose the use of kernel density (Sheather & Jones, 1991) for the estimation of the weights of the opponent's additive utility function. The negotiation model revolves around the idea that a rational agent gradually con- cedes towards its reservation utility, and a rational agent should concede less on the most important issues at the start of the negotiation and concede more on the least important issues. Given this assumption, the agent calculates for each pair of consecutive offers the concession carried out in each issue, and an educated guess of the weight based on such concession. Each tuple, composed of the difference between pairs of consecutive offers, the estimated weight, and the probability density of the weight, forms a three dimensional kernel that is used along the other kernels to calculate an estimation of the real issue weight.

Another set of approaches that heavily rely on offline learning are those approaches based on Artificial Neural Networks (Carbonneau, Kersten & Vahidov, 2008; Carbonneau, Kersten & Vahidov, 2011). In Carbonneau et al. (2008), authors propose a neural network that takes as input the negotiation history of a bilateral negotiation with continuous issues and an offer to make an estimation of the opponent's counter-offer. The major drawback of this approach is that it requires that an artificial neural network is trained per negotiation case. Similarly, the same authors propose an improvement over their previous work in (Carbonneau, Kersten & Vahidov, 2011). It aims to make a predictive model that does not depend on the negotiation case. The model takes pairs of negotiation issues as inputs of the neural network, where one of the issues is considered the primary issue (i.e., independent variable) and the other issue is considered the secondary issue (i.e., dependent variable). The neural network may also take historical information from each issue like the minimum value, maximum value, average value, etc.

Complex Interdependent Utility Functions

Negotiation processes normally consist in the exchange of proposal between the involved parties. One of the key issues in negotiation strategies is the way in which the agents' preferences are represented. This issue strongly affects how proposals are evaluated and how offers should be generated. In processes where just a single issue is involved, it is quite clear how to evaluate and generate proposals: the value of the issue. However, it is not easy to give a valuation when multiple issues are involved. The multi-attribute utility theory (Wallenius, 2008; Keeney & Raiffa, 1993) comes into play in this case. This theory provides mechanisms for the evaluation of proposals composed of multiple issues. Classic multi-attribute theory has considered that issues are independent. Issue independence means that the value of negotiation issues does not affect the valuation of other issues. Hence, a classic way of representing such preferences is by means of linear additive utility functions. Despite the fact that linear additive functions perform well in some simple domains, there are scenarios where they become poorly suited (Klein, Faratin, Sayama & Bar-Yam, 2003). Just as an example, we could think of a water market domain where two parties negotiate over the exploitation of several water resources. One of the parties' desires to satisfy its water needs whereas the other party has rights over several water exploitations. In this negotiation, the different issues are the water exploitations to be included in the deal. Even though the provider offers a proposal whose amount of water may satisfy the buyer, the value of the proposal may turn into a low utility for the buyer if the water sources are too distant. Thus, some issues have a negative effect over the value of others, and preferences can no longer be represented as classic linear additive utility functions. There is a need to provide complex utility functions that are capable of representing interdependences between negotiation issues.

Negotiation strategies that perform well in domains with linear utility functions may not perform equally in the case of complex interdependent utility functions. In fact, the search space for each agent is much more complicated, needing new negotiation strategies adapted to these complex functions. Figure 2 shows an illustrative example of the search space in the case of linear utility functions and complex interdependent utility functions. The left figure shows the search space of a two issues linear utility function, whereas the right figure shows the search space of a two issues complex interdependent utility function using the model introduced by Ito et al. (2008), which will be reviewed later. As it can be observed, the optimization problem faced by each agent is more complex in the case of interdependent utility functions, leading to the need of new mechanisms that tackle these domains.

Figure 2. An example of linear (left) and complex (right) utility functions

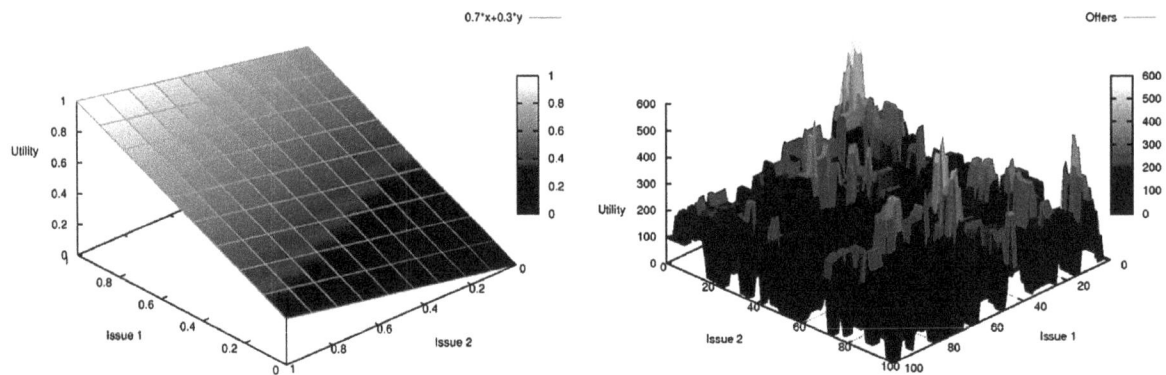

In this section we have review some important works related with automated negotiation, and more specifically in bilateral negotiation. We have analyzed the adequateness of the different models proposed in the literature for conflict resolution, and we identify those mechanisms that may prove more interesting for solving conflicts. Next section introduces argumentation as a complementary technology to achieve success in negotiation processes among intelligent entities.

ARGUMENTATION

The high dynamism of MAS requires agents to have a way of harmonizing the conflicts that come out when they have to collaborate or coordinate their activities. In those situations, agents need a mechanism to argue (persuade other agents to accept their points of view, negotiating the terms of a contract, etc.) and reach agreements. Argumentation provides a fruitful means of dealing with conflicts and knowledge inconsistencies in MAS. Within the history of research done in argumentation in Artificial Intelligence (AI), there have been a wide variety of mutual contributions. The argumentation theory has produced important benefits on many AI research areas, from its first uses as an alternative to formal logic for reasoning with incomplete and uncertain information to its more recent applications in Multi-Agent Systems (MAS) (Bench-Capon & Dunne, 2007; Rahwan & Simari, 2009). Currently, the study of argumentation in this area has gained a growing interest. The reason behind is that having argumentation skills increases the agents' autonomy and provides them with a mechanism to engage in dialogues and to solve conflicts with other agents demonstrating an intelligent behavior.

An autonomous agent should be able to act and reason as an individual entity on the basis of its mental state (beliefs, desires, intentions, goals, etc.). As a member of a MAS, an agent interacts with other agents whose goals could come into conflict with those of the agent. Moreover, if dynamic and open MAS are considered, the knowledge that an agent has about the environment, its neighbors and its mental state can change in the course of time. In addition, agents can have a social context that imposes dependency relations between them and preference orders among a set of potential values to promote/demote. Therefore, agents must have the ability of reaching agreements that harmonize their mental states and that solve their conflicts with other agents by taking into account their social context and values. Argumentation is a natural way of reaching agreements between several parties with opposing positions about a particular issue. The argumentation techniques, hence, can be used to facilitate the agents' autonomous reasoning and to specify interaction protocols between them (Rahwan, 2006).

Argumentation and Artificial Intelligence

From the beginning of AI research, the development of knowledge-bases, reasoning methods and cognitive architectures able to reply human reasoning has been a core area of interest. The work done in such area is typically known as common sense reasoning research. A reasoning method of this kind must include the following features: (i) the ability to reason with knowledge that is assumed to be true or false in the absence of any evidence that shows the opposite, which is called default reasoning; (ii) the ability to manage uncertain knowledge; (iii) the ability to reason quickly over a wide range of domains; and (iv) the ability to reason and take decisions in presence of incomplete knowledge and subsequently, to revise the beliefs and decisions that were taken when concrete knowledge is acquired, which is called non-monotonic reasoning.

Initially, argumentation theory was adopted in AI due to the inability of the classic propositional logic to reason and give explanations in presence of uncertain or imprecise information (Reiter, 1980). The main problem with classical logic is its monotonic condition, which implies that the acquisition of new information cannot modify the conclusions that were inferred to that moment and thus, it is not applicable as common sense reasoning method. This problem already appeared in rule-based expert systems, where several rules could conflict or even be invalidated by the acquisition of new information. The process of drawing conclusions by using rules that can be defeated by new information is called defeasible reasoning. When defeasible rules are linked up to reach to a conclusion, the proofs that support such rules turn into arguments. The arguments can defeat each other, given rise to an argumentation process. To determine the winning arguments, they must be compared by establishing which beliefs are justified. Therefore, argumentation theory has been studied in AI to deal with the process of argument searching and more concretely (Bench-Capon & Dunne, 2007): (i) to distinguish between valid and invalid arguments; (ii) to identify the protocols and rules that manage the argumentation processes; (iii) to define the argument components and their interaction; and (iv) to determine the conditions under which further discussion becomes redundant.

There are several works that provide an extensive review of the argumentation research that has been done in AI throughout history. According to (Bench-Capon & Dunne, 2007) and (Rahwan & Simari, 2009), the foundations of argumentation in AI lie in the studies done to extend non-classical logic to manage argumentation, the argumentation models that are based on dialogue processes and the diagrammatic treatments of the argument structure. We refer the reader to this important work for further details. Nowadays, the argumentation research in AI is experiencing a new reactivation, mainly motivated by recent and interesting contributions developed in MAS. On the one hand, the argumentation theory has been studied in MAS to manage the agent's practical reasoning. Practical reasoning is a well-known area in philosophy, but which historically has received less attention in AI than the theoretical reasoning. This type of reasoning analyses which specific action should be performed in a particular situation, instead of the theoretical reasoning objective of deciding the truthfulness of beliefs. Moreover, practical reasoning does not presuppose, as theoretical reasoning does, that the fact of reaching an objective is always adequate or profitable, but it must select the best objectives to perform and decide afterwards whether their realization is worthwhile. This fits the reality of a MAS, where each individual agent has its own point of view and its particular objectives and interests. However, the theoretical reasoning about the state of the world and the effects of the potential actions to perform is also essential. Therefore, both types of reasoning must be considered in MAS. In (Rahwan & Amgoud, 2006), an argumentation-based approach for practical reasoning has been proposed. In this work, Dung's abstract argumentation framework (Dung, 1995) is instantiated to generate consistent desires and plans to achieve them. Dung's framework is defined as a pair <A, R> where A is a set of arguments and R ⊆ A × A is a binary attack relation on A. The works developed by Atkinson in her thesis and her subsequent research are also other important contributions to the modelling of argumentation processes that allow the agents to reason about what is the best action to execute (Atkinson, 2005).

Argumentation in MAS

Moreover, the argumentation techniques have been applied to manage the agents' autonomous reasoning and the interaction between them (Rahwan, 2006). In open MAS, the introduction of new information may give rise to new arguments that reinforce or weaken certain beliefs. Therefore, the argumentation techniques can be used as a way of revising the agents' beliefs in presence of incomplete or uncertain information. The work proposed in (Capobianco, Chesñevar & Simari, 2005) applies argumentation to keep the consistency of the agents' mental state in changing environments by using an appropriate representation of the environment and a mechanism that integrates the new information in the beliefs update process. Argumentation has also been applied in MAS as a selection means between conflicting desires (Amgoud, 2003) and objectives (Amgoud & Kaci, 2004), as a qualitative means of reasoning about the expected value of the realization of certain actions (Fox & Parsons, 1998) and as generator of plans (Hulstijn & van der Torre, 2004) (Simari, Garcia & Capobianco, 2004).

Argumentation provides MAS with a framework that assures a rational communication. The dialogue typology of Walton and Krabbe (Walton & Krabbe, 1995) has been adopted in MAS to classify the different types of dialogues between the agents depending on the objective of the interaction. Other concepts of the argumentation theory (i.e. dialogue games (Hamblin, 1970) and argumentation schemes (Walton, 1996) have also been applied to structure the dialogue between agents with different points of view according to the interaction rules that have been previously agreed. A wide range of approaches that formalize interaction protocols by using different dialogue games have been published (McBurney & Parsons, 2002).

Some examples of dialogue game protocols about specific types of dialogues are: inquiry, persuasion, negotiation and deliberation. As pointed out before, argumentation schemes have several characteristics that make them very useful in defining the communication between agents. In the case of Walton's argumentation schemes, the critical questions are arguments that can be presented by an opponent to criticize the claim that the scheme poses, thus providing the argument with a clear structure that reduces the computational cost of generating and evaluating arguments. Reed & Walton (2005) propose a formal framework to specify argumentation schemes for agent's communication by using the markup language AML, based on XML. Also, the work presented in Atkinson and Bench-Capon (2007) provides firm foundations for an approach to practical reasoning based on presumptive argument.

Among current research on argumentation in MAS, to study the effect of argumentation strategies in the interaction between agents is also a recent trend. Here, there are different approaches to the study of strategies in argumentation frameworks. On the one hand, preliminary works studied the concept of strategy as developing heuristics for move selection in argumentation dialogues. A first contribution was provided in Bench-Capon (1998). In this work the author defines a Toulmin dialogue game machine and proposes some heuristics for move selection. The acceptability of the arguments is computed by using some Toulmin-like rules. A similar work is the one presented in Amgoud and Maudet (2002), which proposes heuristics for move selection on the context of persuasion and negotiation dialogues. This research defends a three-level approach of strategy, inspired on naturally occurring dialogues between humans. The levels identified are: maintaining the focus of the dispute, building one's point of view or destroying the opponent's one, and selecting the method to fulfil the objective set at levels 1 and 2.

While levels 1 and 2 refer to strategy (planning the line of argumentation), level 3 refers to tactic (the mean to reach the aims fixed at the strategically level). Then, the account for strategy proposed follows three steps to develop strategies: (i) define some agent profile: agreeable (accept whenever possible), disagreeable (only accept when there is no reason not to), open-minded (only challenge when necessary), argumentative (challenge whenever possible), or elephant child (question whenever possible); (ii) choose to build or destroy; and (iii) choose some appropriate argumentative content.

This work computes argument acceptability by using a more general Dung-like argumentation framework. In a subsequent work, the author studied the notion of strategy for selecting offers during a negotiation dialogue (Amgoud & Kaci, 2005), proposing different agent's profiles and different criteria for the notions of acceptability and satisfiability of offers. Also, in (Amgoud & Hameurlain, 2006) it is argued that there is no consensus on the definition of a strategy and on the parameters necessary for its definition. Consequently, there are no methodology and no formal models for strategies. This work defends that a strategy is a two steps decision process: (i) to select the type of act to utter at a given step of a dialogue, and (ii) to select the content, which will accompany the act. Thus, an agent tries to choose among different alternatives the best option, which according to its beliefs will satisfy at least its most important goals. There are two types of goals: strategic goals, which help an agent, on the basis of the strategic beliefs, to select the type of act to utter; and functional goals, which help an agent to select, on the basis of the basic beliefs, the content of a move. Then, the work proposes a formal model for defining strategies. The model takes as input the strategic and the functional goals together with the strategic and basic beliefs and returns the next move (act plus its content) to play. Then, the model assesses each alternative by constructing the set of supporting arguments for each one and evaluating their quality.

The agent profiles of Amgoud and Maudet (2002) were also considered in Kakas, Maudet & Moraitis (2005) to develop different types of strategies. This work proposes an argument-based framework for representing communication theories of agents that can take into account the conformance to society protocols, private tactics of individual agents, strategies that reflect different types of personal attitudes (agents' profiles) and adaptability to the particular external circumstances at the time when the communication takes place. Although the authors do not provide a clear structure and definition for their notion of agent society, social relations between agents are captured in the form of preference rules that affect the tactic component of an agent and help it to decide the next move in a dialogue.

On the other hand, a different approach follows a game-theoretic view to the study of argumentation strategies. This is the case of the work proposed in Roth & Rotolo (2007), where the probability of a conclusion is calculated using a standard variant of defeasible logic, in combination with standard probability calculus. In this approach the exchange of arguments is analyzed with game-theoretic tools, yielding a prescriptive account of the actual course of play. Other game-theoretic approach for the study or argumentation strategies in negotiation dialogues was presented in Rahwan & Larson (2009). This approach uses the paradigm of Argumentation Mechanism Design (ArgMD) for designing and analyzing argument evaluation criteria among self-interested agents using game-theoretic techniques. Mechanism design (MD) is a sub-field of game theory concerned with determining the game rules that guarantee a desirable social outcome when each self-interested agent selects the best strategy for itself.

The approach analyses strategy-proofness under grounded semantics for a specific type of arguments, the so-called focal arguments (the arguments that agents are especially interested in being accepted). In a preliminary work (Rahwan & Larson, 2008), the authors restricted the analysis to the case where agents use a specific type of preference criteria, the individual acceptability maximizing preference criteria. Following these criteria, every agent attempts to maximize the number of its arguments that are accepted. In further research the ArgMD approach has been applied to more realistic situations in which each agent has a single focal argument it wishes to have accepted. Authors demonstrate for both preference criteria that if each agent's type (characterized as the set of argument that an agent can bring up) corresponds to a conflict-free set of arguments which does not include (in)direct defeats, the grounded direct argumentation mechanism for this argumentation framework is strategy-proof. Opposite to the heuristic-based approaches, the goal of this game-theoretic approach is to design rules that ensure, under precise conditions, that agents have no incentive to manipulate the outcome of the game by hiding arguments or lying (how to ensure the truth in an argumentation framework).

Within this section it has been shown how argumentation techniques have been successfully used to reach agreements and solve conflicts that assure the coherence of the agents' mental state and to structure their interaction in disagreement situations. Parsons et al. (1998) proposed a seminal theoretical framework that unifies argumentation-based reasoning and communication for negotiation in MAS. After that, Rahwan et al. (2003) analyzed this and other argumentation-based negotiation frameworks. A wide review of the situation of the argumentation research in AI was also published in the special issue on argumentation of the journal Artificial Intelligence (Bench-Capon & Dunne, 2007) and in the book Rahwan & Simari (2009). Moreover, an effort to consolidate the work done in argumentation languages and protocols, argument visualization and editing tools and, generally, in argumentation frameworks for MAS, was performed by the ASPIC project. As a result, a new standard for argument interchange in MAS, the Argument Interchange Format (AIF), was proposed to serve as a convergence point for theoretical and practical work in this area (Willmott, 2006). All these advances show how the study of argumentation in AI, and more concretely in MAS, is currently a research area that has a high activity and a growing interest.

CONCLUSION

In this chapter, we have reviewed the state-of-the-art in automated negotiation from the point of view of Agreement Technologies. A special emphasis was put to analyze which current negotiation models are more convenient for conflict resolution. The analysis allowed us to identify that from the point of view of negotiation, the use of time-based concession tactics, the use of complex and interdependent utility functions for representing agents' preferences, and the use of similarity heuristics and genetic algorithms as learning mechanisms may be of interest in order to achieve more efficient automated conflict resolution tools.

Moreover, this chapter has also introduced several concepts and works of argumentation technology that have been applied to model the reasoning and behavior of agents in MAS. Argumentation technology has been proved as a powerful tool for solving conflicts in the context of a society in a MAS. Nevertheless, the application of argumentation to agent societies is a new area or research with few contributions to date. Commonly, the term agent society is used in the argumentation and AI literature as a synonym for an agent organization or a group of agents that play specific roles, follow some interaction patterns and collaborate to reach global objectives. Many works in argumentation in MAS that refer to the term 'agent societies' follow this approach, which is not targeted to the study of the structure of agent societies and the underlying social dependencies between agents. The influence of the agent group and the social dependencies between agents in the way agents can argue must be further investigated.

REFERENCES

Amgoud, L. (2003). A formal framework for handling conflicting desires. In *7th European Conference on Symbolic and Quantitative Approaches to Reasoning with Uncertainty, ECSQARU-03*, (LNAI) (vol. 2711, pp. 552–563). Springer. doi:10.1007/978-3-540-45062-7_45

Amgoud, L., & Hameurlain, N. (2006). A formal model for designing dialogue strategies. In *5th International Joint Conference on Autonomous Agents and Multiagent Systems, AAMAS-06*. ACM Press. doi:10.1145/1160633.1160706

Amgoud, L., & Kaci, S. (2004). On the generation of bipolar goals in argumentation-based negotiation. In *Argumentation in Multi-Agent Systems: State of the art survey* (LNAI), (Vol. 3366, pp. 192–207). Springer.

Amgoud, L., & Kaci, S. (2005). On the study of negotiation strategies. In *AAMAS 2005 Workshop on Agent Communication*. ACM Press.

Amgoud, L., & Maudet, N. (2002). Strategical considerations for argumentative agents (preliminary report). In *9th International Workshop on Non-Monotonic Reasoning* (LNAI), (pp. 399–407). Springer.

Argente, E., Botti, V., Carrascosa, C., Giret, A., Julian, V., & Rebollo, M. (2011). An abstract architecture for virtual organizations: The THOMAS approach. *Knowledge and Information Systems*, *29*(2), 379–403. doi:10.1007/s10115-010-0349-1

Argente, E., Botti, V., Carrascosa, C., Giret, A., Julian, V., & Rebollo, M. (2011). An Abstract Architecture for Virtual Organizations: The THOMAS approach. *Knowledge and Information Systems*, *29*(2), 379–403. doi:10.1007/s10115-010-0349-1

Atkinson, K. (2005). *What Should We Do? Computational Representation of Persuasive Argument in Practical Reasoning*. (PhD thesis). Liverpool University.

Atkinson, K., & Bench-Capon, T. (2007). Practical reasoning as presumptive argumentation using action based alternating transition systems. *Artificial Intelligence*, *171*(10-15), 855–874. doi:10.1016/j.artint.2007.04.009

Beam, C., & Segev, A. (1997). Automated negotiations: A survey of the state of the art. *Wirtschaftsinformatik*, *39*(3), 263–268.

Bench-Capon, T., & Dunne, P. (2007). Argumentation in artificial intelligence. *Artificial Intelligence*, *171*(10-15), 619–938. doi:10.1016/j.artint.2007.05.001

Bench-Capon, T. J. (1998). Specification and implementation of Toulmin dialogue game. In *International Conferences on Legal Knowledge and Information Systems*. IOS Press.

Binmore, K., Rubinstein, A., & Wolinsky, A. (1986). The Nash bargaining solution in economic modelling. *The Rand Journal of Economics*, *17*(2), 176–188. doi:10.2307/2555382

Boella, G., Van Der Torre, L., & Verhagen, H. (2006). Introduction to normative multiagent systems. *Computational & Mathematical Organization Theory*, *12*(2), 71–79. doi:10.1007/s10588-006-9537-7

Browder, G. (2000). An analysis of the negotiations for the 1995 mekong agreement. *International Negotiation*, *5*(2), 237–261. doi:10.1163/15718060020848758

Buffett, S., & Spencer, B. (2007). A bayesian classifier for learning opponents' preferences in multi-object automated negotiation. *Electronic Commerce Research and Applications*, *6*(3), 274–284. doi:10.1016/j.elerap.2006.06.008

Bui, H., Venkatesh, S., & Kieronska, D. (1999). Learning Other Agents' Preferences in Multi-Agent Negotiation Using the Bayesian Classifier. *International Journal of Cooperative Information Systems*, *8*(4), 275–293. doi:10.1142/S0218843099000149

Capobianco, M., Chesñevar, C. I., & Simari, G. R. (2005). Argumentation and the dynamics of warranted beliefs in changing environments. *Autonomous Agents and Multi-Agent Systems*, *11*(2), 127–151. doi:10.1007/s10458-005-1354-8

Carbonneau, R., Kersten, G., & Vahidov, R. (2011). Pairwise issue modeling for negotiation counteroffer prediction using neural networks. *Decision Support Systems*, *50*(2), 449–459. doi:10.1016/j.dss.2010.11.002

Carbonneau, R., Kersten, G. E., & Vahidov, R. (2008). Predicting opponent's moves in electronic negotiations using neural networks. *Expert Systems with Applications*, *34*(2), 1266–1273. doi:10.1016/j.eswa.2006.12.027

Choi, N., Song, I. Y., & Han, H. (2006). A survey on ontology mapping. *SIGMOD Record*, *35*(3), 34–41. doi:10.1145/1168092.1168097

Coehoorn, R., & Jennings, N. (2004). Learning on opponent's preferences to make effective multi-issue negotiation trade-offs. In *The 6th International Conference on Electronic Commerce (ICEC'04)*, (pp. 59–68).

Criado, N., Argente, E., & Botti, V. (2013). THOMAS: An Agent Platform For Supporting Normative Multi-Agent Systems. *Journal of Logic and Computation.*, *23*(2), 309–333. doi:10.1093/logcom/exr025

Dung, P. M. (1995). On the acceptability of arguments and its fundamental role in nonmonotonic reasoning, logic programming, and n-person games. *Artificial Intelligence*, *77*(2), 321–357. doi:10.1016/0004-3702(94)00041-X

Esparcia, S., & Argente, E. (2011). *Defining Virtual Organizations Following a Formal Approach. In Agents and Artificial Intelligence 2011*. Revised Selected Papers.

Faratin, P., Sierra, C., & Jennings, N. (1998). Negotiation Decision Functions for Autonomous Agents. *International Journal of Robotics and Autonomous Systems*, *24*(3-4), 159–182. doi:10.1016/S0921-8890(98)00029-3

Faratin, P., Sierra, C., & Jennings, N. (2002). Using Similarity Criteria to Make Issue Trade-Offs in Automated Negotiations. *Artificial Intelligence*, *142*(2), 205–237. doi:10.1016/S0004-3702(02)00290-4

Fatima, S. S., Wooldridge, M. J., & Jennings, N. R. (2004). An agenda-based framework for multi-issue negotiation. *Artificial Intelligence*, *152*(1), 1–45. doi:10.1016/S0004-3702(03)00115-2

Foster, I., Kesselman, C., & Tuecke, S. (2001). The anatomy of the grid: Enabling scalable virtual organizations. *International Journal of High Performance Computing Applications*, *15*(3), 200–222. doi:10.1177/109434200101500302

Fox, J., & Parsons, S. (1998). Arguing about beliefs and actions. In *Applications of Uncertainty Formalisms* (Vol. 1455, pp. 266–302). Springer. doi:10.1007/3-540-49426-X_13

Goldberg, D. E. (1989). *Genetic Algorithms in Search, Optimization and Machine Learning*. Boston, MA: Addison-Wesley Longman Publishing Co., Inc.

Guttman, R. H., Moukas, A. G., & Maes, P. (1998). Agent-mediated electronic commerce: A survey. *The Knowledge Engineering Review*, *13*(2), 147–159. doi:10.1017/S0269888998002082

Hamblin, C. L. (1970). *Fallacies*. Methuen Co. Ltd.

Hewitt, C. (1991). Open information systems semantics for distributed artificial intelligence. *Artificial Intelligence*, *47*(1-3), 79–106. doi:10.1016/0004-3702(91)90051-K

Hindriks, K. V., & Tykhonov, D. (2008). Opponent modelling in automated multi-issue negotiation using Bayesian learning. In *The 7th International Joint Conference on Autonomous Agents and Multiagent Systems (AAMAS'08)*.

Horling, B., & Lesser, V. (2008). Using quantitative models to search for appropriate organizational designs. *Autonomous Agents and Multi-Agent Systems*, *16*(2), 95–149. doi:10.1007/s10458-007-9020-y

Hübner, J. F., Sichman, J. S., & Boissier, O. (2002). A model for the structural, functional, and deontic specification of organizations in multiagent systems. *Advances in Artificial Intelligence*.

Hulstijn, J., & van der Torre, L. (2004). Combining goal generation and planning in an argumentation framework. In *10th International Workshop on Non-Monotonic Reasoning* (LNAI). Springer-Verlag.

In, Y., & Serrano, R. (2003). Agenda restrictions in multi-issue bargaining (II): Unrestricted agendas. *Economics Letters*, *79*(3), 325–331. doi:10.1016/S0165-1765(02)00321-X

Ito, T., Klein, M., & Hattori, H. (2008). A multi-issue negotiation protocol among agents with nonlinear utility functions. *Multiagent and Grid Systems*, *4*(1), 67–83.

Jennings, N. R., Faratin, P., Lomuscio, A. R., Parsons, S., Wooldridge, M. J., & Sierra, C. (2001). Automated negotiation: Prospects, methods and challenges. *Group Decision and Negotiation*, *10*(2), 199–215. doi:10.1023/A:1008746126376

Jennings, N. R., Faratin, P., Lomuscio, A. R., Parsons, S., Wooldridge, M. J., & Sierra, C. (2001). Automated Negotiation: Prospects, Methods and Challenges. *Group Decision and Negotiation, 10*(2), 199–215. doi:10.1023/A:1008746126376

Jonker, C. M., Robu, V., & Treur, J. (2007). An agent architecture for multi-attribute negotiation using incomplete preference information. *Autonomous Agents and Multi-Agent Systems, 15*(2), 221–252. doi:10.1007/s10458-006-9009-y

Jonker, C. M., & Treur, J. (2001). An Agent Architecture for Multi-Attribute Negotiation. In *The 17th International Joint Conference on Artificial Intelligence (IJCAI'01)*.

Kakas, A., Maudet, N., & Moraitis, P. (2005). Modular Representation of Agent Interaction Rules through Argumentation. *Autonomous Agents and Multi-Agent Systems, 11*(2), 189–206. doi:10.1007/s10458-005-2176-4

Keeney, R. L., & Raiffa, H. (1993). *Decisions with Multiple Objectives: Preferences and Value Tradeoffs*. Cambridge University Press. doi:10.1017/CBO9781139174084

Kitano, H., & Tadokoro, S. (2001). RoboCup Rescue: A Grand Challenge for Multiagent and Intelligent Systems. *AI Magazine, 22*(1), 39–52.

Klein, M., Faratin, P., Sayama, H., & Bar-Yam, Y. (2003). Negotiating Complex Contracts. *Group Decision and Negotiation, 12*(2), 111–125. doi:10.1023/A:1023068821218

Kraus, S. (1997). Negotiation and cooperation in multi-agent environments. *Artificial Intelligence, 94*(1-2), 79–97. doi:10.1016/S0004-3702(97)00025-8

Lai, G., Sycara, K., & Li, C. (2008). A decentralized model for automated multi-attribute negotiations with incomplete information and general utility functions. *Multiagent and Grid Systems, 4*(1), 45–65.

Leake, D. B. (1994). Case-based reasoning. *The Knowledge Engineering Review, 9*(01), 61–64. doi:10.1017/S0269888900006585

Lomuscio, A., Wooldridge, M., & Jennings, N. (2003). A Classification Scheme for Negotiation in Electronic Commerce. *Group Decision and Negotiation, 12*(1), 31–56. doi:10.1023/A:1022232410606

Lopes, F., Wooldridge, M., & Novais, A. Q. (2008). Negotiation among autonomous computational agents: Principles, analysis and challenges. *Artificial Intelligence Review, 29*(1), 1–44. doi:10.1007/s10462-009-9107-8

Lopez de Mantaras, R. (2001). Case-Based Reasoning. In Machine Learning and Its Applications (LNCS), (Vol. 2049, pp. 127-145). Springer. doi:10.1007/3-540-44673-7_6

Luck, M., & McBurney, P. (2008). Computing as Interaction: Agent and Agreement Technologies. In *Proc. IEEE Conference on Distributed Human-Machine Systems*.

Matos, N., Sierra, C., & Jennings, N. (1998). Determining Successful Negotiation Strategies: An Evolutionary Approach. In *The 3rd International Conference on Multi Agent Systems (ICMAS '98)*. Washington, DC: IEEE Computer Society. doi:10.1109/ICMAS.1998.699048

McBurney, P., & Parsons, S. (2002). Dialogue games in multi-agent systems. Informal Logic. *Special Issue on Applications of Argumentation in Computer Science*, *22*(3), 257–274.

Nash, J. F. (1950). The bargaining problem. *Econometrica*, *18*(2), 155–162. doi:10.2307/1907266

Noy, N. F. (2004). Semantic integration: A survey of ontology-based approaches. *SIGMOD Record*, *33*(4), 65–70. doi:10.1145/1041410.1041421

Oliver, J. R. (1996). On Artificial Agents for Negotiation in Electronic Commerce. In *The 29 Hawaii International Conference on System Sciences (HICSS'96)*. Washington, DC: IEEE Computer Society. doi:10.1109/HICSS.1996.495355

Osborne, M. J., & Rubinstein, A. (1999). *A Course in Game Theory*. MIT Press.

Ossowski, S. (2013). *Agreement Technologies. In Law, Governance and Technology Series* (Vol. 8). Springer.

Papazoglou, M. P., & Georgakopoulos, D. (2003). Service-oriented computing. *Communications of the ACM*, *46*(10), 25–28.

Parsons, S., Rodriguez-Aguilar, J. A., & Klein, M. (2011). Auctions and bidding: A guide for computer scientists. *ACM Computing Surveys*, *43*(2), 10. doi:10.1145/1883612.1883617

Parsons, S., Sierra, C., & Jennings, N. R. (1998). Agents that reason and negotiate by arguing. *Journal of Logic and Computation*, *8*(3), 261–292. doi:10.1093/logcom/8.3.261

Pinyol, I., & Sabater-Mir, J. (2013). Computational trust and reputation models for open multi-agent systems: A review. *Artificial Intelligence Review, Springer Netherlands.*, *40*(1), 1–25. doi:10.1007/s10462-011-9277-z

Pruitt, D. G. (1981). *Negotiation Behavior*. Academic Press.

Rahwan, I. (2006). *Argumentation in multi-agent systems*. Autonomous Agents and Multiagent Systems. *Guest Editorial*, *11*(2), 115–125.

Rahwan, I., & Amgoud, L. (2006). An argumentation-based approach for practical reasoning. In *5th International Joint Conference on Autonomous Agents and Multiagent Systems, AAMAS-06*. ACM Press. doi:10.1145/1160633.1160696

Rahwan, I., & Larson, K. (2008). Mechanism design for abstract argumentation. In *Proceedings of the 7th international joint conference on Autonomous agents and multiagent systems* (vol. 2, pp. 1031–1038). ACM Press.

Rahwan, I., & Larson, K. (2009). *Argumentation and Game Theory*. Argumentation in Artificial Intelligence.

Rahwan, I., Ramchurn, S. D., Jennings, N. R., Mcburney, P., Parsons, S., & Sonenberg, L. (2003). Argumentation-based negotiation. *The Knowledge Engineering Review*, *18*(04), 343–375. doi:10.1017/S0269888904000098

Rahwan, I., Ramchurn, S. D., Jennings, N. R., McBurney, P., Parsons, S., & Sonenberg, L. (2003). Argumentation-based negotiation. *The Knowledge Engineering Review*, *18*(4), 343–375. doi:10.1017/S0269888904000098

Rahwan, I., & Simari, G. (Eds.). (2009). *Argumentation in Artificial Intelligence*. Springer.

Rebollo, M., Carrascosa, C., & Palomares, A. (2014). Follow the leader in a consensus network as a solution to manage a smart grid: the Balearic Islands case. In *Proceedings of the 2014 international conference on Autonomous agents and multi-agent systems* (AAMAS '14). International Foundation for Autonomous Agents and Multiagent Systems.

Reed, C., & Walton, D. (2005). Towards a formal and implemented model of argumentation schemes in agent communication. *Autonomous Agents and Multi-Agent Systems*, *11*(2), 173–188. doi:10.1007/s10458-005-1729-x

Reiter, R. (1980). A logic for default reasoning. *Artificial Intelligence*, *13*(1-2), 81–132. doi:10.1016/0004-3702(80)90014-4

Roth, B., & Rotolo, A. (2007). Strategic argumentation: a game theoretical investigation. In *Proceedings of the Eleventh International Conference on Artificial Intelligence and Law*. ACM Press.

Rubinstein, A. (1982). Perfect equilibrium in a bargaining model. *Econometrica*, *50*(1), 155–162. doi:10.2307/1912531

Sabater, J., & Sierra, C. (2005). Review on computational trust and reputation models. *Artificial Intelligence Review*, *24*(1), 33–60. doi:10.1007/s10462-004-0041-5

Sanchez-Anguix, V., Julian, V., Botti, V., & García-Fornes, A. (2013). Tasks for agent-based negotiation teams: Analysis, review, and challenges. *Engineering Applications of Artificial Intelligence*, *26*(10), 2480–2494. doi:10.1016/j.engappai.2013.07.006

Sheather, S. J., & Jones, M. C. (1991). A reliable data-based bandwidth selection method for kernel density estimation. *Journal of the Royal Statistical Society. Series B. Methodological*, 683–690.

Sierra, C., Botti, V., & Ossowski, S. (2011). Agreement computing. *KI-Künstliche Intelligenz*, *25*(1), 57–61. doi:10.1007/s13218-010-0070-y

Sierra, C., Botti, V., & Ossowski, S. (2011). *Agreement Computing*. KI-Kunstliche Intelligenz.

Simari, G. R., Garcia, A. J., & Capobianco, M. (2004). Actions, planning and defeasible reasoning. In *10th International Workshop on Non-Monotonic Reasoning* (LNAI), (pp. 377–384). Springer.

Such, J. M., Espinosa, A., Garcia-Fornes, A., & Botti, V. (2011). Partial identities as a foundation for Trust and Reputation. *Engineering Applications of Artificial Intelligence*, *24*(7), 1128–1136. doi:10.1016/j.engappai.2011.06.008

Sycara, K. P. (1989). *Multiagent compromise via negotiation*. In Distributed. *Artificial Intelligence*, *2*, 119–137.

Sycara, K. P. (1990). Negotiation Planning. *An AI Approach*, *46*(1), 216–234.

Sycara, K. P. (1991). Problem restructuring in negotiation. *Management Science, 37*(10), 1248–1268. doi:10.1287/mnsc.37.10.1248

Wallenius, J., Dyer, J. S., Fishburn, P., Steuer, R., Zionts, S., & Deb, K. (2008). Multiple Criteria Decision Making, Multiattribute Utility Theory: Recent Accomplishments and What Lies Ahead. *Management Science, 54*(7), 1336–1349. doi:10.1287/mnsc.1070.0838

Walton, D. (1996). *Argumentation Schemes for Presumptive Reasoning*. Routledge Publishers.

Walton, D., & Krabbe, E. C. W. (1995). *Commitment in Dialogue: Basic Concepts of Interpersonal Reasoning*. State University of New York Press.

Willmott, S., Vreeswijk, G., Chesñevar, C., South, M., McGinnis, J., Modgil, S., & Simari, G. et al. (2006). Towards an argument interchange format for Multi-Agent Systems. In *3rd International Workshop on Argumentation in Multi-Agent Systems, ArgMAS-06*. ACM Press.

Zeng, D., & Sycara, K. (1998). Bayesian learning in negotiation. *International Journal of Human-Computer Studies, 48*(1), 125–141. doi:10.1006/ijhc.1997.0164

KEY TERMS AND DEFINITIONS

Agreement Technologies: All of those technologies that are envisioned to collaborate, directly or indirectly, to the resolution of conflicts in software systems, and specifically in MAS systems.

Argumentation: A verbal, social, and rational activity aimed at convincing a reasonable critic of the acceptability of a standpoint by putting forward a constellation of propositions justifying or refuting the proposition expressed in the standpoint.

Negotiation: Process in which a joint decision is made by two or more parties.

Open Multi-Agent System: A distributed system where heterogeneous agents, with their own goals, can enter and leave the system during the life of the system.

Reputation: What a society says about a target (probably an entity) regarding his behavior.

Trust: An expectation about an uncertain behavior.

Virtual Organization: A set of individuals and institutions that need to coordinate resources and services across institutional boundaries.

Chapter 10
Conflict Resolution Problem Solving with Bio-Inspired Metaheuristics:
A Perspective

P. B. de Moura Oliveira
Universidade de Trás-os-Montes e Alto Douro, Portugal

E. J. Solteiro Pires
Universidade de Trás-os-Montes e Alto Douro, Portugal

ABSTRACT

This chapter addresses nature and bio-inspired metaheuristics in the context of conflict detection and resolution problems. An approach is presented for a generalization of a population-based bio-inspired search and optimization algorithm, which is depicted for three of the most well-known and firmly established methods: the genetic algorithm, the particle swarm optimization algorithm and the differential evolution algorithm. This integrated approach to a basic general population-based bio-inspired algorithm is presented for single-objective optimization, multi-objective optimization and many-objective optimization. A revision of these three main bio-inspired algorithms is presented for conflict resolution problems in diverse application areas. A bridge between feedback controller design, genetic algorithm, particle swarm optimization and differential evolution is established using a conflict resolution approach. Finally, some perspectives concerning future trends of more recent bio-inspired meta-heuristics is presented.

INTRODUCTION

As there are conflicts in all engineering and computer science fields the conflict resolution range of applications is quite wide. Indeed, as it will be reviewed in this chapter, there are conflict resolution problems in areas as diverse as: air-traffic control, train-scheduling, production systems, water management, legal disputes, among many others. This chapter addresses the use of search and optimization techniques, which can be classified as nature or bio-inspired, in conflict resolution problem solving. While

DOI: 10.4018/978-1-5225-0245-6.ch010

the range of nature and bio-inspired metaheuristics is increasing in time, three of the most established techniques are: genetic algorithms, (GAs) (Holland, 1975; Goldberg, 1989), differential evolution, (DE) (Storn and Price, 1997) and particle swarm optimization (PSO) (Kennedy and Eberhart, 1995). Thus, given the application success of the former firmly established techniques, it is not surprising that the same techniques are the most applied within conflict resolution problems.

While there are differences between all bio-inspired search and optimization techniques, population based-bio-inspired algorithm also have many similarities. Three of the most well-known bio-inspired algorithms, which are also the most used in conflict detection and resolution, are reviewed. This revision is based on presenting both the common structures to all methods as well as specific functions and particularities to each algorithm. However, as it will be presented, the different problems diversity and specificity, will always require search and optimization techniques adaptation. The main issues concerning the transition and adaptation of single-objective to multi-objective and many-objective optimization are presented, by using a simplified approach. Which conflict detection and resolution problems have been solved using bio-inspired meta-heuristics? Answer to this question will be provided in this text, focusing in the three main bio-inspired algorithms: GA, PSO and DE. A feedback control design problem, is presented from a conflict resolution perspective, bridging some work done in the last 20 years for proportional integrative and derivative (PID) controller design.

The rest of the chapter is organized sequentially in the following order: Nature and Bio-inspired Search and Optimization techniques- key issues; Applications in Conflict Resolution Problem Solving; Conflict Resolution in Feedback Control Design, Perspectives of Evolution and Conclusion.

NATURE AND BIO-INSPIRED SEARCH AND OPTIMIZATION TECHNIQUES: KEY ISSUES

This section, begins by overviewing three of the most successful bio-inspired search and optimization techniques: genetic algorithm (GA), particle swarm optimization (PSO) and differential evolution (DE). The methodology used to present key issues concerning these algorithms is based in an integrated approach, by focusing firstly in the common issues to all three algorithms and then in the particular differences regarding each meta-heuristic. Due to the huge number of existing variants and refined versions presented in the last decades for all three algorithms, including hybridization techniques, a simplified approach presenting the core of these bio-inspired algorithms is presented here, in order to make it easier their application to solve conflict resolution problems.

Most applications regarding conflict resolution or any other type of problems, require solving an optimization problem with one or more functions, which can be formulated considering the minimization case as follows:

$$\min f(x) = \left(f_1(x), f_2(x), \ldots, f_o(x) \right)$$
$$s.t. \quad g_i(x) \le 0, \quad i = 1, 2, \ldots, k, \tag{1}$$
$$x \in S \subset \mathfrak{R}^n$$

Algorithm 1. General bio-inspired population-based algorithm

```
t=0
initialize population X(t)
evaluate X(t)
while(!(termination criterion))
  modify X(t+1)
  evaluate X(t+1)
  replace X(t)by X(t+1)
  t=t+1
end
```

with: $x(t)=(x_1(t),x_2(t), ...,x_n(t))$ representing a n-dimensional decision variable and a potential solution for the problem, t the evolutionary iteration, S the feasible search space, g_i the ith constraint and f_o an objective function. The number of objective functions is denoted as o, and the number of constraints is denoted as k (for simplicity sake, equality constraints are not represented in (1)). Three of the most relevant aspects, which influence the most the complexity of the search procedure involved in an optimization problem are:

- The number of objective functions. If $o=1$ the problem is single-objective, if $1<o<4$ the problem is known as multi-objective and if $o>=4$ the problem is referenced as many-objective optimization. Naturally, as the number of objectives increases the problem complexity increases as well.
- The number of decision variables, which influence the complexity of the search. The higher the number of decision variables to be optimized, the higher the problem complexity tends to be.
- The number and level of restriction of the search space. Some search spaces are so restricted that finding viable solutions, is a difficult optimization problem by itself.

Bio-inspired meta-heuristics are known to cope very well with the previous search issues. To make the algorithms description as simple as possible, and for generalization purposes, the algorithms issues are described firstly considering single-objective problems. Most of nature and inspired metaheuristics consider a set of potential solutions, denoted as population or swarm, as opposite to single-solution algorithms such as the Simulated Annealing case. Here the population is represented as $X(t)$, with size m. Consider the general bio-inspired algorithm presented in Algorithm 1. Looking at Algorithm 1, the first step is the population initialization. But before describing the initialization, a very important issue which must be addressed is the solution codification methodology used. In the GA case, each solution represents an analogy with a chromosome, which in the original GA formulation proposed by Holland (1975), was encoded using binary strings. The standard PSO algorithm uses a real-based coding scheme, as well as the DE algorithm. However, GA can be used with real-coded chromosomes, as well as other formats such as matrices, integers, and represented using appropriate data structures.

As it will be reviewed in the next section, conflict detection and resolution techniques depends on the specific application, the solution encoding methodology adopted is problem dependent. For instance, in the case of conflict scenarios between aircrafts, attributes such as vertical and horizontal separation between aircrafts, conflict angles, among others (Alam *et al.*, 2009) are encoded into the chromosome. This is related with the problem formulation, which along with the definition of number of decision

Algorithm 2. GA modify

```
selection of progenitors to mate
generate descendants with crossover
mutation of descendants
```

variables, requires setting the variation range for each variable, and depending on the encoding method, decoding and scaling functions. The particle swarm initialization, which uses a real encoding scheme, differs from real encoding based genetic algorithm, as it requires the initialization of another matrix incorporating the initial particles velocity. A particle velocity is represented by $v(t)=(v_1(t),v_2(t), ...,v_n(t))$. The velocity matrix is usually initialized using a uniform based random procedure within a sub-range of the search space.

The population (or swarm) initialization is a very important step in all population-based bio-inspired algorithms. In simple terms this step concerns the initialization of potential solutions for a given problem in the search space, often referred as landscape. This can be performed using several approaches:

- Using a totally random procedure. The solutions are randomly initialized in the search space. No information about the solution viability is provided and no evaluation about their merit performed.
- A random procedure with minimum performance thresholds. In this case the solution is randomly initialized, but it is allowed to incorporate the initial population depending on minimum performance threshold levels and/or viability concerning constraints. This approach requires calling the objective function to test each candidate solution.
- Using an informed procedure. This initialization method assumes that information available which may help solving the specific conflict resolution problem is incorporated in the initial population. For instance, in the legal negotiation (Carneiro *et al.*, 2013), some information regarding the monetary values from items in dispute and weights regarding the users preferences may be incorporated in the GA population initialization.

After the initial population has been created and evaluated, entering in Algorithm 1 evolutionary cycle, the population is modified accordingly to the specific bio-inspired heuristics inherent to each method. The function termed as *modify* in the general bio-inspired Algorithm 1, is presented for elementary GA, PSO and DE algorithms, in Algorithms 2, 3 and 4, respectively.

Algorithm 3. PSO modify

```
evaluate new velocity vectors v(t+1)
evaluate new position vectors x(t+1)
```

Algorithm 4. DE modify

```
generate  the incremental vectors  δ(t+1)
generate new solutions vectors xv(t+1)
crossover
```

The basic GA population modification operations, are inspired on the natural evolution operators: selection, reproduction and mutation. Selection should implement Darwin principle of the survival of the fittest, by providing the most able population elements with higher chances to participate in the breeding process and in this way pass their genetic information to the next generation. There are multiple selection schemes which can be found in the related literature (e.g. Goldberg, 1989). Crossover, as the name indicates, crosses information between the selected progenitors, using a probability threshold (usually high) to generate new descendants. There are several crossover methods, which depends also on the chromosome encoding scheme used. The mutation operator, introduces randomly generated changes in the chromosome using a probability threshold (usually very low).

The basic PSO population modification operations, are much simpler than the GA ones. They consist, for each swarm member, in evaluating the velocity new value, $v(t+1)$, updating the previous velocity value, $v(t)$, by using (2). Then the new particle position is determined applying the new velocity increment in (3). In equations (2) and (3), c_c and c_s represent the cognitive and social constants, respectively (here $c_c = c_s = 2$), φ_c and φ_s represent uniformly distributed random numbers generated in the interval $[0,1]$, p_i represents the current individual i best solution, p_g the entire swarm best solution and ω the inertia weight.

$$v_{id}(t+1) = \omega v_{id}(t) + c_c \phi_c \cdot (p_{id}(t) - x_{id}(t)) +$$
$$c_s \phi_s \cdot (p_{gd}(t) - x_{id}(t)) \quad 1 \leq i \leq m \quad 1 \leq d \leq n \tag{2}$$

$$x_{id}(t+1) = x_{id}(t) + v_{id}(t+1) \quad 1 \leq i \leq m \quad 1 \leq d \leq n \tag{3}$$

The inertia weight influence is crucial to regulate the PSO algorithm convergence. If this parameter is set to a small value (e.g. 0.4) it will promote a faster convergence rate, while if it is set to a higher value (e.g. 0.9) it will promote a slower convergence rate. The setting of this parameter is related to the problem of search space exploration versus exploitation. It is common to vary this parameter by linearly (or non-linearly) decreasing its value gradually along the search, by relating its value to the number of iterations used in the search. Varying the inertia weight between 0.9 and 0.4 will work just fine for most cases.

The basic DE population modification operations consist in the following: for each population member a trial vector x_v is generated in each iteration using (4) and the increment δ is evaluated using (5). Vectors x_{r1}, x_{r2} and x_{r3} are selected randomly from the population X in each iteration, and F is a positive real constant defined prior to the search procedure. Here, x_{r1} is the best vector solution found in the previous iteration.

$$x_{vid}(t+1) = x_{r_1 d}(t) + \delta_{id}(t+1) \quad 1 \leq i \leq m \quad 1 \leq d \leq n \quad r_1 \in [1,m] \neq i \tag{4}$$

$$\delta_{id}(t+1) =$$
$$F\left(x_{r_2 d}(t) - x_{r_3 d}(t)\right) \quad 1 \leq i \leq m \quad 1 \leq d \leq n \quad r_2 \in [1,m] \neq i \neq r_1 \neq r_2 \quad r_3 \in [1,m] \neq i \neq r_1 \neq r_2 \tag{5}$$

The crossover operation (binomial or exponential, Storn and Price, 1997), crosses information from the trial vector x_v with the current population element x_i, based in a predefined probability resulting in a new vector x_{ci}. The evaluation and population replacement steps in the GA case, correspond to the fitness evaluation by calling the objective function. The new population can totally or partially replace the old population, following different biological inspired methods. In the PSO case, for each new generated particle, its fitness is evaluated and the individual best position and global best position updated. Thus, as a new particle position is updated it replaces automatically the previous one, while the individual best position is not necessarily improved. For the DE evolution case, if fitness value for the crossed trial vector, x_v, is better or equal than the value obtained for the current vector, x_i, the latest is replaced by the former. Thus, there is a updating of the population. Regarding the termination criterion, often it is simply a pre-defined number of iterations being reached. However, depending on the case, the termination criterion can adaptively follows the search evolution progress.

Most of the techniques extending single-objective GAs, PSO and DE to multi-objective cases are based on Pareto dominance concepts (see Definition 1). In this case the aim is not to obtain a single solution at the end of the search procedure, but a set of non-dominated optimal solutions regarding all the objectives. This set is usually referred as Pareto front (see Definition 2). A simple illustration of a Pareto-front with some non-dominated solutions along the front, for a two-objective minimization problem is presented in Figure 1.

Definition 1: *Pareto dominance. For two solutions x_1 and x_2, if $\forall j \in \{1,2,...,o\}$: $f_j(x_1) \leq f_j(x_2)$ and $\exists$ $j' \in \{1,2,...,o\}$: $f_{j'}(x_1) < f_{j'}(x_2)$, solution x_1 is said to dominate x_2, denoted $x_1 \succ x_2$.*

Definition 2: *Pareto optimal set and Pareto front. For a solution $x_1 \in S$, if there is no $\boldsymbol{x'} \in S$: $x' \succ x^*$, x^* is said to be non-dominated and called as a Pareto optimal solution. The set consisting of all non-dominated solutions is called the Pareto optimal set. Accordingly, the images of all the Pareto optimal solutions in the objective space form the Pareto front.*

Figure 1. Example of non-dominated solutions in the Pareto front for a two objectives minimization problem

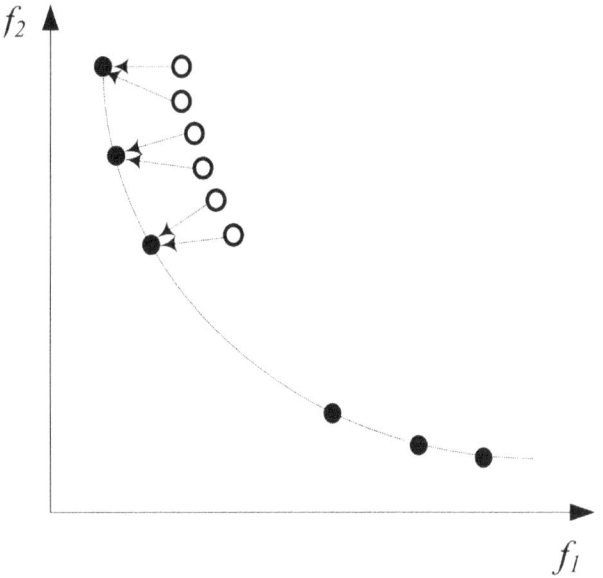

A great deal of multi-objective bio-inspired optimization algorithms use a secondary population, called archive, in which the non-dominated solutions are kept along the evolutionary process. The primary goal is to promote the evolution of non-dominated solutions, with secondary goal of obtaining Pareto-fronts as wide as possible, with a diverse representation of solutions along the front which should be as uniformly distributed as possible. Due to the complexity associated with this type of problem, particularly concerning multi-objective objective problems with multi-modal search landscapes, is quite easy for a multi-objective algorithm to become trapped in a local front instead of the Pareto-front. Also, for a great number of practical problems knowledge about the precise location of the Pareto front does not exist, and it is difficult to measure if the achieved non-dominated front is or not the real Pareto-front. So, a great deal of techniques have been proposed to deal with the archive management and updating of the new population. Reference techniques for the case of multi-objective genetic algorithms are the Strength Pareto Evolutionary Algorithm (SPEA2) (Zitzler *et al.*, 2001) and the non-dominated sorting genetic algorithm (NSGA-II) proposed by Deb *et al.* (2001). A successful and effective maxi-min technique to promote solution uniformity along the Pareto-front has been proposed by Pires *et al.* (2005).

While in terms of a DE algorithm transition from single-objective optimization to multi-objective, the procedure can be the same, or very similar, to the one used for MOGA, this is not the case for the PSO algorithm. Without entering in great detail, not to lose scope of the general perspective which is the aim of this section, one of the key questions is: how to choose global particles in this case? Opposite to the single-objective case in which the global best particle is easy to determine, as it depends only on the neighborhood adopted. In the general case, using a fully connected neighborhood, in which every particle shares information with all the other swarm particles, determining the global best particle is trivial. Considering the example provided in Figure 1, which is the best global particle in terms of non-dominance that the non-filled particle should follow? It makes sense that it selects one of the nearest non-dominated Pareto-front particles, in the objective space, which in this example are better regarding the minimization of objective f_1. However, in terms of diversity promotion and search space exploration it may be advisable in some cases to promote a different selection of a global best. For instance, in the example provided in Figure 1, that the non-filled particle selects as global leader one of the three particles which are better in terms of f_2 minimization. These issues are the ones which makes multi-objective particle swarming optimization (MOPSO) algorithms quite different to tackle than MOGA and multi-objective differential evolution (MODE). Some examples of MOPSO algorithm are: the Speed-Constrained Multi-objective Particle Swarm Optimization (SMPSO), Nebro *et al.* (2009), Maximin MOPSO, Moura Oliveira *et al.* (2009), two-lbests MOPSO, Zhao and Suganthan (2011), while more can be found in the survey papers: Sierra and Coello, (2006) and Lalwani *et al.* (2013). An example of a MODE is Generalized Differential Evolution (GDE3) proposed by (Kukkonen and Lampinen, 2005) and more DE algorithm can be found in the survey presented by Cheng and Zhang (2013).

To conclude this section a brief reference is made to Many-objective optimization algorithm, which refers to the case of considering 4 or more design objectives. Currently, significant research efforts are being devoted to the development of many-objective optimization algorithms. The complexity involved in solving this type of problem is significantly increased compared to the multi-objective case. Some the motives behind the increase of complexity are the following (Freire *et al.*, 2014), considering the use of non-dominated based approaches:

- It is proved that (Corne and Knowles, 2007; Ishibuchi *et al.*, 2008b, Deb and Jain, 2012) there is a tendency to achieve populations with non-dominated solutions, in a very early evolutionary stage. This compromises and deteriorates the search ability.
- The quantity of solutions to approximate the Pareto-front increases exponentially with the number of objectives.
- Visualizing the non-dominated solutions for the many-objective case is more complex. This is a relevant issue as there is no point in achieving multi-dimensional non-dominated Pareto fronts if there is not appropriate tools which enable the decision-maker to easily select the most appropriate solution(s) for its specific problem.

APPLICATIONS IN CONFLICT RESOLUTION PROBLEM SOLVING

The first technique addressed in this applications review is the genetic algorithm (GA). A research and application area involving conflict resolution which has been tackled by using bio-inspired meta-heuristics is aircraft air-traffic related. One of the problems concerns the development of systems which can contribute to improve in finding conflict free aircraft trajectories (and if possible which are optimal or near-optimal). The real time aircraft conflict resolution was addressed by Durand *et al.* (1996), by proposing a genetic algorithm using a simulated annealing tournament selection scheme, a sharing technique and adapted crossover and mutation operators. In the near future, due to the increasing number of flights, air traffic control management will allow more free flights. This will require individual aircrafts to establish their own route and systems which will solve possible conflicts in the optimized trajectories. This problem was addressed by Malaek and Alaeddini (2009) using a GA. In this study different approaches regarding conflicting aircrafts positioning in a web are presented and respective chromosome encoding aspects detailed and a case study considering horizontal maneuvers addressed. A cooperative co-evolutionary approach based on genetic algorithm is proposed by XueJun *et al.* (2013) to address multi-aircraft conflict resolution. In this study, a dynamic approach is proposed to organize the aircrafts in sub-groups which are encoded as GA sub-populations optimized accordingly to criteria such aircraft paths optimization. More studies concerning the use of GA based air traffic management techniques can be found in (Bai & Zhang, 2011; Dougui *et al.*, 2013). Related applications concerning conflict resolution within unmanned vehicles, validated by using experiments with quadrotors are reported in (Granger *et al.*, 2001; Cobano *et al.*, 2011; Conde *et al.*, 2012). Here a GA based technique, involving the cooperation among several aerial vehicles which may have trajectory conflicts, is proposed and tested. Conflict detection and resolution addressed using a multi-objective genetic algorithm (MOGA) approach based on Pareto Optimality was proposed by Alam *et al.* (2009). This study addresses conflict resolution within free flight operations.

Conflict resolution in requirement engineering using GA was proposed by Ramzan *et al.* (2012). In this study the problem, deals with the type of conflict which occurs between stakeholders about system requirements. The GA is used to solve a problem considering a set of requirements which is to be optimized by minimizing a sub-set of conflict requirements. In this technique there is an iterative process which requires clients to assign weights to the identified conflicts, which will determine a weighted sum to be checked by the proposed fitness function. A MOGA approach to research trade-offs between several notions of fairness between multiple clients is proposed by Finkelstein *et al.* (2008). The non-dominated sorting genetic algorithm (NSGA-II) proposed originally by Deb *et al.* (2001), is used to balance the requirements fulfillment among costumers. Other application of the NSGA-II can be found in Niksokhan *et al.* (2009), concerning conflict resolution for trading pollutant discharges permits in rivers. Here the trade-off to be optimized is between treatment costs and risks to violate water quality standards in disputes between decision-makers and stake-holders.

Another interesting research and application area in which GA were deployed as a tool is the conflict resolution within court of law disputes was reported by Carneiro *et al.* (2013). In this work each population member encodes a potential solution to a conflict, regarding for instance the division of items in a divorce dispute. A crucial aspect of the GA in the former study are the fitness functions proposed where the individual preferences and value assigned to each item in dispute, by the different dispute agents.

Regarding the particle swarm optimization (PSO) algorithm, the number of conflict resolution application is increasing. The field of intelligent transportation systems, and the need to increase security by integrating cooperative coordinated techniques among vehicles and infrastructures facilities motivates the proposal of new techniques for conflict resolution. This is the case of the PSO based technique proposed by Lui *et al.* (2013) concerning the problem of vehicle safety at unsignalized intersections. Conflict resolution within the free flight problematic is addressed with a PSO algorithm by Emami and Derakhshan (2014), using a multi-agent framework. Following the framework presented for GAs by the same research group, Alejo *et al.* (2012), addressed conflict resolution problems for ensuring collision free trajectories. In this case, once collisions are detected for current planned trajectories, the technique proposes a feasible non-optimal solution, which is then refined by the PSO algorithm. Another PSO application is reported by Wang (2011) to solve conflict resolution problems in collaborative product design. In this case the use of varying decaying inertia weights is explored as well as an adaptive weighting version.

A general integrating paper from Maier *et al.* (2014) integrates several evolutionary algorithms and other metaheuristics, also addressing conflict resolution issues in water resources optimization. Specific issues concerning the understanding of fitness landscape properties and their influence in the algorithm performance are studied. An attempt to benchmark conflict resolution algorithms for air traffic (centralized and autonomous approaches) is reported by Vanaret *et al.* (2013). In this study, GAs, PSO and the differential evolution algorithm (DE) are applied to two problems.

CONFLICT RESOLUTION IN FEEDBACK CONTROLLER DESIGN

In this section a different approach regarding the design of feedback controllers is addressed. The type of industrial controller considered is the most popular industrial controller: the proportional integrative and derivative (PID) controller. Considering the block diagram representation of a single-input single

Figure 2. Single-input single-output feedback control system representation

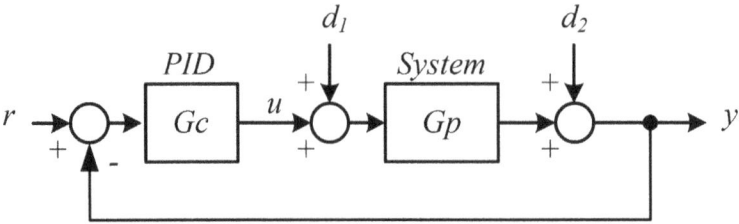

output control system, with *r* representing the reference input (also known as set-point), y the system controlled output, d_1 a load disturbance, d_2 an output disturbance, *u* the controller output, *Gc* the PID controller and *Gp* the system to be controlled.

The PID design problem is quite simple to state; The controller has three control actions: i) proportional to the error signal (u_p) ii) proportional to the integral of the error (u_i) and iii) proportional to the derivative of the error (u_d). The final control signal, *u*, can be evaluated as a weighted sum of the three components as follows: $u = K_p u_p + K_i u_i + K_d u_d$. The weights are known as gains: *K*p represents the proportional gain, K_i the integrative gain and K_d the derivative gain. Thus, the PID design consist in determining the best set for $\{K_p, K_i, K_d\}$ for a specific system to be controlled, regarding pre-specified criteria. Classical design of PID controllers is generally based on a single design criterion. As two of the most relevant control design criteria are: i) the system controlled output, *y*, should track as close as possible the input command signal, r. This control design objective is generally known as set-point tracking; ii) the system controlled output should reject as much as possible all the undesired system disturbances (and signal noise, input not represented in Figure 1, for simplicity sake). This control design objective is generally known as disturbance rejection. At this point the reader, may be asking itself: where is the conflict in this case? The conflict may arise, when the settings selected for the PID controller for optimally rejecting disturbances, have poor performance for set-point tracking and vice-versa. Single-criteria design of PID controller (considering different control structures configurations) with bio-inspired algorithm has been studied over the last 20 years by the first author: using GAs (Jones and Moura Oliveira, 1995, 1996, 1997; Moura Oliveira and Jones, 2001), using PSO (Moura Oliveira *et al.*, 2002; Coelho *et al.*, 2006), using DE (Moura Oliveira, 2005).

There are cases in which there are variations in the dynamics of the system to be controlled. These changes may be represented in the system model, by assuming parametric variations. In these cases, a fixed gain parameter PID controller performance will vary with the model parameter set. Designing controllers to hold a minimum performance value in all the plant parametric envelope is a desirable feature. This problem was formulated as representing a conflict between controllers and plants. A competitive co-evolutionary approach was proposed by (Moura Oliveira and Jones, 1997; 2000) to solve this problem. The general idea is to use two populations: one representing potential solutions for PID controllers and the other representing potential solutions for the plant model parameters. Each population is evolved using a GA. The objective function of the controller's population is to minimize a time-domain error based criterion and the objective of the plant population is to maximize the same criterion. As in natural competitive co-evolution, with the arms race between predators and preys, when properly balanced by nature, improve the average fitness of both populations over time, the artificial competitive co-evolution has the same effect. While the controller GA tries to find the best controllers, the plant GA tries to find the worth possible plants to be controlled. A technique detailed in (Moura Oliveira and Jones, 1997; 2000) is proposed in order to ensure that the resulting controller can control all possibilities evolved in the plant population, with a minimum performance value guarantied in the entire parameter envelope.

Another approach which can be considered as a conflict resolution problem for PID controller design, is when more than one design criterion is considered. Indeed, it only makes sense to consider multi-objective optimization if the design objectives are conflicting, meaning that when one is optimize regarding its objective function this will make the performance of the other objective function to be worth. The problem described based on Figure 1 for set-point tracking and disturbance rejection is one these cases. Thus, a MOPSO was proposed by (Moura Oliveira *et al.*, 2009) to design PID controllers regarding two design objectives. More recently the number of control design objectives considered was increased and a many-objective MOPSO was proposed by (Freire *et al.*, 2014) to design PID controllers to deal simultaneously with four design objectives.

PERSPECTIVES OF EVOLUTION

In this section a perspective of future trends of bio-inspired metaheuristics is presented. As stated previously, there is an enormous success of application of this type of search and optimization methods in conflict detection and resolution problems. This is not surprising, as the same occurs in almost all the engineering and computer science research and development areas. Indeed these techniques: GA, PSO and DE, have been applied to a wide and broad application scope transversal to all research fields. Why? Because most of these techniques can be implemented with "no knowledge" about the problem to be solved, meaning that they primarily require a solution cost evaluation. However, in practice, in order to be successful, there are certain adjustable heuristics in every algorithm which may benefit from problem specific knowledge, and can be fine-tuned by experts in the fields. Also the problem formulation is of crucial importance.

So, what are (in the author's view) the main evolutionary tracks concerning (but not restricted) conflict resolution problem solving? The following points summarizes potential answers to this question:

- *Multi-objective and Many-objective.* Clearly there are opportunities to extend most of the work done in conflict resolution, to problems dealing with single-criterion optimization problems to multi-criteria, by using multi-objective bio-inspired algorithms. As presented before, while there are some reports addressing multi-objective optimization in this area, there is still a lot of open research issues. In practice, most of the problems are multi-criteria, but treated as single-objective problems to simplify the optimization process. This is possible because, often there is one criterion which is by far the most relevant to be optimized. However, neglecting other design criteria may compromise the quality of the final optimal solution achieved. With future advances in the ever increasing computational power, the natural evolution is that these techniques will tend to deal with many-objective optimization cases, fast and effectively. The decision-maker will be provided with user-friendly software which will enable and help him to select the most appropriate optimal solution for their specific problem.
- *Exploration of other nature and bio-inspired algorithms.* Some of the more recently introduced methods such as: firefly algorithm Yang (2008), cuckoo search algorithm (Yang and Deb, 2009), gravitational search algorithm (Rashedi *et al.*, 2009), bacterial foraging (Passino, 2002), can also be explored by incorporating them into conflict resolution problem solving. The authors of this chapter are firmly convicted that there is still a large improvement margin concerning the development and use of bio-inspired metaheuristics.

CONCLUSION

In this chapter the use of population-based nature and bio-inspired metaheuristics was addressed in the context of conflict detection and resolution problem solving. Three of the most popular and well-established techniques were reviewed: genetic algorithm, particle swarm optimization algorithm and differential evolution. For the former three techniques, the very basic and elementary algorithms were presented in an integrated form, which provides an easy understanding of the existing similarities and differences. This simplified approach, tries to clarify some key issues, and provide the reader with the elementary concepts which may enable their fast implementation using any programing language. The GA, PSO and DE algorithms were reviewed in terms of current applications in conflict resolution problem solving. The applications reviewed cover a wide set of different types of conflicts, ranging from air traffic management and control to water management systems. One of the main strengths of nature and bio-inspired techniques is that can be interpreted as "blind" to the specific problem to be solved, as they only require the merit evaluation of potential solutions to a specific problem. This also explains the diversity of applications.

A perspective of conflict resolution within feedback controller design was presented, bridging several of the population-based bio-inspired techniques addressed. The connection from single-objective to multiple-objective and many-objective search and optimization methods was presented, based on the concepts of Pareto non-dominance optimality.

Finally some perspectives of evolution concerning possible advances in the use of bio-inspired metaheuristics were presented, outlining some of more recently introduced algorithms.

REFERENCES

Alam, S., Shafi, K., Abbass, H. A., & Barlow, M. (2009). An ensemble approach for conflict detection in Free Flight by data mining. *Transportation Research*, *17*(Part C), 298–317. doi:10.1016/j.trc.2008.12.002

Alejo, D., Cobano, J. A., Heredia, G., & Heredia, G. (2013). Particle Swarm Optimization for collision-free 4D trajectory planning in Unmanned Aerial Vehicles. *International Conference on Unmanned Aircraft Systems (ICUAS)*. doi:10.1109/ICUAS.2013.6564702

Bai, C., & Zhang, X. (2011). Aircraft Landing Scheduling in the Small Aircraft Transportation System. *IEEE International Conference on Computational and Information Sciences*. doi:10.1109/ICCIS.2011.65

Carneiro, D., Novais, P., & Neves, J. (2013). Using genetic algorithms to create solutions for conflict resolution. *Neurocomputing*, *109*, 16–26. doi:10.1016/j.neucom.2012.03.024

Cheng, J., & Zhang, G. (2013). Multi-objective Differential Evolution: A Recent Survey. *Soft Computing with Applications*, *1*(1). doi:10.4156/sca.vol1.issue1.1

Cobano, J. A., Conde, R., Alejo, D., & Ollero, A. (2011). Conflict detection and resolution algorithm for en-route conflicts in dense non-segregated aerial traffic. *1st Int. Conf. on Application and Theory of Automation in Command and Control Systems (ATACCS 2011)*.

Coelho, J. P., Moura Oliveira, P. B., Boaventura Cunha, J., & Vrancic, D. (2006). On-Line Control using the Particle Swarm Optimisation Algorithm. *The 6th Asian Control Conference*.

Conde, R., Alejo, D., Cobano, J. A., Viguria, A., & Ollero, A. (2012). Conflict Detection and Resolution Method for Cooperating Unmanned Aerial Vehicles. *Journal of Intelligent & Robotic Systems*, *65*(1-4), 495–505. doi:10.1007/s10846-011-9564-6

Corne, D., & Knowles, J. (2007). Techniques for Highly Multiobjective Optimisation: Some Nondominated Points are Better than Others. Academic Press.

Deb, K., & Jain, H. (2012). Handling many-objective problems using an improved NSGA-II procedure. In *IEEE Congress on Evolutionary Computation (CEC)*. doi:10.1109/CEC.2012.6256519

Deb, K., Pratap, A., Agarwal, S., & Meyarivan, T. (2002). A Fast and Elitist Multiobjective Genetic Algorithm: NSGA–II. *IEEE Transactions on Evolutionary Computation*, *6*(2), 182–197. doi:10.1109/4235.996017

Dougui, N., Delahaye, D., Puechmorel, S., & Mongeau, M. (2013). A light-propagation model for aircraft trajectory planning. *Journal of Global Optimization*, *56*(3), 873–895. doi:10.1007/s10898-012-9896-1

Durand, N., Alliot, J. M., & Noailles, J. (1996). Automatic aircraft conflict resolution using genetic algorithms. In *Proceedings of the 1996 ACM symposium on Applied Computing*, (pp. 289-298).

Emami, H., & Derakhshan, F. (2014). Multi-Agent Based Solution for Free Flight Conflict Detection and Resolution using Particle Swarm Optimization Algorithm. *U.P.B. Sci. Bull., Series C, 76*(3), 49-64.

Finkelstein, A., Harman, M., Mansouri, S. A., Ren, J., & Zhang, Y. (2008). Fairness Analysis. In *Requirements Assignments, 16th IEEE International Requirements Engineering Conference*, (pp. 115-124). Doi:10.1109/RE.2008.61

Freire, H. F., Moura Oliveira, P. B., Solteiro Pires, E. J., & Bessa, M. (2014). Many-Objective PSO PID Controller Tuning. In *Proceedings of the 11th Portuguese Conference on Automatic Control Lecture Notes in Electrical Engineering*. Springer. doi:10.1007/978-3-319-10380-8_18

Goldberg, E. D. (1989). *Genetic Algorithms in Search*. Optimization and Machine Learning, Adison Wesley P.C.

Granger, G., Durand, N., & Alliot, J. M. (2001). *Optimal Resolution of En Route Conflicts*. 4th ATM R&D Seminar, Santa Fe, NM.

Holland J. H., (1975). *Adaptation in Natural and Artificial Systems*. MIT Press.

Ishibuhi, H., Tsukamoto, N., & Nojima, Y. (2008). Evolutionary many-objective optimization: A short review. *IEEE Congress on Evolutionary Computation. IEEE World Congress on Computational Intelligence.*

Jones, A. H., & Moura Oliveira, P. B. (1995). Genetic Auto-Tuning of PID Controllers. In *Proceedings of the First IEE Conference on Genetic Algorithms in Engineering Systems: Innovations and Applications* (GALESIA'95). doi:10.1049/cp:19951039

Jones, A. H., & Moura Oliveira, P. B. (1996). Auto-Tuning of PI Smith Predictor Controllers using Genetic Algorithms. *Control'96: UKACC International Conference on Control*. doi:10.1049/cp:19960595

Kennedy, J., & Eberhart, R. C. (1995). Particle swarm optimization. *Proc. IEEE Int. Conf. on Neural Networks, 4*, 1942–1948. doi:10.1109/ICNN.1995.488968

Lalwani, S., Singhal, S., Kumar, R., & Gupta, N. (2013). A comprehensive survey: Applications of multi-objective particle swarm optimization (MOPSO) algorithm. *Transactions on Combinatorics, 2*(1), 39-101.

Liu, J., Cai, B., Wang, Y., & Wang, J. (2013). A lane level positioning-based cooperative vehicle conflict resolution algorithm for unsignalized intersection collisions. *Computers & Electrical Engineering, 39*(5), 1381–1398. doi:10.1016/j.compeleceng.2013.04.011

Maier, H. R., Kapelan, Z., Kasprzyk, J., Kollat, J., Matott, L. S., Cunha, M. C., & Reed, P. M. et al. (2014). Evolutionary algorithms and other metaheuristics in water resources: Current status, research challenges and future directions. *Environmental Modelling & Software, 62*, 271–299. doi:10.1016/j.envsoft.2014.09.013

Malaek, M. B., & Alaeddini, A. (2009). Conflict Resolution Maneuvers Based on Genetic Algorithm Modified Webs. *IEEE Aerospace Conference*. doi:10.1109/AERO.2009.4839430

Margarita, R. S., & Coello, C. A. C. (2006). Multi-objective particle swarm optimizers: A survey of the state-of-the-art. *International Journal of Computational Intelligence Research, 2*(3).

Moura Oliveira, P. B. (2001). Design of Discrete Non-linear Two-degrees-of-freedom PID Controllers using Genetic Algorithms. In *Fifth International Conference on Artificial Neural Networks and Genetic Algorithms*, (pp. 320-323). Springer Computer Science. doi:10.1007/978-3-7091-6230-9_79

Moura Oliveira, P. B. (2005). Modern Heuristics Review for PID Control Systems Optimization: a Teaching Experiment. *IEEE-International Conference on Control and Automation* (ICCA2005), (pp. 828-833). doi:10.1109/ICCA.2005.1528237

Moura Oliveira, P. B., Boaventura Cunha, J., & Coelho, J. P. (2002). Design of PID Controllers using the Particle Swarm Algorithm. *23rd IASTED International Conference in Modelling, Identification and Control (MIC 2002)*, (pp. 263-268).

Moura Oliveira, P. B. & Jones, A. H. (1997). Evolutionary Approaches to the Design of Cascade Controllers. *5as Jornadas Hispano-Lusas de Ingeniería Eléctrica, 3*, pp. 1745-1752.

Moura Oliveira, P. B., & Jones, A. H. (1997). Robust Co-evolutionary Design of SISO Smith Predictor for PID Controllers. *2nd IEE Conference on Genetic Algorithms in Engineering Systems: Innovations and Applications*. doi:10.1049/cp:19971231

Moura Oliveira, P. B., & Jones, A. H. (2000). Co-Evolutionary Design of PID Control Structures. In *Proceedings of the IFAC Workshop on Digital Control: Past, Present and Future of PID Control- PID'00*. Pergamon.

Moura Oliveira, P. B., Boaventura, J., Solteiro Pires, E. J., & Vrancic, D. (2009). Multi-objective Particle Swarm Optimization Design of PID Controllers. *Workshop on Soft Computing Models in Industrial Applications (SOCO'09), Part II* (LNCS), (vol. 5518, pp. 1222-1230). Springer-Verlag.

Passino, K. M. (2002). Biomimicry of bacterial foraging for distributed optimization and control. *IEEE Control Systems Magazine, 22*(3), 52–67. doi:10.1109/MCS.2002.1004010

Pires, E. J. S., Moura Oliveira, P. B., & Machado, J. A. T. (2005). *Multi objective MaxiMin Sorting Scheme*, (Vol. 3410). Notes in Comp. Science.

Ramzan, M., Khan, Q. M., Iqbal, M. A., Aasem, M., Jaffar, A., Anwar, S., & Alam, M. et al. (2012). A genetic algorithms based approach for conflicts resolution in requirement. *International Journal of the Physical Sciences*, 6(4), 828–836.

Rashedi, E., Nezamabadi-pour, H., & Saryazdi, S. (2009). GSA: A Gravitational Search Algorithm. *Information Sciences*, 179(13), 2232–2248. doi:10.1016/j.ins.2009.03.004

Storn, R., & Price, K. (1997). Differential Evolution: A Simple and Efficient Adaptive Scheme for Global Optimization Over Continuous Spaces. *Journal of Global Optimization*, 11(4), 341–349. doi:10.1023/A:1008202821328

Vanaret, C., Gianazza, D., Durand, N., & Gotteland, J. B. (2012). *Benchmarking conflict resolution algorithms*. ICRAT 2012, 5th International Conference on Research in Air Transportation, Berkeley, CA.

Xue, J. Z., Xiang, M. G., Inseok, H., & Kai, Q. C. (2013). A hybrid distributed-centralized conflict resolution approach for multi-aircraft based on cooperative co-evolutionary. *Science China, 56*. DOI: 10.1007/s11432-013-4836-3

Yang, X. S. (2008). Firefly algorithm. In X.-S. Yang (Ed.), *Nature-inspired metaheuristic algorithms* (pp. 79–90). Wiley Online Library.

Yang, X. S., & Deb, S. (2009). Cuckoo Search via Lévy flights. In *NaBIC World Congress on Nature & Biologically Inspired Computing*.

Zhao, S. Z., & Suganthan, P. N. (2011). Two-lbests based multi-objective particle swarm optimizer. *Engineering Optimization*, 43(1), 1–17. doi:10.1080/03052151003686716

Zitzler, E., Laumanns, M., & Thiele, L. (2001). *SPEA2: Improving the Strength Pareto Evolutionary Algorithm*. Technical Report 103, Computer Engineering and Networks Laboratory (TIK), Swiss Federal Institute of Technology (ETH) Zurich.

KEY TERMS AND DEFINITIONS

Conflicting Objectives in Feedback Control: Refers to design objectives, that when one is optimized it degrades the performance of at least one other objective.

Many-Objective: Refers to problem requiring the optimization of more than four criteria.

Multi-Objective: Refers to a problem requiring the optimization of several optimization criteria.

Nature and Bio-Inspired Metaheuristics: Techniques and/or algorithms inspired in natural and biological phenomena used to solve iteratively search and optimization problems.

Pareto Front: Refers to images of all the Pareto optimal solutions in the objective space.

Pareto Optimal Set: Refers to a set consisting of all non-dominated solutions.

Population-Based Algorithms: Based on the use of a set of potential solutions for a given problem.

Single-Objective: Refers to a problem requiring the optimization of a single criterion.

Chapter 11

Opinion Aggregation and Conflict Resolution in E–Government Platforms:
Contrasting Social Media Information through Argumentation

Carlos Ivan Chesnevar
Universidad Nacional del Sur, Argentina

María Paula González
Universidad Nacional del Sur, Argentina

Ana Gabriela Maguitman
Universidad Nacional del Sur, Argentina

Elsa Estevez
United Nations University, Japan

ABSTRACT

This chapter presents an account of recent advances in the development of a novel e-participation frame-work which integrates social networks, intelligent information retrieval and argumentation techniques. We discuss a novel conceptualization for Electronic Empowerment Participation (E2P), a radically new perspective on e-Participation, where collective thinking patterns can be identified under the generic form of "arguments", being contrasted automatically and enhancing thus the abilities of the different stakeholders to engage in creative participatory processes. The underlying machinery that makes E2P possible is given by agreement technologies, a new metaphor that integrates several aspects from database theory, artificial intelligence, multi-agent systems and social infrastructures. A core component in this conceptualization is an underlying argument-based approach, which allows to mine opinions from text-based information items based on incrementally generated topics.

INTRODUCTION AND MOTIVATION

At the dawn of the United Nations (UN) Agenda for Post 2015 (UN General Assembly, 2014), governments around the world have already recognized that the current development paths are unsustainable and that new governance mechanisms need to be envisioned to promote sustainable development - sustained

DOI: 10.4018/978-1-5225-0245-6.ch011

and inclusive economic growth, social development and environmental protection. In particular, one of the major governance goals for achieving sustainable development is to develop more fair, equitable and inclusive societies, where the voice and needs of all stakeholders are heard and considered. For this reason, stakeholder engagement is at the core of most government initiatives in the post-2015 age.

The voice and needs of government stakeholders are usually contradictory, since they usually represent opposed interest from different groups - e.g. on the one hand, businesses are interested in pursuing economic development, while on the other hand, environmentalists are concerned with protecting natural resources against blind economic interests. Developing new governance mechanisms contributing to bridge differences among stakeholders' needs post various types of challenges - technical, political, organizational, etc.; that governments need to overcome. At the same time, Information and Communication Technologies (ICTs) offer new and innovative solutions that governments can adopt to resolve some of such technical and governance-related challenges.

Within the scenario described above, a fundamental need for policy makers and government decision makers is to back their decisions and agreements on arguments and opinions provided by citizens. They might even argue with other policy makers about why making a particular decision is advisable (e.g. "according to the last poll, 80% of the people are against the health system reform; therefore, the reform should not be carried out"). From this perspective, new ITCs used by citizens in their daily lives, like Facebook and Twitter provide a unique opportunity for governments to leverage on technologies already infused and adopted by the society, providing a knowledge base from which information could be collected and analyzed in order to provide inputs and partially automatize government decision making processes. In particular, tweets have a rich structure, providing a number of record fields which allow to detect provenance of the tweet (author), number of re-tweets, followers, etc.

Aware about the need for citizen participation, governments at different levels - national, regional and local, in most countries are seeking their participation through the use of ICTs (Electronic Participation or e-Participation). Most e-Participation initiatives nowadays take place within ad-hoc platforms which provide suitable channels for efficient electronic communication and coordination connecting the involved stakeholders (e.g. government-citizens, government-business, citizens-citizens, partnerbusiness, etc.). Nevertheless, such platforms do not provide suitable and generic components to model and process emerging *collective thinking patterns* in communities; although understanding such patterns is a mainstream trend nowadays in daily life, particularly through the widespread use of social media and their support by mobile technologies. Collective thinking patterns could correspond to ideas, proposals, criticisms or viewpoints, which decision makers can identify and confront based on atomic, individual inputs from citizens and users, such as tweets, Facebook posts, web-based product reviews, etc. Such patterns can take place in different policy contexts associated with social innovation and change, e.g. crowdfunding initiatives, citizen journalism, cyberactivism, etc.

Government 2.0 refers to government's adoption of Web 2.0 technologies to socialize government services, processes, and data, improving relationships between government and the governed. Enabling new communication channels - such as social media, wikis, blogs, and others; and two-way communication - enabling to push and pull information to and from citizens; Government 2.0 provides new mechanisms for government agencies to: 1) increase transparency –bringing public sector agenda and government activities closer to citizens; 2) facilitate participation –engaging citizens in government decision- and policy-making processes; and 3) enhance service delivery –pushing service-related information and gathering citizens' opinions about service delivery to design customer-oriented public services that better serve their needs.

To materialize the benefits promised by Government 2.0, public institutions must resolve several issues related to privacy, security, data management, accessibility, digital divide, governance and policy, among many others. Focusing on the data management perspective, the aggregation of information from data streams in social media tools (such as Facebook or Twitter) requires solving two important issues: 1) the magnitude of the information flow associated with such data streams (e.g. Twitter disseminates 55 million tweets a day), and 2) the extraction of meaningful information and the determination of potential conflicting views (viewpoints emerging from social media data streams are usually in conflict, as citizens might have different views on a certain issue).

In this context, over the last few years *argumentation systems* (Rawhan, & Simari, 2009; García, & Simari, 2004; Besnard, & Hunter, 2008; Modgil et al, 2012) have been gaining increasing importance in several areas of Artificial Intelligence, mainly as a vehicle for facilitating rationally justifiable decision making when handling incomplete and potentially inconsistent information. Argumentation provides a sound model for dialectical reasoning, which underlies discussions or opinion confrontation in social networks. Argumentation systems are increasingly being considered for applications in developing software engineering tools, constituting an important component of multi-agent systems for negotiation, problem solving, and for the fusion of data and knowledge. Such systems implement a dialectical reasoning process by determining whether a proposition follows from certain assumptions, analyzing whether some of those assumptions can be disproved by other assumptions in our premises. In this way, an argumentation system provides valuable help to analyze which assumptions from our knowledge base are really giving rise to inconsistency and which assumptions are harmless.

The underlying idea of applying argumentation systems for mining citizens' opinions on a given topic is the following. Given a topic, we will model the notion of opinion supporting it as a collection of atomic opinions, which can be aggregated according to certain specific criteria. Based on topic specificity and preferences defined on different dimensions or features, opinions can be contrasted with counter-opinions, which have to be preferred (according to a partial order) with respect to the opinion at issue. As a result, we will be able to obtain an "opinion analysis tree", rooted in the first original topic. Distinguished, conflicting elements in an opinion tree lead to so-called "conflict opinion analysis trees", which resemble dialectical trees as those used traditionally in argumentation theory. In our analysis, we distinguish a particular function for abstracting away the "sentiment" associated with a particular piece of information. Different sentiments can be established as a reference value (e.g. anger, joy, etc.), in a modular way independent from the general framework. By aggregating single pieces of information the general sentiment of the emerging "opinion" can be established. Every opinion is rooted in a particular set of keywords, which is expanded into larger sets in order to get possible counter-opinions, counter-counter-opinions, and so on. We also provide theoretical results which account for an algebraic characterization of our proposal, using equivalence classes to minimize the representation space to be analyzed when contrasting arguments. As a case study, we will present different real-world examples from Twitter, showing the emerging argument-based characterization obtained from our proposal, based on a prototypical implementation of the underlying algorithm in Java.

Bringing argumentation into the scene provides enormous advantages for the analysis of e-Participation scenarios. Rather than simply collecting statistics showing the amount of people that support certain views, the proposed approach makes it possible to aggregate reasoned explanations of why certain groups of people adhere to or go against an issue or initiative. In doing so, recognizing the preferences of the crowds will be important but even more important will be the possibility of getting a structured picture of how different opinions interrelate. This allows analyzing how opinions change through time, or across communities, or when the topic under analysis becomes more specific, providing a powerful approach to conflict resolution. Contrary arguments can be incrementally incorporated by individuals, giving rise to arguments pro and con an issue. By exposing the individuals to the set of arguments, individuals can both update their statements, and critically understand why specific decisions were made, or conclusions were reached. At a societal level, this approach enables more people to participate in large-scale decision making processes through opinion provision. This helps to ensure that the opinions advanced by individuals are well-informed and legitimate and that any decisions made are acceptable and understood by the society.

This book chapter presents an account of recent advances in the development of a novel e-participation framework which integrates social networks (particularly Twitter), intelligent information retrieval and argumentation techniques. This research started within the LACCIR Project DECIDE 2.0 (funded by Microsoft Research Latin America and the Inter-American Development Bank), which aims at integrating Artificial Intelligence and Software Engineering techniques and tools with Electronic Governance models and principles to design innovative tools for conflict resolution in e-Government contexts. We discuss a novel conceptualization for Electronic Empowerment Participation (E^{2}P), a radically new perspective on e-Participation, where collective thinking patterns can be identified under the generic form of "arguments", being contrasted automatically and enhancing thus the abilities of the different stakeholders to engage in creative participatory processes. The underlying machinery that makes E^{2}P possible is given by agreement technologies, a new metaphor that integrates several aspects from database theory, artificial intelligence, multi-agent systems and social infrastructures. A core component in this conceptualization is an underlying argument-based approach, which allows to mine opinions from text-based information items based on incrementally generated topics.

Following this introduction, the rest of this chapter is structured as follows. Section 2 explains the fundamentals about argumentation technologies. Section 3 presents the proposed E^{2}P framework. Section 4 introduces the algorithms implemented in the E^{2}P framework tools, and Section 5 illustrates the application of the tools in two case studies. Finally, Section 6 discusses related work, while Section 7 draws some conclusions and future work.

ARGUMENTATION TECHNOLOGY: FUNDAMENTALS

Argumentation is an important aspect of human decision making. In many situations of everyday life, when faced with new information people need to ponder its consequences, in particular when attempting to understand problems and come to a decision. Argumentation systems (Rawhan & Simari, 2009; García & Simari, 2004; Besnard & Hunter, 2008) are increasingly being considered for applications in developing software engineering tools, constituting an important component of multi-agent systems for negotiation, problem solving, and for the fusion of data and knowledge. Such systems implement a dialectical reasoning process by determining whether a proposition follows from certain assumptions, analyzing whether some of those assumptions can be disproved by other assumptions in our premises. In this way, an argumentation system provides valuable help to analyze which assumptions from our knowledge base give rise to inconsistencies and which assumptions are harmless.

In defeasible argumentation, an *argument* is a tentative (defeasible) proof for reaching a conclusion. Arguments may compete, rebutting each other, so a *process* of argumentation is a natural result of the search for arguments. Adjudication of competing arguments must be performed, comparing arguments in order to determine what beliefs are ultimately accepted as *warranted* or *justified*. Preference among conflicting arguments is defined in terms of a *preference criterion* which establishes a partial order "$\preceq$" among possible arguments; thus, for two arguments A and B in conflict, it may be the case that A is strictly preferred over B ($A \succ B$), that A and B are equally preferred ($A \succeq B$ and $A \preceq B$) or that A and B are not comparable with each other. For the sake of example, let us consider the well-known example of nonmonotonic reasoning in AI about the flying abilities of birds, recast in argumentative terms. Consider the following sentences: (1) Birds usually fly; (2) Penguins usually do not fly; (3) Penguins are birds. The first two sentences correspond to *defeasible rules* (rules which are subject to possible exceptions). The third sentence is a *strict rule*, where no exceptions are possible. Given now the fact that *Tweety is a penguin* two different arguments can be constructed:

1. Argument A (based on rules 1 & 3): Tweety is a penguin. Penguins are birds. Birds usually fly. So Tweety flies.
2. Argument B (based on rule 2): Tweety is a penguin. Penguins usually do not fly. So Tweety does not fly.

In this particular situation, two arguments arise that cannot be accepted simultaneously (as they reach contradictory conclusions). Note that argument B seems rationally preferable over argument A, as it is based on more *specific* information. As a matter of fact, specificity is commonly adopted as a syntax-based criterion among conflicting arguments, preferring those arguments which are *more informed* or *more direct* (Besnard & Hunter, 2008). In this particular case, if we adopt specificity as a preference criterion, argument B is justified, whereas A is not (as it is defeated by B). The above situation can easily become much more complex, as an argument may be defeated by a second argument (a defeater), which in turn can be defeated by a third argument, *reinstating* the first one. As a given argument might have many defeaters, the above situation results in a tree-like structure, rooted in the first argument at issue, where every argument in a branch (except the root) defeats its parent.

Over the last few years, argumentation has been gaining increasing importance as a vehicle for facilitating "rational interaction" (i.e., interaction which involves the giving and receiving of reasons). This is because argumentation provides tools for designing, implementing and analysing sophisticated forms of interaction among rational agents. Argumentation has made solid contributions to the practice of multi-agent dialogues, and its application domains include: legal disputes, business negotiation, labor disputes, team formation, scientific inquiry, deliberative democracy, ontology reconciliation, risk analysis, scheduling, and logistics. A single agent may also use argumentation techniques to perform its individual reasoning because it needs to make decisions under complex preferences policies, in a highly dynamic environment.

In this context, different opinion groups may emerge, using online conversations and social media to coordinate and support decision-making. A fundamental need is to identify possible claims and the information provided to support them, as well as the user communities which are arguing pro and against different issues, within particular constraints (time, geographical location, etc.). This will lead to the generic characterization of collective thinking patterns as arguments, which will be presented in the next sections, providing a central component for the inference machinery used in the E2P framework.

THE E²P FRAMEWORK

Electronic Empowerment Participation (E²P) (Chesñevar et al, 2013; Chesñevar et al, 2014) captures a radically new perspective on e-Participation, where collective thinking patterns can be identified under the generic form of *"arguments"*, being contrasted automatically, enhancing thus the abilities of the different stakeholders to engage in creative participatory processes. The underlying machinery that makes E²P possible is given by agreement technologies (Ossowski, 2013), a new metaphor that integrates several aspects from database theory, artificial intelligence, multi-agent systems and social infrastructures.

The E²P framework relies on social media platforms as a generic communication platform, incorporating novel algorithms for performing intelligent aggregation and reasoning from the inputs of individual citizens and users in order to identify collective thinking patterns to assist in particular government-decision- and policy- makers in understanding public opinion. In particular, three main technologies are involved: 1) *Argumentation mechanisms* [6], which will help assess which arguments in online interactions and discussions have stronger grounds; 2) *Trust and reputation models* [2], which will be coupled with the argumentation mechanism to help assess the reliability of information and information sources; and (3) *Natural language processing*, which will be used in structuring online information by building argumentation graphs which provide the needed bases for argumentation mechanisms. The above three technologies will add structure to online information by linking scattered and unorganized information into coherent discussions; noise resulting from redundancy will be reduced through grouping related information together ; noise resulting from spam, lies and bias will be reduced by assessing the reliability of information.

The E²P Framework comprises a knowledge base storing users' opinions (UOK) and 6 major software components: 1) *NLP Component* – provides various Natural Language Processing (NLP) tools to extract terms, relations and entities, to parse text and do semantic annotation and semantic analysis; 2) *Argument Generation Component* – given a context C for analyzing opinions, the component generates pro and con arguments based on the opinions stored in UOK; 3) *Organization Ontology Component* – provides an ontology defining domain knowledge, such as information sources, concept hierarchies, social relations, etc.; 4) *Trust and Reputation Component* – implements a trust and reputation system to weigh arguments based on provenance and domain knowledge; 5) *Argument Assessment Component* – based on the status assigned to individual arguments, assesses and contrasts arguments considering various criteria, like attacked argument, accrual, user expertise; and 6) *Argument Visualization Component* – based on graphic user interfaces (GUI), the component enables to visualize dialectical analysis of arguments to support and facilitate decision-makers' tasks. In addition, the E²P framework includes an *Instantiation Procedure* providing guidelines to instantiate the framework for a given use case.

As can be seen from Figure 1, the E²P framework encompasses many components, many of which are currently under development. In line with the focus of this chapter concerning opinion aggregation and conflict resolution in e-government platforms, we will focus on the conceptualization of the Argument Generation Component and the Argument Assessment Component, using Twitter as underlying social network.

Figure 1. The E² participation framework

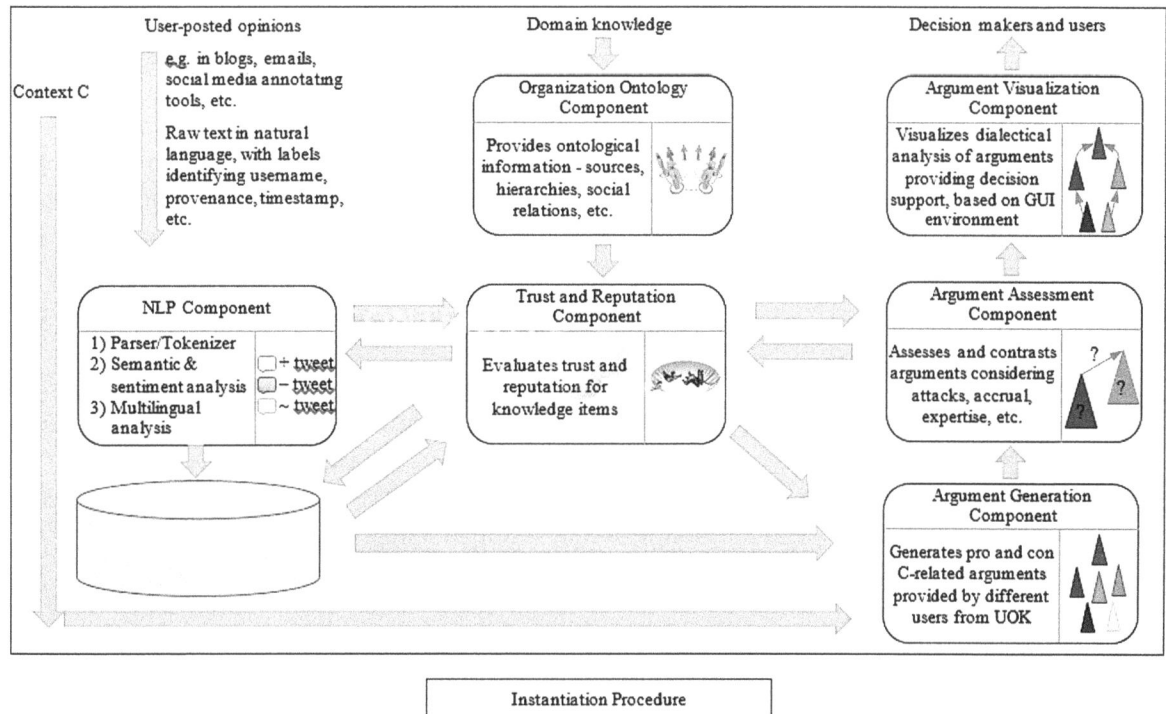

OPINION TREES IN E²P: CONTRASTING VIEWPOINTS AND SENTIMENTS

In this section we will summarize some of the major elements under consideration in E²P for formalizing argument construction and assessment, in particular when analyzing a particular, restricted form of input, namely tweets provided by users in a certain context.

Twitter messages (Tweets) are 140 character long, with a number of additional fields which help identify relevant information within a message (sender, number of retweets associated with the message, etc.). In particular, we will focus on the presence of descriptors which are either hashtags (words or phrases prefixed with the symbol #, a form of metadata tag) or terms that tend to occur often in the context of a given topic. Consider for example the issue "abortion". Some tweets on that topic could be as follows:

$Tweet_1$ = "government should ban #abortion, it means killing babies"
$Tweet_2$ = "#abortion is debatable, not all cases are to be equally considered"
$Tweet_3$ = "#abortion is a right every woman has. Defend it"
$Tweet_4$ = ...

We will assume that a tweet is just a "bag" of words, not taking into account the actual order of terms in the tweet. Additionally, we assume that the set of all currently existing tweets corresponds to a snapshot of Twitter messages at a given fixed time, as the Twitter database (i.e., the universe of tweets within a certain time frame) is highly dynamic. In our approach, a *query* Q is any set of descriptors used for filtering some relevant tweets from the set of existing tweets based on a given criterion C. In order to abstract away how such selection is performed, we will define an *aggregation operator* Agg(Q,C). There are several alternative definitions for Agg(Q,C). For instance, suppose that C_1 is a criterion that indicates that only tweets posted between timestamp T_1 and T_2 are to be selected. Then Agg(Q,C_1) will select only those tweets that contain all the terms of query Q and have been posted in the time period $[T_1,T_2]$. Other examples of criteria that can be naturally applied are, for instance, requiring that those tweets were retweeted more than n times, requiring that every user that posted tweets T has at least m followers, etc. Finally, we will also assume a set S of possible *sentiments*. A possible range for S could be *positive*, *negative* and *neutral* (as done for example in commercial platform sentiment140.com; in this platform, prevailing sentiments associated with a tweet set are expressed by percentages). For the sake of example, $Tweet_1$ could be considered as a negative tweet towards abortion, whereas Tweet3 corresponds to a positive tweet on that topic.

We will generalize the notion of sentiment associated with a single tweet to the notion of *prevailing sentiment* in a bunch of tweets (i.e., the sentiment that prevails, according to some criterion, e.g. percentage). In the same way, we will assume that sentiments might convey conflicting feelings or emotions (e.g. anger vs. happiness; boredom vs. excitement, positive vs. negative, etc.). We will abstract away which is the prevailing sentiment as well as existing conflicts through mapping functions *Sent* and *Conflict*, respectively.

Logical Language for Expressing Twitter Messages

Twitter messages (Tweets) are 140 character long, with a number of additional fields (metadata) which help identify relevant information within a message (sender, number of retweets associated with the message, etc.). In particular, we will focus on the presence of *descriptors,* which are either *hashtags* (words or phrases prefixed with the symbol #, a form of metadata tag) or terms that tend to occur often in the context of a given topic. Stopwords (such as "a", "this", "and", etc.) will not be considered descriptors and will be ignored in our analysis. Hashtags are used within IRC networks to identify groups and topics and in short messages on microblogging social networking services such as Twitter, identi.ca or Google+ (which may be tagged by including one or more with multiple words concatenated). Other good descriptors can be dynamically found by looking for terms that are frequently used in tweets related to the topic at hand. In the sequel we will assume that the term "descriptor" refers to either actual hashtags in Twitter or to relevant keywords found in tweets.

We define a tweet T as a bag (or multiset) of descriptors {d1, d2,. . . dk}. We will consider a distinguished subset Q of T, where Q is a set of descriptors and will be denoted query. Let Tweets be the set of all currently existing tweets. Given a query Q, we will write *TweetQ* to denote the subset of distinguished elements (tweets) in Tweets associated with Q. In our approach, a query Q is any set of descriptors used for filtering relevant tweets *TweetQ* from Tweets. In order to select those tweets relevant for a particular query Q, we will consider an aggregation operator Agg(Q,C) which returns a subset of tweets associated with Q according to some criterion C. This operator could be defined in several ways, e.g. Agg($Q,C1$) = { $T \in$ Tweets such that $Q \subseteq T$ }, or Agg($Q,C2$) = { $T \in$ Tweets such that $Q \subseteq T$ and T was retweeted more than 5 times }. Note that for the same query Q, different alternative criteria ($C1, C2, \ldots, Ck$) can lead to different distinguished subsets in Tweets. An example of such a criterion C could be a timestamp, or/and further restrictions, such as only using Tweets from UK, etc.

As explained before, tweets can be associated with different feelings or sentiments. Even if in real life there may be a lot of emotions in tweets (like anger, happiness, and so on), we will assume here that there is only a set S of three possible sentiments, which are positive, negative and neutral ones (as done for example in platform Sentiment140.com). Thus our assumption is to a have a mapping *s* that maps a set of given tweets into a set S of three sentiments (i.e. S = *{positive, negative, neutral}*). Note that we are not going into detail on how this is computed, and that we are aware that there may be other ways to rate tweets (such as the number of followers, etc.).

Next we will formalize the previous notions. Let *s*: $2^{Tweets} \rightarrow$ S be a mapping. We should clarify that the mapping *s* is indented to take a set of tweets (i.e, an aggregation of tweets) and not an individual tweet to determine its associated prevailing sentiment. We must remark that we are not interested in analyzing a single tweet at a time but all those tweets associated with a given query *Q* and a given criterion *C*. Two sentiments *Sent1; Sent2* $\in$ S will be "in conflict" whenever *Sent1/= Sent2*. (e.g. *positive* will be in conflict with *negative*; *neutral* will be in conflict with *negative*). According to this, we can say that a set of tweets Tweets$_1 \subseteq$ Tweets is in conflict with a set of tweets Tweets$_2 \subseteq$ Tweets whenever s(Tweets$_1$)/= s(Tweets$_2$). We further assume that all possible conflicts are "equally preferred" in the sense that a conflict between positive and negative is as strong as a conflict between positive and neutral; the underlying idea is to identify when the prevailing sentiments are not the same.

Formalizing a Twitter-Based Framework and Twitter-Based Arguments

The preceding elements provide the background required to define a Twitter-Based (TB) Argumentation Framework, and the notion of TB-argument (or TB-opinion). A *TB-argumentation framework* is a 5-tuple *(Tweets, C, S, Sent, Conflict)*, where *Tweets* is the set of available tweets, *C* is a selection criterion, *S* is a non-empty set of possible sentiments and *Sent* and *Conflict* are sentiment prevailing and conflict mappings. A *TB-argument* for a query Q is a 3-uple <Arg, Q, *Sent*>, where

- Arg corresponds to a bunch of tweets associated with a query Q, obtained through Agg(Q,C)
- *Sent* is the prevailing sentiment associated with Agg(Q,C), as discussed before.

Example: Consider a TB-framework *(Tweets, C, S, Sent, Conflict)*, where Q = {"abortion","murder"}, *C* is defined as all tweets after Jan 1, 2012, and S = {pos, neg, neutral}, such that: *Conflict*(pos) = { neg, neutral}, *Conflict*(neg) ={pos, neutral} and *Conflict*(neutral) ={ pos,neg}. Then Arg = Agg(Q,C) is the set of all possible tweets containing {"abortion", "murder"} that have been published since Jan. 1, 2012. Suppose that *Sent*(AggTweets(Q,C)) = negative (i.e., the prevailing sentiment involved is negative). Then <Arg; {"abortion","murder"},negative> is a TB-argument.

Contrasting Arguments and Counter-Arguments: Opinion Trees and Conflict Trees

We have shown how to express arguments for queries associated with a given prevailing sentiment. Such arguments might be *attacked* by other arguments, which on their turn might be attacked, too. In argumentation theory (Rahwan&Simari, 2009), this leads to the notion of *dialectical analysis*, which can be

Algorithm 1. Algorithm BuildOpinionTree

```
Input: Q
Output: Opinion Tree OT_Q rooted in <Arg, Q, Sent>
1. We start with a TB-argument A obtained from the original query Q (i.e.,
<Arg,Q,Sent>), which will be the root of the tree.
2. Next, we compute within A all relevant descriptors that might be used to
"extend" Q, by adding a new element (d) to the query, obtaining Q' = Q U {d}.
3. Then, a new argument for Q' is obtained, which will be associated with
a subtree rooted in the original argument A (i.e., the tree resulting from
BuildOpinionTree(Q')).
```

associated with a tree-like structure in which arguments, counter-arguments, counter-counter-arguments, and so on, are taken into account. The central idea underlying the exploration of possible attacks for a given argument is given by the notion of *specificity*.

Suppose that a TB-argument supporting the query Q="abortion" is obtained, with a prevailing *negative* sentiment. If the original query Q is extended in some way into a new query Q' that is more specific than Q (i.e. Q' = Q U {d}, for some descriptor d), it could be the case that a TB-argument supporting Q' has a different (possibly conflicting) prevailing sentiment. For example, more specific opinions about abortion are related to other topics, like for example ethics, social problems or programs, religious issues, etc. To explore all possible relationships associated with TB-arguments returned for a specified query Q and criteria C, we can define an algorithm to construct an *opinion tree* recursively as follows (Algorithm 1).

It is also easy to see that for any query Q, the algorithm BuildOpinionTree finishes in finite time: given that a tweet may not contain more than 140 characters, the number of contained descriptors is finite, and therefore the algorithm will eventually stop, providing an opinion tree as an output.

Given an opinion tree we might be interested in finding a minimal structure that reflects all existing conflicts between opinions it the tree. In other words, we might want to build a minimal tree such that arguments and counter-arguments are easy to visualize. To accomplish this, we apply a partitioning algorithm to generate a minimal structure that preserves the conflicts between arguments existing in the original opinion tree. The application of this algorithm results in a natural grouping of arguments that are related to and no conflicting with each other, forming equivalence classes of arguments. The resulting minimal structure also has a tree structure and we will refer to it as *conflict tree*. The notion of lowest common ancestor (LCA) of two nodes in a tree is used to compute a conflict tree. The LCA of two nodes n_1 and n_2 in a tree is the lowest (most specific) node that has both nodes n_1 and n_2 as descendants. Algorithm 2 describes the steps involved in the transformation of an opinion tree (OT_Q) into a conflict tree (CT_Q).

To illustrate this algorithm, consider the opinion tree presented on the left-hand side of Figure 2. In this figure, we use the label Q_i as a shorthand for $\langle Arg_i, Q_i, Sent_i \rangle$. The partitioning algorithm BuildConflictTree will identify eight equivalence classes: $\{Q_1,Q_2,Q_3,Q_8,Q_{10},Q_{11},Q_{12},Q_{13},Q_{14},Q_{19}\}$, $\{Q_4,Q_6,Q_7\}$, $\{Q_5\}$, $\{Q_9\}$, $\{Q_{15},Q_{16},Q_{17}\}$, $\{Q_{18}\}$, $\{Q_{20},Q_{22}\}$ and $\{Q_{21}\}$. By taking exactly one element from each equivalence class, we obtain the conflict tree depicted on the right-hand side of Figure 2.

Algorithm 2. Algorithm BuildConflictTree

```
Output: Conflict Tree CT_Q

1. For each pair of TB-arguments ⟨Arg_i,Q_i, Sent_i⟩  and  ⟨Arg_j, Qj, Sent_j⟩  in
the Opinion Tree  OT_Q, we define the ~_0 equivalence relation as follows:
 ⟨Arg_i,Q_i, Sent_i⟩  ~_0  ⟨Arg_j, Qj, Sent_j⟩  if and only if Sent_i = Sent_j
2. n = 0; compute the 0-equivalence classes based on the ~_0 equivalence rela-
tion
3. REPEAT
         n = n + 1
         Compute the n-equivalence classes as a refinement of the (n –
1)-equivalence classes:
             ⟨Arg_i,Q_i, Sent_i⟩  ~_n  ⟨Arg_j, Qj, Sent_j⟩ if and only if
             (1)  ⟨Arg_i,Q_i, Sent_i⟩  ~_(n-1)  ⟨Arg_j, Qj, Sent_j⟩, and
             (2) For all ⟨Arg_k,Q_k, Sent_k⟩ in OT_Q
                 LCA(⟨Arg_i,Q_i, Sent_i⟩, ⟨Arg_k,Q_k, Sent_k⟩)  ~_(n-1) LCA(⟨Arg_j, Qj, Sent_j⟩,
⟨Arg_k,Q_k, Sent_k⟩)
    UNTIL the n-equivalence classes are equal to the (n – 1)-equivalence class-
es
4. Define CT_Q by taking exactly one element from each of the equivalence class-
es defined for OT_Q .
5. RETURN CT_Q
```

Figure 2. From an opinion tree to a conflict tree

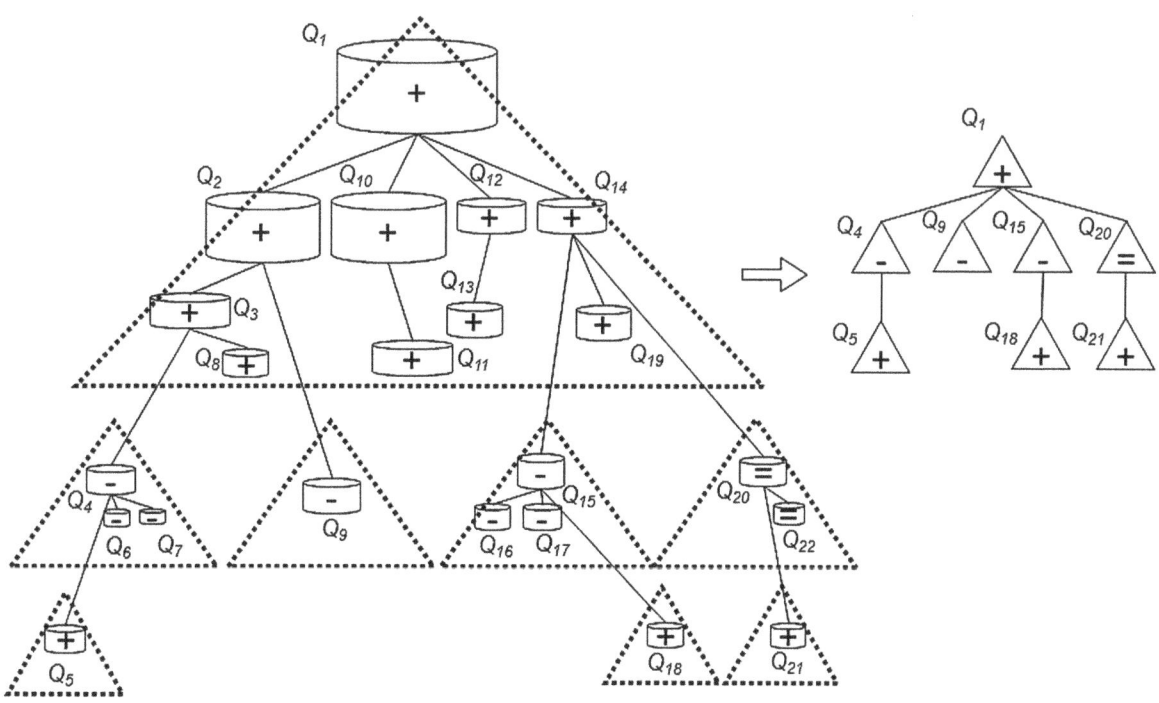

TWO APPLICATION CASES: THE ABORTION ISSUE AND USER SEGMENTATION

Next we show how the proposed approach can be used to handle two different case studies: the abortion issue (based on tweets related to that topic in December 2012), and the user segmentation problem.

The Abortion Issue

A case study based on the abortion issue, obtained from Twitter in December 2012, when Michigan legislature was debating several regulations on abortion practices.

Consider the query Q = "abortion", and a criterion C = {tweets posted less than 48 hours ago}. A root TB-argument is computed for Q and C, obtaining an associated prevailing sentiment (negative). It should be remarked that the algorithm for building opinion trees avoids the repetition of any new descriptor used to extend the query associated with a node. The construction is performed depth-first, so that new descriptors are gradually introduced using a technique specifically designed to guide term selection (outside the scope of this paper, for a detailed description see (Gosse, González, Chesñevar, & Maguitman, 2015)).

Figure 3 illustrates how the construction of an opinion tree for the query Q = "abortion" looks like. Distinguished symbols (+, -, =) are used to denote positive, negative and neutral sentiments, respectively. Note that the original query Q has cardinality 1, and further levels in the opinion tree refer to incrementally augmented queries (e.g. {"abortion", "michigan"}, or {"abortion", "murder"}). Leaves correspond to arguments associated with a query Q' which cannot be further expanded, as the associated number of tweets is too small for any possible query Q' U {d}, for some d. Furthermore, we can identify some subtrees in the Opinion Tree rooted in "abortion" which consist of nodes having all the same sentiment.

Figure 3. An opinion tree for the abortion issue (computed from Twitter, 2012)

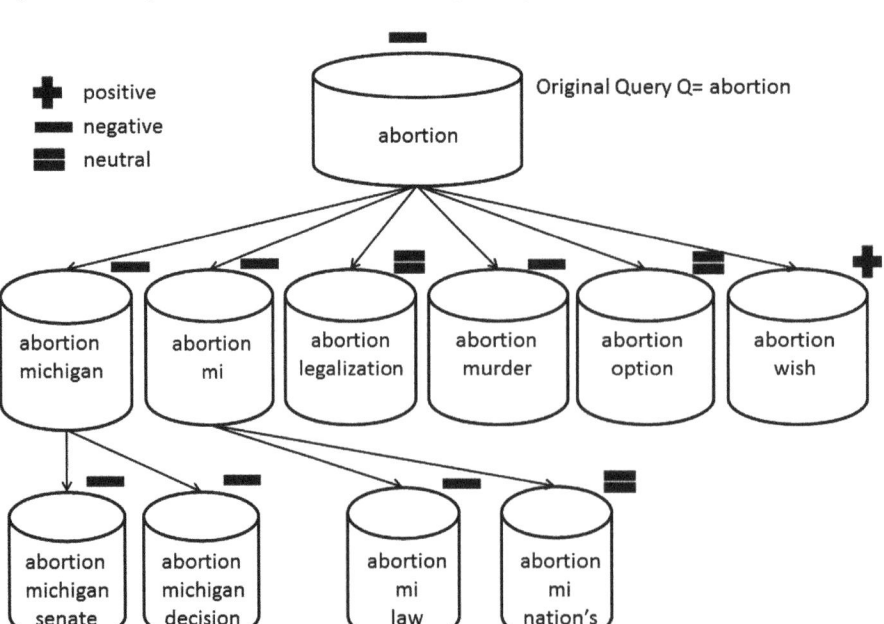

Figure 4. Conflict tree derived from the opinion tree for the abortion issue

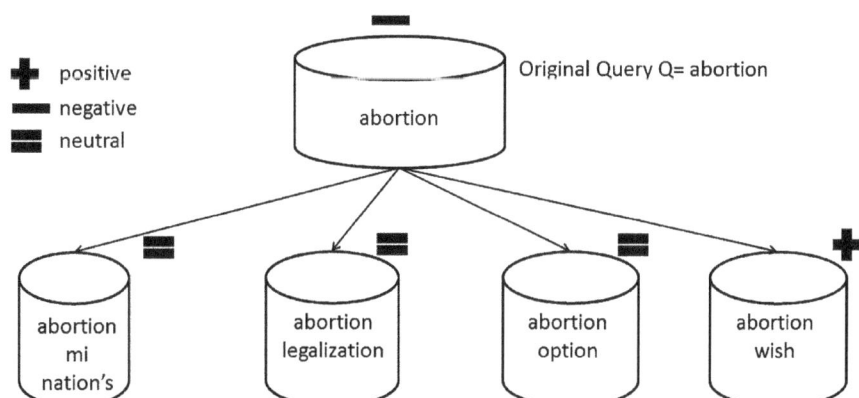

In other words, further expanding a query into more complex queries does not change the prevailing sentiment associated with the root node. In other cases, expanding some queries results in a sentiment change (e.g. from "abortion" into {"abortion", "option"} or {"abortion", "wish"}).

Following the BuildConflictTree algorithm it is possible to derive a minimal structure (conflict tree) where conflicts among opinions are readily available for analysis. The conflict tree resulting from applying the BuildConflictTree algorithm to the opinion tree of Figure 3 is presented in Figure 4. Note that the resulting conflict tree only contains a representative element from each equivalence class of queries. Therefore, immediate descendants of a node will necessarily have a different polarity from that of their parent. This results in a tree that resembles dialectical trees as those used traditionally in argumentation.

The User Segmentation Problem

The abortion issue example sketched the use of the E^{2}P framework in a real case when both the query Q and the criteria C were previously stated. However, in many cases even if the query Q is clearly known, the challenge is related to the specification of some accurate criterion C.

A relevant example is the practice of audience segmentation when studying user's behavior in the current e-scenario from a User Centered Design (UCD) perspective. UCD is a broad term to describe design processes in which end-users influence how a design takes shape. It is both a broad philosophy and variety of methods. There is a spectrum of ways in which users are involved in UCD but the important concept is that users are involved one way or another (Abras, C., Maloney-Krichmar, D., & Preece, J. 2004). Thus UCD enhances e-participation in the e-government context.

Audience segmentation is a practice of clustering an audience based on mutually exclusive subsets of individuals that are similar in specific ways to make up hypothetical archetypes of actual users. Audience segmentation has been defined as ``the process of identifying groups of customers who are relatively homogenous in their response to marketing stimuli, so that the market offering can be tailored more closely to meet their needs" (Brennan, R., Baines, P., & Garneau, P., 2008). The goal is to find new, previously unaddressed target groups of customers to better design communication strategies catering them in a suitable way according with their specific needs to increase their satisfaction and loyalty. The segmentation could be based on demographic issues (i.e. age, gender, region, ethnic); social-economical features (i.e. sector, services access, income); psychographic data (i.e. lifestyle, values, attitudes, interests, activities, opinions), physical characteristics (disabilities, perceptual abilities, motor skills abilities), psychological profiles, and all other measurable criteria that will affect the target.

With the advent of the Digital Society, the idea that people behave differently during the purchase process has been extended beyond the business industry to other fields. In particular, audience segmentation provides key insights to the field of UCD, where achieving and accurate understanding of user's behavior is becoming a complex task (Liu, Y., Osvalder, A., & Karlsson, M., 2010). An adequate user classification will enhance later definition of user profiles, flexible targeting requirements, personalized design, test cases design, and prediction of user navigation patterns and habits, among others UCD oriented activities.

In the above context, the psychographic and psychological factors (emotions and feeling) treatment is sometimes avoided for considering them too difficult and subjective (Panagiotis, Tsianos, Lekkas, Mourlas, & Samaras, 2008). Indeed, obstacles related to the criteria for segmentation itself emerge, including what data to select, how many clusters to produce and how to evaluate the clustering results. In addition, even some proposals deal with with vagueness and uncertainty (Lefait, G., & Kechadi, T., (2010) (Hiziroglu, A., 2013), coping with the treatment of incomplete, contradictory or potentially inconsistent information is still a challenge to address.

Based on E^{2}P, a novel UCD-oriented strategy for the automatic detection of critical US factors regarding psychological factors towards a particular topic was proposed (González, Chesñevar, & Brena, 2015). The goal is to enhance E^{2}P by adding to traditional construction process novel tools to support the computational treatment of incomplete, contradictory or potentially inconsistent information, as well as novel mechanisms to discover segmentation issues when dealing with user's feelings and opinion.

Figure 5 illustrates how the construction of an opinion tree for the query Q= ``Windows 8'' looks like (computed in 2014). As in the abortion example, the original query Q has cardinality 1, and further levels in the opinion tree refer to incrementally augmented queries that may or may not change the prevailing sentiment associated with the root node. Leaves correspond to arguments associated with a query Q which cannot be further expanded. Instead of assuming a probable segmentation criterion when dealing with people emotions, factors determining internal branches of the computed trees showed both the most significant segmentation criteria (expressed in the root of the obtained tree) and the more specific segmentation criteria (such as ``stability'' or ``usability''). This way, novel and non-evident or unexplored segmentation criteria should emerge, showing the real factors that are determining the user's feeling toward a topic without previous conjectures or assumptions.

Besides, the E^{2}P automatic calculation provides a reasonable resource to re-calculate the same query at different times, thus providing evidence about the evolution of psychographic and psychological factors over time. Figure 6 presents the conflict tree derived from the opinion tree shown in Figure 5.

RELATED WORK

Our approach is inspired by recent research in integrating argumentation, social networks and e-democracy. In the last years, there has been growing interest in assessing meaning to streams of data from microblogging services such as Twitter, as well as research in using argumentation in e-government contexts. In (Cartwright & Atkinson, 2009), Cartwright et al. presented different issues related to exploiting argument representation in systems for e-democracy. In particular, the authors discuss the contributions of the Parmenides software tool, which is intended as a system for deliberative democracy whereby the

Figure 5. Opinion tree for the query "Windows 8" (computed from Twitter, 2014)

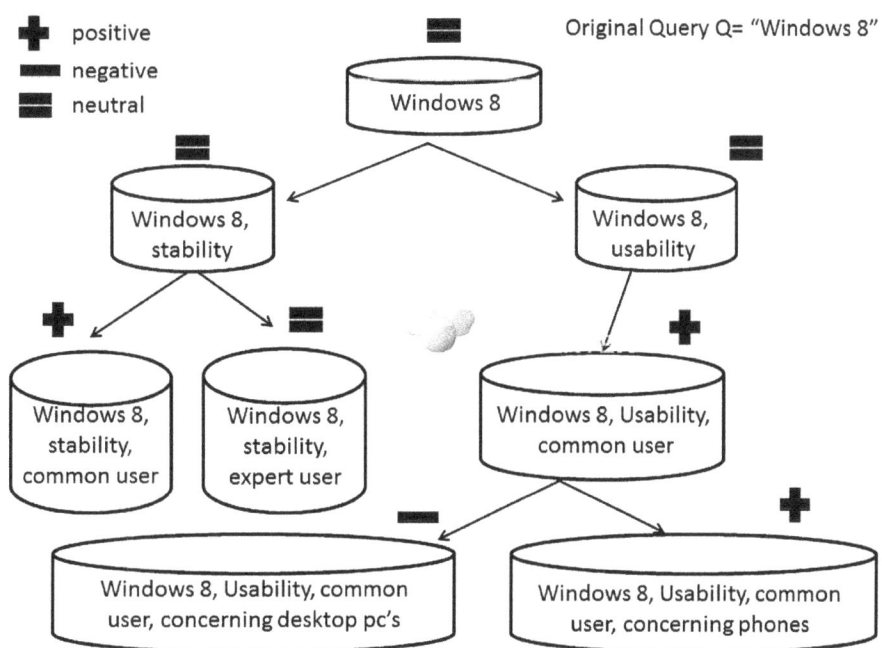

Figure 6. Conflict tree derived from the Opinion tree for the query "Windows 8"

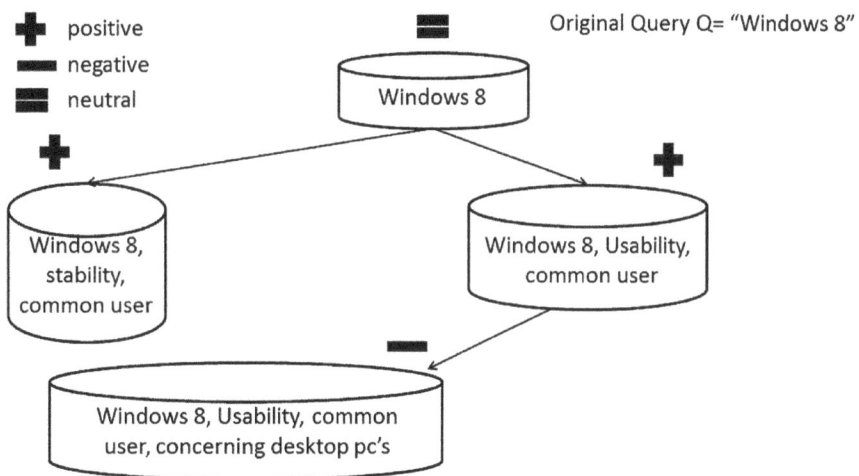

government is able to present policy proposals to the public so that users can submit their opinions on the justification presented for the particular policy. In contrast with our approach, this research work assumes that argument schemas are established beforehand, and are not detected as emerging patterns from social network activities.

Torroni & Toni (Torroni & Toni, 2011) coined the term *bottom-up argumentation*, as they take a grassroot approach to the problem of deploying computational argumentation in online systems. In this novel view, argumentation frameworks are obtained bottom-up starting from the users' comments, opinions and suggested links, with no top-down intervention of or interpretation by "argumentation engineers". As the authors point out "topics emerge, bottom-up, during the underlying process, possibly serendipitously". We generalize this view by identifying two issues: on the one hand, a metalevel characterization of rule-based argument processes, based on social network knowledge bases. On the other hand, we distinguish schema-based argumentation as an alternative for bottom-up argumentation, also obtained in a similar way as for rule-based argumentation.

In (Heras et al, 2010), the authors show how the theory of argumentation schemes can provide a valuable help to formalize and structure online discussions and user opinions in decision support and business oriented websites that hold social networks among their users. In their investigation real case studies are considered and analyzed, establishing as well guidelines for website and system design to enhance social decision support and recommendations with argumentation. Their research pinpoints several issues presented in our approach, but does not aim at a particular applicability for e-Government issues, nor for identifying emerging patterns in network traffic and associating them with high-level arguments. (Klein & Iandoli, 2008) describe Collaboratorium, a system that enables collaborative deliberation where users can create networks of posts organized as an argument map. In this sense, this system resembles our proposal in that it adopts knowledge sharing technologies to facilitate logic-based knowledge organization.

However, differently from our proposal, it is not intended to mine social media to automatically identify conflicting positions but to support large-scale argumentation, where users are allowed to enter arguments and a moderator takes a key role. Finally, (Abbas & Sawamura, 2012) formalize argument mining from the perspective of intelligent tutoring systems. In contrast with our approach, they rely on a relational database, and their aim is not related with identifying underlying arguments in social networks as done in this paper.

Finally, we argue that the application of the framework presented in this chapter serves as an important novel tool for governments to process and create public value from citizens' opinion, addressing an important problem, such as conflict resolution raised by contradictory opinions in the society, in government decision making processes. We argue that the solution presented here, is a seminal work for a very promising area - Electronic Governance (EGOV) for Conflict Resolution. As shown in Figure 7, the area of conflict resolution presents the problem domain - raising problems related to stakeholders' conflict of interests, social or other type of conflicts, to be solved by EGOV - technology-enabled governance

Figure 7. Conflict Resolution (CR) in the context of EGOV

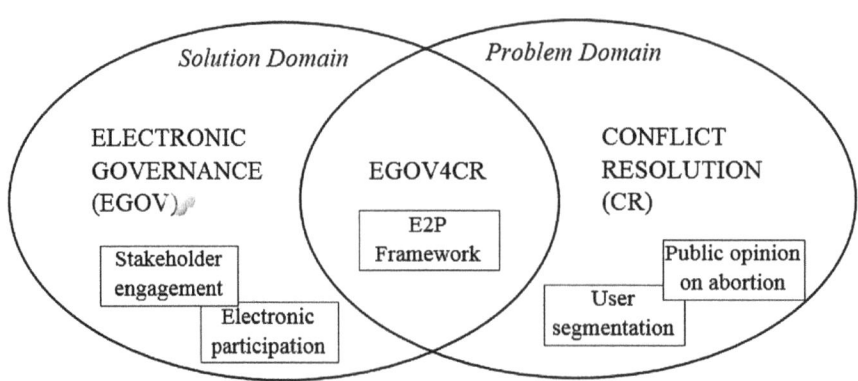

mechanisms, which in turns defines the solution domain. We justify the novelty of the area, since searches in the SCOPUS database with the following keywords: 1) "conflict resolution" and "electronic government"; 2) "conflict resolution" and "electronic governance"; and 3) "conflict resolution" and "digital government", in the articles titles, abstracts, and keywords of the database produced zero results in all three cases. The same searches in Google Scholar produced 579, 143, and 313 results, respectively, compared with the over 2 million results that are obtained when searching separately for "electronic government", "electronic governance" and "conflict resolution", and more than 1.9 million results for "digital government". The figure illustrates two case studies of conflict resolution illustrated in Section 5, example of governance mechanisms available to solve such issues as explained in the Introduction, and a concrete solution - the tools provided by the E^2P framework introduced in sections 3 and 4.

CONCLUSION: FUTURE WORK

In this chapter we have presented a first approach towards integrating argumentation and microblogging technologies, with a particular focus on Twitter. We have shown how the different elements in argumentation theory can be conceptualized in terms of Twitter messages, according to relevant fields present in those messages (number of retweets, provenance, etc.). We have also presented a definition of argument that considers as a support the bunch of Tweets which are associated with a particular set of terms (hashtags). For such an argument, we also define a polarity (positive, negative, neutral), obtained in terms of sentiment analysis tools. Such polarity allowed us to characterize the notion of conflict between arguments, establishing as well as the backgrounds for formalizing defeat. We showed how this idea could be exploited in terms of so-called "opinion trees", which resemble argumentative dialectical trees. Their aim, in contrast, is to explore the space of possible confronting opinions associated with a given opinion, in terms of the specificity principle used in argumentation for preferring arguments.

Part of our future work is associated with deploying the ideas presented in this paper in a software product. As a basis for such deployment, visual tools for displaying and analyzing dialectical trees have been already developed for Defeasible Logic Programming (García & Simari, 2004). We expect to use the underlying algorithms from this tool in our framework. Additionally, we expect to perform different experiments with hashtags associated with relevant topics, assessing the applicability of our approach in a real-world context. In addition, there exists also the possibility of not only expanding hashtags of one set of tweets, but always looking for all tweets given a new hashtag. Thus not a tree but a graph would be built up, and connections between different topics (hashtags) become clear. This would give us the advantage of being able to observe if a special hashtag is positive/negative only together with some other hashtags or by itself (leaving apart indicator words such as "good", "bad", etc.). Research in this direction is currently being pursued.

ACKNOWLEDGMENT

This research is funded by Projects LACCIR R1211LAC004 (Microsoft Research, CONACyT and IDB), PIP 112-200801-02798, PIP 112-200901-00863 (CONICET, Argentina), PGI 24/ZN10, PGI 24/N006 (SGCyT, UNS, Argentina), PGI 24/N030 (SGCyT, UNS, Argentina) and Universidad Nacional del Sur.

REFERENCES

Abbas, S., & Sawamura, H. (2012). Argument mining based on a structured database and its usage in an intelligent tutoring environment. *Knowledge and Information Systems*, *30*(1), 213–246. doi:10.1007/s10115-010-0371-3

Abras, C., Maloney-Krichmar, D., & Preece, J. (2004). User-centered design. In Encyclopedia of Human-Computer Interaction. Thousand Oaks, CA: Sage Publications.

Bertot, J. C., Jaeger, P. T., & Hansen, D. (2012). The Impact of Polices on Government Social Media Usage: Issues, Challenges, and Recommendations. *Government Information Quarterly*, *29*(1), 30–40. doi:10.1016/j.giq.2011.04.004

Besnard, P., & Hunter, A. (2008). *The elements of argumentation*. The MIT Press. doi:10.7551/mitpress/9780262026437.001.0001

Bonson, E., Torres, L., Royo, S., & Flores, F. (2012). Local e-Government 2.0. Social Media and Corporate Transparency in Municipalities. *Government Information Quarterly*, *29*(2), 123–132. doi:10.1016/j.giq.2011.10.001

Brennan, R., Baines, P., & Garneau, P. (2008). *Contemporary strategic marketing*. Palgrave Macmillan.

Cartwright, D., & Atkinson, K. (2009). Using Computational Argumentation to Support E-participation. *IEEE Intelligent Systems*, *24*(5), 42–52. doi:10.1109/MIS.2009.104

Chesñevar, C., Maguitman, A., Estévez, E., & Brena, R. (2012). Integrating Argumentation Technologies and Context-Based Search for Intelligent Processing of Citizens' Opinion in Social Media. In *Proceedings of 6th International Conference on Theory and Practice of Electronic Governance, ICEGOV '12*, (pp. 171-174). ACM Press. doi:10.1145/2463728.2463762

Chesñevar, C., Maguitman, A., Estevez, E., Osman, N., & Sierra, C. (2013) E2 participation: electronically empowering citizens for social innovation through agreement technologies. In *Proceeding of 14th Annual International Conference on Digital Government Research DG.O 2013*. ACM Press. doi:10.1145/2479724.2479772

Chesñevar, C., Maguitman, A., & González, M. (2014). Empowering citizens through opinion mining from twitter-based arguments. In *Proceedings of 6th International Conference on Theory and Practice of Electronic Governance, ICEGOV '12*, (pp. 275-278). ACM Press. doi:10.1145/2691195.2691282

Chesñevar, C., Maguitman, A., & Simari, G. (2007). Recommender Systems based on Argumentation. in Emerging Artificial Intelligence Applications in Computer Engineering. IOS Press.

DiMaio, A. (2009). *Government 2.0: A Gartner Definition*. Retrieved February 28, 2014, from http://blogs.gartner.com/andrea_dimaio/2009/11/13/government-2-0-a-gartner-definition/

Galitsky, B., & McKenna, E. (2009). *Sentiment Extraction from Consumer Reviews for Providing Product Recommendations*. US Patent Application US 2009/0282019 A1

García, A., & Simari, G. (2004). Defeasible Logic Programming: An Argumentative Approach. *Theory and Practice of Logic Programming*, *4*(1-2), 95–138. doi:10.1017/S1471068403001674

González, M. P., Chesñevar, C., & Brena, R. (2015). Modeling User's Sentiment in User Segmentations: An Argumentation Approach for User Centered Design. *Lecture Notes in Computer Science Series*, *9172*, 595–606. doi:10.1007/978-3-319-20612-7_56

Grosse, K., González, M. P., Chesñevar, C., & Maguitman, A. G. (2015). Integrating argumentation and sentiment analysis for mining opinions from Twitter. *AI Communications*, *28*(3), 387–401. doi:10.3233/AIC-140627

Guo, L., & Lease, M. (2011). Personalizing Local Search with Twitter (2011). In *Proceedings of the Workshop on Enriching Information Retrieval. 34th International ACM SIGIR Conference on Research and Development in Information Retrieval, SIGIR 2011*. ACM Press.

Heras, S., Atkinson, K., Botti, V., Grasso, F., Julian, V., & McBurney, P. (2010). How argumentation can enhance dialogues in social networks. In *Frontiers in Artificial Intelligence and Applications. Proceedings of COMMA*.

Hiziroglu, A. (2013). Soft Computing Applications in Customer Segmentation: State-of-Art Review and Critique. *Expert Systems with Applications*, *40*(16), 6491–6507. doi:10.1016/j.eswa.2013.05.052

Klein, M., & Iandoli, L. (2008). *Supporting collaborative deliberation using a large-scale argumentation system:* The MIT Collaboratorium. Technical Report 4691-08, MIT Sloan.

Lefait, G., & Kechadi, T. (2010). *Customer Segmentation Architecture Based on Clustering Techniques*. Digital Society, 2010. ICDS '10. Fourth International Conference on Digital Society. doi:10.1109/ICDS.2010.47

Liu, B. (2010). Sentiment Analysis: A Multifaceted Problem. *IEEE Intelligent Systems*, *25*(3), 76–80.

Liu, Y., Osvalder, A., & Karlsson, M. (2010). Considering the Importance of User Profiles in Interface Design. In R. Matrai (Ed.), *User Interfaces*. InTech. doi:10.5772/8903

Lorenzetti, C., & Maguitman, A. (2009). A Semi-supervised Incremental Algorithm to Automatically Formulate Topical Queries. *Information Science*, *179*(12), 1881–1892. doi:10.1016/j.ins.2009.01.029

Maguitman, A., Leake, D., & Reichherzer, T. (2005). Suggesting novel but related topics: towards context-based support for knowledge model extension, In *Proceedings of the 2005 International Conference on Intelligent User Interfaces* (pp. 207-214). ACM Press. doi:10.1145/1040830.1040876

Maguitman, A., Leake, D., Reichherzer, T., & Menczer, F. (2004). Dynamic Extraction of Topic Descriptors and Discriminators: Towards Automatic Context-Based Topic Search. In *Proceedings of 2004 ACM CIKM International Conference on Information and Knowledge Management*, (pp. 463-472). ACM Press. doi:10.1145/1031171.1031260

Modgil, S., Toni, F., Bex, F., Bratko, I., Chesñevar, C., Dvorak, W., . . . Woltran, S. (2012). The Added Value of Argumentation. In Agreement Technology Handbook. Academic Press.

O'Reilly, T. (2010). Government as a Platform. *Innovations*, *6*(1), 13–40. doi:10.1162/INOV_a_00056

Osman, N., Sierra, C., McNeill, F., Pane, J., & Debenham, J. (2013). Trust and Matching Algorithms for Selecting Suitable Agents. *ACM Transactions on Intelligent Systems and Technology*, *5*(1), 16–16. doi:10.1145/2542182.2542198

Ossowski, S. (Ed.). (2013). *Handbook of Agreement Technologies (vol. 8)*. New York: Springer Verlag.

Panagiotis, G., Tsianos, N., Lekkas, Z., Mourlas, C., & Samaras, G. (2008). Capturing Essential Intrinsic User Behaviour Values for the Design of Comprehensive Web-based Personalized Environments. *Computers in Human Behavior*, *24*(4), 1434–1451. doi:10.1016/j.chb.2007.07.010

Rahwan, I., & Simari, G. (Eds.). (2009). *Argumentation in Artificial Intelligence*. Springer.

Schneider, J., Groza, T., & Passant, A. (2013). A review of argumentation for the Social Semantic Web. *Semantic Web*, *4*(2), 159–218.

Steibel, F., & Estevez, E. (2012). Designing argumentative metrics for online consultation portals in Brazil. In *Proceedings of the 13th Annual International Conference on Digital Government Research DG.O 2012* (pp. 272-273). ACM Press. doi:10.1145/2307729.2307781

Torroni, P., & Toni, F. (2011). Bottom up argumentation. In *Proceedings of First Intl. Workshop on Theoretical and Formal Argumentation (TAFA). IJCAI 2011* (LNCS), (pp. 249-262). Springer Verlag.

Toulmin, S. (1959). *The uses of argument*. Cambridge, UK: Cambridge University Press.

UN General Assembly. (2014). *Report of the Open Working Group of the General Assembly on Sustainable Development Goals*. Retrieved December 16, 2015, from http://www.un.org/ga/search/view_doc.asp? symbol=A/68/970&Lang=E

KEY TERMS AND DEFINITIONS

Agreement Technologies: Computer systems in which autonomous software agents negotiate with one another, typically on behalf of humans, in order to come to mutually acceptable agreements.

Argument: In logic and philosophy, an argument is a series of statements typically used to persuade someone of something or to present reasons for accepting a conclusion.

Argumentation: The interdisciplinary study of how conclusions can be reached through logical reasoning; that is, claims based, soundly or not, on premises. It includes the arts and sciences of civil debate, dialogue, conversation, and persuasion.

Electronic Government (or E-Government): The utilization of Information and Communication Technologies (ICTs) and other web-based telecommunication technologies to improve and/or enhance on the efficiency and effectiveness of service delivery in the public sector.

Electronic Participation (or E-Participation): Participation supported by Information and Communication Technologies (ICTs) in processes involved in government and governance. Processes may concern administration, service delivery, decision making and policy making.

Sentiment Analysis: Also known as Opinion Mining, it is the use of natural language processing, text analysis and computational linguistics to identify and extract subjective information in source materials.

Twitter: An online social networking service that enables users to send and read short 140-character messages called "tweets". Registered users can read and post tweets, but unregistered users can only read them.

User-Centred Design (UCD): Discipline in which the needs, wants, and limitations of end users of a product, service or process are given extensive attention at each stage of the design process (not restricted to interactive interfaces sign or technology design. In the context of this chapter User-Centred Design is related to Human-Computer Interaction and Participatory Design.

Section 3
Applications for Conflict Resolution

As shown in Sections 1 and 2, conflicts are virtually everywhere. This undoubtedly calls for interdisciplinary approaches for not only perceiving and modeling conflicts as already addressed but most of all for solving these conflicts. This section describes new processes for solving new forms of conflict that emerged in the recent years as a result of an unprecedented technological and social evolution.

Chapter 12
Intelligent Tutoring:
Active Monitoring and Recommendation

Manuel Fernando Rodrigues
Polytechnic Institute of Porto, Portugal

Ricardo Santos
Polytechnic Institute of Porto, Portugal

Sérgio Manuel Gonçalves
University of Vigo, Spain

Florentino Fdez-Riverola
University of Vigo, Spain

Davide Carneiro
University of Minho, Portugal

ABSTRACT

Society has been changing dynamically over the years and technology has been boosting that change. Teaching, as a social activity has not been changing at the same speed. Technology enhanced learning, arises as a way to cope with that challenge, opening new paths for learning. However, sometimes it becomes difficult to cope with student´s challenges: interest, motivation, attention, are difficult to achieve with the so called net-generation. With an amazing new world at the touch of their fingers, the focus is on new, challenging and interesting things, leaving very little room to other activities. Keeping students in the right track, interested and motivated is in fact an enormous challenge. Fatigue and stress play an important role in this equation: they can dramatically decrease students' performance. Controlling these factors, in such a way that´s unaware by students, is the best way to achieve better results, as the data gathering process does not interfere with the parameters being monitored. The aim is to forecast negative situations taking some actions to mitigate them.

INTRODUCTION

Modern society needs to be constantly fed with new knowledge, putting an enormous amount of pressure into the formation/requalification of their citizens. The need for qualified people is growing quickly, thus requiring a more efficient use of the limited resources that are allocated to education/training. Technology emerges as a way to enhance this learning/teaching process, providing new ways to achieve better results, and overcoming some known constraints such as qualified instructors availability, time restrictions or individual monitoring. Nonetheless, when using technology-enhanced learning, some

DOI: 10.4018/978-1-5225-0245-6.ch012

drawbacks need to be carefully analysed. When a student engages into an electronic course, the interaction between student and teacher, without all its non-verbal interactions, is poorer. Thus the assessment of feelings and attitudes by the teacher becomes more difficult. In that sense, the use of technological tools for teaching, with the consequent teacher-student and student-student separation, may represent a risk as a significant amount of context information is lost.

Indeed, the teacher/student relationship is a crucial aspect in order to succeed in learning, both for the student and teacher, and is one of the main aspects determining the success or failure of teaching. Positive relationships, both in terms of respect and empathy, enhance students' abilities and commitment throughout the learning process (Hamre et al., 2006).

There are several studies that support the fact that a positive relationship between teacher and student, measurable by, among others, the number of conflicts, the degree of closeness or the support and dependency, is directly related to greater and easier adaptation to school, increase of social skills and improved academic performance (Battistich, Schaps & Wilson, 2004). Moreover teachers feel that these positive relationships have resulted in reduced levels of absenteeism and increased levels of cooperation and motivation from students (Klem & Connell, 2004).

As communication processes evolve to other levels, they shift increasingly to online platforms, in the so-called e-learning tools. These tools still have gaps that do not allow a rich environment regarding the communication between the teacher and the student. Moreover, managing possible conflicts and negative situations is much more difficult.

It is credible that the technology that physically separates and distances human relations, can be developed to levels similar to those in traditional methods of classroom teaching.

To accomplish this task, different fields of knowledge must intersect, such as Behavioural Biometrics (Yampolskiy & Govindaraju, 2008), Ambient Intelligence (Aarts & Wichert, 2009) and Behaviourism (Bouton, 2009), to develop a classification of the students' state, namely by observing their interaction with computers, and more specifically with e-learning platforms.

Since students' effectiveness and success in learning is highly related to their mood while doing it, such issues should be taken into account when in an e-learning environment. Aspects such fatigue and stress significantly influence students' performance and need to be taken into consideration (Rodrigues, Riverola & Novais, 2011).

The fundamental goal of any teacher is to develop and deliver instruction that inspire and invoke learning in their students. To achieve this, an understanding of how learning occurs is strictly necessary. Learning theories provide insight into the complex process of learning and so, they must be known by instructors. This is also especially true in e-learning environments, where it can even be considered if a new learning theory is required, or just the best selection and use of existing theories for each particular situation (Alzaghoul, 2012).

With all these constraints, monitoring the students' behaviour and providing recommendations in order to improve the learning process needs to be continually addressed, and especially in an online environment. Stress and emotions, in particular, can play an important (usually negative) role in education (Hwang & Yang, 2009; Williamson et al., 2005). In that sense, its analysis in an e-learning environment assumes greater importance in the sense that no other approaches can be used, such as in face-to-face, in which we easily understand contextual cues. The role of stress, frustration or fatigue on the emergence of conflicts between students and between students and teachers should also not be neglected. Thus, one of the key notions of this chapter can be put forward: the continuous assessment of the student's level of stress while using an e-Learning tool as a way to minimize conflicts. The conviction is that a teacher with access to contextual information about students will be in a better position to take decisions that influence the students' performance, commitment and relationships, thus decreasing conflict.

Generally, stress assessment is done either through questionnaires (an easily misleading approach and certainly not a dynamic one) or through physiological sensors (very accurate but intrusive to the point of making them impractical in e-Learning). Attention, as one of the utmost important mechanisms when acquiring new knowledge needs to be monitored too. It is strongly connected with learning and assimilating new concepts. The lack of attention can thus be very problematic (Pimenta et al., 2013). Also, when working in a challenging cognitive task for a long period of time, it is very likely that students suffer from the effects of fatigue, reflected in reduced motivation to continue working on the task at hand.

All these factors can also increment the level of possible conflicts, putting the focus on the acute management of those conflicts. Regarding stress, fatigue and distraction, a carefully motorization can improve the teaching/learning process, as some negative situations can be foreseen and actions to mitigate them can be triggered. The monitoring of these features is usually done as previously mentioned, by means of physiological sensors or questionnaires.

We believe that such an approach causes, by itself, significant changes in the monitored variables, so a non-intrusive way to obtain reliable data is needed. The high-level information that can be compiled with this data will support actions that can mitigate potential problems and avoid new ones, especially those related to conflicts. We put forward an approach in which the acquisition of this data is implemented by a monitoring system that, by taking as input the interaction patterns of the students, allows to classify fatigue, stress and attention. It thus so through the use of behavioural biometrics, specifically keystroke dynamics and mouse dynamics.

This approach can be deemed both non-invasive and non-intrusive as it relies solely on the observation of the individual's use of the mouse and keyboard, and allows for recommendations to be issues in real-time to the teacher, aimed at continuously improving the state of the students, especially to prevent the emergence of conflicts.

E-LEARNING: CONTEXTUALIZATION

E-learning is a concept that emerged and evolved in recent years. It is a trend in virtually all educational organizations nowadays, and there are several good reasons to use it. In the past years, significant efforts were carried out regarding standardization, which enables reusing e-learning objects in different platforms, thus increasing its usage. Three main "eras" can be established regarding e-learning.

E-Learning 1.0

The web 1.0 is characterized by providing content online. This was a significant development because it allowed easy access to the information provided. However, this access is limited to read-only access and visualization, a reason why the web 1.0 is referred to as a "read-only web" (Richardson, 2005). E-learning 1.0 quickly followed this new technology, with the motto "anytime, anywhere and to anyone" as its main feature, providing easy and convenient access to learning content (Ebner, 2007). E-learning 1.0, focuses on the creation and administration to the essence of content for online visualization. The concept of "learning object" was created to ensure the quality and usefulness of the "read-only "contents. These objects were thought as Lego blocks, which allow sequencing and organization of content blocks in courses that are available for delivery as books or manuals (Downes, 2005).

E-Learning 2.0

The ongoing changes in the internet and the ways it was used by people originated the term Web 2.0, which could not fail to have a strong impact on education and learning. This change promoted a transition from a somewhat grey scenario to another form that, following the movement and the dominant characteristics of Web 2.0, would give a greater autonomy and control to the learner. It is this intersection between Web 2.0 and e-learning that Downes called e-learning 2.0 (U.S. Dep. Education, 2009).

One of the most important aspects in this change is related to the ways in which a new type of users, born and raised in a digital world and deemed "digital natives" by Prensky (2001) "or n-gen" (net generation) by Tapscott (1998), interact with information and face communication and the media. They absorb information quickly, in images and video as well as text, from multiple sources simultaneously. They operate at "twitch speed", expecting instant responses and feedback. They prefer random "on-demand" access to media, expect to be in constant communication with their friends (who may be next door or around the world), and they are the likely to create their own media (or download someone else's) then to purchase the book or the CD [17].

In terms of learning, this trend results in a shift of control to students, with pedagogical approaches that focus on the students and their expectations, needs and characteristics. This perspective allows them a much greater autonomy on one the hand and, on the other, gives great prominence to active learning, based on the creation, communication and participation.

E-Learning 3.0

The predictions of the future of e-learning vary due to different opinions about what is Web 3.0 and the technologies that best meet the needs in the field of learning. Wheeler (2011) believes that Web 3.0 is the "Read/Write/Collaborate" web.

E-learning 3.0 will have at least four key factors: distributed computing, extended mobile technology intelligence, intelligent collaborative filtering and visualization and 3D interaction. The distributed computing technology combined with mobile intelligence will allow students to approach the school "anytime anywhere" and will provide smart solutions for web searches, document management and content organization.

It will also lead to an increase in self-organized learning, driven by easy access to tools and services that allow to customize learning recursively. Intelligent collaborative filtering performed by intelligent agents will allow users to work smarter and more collaboratively. 3D visualization and interaction will promote rich learning, making a series of tasks easier including the exploration of virtual spaces and virtual objects manipulation. Goroshko and Samoilenko (2011) consider that e-learning 3.0 is both "collaboration" as "intelligence", with intelligent agents will facilitating human thought. Moravec (2008) suggests that in e-learning 3.0, the meaning is socially constructed and contextually reinvented, and teaching will be done in a co-constructivist. The focus of learning will shift from "what to learn" to "how to learn".

Figure 1. E-learning evolution

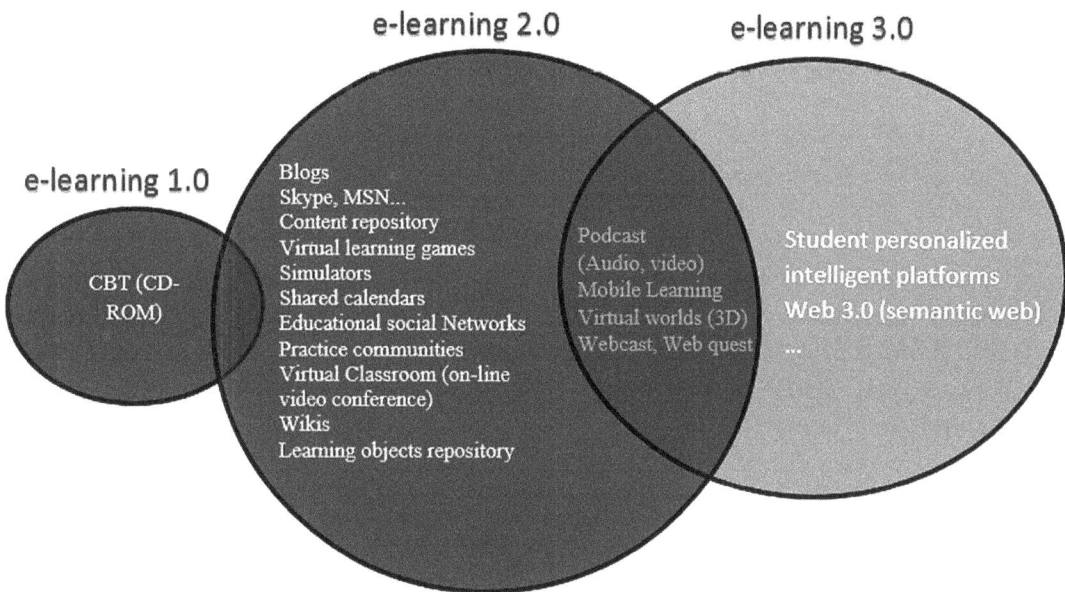

Technology will play a central role, despite being in the background and in an invisible way. Technology will connect knowledge, knowledge brokering, and allow the translation of knowledge into beneficial and useful applications. Rego et al. (2010) consider that the concept of e-learning "anytime, anywhere and anyone" will be complemented with "anyway", i.e. it should be accessible to all types of devices. Figure 1 summarizes these concepts.

The approach put forward in this chapter is thus fully in-line with the so-called e-learning 3.0. Indeed, we propose the invisible collection of very important knowledge about the students, to be used by the teacher with the aim of improving both the communication process as well as the teaching-learning relationship. Our aim is that e-learning environments for learning can have significantly less conflicts that their physical and traditional counterparts, thus being more harmonious environments and potentiating learning.

LEARNING THEORIES AND E-LEARNING

Teaching should be solidly grounded to the absolute understanding of how the process of learning occurs, so that instructional strategies can be efficient and lead to persistent knowledge. This is especially true when in e-learning environments, where some of the previously mentioned issues can negatively affect the acquisition of knowledge and the persistence of that same knowledge.

Learning theories are thus crucial to improve the learning process and to mitigate the conflicts and problems that might (and surely will) occur in a technology-enhanced learning environment, as they do in physical environments. Learning theories provide insights into the very complex processes and factors that influence learning and provide precious information that can be used to design teaching methodologies that will produce better results.

Moreover, each student has a personal and specific way of assimilating knowledge, i.e., the student's personal learning style. Knowledge about learning styles is important in the sense that a student that has a specific learning style may face difficulties in learning when submitted to another learning style (Smith & Renzulli, 1984). When the presenting instruction style matches the student's learning style, the efficiency of the process is maximized, that is, the student learns more and better.

Technology-enhanced learning environments are ideal for generating instructional materials based on learning styles, especially in large classes, as they do not have the same limitations as human instructors do. They are especially advantageous when there is lack of resources and time for focusing on individual students and on their individual needs. In this regard, learning theories and learning styles gain a significant importance.

Regarding learning theories, there are four main theories or philosophical frameworks under which all learning theories fall: behaviourism, cognitivism, constructivism, and connectivism. Table 1 summarizes all four, regarding some important aspects. A successful online learning experience would incorporate a combination of components from each of the four learning theories. Behaviorism can be used to teach the *what*, Cognitivism can be used to teach the *how*, Constructivism can be used to teach the *why*, while Conectivism redefines a new way by building a network of knowledge sources which are accessible as the need for it grows, recognizing meaningful patterns among distributed sets of information.

A combination of the four theories is important as it allows to cover all the bases and ensure that the best possible learning experience is provided to the student. The next step would be the so-called PLE – Personal Learning Environments, that are unique for each student, suiting individual needs and goals. It is here that we frame the proposed automatic and non-intrusive monitoring of the student's state, namely to avoid conflict, especially because the actions taken by the professor, as well as the compiled information, must also be individual and personalized.

Table 1. Learning theories and e-learning

Learning Theories	Explanation	Implications on E-Learning
Behaviorism	Stimulus and response: • Students remember and respond (change in clear behaviour due to conditioning) • Teachers present and provide for practice and feedback	Sees mind as a "black box, so very little effect on –e-learning courses
Cognitivism	Information transmission and processing: • Students rem strategies, rules and patterns • Teachers plan for cognitive learning strategies	The mind should be opened and understand. Therefore, it has high effect on e-courses
Constructivism	Personal discovery of knowledge: • Discover relationships between concepts, e.g. addition and subtraction. • Teachers provide instructional context for active and self-regulated students.	Sees each learner as a unique individual with unique needs and backgrounds, so it has very high effect on e-learning courses
Conectivism	Deemed as "A learning theory for the digital age". In today's world, there is simply too much knowledge to take in. Moreover, it changes too quickly. So one should forget about trying to know everything, focusing instead on exploiting technology to extend your knowledge beyond our own brain, building a network of knowledge sources that can be accessed on-demand.	Learner autonomy, in terms of choice of content and how they choose to learn openness, in terms of access to the course, content, activities and methods of assessment diversity: varied content, individual perspectives and multiple tools, especially for networking learners and creating opportunities for dialogue and discussion interactivity: 'massive' communication between learners and co-operative learning, resulting in emergent knowledge

AFFECTIVE COMPUTING AND E-LEARNING

Affection means, in a few words, the whole realm of emotions properly said, the feelings of emotions, sensory experiences, and especially the ability to be able to get in touch with the sensations (Bercht, 2001). Affective computing has thus emerged as a field of Artificial Intelligence, whose objective is the study of emotions and their application in computer systems. According to Picard (2000), the discipline studies how computing systems can detect classify and respond to human emotions. Affective computing in Human-Computer Interaction can be defined as "computing that relates to, arises from, or deliberately influences emotion" (Picard, 2000). Various studies support that affect plays a critical role in learning performance, as well as significant influencing cognitive processes (Given & Barbara, 1998).

Goleman (1995) stats that the extent to which emotional upsets can interfere with mental life is no news to teachers, as it is common knowledge that students who are angry, anxious, or depressed have difficulties in learning. Indeed, people who are caught in these states do not take information efficiently or deal with it very well. Hence the need to acquire this kind of information, and especially in online environments in which the lack of face-to-face communication makes it harder for the teacher to know the state of the student. However, the relationship between learning and emotions is far from being that simple and linear.

Positive and negative affect states produce different kind of thinking and this might hold important implications from educational and training perspective. A consistent theory of learning that integrates effectively cognitive and emotional factors is strongly needed (Kort & Reilly, 2001).

A wide range of emotions occurs naturally in a real learning processes, from positive ones (e.g. joy, satisfaction) to negative ones (e.g. frustration, sadness, confusion, stress, fatigue) or to emotions more related to interest, curiosity and surprise in front of a new topic. There are a numerous emotions along with their combinations, variations and mutations. In fact, there are more subtleties of emotions than the words we have to define them.

Emotions have a close relationship with education, because the affective state of the student directly affects the motivation and aptitude to learn something. Thus, knowing the user's affective state might play an important role improving the effectiveness and efficacy of e-learning. The unawareness of emotional states has been considered one of the core limitations of the traditional e-learning tools. Skilled teachers modify the learning path and their teaching style according to students feedback signals (which include cognitive, emotional and motivational aspects) while e-learning platforms generally do not take into account these feedbacks, becoming too rigid and weakened as they perform in the same manner for all students.

AFFECTIVE STATES IN E-LEARNING

Most of the e-learning systems focus attention towards knowledge acquisition or cognitive processing. When building such a system, affective states (such as motivation and emotion for instance), are considered only in terms of how the content is structured and presented. To make learning efficient and to deliver personalized content, adaptive systems are based on student's goals models, knowledge, and preferences. Thus, a student model that integrates the cognitive processes and motivational states would lead to more efficient and personalized adaptation (Cocea & Weibelzahl, 2007). Transforming a non-affect sensitive e-learning system into a system that includes user's affective states requires the modelling of a cycle known as the affective loop.

As stated before, affection influences the learning performance and decision-making. This means that students who become caught in affective states such as anger or depression do not process and absorb information efficiently. From this, it can be inferred that a user's affective state has a major role in improving the effectiveness of e-learning (Weimin & Wenhong, 2007).

In (Khan et al., 2010), four methods to infer the student's affective states are proposed, namely:

1. Verbal approach, where a questionnaire or self-report instrument is presented to the student;
2. Nonverbal approach, where psycho-physiological instrument measures physical states;
3. Physiological sensors, an approach based on intrusive instruments to measure affective states; and
4. Non-intrusive approach, where the affective state is identified through the interaction with the system.

This last approach, seems to be the most desirable, as the monitoring process is done without the user's knowledge, thus the results are not contaminated by the process itself. That is, a student will not become stress by knowing that the level of stress is being monitored. Moreover, the student does not need to be connected to sensors or to carry out any specific action.

FATIGUE, STRESS, AND DISTRACTION

In all kinds of activities there are several factors that influence the normal achievement of the established objectives. Learning is no exception, especially being the social activity that it is, in which these factors are numerous and complex. When in an e-learning platform, these factors assume even greater importance, due to the absence of the daily and personal contact between the teacher and the student. Thus, the analysis of the feelings, state and attitudes of the student by the teacher become more difficult (Skinner & Belmont, 1993; Epp, et al., 2011).

In this sense, the use of technological tools for teaching, with the consequent teacher-student and student-student separation, may represent a risk as a significant amount of context information is lost. Since students' effectiveness and success in learning is much related and can be somewhat explained by their mood while doing it, these issues should be taken into consideration when in an e-learning environment.

When in such an environment, the teacher can't detect or foresee that some negative situation is about to occur (such as a conflict) and take measures accordingly to mitigate it. Affective states thus need to be monitored. Specifically, this work tries to monitor and detect stress, fatigue and distraction, which are root causes for the different types of conflict that can emerge between students or between student and teacher.

The definition of concepts such as Fatigue, Stress and Distraction from a scientific point of view is particularly difficult and very subjective. Fatigue may be defined as a combination of several symptoms, among which we can include performance decrease (e.g. attention loss, slow reaction to a particular event, or low performance in activities to which the individual has the necessary skills), and subjective feelings of drowsiness and tiredness. From an abstract point of view, fatigue may be seen as two-dimensional perspective, namely mental and physical. Despite the frequent inter-dependence of these two dimensions, they may be analysed independently (Horvitz, Jacobs & Hovel, 1999).

In studying fatigue one must acknowledge the major role of the biological clock, which goes beyond compelling the body to fall asleep and to wake up again. It also modulates our hour-to-hour waking behaviour, which in turn affects our sense of fatigue, alertness and performance, generating circadian rhythmicity in almost all neuro-behavioural variables. This means that there is a natural oscillation of the level of fatigue that we experience during the day that is independent of the intensity of the tasks being performed: the base level of fatigue

A user profile provides very important and valuable information with respect to the potential level of fatigue (Faber et al., 2012). It helps to build a predicted base level of fatigue in the sense that it establishes a baseline, according to the lifestyle of the individual. These aspects have been widely studied, mostly by psychologists. The most important aspects include:

- **Age:** Defines the mental age of the individual. It is crucial to understand the expected cognitive abilities, which may have a tendency to degrade over time;
- **Gender:** The mental states are different between men and women;
- **Professional Occupation:** Important to understand possible causes of mental fatigue, since many occupations are intrinsically more exasperating or exhausting than others;
- **Consumption of Addictive Substances:** The use of certain substances for short or prolonged periods of time may cause dependencies and other effects that lead to a state of mental fatigue;
- **Health Problems:** Hearing or vision problems may significantly influence the progress in the proposed tasks.

Stress is also a significant factor. It can play a pertinent (usually negative) role in education, even more in e-learning. Stress can change the learning style and is essentially felt when the perceived pressure exceeds the perceived ability to cope. Stress represents an abnormal condition that disrupts the normal functions of the body or mind. In other words, human stress is a state of tension that is created when a person responds to demands and pressures (Palmer et al., 2003). Stress is thus always perceived; a situation is stressful for an individual – not for all individuals. Given a particular situation, one student may feel it like a stressful one, whilst another student may feel it like an enjoyable situation. Likewise, in a same situation but for different students, a conflict may or may not emerge. Given the complexity of the phenomena and the different dimensions that are affected, a multi-modal approach should be considered when dealing with stress so as to acquire input from a broad series of markers (Figure 2).

Figure 2. Multimodal approach to stress

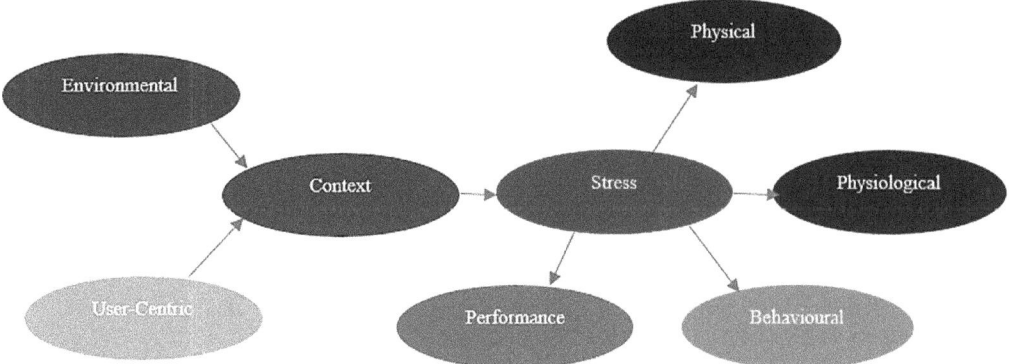

Attention is also one of the most important mechanisms when it comes to acquiring new knowledge: being a cognitive process, attention is strongly connected with learning and the assimilating of new concepts (Horvitz et al., 1999). Lack of attention can thus be very problematic in learning, and especially in e-learning (Mayer & Moreno, 1998). Attention is also very important to perform any task efficiently and in an adequate way, or to distinguish between important and superfluous information for a given task at hand. When engaged in e-learning, the lack of attention can have very negative effects. The ability to focus on a task for extended periods is however at risk in a time in which students are constantly tempted with new things from the digital world, available just around the corner and at the touch of their fingers.

In order to detect and prevent potential conflicts, monitoring these three factors is crucial. In order to get valuable data and results, the process of acquiring data should be completely transparent to the user, carried out in a non-intrusive way.

CONFLICT MANAGEMENT IN E-LEARNING PLATFORMS

When considering conflicts in the context of e-learning platforms, fatigue, stress or distraction can act as catalytic agent. It is common sense that a stressed and fatigued student or teacher is more prone to conflict than a calm and wake one. Conflicts may still emerge without stress or fatigue, as they emerge naturally from the complexity of our social relationships and our often conflicting goals. When in such virtual millieus, foreseeing that a conflict is about to occur is thus a major issue. When that predictability is not possible or achieved, it is still possible to try to mitigate the negative consequences of the conflict. However, the main focus resides on the prediction of aggregated factors, that combined can lead to a possible conflict situation.

E-learning platforms lack the mechanisms to cope with the vast and heterogeneous nature of students that interact with them. Several critical issues were previously identified, that need comprehensive attention in order to improve students success, and reduce conflicts. The need for an accurate and transparent monitoring of these issues is needed. It must also be kept in mind that in order to minimize conflict, each student must be addressed individually. Specifically, new e-learning systems must personalize instruction and make individually useful recommendations, successfully guiding students to success. In this path, learning theories, affective states and contextualization is paramount. Such an approach is proposed in this chapter, as depicted in Figure 3.

This framework proposes a dynamic student monitoring tool that analyses the context of the student/ platform interaction, namely attitudes, behaviours and emotions, taking into account learning theories and affective computing to build and adapt strategies in order to propose personalized instruction and thus improving the abilities of the e-learning platforms to promote individual success. Moreover, given that an active monitoring of the students is being carried out, possible conflicts can be foreseen and actions taken to mitigate them. As a first approach, and to keep things into a manageable scope, stress, fatigue and distraction will be monitored, as detailed next. These factors were identified as significant concerning conflicts and learning performance.

Figure 3. Intelligent learning environment

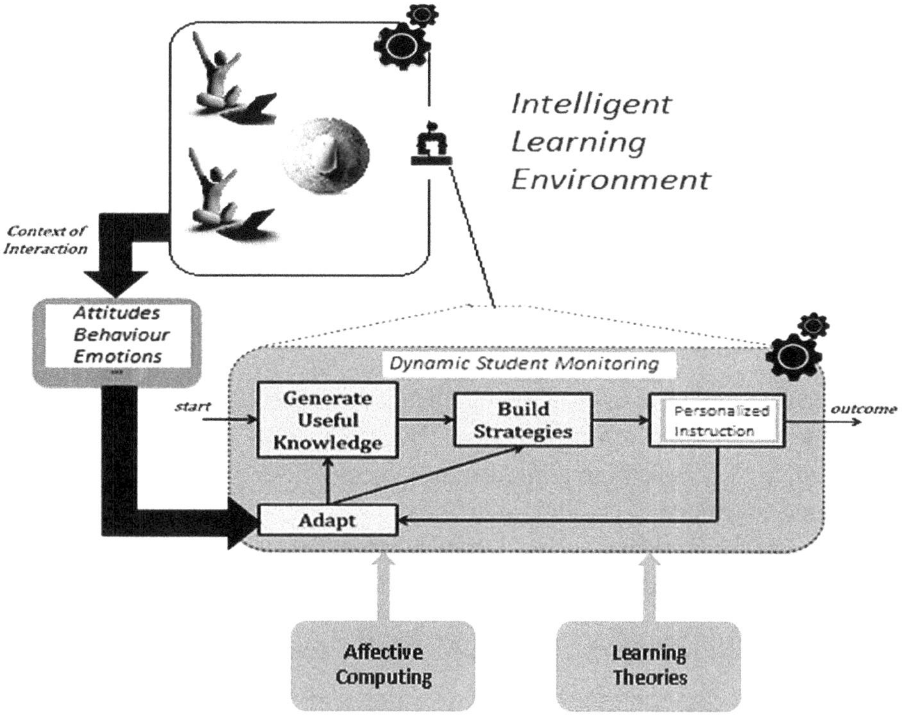

A DYNAMIC APPROACH TO MONITOR FATIGUE, STRESS AND DISTRACTION

In this chapter we have already addressed potential problems that may arise from abnormal levels of fatigue or stress in the context of e-learning. To cope with these problems in this context, monitoring certain indicators becomes essential.

However, this process needs to be completely transparent and non-intrusive, taking place at the same time that the student is working. Specifically, we developed an approach that is based on the observation of the student's interaction with the computer. These interactions occur, as in other domains, mostly by means of the keyboard and mouse.

We thus look at these devices in order to collect potentially interesting information to classify the student's state. Mobile devices (e.g. smartphones, tablets) were also considered, namely due to the sensors that this kind of devices generally includes, and that may provide additional interesting information. Nonetheless, given that the computer is more commonly used when interacting with e-learning tools, in this chapter we consider only the use of keyboard and mouse. In previous work we have also explored, with success, the use of video cameras for classifying stress and fatigue. However, in this sensitive domain, which often involves children, we definitely exclude its use.

The use of the mouse and keyboard allows to acquire diverse and thorough contextual features that describe the interaction patterns of the user with the computer, as addressed in (Rodrigues et al., 2012). These features reflect the behaviour of the user and how it changes under certain conditions, such as when the user is fatigued, stressed or distracted.

Table 2. Mouse and keyboard events

Event	Description
MOV	Mouse movement, in a given time, to coordinates (posX, posY)
MOUSE_DOWN	Mouse button pressed down (left or right), in a given time and position (posX, posY)
MOUSE_UP	An event similar to the previous one but describing the second part of the click, when the mouse button is released
MOUSE_WHEEL	This event describes a mouse wheel scroll of a given amount, in a given time
KEY_DOWN	The event of pressing down a given key, at a given time
KEY_UP	The event of releasing a given key, at a given time

To monitor students, a tool developed at the Intelligent Systems Lab of the University of Minho was incorporated into the e-learning platform and used. This tool records all events of interaction with the mouse and keyboard, as they happen (e.g. mouse movement, clicks, key presses or releases). Table 2 summarizes the events registered.

From logs containing these events, a transformation process is carried out on the data that results in high-level information that characterizes the behaviour of the student. Namely, the following features are extracted.

- **Time between Keys:** The timespan between two consecutive KEY_UP and KEY_DOWN events, i.e., how long did the individual took to press another key.
- **Mouse Velocity:** The distance travelled by the mouse (in pixels) over the time (in milliseconds). The velocity is computed for each interval defined by two consecutive MOUSE_UP and MOUSE_DOWN events.
- **Mouse Acceleration:** The velocity of the mouse (in pixels/milliseconds) over the time (in milliseconds). A value of acceleration is computed for each interval defined by two consecutive MOUSE_UP and MOUSE_DOWN events, using the intervals and data computed for the Velocity.
- **Time between Clicks:** The timespan between two consecutive MOUSE_UP and MOUSE_DOWN events, i.e., how long did it took the individual to perform another click.
- **Double Click Duration:** The timespan between two consecutive MOUSE_UP events, whenever this timespan is inferior to 200 milliseconds. Wider timespans are not considered double clicks.
- **Average Excess of Distance:** This feature measures the average excess of distance that the mouse travelled between each two consecutive MOUSE_UP and MOUSE_DOWN events.
- **Average Distance of the Mouse to the Straight Line:** In a few words, this feature measures the average distance of the mouse to the straight line defined between two consecutive clicks.
- **Distance of the Mouse to the Straight Line:** This feature is similar to the previous one in the sense that it will compute the distance between two consecutive MOUSE_UP and MOUSE_DOWN events. However, it returns its sum rather than the average value during the path.
- **Signed Sum of Angles:** The aim of this feature is to determine if the movement of the mouse tends to "turn" more to the right or to the left
- **Absolute Sum of Angles:** This feature is very similar to the previous one. However, it seeks to find only how much the mouse "turned", independently of the direction to which it turned.

- **Distance between Clicks:** Represents the total distance travelled by the mouse between two consecutive clicks, i.e., between each two consecutive MOUSE_UP and MOUSE_DOWN events.

Previous work on this data collection and reporting tool can be found in (Rodrigues et al., 2013) where a more detailed analysis of the process is provided. From these features it is possible to obtain a measure of the user's performance (e.g. an increased distance between clicks or sum of angles represents decreased performance).

Once information about the individual's performance exists in these terms, it is possible to start monitoring fatigue and stress, in real-time, and without the need for any explicit or conscious interaction. This makes this approach especially suited to be used in e-learning environments in which people use computers as it requires no change in their working routines. This is the main advantage of this work, especially when compared to more traditional approaches that still rely on questionnaires (with issues concerning wording or question construction), special hardware (that has additional costs and is frequently intrusive) or the availability of human experts. The monitoring of these indicators, especially stress, as described in the following section, is paramount for the real-time prevention of the emergence of conflicts.

MONITORING TOOL

In this monitoring tool, the mouse and keyboard can be seen as sensors (Figure 4), more specifically, soft-sensors. Given that these peripherals are always used while interacting with the computer, they constitute optimal interaction sensors.

Figure 4. Monitoring tool architecture

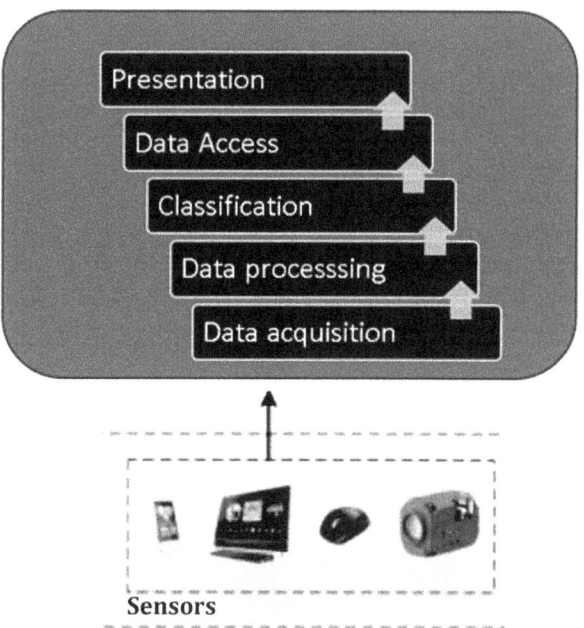

The proposed framework includes not only the sheer acquisition and classification of the data, but also a presentation tier that will support the human-based or autonomous decision-making and reporting mechanisms that are now being implemented, specifically targeted at the teacher (e.g. pointing out a student or group of students in which a potential conflict is emerging). The framework is built on top of a layered architecture, composed of five main layers.

The Data Acquisition layer is responsible for capturing information describing the behavioural patterns of the user, receiving data of events from the use of the mouse and the keyboard. This layer encodes each event with the corresponding necessary information (e.g. timestamp, coordinates, type of click, code of the key pressed).

The Data Processing layer is responsible for processing the data received from the Data Acquisition layer in order to evaluate the data according to the features presented. It is also in this phase that outlier values are filtered to eliminate possible negative effects on the analysis (e.g. the continuous pressing of the backspace key to delete multiple characters should not be considered as a regular key press).

The Classification layer is where the collected data is used to build behavioural models that shape the user's interaction patterns in different scenarios and states. These models can then be used, in real-time, to classify the state of the students taking as input their interaction with the computer.

After the classification, the Data Access layer is responsible for providing access to the lower layer. Thus, this layer facilitates the access to the trained classifiers in real-time, taking as input logs of interaction events and providing as output a classification of the state of the student.

Finally, at the top there is the Presentation layer, which includes the mechanisms to build intuitive and visual representations of the mental states of the users, abstracting from the complexity and lack of information of the data level (Figure 5). This layer is also responsible for the generation of warnings

Figure 5. Part of the interfaces that make up the Presentation layer of the monitoring tool

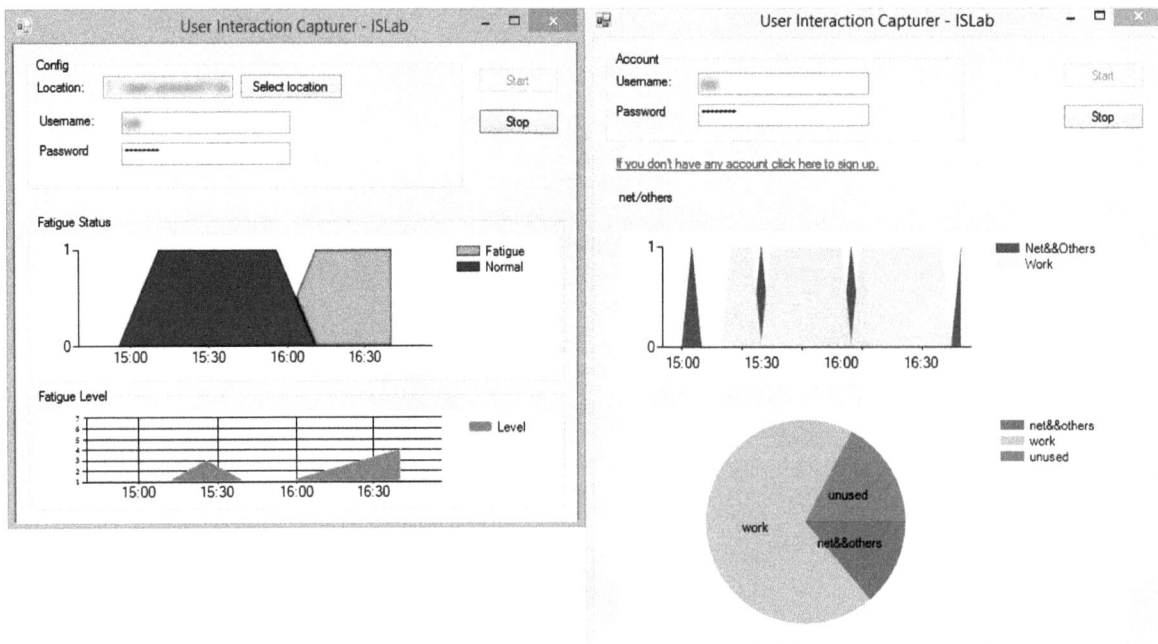

and notifications especially targeted at the teacher, namely to point out students or group of students that show potential negative signs. The teacher can then take the appropriate actions towards the prevention of the emergence of conflicts or other problems in the teacher/student relationship.

CASE STUDY

To assess and validate the developed tool and its ability to point out potentially negative states so that conflicts can be avoided, a study was conducted in a real setting, with the participation of 34 volunteer students. These students were simply asked to perform a group of tasks, without any difference from the tasks they were used to carry out in the context of their course, in two different moments in time, separated by a week. In the first moment, students were told that this was a regular progress task, as many others before. In the second moment, students were told that this task was for evaluation purposes, with a significant impact on their final score. Students were thus more relaxed and calm in the first moment of data collection.

During both data collection events, the previously described tool was used to collect data from the two experiments. It was a completely transparent process and students were only briefed about this data collection after the second moment.

The collected data was used to train one model whose main aim was to distinguish between positive (first moment of data collection) and negative (second moment of data collection) states.

However, before the actual training of the classifier and in order to assess the extent the potential differences found between the two moments, the data collected was organized in two groups in order to be compared, feature by feature.

Given that most of the distributions of the collected data were not normal, the Mann-Whitney test was used to perform this analysis. This test is a non-parametric statistical hypothesis test for assessing whether one of two samples of independent observations tends to have larger values than the other. The null hypothesis is thus: H_0 = the medians of the two distributions are equal. For each two distributions compared, the test returns a p-value, with a small p-value suggesting that it is unlikely that H_0 is true. Thus, for every Mann-Whitney test whose p-value $< \alpha$, the difference is considered to be statistically significant, i.e., H_0 is rejected. A commonly adopted value of $\alpha = 0.05$ was used in this test.

The results showed that in all students there was a varying but significant number of features affected by the conditions of the second moment. Interestingly enough, features extracted from both the mouse and the keyboard were affected, showing that both peripherals can effectively be used for this purpose. Specifically, we focused on the mean and median values of each feature, to find not only statistically significant differences between the distributions of the data but also to determine if the observed differences between the two moments were consistent among students.

Figure 6 depicts some of the statistically significant differences observed. Each set of box-and-whisker plots shows the distribution of the data collected for all students and for a given feature, in the two moments of data collection (Baseline designates moment 1 and Stressed designates moment 2). Four specific features are detailed: Click duration (a), absolute sum of angles (b), distance of the mouse to the straight line (c) and average excess of distance (d).

Figure 6. Comparison of the distribution of data of four features in the two moments of data collection (a - Click duration, b - absolute sum of angles, c- distance of the mouse to the straight line, d- average excess of distance)

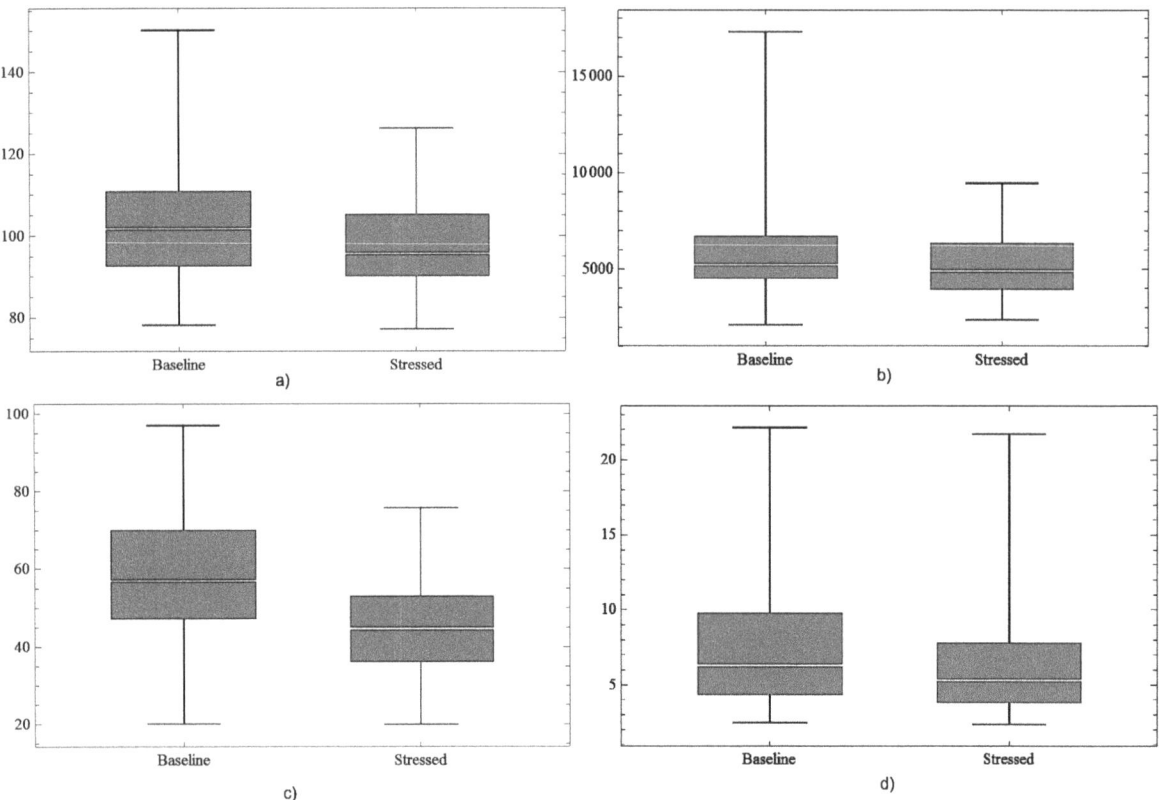

The four plots included in Figure 6 show a consistent trend in the second moment of data collection: the mean and median of the four features decreased. This actually points out an increase in the performance of the interaction, showing that when under stress students tend to interact in a more efficient way with the mouse and the keyboard.

It also shows that changes in the students' inner state affect their interaction patterns, which opens the door to the development of a solution such as the one proposed in the first sections of this chapter, which can actively be used by the teacher to prevent conflicts in the e-learning environment by promoting better states between students and between students and teacher.

CONCLUSION AND FUTURE WORK

As stated, modern society puts an enormous amount of pressure into the formation/requalification of their citizens. Technology arises as a way to enhance these learning/teaching processes, overcoming constraints such as qualified instructors availability, time restrictions, and individual monitoring for instance. However, important context information is lost, which calls for new methods in order to get useful information to monitor and personalise instruction.

When engaging with e-learning platforms, students affective states, together with the proper way of presenting content (Learning theories), must be considered, to enhance learning. A framework is proposed to address these issues, specially do dynamically monitor students. Narrowing the scope of the study, a model to detect stress fatigue and distraction is proposed, through the use of a monitoring tool. With this tool it is possible to detect those factors dynamically and non-intrusively, making it possible to foresee negative situations, and taking actions to mitigate them. This also represents an important step towards the decrease or avoidance of conflicts in the learning environment, that often emerge due to stress or fatigue.

The door is then open to intelligent e-learning platforms that allow to analyse the students' inner state, taking into account their individual characteristics, and to propose new strategies and actions, minimizing issues such as stress, fatigues and distraction, which in turn can influence students' performance and are closely related to the occurrence of conflicts. We will enlarge this study to the use of smartphones and tablets, taking advantage of their new characteristics, including soft and hard sensors, motivated by the role that these devices have nowadays in the students' lives. This next step will make it possible to perform a wider characterization of the student, resulting in an enhanced learning experience, though better recommendation and personalization.

REFERENCES

Aarts, E., & Wichert, R. (2009). Ambient intelligence. In *Technology Guide* (pp. 244–249). Springer Berlin Heidelberg. doi:10.1007/978-3-540-88546-7_47

Alzaghoul, A. F. (2012). The implication of the learning theories on implementing e-learning courses. *The Research Bulletin of Jordan*, 2(2), 27–30.

Battistich, V., Schaps, E., & Wilson, N. (2004). Effects of an elementary school intervention on students' "connectedness" to school and social adjustment during middle school. *The Journal of Primary Prevention*, 24(3), 243–262. doi:10.1023/B:JOPP.0000018048.38517.cd

Bercht, M. (2001). *Em direção a agentes pedagógicos com dimensões afetivas. Tese de Doutorado (Doutorado em Ciência da Computação)*. Porto Alegre: Universidade Federal do Rio Grande do Sul.

Bouton, M. E. (2009). Behaviourism, thoughts, and actions. *British Journal of Psychology*, 100(S1), 181–183. doi:10.1348/000712609X415140 PMID:19351440

Cocea, M., & Weibelzahl, S. (2007). Eliciting motivation knowledge from log files towards motivation diagnosis for Adaptive Systems. *User Modeling 2007* (LNCS). Springer Berlin / Heidelberg.

Downes, S. (2005, October). E-learning 2.0. *eLearn*.

Ebner, M. (2007). E-learning 2.0 = e-learning 1.0 + web 2.0? *Availability, Reliability and Security, International Conference on*.

Epp, C., Lippold, M., & Mandryk, R. L. (2011). Identifying emotional states using keystroke dynamics. In *Proceedings of the SIGCHI Conference on Human Factors in Computing Systems*, (pp. 715–724). ACM. DOI doi:10.1145/1978942.1979046

Faber, L. G., Maurits, N. M., & Lorist, M. M. (2012). Mental fatigue affects visual selective attention. *PLoS ONE*, *7*(10), e48073. doi:10.1371/journal.pone.0048073 PMID:23118927

Given, B. K. (1998). Psychological and neurobiological support for learning-style instruction: Why it works. *National Forum of Teacher Education Journal, 8.*

Goleman, D. (1995). *Emotional Intelligence.* Bantam Books.

Goroshko, O. I. & Samoilenko S. A. (2011). Twitter as a Conversation through e-learning Context. *Revista de Informatica Sociala*, (15).

Hamre, B. K., Pianta, R. C., & Bear, G. (Eds.). (2006). Student-Teacher Relationships. In Children's needs III: Development, prevention, and intervention, (pp. 59-71). Washington, DC: National Association of School Psychologists.

Horvitz, E., Jacobs, A., & Hovel, D. (1999). Attention-sensitive alerting. In *Proceedings of the Fifteenth Conference on Uncertainty in Artificial Intelligence*, (pp. 305–313). Morgan Kaufmann Publishers Inc.

Hwang, K., & Yang, C. (2009). Automated Inattention and Fatigue Detection System in Distance Education for Elementary School Students. *Journal of Educational Technology & Society*, *12*, 22–35.

Khan, F. A. (2010). Identifying and Incorporating Affective States and Learning Styles in Web-based Learning Management Systems. *Interaction Design and Architecture(s) Journal, 9-10*, 85-103.

Klem, A. M., & Connell, J. P. (2004). Relationships matter: Linking teacher support to student engagement and achievement. *The Journal of School Health*, *74*(7), 262–273. doi:10.1111/j.1746-1561.2004.tb08283.x PMID:15493703

Kort, B., & Reilly, R. (2001). *Analytical Models of Emotions, Learning and Relationships: Towards an Affect-sensitive Cognitive Machine.* MIT Media Lab Tech Report No 548.

Mayer, R. E., & Moreno, R. (1998). A split-attention effect in multimedia learning: Evidence for dual processing systems in working memory. *Journal of Educational Psychology*, *90*(2), 312–320. doi:10.1037/0022-0663.90.2.312

Moravec, J. W. (2008). A new paradigm of knowledge production in higher education. *On the Horizon*, *16*(3), 123–136. doi:10.1108/10748120810901422

Picard, R. W. (2000). *Affective Computing.* The MIT Press.

Pimenta, A., Carneiro, D., Novais, P., & Neves, J. (2013). Monitoring mental fatigue through the analysis of keyboard and mouse interaction patterns. LNAI, 8073, 222–231. Doi: doi:10.1007/978-3-642-40846-5_23

Prensky, M. (2001). Digital natives, digital immigrants. On the Horizon, 9(5).

Williamson, R., Purcell, S., Sterne, A., Hotopof, M., Farmer, A., & Sham, P. (2005). The relationship of fatigue to mental and physical health in a community sample. *Social Psychiatry and Psychiatric Epidemiology*, *2*(2), 126–135. doi:10.1007/s00127-005-0858-5 PMID:15685404

Rego, H., Moreira, T., Morales, E., & Garcia, F. J. (2010). Metadata and Knowledge Management driven Web-based Learning Information System towards Web/e-learning 3.0. [iJET]. *International Journal of Emerging Technologies in Learning*, *5*(2), 36–44.

Richardson, W. (2005). The educator's guide to the read/write web. *Educational Leadership*, *63*(4), 24.

Rodrigues, M., Gonçalves, S., Carneiro, D., Novais, P., & Fdez-Riverola, F. (2013). Keystrokes and Clicks: Measuring Stress on E-learning Students. In *Management Intelligent Systems, Second International Symposium*. Springer.

Rodrigues, M., Fdez-Riverola, F., & Novais, P. (2012). An approach to assessing stress in e-learning students. *ECEL-2012 – 11th European Conference on E-Learning*. Retrieved from http://repositorium.sdum.uminho.pt/handle/1822/23894

Rodrigues, M., Fdez-Riverola, F., & Novais, P. (2011). Moodle and Affective Computing –Knowing Who's on the Other Side. *ECEL-2011 – 10th European Conference on Elearning*. University of Brighton.

Palmer, S., Cooper, C., & Thomas, K. (2003). *Creating a Balance: Managing Stress*. London: British Library.

Smith, L. H., & Renzulli, J. S. (1984). Learning style preferences: A practical approach for classroom teachers. *Theory into Practice*, *23*(1), 44–50. doi:10.1080/00405848409543088

Skinner, E. A., & Belmont, M. J. (1993). Motivation in the classroom: Reciprocal effects of teacher behavior and student engagement across the school year. *Journal of Educational Psychology*, *85*(4), 571–581. doi:10.1037/0022-0663.85.4.571

Tapscott, D. (1998). *Growing Up Digital. The Rise of the Net Generation*. New York: McGraw Hill. Retrieved from http://www.growingupdigital.com/index.html

U.S. Department of Education. (2009). *Evaluation of Evidence-Based Practices in Online Learning: A Meta-Analysis and Review of Online Learning Studies*. Retrieved from http://www.ed.gov/rschstat/eval/tech/evidence-based-practices/finalreport.pdf

Weimin, X., & Wenhong, X. (2007). *E-Learning Assistant System Based on Virtual Human Interaction Technology, ICCS 2007* (LNCS). Springer Berlin / Heidelberg.

Wheeler, S. (2011). *E-learning 3.0: Learning through the eXtended Smart Web*. In National IT Training Conference.

Yampolskiy, R. V., & Govindaraju, V. (2008). Behavioural biometrics: A survey and classification. *International Journal of Biometrics*, *1*(1), 81–113. doi:10.1504/IJBM.2008.018665

KEY TERMS AND DEFINITIONS

Affective Computing: A sub-field of Artificial Intelligence that seeks the development of systems that are aware of user emotions.

Behavioral Analysis: A group of processes that allow to acquire and process information about one's behaviors, tendentiously in a non-intrusive way.

Behavioral Biometrics: A field of science that looks at the individuals' behaviors as unique, allowing identification based on behavioral analysis.

Classification: A general process that attributes one known category, from a discrete set, to an observation of data.

E-Learning: The use of technological tools, especially those related to ICT, for the purpose of facilitating or supporting learning, either in the classroom or remotely.

Information Fusion: The process of integration of multiple data and knowledge sources, describing one real-world object.

Non-Intrusive Monitoring: The ability to continuously monitor variables of interest, in a way that does not interfere with the users' routines.

Chapter 13
Real–Time Detection of Pedestrians:
A Comparison of Three Segmentation Algorithms in Infrared Video

Juan Serrano-Cuerda
Universidad de Castilla – La Mancha, Spain

María T. López
Universidad de Castilla – La Mancha, Spain

José Carlos Castillo
Universidad Carlos III de Madrid, Spain

Antonio Fernández-Caballero
Universidad de Castilla – La Mancha, Spain

ABSTRACT

Real-time pedestrian detection is a key technology for video surveillance. A widespread approach for detecting pedestrians is the use of color information. In recent times, the use of thermal infrared cameras has revealed to be an excellent alternative that offers good results in people segmentation. Nonetheless, thermal infrared cameras are very sensitive to the overall heat detected at each image. Moreover, a great amount of infrared images has low spatial resolution and lower sensitivity than visible spectrum images due to the technological limitations of infrared cameras. This chapter introduces a comparison of three different algorithms for real-time and robust pedestrian detection in the infrared spectrum. The aim of the paper is to look for the best algorithms prepared to resolve the conflicts that arise in the detection process in image sequences. We propose to use simple rules as conflict resolution mechanism when the outputs of the three algorithms do not coincide.

INTRODUCTION

Electronic surveillance deals with observing or listening to persons, places, or activities with the aid of electronic devices such as cameras, microphones, and tape recorders, among others. Electronic surveillance serves several purposes, such as (1) enhancement of security for persons and property; (2) detection and prevention of criminal, wrongful, or impermissible activity; and (3) interception, protection, or appropriation of valuable, useful, scandalous, embarrassing, and discrediting information.

DOI: 10.4018/978-1-5225-0245-6.ch013

Conflicts in electronic surveillance use to arise when the information gathered from technological artefacts does not provide enough evidence of the accuracy in the events related to people identification. In vision-based electronic surveillance, a first crucial step towards identification is a very precise and efficient detection of people. Here, conflict resolution is the process in which different computer vision algorithms demonstrate their consistency in the segmentation performance in case there is a conflict. A conflict arises when the algorithms hold incompatible views on the segmentation of people in a sequence of images.

Concretely, this chapter faces the comparison of robust algorithms for real-time people detection, a key technology for electronic surveillance. A widespread approach for detecting people is the use of color information. In recent times, the use of thermal infrared cameras has revealed to be an excellent alternative that offers excellent results in people segmentation. This chapter introduces a comparison of three different algorithms for real-time and robust people detection in the infrared spectrum. It is appreciated that people detection based on combining thermal properties and motion information is the best choice among the tested approaches.

This mixed approach is very helpful in reducing conflicts in camera-based electronic people surveillance, as accurate people segmentation is mandatory to achieve further solid people identification. In this sense, this chapter introduces a comparison of three different algorithms for real-time and robust pedestrian detection in the infrared spectrum.

BACKGROUND

Detecting pedestrians is a key technology for many applications, especially in the video surveillance domain (Dollár, Wojek, Schiele, & Perona, 2012). At the same time, it is one of the most challenging problems in computer vision and remains a scientific challenge for realistic and dynamic scenes. Indeed, visual processing of pedestrians, including detection, tracking, recognition, and behavior interpretation, is a key component of intelligent video surveillance systems. A number of surveillance applications require the detection and tracking of people to ensure security and safety (Navarro, Fernández-Caballero, & Martínez-Tomás, 2014), (Costa, Guedes, Vasques, & Portugal, 2013). That is, many video surveillance systems require the ability to determine if an image region contains pedestrians. This is none but a specific case of object classification in which there are only two object classes: pedestrian and non-pedestrian. Object classification in general is difficult and people detection is even harder. In addition, video-surveillance systems must run at video-rate and thus require a trade-off between precision and computing time. Moreover, any pedestrian detection method highly depends on segmentation, which remains a primitive problem. A widespread approach for detecting pedestrians is the use of gray scale (Enzweiler & Gavrila, 2009) and color information (Wan & Liu, 2009; Rodriguez & Shah, 2007), (Schwartz, Kembhavi, Harwood, & Davis, 2009). These are usually problematic when facing changes in lighting in a scene or visibility problems therein. To guard against these failures, you can find an alternative in the use of the infrared spectrum (Sun & Park, 2007).

Thermal infrared images have a number of distinctive features compared to frames acquired by a visible spectrum camera (Li, Gong, Li, & Liu, 2010; Olmeda, de la Escalera, & Armingol, 2011). The gray level value of the objects is usually set by their temperature and radiated heat, and is independent from lighting conditions. This is why a detection system in this spectrum can be applied under day and night conditions. Thus, the most intuitive idea when performing a pedestrian detection algorithm in the thermal infrared spectrum is to take advantage of the fact that humans appear warmer than other objects in the scene. However, this is not always the case (Goubet, Katz, & Porikli, 2006). The condition is usually satisfied during winter and at night, when it is easy to detect humans after applying a simple threshold. In summer conditions, it is also possible to perform a threshold following a background subtraction algorithm, but it is harder to classify humans according to their body features and shape. The reason is that some properties of the objects present in the scene (such as emissivity, reflectivity and transmissivity) as well as their wavelength affect the intensity of thermal infrared images. Non-human objects such as cars or lampposts have bright areas in those images, especially in summer afternoons, making human detection almost impossible when it is based on the objects' gray level values. On the other hand, a great amount of infrared images has low spatial resolution and lower sensitivity than visible spectrum images due to the technological limitations of infrared cameras. These defects often result in low image quality and a great amount of image noise. Many approaches in this spectrum combine appearance and shape properties since humans are initially detected according to the former (their appearance is usually brighter than other objects in the scene) and are filtered and classified based on the latter.

A combination of histograms of oriented gradients (HOGs) and a classifier based on a conventional support vector machine (SVM) is a common trend. An application of this technique segments humans by using a region growing approach with high intensity seeds (O'Malley, Jones, & Glavin, 2010). Then a HOG is created for the candidate regions found and a series of features are extracted from the histogram. A SVM classifier finally uses these features. HOGs are also used in (Chang, Yang, Wu, Cho, & Chen, 2011), where firstly a background subtraction is performed. The Otsu algorithm is applied over the subtraction results, as well as a number of morphological opening and closing operators. Next, regions without humans are filtered out by applying size and shape restrictions.

Finally, the recognition is enhanced by using features extracted by HOGs, such as magnitude and gradient orientation. In a later approach (Wang, Chen, Chen, & Yan, 2012), the scene background is built using a mixture of Gaussians technique and performing a partial vertical sloping operation over human candidates to correct distortions due to clothing. A weighting is applied in order to differentiate humans from other objects. An SVM classifier is applied after these features models are obtained to classify human and non-human candidates.

This chapter introduces three different real-time pedestrian detection algorithms that are not based on HOG and SVM, but only take advantage of the heat information provided by the infrared image and the motion calculated between consecutive video frames. Then, a comparison is done to conclude which of them shows a better performance in terms of sensitivity, precision and F-Score.

ALGORITHMS FOR PEDESTRIAN SEGMENTATION IN INFRARED

The infrared spectrum possesses many interesting features which can be exploited for robust pedestrian detection. Two of these properties are clearly important for this purpose: (1) the independence of lighting conditions of the scene, and specially, (2) the fact that people tend to be clearly highlighted respect to the background of the picture. A human's head also uses to appear hotter than the rest of the body covered with clothing.

A first pedestrian detection algorithm based on a single frame - the current infrared frame IIR (t) - and that uses these properties is developed. Afterwards, a second algorithm is proposed. It adds motion information between the current frame IIR (t) and the previous frame IIR (t- Δt) to the first algorithm.

In this second case, frame subtraction is used to extract moving elements in the scene; pedestrians detected due to motion information are added to those detected based on a single frame. Finally, a third algorithm tested in this proposal is based on using optical flow on the people previously detected in the single frame detection algorithm.

A visual representation of the three approaches is provided in Figure 1. Notice that pedestrian detection based on frame subtraction directly adds its information to the results of the pedestrian detection based on a single frame, while pedestrian detection based on optical flow directly affects the outcome of previous stages of the approach based on a single frame.

The results of the three approaches are compared in the results section to assess which algorithm fits better to the test scenario where the overall system is evaluated. Once the experimental environment is established, all these approaches are compared to establish the algorithm which suits better for the particular needs of a selected test scenario. Each one of the approaches has an initial stage where a list of pedestrian candidates (possible pedestrians) is extracted. The candidates (enlisted through their representing blobs) are analyzed and refined in later stages in order to separate possible groups of pedestrians or to remove false positives (non-pedestrians) which could not be filtered in the previous stages. The results of each algorithm are finally obtained in a new list of blobs. Both lists are later compared to obtain a final list LIR of pedestrians in the infrared spectrum.

Human Detection in Infrared Based on a Single Frame

A pedestrian detection system based on a single frame has initially been developed in the infrared spectrum using the already mentioned properties (Fernández-Caballero, Castillo, Serrano-Cuerda, & Maldonado-Bascón, 2011). Firstly, a set of human candidates are extracted from the scene, based on their thermal properties. A series of adjustments are performed on the initial candidates to obtain a better characterization of their size and location. A series of restrictions on size and shape are finally applied over the adjusted candidates to eliminate potential false positives that may have appeared in the algorithm. Each one of the stages is now explained in more detail.

Detection of Human Candidate Blobs

The algorithm starts with the analysis of input image, $I_{IR}(t)$, captured at time t by the acquisition system, as shown in Figure 2a. A threshold θ_c is used to perform a binarization for the aim of isolating the human candidate spots. This threshold obtains the image areas containing moderate heat blobs, thus belonging to pedestrian candidates. Therefore, warmer zones of the image where humans could be present are isolated. The threshold is calculated as shown in equation (1), where σ_{IIR} is the standard deviation of image $I_{IR}(t)$.

In addition, a base threshold γ, which is experimentally fixed based on the features of each scenario, is used. This base threshold is added to the product of the standard deviation σ_{IIR} and an augmentation percentage factor τ experimentally fixed according to the features of the scenario.

Now, image $I_{IR}(t)$ is binarized using the obtained threshold θ_c. Pixels above the threshold are set as maximum value *max* = 255 (the maximum pixel intensity for a gray level 8 bits image) and pixels below are set as minimum value *min* = 0. This process is shown in equation (2) while the results can be seen in Figure 2b.

Figure 1. Overview of the infrared segmentation system

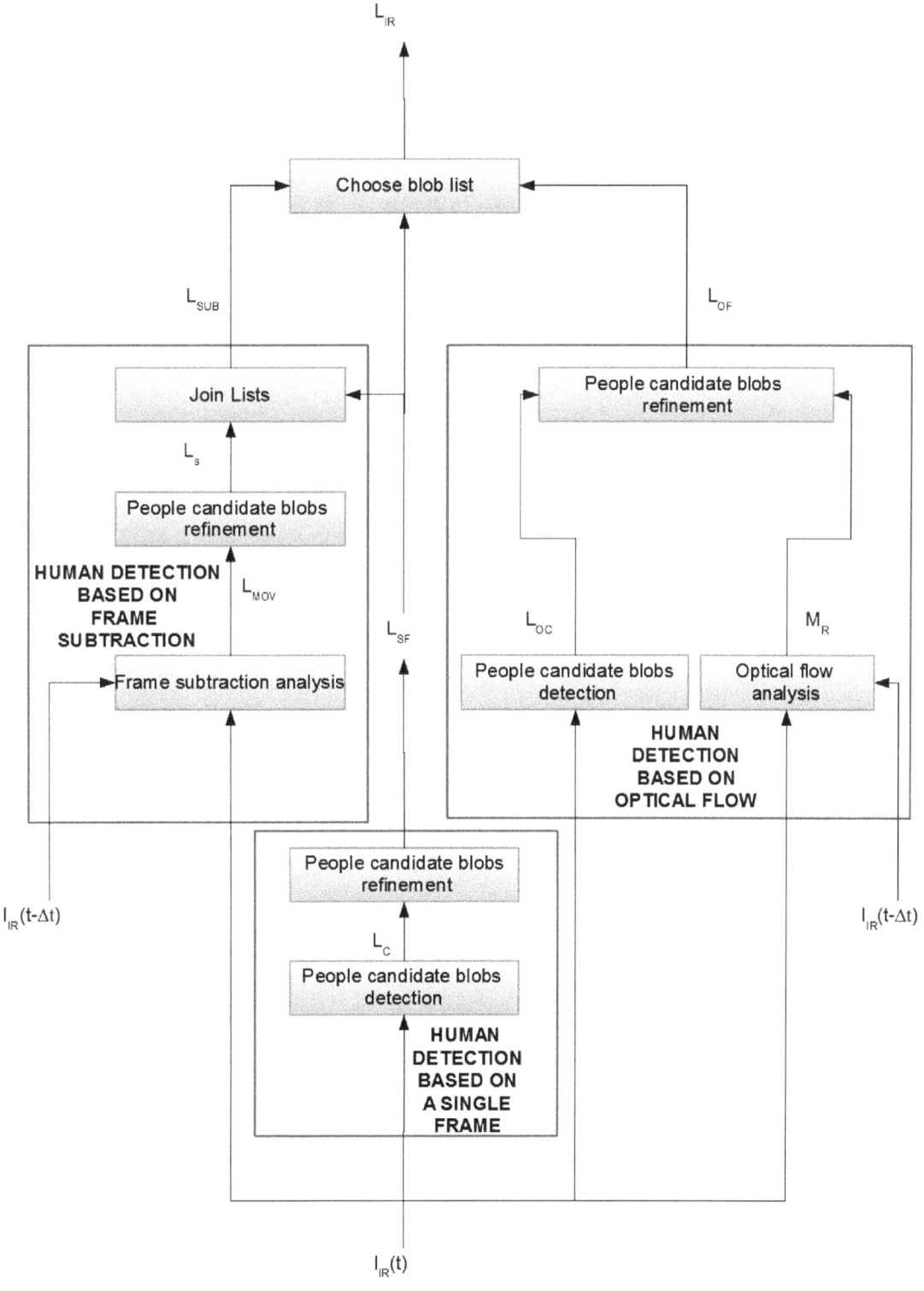

Figure 2. Detection of human candidate blobs in the infrared spectrum. (a) Infrared input frame. (b) Thresholded frame. (c) Frame after morphological operations.

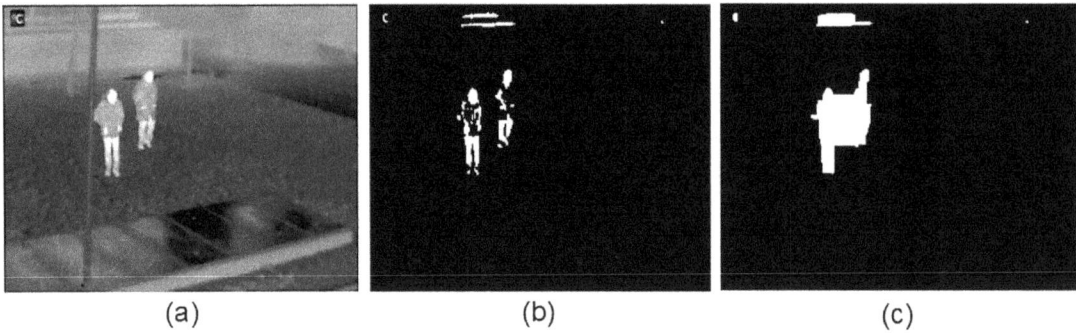

(a)   (b)   (c)

$$\theta_c = \left(\gamma + \tau \times \sigma_{IIR}\right)$$

$$I_b\left(x,y,t\right) = \begin{cases} \min, \textit{if } I_{IR}\left(x,y,t\right) \leq \theta_c \\ \max, \textit{otherwise} \end{cases}$$

Next, the algorithm performs morphological opening and closing operations to eliminate isolated pixels and to unite areas split during the binarization, obtaining image I_c. These operations join small artefacts that could be part of the shapes, as shown in Figure 2c.

Once the binarized image has been obtained, the blobs contained in the image are extracted. A minimum area, A_{min}, -function of the image size- is established for a blob to be considered to contain humans. A_{Ic} is the area of image I_c, as shown in equation (3).

$$A_{min} = \frac{A_{Ic}}{400}$$

This value is experimentally fixed as $\frac{1}{400}$ of the area of I_c. As a result, the list of blobs, L_c containing people candidates in form of blobs b_λ [(x_{start}, y_{start}), (x_{end}, y_{end})] is generated. λ stands for the number (index) of people candidate blob in image $I_c(x,y)$ and (x_{start}, y_{start}) and (x_{end}, y_{end}) are the upper left and lower right coordinates, respectively, of the minimum rectangle containing the blob.

Refinement of Human Candidate Blobs

In this part, the algorithm works with the list of blobs L_c present in image I_c This list was obtained at the end of the previous section. At this point, there is a need to validate the content of each blob to find out if it contains one single human candidate or more than one. Therefore, each detected blob is individually processed.

Let us define a region of interest (ROI) as the minimum rectangle containing one blob of list L_c (obtained from I_c). A ROI may be defined as $R_\kappa = R_\kappa (i,j)$, when associated to blob $b_\kappa [(x_{start}, y_{start}), (x_{end}, y_{end})]$ Notice that $i \in [1..max_i=x_{end}-x_{start}+1]$ and $j \in [1..max_j=y_{end}-y_{start}+1]$.

The next step consists in scanning R_κ by columns, adding the gray level value corresponding to each pixel in that column, as shown in equation (4). This way, a histogram $H_\kappa [i]$ showing which zones of the current ROI own greater heat concentrations, is obtained. A double purpose is pursued when computing the histogram. In first place, we want to increase the certainty of the presence and situation of human heads.

Secondly, as a ROI may contain several persons that are close enough to each other, the histogram helps separating human groups (if any) into single humans. This method, when looking for maxima and minima within the histogram allows differentiating among the people present in the particular ROI.

$$H_\kappa [i] = \sum_{j=1}^{max_j} R_\kappa (i,j) \forall i \in [1,2,\ldots,max_j]$$

Now the histogram, $H_\kappa [i]$, is scanned to separate grouped humans, if any. Local maxima and local minima are searched in the histogram to establish the different heat sources (see Figure 3a) with this purpose. To assess whether a histogram column contains a local maximum or minimum, a new threshold θ_{vmin} is fixed. Experimentally we went to the conclusion that the local maximum threshold must be set as shown in equation (5) where θ_{vmin} indicates those regions of the ROI where the sum of the heat sources are really low. We are looking for columns where the 60% of their pixels are below the mean gray value of R_κ, since those regions are supposed to belong to gaps between two humans. Figure 3b shows the histogram for input ROI of Figure 3a. Figure 3c shows the two humans as separated by the algorithm into sub-ROIs, $sR_{\kappa, \alpha}$.

$$\theta_{vmin} = \left(0,6 \times \overline{R_\kappa} \times max_j \right)$$

All humans contained in a sub-ROI, $sR_{\kappa, \alpha}$ still possess the same height, namely the height of the original ROI. Now, we want to fit the height of each sub-ROI to the real height of the human contained. For this purpose row adjustment is performed for each new sub-ROI, $sR_{\kappa, \alpha}$ generated after the previous column adjustment, by applying a new threshold, θ_h. The calculation is done separately on each sub-ROI to avoid the influence of the rest of image pixels on the result. This threshold uses the value of the sub-ROI mean gray level, $\theta_r = \overline{sR_{\kappa, \alpha}}$. Thus, sub-ROI, $sR_{\kappa, \alpha}$ is binarized in order to delimit its upper and lower limits, obtaining, $sR_{\beta, \kappa, \alpha}$ as shown in equation (6) similarly to equation (2). The result of the threshold application over the input sub-ROI shown in Figure 4a can be seen in Figure 4b.

$$sR_{\beta,\kappa, \alpha} = \begin{cases} min, & if \ sR_{\kappa, \alpha} \leq \theta_r \\ max, & otherwise \end{cases}$$

Figure 3. Vertical delimiting of humans in the infrared spectrum. (a) Input ROI containing a group of humans. (b) Histogram. (c) Column adjustment to obtain two human candidates.

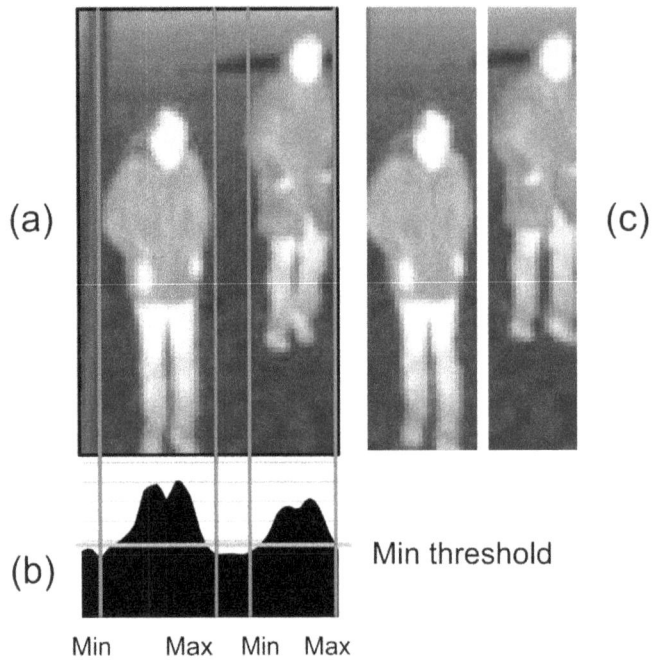

Figure 4. Horizontal delimiting of humans in the infrared spectrum. (a) Input sub-ROI. (b) Thresholded sub-ROI. (c) Row adjustment to obtain two human candidates.

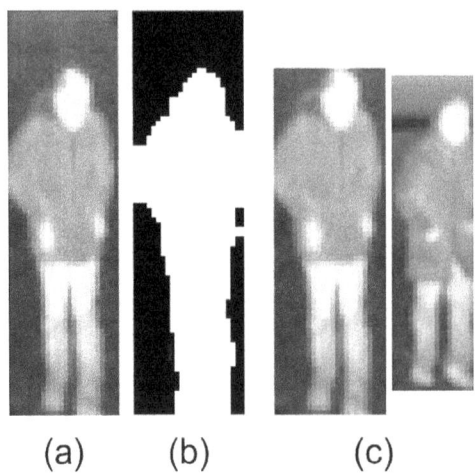

After this, a closing operation is performed to unite spots isolated in the binarization, getting $sR_{\varsigma, \kappa, \alpha}$ (see Figure 4b). Next, $sR_{\varsigma, \kappa, \alpha}$ is scanned, searching pixels with values superior to *min*. The upper and lower rows of the human are equal to the first and last rows, respectively, containing pixels with a value set to *max*. The final result may be observed in Figure4c.

Now a final stage is needed for each sub-ROI sR$_{\varsigma,\kappa,\alpha}$ to confirm if the human candidate contained in it is actually a human. At this point, it is interesting to remind that every sub-ROI is defined by its coordinates (x_{start}, y_{start}) and (x_{end}, y_{end}). In first place, let us define the basic parameters needed for human confirmation for every sub-ROI, sR$_{\varsigma,\kappa,\alpha}$, in equations (7), (8), (9) and (10).

$$h_{sR} = y_{end} - y_{start}$$

$$w_{sR} = x_{end} - x_{start}$$

$$A_{sR} = h_{sR} \times w_{sR}$$

$$hwR = \frac{h_{sR}}{w_{sR}}$$

Some of the incandescent spots in the image (such as light bulbs or big heat sources in general) can still be confused under certain circumstances with humans due to their heat properties, so another important step consists in verifying if one of these spots is being scanned instead of a human. First, the human candidate's shape is checked. The first check consists in testing its height/width ratio as shown in equation (10). The restrictions applied are not specifically fixed since they will be relaxed when the scene has low contrast.

The human candidate's area A_{sR} is also required to be above a minimal area A_{sRmin} experimentally fixed according to features such as the camera height or the extension of the scenario. Area A_{sR} is calculated as shown in equation (9) where h_{sR} and w_{sR} are the height and width of the subROI and are obtained as shown in equations (7) and (8), respectively.

Next, if the human candidate's width w_{sR} is longer than its height $h_{sR,}$ its standard deviation (σ_{sR}) is checked. This is due to the fact that incandescent spots such as lamps or fuses have a low standard deviation since their heat distribution is uniform, while humans, as it has been previously said, have different heat concentrations in their body parts, such as the head being warmer than the rest of the body. We have determined experimentally that σ_{sR} must be greater than 12 to be a human candidate.

The final check scans if the human candidate has zones warmer than the hard threshold θ_h, calculated in equation (11), similarly to equation (1). The standard deviation of image I_{IR} is replaced by the sub-ROI sR$_{\varsigma,\kappa,\alpha}$ standard deviation in order to use only the features of the human candidate and γ has been experimentally fixed to approximately a 60% of the maximum value of a 256 gray level image, i.e., 150. The final zones obtained indicate the presence of human heads.

$$\theta_h = \left(\gamma + \sigma_{sR}\right)$$

Finally, the blobs associated to the split ROIs that have satisfied these criteria are enlisted into the final list of humans, L_{SF}.

Human Detection in Infrared Based on Frame Subtraction

We have previously explained that certain environmental conditions affect negatively the visual contrast in the infrared spectrum. For example, humans are very hard to find in warm environments where the scene temperature is similar to the people temperature. An example of this situation can be appreciated in Figure 5, where the human has been manually highlighted because it cannot be easily seen in this single frame. Yet, if we use the motion information in the scene, we can find the humans in it since they do not tend to be static during long periods of time.

Therefore, an extension for the human detection based on a single frame is developed using the motion information in the scene. While the list L_{SF} of humans obtained from detection based on a single frame is used, information from two new stages is added to the previous list. A new phase, called frame subtraction analysis, is introduced in this extension in order to take advantage of the motion information in the scene. The results L_{MOV} from this new stage are later refined into a new list L_S which will be joined with the list L_{SF} in order to reduce the number of false negatives in the scene.

Frame Subtraction Analysis

In this new phase, the previous image $I_{IR}(t-\Delta t)$ and the current one, $I_{IR}(t)$ are used. An image subtraction and thresholding is performed on these frames as shown in equation (12) where θ_{sub} is experimentally fixed as a 16% of the maximum value of a 256 gray levels image, obtaining I_s. This binarized image is combined with I_c by an "AND"' operation, obtaining binary image I_{sc}. This way, false positives due to small illumination changes are discarded, by ensuring that the zones with motion have also warm heat concentrations similar to humans. Now, ROIs with area superior to A_{min} (calculated as shown in equation (3)) and with a percentage of pixels set to *max* greater than a rate threshold ψ (experimentally fixed at a 5% of the area of the ROI) are extracted from I_{sc} in the list of blobs L_{MOV}.

Figure 5. Example of a human hard to be detected in the infrared spectrum

$$I_s = \begin{cases} max, & if \left| I_{IR}\left(x,y,t-\Delta t\right) - I_{IR}\left(x,y,t-\Delta t\right)\right| > \theta_{sub} \\ min, & otherwise \end{cases}$$

Refinement of Human Candidate Blobs

ROIs obtained from the blobs in L_{MOV} are vertically and horizontally delimited in the same way as the ROIs are refined in the human detection based on a single frame. The humans are also confirmed exactly the same way. The main difference is that human candidates are here enlisted in a list L_s. This list is finally checked along with L_c (obtained from human detection based on a single frame) to remove redundancies encountered in both lists. This way, humans that can only be found through motion information are added to the initial algorithm. These humans are enlisted into the final list L_{SUB}.

Human Detection in Infrared Based on Optical Flow Calculation

An extension of the algorithm for human detection based on a single frame is developed with the objective of using the motion information that can be extracted from a scene acquired from a moving camera. This information can be especially useful when capturing images from a surveillance robot or a moving vehicle that must detect pedestrians with the aim of warning the driver about them. Image subtraction is not used in this new approach, since there are differences between every pixel in the scene due to the camera motion. Optical flow has been selected as it discards the scene movement due to the proper vehicle motion. A simple subtraction-based approach would indicate that everything is in movement, making impossible to really differentiate moving objects in the completely moving scene. Thus, as the majority motion is the scene movement, optical flow discards it to only focus in other different direction movements (Lucas & Kanade, 1981). Although this algorithm was originally designed for a not static location, it was tested to assess another way of the influence of motion in the scene.

Detection of Human Candidate Blobs

This initial phase is performed exactly in the same way described in the algorithm for human detection based on a single frame with the obtained blows enlisted into a list L_{oc}. Indeed, notice that those ROIs without motion detected in the next stage run through the same stages as in the original algorithm.

Optical Flow Analysis

This phase uses two image frames, the previous image, I_{IR} (t- Δt) and the current one, I_{IR} (t) (see Figure 6a and Figure 6b). In first place, the current and the previous frames are multiplied to enhance the contrast, such that the dark values become darker and the bright values become brighter (see Figure 6c and Figure 6d). This way, the calculation of the optical flow is facilitated.

The dynamic analysis requires the calculation of the moments corresponding to each pixel movement on the input images I_{IR} (t- Δt) and I_{IR} (t). The optical flow calculation results into two gray level images, where each pixel reflects the angular moment detected, storing the movements in X and Y axes. Firstly, the algorithm performs the speed calculation of the optical flow. The selected optical flow approach is Lucas-Kanade without pyramids algorithm. This algorithm is fast and offers an excellent success vs. speed ratio. The calculated speeds, as a result of the optical flow, are turned into angles, α (x,y,t), and magnitudes, m (x,y,t).

Figure 6. Images obtained in the human detection based on optical flow. (a) Previous frame. (b) Current frame. (c) Multiplied previous frame. (d) Multiplied current frame. (e) Soft thresholded moments. (f) Hard thresholded moments. (g) Matched thresholds.

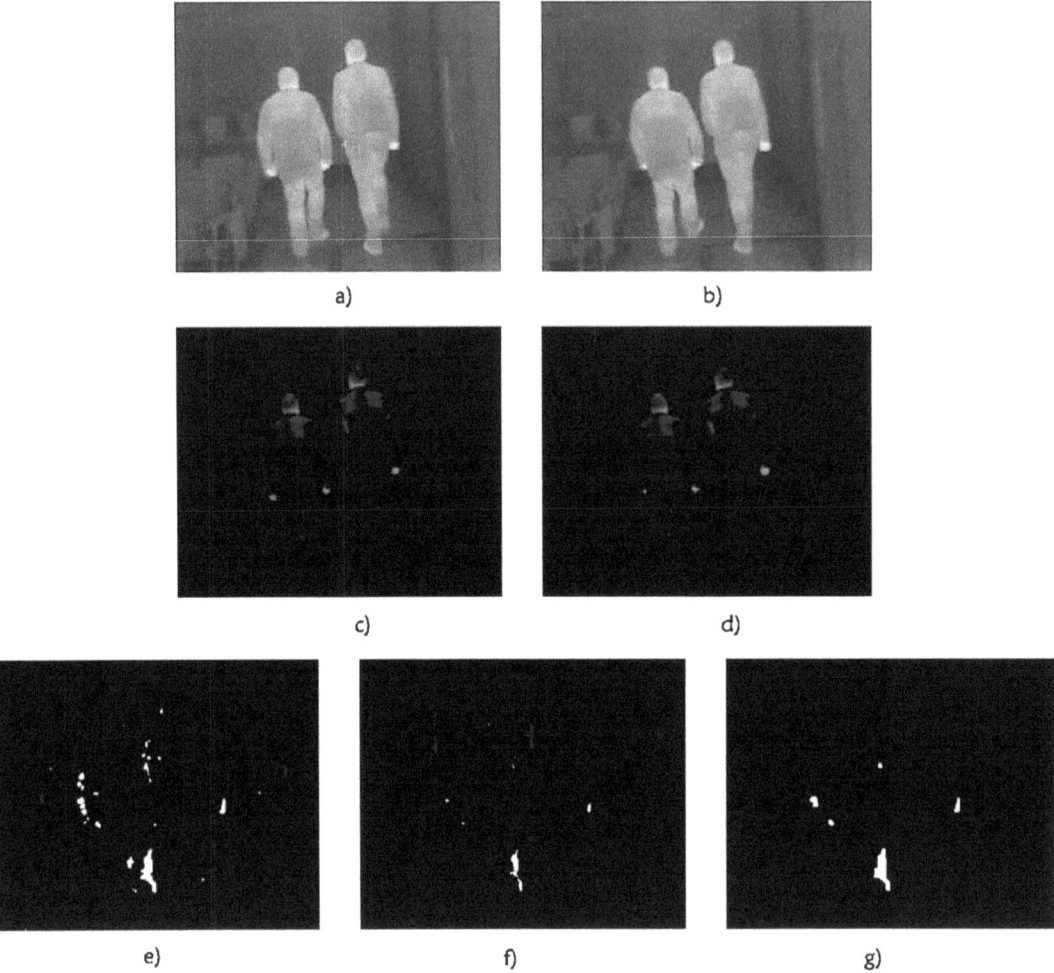

Figure 7a shows the magnitudes (moments), that is to say, the amount of movement at each pixel (x,y) between I_{IR} (t- Δt) and I_{IR} (t), in form of a moments image, M(x,y,t). Similarly, Figure 7b shows the direction of the movement (angles). The results clearly indicate that angles are less important than moments. Indeed, on the one hand, non-rigid objects' movements go into very different directions, and, on the other side, angles with low moments may be caused by image noise.

To efficiently use the moments image M(x,y,t), its histogram, as shown in Figure 7c has been studied for many cases. As you may observe, most values are in the [0, 64] interval, but very close to 0. Indeed, the average value is close to 1 in these moments images. Therefore, two thresholds, a moments soft threshold μ_s = 10 and a moments hard threshold μ_h = 25, are used to delimit the blobs of possible (candidate) humans. The aim of the soft threshold, μ_s, is to obtain the most representative values, whereas the hard threshold, μ_h, is used to refine a better matching between zones that show an elevated movement and zones with less movement but connected to the previous ones. Thus, the zones where movement has been detected are extended, and the zones with reduced movements are eliminated.

Figure 7. Optical flow calculation. (a) Moments. (b) Angles. (c) Histogram of the optical flow moments.

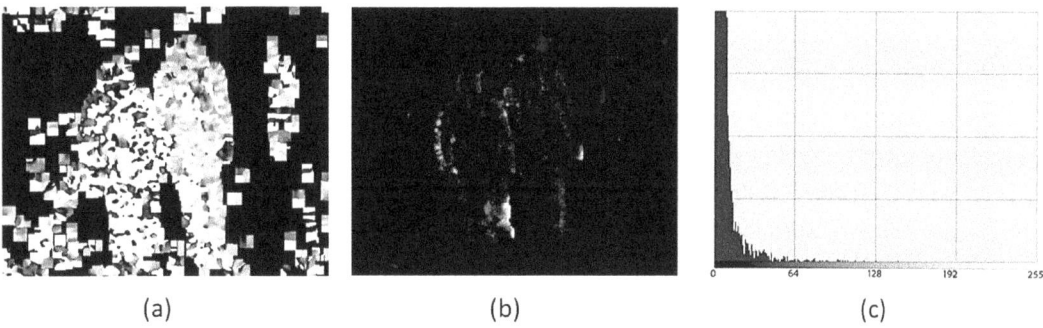

(a)   (b)   (c)

Therefore, firstly, the moments soft threshold μ_s is applied to the moments image M(x,y,t) to obtain image M_s(x,y,t), as shown in previous Figure 6e. The related formula is shown in equation (13).

$$M_s\left(x,y,t\right) = \begin{cases} min, & if\ M\left(x,y,t\right) \leq \mu_s \\ max, & otherwise \end{cases}$$

Afterwards, an opening filter is applied to erase isolated pixels, getting M_o. In this case, disconnected areas can arise, as parts of the image may have gone in different directions. After this, the moments hard threshold, μ_h =25 is applied to M in order to obtain image M_h (see Figure 6f and equation (14)).

$$M_h\left(x,y,t\right) = \begin{cases} min, & if\ M\left(x,y,t\right) \leq \mu_h \\ max, & otherwise \end{cases}$$

Now, the list of blobs L_o present in M_o is compared to the list of blobs L_h found in M_h. The aim is to verify if each blob detected with the hard threshold is contained in a spot detected with the soft threshold. The spots that do not meet this condition are discarded. Finally, the common blobs are depicted as white areas over a black background in a resulting binary image, called refined moments image M_r, and shown in Figure 10g, only contains the blobs that have met the previous condition. This image is used during the people candidate blobs refinement phase to improve the certainty about the human presence.

Refinement of Human Candidate Blobs

The first two stages of this phase (the people vertical and horizontal delimiting for every sub-ROI) are performed in exactly the same way as in the people detection in a single frame. However, a major change occurs at the end of the people horizontal delimiting stage. At this point, the equivalent region of the sub-ROI sR $_{\varsigma,\kappa,\alpha}$ is scanned in the image M_R obtained at the end of the image motion analysis stage. If any pixels are found which value is set to *max*, the hard threshold is not applied in the human confirmation stage, since a warm human candidate has been detected whose movement is different to the majority motion in the scene, so a major trust in that candidate is assumed. If there were no pixels found with value set to *max*, the human candidate is treated the same way as it was in the human detection based on a single frame algorithm. The humans found are finally enlisted into the list L_{OF}.

RESULTS AND DISCUSSION

Our test environment is an outdoor scenario, with the camera placed at 6 meters over the ground level. The decision to use an outdoor environment is because these scenarios have a greater number of variations in temperature and lighting conditions whereas an indoor environment is usually more controlled. The scenario does not have any predefined access and a pedestrian can appear in the lower limits of the image, as well as at the left or right sides of the frame. A concrete platform is located in the lower part of the scene. This material quickly absorbs the temperature of the environment. This property is also present in the building placed in the scene background. The building shows additional problems for infrared human detection since the camera also has thermal attenuation which results in the objects' temperature distinguished at a lower accuracy as they are placed farther from the camera. This attenuation causes the human thermal readings to be confused with the temperature of the building, hardening their isolation from the scene background.

Three different sequences were recorded. The sequence *3°Sunny* features a human walking in the environment and performing some movements such as crouching. Later, a second human is walking in different trajectories. Finally, both humans cross their path, meeting on the concrete platform. In the sequence *15°Cloudy* some more complex actions are performed by a single human, such as sitting in the central platform. The temperature rise causes the apparition of human reflections on the concrete platform. The final sequence *23°Sunny* augments the difficulty of the pedestrian detection algorithms with the apparition of up to three people walking in the scene and performing actions such as sitting, crossing their paths or meeting. The high temperature makes it quite difficult to distinguish humans, especially on the concrete platform.

Some measures widely used by the computer vision community, such as sensitivity, precision and F-Score, were considered to evaluate the performance of the different algorithms. These measures are calculated as shown in equations (15), (16) and (17), respectively.

$$Sensitivity = \frac{TP}{TP + FN}$$

$$Precision = \frac{TP}{TP + FP}$$

$$F - Score = 2 \times \frac{Precision \times Sensitivity}{Precision + Sensitivity}$$

where TP (true positives) is the amount of correct detections of the system in the sequence, FP (false positives) are the mistaken detections gotten by the system and FN (false negatives) is the amount of humans really present in the scene but not detected by the system.

The precision shows the percentage of true positives with respect to the total number of detections, i.e., the probability of detections of a system which really correspond to a human. On the other hand, the sensitivity shows the probability of a human on the scene to be really detected. Finally, F-Score provides an overall vision of the system performance, considering precision and sensitivity. F-Score is as a weighted average; an ideal system will show an F-Score of 1.

Table 1. Results of the three algorithms

Sequence	Algorithm	TP	FP	FN	Sensitivity	Precision	F-Score
	IR-SF	2703	287	243	0,92	0,90	0,91
	IR-OF	2783	399	163	0,94	0,88	0,91
3°Sunny	IR-(SF+FS)	2901	295	45	**0,98**	**0,91**	0,94
	IR-SF	1321	21	523	0,72	**0,98**	0,83
	IR-OF	1647	203	197	0,89	0,89	0,89
15°Cloudy	IR-(SF+FS)	1684	51	160	**0,91**	0,97	0,94
	IR-SF	927	136	2695	0,26	0,87	0,40
	IR-OF	952	131	2670	0,31	**0,92**	0,74
23°Sunny	IR-(SF+FS)	2174	363	1448	**0,60**	0,86	0,71

The infrared pedestrian detection algorithms described were tested using these different sequences recorded in the described environment. The results are shown in Table 1.

For the sake of clarity, human detection based on a single frame will be noted as *IR-SF*, human detection based on frame subtraction will be noted as *IR-(SF+FS)* and human detection based on optical flow will be written as *IR-OF*. The first conclusion extracted is that infrared spectrum is generally suitable to detect humans in sequences recorded at low and medium temperatures. However, when the scene is recorded at a temperature over 20°C, the results worsen drastically. This problem is due to the similarity between thermal radiation of the building, the concrete platform and the humans' thermal readings.

Next, the three algorithms are compared among themselves. In accordance to the results shown in Table 1, human detection algorithms *IR-OF* and *IR-(SF+FS)* always work better than the *IR-SF* approach. This is partially because the former approaches add new information to improve the amount of performed detections without discarding any human detected by the *IR-SF* approach. When humans remain a long time close to the background building or in the sequence recorded at a high temperature (where the scene contrast is low), thermal readings of humans make it difficult to distinguish their limits from the scene background. This difficulty usually results in false negatives for the human detection based on a single frame because many human candidates are discarded due to their dimensions or proportions.

However, the *IR-OF* and *IR-(SF+FS)* approaches use motion information to enhance human detections based on single frame, since shapes and dimensions of the humans found using these approaches are usually more accurate than those found using *IR-SF*. As an inconvenient, precision is higher in the first approach since a lower amount of detections is also associated to a lower false positives rate.

Finally, the three different proposals are analyzed separately.

- *IR-SF* usually has a lower sensitivity rate than the other two approaches, since it only uses information from the current frame. This worsens the amount of detections when the scene has a low contrast or the pedestrians are hard to differentiate from the background, especially at high temperatures or when the human is far away from the camera, as shown in Figure 8b, where the humans are hard to distinguish from the scene environment.

- *IR-OF* usually shows a significant improvement over *IR-SF* since it adds motion information and optical flow detects moving objects on the scene, although with lower sensitivity than *IR-(SF+FS)*, since in certain conditions (such as the human placed far away from the camera) the motion information added by the optical flow calculation is not significant enough, as shown in Figure 8c. Precision also shows a minor drawback due to detected motion of objects such as tree leaves.

- Lastly, *IR-(SF+FS)* usually shows a major improvement since it directly adds information obtained from background subtraction between the current frame and previously acquired image. Also more subtle movements can be detected. These detections are combined with those realized by the *IR-SF* approach. Yet, these detections can also result in apparition of a greater amount of false positives due to occasional detections of small thermal infrared reflections or motion of human body parts such as arms or legs, as shown in Figure 8c.

After these tests, it can be appreciated that pedestrian detection based on frame subtraction, *IR-(SF+FS)*, is the best choice between our tested approaches since it has a great sensitivity enhancement without drastically worsening the achieved precision.

Figure 8. Examples of segmentation results for different sequences. (a) 3°Sunny (b) 15°Cloudy (c) 23°Sunny.

Nevertheless, let us highlight that none of the algorithms is perfect in segmenting people under all conditions. This is why we propose to use simple rules as conflict resolution mechanism when the outputs of the three algorithms do not coincide. After studying different weather conditions, the decision on what is the best people detection will be the result of the algorithm or algorithms that hold(s) better combined performance in terms of sensitivity and precision. For instance, in sequence *3°Sunny* the conflict is resolved through using only the *IR-(SF+FS)* algorithm. Sequence *15°Cloudy* will resolve the conflict by using algorithms *IR-SF* and *IR-(SF+FS)*, whereas sequence *23°Sunny* should use algorithms *IR-OF* and *IR-(SF+FS)*.

CONCLUSION

This chapter has introduced three algorithms for real-time and robust pedestrian detection in infrared video. The idea of comparing three different algorithms for real-time and robust people detection in the infrared spectrum is thought to reduce conflicts in camera-based electronic people surveillance, as accurate people segmentation is mandatory to achieve further solid people identification. The three algorithms can be used in parallel in order to produce three different people segmentation results before taking the best decision.

In first place, a pedestrian detection system based on a single frame (*IR-SF*) has initially been developed. A set of human candidates are extracted from the scene based on their thermal properties. Some series of adjustments are performed on the initial candidates to obtain a better characterization of their size and location. A series of restrictions on size and shape are finally applied over the adjusted candidates to eliminate potential false positives that may have appeared in the algorithm. Secondly, an extension for the human detection based on a single frame is developed using the motion information in the scene (*IR-(SF+FS)*). Although the list of humans obtained from IR-SF is used, information from two new stages is added to the previous list. A new phase, called frame subtraction analysis, is introduced in this extension in order to take advantage of the motion information in the scene. The results from this new stage enable reducing the number of false negatives in the scene. Lastly, an optical flow based approach is used (*IR-OF*).

The three algorithms were tested in an outdoor scenario with changing temperature and lighting conditions. Three different sequences were recorded, namely *3°Sunny*, *15°Cloudy* and *23°Sunny* to demonstrate the validity of the approach under very different thermal conditions. Although the three algorithms offer excellent results in pedestrian segmentation in infrared video, we conclude that pedestrian detection based on frame subtraction, *IR-(SF+FS)*, is the best choice.

ACKNOWLEDGMENT

This work was partially supported by FEDER / Spanish Ministerio de Economía y Competitividad grant under project TIN2013-47074-C2-1-R.

REFERENCES

Chang, S. L., Yang, F. T., Wu, W. P., Cho, Y. A., & Chen, S. W. (2011). Nighttime pedestrian detection using thermal imaging based on HOG feature. In *International Conference on System Science and Engineering* (pp. 694-698). Macao: IEEE. doi:10.1109/ICSSE.2011.5961992

Costa, D. G., Guedes, L. A., Vasques, F., & Portugal, P. (2013). Adaptive monitoring relevance in camera networks for critical surveillance applications. *International Journal of Distributed Sensor Networks*, *2013*, 836721. doi:10.1155/2013/836721

Dollár, P., Wojek, C., Schiele, B., & Perona, P. (2012). Pedestrian detection: An evaluation of the state of the art. *IEEE Transactions on Pattern Analysis and Machine Intelligence*, *34*(4), 743–761. doi:10.1109/TPAMI.2011.155 PMID:21808091

Enzweiler, M., & Gavrila, D. M. (2009). Monocular pedestrian detection: Survey and experiments. *IEEE Transactions on Pattern Analysis and Machine Intelligence*, *31*(12), 2179–2195. doi:10.1109/TPAMI.2008.260 PMID:19834140

Fernández-Caballero, A., Castillo, J. C., Serrano-Cuerda, J., & Maldonado-Bascón, S. (2011). Real-time human segmentation in infrared videos. *Expert Systems with Applications*, *38*(3), 2577–2584. doi:10.1016/j.eswa.2010.08.047

Goubet, E., Katz, J., & Porikli, F. (2006). Pedestrian tracking using thermal infrared imaging. *SPIE Conference on Infrared Technology and Applications*, *6206*, 797-808.

Li, J., Gong, W., Li, W., & Liu, X. (2010). Robust pedestrian detection in thermal infrared imagery using the wavelet transform. *Infrared Physics & Technology*, *53*(4), 267–273. doi:10.1016/j.infrared.2010.03.005

Lucas, B. D., & Kanade, T. (1981). An iterative image registration technique with an application to stereo vision. In *Proceedings of the 1981 DARPA Image Understanding Workshop* (pp. 121-130). Palo Alto, CA: DARPA.

Navarro, E., Fernández-Caballero, A., & Martínez-Tomás, R. (2014). Intelligent multisensory systems in support of information society. *International Journal of Systems Science*, *45*(4), 711–713. doi:10.1080/00207721.2014.844916

O'Malley, R., Jones, E., & Glavin, M. (2010). Detection of pedestrians in far-infrared automotive night vision using region-growing and clothing distortion compensation. *Infrared Physics & Technology*, *53*(6), 439–449. doi:10.1016/j.infrared.2010.09.006

Olmeda, D., de la Escalera, A., & Armingol, J. M. (2011). Far infrared pedestrian detection and tracking for night driving. *Robotica*, *29*(4), 495–505. doi:10.1017/S0263574710000299

Rodriguez, M. D., & Shah, M. (2007). Detecting and segmenting humans in crowded scenes. In *Proceedings of the 15th International Conference on Multimedia* (pp. 353-356). Augsburg: ACM. doi:10.1145/1291233.1291310

Schwartz, W. R., Kembhavi, A., Harwood, D., & Davis, L. S. (2009). Human detection using partial least squares analysis. In *Proceedings of the IEEE 12th International Conference on Computer Vision* (pp. 24-31). Kyoto: IEEE. doi:10.1109/ICCV.2009.5459205

Sun, S. G., & Park, H. (2001). Segmentation of forward-looking infrared image using fuzzy thresholding and edge detection. *Optical Engineering (Redondo Beach, Calif.)*, *40*(11), 2638–2645. doi:10.1117/1.1409563

Wan, J., & Liu, L. (2013). Distributed Bayesian inference for consistent labeling of tracked objects in nonoverlapping camera networks. *International Journal of Distributed Sensor Networks*, *2013*, 613246. doi:10.1155/2013/613246

Wang, J. T., Chen, D. B., Chen, H. Y., & Yan, J. Y. (2012). On pedestrian detection and tracking in infrared videos. *Pattern Recognition Letters*, *33*(6), 775–785. doi:10.1016/j.patrec.2011.12.011

KEY TERMS AND DEFINITIONS

Electronic Surveillance: Observing or listening to persons, places, or activities (usually in a secretive or unobtrusive manner) with the aid of electronic devices such as cameras, microphones, tape recorders, or wire taps.

Frame Subtraction: A process whereby the digital numeric value of a whole image frame is subtracted from another image frame.

F-Score: A measure of a test's accuracy. The F-score can be interpreted as a weighted average of the precision and recall, where an F-score reaches its best value at 1 and worst at 0.

Optical Flow: The pattern of apparent motion of objects, surfaces, and edges in a visual scene caused by the relative motion between an observer (an eye or a camera) and the scene.

People Detection: People (or pedestrian detection) is an essential and significant task in any intelligent video surveillance system, as it provides the fundamental information for semantic understanding of the video footages.

Precision: A description of a level of measurement that yields consistent results when repeated.

Sensitivity: Sensitivity (or recall) measures the proportion of positives that are correctly identified as such.

Thermal Infrared Camera: A device that forms an image using infrared radiation, similar to a common camera that forms an image using visible light. Instead of the 400–700 nanometer range of the visible light camera, infrared cameras operate in wavelengths as long as 14,000 nm (14 μm).

Thresholding: Thresholding is the simplest method of image segmentation. From a grayscale image, thresholding can be used to create binary images.

Chapter 14
Conflict Resolution with Agents in Smart Cities

Pablo Chamoso
University of Salamanca, Spain

Javier Bajo Pérez
Polytechnic University of Madrid, Spain

Fernando De la Prieta
University of Salamanca, Spain

Juan Manuel Corchado Rodríguez
University of Salamanca, Spain

ABSTRACT

Today, there is a common trend to use tools and methodologies that allow the development of Multi-Agent Systems (MAS) with capabilities of reorganization and adaptation to determine changes in their environments. This work presents an architecture based on different levels and whose key level is the one corresponding to the semi-open type of MAS, structured in such a way that it is able to solve conflicts. In addition, a case study is introduced with the objective of showing the possibilities on conflict resolution basis, where a specifically designed architecture is utilized for that purpose. In particular, the system is applied to the resolution of the conflict raised by the decision of the technology to be used in order to obtain or to measure information in smart cities.

INTRODUCTION

Recent technological developments have shown a rapid evolution in wireless communications, sensors, information distributed processing, and other new technologies, all of which are mainly associated to a new paradigm known as the Internet of Things (Weber, 2010, pp. 23-30). This technological evolution has resulted in an increase in the features and services available through the Internet. Accordingly, there is not only an increase in online services, but also an increase in new services in the real world, mainly in large urban areas, which use the technological base provided by the Internet of Things paradigm. In effect, we are talking about smart cities, which have emerged as a response to the challenges experienced by cities in meeting objectives regarding the socio-economic development and quality of life of their citizens (Schaffers et al., 2011, pp. 431-446).

DOI: 10.4018/978-1-5225-0245-6.ch014

Smart cities have become quite significant, and are currently one of the main objectives of research in America as well as in the European Union (Caragliu, Del Bo, & Nijkamp, 2011, pp. 65-82). The main interest currently consists of directly or indirectly increasing the well-being of the population. *Direct* measures include offering new services or improving existing ones. Some of the ways to achieve this objective consist of tele-care services for the elderly or dependent persons, the use of traffic optimization techniques, actively controlling energy supplies, etc. *Indirect* measures include offering the same services, as perceived by the citizens, but changing the way they are managed or their internal performance in order to increase the economic savings of the city. This will definitely imply an indirect increase in the quality of life for the citizens (tax savings, new services offered as a result of the economic savings, etc.). An example of the latter would be the replacement of older light bulbs in public light fixtures with new bulbs with a lower power requirement (LED bulbs for instance). Thus, new technological advances make it possible to rapidly increase the ability to enhance the social well-being of a city. While this may result in greater benefits for the cities, it is not without some disadvantages.

The reasons why emerging technologies are a major benefit are self-evident: the majority of the advances are going to be useful to improve any factor, whether in data acquisition, information transmission or information processing. However, the unstoppable technological evolution means that in most of the cases different alternative technologies, with similar characteristics and capabilities, will be required to cohabitate at the same time and in the same environment. On the other hand, the constantly evolving technology makes it necessary, in some cases, to dismiss the existing infrastructure.

Thus, one of the main current concerns for most cities is the integration of new technologies in everyday environments and their ability to improve the well-being of each citizen. With the objective of solving the problems associated with the technological evolution, we turn to Agent technologies, in particular, those following a design model based on roles, objectives and norms.

There is no doubt that Multi-Agent Systems (MAS) have become tremendously significant during the last years within the environment of Distributed Artificial Intelligence (DAI). MAS allow solving problems in a distributed manner by taking advantage of social behaviors as well as the individual behavior of the agents. Since a smart city requires the features of an open system (dynamic, heterogeneous and with uncertainty), MAS have been applied in this environment with promising results, for example to address multiple aspects in the management of smart cities (Roscia, Longo, & Lazaroiu 2013, pp. 371-376).

Recently, the design theories of MAS promote their grouping into organizations or societies, thus sharing features, norms and objectives. These societies can be open or closed societies depending on their flexibility to admit new members. These capabilities, similar to those of human societies, are perfectly suited to the new open context of smart cities. One example of these capabilities is the use of a semi-open society, as the design model would be able to evolve and auto adapt to new situations. Another example is allowing different members, independently of the technology used, to enter the society to provide the services of a specific role. For example, given the task of regulating city traffic, two roles, which would be technologically independent, might include counting the number of vehicles on the road and regulating traffic lights according to available information.

This ability would make it possible to obtain a system capable of making the best decision regarding the technologies to be used. This system also prevents possible changes from negatively impacting the management, or the services offered. This means that a change in technology will not affect the way the system uses or presents the information. It tremendously facilitates tasks requiring a human operator without needing to adapt the software that manages the information gathered by the sensors.

This present work provides a multi-level agent-based architecture whose main functionality resides in the layer in which an organizational MAS resolves conflicts regarding the selection of the best technology at each moment. More specifically, the work focuses on the resolution of conflicts when considering the technological solution, where all the options can be valid, but only one will be the most suitable for the global system at each moment. However, the system is completely adaptable to the resolution of more conflicts related to smart cities as well as to other environments.

The rest of the section presents the current state of the art of the main technologies, theories and tools applicable to the development of the system, followed by a presentation of the main existing technology conflicts in smart cities and their potential solutions. The decisions and techniques followed to deal with this conflicts are then presented. After that, a case study, where the solution has been applied, is explained. The chapter ends by identifying certain keys required to continue the research and the conclusion to the present work.

BACKGROUND

Autonomy, robustness, flexibility and adaptability are among the most desirable characteristics with regard to the design of software applications. They are also some of the characteristics that platform must have in order to manage smart cities. To do so, there is a need for theories, models, mechanisms, methodologies and tools that can develop a system capable of reorganizing and adapting itself to possible future changes in the environment.

For this reason, the present work proposes a combination of technologies, such as organized-models based open MAS, Cloud Computing (CC) and Wireless Sensor Networks (WSN), such as the key technological context to confront the existing needs within smart cities environments.

Multi-Agent Systems

There is extensive literature about Agent Theory. For decades, the concept of agent has been that of an autonomous entity capable of interacting with the surrounding environment. However, there are some complex problems a single entity is not able to solve, and the use of a set of at least two entities collaborating to achieve a common objective is required. This set may include a MAS, which has also been extensively studied in literature (Chopra, & Singh, 2013, pp. 101-141).

The main objective of MAS is to construct systems capable of autonomous and flexible decision-making, and cooperate with other systems as a society. This chapter is going to focus on the part of MAS above agents. It is commonly understood that MAS contain agents and establish relationships between them, including a set of operations that can be performed according to their observations with regards on the the external changes in the environment along the time (Ferber, 1999).

A way to analyze MAS is to compose a number of autonomous entities that interact together, or in terms of a society, an organized society of individuals, where each entity plays at least one specific role (Zambonelli, Jennings, & Wooldridge, 2001, pp. 303-328). One of the main challenges of MAS is to both maintain the heterogeneity and the autonomy of the system components and provide guarantees about the behavior and outcomes of individual agents and of the system as whole (Vasconcelos, Kollingbaum, & Norman, 2009, pp. 124-152).

But beyond its definition, a MAS can be represented in different ways or have multiple configurations. Artificial societies and Virtual Organizations (VO) are important terms associated to the MAS and form the base of the current work (Zato, et al. 2012, pp. 10389-10401).

Both terms are closely related. Artificial societies can be defined as a set of interrelated and interacting artificial entities, which are governed by certain rules and conditions (Annunziato, & Pierucci, 2003). These rules and conditions can be classified according to different criteria: openness, flexibility, stability and reliability. Openness is the possibility of an agent joining the society. Flexibility indicates the grade of constraint of the agent in its behavior due to the norms of the society. Stability measures the predictability of the actions. Finally, reliability measures the grade by which the agents can rely on the society (Davidsson, & Johansson, 2006). From these criteria, the following types of societies can be established:

- **Open Societies:** Characterized by having high flexibility, which makes them a bit unstable, and not very reliable.
- **Closed Societies:** As opposed to the open societies, they are stable and reliable, but not flexible; that is, they are fixed or unalterable societies.
- **Semi-Open Societies:** The concept of gatekeeper is introduced to require external societies to communicate in advance and demonstrate they are safe to enter the system without altering the reliability and stability of the society.
- **Semi-Closed Societies**: These societies do not allow the authorization of external agents, but they do allow an agent of the society to perform the tasks of an external agent.

For the development of organizational systems, the most appropriate types of society would be semi-open and semi-closed, due to their inherent constraints of either flexibility or lack thereof.

Returning to the concept of organization, it can be defined as a set of entities regulated by social order mechanisms, in a way that they facilitate the achievement of common objectives. An organization must be composed of individual agents manifesting their behavior and relating to each other in a dynamic way. It can be split in sub-organizations, which can be further divided into sub-sub organizations. The behavior of these agents needs to be related, in functional terms, to the organization. Finally, its functionality has to be defined as a role to be taken into consideration within the organization (Ferber, Gutkenecht, & Michel, 2004, pp. 65-82). The role is the key concept which represents an abstract description of the behavior of the agents. This includes their obligations, constraints and qualities. It must also include the description of the interaction procedures among the different roles that make up the system.

The chance of a conflict occurring and requiring a solution increases when agents with different roles have to cooperate and coordinate their activities. It is precisely these situations that require mechanisms to allow an efficient argument on behalf of each agent in order to make it possible to achieve an agreement.

As indicated in (Daft, 2012), decision making and the control that governs the organization follow a collaborative strategy. When a conflict occurs, each agent has to propose its solutions and attempt to find the best common solution. Each agent will try its proposed solution and must defend it before reaching the agreement. Therefore, the organizations play an important role in the resolution of conflicts.

Cloud Computing

In recent years, the term Cloud Computing (CC) has become increasingly prevalent, especially in environments or applications where the required processing power, storage and infrastructure to supply services. CC refers to both the applications delivered as services over the Internet and the hardware capabilities and system software in the data centers that provide those services (Ambrust et al., 2010).

The theory of agents and multiagent systems (MAS) can provide a new model for the usage of CC. However, joining both computational models (MAS and CC) is a great challenge, given the difference between the two models. However, since the CC system is considered an open system and the application of MAS in open systems is a recognized challenge in which there has already been a notable rate of success. Nowadays, there is an important relationship between the way MAS work and the way in which the CC environments work. CC environments offer a high capability and high performance technology, along with high availability and scalability (De la Prieta, Rodríguez, Bajo, Corchado, 2013, pp. 37-48) (Talia, 2012), which makes it easy to apply MAS to a new group of complex applications.

The combination of CC, MAS and sensors allow to apply the solution to smart cities provides a more than adequate infrastructure (Mitton, Papavassiliou, Puliafito, & Trivedi, 2012). First of all, CC environments can cover the computational needs for persistence of information and the computing potential that MAS require for different applications such as data mining, management of complex services, etc. The use of these technologies applied to the work described in this chapter, and as argued below, provides multiple benefits when offering cities a system capable of managing the totality of the deployed sensors and the services it offers.

Wireless Sensor Networks in Smart Cities

It may be difficult to define exactly the term 'smart city'. However, a preliminary approach could imply the use of networked infrastructure to improve economic and political efficiency and enable social, cultural and urban development (Hollands, 2008, pp. 303-320). In line with this definition, the most important technological part of smart cities is their networked infrastructure. The design of this networked infrastructure plays an important role when saving money, automating processes and determining which sensors have to be used for meeting the city goals.

The process of building automation and control systems through sensor networks, which started with wired technology, has now entered the era of wireless technology, having produced technologies such as ZigBee, Z-Wave, EnOcean, and others. WSNs are used for gathering the information needed by intelligent environments, whether in urban construction and Smart Cities, home and building automation, industrial applications or smart hospitals and so on (Liu, Seet, & Al-Anbuky, 2013, pp. 653-674). WSNs support current requirements related to the deployment of networks that cover communication needs, and flexibly in time, space and autonomy, without requiring a fixed structure (Navarro, Bhatnagar, & Liang, 2011, pp. 819-824). There are several wireless technologies that enable easier deployments than their wired counterparts by avoiding the need to wire buildings and decreasing the costs and drawbacks of the setup phase. However, the growing heterogeneity of this type of wireless network protocols makes it difficult to use them. WSNs make it possible to build a wide range of applications, such as the control of energy costs, monitoring environmental data, security and access control in buildings, as well as industrial and home automation, etc. Therefore, WSNs have multiple potential applications in military, industrial, environmental, biomedical and residential fields. The latter is the focus of this chapter. The implementation of these sensor networks tends to require sophisticated and efficient communication protocols, low-power consumption, and low cost (Akyildiz, & Vuran, 2010). Furthermore, sensor nodes should be small and deployed in large quantities, emphasizing the need for low-cost and eco-friendly, especially in the case of smart cities.

Due to the natural evolution of technology, as a result of a vast effort in research activities and industrial investments on this field since last decade (Buratti, Conti, Dardari & Verdone, 2009), a new conflict has emerged and is in need of a resolution. This evolution has led to the cohabitation of different technologies capable of providing valid solutions to transmit the measured information. This circumstance implies a short-term advantage for new systems, as they will always be constructed following the best option. The problem arises when maintaining those systems or when adapting working systems that are already deployed. Having to change one technology for another, seemingly better, will not provide optimal results for every case. Thus, in order to choose the best measure for the technology selection, multiple existing options must be evaluated, along with their corresponding weaknesses and strengths for the system. To do so, next section introduces an approach based on open MAS that deals with these issues.

CONFLICTS IN SMART CITIES

Issues, Controversies, Problems

Despite the ongoing efforts in the process of standardizing technologies for information and communications technology, the reality is that to date, there are multiple techniques, tools and technological protocols, which, in some cases, are not even compatible among each other. Of course, this also implies the advantage of having the opportunity to choose the technology that best suits a specific purpose, considering performance, ease of implementation, inherent characteristics, etc. However, some disadvantages can also be observed, such as the challenge of the integration and compatibility between technologies (Lian, Hsiao, & Sung, 2013, pp. 756-767), which occurs because systems of a certain size (or even in home environments) tend to work with multiple technologies in a simultaneous way (Hafeez et al., 2014).

For an environment such as smart cities, which involve such a wide variety of information to process, the advantage of having the latest technology gets transformed into an important problem when making a decision in favor of one technology over another, especially when the system is already developed and performing, or the city is using a sensor network that has already been deployed. Thus, even though there are different inherent characteristics in technology, which could consider one of the multiple existing options to be better than the others, it does not only depend on the technology to be used, but also on external aspects.

Despite considering all the factors affecting the decision of using one technology as opposed to the others, the situation could change over time. This fact could lead to a need to partially or totally change the deployed sensor network.

Thus, the integration in the global system must first comply with the specific norms or rules for the system to admit it. In the case of the MAS, this problem is solved because it is based on a semi-open architecture that guarantees the heterogeneity of the system. So the problem disappears due to the fact any entity who wants to enter in the systems have to follow a series of the norms in order to be admitted into the system.

In addition to integration, other problems may occur when the technology is used as the base, causing certain technologies to be discarded or chosen. These problems are influenced by factors such as the reliability of the regulatory entity for example support, API (*Application Programming Interface*), etc., the cost of deployment, the cost of maintenance, the consumption of resource, compatibility with already deployed infrastructures, portability, scalability or ease of use.

SOLUTIONS AND RECOMMENDATIONS

The following sub-sections present the main techniques that should be used in order to solve the problems described in the previously. So, next it is described how these techniques have been applied to the global system, which is structured in a way that follows a multi-layer, or multilevel, architecture.

Global Architecture

To achieve a better understanding of the global architecture of the system, it is necessary to have a preliminary global view of it. Each one of the levels constituting the system will be explained in detail later on. The diagram in Figure 1 shows the main layers that constitute the proposed system.

Figure 1 shows the architecture proposed to solve the problem derived from the combination or changes in technologies deployed in a smart city environment, which overcome the shortcomings of current systems. For a better understanding, the analysis starts from the lowest layers. The sensor network is deployed in the first level to gather information from the environment. This information is required to fully guarantee the services offered to citizens and allowing them to effectively become beneficiaries of the society. On top of this sensor network we can find a middleware (MW), which allows the encapsulation of this information by separating it from the used technology. Its communication protocol is also transformed into a common protocol for the system, allowing the highest levels to be able to obtain the data, no matter how they do it. Such MW and successive processing layers are executed in a CC platform that allows the system to be distributed and adaptable according to the needs of the cities. The next level, which is also executed in the CC platform of the MW, is associated to the MAS. The MAS is the most important part within the system and its objective is, depending on the situation, to act autonomously or to offer certain services the end user (software or authorized human) can use. These services constitute the last layer in the developed architecture. Next sections present in detail each of these layers and the proposed algorithm in order to resolve technological conflicts on smart cities.

Sensor Network

Starting from the lowest layer, the first level corresponds to the sensor network. This sensor network may be composed of multiple sets, possibly heterogeneous, of individual sensors. These sensors are in charge of automatically gathering the information of the nearest environment by themselves. They must also incorporate some kind of mechanism to transmit this information in order to integrate it in the global system for future use. On many occasions, the cities already use sensor networks that have

Figure 1. Design of the multi-layer architecture that provides support for smart city management and the offered services

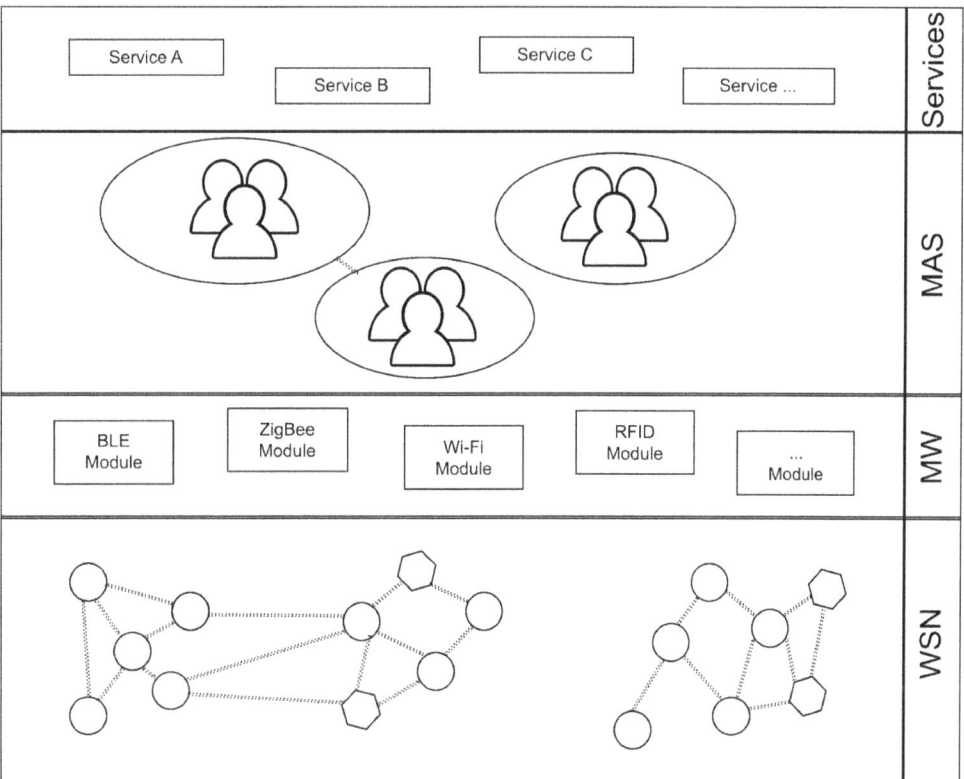

been incorporated in order to develop studies or to take measures. They could also have been added due to some other reasons, prior to the process of transforming the city into a smart city. In addition to the previously commented evolution in technology, this could result in the cohabitation of different kinds of sensors, gathering the information associated to a same environment.

To enhance its management, these sensor networks in the cities get organizationally divided into sets, where each one of them is specifically applied to a particular environment of the city. Thus, it may be the case that different sets, dedicated to a same environment, cohabitate together, which makes the system even more heterogeneous. In a practical case study, a city could require a set of sensors involved in the management of the traffic lights in the city and another set of sensors to perform vehicle-counting tasks. In such a case, both sets of sensors are involved in traffic management.

The heterogeneity of the sensor sets needs to be emphasized, as it plays an important role in this system. Similarly, as will be seen later, this structure will be associated to the roles within the MAS organizations.

Middleware

Large-scale systems typically include MW to collect information coming from the sensors. The main task of this MW is to allow the information gathered by the sensors to be standardized within the system. To do so, the system includes an intermediate layer specialized in collecting information by using the required protocol for each technology. Once the information is obtained by the sensor and transmitted, the MW collects it and processes it (without interruption) to produce a new encapsulation to a common protocol for the whole system.

This way, the inclusion of new technologies, which may appear in the future to offer new or better features, prevents the bulk of the smart-cities management system from being affected in the case of using them. In such cases, the procedure would be based, as a general rule, on creating a new module incorporating the MW, as a driver. This module shall include the programming associated to the conversion of information formats and communication protocols. In turn, it shall allow the definition of every configuration parameter that such technology requires.

Henceforth, the inclusion of an MW with such characteristics is necessary in the system, as it means a reduction in risk of some factors that affect the conflict of decision making regarding the technology to be used in a city. In particular, the communication protocol directly affects important factors such as sustainability, adaptability and system maintenance over time.

Support to the hosting and processing of information is performed in a CC environment; therefore, such environments support this and subsequent levels. The application of CC technology, particularly to smart city management, provides the deployed system with different benefits. To begin, the initial investment gets reduced due to the fact that there is no need to acquire hardware and software to deploy the system. The flexibility is the other main advantage provided by CC because the service is capable of adapting itself to the demand and always providing the necessary resources. Thanks to this, the size of the city is downplayed.

Using a practical case taken from this work as an example, the MW is divided into a series of modules. Each one gets associated to a different technology. For example, to communicate through Bluetooth 4.0 (BLE - *Bluetooth Low Energy*), there is a module in charge of requiring the technology-specific information needed to register a sensor of this kind. For the case of BLE, this information only includes the MAC (*Media Access Control*) address. Once the configuration has been stored, the library *Gatttool* is internally used. This library makes it possible to use any BLE device through a series of simple commands. Similarly, there are specific modules to communicate through ZigBee, RFID or Wi-Fi technology, as well as through wired sensors, independently of their protocol or API. In every particular case, the specific de-encapsulation, associated to the technology, is performed. To do so, the needed information is extracted and the encapsulation to the protocol required by the higher layers in the system is performed. All these processes are performed remotely (in the CC environment), which allows us to take advantage of the benefits each technology offers regarding consumption, range or duration, without affecting the gathering of data by the higher levels of the architecture.

Thus, it is necessary to include a MW with such features in the system, as it implies the resolution of the protocol incompatibility conflict, which directly affects the stability of the entire system. However, despite using these techniques, additional conflicts still remain.

Multi-Agent System Structure

The MAS, which is based on VO, gets deployed in the third level of the proposed architecture and constitutes the kernel of the system, where most of the efforts have been directed. It is critical to ensure this level supports tools and methodologies to provide the system with openness, reorganization and auto-adaptation capabilities to certain kinds of changes in the environment. These features are highly important within MAS, which are placed in open systems such as a smart city due to their inherent characteristics (dynamism and heterogeneity). This approximation, with a MAS semi-open society, was selected as the central technology for this work as it adapts itself perfectly to the evolutionary model of a smart city.

The proposed structure is capable of solving conflicts when adding agents to a VO. Consequently, it is not only restricted to the case study in this chapter and may be used for different functionalities. However, we will focus on conflict resolution when the system needs to add a new technology.

Figure 2 shows a schema of the internal architecture of VO-based MAS, which allows the system to solve the problem of choosing the most suitable technology. These technologies are represented as external agents with the intention of entering the society to play a particular role within it. With that in mind, the presence of two or more possible technologies is said to produce a conflict between them, which needs to be solved. So, the first step consists of describing the term *conflict* within this work. A conflict arises when the agent society contains a set of tasks that are associated to a specific role within the MAS; the task must be satisfied by an external entity, but there are different external entities with the capability to do so. The first step is to find the *External Candidate Entities (ECE)* representing the

Figure 2. Proposed schema for the MAS, focused on the need for conflict resolution when choosing a sensor associated to a specific technology

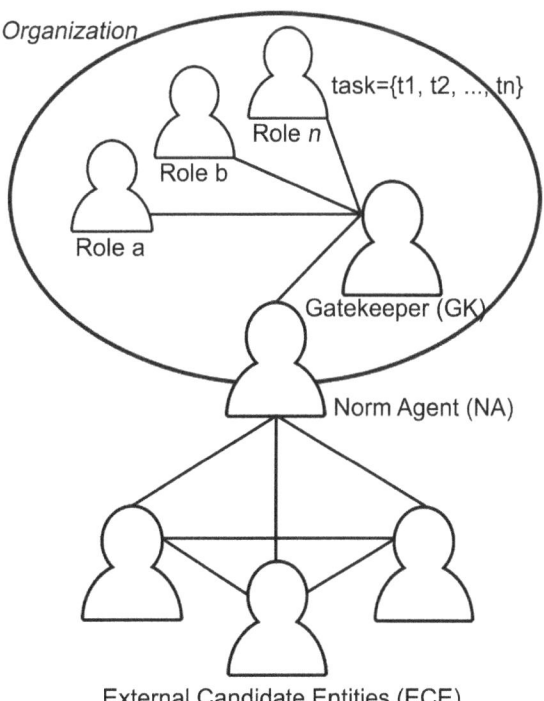

different existing options in the environment (different technologies to use), each one perfectly valid to satisfy the system's need (society) when interacting with the environment. At the beginning of the existence of a conflict, every possible solution is initially considered to be compatible with the global system. However, it is necessary to determine which ECE is the most suitable to perform the required tasks. This ECE will be integrated in the existing MAS, solving the conflict and acquiring a role within the society during a limited time needed to perform the task.

However, previously an agreement between these candidate entities must first be reached. To do so, the first step is to find out which external entities are compatible with the society. In other words, which ones comply with the norms of the society they want to enter, and in so doing will not constitute a risk in the stabilization of the MAS as a whole. The first agent they communicate with is the one with the role of Norm Agent (NA), which determines whether or not an ECE complies with the norms defined in the organization. Norms represent the obligations, constraints and qualities each agent in such an organization must somehow comply with. Each norm has an associated weight to be accumulated in a parameter to measure the incompatibility of the entity in the organization and, which should not exceed a maximum defined in the organization. For example, it guarantees that the gathered information can be communicated within the system, and does so in a stable manner, without disrupting the organization. If an ECE does not comply with the requirements, it ceases to be a candidate and will no longer take part in the negotiation process that occurs in subsequent steps.

The entities that are taken into consideration to participate in the system are considered reliable or safe, and must accept a series of factors which they must comply with to some degree. In other words, they need to be functional as well as reliable. The agent playing the Gatekeeper (GK) role is in charge of determining those factors. It does so by considering the needs of the system at any time. This agent formalizes any needs of the organization, breaking them down into a set of parameters with an associated value. This list of parameters forms the basis of negotiations the candidate entities will have to develop. The winning ECE will acquire access to the society. The value assigned to each parameter, *Degree of Need (DfN)*, is accompanied by a second value to define the priority of the parameter in question. The priority has a range of three possible nominal values depending on its grade: high (3), medium (2) and low (1).

The *DfN* could be a positive or a negative concept depending on whether it increases or decreases. In other words, it depends on whether the fact of exceeding the value of the *DfN* means the parameter is complying with the need or even improving the performance (an increasing parameter). On the other hand, if the *DfN* improves when the value decreases, it is considered a negative concept. For instance, according to the example of the sensors in the city, an increasing parameter would be the sensor range because a higher range means a benefit. On the other hand, a decreasing parameter could be the consumption because the lower the consumption, the higher the autonomy or the lower the associated economic expense. These factors, which are required by the society, are communicated through the GK to different ECEs complying with the norms required by the NA. Once the requirements are received, it starts the negotiation process among the ECEs, where each one indicates to the others, in the form of an argument, the in the degree to which they provide the required factors.

A simplified way in which the entities argue the reasons why they should be chosen as part of the system is shown in Figure 3. It is based on the three following rules:

Figure 3. State diagram to reflect the way of analyzing the rules on which the arguments of the ECEs are based

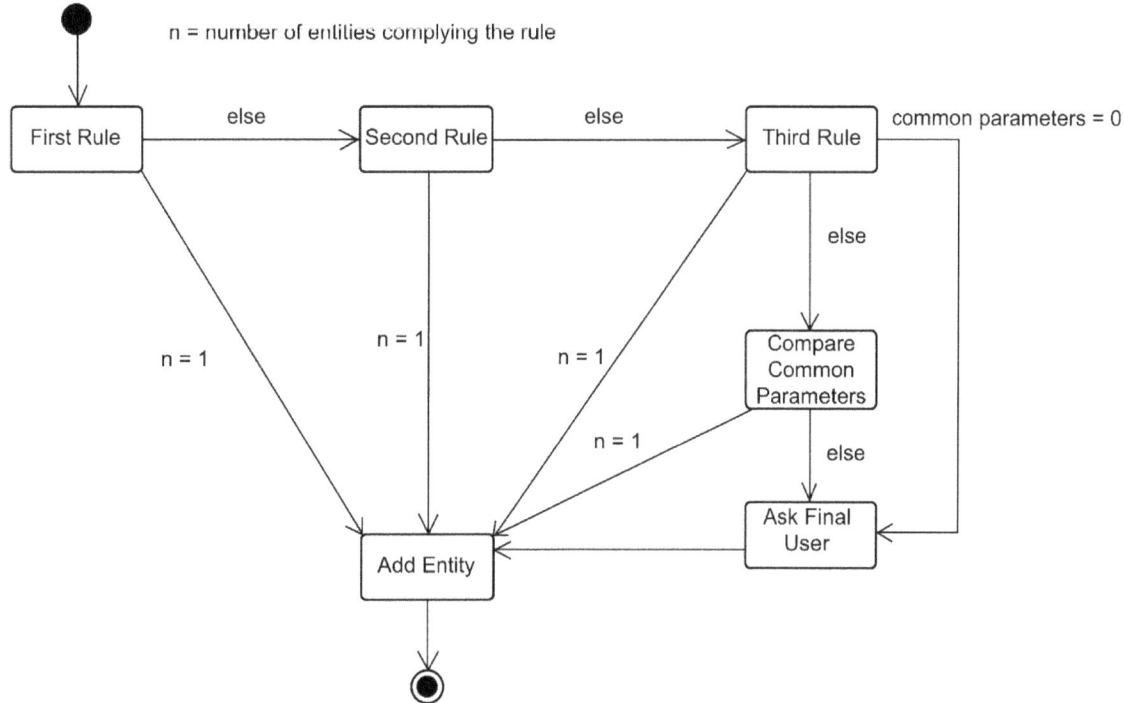

1. **First Rule:** Determines whether all the parameters ($R = \{1..n\}$) proposed by an ECE (p_i) satisfy, in a positive way, or at least match all the parameters required by the Organization (r_i). If only one candidate entity fulfills the rule, it will enter the system. When two or more ECEs fulfill the rule, these entities will evaluate the following rule. Finally, when no entity satisfies the first rule, every candidate entity moves on to evaluate the second rule.

$$\forall i \in R / p_i - r_i \geq 0, R = \{1..n\}$$

2. **Second Rule:** Calculates the degree to which the parameters ($R = \{1..n\}$) proposed by each ECE (p_i) solve the requirements of the system (r_i). If the greatest value obtained is associated to a single entity, this entity will become part of the system. But, if two or more entities share the obtained maximum value, they move on to evaluate the following rule.

$$\sum_{i=1}^{n} \left(p_i - r_i \right)$$

3. **Third Rule:** The concept of the priority of each parameter (y_i) is considered when evaluating this rule. Following the logic of the previous rule, the entity with the maximum value will enter the system.

$$\sum_{i=1}^{n} \left(\left(p_i - r_i \right) \cdot y_i \right)$$

If as a result of the last rule, there appears to be an entity plurality, there are two possible solutions. The first solution compares the values of the not required by the system but common to those entities parameters, arguing the reason that it should be the chosen entity. When it is not possible to solve the conflict, the system autonomously asks the final user to select a decision among those the system has already pre-selected.

Services

The services offered by the architecture are based on offering multiple possibilities to the end user. These possibilities range from monitoring the state of the whole system, where the state of each element participating in the system can be observed, to individually or collectively controlling such elements.

This type of control can be performed by defining a series of guidelines for the system to autonomously be able to replicate them when in similar situation. These guidelines to follow may be, for example, based on data mining or any other Artificial Intelligence (IA) technology to maximize the energetic efficiency of public lighting in the city.

Entrance services are also provided for the elements to be registered and for the existing possibilities to be presented. The conflict resolution is described and the most efficient solution for the system is provided to the end user. It is precisely at this moment that the city begins to achieve efficiency.

Study Case and Preliminary Evaluation

One example of applying this approach to solving conflicts in the proposed case study is traffic management. Sensors with different functionalities participate during the performance of this task. For example, an organization with this purpose could be called "Traffic Organization". In this organization, there are different types of roles apart from the GK role and the NA role. In this case, there are agents to obtain information (vehicle-counting role, pedestrian flow detection role, etc.), decision-making roles for the criteria related to traffic (size of roads, timetables, information gathered by the sensors, etc.) and actuators (role in charge of modifying the state of the traffic lights).

The feature of information acquisition and actuation is directly related to that of technology, for which this work attempts to offer a solution (we are not taking into consideration the AI issues related to decision making).

As an example, when adopting a technology as a solution to the vehicle-counting role, a case is presented with the following possibilities (real alternatives are simplified to facilitate the comprehension of the example):

- **Sensor on the Road:** Pressure sensors are deployed along the roads (underneath the asphalt or with bands adhered to it). The following technologies are available for this kind of sensor:
  - Bluetooth.
  - RFID.
  - ZigBee.
  - 6lowpan.
- **Optical IP Camera:** It may be placed over a traffic light or on the side of the road. It allows the following technologies
  - Wi-Fi.
  - Ethernet (with Power over Ethernet).

For this particular example, the system will only require three parameters (*DfN*). The parameters chosen for our consideration are:

- **Range:** A minimum range of 10 meters is required so that it can be assigned the value 10. High priority, as it is mandatory to guarantee the information can arrive from one side of the road to the other, in case an intermediate node fails. It is an increasing parameter.
- **Consumption:** The sensors should not drain more than 200 mA as an average when transmitting. Medium priority, as a lower priority than the range priority is assigned. It is a decreasing parameter so its value is negative.
- **Price:** The price of the sensors for smart cities is a relevant factor to be taken into consideration because of the large number of sensors to be used in a smart city. For our case, a maximum price of 40€ per unit is established, taking into account the criteria based on the city budget. If the main idea is to save money, we should not discount the installation costs. Medium priority. It is a decreasing parameter (negative values).

Clearly there are more influencing parameters, such as the deployment cost and maintenance cost, but again, a reduced view is provided for a better understanding. Table 1 shows the values for each of the candidate entities vying to become part of the system.

Table 1. Candidate technologies and values provided for the system degree of need

Technology	Range	Consumption	Price
Bluetooth 4.0	10 m	25 mA	30 €
RFID	30 m	24 mA	40 €
ZigBee	15 m	30 mA	30 €
6lowpan	60 m	24 mA	20 €
Wi-Fi	50 m	1000 mA	80 €
Ethernet	100 m	600 mA	70 €

Table 2. Arguing table for each candidate technology

Technology	First Rule	Second Rule	Third Rule
Bluetooth 4.0	≥ 0 ; ≥ 0 ; ≥ 0	185	370
RFID	≥ 0 ; ≥ 0 ; ≥ 0	196	412
ZigBee	≥ 0 ; ≥ 0 ; ≥ 0	185	375
6lowpan	≥ 0 ; ≥ 0 ; ≥ 0	**246**	**542**
Wi-Fi	≥ 0 ; < 0 ; < 0	-800	-1600
Ethernet	≥ 0 ; < 0 ; < 0	-340	-590

Assuming that every entity complies with the access norms to the system, each one will use the values described in Table 2 when arguing its case for accessing the system.

Based on the arguing criteria, the entity that will become part of the system following the vehicle-counting role from the "Traffic Organization" is, in this case, the entity associated to the 6lowpan technology. This is because it has the highest value in the application of the second rule.

One of the main disadvantages of the 6lowpan technology is that it is not very widespread among users, which means the selection of the parameters to be considered is very important. For instance, had we only used an extra parameter, in addition to the other three required parameters, to refer to support, it is possible that the 6lowpan would not have been the chosen technology. In order to guarantee the technological decisions are adequate, we suggest analyzing, apart from those already used, at least the following parameters: maintenance cost, deployment cost, upgradability and maximum size of the network.

To test the proper performance of the architecture, the system was applied to the simulation environment of a smart city, as a preliminary evaluation. This environment recreates the main characteristic elements of this kind of city in a model of a city. The model was almost entirely 3D printed, having an area of 2 x 2 meters. This model can be seen in Figure 4. By using this architecture as the base, it is possible to manage every element on the model: luminaries, solar panels, traffic lights, containers,

Figure 4. Simulation environment used to develop the architecture testing (left), along with the management software and monitoring of the smart city (right)

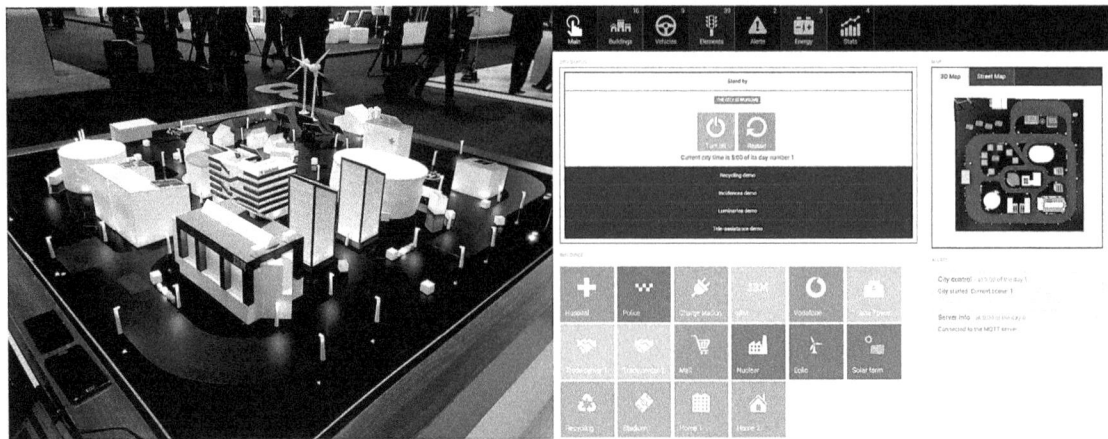

aero-generators and even vehicles. This way, although the number of sensors is lower than in a real smart city, some testing on the offered services, such as the decision making when choosing the sensor to be used, was developed

FUTURE RESEARCH DIRECTIONS AND CONCLUSION

This work has created a platform capable of solving conflicts, with a special focus on smart cities management. The problems in this study have focused on technology used as a base to gather and merge the information of everything happening on it, as it is the first conflict posed when designing a platform with such features.

Nevertheless, the schema can be extrapolated to superior levels in the architecture where decisions are taken to a higher level. For instance, for reaching an agreement and achieving conflict resolution, it is possible to apply the proposed schema to the distribution of street lighting between the streets in a city, taking multiple factors into account (pedestrian flow, traffic, location, businesses, etc.). The efforts made have not quite finished and more efforts will be made in order to apply the system to new case studies within the smart city environment.

In the long term, the results of the architecture can be measured by quantifying the savings produced in a city using this system, as opposed to other cities with similar characteristics (size, number of citizens, institutions and number of sensors) but a different management system.

Moreover, this system is not just limited to smart cities. For example, it could be extrapolated as a system to manage data from a WSN in a residential home, in addition to many other fields of application. Therefore, it is possible to continue applying the architecture to different environments, which would allow its functionality to increase.

This work has presented a platform capable of solving conflicts in the management of smart cities, which, and has focused on the technology to be used as a base to gather and merge information regarding all events occurring on it. This feature is practically vital when centralizing all activities taking place in a city into a stable system within a project with continuity. While a standardized and common sensor protocol is not presented, the offered solution remains an alternative capable of isolating the part of communication with the sensor from the result of the global system. The platform can also adapt itself to changes in technology when the existing system becomes more inefficient, which permits making the most of the advantages coming from the currently offered technologic diversity and the benefit of gathering the information in a unique manner.

ACKNOWLEDGMENT

This work has been supported by the European Commission H2020 MSCA-RISE-2014: Marie Skłodowska-Curie project DREAM-GO Enabling Demand Response for short and real-time Efficient And Market Based Smart Grid Operation - An intelligent and real-time simulation approach ref 641794

REFERENCES

Akyildiz, I. F., & Vuran, M. C. (2010). *Wireless sensor networks* (Vol. 4). John Wiley & Sons. doi:10.1002/9780470515181

Annunziato, M., & Pierucci, P. (2003). The emergence of social learning in artificial societies. In *Applications of evolutionary computing* (pp. 467–478). Springer Berlin Heidelberg. doi:10.1007/3-540-36605-9_43

Armbrust, M., Fox, A., Griffith, R., Joseph, A. D., Katz, R., Konwinski, A., & Zaharia, M. et al. (2010). A view of cloud computing. *Communications of the ACM*, *53*(4), 50–58. doi:10.1145/1721654.1721672

Buratti, C., Conti, A., Dardari, D., & Verdone, R. (2009). An overview on wireless sensor networks technology and evolution. *Sensors (Basel, Switzerland)*, *9*(9), 6869–6896. doi:10.3390/s90906869 PMID:22423202

Caragliu, A., Del Bo, C., & Nijkamp, P. (2011). Smart cities in Europe. *Journal of Urban Technology*, *18*(2), 65–82. doi:10.1080/10630732.2011.601117

Chopra, A. K., & Singh, M. P. (2013). *Multiagent Systems: A Modern Approach to Distributed Artificial Intelligence. In Agent Communication* (pp. 101–141). The MIT Press.

Daft, R. (2012). *Organization theory and design*. Cengage Learning.

Davidsson, P., & Johansson, S. (2006). On the potential of norm-governed behavior in different categories of artificial societies. *Computational & Mathematical Organization Theory*, *12*(2-3), 169–180. doi:10.1007/s10588-006-9542-x

De la Prieta, F., Rodríguez, S., Bajo, J., & Corchado, J. M. (2013). A multiagent system for resource distribution into a Cloud Computing environment. In *Advances on Practical Applications of Agents and Multi-Agent Systems* (pp. 37–48). Springer Berlin Heidelberg. doi:10.1007/978-3-642-38073-0_4

Ferber, J. (1999). *Multi-agent systems: an introduction to distributed artificial intelligence* (Vol. 1). Reading: Addison-Wesley.

Ferber, J., Gutknecht, O., & Michel, F. (2004). From agents to organizations: an organizational view of multi-agent systems. In *Agent-Oriented Software Engineering IV* (pp. 214–230). Springer Berlin Heidelberg. doi:10.1007/978-3-540-24620-6_15

Hafeez, A., Kandil, N. H., Al-Omar, B., Landolsi, T., & Al-Ali, A. R. (2014). Smart Home Area Networks Protocols within the Smart Grid Context. *Journal of Communication*, *9*(9).

Hollands, R. G. (2008). Will the real smart city please stand up? Intelligent, progressive or entrepreneurial? *City*, *12*(3), 303–320. doi:10.1080/13604810802479126

Lian, K. Y., Hsiao, S. J., & Sung, W. T. (2013). Intelligent multi-sensor control system based on innovative technology integration via ZigBee and Wi-Fi networks. *Journal of Network and Computer Applications*, *36*(2), 756–767. doi:10.1016/j.jnca.2012.12.012

Liu, Y., Seet, B. C., & Al-Anbuky, A. (2013). An ontology-based context model for Wireless Sensor Network (WSN) management in the internet of things. *Journal of Sensor and Actuator Networks*, 2(4), 653–674. doi:10.3390/jsan2040653

Mitton, N., Papavassiliou, S., Puliafito, A., & Trivedi, K. S. (2012). Combining Cloud and sensors in a smart city environment. *EURASIP Journal on Wireless Communications and Networking*, (1): 1–10.

Navarro, M., Bhatnagar, D., & Liang, Y. (2011, October). An integrated network and data management system for heterogeneous WSNs. In *Mobile Adhoc and Sensor Systems (MASS), 2011 IEEE 8th International Conference on* (pp. 819-824). IEEE. doi:10.1109/MASS.2011.94

Roscia, M., Longo, M., & Lazaroiu, G. C. (2013, October). Smart city by multi-agent systems. In *Renewable Energy Research and Applications (ICRERA), 2013 International Conference on* (pp. 371-376). IEEE. doi:10.1109/ICRERA.2013.6749783

Schaffers, H., Komninos, N., Pallot, M., Trousse, B., Nilsson, M., & Oliveira, A. (2011). Smart Cities and the Future Internet: Towards Cooperation Frameworks for Open Innovation. *Future Internet Assembly*, 6656, 431–446. doi:10.1007/978-3-642-20898-0_31

Talia, D. (2012). Clouds meet agents: Toward intelligent cloud services. *IEEE Internet Computing*, 16(2), 78–81. doi:10.1109/MIC.2012.28

Vasconcelos, W. W., Kollingbaum, M. J., & Norman, T. J. (2009). Normative conflict resolution in multi-agent systems. *Autonomous Agents and Multi-Agent Systems*, 19(2), 124–152. doi:10.1007/s10458-008-9070-9

Weber, R. H. (2010). Internet of Things–New security and privacy challenges. *Computer Law & Security Report*, 26(1), 23–30. doi:10.1016/j.clsr.2009.11.008

Zambonelli, F., Jennings, N. R., & Wooldridge, M. (2001). Organisational rules as an abstraction for the analysis and design of multi-agent systems. *International Journal of Software Engineering and Knowledge Engineering*, 11(03), 303–328. doi:10.1142/S0218194001000505

Zato, C., De Paz, J. F., de Luis, A., Bajo, J., & Corchado, J. M. (2012). Model for assigning roles automatically in egovernment virtual organizations. *Expert Systems with Applications*, 39(12), 10389–10401. doi:10.1016/j.eswa.2012.01.185

KEY TERMS AND DEFINITIONS

Agent: In a global and reduced way, as there are loads of versions to define the term as well as possible classifications characteristics to comply with, it is a physical or virtual entity that acts by responding to collected stimuli from its environment. This response needs to be rational, tending to maximize the desired result.

Cloud Computing: It is a kind of computation where all the resources from a computational system are offered as a service through the Internet. This way, the demander gets unlinked from the way those resources are managed, focusing only in its use. So the user does not need any knowledge on the way those resources need to be managed, saving time, and in many occasions money.

Gatekeeper: It defines an access point to organizations in semi-open type of MAS trough which all the external entities have to contact in order to enter the society. Its purpose is to guarantee every entity in the system complies with a degree of security. This is what guarantees it is a reliable and stable system even when having some degree of openness.

Multi-Agent System: It is composed of agents and their environment. This kind of systems is usually used to solve problems that are difficult or even impossible for single agents to solve.

Role: It defines the position and the set of responsibilities an agent within the global system has. An agent is capable of adopting different roles depending on the context.

Smart City: It is an emerging term during the last decade. It represents the concept of efficient and sustainable city, capable of responding in the most adequate way to the basic needs of the city. This response to the needs is mainly based on the economic, environmental, social and operative fields. To do so, an efficient and lasting infrastructure needed to manage water, energy, tele-communications, transportation, emergency services, etc.

Virtual Organization: It could be seen as a set of roles with a certain relationship among them, with the capability of interacting with other roles trough certain patterns. They are a way of interpreting the MAS from a sociologic point of view.

Wireless Sensor Network: It is a spatially distributed network of autonomous sensors used to monitor physical or environmental conditions, for example, in a smart city. In general, they are composed of a series of nodes connected together in a way that the network allows knowing the information each one of those nodes gathers.

Chapter 15
Conflict Resolution in Robotics:
An Overview

Ester Martinez-Martin
Jaume-I University, Spain

Angel P. del Pobil
Jaume-I University, Spain

ABSTRACT

A long-term goal in Robotics is developing autonomous systems able to assist and support human beings, especially in hazardous and/or repetitive tasks. So, these robotic systems will share their workspace with other robots, people or both of them, possibly having different goals and needs. This fact may result in a conflict that should be solved for properly achieving the intended goals. However, there is no a universal way to do it since different scenarios and behaviours lead to different kinds of conflicts. In addition, execution time is a critical issue in the Robotics field and has to be taken into account when a conflict resolution technique is developed. In this chapter we will discuss the state-of-the-art algorithms applied to several robotic tasks from assembly and disassembly in industrial settings to multi-robot cooperation through collision avoidance in unstructured, crowded environments. So, a deep analysis will highlight approach's applications and utilities, as well as their limitations.

INTRODUCTION

Technological advances are currently being directed to assist human population in performing daily tasks in real scenarios. So, the robot systems should be able to properly reach a variety of tasks in different kinds of environments. In this context, conflict resolution is a key issue since the way to resolve conflicts between the multiple tasks to be performed simultaneously and/or several robots cooperating to achieve a common goal, will determine the success/failure of the robot system.

From a biological point of view, people handle conflicts in five different styles (Kilmann & Thomas, 1977):

DOI: 10.4018/978-1-5225-0245-6.ch015

- **Avoiding:** This is an unassertive and uncooperative style. When avoiding, the issue is simply not addressed. So, it can be appropriate when the victory is impossible, when the controversy is trivial, or when someone else is in a better position to solve the problem. However, avoiding is not a good long term strategy in general.
- **Competitive:** This is the "win-lose" approach. That is, this is assertive, uncooperative and a power-oriented mode. This style can be useful when there is an emergency and a decision needs to be made fast, when the decision is unpopular, or when defending against someone trying to exploit the situation selfishly.
- **Accommodating:** This mode takes place when there is high-degree cooperation, even at the individual's own expense. Actually, there is an element of self-sacrifice in this style. So, this unassertive and cooperative (not competitive) approach is effective when the other party is the expert or has a better solution.
- **Collaborative:** This style is both assertive and cooperative. Therefore, when collaborating, an individual attempts to work with the other person to find a solution that fully satisfies the concerns of both. So, the individual breaks free of the "win-lose" paradigm and seeks the "win-win" approach. This style is useful when it is necessary to bring together a variety of viewpoints to get the best solution, when there have been previous conflicts in the group, or when the situation is too important for a simple trade-off.
- **Compromising:** This mode is intermediate in both assertiveness and cooperativeness, and addresses an issue more directly than avoiding. Thus, when compromising, the goal is to find a mutually acceptable solution partially satisfying both parties. This style is useful when the cost of the conflict is higher than the cost of losing ground, when equal strength opponents are at a standstill, or when there is a deadline looming.

Ideally, a system should adopt the proper approach that meets the situation at hand at any time. However, this is not straightforward since it depends on different factors such as the environment, the goal to be achieved and the kind of partners the system has (i.e. other robots and/or people). In addition, the conflict resolution technique must be fast and must result in a reliable negotiation of the shared resources and energy management. So, this chapter reviews those techniques for conflict resolution used in three different fields of Robotics: multi-robot cooperation, human-robot collaboration and multi-tasking assignation.

CONFLICT RESOLUTION IN MULTI-ROBOT COOPERATION

Advances in swarm robotics make it possible to use (large) teams of robots in many applications such as air-traffic control, factory automation, agriculture, logistics, etc. However, despite the popularity of cooperative robotics in the last decades, the problem of conflict resolution is still a challenge, especially when the number of the integrating robots is variable.

In this context, two different issues have been addressed: path planning, where several robots share a workspace and have to avoid collision with obstacles as well as with fellow robots; and, object manipulation.

Path Planning

The goal of path planning is to find a continuous trajectory for a robot from the initial state to the goal state without colliding with obstacles (including other robots and/or people), while maintaining robot-specific constraints (Kala, Shukla & Tiwari, 2010).

A wide research has been aimed to efficient motion planning algorithms for robot teams in different scenarios. However, these approaches can be roughly classified into two different categories: (1) centralised and hierarchical control solutions, which optimize the performance; and, (2) distributed paradigms (with advantages such as scalability and flexibility).

So, the centralised approaches consider the multiple robots as a single system, rather than independent entities. For that reason, this kind of approaches allows the system to perform global optimization and develop complete solutions. Nevertheless, the problem complexity increases exponentially as a function of the number of the integrating robots and their Degrees of Freedom (DoFs). So, the cost of the multi-robot path planning can be prohibitively high even for a relatively small number of robots. As a consequence, some approaches relax the completeness requirement to compute a solution in a reasonable amount of time. This is the case of the sampling-based approaches, which build an implicit representation of a robot configuration space by sampling this space for valid robot placements and connecting nearby samples (Kavraki, Svestka, Latombe, & Overmars, 1996; Kuffner & Lavalle, 2000). So, the connections between samples form a *roadmap* whose vertices describe valid placements for each robot and the edges represent valid paths from one position to the other. This implicit representation of the configuration space and its simplicity make these algorithms be much faster than complete planners in practice and be applicable with a large number of DoFs such as the multi-robot problem. Actually, a wide variety of these algorithms can be found in the literature (Solovey & Halperin, 2014; Cui, Gao, & Guo, 2012; La-Valle, 2006; Basu, Pollack, & Roy, 2000; Svestka & Overmars, 1998; Canny, 1991). Furthermore, some combinations are presented like in (Wagner, Kang, & Choset, 2012) where the multi-agent path-finding in discrete environments is coupled with an implicit representation of a *roadmap* with the purpose to yield an efficient algorithm for the fully coloured multi-robot motion planning problem.

As an alternative, some efforts were made in the direction of reducing the effective number of DoFs. For example, Aronov et al. (1999) showed that it is possible to reduce the number of DoFs by one or two when pairs or triples of robots are used in low-density workspaces and under the assumption that the robots move while keeping contact. Another solution is decomposing the multi-robot problem into a sequence of subproblems such that every subproblem can be solved separately and all the obtained results are combined into a solution for the original problem (van Den Berg, Snoeyink, Lin, & Manocha, 2009). In this way, the number of DoFs is reduced to the number of DoFs of the largest subproblem. However, this approach is constrained in the sense that an exact representation of both the robot geometry and the workspace is required. Another possibility is to decompose a large map into subgraphs, and plan robot paths between subgraph segments before coordinating motion within each subgraph (Ryan, 2007).

Despite the efforts in designing centralised algorithms, they are not usually suitable for dynamic applications since they take many resources when the solution is computed (online recomputation becomes unachievable). This complexity led to the emergence of decoupled approaches for multi-robot planning, where completeness is sacrificed in favour of complexity.

Mainly, a decoupled approach typically generates paths for each robot independently, and then it considers the interactions between the integrating robots, by trading completeness with efficiency. Therefore, the planning is basically done in two decouple stages: (1) a collision-free path with respect to the environment obstacles (excluding the other robots) is computed; and, (2) *velocity tuning*, that is, inter-robot collisions are avoided by assigning time along the robot paths estimated in the first stage (Chiddarwar & Babu, 2011; Purwin, D'Andrea, & Lee, 2008; Peng & Akella, 2005; Guo & Parker, 2002; Leroy, Laumond, & Simeon, 1999). As an alternative other schemes such as coordination graphs (Li, Gupta, & Payandeh, 2005), incremental planning (Saha & Isto, 2006), or minimal communication (Krontiris & Bekris, 2011) can help to ensure that no collisions occur along the paths.

A variant of the basic decoupled approach is the prioritized planning technique (Cap, Novak, Kleiner, Selecky, & Pechoucek, 2015; Yu, Peng, Zhang, & Lin, 2014; Velagapudi, Sycara, & Scerri, 2010; Erdmann & Lozano-Perez, 1986). In this case, every robot is given a priority and the robot motion path is sequentially computed to avoid collision with both static obstacles and lower-priority robots, considered as moving obstacles, in the specified order. Nevertheless, a key issue is how to choose the priorities since they can have a large impact on the algorithm's performance (van den Berg & Overmars, 2005). Consequently, some approaches include a search through a space of prioritizations (Bennewitz, Burgard, & Thrun, 2001, 2002; Buckley, 1989).

Another option is the *coordination-diagram approach* (O'Donnell & Lozano-Perez, 1989), which independently combines generated paths of many robots while avoiding collisions (Siméon, Leroy, & Laumond, 2002); decentralized state machines defining the robot behaviour (Ferrera, Castaño, Capitán, Marrón, & Ollero, 2014); or augmented time-expanded network (Ferrati & Pallotino, 2013).

Although decentralised approaches can be efficient in some cases, they do not guarantee finding a solution (in case one exists) and usually work only for a restricted set of problems.

In addition, hybrid methods combine aspects of both centralised and decoupled approaches in order to obtain techniques that are more reliable or offer completeness but also scale better than coupled approaches. For instance, Alami et al. (1995) proposed an approach based on the *Plan-Merging Paradigm*, where robots incrementally merge their plans into a set of already coordinated plans from a continuous information exchange about the robot's current state and their future actions. Alternatively, LaValle and Hutchinson (1998) presented a multi-robot motion planning approach derived from the principle of optimality, by *filtering out* all the motion plans that are not worth considering and presenting a small set of the best alternatives. This coordination on *roadmaps* provides enough maneuverability for most robotic swarms, although its completeness with respect to the original problem is lost when constrained to *roadmaps*. Other approach based on a topological graph of the environment (i.e. a *roadmap*) and a spanning tree representation is the multiphase approach presented by (Peasgood, Clark, & McPhee, 2008). In addition, the used *roadmap* can be adaptive by using deformable links (Gayle, Sud, Lin, & Manocha, 2007), although it is susceptible to leave a robot in a state where a collision is inevitable and the optimality of the computed paths is not guaranteed.

Other possibilities include independent planning-based methods such as multi-objective evolutionary algorithms (Pohl & Lamont, 2008), particle swarm optimization (Alejo, Cobano, Heredia, & Ollero, 2013), maze searching (Lumelsky & Harinarayan, 1997), potential fields (Ge & Cui, 1997; Barraquand & Latombe, 1991), neural networks (Kaidi, Lazaar, & Ettaouil, 2014), dynamic networks (Clark, Rock, & Latombe, 2003), or the iteratively addition of new plans as obstacles into the configuration space-time (Erdmann & Lozano-Perez, 1987).

A comparison between centralised and decoupled approaches (Sanchez & Latombe, 2002) concluded that the decoupled planners are very unreliable in practice because of their inherent incomplete nature since fewer degrees of freedom are considered at one time. Consequently, they suggest that a centralised approach should usually be the preferred choice, although they are slower. On the contrary, Isto and Saha

(2006) demonstrated that the decoupled performance could be improved by exploiting the decoupled nature of multi-robot. Therefore, the suitability of one approach over the other is usually determined by the trade-off between the computational complexity associated with the task at hand and the amount of completeness that can be lost.

Object Manipulation

Robot sensing and object manipulation can be noisy and uncertain in some domains. However, the partial knowledge about the world could be overcome by using a team of robots, becoming more efficient through cooperation. Furthermore, using multiple robots versus a single robot has the advantage of distributing a load among several smaller and less expensive robots, and tighter control of the internal force of the payload. For that, the robot cooperative manipulation is socially desired.

A wide research has been done for the motion control of multiple robot systems manipulating an object in coordination. So, as in the case of path planning, centralised and decoupled control algorithms have been proposed in the literature.

In this case, the centralised control approaches mainly use a single controller that coordinates all the other robots based on global information (Wang, Nakano, & Matsukawa, 1994; Kawauchi, Inaba, & Fukuda, 1993). Among their variants, we can find a passivity-based motion control strategy combined with integral force control (Wen & Kreutz-Delgado, 1992), an event-based control scheme where the internal force is regulated by modifying the desired trajectory at a supervisory level (Munawar & Uchiyama, 1999) or the use of payload dynamics (mass/inertia, location of the centre of mass) in the control law (Zribi & Ahmed, 1991).

Note that the centralised control system can be effective in case of coordinated motion control for object handling when the number of the robots (manipulators) in coordination is limited. Nevertheless, the problem becomes impractical when the number of the involved robots (manipulators) is variable and/or large. Furthermore, the kinematics and dynamics information may not be fully available.

On the contrary, each robot could be provided with the ability to estimate the position of their neighbours and to be controlled by its own controller, leading to decoupled approaches like (Mellinger, Shomin, Michael, & Kumar, 2013). An example is the application of the classical leader-follower algorithm to this problem (Kosuge & Oosumi, 1996). A further implementation assumes that the geometry is precisely known and the contact forces are not measured. In this way, a robot leader broadcasts its estimated position and velocity, while the followers simply try to keep up by using the known relative geometry (Sugar, Desai, Ostrowski, & Kumar, 2001; Chaimowicz, Sugar, Kumar, & Campos, 2001). Nevertheless, in this kind of approaches the communication delay is not considered and there is no internal force control. A similar leader/follower scheme for multiple mobile manipulators motivated by caster wheels was proposed in (Hirata, Kume, Wang, & Kosuge, 2003; Kume, Hirata, Wang, & Kosuge, 2002).

In contrast to these approaches, other authors present an approach where all the robots participate in both the motion and the force control resulting in a tighter force regulation and a higher motor speed (Montemayor & Wen, 2005). On the contrary, other approaches use potential fields for planning and control (Song & Kumar, 2002); cluster control (Neumann, Chin, & Kitts, 2014; Mas & Kitts, 2012); or communication to minimize the need for explicit modelling and prediction like (Mataric, Nilsson, & Simsarin, 1995). Others are based on object closure condition (Pereira, Campos, & Kumar, 2004) or on action extraction (Kubo & Ohnishi, 2006).

Again, the lack of a successful performance under all the scenarios has resulted in the development of hybrid approaches by focusing on precision manipulation for complex tasks (Michelman, 1998), controlling the motion of the object under constraint while taking into account the contact with the environment (Yoshikawa & Zheng, 1990) or by using the Discrete Fourier Transform for grasping and manipulation (Kubo & Ohnishi, 2006b).

CONFLICT RESOLUTION IN HUMAN-ROBOT COOPERATION

Human-Robot collaboration can be a difficult task due to conflicts in beliefs, plans or goals between cooperating partners. Thus, humans and robot systems must collaborate in the dynamic physical world while dealing with conflicting information and uncertainty. For that, communication is required. However, current research on this topic primarily addresses the "how to say" and "when to say it" issues. The "how to say it" problem aims to the best way for a robot to deliver dialogue content (e.g., using speech, text or a different modality) (Mutlu, 2011). On the contrary, the "when to say it" issue considers the timing of dialogue delivery. On the way of finding a balance between them, many HRI systems utilize scripted dialogue management modules as the robot receptionist (Kirby et al., 2005). Nevertheless, a scripted dialogue model is not sufficient for robots operating in a highly dynamic and changing environment shared by human and robots, working together.

As a solution Azhar et al. (2013) proposed a dialogue framework (*ArgHRI*) integrated into planning and decision-making for a human-robot collaborative task. This framework mainly consists in four components: an ontology describing the robot's environment and capabilities; a memory system to maintain the robot's beliefs; an argumentation engine, *ArgTrust*, adopted from (Tang, Cai, McBurney, Sklar, & Parsons, 2012), supporting the robot's internal decision-making; and a dialogue system for interacting with a human. Despite the good obtained results, its current implementation only considers a one-robot team.

CONFLICT RESOLUTION IN MULTI-TASKING ASSIGNATION

Another important issue to be solved refers to implement a mechanism for task allocation, that is, an efficient assignment of tasks to robots. The Task Assignment Problem is a common problem in many different domains from pick-up and delivery (Giordano, Zhang, Naso, & Lewis, 2008; Naso & Turchiano, 2005; Savelsbergh & Sol, 1995) to environmental surveillance and monitoring (Di Paola, Naso, Milella, Cicirelli, & Distante, 2010; Di Paola, Naso, Turchiano, Cicirelli, & Distante, 2009), from operation research (Hillier & Lieberman, 2009) to transportation (Naso & Turchiano, 2007), or vehicle routing (Golden, Raghavan, & Wasil, 2008; Toth & Vigo, 2001).

Basically, this problem can be defined as follows: *given a list of N_t tasks and N_a agents, the allocation problem is to find a conflict-free and constraint-fulfilling assignment that maximizes a pre-defined score function. The score function is the sum of local rewards determined as a function of the tasks assigned to each agent. An assignment is free of conflicts if each task is assigned to no more than one agent* (Binetti, Naso, & Turchiano, 2013).

In this context, the area of multi-robot systems is undoubtedly one of the most active research fields. So, in the literature we can find systems that use an explicit task allocation mechanism by assuming either that a static set of tasks is given to the system as input (Botelho & Alami, 1999; Golfarelli, Maio,

& Rizzi, 1997), or that the different tasks arrive dynamically, from external (Zlot & Stentz, 2005; Dias, 2004; Gerkey & Mataric, 2002) or internal (Zlot, Stentz, Dias, & Thayer, 2002; Simmons et al., 2000) sources. In most of cases, such approaches search for an efficient assignment of the current task set to robots, assuming that all tasks are indivisible. Consequently, when a complex task is considered, the robot assigned that task can decompose it and then perform the resulting simple tasks.

A common alternative for explicitly handling complex tasks is a two-stage approach such that the first step is to decompose all tasks and secondly the algorithm distributes the resulting set of subtasks (Aylett & Barnes, 1998). However, the task decomposition method represents its main shortcoming since it is performed without any knowledge of the eventual task allocation. Consequently, the cost of the final plan cannot be completely considered and, given that no backtracking is performed, it is not possible to rectify the costly mistakes in the central decompositions. As a solution, some approaches intentionally leave the central plan vague, providing the system with a limited flexibility to modify it afterwards. This is the case of GOFER (Caloud, Choi, Latombe, Pape, & Yim, 1990), where the central planner generates an overall plan structure with some variables that can be later instantiated by the individual robots. Another example is the *playbook system* (Simmons et al., 2000b). In this case, the planner depends on a central manager for both allocating tasks and filling in some plan details.

On its behalf, some reallocation of subcomponents of complex tasks is allowed by the M+ cooperative task achievement scheme (Botelho & Alami, 2000). In this approach, the tasks are firstly allocated by means of a bidding protocol to distribute predefined abstract tasks among the robot team (i.e. the M+ task allocation mechanism (Botelho & Alami, 1999)). Then, each robot locally decomposes its tasks into actions viewed as primitive subtasks. In addition, the task achievement scheme allows the system to suppress or transfer actions between robots with the aim of removing some inefficiencies or redundancies in the global plan. In this way, the solution quality can be potentially improved to some degree since the initial task allocation does not consider how the actions are to be shared among the team robots, nor does the decomposition step consider the eventual allocation of its resulting actions. Moreover, the task achievement scheme does not explicitly model the costs of reassigning or cancelling actions.

On the other hand, decentralised approaches can also be applied. In this case, the tasks are related to goals to be reached by the agents (Smith & Bullo, 2009; Michael, Zavlanos, Kumar, & Pappas, 2008). Consequently, research on this topic has focused on specific aspects such as precedence constraints among tasks (Casbeer & Holsapple, 2011), uncertainty and robustness (Liu & Shell, 2011), energy efficiency (Krieger & Billeter, 2000), temporal deadline (Guerrero & Oliver, 2012), heterogeneous robots (Binetti et al., 2013; Kiener & von Stryk, 2010), large-scale systems (Liu & Shell, 2012), or coalition formation with constrained resources (Chen & Sun, 2012). Nevertheless, these approaches only properly work achieving certain requirements (e.g. the agent capacity (i.e. the maximum number of tasks that can be assigned to a single agent) is fixed a priori and based on its physical limitations; the existence of different agent features like storage or sensory/actuating equipment; the mandatory need of assuring the allocation of some critical; …) what considerably restricts the functionality of the multi-robot system.

CONCLUSION

Robots are increasingly broadening their horizons beyond the factory settings. So, one of the ultimate goals of the Robotics research is to build robots able of autonomous actions while requiring little or no human supervision. In this way, these systems could assist human beings in a countless number of applications such as agriculture, urban search and rescue, surveillance, transport, traffic, space exploration, surgery, etc. However, this is a challenging topic since robots must share their workspace with humans and other robots. In addition, the dynamism of real world provides so much complexity that demands extremely high computational costs, leading to an unacceptable time consumption for useful robotics applications.

Alternatively, it has long been recognised that there are several tasks that can be performed more efficiently and robustly using multiple robots. In fact, in the last decades there has been a wide research on this topic, analysing different issues such as group architecture, geometric problems, learning, resource conflict, and cooperation. However, although significant progress has been done in this area, it is still difficult to design a fast, optimal cooperative strategies to accomplish efficient robot tasks, while accommodating environment complexity (e.g. obstacles), and hardware and robot configuration constraints (e.g. speed and steering angle limitations).

In this chapter, a review of the existing approaches regarding three fundamental robotic tasks (i.e. path planning, human-robot cooperation and task assignment) has been presented. As observed, the up-to-date developments are still in their formative stages. Nevertheless, they are stepping stone for achieving larger-scaled and more complicated tasks.

ACKNOWLEDGMENT

This work has been partially funded by Ministerio de Economía y Competitividad (DPI2015-69041-R), by Generalitat Valenciana (PROMETEOII/2014/028), and by Jaume-I University (P1-1B2014-52).

REFERENCES

Alami, R., Robert, F., Ingrand, F., & Suzuki, S. (1995). Multi-robot cooperation through incremental plan-merging. In *IEEE International Conference on Robotics and Automation* (ICRA), (pp. 2573–2579).

Alejo, D., Cobano, J. A., Heredia, G., & Ollero, A. (2013). Particle Swarm Optimization for collision-free 4D trajectory planning in Unmanned Aerial Vehicles. In *International Conference on Unmanned Aircraft Systems* (ICUAS), (pp. 298 – 307). doi:10.1109/ICUAS.2013.6564702

Aronov, B., de Berg, M., van der Stappen, A. F., Svestka, P., & Vleugels, J. (1999). Motion planning for multiple robots. *Discrete & Computational Geometry*, 22(4), 505–525. doi:10.1007/PL00009476

Aylett, R., & Barnes, D. (1998). A multi-robot architecture for planetary rovers. In *5th ESA Workshop on Advanced Space Technologies for Robotics and Automation*.

Azhar, M. Q., Parsons, S., & Sklar, E. (2013). An Argumentation-based Dialogue System for Human-Robot Collaboration (Demonstration). In *12th International Conference on Autonomous Agents and Multiagent Systems* (AA-MAS), (pp. 1353–1354).

Barraquand, J., & Latombe, J.-C. (1991). Robot motion planning: A distributed representation approach. *The International Journal of Robotics Research*, 10(6), 628–649. doi:10.1177/027836499101000604

Basu, S., Pollack, R., & Roy, M.-F. (2000). Computing Roadmaps of Semi-algebraic Sets on a Variety. *Journal of the American Mathematical Society*, 13(01), 55–82. doi:10.1090/S0894-0347-99-00311-2

Bennewitz, M., Burgard, W., & Thrun, S. (2001). Optimizing schedules for prioritized path planning of multi-robot systems. In *IEEE International Conference on Robotics and Automation* (ICRA), (pp. 271–276). doi:10.1109/ROBOT.2001.932565

Bennewitz, M., Burgard, W., & Thrun, S. (2002). Finding and optimizing solvable priority schemes for decoupled path planning techniques for teams of mobile robots. *Robotics and Autonomous Systems*, *41*(2), 89–99. doi:10.1016/S0921-8890(02)00256-7

Binetti, G., Naso, D., & Turchiano, B. (2013). Decentralized task allocation for surveillance systems with critical tasks. *Robotics and Autonomous Systems*, *61*(12), 1653–1664. doi:10.1016/j.robot.2013.06.007

Botelho, S. S. C., & Alami, R. (1999). *M+:* A scheme for multi-robot cooperation through negotiated task allocation and achievement. In *International Conference on Robotics and Automation* (ICRA), (vol. 2, pp. 1234–1239). doi:10.1109/ROBOT.1999.772530

Botelho, S. S. C., & Alami, R. (2000). Robots that cooperatively enhance their plans. In *5th International Symposium on Distributed Autonomous Robotic Systems* (DARS).

Buckley, S. (1989) Fast motion planning for multiple moving robots. In *IEEE International Conference on Robotics and Automation* (ICRA), (pp. 322–326). doi:10.1109/ROBOT.1989.100008

Caloud, P., Choi, W., Latombe, J.-C., Pape, C. L., & Yim, M. (1990). Indoor automation with many mobile robots. In *International Workshop on Intelligent Robotics and Systems* (IROS).

Canny, J. F. (1991). Computing roadmaps of general semi-algebraic sets. *Applied Algebra, Algebraic Algorithms and Error–Correcting Codes. Lecture Notes in Computer Science*, *539*, 94–107. doi:10.1007/3-540-54522-0_99

Cap, M., Novak, P., Kleiner, A., Selecky, M., & Pechoucek, M. (2015). *Prioritized Planning Algorithms for Trajectory Coordination of Multiple Mobile Robots. IEEE Transactions on Automation Science and Engineering*.

Casbeer, D. W., & Holsapple, R. W. (2011). Column generation for a UAV assignment problem with precedence constraints. *International Journal of Robust and Nonlinear Control*, *21*(12), 1421–1433. doi:10.1002/rnc.1722

Chaimowicz, L., Sugar, T., Kumar, V., & Campos, M. (2001). An architecture for tightly couple multi-robot cooperation. In *IEEE International Conference on Robotics and Automation* (ICRA), (pp. 2992–2997).

Chen, J., & Sun, D. (2012). Coalition-based approach to task allocation of multiple robots with resource constraints. *IEEE Transactions on Automation Science and Engineering*, *9*(3), 516–528. doi:10.1109/TASE.2012.2201470

Chiddarwar, S. S., & Babu, N. R. (2011). Conflict Free Coordinated Path Planning for Multiple Robots Using a Dynamic Path Modification Sequence. *Robotics and Autonomous Systems*, *59*(7–8), 508–518. doi:10.1016/j.robot.2011.03.006

Clark, C., Rock, S., & Latombe, J.-C. (2003). Motion planning for multiple robot systems using dynamic networks. In *IEEE International Conference on Robotics and Automation* (ICRA), (pp. 4222–4227).

Cui, R., Gao, B., & Guo, J. (2012). Pareto-optimal coordination of multiple robots with safety guarantees. *Autonomous Robots*, *32*(3), 189–205. doi:10.1007/s10514-011-9265-9

Di Paola, D., Naso, D., Milella, A., Cicirelli, G., & Distante, A. (2010). Multi-sensor surveillance of indoor environments by an autonomous mobile robot. *International Journal of Intelligent Systems Technologies and Applications*, *8*(1–4), 18–35. doi:10.1504/IJISTA.2010.030187

Di Paola, D., Naso, D., Turchiano, B., Cicirelli, G., & Distante, A. (2009). Matrix-based discrete event control for surveillance mobile robotics. *Journal of Intelligent & Robotic Systems*, *56*(5), 513–541. doi:10.1007/s10846-009-9326-x

Dias, M. B. (2004). *TraderBots: A New Paradigm for Robust and Efficient Multirobot Coordination in Dynamic Environments*. (PhD thesis). Robotics Institute, Carnegie Mellon University.

Erdmann, M., & Lozano-Perez, T. (1986). On multiple moving objects. In *IEEE International Conference on Robotics and Automation* (ICRA), (pp. 1419–1424).

Erdmann, M., & Lozano-Perez, T. (1987). On multiple moving objects. *Algorithmica*, *2*(1-4), 477–521. doi:10.1007/BF01840371

Ferrati, M., & Pallottino, L. (2013). A time expanded network based algorithm for safe and efficient distributed multi-agent coordination. In *IEEE Conference on Decision and Control*, (pp. 2805–2810). doi:10.1109/CDC.2013.6760308

Ferrera, E., Castaño, A. R., Capitán, J., Marrón, P. J., & Ollero, A. (2014). Multi-robot Operation System with Conflict Resolution. In *ROBOT2013: First Iberian Robotics Conference Advances in Intelligent Systems and Computing*, (vol. 252, pp. 407–419).

Fink, J., Hsieh, M. A., & Kumar, V. (2008). Multi-Robot Manipulation via Caging in Environments with Obstacles. In *IEEE International Conference on Robotics and Automation* (ICRA), (pp. 1471–1476). doi:10.1109/ROBOT.2008.4543409

Gayle, R., Sud, A., Lin, M. C., & Manocha, D. (2007). Reactive deformation roadmaps: motion planning of multiple robots in dynamic environments. In *International Conference on Intelligent Robots and Systems* (IROS), (pp. 3777–3783). doi:10.1109/IROS.2007.4399287

Ge, S. S., & Cui, Y. J. (1997). Dynamic motion planning for mobile robots using potential field method. *Autonomous Robots*, *13*(3), 207–222. doi:10.1023/A:1020564024509

Gerkey, B. P., & Mataric, M. J. (2002). Sold! Auction methods for multi-robot control. *IEEE Transactions on Robotics and Automation. Special Issue on Multi-Robot Systems*, *18*(5), 758–768.

Giordano, V., Zhang, J. B., Naso, D., & Lewis, F. L. (2008). Integrated supervisory and operational control of a warehouse with a matrix-based approach. *IEEE Transactions on Automation Science and Engineering*, *5*(1), 53–70. doi:10.1109/TASE.2007.891472

Golden, B., Raghavan, S., & Wasil, E. (2008). *The Vehicle Routing Problem: Latest Advances and New Challenges* (Vol. 43). Springer. doi:10.1007/978-0-387-77778-8

Golfarelli, M., Maio, D., & Rizzi, S. (1997). *A task-swap negotiation protocol based on the contract net paradigm*. Technical Report 005-97, Research Center for Informatics and Telecommunication Systems (CSITE), University of Bologna.

Guerrero, J., & Oliver, G. (2012). Multi-robot coalition formation in real-time scenarios. *Robotics and Autonomous Systems*, *60*(10), 1295–1307. doi:10.1016/j.robot.2012.06.004

Guo, Y., & Parker, E. (2002). A Distributed and Optimal Motion Planning Approach for Multiple Mobile Robots. In *IEEE International Conference on Robotics and Automation* (ICRA), (pp. 2612–2619).

Hillier, F. S., & Lieberman, G. J. (2009). *Introduction to Operations Research* (9th ed.). McGraw-Hill.

Hirata, Y., Kume, Y., Wang, Z., & Kosuge, K. (2003). Decentralized control of multiple mobile manipulators based on virtual 3-D caster motion for handling an object in cooperation with a human. In *IEEE International Conference on Robotics and Automation* (ICRA), (vol. 1, pp. 938–943). doi:10.1109/ROBOT.2003.1241713

Isto, P., & Saha, M. (2006). A slicing connection strategy for constructing PRMs in high-dimensional cspaces. In *International Conference on Robotics and Automation* (ICRA), (pp. 1249–1254). doi:10.1109/ROBOT.2006.1641880

Kaidi, R., Lazaar, M., & Ettaouil, M. (2014). Neural Network Apply to predict aircraft trajectory for conflict resolution. In *International Conference on Intelligent Systems: Theories and Applications* (SITA). doi:10.1109/SITA.2014.6847309

Kala, R., Shukla, A., & Tiwari, R. (2010). Dynamic Environment Robot Path Planning Using Hierarchical Evolutionary Algorithms. *Cybernetics and Systems: An International Journal*, *41*(6), 435–454. doi:10.1080/01969722.2010.500800

Kavraki, L. E., Svestka, P., Latombe, J. C., & Overmars, M. (1996). Probabilistic roadmaps for path planning in high dimensional configuration spaces. *IEEE Transactions on Robotics and Automation*, *12*(4), 566–580. doi:10.1109/70.508439

Kawauchi, Y., Inaba, M., & Fukuda, T. (1993). A Principle of Distributed Decision Making of Cellular Robotic System (CEBOT). In *International Conference on Robotics and Automation* (ICRA), (vol. 3, pp. 833–838). doi:10.1109/ROBOT.1993.292248

Kiener, J., & von Stryk, O. (2010). Towards cooperation of heterogeneous, autonomous robots: A case study of humanoid and wheeled robots. *Robotics and Autonomous Systems*, *58*(7), 21–929. doi:10.1016/j.robot.2010.03.013

Kilmann, R. H., & Thomas, K. W. (1977). Developing a Forced-Choice Measure of Conflict-Handling Behavior: The "Mode" Instrument. *Educational and Psychological Measurement*, *37*(2), 309–325. doi:10.1177/001316447703700204

Kirby, R., Broz, F., Forlizzi, J., Michalowski, M. P., Mundell, A., Rosenthal, … Wang, J. (2005). Designing Robots for Long-Term Social Interaction. In *IEEE/RSJ International Conference on Intelligent Robots and Systems* (IROS), (pp. 2199–2204).

Kornhauser, D., Miller, G., & Spirakis, P. (1984). Coordinating pebble motion on graphs, the diameter of permutation groups, and applications. In *Foundations of Computer Science (FOCS)* (pp. 241–250). Los Alamitos, CA: IEEE Computer Society Press. doi:10.1109/SFCS.1984.715921

Kosuge, K., & Oosumi, T. (1996). Decentralized Control of Multiple Robots Handling an Object. In: *International Conference on Intelligent Robots and Systems* (IROS), (pp. 318–323). doi:10.1109/IROS.1996.570694

Krieger, M. J. B., & Billeter, J. B. (2000). The call of duty: Self-organised task allocation in a population of up to twelve mobile robots. *Robotics and Autonomous Systems*, *30*(1–2), 65–84. doi:10.1016/S0921-8890(99)00065-2

Krontiris, A., & Bekris, K. E. (2011). Using Minimal Communication to Improve Decentralized Conflict Resolution for Non-holonomic Vehicles. In *IEEE/RSJ International Conference on Intelligent Robots and Systems*, (pp. 3235–3240).

Kubo, R., & Ohnishi, K. (2006). An Extraction Method of Environmental Surface Profile Using Planar End-Effectors. In *IEEE International Workshop on Advanced Motion Control*, (pp. 368–373). doi:10.1109/AMC.2006.1631686

Kubo, R., & Ohnishi, K. (2006b). Hybrid Control for Multiple Robots in Grasping and Manipulation. In *IEEE International Power Electronics and Motion Control Conference*, (pp. 367–372). doi:10.1109/EPEPEMC.2006.283187

Kuffner, J. J., & Lavalle, S. M. (2000). RRT-Connect: An efficient approach to single-query path planning. In *International Conference on Robotics and Automation* (ICRA), (pp. 995–1001). doi:10.1109/ROBOT.2000.844730

Kume, Y., Hirata, Y., Wang, Z., & Kosuge, K. (2002). Decentralized control of multiple mobile manipulators handling a single object in coordination. In *IEEE/RSJ International Conference on Intelligent Robots and Systems* (IROS), (vol. 3, pp. 2758–2763). doi:10.1109/IRDS.2002.1041687

La Valle, S. M. (2006). *Planning Algorithms*. Cambridge, UK: Cambridge University Press. doi:10.1017/CBO9780511546877

LaValle, S. M., & Hutchinson, S. A. (1998). Optimal Motion Planning for Multiple Robots Having Independent Goals. *IEEE Transactions on Robotics and Automation*, *14*(6), 912–925. doi:10.1109/70.736775

Leroy, S., Laumond, J. P., & Simeon, T. (1999). Multiple path coordination for mobile robots: A geometric algorithm. In *International Joint Conference on Artificial Intelligence* (IJCAI), (pp. 1118–1123).

Li, Y., Gupta, K., & Payandeh, S. (2005). Motion planning of multiple agents in virtual environments using coordination graphs. In *IEEE International Conference on Robotics and Automation* (ICRA), (pp. 378–383).

Liu, L., & Shell, D. A. (2011). Assessing optimal assignment under uncertainty: An interval-based algorithm. *The International Journal of Robotics Research*, *30*(7), 936–953. doi:10.1177/0278364911404579

Liu, L., & Shell, D. A. (2012). Large-scale multi-robot task allocation via dynamic partitioning and distribution. *Autonomous Robots*, *33*(3), 291–307. doi:10.1007/s10514-012-9303-2

Lumelsky, V. J., & Harinarayan, K. R. (1997). Decentralized motion planning for multiple mobile robots: The cocktail party model. *Journal of Autonomous Robots*, *4*(1), 121–135. doi:10.1023/A:1008815304810

Mas, I., & Kitts, C. A. (2012). Objcct manipulation using cooperative mobile multi-robot systems. In *World Congress on Engineering and Computer Science*, (vol. 1, pp. 324–329).

Mataric, M. J., Nilsson, M., & Simsarin, K. T. (1995). Cooperative multi-robot box-pushing. In *IEEE/RSJ International Conference on Intelligent Robots and Systems* (IROS), (vol. 3, pp. 556–561).

Mellinger, D., Shomin, M., Michael, N., & Kumar, V. (2013) Cooperative Grasping and Transport Using Multiple Quadrotors. In *International Symposium on Distributed Autonomous Robotic Systems* (DARS), (pp. 545–558). doi:10.1007/978-3-642-32723-0_39

Michael, N., Zavlanos, M. M., Kumar, V., & Pappas, G. J. (2008). Distributed multi-robot task assignment and formation control. In *International Conference on Robotics and Automation* (ICRA), (pp. 128–133). doi:10.1109/ROBOT.2008.4543197

Michelman, P. (1998). Precision Object Manipulation with a Multifingered Robot Hand. *IEEE Transactions on Robotics and Automation*, *14*(1), 105–113. doi:10.1109/70.660851

Montemayor, G., & Wen, J. T. (2005). Decentralized Collaborative Load Transport by Multiple Robots. In *IEEE International Conference on Robotics and Automation* (ICRA), (pp. 372–377). doi:10.1109/ROBOT.2005.1570147

Munawar, K., & Uchiyama, M. (1999). Experimental verification of distributed event-based control of multiple unifunctional manipulators. In *IEEE International Conference on Robotics and Automation* (ICRA), (pp. 1213–1218). doi:10.1109/ROBOT.1999.772527

Mutlu, B. (2011). Designing embodied cues for dialog with robots. *AI Magazine*, *32*(4), 17–30.

Naso, D., Surico, M., & Turchiano, B. (2007). Reactive scheduling of a distributed network for the supply of perishable products. *IEEE Transactions on Automation Science and Engineering*, *4*(3), 407–423. doi:10.1109/TASE.2006.884672

Naso, D., & Turchiano, B. (2005). Multicriteria meta-heuristics for AGV dispatching control based on computational intelligence. *IEEE Transactions on Systems, Man, and Cybernetics. Part B, Cybernetics*, *35*(2), 208–226. doi:10.1109/TSMCB.2004.842249 PMID:15828651

Neumann, M. A., Chin, M. H., & Kitts, C. A. (2014). Object Manipulation through Explicit Force Control Using Cooperative Mobile Multi-Robot Systems. In *World Congress on Engineering and Computer Science* (WCECS), (vol. 1, pp. 364–369).

O'Donnell, P. A., & Lozano-Perez, T. (1989). Deadlock-free and collision-free coordination of two robot manipulators. In *IEEE International Conference on Robotics and Automation* (ICRA), (pp. 484–489).

Peasgood, M., Clark, C., & McPhee, J. (2008). A Complete and scalable strategy for coordinating multiple robots within roadmaps. *IEEE Transactions on Robotics*, *24*(2), 283–292. doi:10.1109/TRO.2008.918056

Peng, J., & Akella, S. (2005). Coordinating multiple robots with kinodynamic constraints along specified paths. *The International Journal of Robotics Research*, *24*(4), 295–310. doi:10.1177/0278364905051974

Pereira, G. A. S., Campos, M. F. M., & Kumar, V. (2004). Decentralized Algorithms for Multi-Robot Manipulation via Caging. *The International Journal of Robotics Research*, *23*(7–8), 783–795. doi:10.1177/0278364904045477

Pohl, A. J., & Lamont, G. B. (2008). Multi-objective UAV mission planning using evolutionary computation. In *Winter Simulation Conference*, (pp. 1268–1279). doi:10.1109/WSC.2008.4736199

Purwin, O., D'Andrea, R., & Lee, J. W. (2008). Theory and implementation of path planning by negotiation for decentralized agents. *Robotics and Autonomous Systems*, *56*(5), 422–436. doi:10.1016/j.robot.2007.09.020

Ryan, M. R. K. (2007). Graph decomposition for efficient multi-robot path planning. In *International Joint Conference on Artificial Intelligence* (IJCAI), (pp. 2003–2008).

Saha, M., & Isto, P. (2006). Multi-robot motion planning by incremental coordination. In *IEEE/RSJ International Conference on Intelligent Robots and Systems* (IROS), (pp. 5960–5963).

Sanchez, G., & Latombe, J. C. (2002). Using a PRM planner to compare centralized and decoupled planning for multi-robot systems. In *International Conference on Robotics and Automation* (ICRA), (Vol. 2, pp. 2112–2119). doi:10.1109/ROBOT.2002.1014852

Savelsbergh, M. W. P., & Sol, M. (1995). The general pickup and delivery problem. *Transportation Science*, *29*(1), 17–29. doi:10.1287/trsc.29.1.17

Siméon, T., Leroy, S., & Laumond, J.-P. (2002). Path coordination for multiple mobile robots: A resolution complete algorithm. *IEEE Transactions on Robotics and Automation*, *18*(1), 42–49. doi:10.1109/70.988973

Simmons, R., Apfelbaum, D., Burgard, W., Fox, D., Thrun, S., & Younes, H. (2000). Coordination for multi-robot exploration and mapping. In *National Conference on Artificial Intelligence*.

Simmons, R., Apfelbaum, D., Fox, D., Goldman, R. P., Haigh, K. Z., Musliner, D. J., … Thrun, S. (2000b). Coordinated deployment of multiple heterogeneous robots. In *International Conference on Intelligent Robotics and Systems* (IROS), (*vol. 3*, pp. 2254–2260).

Smith, S. L., & Bullo, F. (2009). Monotonic target assignment for robotic networks. *IEEE Transactions on Automatic Control*, *54*(9), 2042–2057. doi:10.1109/TAC.2009.2026926

Solovey, K., & Halperin, D. (2014). k-color multi-robot motion planning. *The International Journal of Robotics Research*, *33*(1), 82–97. doi:10.1177/0278364913506268

Song, P., & Kumar, V. (2002). A potential field based approach to multi-robot manipulation. In *IEEE International Conference on Robotics and Automation* (ICRA), (vol. 2, pp. 1217–1222). doi:10.1109/ROBOT.2002.1014709

Sugar, T., Desai, J., Ostrowski, J., & Kumar, V. (2001). Coordination of multiple mobile manipulators. In *IEEE International Conference on Robotics and Automation* (ICRA), (pp. 3284–3289).

Svestka, P., & Overmars, M. H. (1998). Coordinated path planning for multiple robots. *Robotics and Autonomous Systems*, *23*(3), 125–152. doi:10.1016/S0921-8890(97)00033-X

Tang, Y., Cai, K., McBurney, P., Sklar, E., & Parsons, S. (2011). Using argumentation to reason about trust and belief. *Journal of Logic and Computation, 22*(5), 979–1018.

Toth, P., & Vigo, D. (2001). *The Vehicle Routing Problem*. Philadelphia, PA: Society for Industrial and Applied Mathematics.

van den Berg, J., & Overmars, M. (2005). Prioritized motion planning for multiple robots. In *International Conference on Intelligent Robots and Systems* (IROS), (pp. 430–435).

van den Berg, J., Snoeyink, J., Lin, M., & Manocha, D. (2009). Centralized Path Planning for Multiple Robots: Optimal Decoupling into Sequential Plans. In Robotics: Science and Systems (RSS).

Velagapudi, P., Sycara, K. P., & Scerri, P. (2010). Decentralized prioritized planning in large multirobot teams. In *International Conference on Intelligent Robots and Systems* (IROS), (pp. 4603–4609). doi:10.1109/IROS.2010.5649438

Wagner, G., Kang, M., & Choset, H. (2012). Probabilistic path planning for multiple robots with subdimensional expansion. In *International Conference on Robotics and Automation* (ICRA), (pp. 2886–2892). doi:10.1109/ICRA.2012.6225297

Wang, Z., Nakano, E., & Matsukawa, T. (1994). Cooperating Multiple Behavior-Based Robots for Object Manipulation. In *International Conference on Intelligent Robots and Systems* (IROS), (vol. 3, pp. 1524–1531). doi:10.1007/978-4-431-68275-2_33

Wen, J., & Kreutz-Delgado, K. (1992). Motion and force control of multiple robotic manipulators. *Automatica, 28*(4), 729–743. doi:10.1016/0005-1098(92)90033-C

Yoshikawa, T., & Zheng, X. (1990). Coordinated Dynamic Hybrid Position/Force Control for Multiple robot Manipulators Handling One Constrained Object. In *IEEE International Conference on Robotics and Automation* (ICRA), (vol. 2, pp. 1178–1183). doi:10.1109/ROBOT.1990.126156

Yu, W., Peng, J., Zhang, X., & Lin, K.-c. (2014). A Cooperative Path Planning Algorithm for a Multiple Mobile Robot System in a Dynamic Environment. *International Journal of Advanced Robotic Systems, 11*, 136.

Zlot, R., & Stentz, A. (2005). Complex Task Allocation for Multiple Robots. In *International Conference on Robotics and Automation* (ICRA), (pp. 1515–1522).

Zlot, R., Stentz, A., Dias, M. B., & Thayer, S. (2002). Multi-robot exploration controlled by a market economy. In *International Conference on Robotics and Automation* (ICRA), (pp. 3016–3023). doi:10.1109/ROBOT.2002.1013690

Zribi, M., & Ahmed, S. (1991). Predictive adaptive control of multiple robots in cooperation motion. In *IEEE Conference on Decision and Control*, (pp. 2416–2421). doi:10.1109/CDC.1991.261787

KEY TERMS AND DEFINITIONS

Conflict: When different systems or tasks compete for the same resource.

Cooperative Robotics: A multiple-robot system that work together to increase the total utility of the whole system.

Degree-Of-Freedom (DoF): Defines modes in which a system can move (possible positions and orientations of each robot joint).

Human-Robot Collaboration: When a robot is used as a human assistant to successfully achieve a specific task.

Multi-Robot Cooperation: A team of robots working together to achieve a common goal.

Multi-Tasking Assignation: How to determine what tasks will be simultaneously performed in a system.

Negotiation: Discussion between the tasks or systems involved in a conflict in search for an agreement.

Chapter 16
Crowdsourcing Dispute Resolution:
Survey and Challenges

Nuno Luz
Polytechnic of Porto, Portugal

Marta Poblet
RMIT University, Australia

Nuno Silva
Polytechnic of Porto, Portugal

ABSTRACT

After almost one decade of active research into human computation and crowdsourcing, several approaches and business models based on crowdsourcing have emerged, managing and distributing work to the crowd. Dispute resolution approaches may incorporate crowdsourcing as a step to retrieve relevant data. The reverse relationship has also become a tendency, where crowdsourcing approaches are close to incorporate dispute resolution techniques to perform quality control and data aggregation or filtering. This chapter provides an introduction to crowdsourcing and its relationship with dispute resolution. A discussion regarding the apparent symbiotic relationship between these two research domains is also presented, along with an overview of several approaches and use cases of particular interest.

INTRODUCTION

As suggested by Levine and Kurzban (2006), humans have developed sophisticated mechanisms to extract benefits from the social world, which are expected to be the product of several adaptations designed to generate mutual benefits to the actors involved.

The Web has opened unprecedented venues for studies on human cooperation and behavior, since much of the information that flows through the Internet contains or represents, either explicitly or implicitly, social interactions. These interactions manifest themselves through technologies like e-mail, mailing list

DOI: 10.4018/978-1-5225-0245-6.ch016

archives, hyperlink structure of homepages, co-authorship of documents, chat sessions and many others (Erétéo, Gandon, Corby, & Buffa, 2009). Also, the Web 2.0 came to introduce social features in most web applications and tools, giving birth to multiple explicit social networks for functional or entertainment purposes (Yun & Kim, 2009).

Online social networks seem to be triggering yet another adaptation to the way humans cooperate, bringing forth new tools for interaction that help to either maintain existent social relationships or establish new ones. They also leverage the emergence of collective intelligence (Segaran, 2007) from the combined behavior, ideas and preferences of thousands or even millions of people (Porter, 2008), attracting even more participants on a world-wide scale.

Over the last decades, researchers have been trying to build machines that emulate the creative and cognitive capabilities of humans. This has led to the development of multiple branches of artificial intelligence, such as multi-agent systems, reasoning and negotiation. Back in the 1960s, however, Licklider (1960) believed that machines and computers were just part of a scale which weights humans on one side, and computers on the other. His vision was that computers and humans should work together performing complementary roles (Licklider, 1960; Quinn & Bederson, 2011).

It was only recently that relevant research emerged and brought humans into computer affairs. The early factors contributing to this retake on Lickliders' vision are the social Web and the harnessing of collective intelligence (Gruber, 2008). These new developments have proved that humans can successfully complement computers with their abilities, and that they can act as guided computational units. Some examples include the use of CAPTCHAs to digitize texts and micro-task crowdsourcing (e.g. Mechanical Turk).

As a part of collective intelligence, human computation re-emerged as a relevant research field. Shortly after, the term crowdsourcing was coined by Jeff Howe, leading to yet another field of business and research highly connected to human computation (Howe, 2006; Poblet, García-Cuesta, & Casanovas, 2014; Quinn & Bederson, 2011; Von Ahn, 2009). One decade after, several approaches and business models based on crowdsourcing have emerged, managing and distributing work to the crowd (Doan, Ramakrishnan, & Halevy, 2011; Quinn & Bederson, 2011; Yuen, King, & Leung, 2011).

Dispute resolution approaches may incorporate crowdsourcing as a step to retrieve relevant data. The reverse relationship has also become a tendency, where crowdsourcing approaches are close to incorporate dispute resolution techniques to perform quality control and data aggregation or filtering.

Constitution-making (Landemore, 2014; Luz, Poblet, Silva, & Novais, 2015) is an application scenario where crowdsourcing is an important step in retrieving relevant data, but also a scenario where dispute resolution techniques can be incorporated into the crowdsourcing process in order to (semi-)automatically reach an adequate constitution document.

This chapter provides an introduction to crowdsourcing and its relationship with dispute resolution. A discussion regarding the apparent symbiotic relationship between these two research domains is also presented, along with an overview of both crowdsourcing and dispute resolution approaches and use cases that are of particular interest. Finally, a systematization of the discussed approaches that captures the main challenges and directions for mixed dispute resolution and crowdsourcing approaches is given.

APPLICATIONS OF CROWDSOURCING

Humans are innately social and the intrinsic aspects of human cooperation have been the subject of great research efforts (Porter, 2008). We, humans, not only tend to form a clustered structure of relationships (social circle), but also extract individual benefits from them (Levine & Kurzban, 2006). Social circles have a great impact on our lives, influencing our ideas and behaviour (Konstas, Stathopoulos, & Jose, 2009). Not so long ago, the information that a person had access to was mostly the information flowing inside each ones' social circle. Nowadays, this social circle also acts as a filter for all the vast amounts of information and choices delivered every day (Ma, Zhou, Liu, Lyu, & King, 2011) by multiple means (e.g. social media, internet).

The emergence of the social Web has brought new powerful Web applications that connect people on a global scale, and allow them to reap the benefits of social life from online virtual environments in a global scale. Along with their huge popularity, online social networks allow the retrieval of significant amounts of important social data, which can be used to promote social benefits (Levine & Kurzban, 2006).

One of the most straightforward benefits we extract from society comes from asking our friends for an opinion or advice (Ma et al., 2011). It is possible to apply a similar mechanism to online social networks by automatically filtering data, and providing the user with relevant and personalized results according to the opinions coming from her/his online social circle. The difference is that, unlike humans alone, the introduction of machines allows that procedure to be performed for millions of items, covering a wide social circle.

Online social networks blur geographical barriers, thus promoting the combination of behaviours and ideas on a global scale (Porter, 2008). This combination is often referred to as collective intelligence (Luo, Xia, Yoshida, & Wang, 2009).

An interesting example of the importance of collective intelligence is what Porter (2008) regards as the Amazon Effect. To explain the Amazon Effect, he describes a usability study where people were asked to buy a product at a certain online store. A lot of people wanted to go to Amazon first, and when they were asked why, they just answered that they would like to do some research on the product, even if they were not buying it on Amazon.

(Brabham, 2008a) follows Surowieckis' (2004) view on the wisdom of crowds (often referred in the context of the Web as collective intelligence), as emerging from aggregating individual solutions instead of averaging them. This view is particularly relevant in the context of problem solving, where aggregating individual solutions often leads to a better solution than any of the best originally proposed individual solutions. The average, however, is mediocrity, and will never be better than the best proposed solution. Following this view, Brabham argues that crowdsourcing is a distributed model achieved through the Web that is "capable of aggregating talent, leveraging ingenuity while reducing costs and time formerly needed to solve problems".

Crowdsourcing, and in particular micro-task crowdsourcing, can be considered to be a form of human computation that harnesses collective intelligence.

Definitions

The term crowdsourcing was coined by Howe in the context of a paradigm shift in business models (Howe 2006, 2008). The shift originated from companies that started to provide outsourcing services relying on anonymous communities or crowds throughout the Web (e.g. iStockPhoto, InnoCentive and Amazon's Mechanical Turk). By 2006, these communities were growing into incredible valuable work forces capable of performing several specific tasks in exchange for small monetary rewards.

Since then, several different definitions have been given to the term crowdsourcing. According to Howe (2008), "crowdsourcing is the act of taking a task traditionally performed by a designated agent (such as an employee or a contractor) and outsourcing it by making an open call to an undefined but large group of people". Doan *et al.* (2011) define crowdsourcing as a system that "enlists a crowd of humans to help solve a problem defined by the system owners, and if in doing so, it addresses" the challenges of recruiting and retaining users, defining which contributions can be made by users, combining these contributions and evaluating user performance.

Quinn and Bederson (2011) not only provide a definition for crowdsourcing, but also compare it to terms such as human computation, social computing and collective intelligence. They aggregate several definitions found in the literature and state that crowdsourcing is a form of collective intelligence that overlaps human computation.

The term human computation dates back to the early years of artificial intelligence, in the 1960s, where it was envisioned that computers and humans should work together performing complementary roles (Licklider, 1960; Quinn & Bederson, 2011). Still, the vision of human-computer collaboration only started to be properly explored after 2005, the year Von Ahn published his doctoral thesis entitled Human Computation (Von Ahn, 2009). Von Ahn proposes the use of human algorithm games to harness the distributed processing power of humans to perform specific tasks. In accordance, human computation can be defined as a computational process that involves humans and their cooperation in order to solve problems that computers cannot yet solve (Quinn & Bederson, 2011). This definition is complemented by stating that "human computation does not encompass online discussions or creative projects where the initiative and flow of activity are directed primarily by the participants' inspiration, as opposed to a predetermined plan designed to solve a computational problem".

Quinn and Bederson (2011) argue that while human computation requires humans to act as managed units that merely perform a computation, crowdsourcing requires several humans to cooperate in a process by performing a computation or a creative task that is not always managed by computers (e.g. Wikipedia).

Crowds have an important role in human computation. Besides providing good amounts of computational power, applicable in tasks that machines can barely solve with efficiency and efficacy, they can also be used for redundancy.

Typical Domains of Application

Several experiments in different domains have shown that crowdsourcing and human computation have great potential for solving large scale problems that are often difficult for computers to solve automatically, on their own (Von Ahn, 2009). These problems usually require a degree of creativity or just common sense plus some background knowledge (Chklovski, 2003; Singh et al., 2002). The interpretation and recognition of images and natural language are two examples of such problems.

One of the applications of crowdsourcing lies in harnessing geographical information. Recently, the production of geo-referenced data, maps, and atlases has moved from mapping agencies and corporations to non-expert users (Goodchild & Glennon, 2010). Some of the services that allow this include Flickr, Google's MyMaps, OpenStreetMap, and Wikimapia. Following this trend, Goodchild and Glennon (2010) discuss the applications of crowdsourcing to harnessing geographical information for disaster response. They argue about the importance of quality in harnessing geographical information and present an analysis of non-expert user generated geographical information from occurrences of wildfires in Santa Barbara, California. Further research on volunteered geographic information (VGI) has proved that there is great potential for quickly generating and spreading disaster-related information through a crowdsourcing system (Elwood, Goodchild, & Sui, 2013; Sui & Goodchild, 2011; Sui, Goodchild, & Elwood, 2013).

The potential and importance of crowdsourcing in harnessing geographical information has also been successfully noted and put into practice by Safecast, a project that emerged one week after the earthquake that led to the Fukushima Japanese nuclear accident. Safecast is a "global sensor network for collecting and sharing radiation measurements to empower people with data about their environments". In order to collect data, different types of radiation sensors are distributed through volunteers that later use them to collect geo-referenced radiation measurements during their travels. The results are collected and published by Safecast, which provides free access to the data.

Several crowdsourcing-based businesses have emerged since the advent of crowdsourcing platforms. While some maintain their own community of workers (e.g. MicroWorkers, ShortTask), others interact with one or more crowdsourcing platforms (e.g. CrowdFlower) offering their services in designing and managing projects and tasks, for obtaining reliable results. Brabham (2008a) discusses several successful applications of crowdsourcing as business models, including Threadless, InnoCentive and iStockPhoto. Threadless crowdsources the design process of t-shirts by promoting online competition. InnoCentive crowdsources the research and development of scientific problems as challenges. The last, iStockPhoto sells photographs, animation and video clips produced by its crowd of artists. Interestingly, surveys of the iStockPhoto crowd show that the main motivations behind their time and effort are not only monetary but also enjoyment and the development of individual skills (Brabham, 2008b).

In 2010, Dawson published a diagram distinguishing up to 13 categories of crowdsourcing operating in different domains (business ideas, 3D and graphic design, data analysis, research, tagging, translation, writing and editing, reviewing and software development) (Dawson & Bynghall, 2015). Categories included: crowdsourcing aggregators (e.g. CrowdFlower), content markets (e.g. iStockPhoto), prediction markets (e.g. Crowdcast), question answering (e.g. Yahoo! Answers), innovation prizes (e.g. XPrize), service marketplaces (e.g. Freelancer), distributed innovation (e.g. InnoCentive), crowdfunding (e.g. KickStarter), competition platforms (e.g. 99 Designs), content-rating (e.g. Delicious), idea platforms (e.g. IdeaScale), data sharing (e.g. Dead Cellzones), reference content (e.g. Wikipedia), cycle sharing (e.g. SETI@Home) and micro-tasks (e.g. Mechanical Turk and ShortTask.

From all the crowdsourcing systems and common types of crowdsourced tasks enumerated by Dawson, just a few qualify as human computation systems. This is the case of crowdsourcing systems under the micro-tasks category. However, even if crowdsourcing systems such as Mechanical Turk and ShortTask provide a platform for building any type of tasks, some types of tasks have become widely popular for being particularly appropriate to micro-task representation, and for being easily accepted by workers. These specific types of tasks are often (as presented in CloudCrowd) writing, editing, categorization, searching, data entry and translation tasks.

In this sense, most crowdsourcing micro-task systems feature the creation of task templates that can be used to request multiple similar tasks. These systems often provide a predefined set of templates for commonly requested types of tasks. Some of the predefined templates provided by Mechanical Turk and ShortTask include:

- Categorization, classification;
- Data verification (e.g. provide correct spelling);
- Data extraction (e.g. finding a website address);
- Moderation and tagging of multimedia content (e.g. tagging images or videos with adult content);
- Transcription from multimedia content (e.g. audio, video and images);
- Sentiment analysis and surveys;
- Search relevance (e.g. evaluate relevance of search results).

Around these crowdsourcing systems that manage their own community of workers, crowdsourcing-oriented businesses have started to emerge. For instance, MobileWorks, a crowdsourcing-oriented company, groups its services into categories such as digitalization of documents, categorization and classification, researching, and harnessing feedback (e.g. through surveys).

Some of these application domains can be easily modelled and managed with single and independent crowdsourced micro-tasks. Recently, however, a special interest in employing crowdsourcing towards solving more complex tasks has emerged (Ahmad, Battle, Malkani, & Kamvar, 2011; Kittur, Smus, Khamkar, & Kraut, 2011; Kulkarni, Can, & Hartmann, 2011; Little, Chilton, Goldman, & Miller, 2010; Luz, Silva, Maio, & Novais, 2012; Sarasua, Simperl, & Noy, 2012). This interest has led to several approaches being built upon workflows of micro-tasks. The modelling of such workflows allows the crowdsourcing of a new kind of more complex processes, such as dispute resolution processes.

MICRO-TASK CROWDSOURCING AND DISPUTE RESOLUTION

Over the last years, online dispute resolution (ODR) has been applied in a variety of situations and domains such as law, conflict resolution and knowledge management. The process involves the use of Web technologies to facilitate the resolution of disputes between parties. Generally, the resolution occurs through an additional "fourth party" that assists in the assessment and identification of common interests and in establishing a consensual solution (Poblet, 2011; Poblet & Casanovas, 2007).

As stated by Rule and Nagarajan (2011), "the field of Online Dispute Resolution has always been driven by technology". It has continually evolved to exploit and absorb new emergent technologies and approaches that improve its efficacy (e.g. Web conferencing, shared whiteboards, mind mapping platforms, social networking). More recently, these approaches include mobile devices and crowdsourcing (Van Den Herik & Dimov, 2012).

In the particular case of micro-task crowdsourcing, there is a close relationship to dispute resolution due, not only to its data collection capabilities, but also to the existence of multiple results for the same micro-task (redundancy). This is often necessary to increase the quality of the micro-task results. Nevertheless, a process that tends to resemble a dispute resolution process is required to aggregate these data.

In this sense, a two way relationship between crowdsourcing and dispute resolution can be identified (where one exploits the other), which manifests in:

- The use of dispute resolution approaches to aggregate micro-task output data;
- The use of crowdsourcing to retrieve relevant information for the dispute resolution process;
- The use of crowdsourcing to model a dispute resolution process through workflows of micro-tasks.

While the first is a manifestation of crowdsourcing exploiting dispute resolution, the other two are manifestations of dispute resolution approaches exploiting crowdsourcing.

Data Aggregation and Quality Control as Dispute Resolution

Over the years, several researchers have dedicated their efforts to evaluating the quality of the results obtained through crowdsourcing micro-tasks (Brabham, 2008b; Goodchild & Glennon, 2010; Kittur, Chi, & Suh, 2008; Paolacci, Chandler, & Ipeirotis, 2010; Willett, Heer, & Agrawala, 2012).

Kittur et al. (2008) present an analysis of crowdsourcing user evaluations and surveys using Mechanical Turk. These user evaluations include "surveys, usability tests, rapid prototyping, cognitive walkthroughs, quantitative ratings, and performance measures". By performing two different experiments they concluded that although promising, special care is required when formulating user evaluation micro-tasks. In the first experiment, workers were asked to rate the quality of a Wikipedia article according to questions formulated from the Wikipedia article guidelines. Results showed that nearly 48.6% of the answers were invalid and 30.5% were given in less than one minute. In the second experiment, questions that guided the worker through the article evaluation process (e.g. how many references and images does the article have?) were added to the micro-task. This resulted in a significant reduction of invalid responses (now around 2.5%) and in an increase of the micro-task execution time.

Willett et al. (2012) discuss the quality of results in social data analysis tasks. This kind of task focuses on harnessing explanations and interpretations of data, thus requiring diverse justified analytical answers. The crowdsourcing process (Figure 1) starts after the selection of a set of charts by an analyst. An analysis micro-task is then created for crowdsourcing workers to provide explanations for each chart. The analysis is followed by a micro-task where workers assess the quality of the submitted explanations according to relevance, clarity and plausibility. The results of this task aid the analyst in filtering low quality explanations.

Implementing this workflow of micro-tasks, Willett et al. (2012) describe seven strategies to improve the quality of explanations, tackling issues like irrelevant, unclear and speculative explanations, inattention to chart details and lack of diversity. These strategies are: i) to use feature-oriented prompts, ii) to provide good examples, iii) to include reference gathering subtasks, iv) to add chart reading subtasks, v) to include annotation subtasks, vi) to use pre-annotated charts, and vii) to elicit explanations iteratively.

Figure 1. The crowdsourcing process of data analysis proposed by Willet et al. (2012)

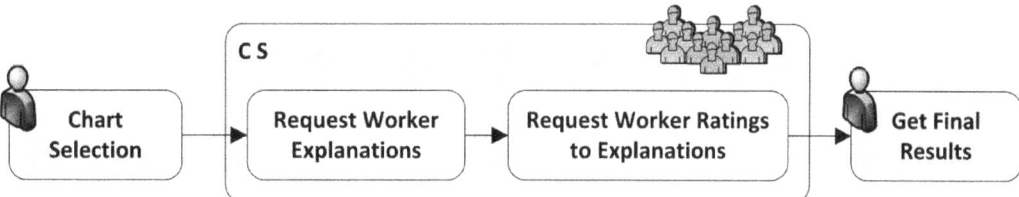

Experiments by Willett et al. show that around 63% of the given explanations are good, and that the described strategies significantly improve the quality of explanations.

Although quality evaluation and control is often a highly domain-specific process, Ipeirotis *et al.* propose an algorithm that evaluates the quality of workers for general tasks in Mechanical Turk and attributes a score to each worker (Ipeirotis, Provost, & Wang, 2010). Following the assumption that biased workers can still provide relevant (although often considered wrong) answers, the algorithm tries to distinguish between error and bias in worker answers.

These processes are similar to common dispute resolution processes. Furthermore, the involved data is highly relevant for situations of conflict and for assessing and establishing a consensual solution.

Dispute Resolution through Micro-Task Crowdsourcing

So far, crowdsourcing has been introduced into dispute resolution processes where "the crowd is a (generally large) group of people who participates in the dispute resolution process through an open call" (Van Den Herik & Dimov, 2012). This kind of crowdsourcing is referred to as Crowdsourced Online Dispute Resolution (CODR).

Van den Herik and Dimov (2012) provide an overview of the currently existing approaches to CODR, which include (i) online opinion polls, (ii) online mock trials and (iii) CODR procedures rendering decisions enforced by private authorities.

The concerns regarding CODR are mostly inherited from general crowdsourcing approaches. However, there is a special concern in the screening of users/workers and in the harnessing of unbiased results. Nevertheless, crowd incentives and quality control, in general, are still issues that must be tackled in every CODR approach.

More recently, workflow approaches to micro-task crowdsourcing have emerged (cf. bellow). These approaches are a typical manifestation of human-machine computation, where humans are guided to act as computational units and their efforts are integrated with the effort of machine algorithms and routines.

The WfMC (Workflow Management Coalition) defines a workflow as "the automation of a business process, in whole or part, during which documents, information or tasks are passed from one participant to another for action, according to a set of procedural rules" (Lawrence, 1997; Van Der Aalst, Ter Hofstede, & Weske, 2003). Similar definitions describe a workflow as "a collection of tasks organized to accomplish some business process" (Mentzas, Halaris, & Kavadias, 2001) and even as a process that "supports the coordination and collaboration of people that implement a process" (Georgakopoulos, Hornick, & Sheth, 1995). Dispute resolution processes can be modeled and represented as crowdsourced micro-task workflows.

So far, several approaches to the crowdsourcing of micro-task workflows have been proposed. These include Turkit, Turkomatic, CrowdForge, CrowdWeaver, Jabberwocky and CompFlow.

Turkit

TurKit is an API, built on top of Mechanical Turk, for running iterative tasks, which provides an environment for the creation of workflows that connect multiple dependent tasks (Little et al., 2010).

Using the crash and rerun model, it provides an abstraction over the specificities and synchronization issues of Mechanical Turk, allowing the developer to focus on imperative ordinary function calls.

The crash and rerun model follows the premise that it is cheap to rerun an entire program up to the point where it crashed, as long as it runs locally. For remote and costly operations (e.g. Human Intelligence Task requests) the results must be stored in a database so that they will be accessible in future reruns.

Turkomatic

Turkomatic follows a divide-and-conquer approach to plan work featuring micro-task workflows partially designed by workers. It works over Mechanical Turk and is defined as "a crowdsourcing interface that consults the crowd to design and execute workflows based on user requests" (Kulkarni et al., 2011).

Workers start by dividing the requested task into subtasks that will be solved by other workers. This process can be iterative, generating a tree of subtasks. The final results are later combined by workers into an adequate solution.

CrowdForge

CrowdForge is a general purpose framework for distributed processing that provides scaffolding for complex human computation tasks (Kittur et al., 2011). The approach features a set of task coordination strategies that allow multi-level and dynamic partitioning of tasks, the specification of task workflows, quality control tasks and aggregation of results.

Finding inspiration in Googles' Map Reduce framework, CrowdForge defines three types of subtasks: (i) partition tasks, (ii) map tasks and (iii) reduce tasks. Partition tasks divide a larger task into smaller subtasks. In map tasks, one or more workers process a task. Finally, in reduce tasks the processing results of multiple workers are merged into a single output.

The CrowdForge prototype presented in (Kittur et al., 2011) consists in a Web application allowing the design of complex tasks, along with a back-end server that interacts with Mechanical Turk. The system manages a workflow of Mechanical Turk HIT (Human Intelligence Task) templates, which can represent partition map or reduce tasks.

CrowdWeaver

TurKit, CrowdForge and Jabberwocky provide an environment for the design and execution of complex tasks through structured languages and non-visual representations. With the current trend on micro-task workflows, work on their management and visualization has started to emerge. Kittur et al. (2012) state that one of the major issues faced by employers working with crowds lies in the complexity of linking tasks and forming workflows. In this sense, they identify several challenges in visually managing crowdsourced workflows and present a system for visualization and management of complex tasks, entitled CrowdWeaver.

CrowdWeaver works on top of CrowdFlower and features the creation and monitoring of task workflows, the management and reuse of templates with human and machine tasks, the tracking and notification of crowd factors such as price and quality, and support for real-time experimentation. The interface provides a mental representation of the task workflow, which can be saved and re-used in further instantiations of the workflow.

Several machine tasks, which mainly manipulate input and output, are supported. These include divide, concatenate, pair, and permute. Additionally, custom machine tasks are allowed.

Jabberwocky

Similarly, Jabberwocky (Ahmad et al., 2011) also employs the MapReduce approach in a framework featuring a high-level abstraction task modelling language. It allows the modelling of complex tasks and workflows in which the advantages of multiple worker communities can be harnessed. These communities can be local or found in social networks and other crowdsourcing systems. In the case of local communities, workers can be identified during the crowdsourcing process. For social network communities, expertise data may be extracted from the social network API.

Jabberwocky is formed by three layers: the (i) base layer is called Dormouse, followed by the (ii) ManReduce layer, with the (iii) Dog layer on top. The Dormouse layer provides an abstraction over human (crowd workers) and machine computational units. Unlike other crowdsourcing frameworks such as Mechanical Turk and CrowdFlower, each computational unit registered under Dormouse can be uniquely identified during workflow executions. Besides featuring its own worker community, Dormouse can crowdsource tasks to external crowdsourcing platforms.

The ManReduce layer is a programming framework, written in Ruby, responsible for facilitating complex data processing tasks in Dormouse. It features map and reduce steps which can be computed by either humans or machines.

The top layer, called Dog, represents an abstraction scripting language for modelling tasks. Dog works over the low-level ManReduce framework and focuses on reusability, maintainability and ease-of-use.

CompFlow

CompFlow (Luz, 2015) is a method for the representation, construction, instantiation and execution of human-machine computation task workflows through ontologies. The representation captures the structure and semantics of the tasks and their domain, while remaining close to the human conceptual level. Workflows are built according to two dimensions: the domain dimension and the operational (task) dimension. This allows the input and the output of workflows to be described according to a domain ontology, completely independent from the workflow representation. The instantiation and execution of the represented workflow can be performed through the implemented workflow engine.

To aid the requester in the creation of new workflow representations (or workflow-definitions), a semi-automatic construction process based on domain ontologies is also proposed. The process has been implemented into a construction framework that allows the aided, iterative and visual construction of workflow-definitions.

Applications to Dispute Resolution

The approach proposed by Willett et al. (2012) is a typical example of CODR through micro-task workflows.

Van der Herik and Dimov (2012) identify four types of CODR, classified according to the dispute resolution approach, i.e. through litigation, arbitration, meditation and negotiation.

Forms of CODR that solve disputes through litigation (Marder, 2005) demand a workflow analysis and representation of the roles of traditional juries and civil procedures. Such approaches are yet to be fully exploited and require a broader community of participants than the one found in traditional litigation procedures.

The process of solving disputes through arbitration (Schmitz, 2010) can be easily adapted to crowd-sourcing if the group of workers or micro-task participants performs an impartial judgement of the case presented by the involved parties. In this case, the focus is given to appropriate selection of the group of workers.

Similarly to litigation processes, heuristic-based mediation processes (Sycara, 1989) can be modelled and represented as micro-task workflows. Nevertheless, mediation can be a typically unstructured and creative process that may not adapt and scale well in the strict structure of a micro-task workflow representation.

Multi-agent negotiation approaches (Maio & Silva, 2011) are well known and often resemble workflows of actions. Such workflows can also be modelled as micro-task workflows for crowdsourcing that exploit and harness collective intelligence.

Although several ideas and approaches have been suggested over the last decade, "the process of solving disputes by collective intelligence is in its infancy" (Van Den Herik & Dimov, 2012). With the emergence of micro-task workflow approaches, new applications of CODR are also possible.

CHALLENGES

Since the appearance of the first crowdsourcing systems for micro-tasks, many more have emerged. Their continuous use has led to several experiments and studies that often focus on user motivation and quality control (Yuen et al., 2011).

User motivation has been addressed in several ways, from providing enjoyment and relying on altruism, to giving monetary rewards (Faridani, Hartmann, & Ipeirotis, 2011). The latter has been the subject of some criticism due to the creation of cheap labor marketplaces (Harris, 2011). In the specific case of task crowdsourcing systems, the current monetary rewards are not sufficient to be a primary source of income, and often they are not enough to serve as a motivator (Mason & Watts, 2010; Paolacci et al., 2010). In these cases, workers actually participate out of altruism, curiosity or simply to keep themselves busy. Still, motivating and retaining workers over time remains a challenge for any crowdsourcing system.

Quality control has been studied in different application domains and addressed differently by a variety of crowdsourcing systems. In general, assessment methods are employed either before (during the worker selection step) or after (during the worker assessment step) the participation of the worker. Among the current assessment strategies are expertise tests in certain domains, asking questions for which the answer is known and analyzing performance in previous tasks.

Although several quality control strategies already exist, the advent of crowdsourcing of complex tasks has brought new challenges to different dimensions of the crowdsourcing process, including specification, flow control, quality control and visualization.

In the specific case of quality control, and due to the presence of a micro-task workflow structure, a deviation or error in one task can accumulate with those of the following tasks.

Besides quality control, the flow control assumes special relevance. In fact, the crowdsourcing of complex tasks establishes requirements regarding worker selection that are often discarded in simple micro-task crowdsourcing systems. One of these requirements is worker identity. The fact that most crowdsourcing systems regard the micro-task as the top-level unit of work, leads to loss of identity information from one micro-task to the other. This can easily become a challenge when the worker, as an identifiable individual, is required to participate in different steps of the task workflow.

Another challenge when dealing with complex tasks is the aggregation and visualization of results. At some point, since multiple micro-tasks are involved in a workflow, tracing a specific result and asserting the causes and facts that led to it becomes a necessity. Enforcing structured machine-readable data also facilitates the implementation of strategies for tracing workflow results. Still, special care is needed so that such a structure does not increase the complexity and cumbersome nature of solving tasks from the worker's perspective.

Overall, the following main challenges were identified:

- Specification of complex tasks, namely:
  - Iterative, interactive and incremental tasks;
  - Support for complex flow control conditions, both internal and external;
  - Structuring the task specification, including its domain knowledge, in a way understandable and interpretable by both workers and machines;
- Specification of the human-machine interaction, namely:
  - Specifying worker selection restrictions for different phases of the workflow;
  - Identifying workers across the workflow in order to permit iterative workflows;
  - Tracing results and obtaining and providing justifications;
- Control quality in complex task workflows:
  - Assessing and reducing the impact of low quality answers across the workflow;
  - Using (social) profile information to assess worker's expertise and relevance, and to enhance context;
- Visualization and reporting.

FUTURE RESEARCH DIRECTIONS

There are several aspects of CODR that are particularly relevant since they affect the dispute resolution process and its results:

- Participant selection, which requires an enriched model of the participant, including the participant's background, expertise and social network;
- Contextual micro-task information, i.e. establishing the context of the dispute along with the facts;
- Tracing results and obtaining justifications, i.e. reaching a justifiable solution based on the output of previous micro-tasks;
- Formal structure and semantics for further automatic processing of data (e.g. the participation of machine agents in the dispute resolution process).

The selection of participants based on social network properties such as homophily (the tendency to bond with similar others) and centrality (Wasserman & Faust, 1994) is particularly interesting and may reveal social patterns and tendencies.

Micro-task crowdsourcing is a research field with a wide variety of application domains. Also, given the complexity of the dimensions involved in the crowdsourcing process, there is room for many different approaches. In this sense, the proposed ideas and possible directions are but a fraction of the future research and development possibilities.

CONCLUSION

Over the last decade, human computation and crowdsourcing approaches have been employed in the creation of multiple systems for problem solving on a wide scale. These systems are starting to facilitate the man-computer symbiosis envisioned by Licklider (1960) in the 1960s.

The increasing popularity of crowdsourcing has led to a variety of commercial and non-commercial applications in different domains. Among these applications, a small set of crowdsourcing platforms oriented towards problem (task) solving has emerged. These platforms regard the problem as micro-tasks that can be solved redundantly in one step by multiple users. In more complex processes (such as dispute resolution) where a workflow of micro-tasks is often required, new challenges emerge. This new trend in crowdsourcing has led to some interesting workflow oriented systems such as CrowdForge and Jabberwocky.

Nevertheless, several challenges regarding CODR still need to be tackled through further research and implementation in different areas such as knowledge representation, visualization and user interaction.

REFERENCES

Ahmad, S., Battle, A., Malkani, Z., & Kamvar, S. (2011). The Jabberwocky Programming Environment for Structured Social Computing. In *Proceedings of the 24th Annual ACM Symposium on User Interface Software and Technology* (pp. 53–64). Retrieved from http://dl.acm.org/citation.cfm?id=2047203

Brabham, D. C. (2008a). Crowdsourcing as a model for problem solving an introduction and cases. *Convergence (London)*, *14*(1), 75–90. doi:10.1177/1354856507084420

Brabham, D. C. (2008b). Moving the crowd at iStockphoto: The composition of the crowd and motivations for participation in a crowdsourcing application. *First Monday*, *13*(6), 1–22. doi:10.5210/fm.v13i6.2159

Chklovski, T. (2003). Learner: A System for Acquiring Commonsense Knowledge by Analogy. In *Proceedings of the 2nd ACM International Conference on Knowledge Capture* (pp. 4–12). Retrieved from http://dl.acm.org/citation.cfm?id=945650

Dawson, R., & Bynghall, S. (2015). *Crowdsourcing landscape*. Retrieved from http://rossdawson.com/frameworks/crowdsourcing-landscape-version-2/

Doan, A., Ramakrishnan, R., & Halevy, A. Y. (2011). Crowdsourcing systems on the world-wide web. *Communications of the ACM*, *54*(4), 86–96. doi:10.1145/1924421.1924442

Elwood, S., Goodchild, M. F., & Sui, D. (2013). Prospects for VGI research and the emerging fourth paradigm. In *Crowdsourcing Geographic Knowledge* (pp. 361–375). Springer. doi:10.1007/978-94-007-4587-2_20

Erétéo, G., Gandon, F. L., Corby, O., & Buffa, M. (2009). *Semantic Social Network Analysis*. Presented at the Web Science. Retrieved from http://hal.inria.fr/inria-00378174

Faridani, S., Hartmann, B., & Ipeirotis, P. G. (2011). What's the right price? pricing tasks for finishing on time. In *Proceedings of AAAI Workshop on Human Computation*. Retrieved from http://www.aaai.org/ocs/index.php/WS/AAAIW11/paper/download/3994/4269

Georgakopoulos, D., Hornick, M., & Sheth, A. (1995). An overview of workflow management: From process modeling to workflow automation infrastructure. *Distributed and Parallel Databases*, *3*(2), 119–153. doi:10.1007/BF01277643

Goodchild, M. F., & Glennon, J. A. (2010). Crowdsourcing geographic information for disaster response: A research frontier. *International Journal of Digital Earth*, *3*(3), 231–241. doi:10.1080/17538941003759255

Gruber, T. (2008). Collective knowledge systems: Where the social web meets the semantic web. *Web Semantics: Science, Services, and Agents on the World Wide Web*, *6*(1), 4–13. doi:10.1016/j.websem.2007.11.011

Harris, C. G. (2011). Dirty Deeds Done Dirt Cheap: A Darker Side to Crowdsourcing. In *IEEE International Conference on Privacy, Security, Risk and Trust* (pp. 1314–1317). Retrieved from http://ieeexplore. ieee.org/xpls/abs_all.jsp?arnumber=6113302

Howe, J. (2006). The rise of crowdsourcing. *Wired Magazine*, *14*(6), 1–4.

Howe, J. (2008). *Crowdsourcing: Why the Power of the Crowd is Driving the Future of Business*. Century.

Ipeirotis, P. G., Provost, F., & Wang, J. (2010). Quality management on amazon mechanical turk. In *Proceedings of the ACM SIGKDD Workshop on Human Computation* (pp. 64–67). Retrieved from http://dl.acm.org/citation.cfm?id=1837906

Kittur, A., Chi, E. H., & Suh, B. (2008). Crowdsourcing user studies with Mechanical Turk. In *Proceedings of the SIGCHI Conference on Human Factors in Computing Systems* (pp. 453–456). Retrieved from http://dl.acm.org/citation.cfm?id=1357127

Kittur, A., Khamkar, S., André, P., & Kraut, R. (2012). CrowdWeaver: visually managing complex crowd work. In *Proceedings of the ACM 2012 Conference on Computer Supported Cooperative Work* (pp. 1033–1036). Retrieved from http://dl.acm.org/citation.cfm?id=2145357

Kittur, A., Smus, B., Khamkar, S., & Kraut, R. E. (2011). Crowdforge: Crowdsourcing Complex Work. In *Proceedings of the 24th Annual ACM Symposium on User Interface Software and Technology* (pp. 43–52). Retrieved from http://dl.acm.org/citation.cfm?id=2047202

Kulkarni, A. P., Can, M., & Hartmann, B. (2011). Turkomatic: Automatic Recursive Task and Workflow Design for Mechanical Turk. In *Proceedings of the 2011 Annual Conference on Extended Abstracts on Human Factors in Computing Systems* (pp. 2053–2058). Retrieved from http://dl.acm.org/citation. cfm?id=1979865

Landemore, H. (2014). Inclusive Constitution-Making: The Icelandic Experiment. *Journal of Political Philosophy*. Retrieved from http://onlinelibrary.wiley.com/doi/10.1111/jopp.12032/full

Lawrence, P. (1997). *Workflow handbook 1997*. John Wiley & Sons, Inc. Retrieved from http://dl.acm. org/citation.cfm?id=272945

Levine, S. S., & Kurzban, R. (2006). Explaining Clustering in Social Networks: Towards an Evolutionary Theory of Cascading Benefits. *Managerial and Decision Economics*, *27*(2-3), 173–187. doi:10.1002/mde.1291

Licklider, J. C. R. (1960). Man-computer symbiosis. *IRE Transactions on Human Factors in Electronics*, (1), 4–11.

Little, G., Chilton, L. B., Goldman, M., & Miller, R. C. (2010). Turkit: Human Computation Algorithms on Mechanical Turk. In *Proceedings of the 23rd Annual ACM Symposium on User Interface Software and Technology* (pp. 57–66). Retrieved from http://dl.acm.org/citation.cfm?id=1866040

Luo, S., Xia, H., Yoshida, T., & Wang, Z. (2009). Toward collective intelligence of online communities: A primitive conceptual model. *Journal of Systems Science and Systems Engineering*, *18*(2), 203–221. doi:10.1007/s11518-009-5095-0

Luz, N. (2015). *Ontology-based Representation and Generation of Workflows for Micro-Task Human-Machine Computation*. Universidade do Minho.

Luz, N., Poblet, M., Silva, N., & Novais, P. (2015). Defining Human-Machine Micro-Task Workflows for Constitution Making. Lecture Notes in Business Information Processing, 218. doi:10.1007/978-3-319-19515-5_26

Luz, N., Silva, N., Maio, P., & Novais, P. (2012). *Ontology Alignment through Argumentation*. Presented at the AAAI Spring Symposium - Wisdom of the Crowd, Palo Alto, CA.

Ma, H., Zhou, D., Liu, C., Lyu, M. R., & King, I. (2011). Recommender systems with social regularization. In *Proceedings of the fourth ACM international conference on Web search and data mining* (pp. 287–296). Retrieved from http://dl.acm.org/citation.cfm?id=1935877

Maio, P., & Silva, N. (2011). A Three-Layer Argumentation Framework. In *First International Workshop on the Theory and Applications of Formal Argumentation (TAFA) at IJCAI*.

Marder, N. S. (2005). Cyberjuries: The Next New Thing? *Information & Communications Technology Law*, *14*(2), 165–198. doi:10.1080/13600830500042756

Mason, W., & Watts, D. J. (2010). Financial incentives and the performance of crowds. *ACM SigKDD Explorations Newsletter*, *11*(2), 100–108. doi:10.1145/1809400.1809422

Mentzas, G., Halaris, C., & Kavadias, S. (2001). Modelling business processes with workflow systems: An evaluation of alternative approaches. *International Journal of Information Management*, *21*(2), 123–135. doi:10.1016/S0268-4012(01)00005-6

Paolacci, G., Chandler, J., & Ipeirotis, P. (2010). Running experiments on amazon mechanical turk. *Judgment and Decision Making*, *5*(5), 411–419.

Poblet, M. (2011). *Mobile Technologies for Conflict Management: Online Dispute Resolution, Governance, Participation* (Vol. 2). Springer Science & Business Media. Retrieved from https://www.google.com/books?hl=pt-PT&lr=&id=RDwp2TrEaKQC&oi=fnd&pg=PR5&dq=introduction+to+mobile+technologies,+conflict+management,+and+odr&ots=m8yvuJ8Kph&sig=PCPszF7-W44V0mkqFUSb-sRL1XRE

Poblet, M., & Casanovas, P. (2007). Emotions in ODR. *International Review of Law Computers & Technology*, *21*(2), 145–156. doi:10.1080/13600860701492146

Poblet, M., García-Cuesta, E., & Casanovas, P. (2014). Crowdsourcing Tools for Disaster Management: A Review of Platforms and Methods. In *AI Approaches to the Complexity of Legal Systems* (pp. 261–274). Springer. Retrieved from http://link.springer.com/chapter/10.1007/978-3-662-45960-7_19

Porter, J. (2008). *Designing for the Social Web*. Peachpit Press.

Quinn, A. J., & Bederson, B. B. (2011). Human Computation: A Survey and Taxonomy of a Growing Field. In *Proceedings of the SIGCHI Conference on Human Factors in Computing Systems* (pp. 1403–1412). New York, NY: ACM. http://doi.org/ doi:10.1145/1978942.1979148

Rule, C., & Nagarajan, C. (2011). Crowdsourcing Dispute Resolution over Mobile Devices. In *Mobile Technologies for Conflict Management* (pp. 93–106). Springer. doi:10.1007/978-94-007-1384-0_8

Sarasua, C., Simperl, E., & Noy, N. F. (2012). CrowdMap: Crowdsourcing Ontology Alignment with Microtasks. In *The Semantic Web – ISWC 2012* (pp. 525–541). Springer. Retrieved from http://link.springer.com/chapter/10.1007/978-3-642-35176-1_33

Schmitz, A. (2010). "Drive-Thru"Arbitration in the Digital Age: Empowering Consumers Through Regulated ODR. *Baylor Law Review*, *62*, 178.

Segaran, T. (2007). *Programming Collective Intelligence: Building Smart Web 2.0 Applications*. O'Reilly Media.

Singh, P., Lin, T., Mueller, E. T., Lim, G., Perkins, T., & Zhu, W. L. (2002). Open Mind Common Sense: Knowledge Acquisition from the General Public. In *On the Move to Meaningful Internet Systems 2002: CoopIS, DOA, and ODBASE* (pp. 1223–1237). Springer. Retrieved from http://link.springer.com/chapter/10.1007/3-540-36124-3_77

Sui, D., & Goodchild, M. (2011). The convergence of GIS and social media: Challenges for GIScience. *International Journal of Geographical Information Science*, *25*(11), 1737–1748. doi:10.1080/13658816.2011.604636

Sui, D., Goodchild, M., & Elwood, S. (2013). Volunteered geographic information, the exaflood, and the growing digital divide. In *Crowdsourcing geographic knowledge* (pp. 1–12). Springer. doi:10.1007/978-94-007-4587-2_1

Surowiecki, J. (2004). *The Wisdom of Crowds: Why the Many Are Smarter Than the Few and How Collective Wisdom Shapes Business, Economies, Societies and Nations*. New York: Doubleday.

Sycara, K. (1989). Multi-agent compromise via negotiation. *Distributed Artificial Intelligence*, *2*(1), 119–139.

Van Den Herik, J., & Dimov, D. (2012). Towards Crowdsourced Online Dispute Resolution. *J. Int'l Com. L. & Tech.*, *7*, 99.

Van Der Aalst, W. M., Ter Hofstede, A. H., & Weske, M. (2003). Business process management: A survey. In *Business process management* (pp. 1–12). Springer. doi:10.1007/3-540-44895-0_1

Von Ahn, L. (2009). Human Computation. In *46th ACM IEEE Design Automation Conference* (pp. 418–419). Retrieved from http://ieeexplore.ieee.org/xpls/abs_all.jsp?arnumber=5227025

Wasserman, S., & Faust, K. (1994). *Social Network Analysis: Methods and Applications*. Cambridge University Press. doi:10.1017/CBO9780511815478

Willett, W., Heer, J., & Agrawala, M. (2012). Strategies for crowdsourcing social data analysis. In *Proceedings of the 2012 ACM Annual conference on Human Factors in Computing Systems* (pp. 227–236). Retrieved from http://dl.acm.org/citation.cfm?id=2207709

Yuen, M.-C., King, I., & Leung, K.-S. (2011). A Survey of Crowdsourcing Systems. In *IEEE International Conference on Privacy*. Boston, MA: Security, Risk and Trust. doi:10.1109/PASSAT/SocialCom.2011.203

Yun, S., & Kim, H.-G. (2009). *Modeling User Interactions in Online Social Networks*. Presented at the Asian Workshop of Social Web and Interoperability, Shanghai, China. Retrieved from http://www.slideshare.net/Channy/modeling-user-interactions-in-online-social-networks

KEY TERMS AND DEFINITIONS

Collective Intelligence: The result of the combined behaviour, effort and ideas of different people on a global scale.

Crowdsourcing: A problem-solving approach that consists in enlisting a crowd of human workers to solve a particular problem defined by an owner.

Dispute Resolution: The process of solving a dispute between entities.

Human Computation: An approach where humans perform computational tasks often performed by machines.

Human-Machine Computation: An approach where both humans and machines collaborate to perform both creative and computational tasks.

Micro-Task Crowdsourcing: A crowdsourcing approach that divides the problem into small computational tasks that are then distributed through a crowd of human workers.

Ontology: A formal, explicit specification of a shared conceptualization.

Workflow: The automation of a business process through the organized execution of tasks.

Chapter 17
Management Conflicts in E-Learning Environment:
Vulnerabilities in E-Learning Environments

Tomás Sola Martínez
Granada University, Spain

Francisco Javier Hinojo Lucena
Granada University, Spain

Dalila Alves Durães
Caldas das Taipas Higher School, Portugal

José Javier Romero Díaz de la Guardia
International University of La Rioja (UNIR), Spain

ABSTRACT

The development and technological revolution has contributed to a remarkable increase in the supply of training processes in e-learning educational institutions. The interaction and participation in educational activities under this paradigm involves a series of implications from the point of view of safety and privacy. This chapter presents the main vulnerabilities of e-learning systems and their involvement in the emergence of conflicts for the participants from online training activities and for the educational institutions. The study develops from three types of conflicts: the availability and system integrity, the privacy of the information that is exchanged in virtual environment and the process of authentication of the participants. The authors emphasize the main conflicts that can occur and the actions to take into account in e-learning environments to avoid or mitigate the effect of these vulnerabilities, to ensuring design and topology of systems, application code, and communications that are exchanged in training processes.

INTRODUCTION TO E-LEARNING ENVIRONMENTS

Lifelong Learning and ICT

Currently, society in permanent change requires continuous adaptation of the human being to the surrounding environment. We live in a global, multicultural and hyper-connected world where technology is present in all spheres of life and is the backbone for the transformation of society (Telefónica Foundation, 2004).

DOI: 10.4018/978-1-5225-0245-6.ch017

The development of the information society is linked to a permanent need for learning by individuals. In this sense, we can speak of learning throughout life in all areas of knowledge, either when it is formal, non-formal or casual learning. It is a continuous process focused on the particular needs of the individual. "The aim of lifelong learning is to improve knowledge, skills and competence with a personal, civic, social or employment-related perspective" (Yamat et al. Cited by Nordin, Embi & Yunus, 2010, p. 131).

Today, the Information and Communication Technology (ICT) has provided the opportunity to experience learning situations at any time, without the necessity of being present, no matter the place or device.

The globalization of education allowed the increase in distance learning programs, supported by the growing use of e-learning systems.

The ICT has expanded the range of possibilities of teaching and implementing innovative methodologies. An example is the organization of cooperative learning with the mediation of virtual scenarios (Trujillo, Cáceres, Hinojo & Aznar, 2011).

The acceptance and use of these e-learning systems enable the success of such educational programs.

E-Learning

It seems there is no consensus regarding what should be the universal definition for e-learning term. Some authors have emphasized the characteristics of a technological nature, and others, on the contrary, highlight the pedagogical issues, depending on the duality of their academic and scientific profile.

After analyzing different definitions from different perspectives like technology, access to information, communication and the educational paradigm, a new definition of e-learning was obtained from a recent international research in which they have used the Delphi method (Sangrà, Vlachopoulos & Cabrera, 2012):

E-learning is an approach to teaching and learning, representing all or part of the educational model applied, that is based on the use of electronic media and devices as tools for improving access to training, communication and interaction and that facilitates the adoption of new ways of understanding and developing learning. (p.152)

Regarding the methodological potential presented by e-learning, Trujillo, Hinojo y Aznar (2011) provide an overview of e-learning as an engine of networking, interaction and collaboration among peers and emphasize the new role of students participating in online training activities which increases their prominence and matters them develop a greater commitment to learning. To implement this methodological change an adaptation of the current teaching practices and the consequent improvement of the teachers´ professional skills is required (Romero, Moreno & Sola, 2012).

Recently, in a review and redefinition paper of the concept of e-learning, García-Peñalvo & Seoane-Pardo (2015) have defined the term from a holistic perspective:

The training process, of intentional or unintentional nature, aimed at the acquisition of a number of competences and skills in a social context, developed in a technological ecosystem in which different profiles of users share content, activities and experiences and interact in situations of formal learning; it must be supervised by teaching actors whose activities contribute to ensure the quality of all the factors involved. (p. 132)

From these definitions a number of key factors of the teaching and learning processes that take place in e-learning environments are derived:

- It includes any learning situation, formal or informal, even simultaneously, in order to acquire certain competences or skills.
- The training process is organized in a technological environment where the individual's interaction occurs in the system, and among individuals.
- It involves the use of electronic devices.
- In formal learning situations there should be a tutor to guide students and ensure the achievement of objectives, furthermore it is also possible to establish cooperative learning processes where a peer-tutoring scenario is followed.

In e-learning we have learning activities conducted through electronic means online and where the knowledge is construct with collaborative approaches. The challenge in e-learning is to build lessons that are compatible with human learning processes (Clark, R.C., Mayer, R.E., 2011).

LEARNING MANAGEMENT SYSTEMS

Currently, institutions that offer e-learning activities are sustained by information systems that support the educational processes which are developed in the institution. In this sense, the learning management systems (LMS) are centralized systems where all courses and learning content are managed, and all training activities both formal and informal are organized (Stone & Zheng, 2014).

From the point of view of educational institutions and teachers, the LMS have been a valuable tool for deploying educational content, set teaching-learning activities, and they permit having a high level of monitoring information of the participants in the activity, and the degree of acquiring skills to be developed.

In recent years, the development of ICT and its applications in the field of education, is charging a number of features to LMS in a way to adapt the current needs of technological and pedagogical measures (Stone & Zheng, 2014):

- **Information Exchange:** Understood from several points of view:
  - The export of internal resources (course materials), thus encouraging lifelong learning, following the accomplishment of an e-learning activity.
  - The import of other educational resources on open formats (Open Educational Resources – OER).
  - The integration with other systems of the educational institution (databases of student information, repositories, etc.).
  - The flexibility to admit changes and adaptations, especially LMS distributed through open source licenses.
- **Personal:** Non-centred in the institution, but in the individual, with own characteristics of the Personal Learning Environments (PLE).
- **Social:** LMS that allow interaction between the parties in a more natural way and the schemes of collaborative or cooperative work.

- **Flexible:** In several ways:
  - ○ In terms of the underlying mode (courses, learning objects entirely or partially visible from the outside of the LMS, etc.).
  - ○ Regarding the system of recognition and evaluation (skills, badges, etc.).
  - ○ Regarding the inherent methodological approach to the training activity (gamification, co-operation, etc.).
- **Learning Analytics:** LMS allowing carrying out collection and analysis of information about students and activities aiming to optimize learning results and processes.
- **Mobile:** LMS adaptable and with specific features to the diversity of mobile devices available today.

The educational institutions must create system that allows the students to have the possibility of using this several systems.

SECURITY IN E-LEARNING ENVIRONMENTS: THE SOURCES OF CONFLICT

The technological evolution of LMS and other e-learning systems, in order to converge for current educational demands, involves the emergence of difficulties and conflicts in the field of security and confidentiality. These conflicts can affect all agents involved in the process: manufacturers of virtual training environments, educational institutions that provide training online, publishers and authors of digital content, as well as, all participants in an online training activity, regardless their role (students, mentoring, coordination, etc.).

When we talk about conflicts, we face a polysemous concept which, in the field of e-learning, can be analysed from different perspectives. We can distinguish different conflicts: social, psychological, behavioural and academic, arising from the peculiarities of the human condition and relationships that are kept in virtual scenarios (De Barros, 2011).

On the other hand, we focus on conflicts that can occur in online training activities, whose nature and origin are related to computer systems that support the training activities and its manipulation by the participants. In this sense, it is possible to classify different levels of conflicts:

- System availability;
- System integrity;
- Confidentiality;
- Authentication.

This different levels of conflicts must be reduced in order to lowest the vulnerabilities of the system.

System Availability

The technical quality of an e-learning system and its level of response to requests from users are a determining factor for the success of the training activities. User satisfaction in their daily operations with the virtual environment is linked to their motivation and to the follow-up of the training activity. In a study that analysed the role of technology in relation to the success of online training activities, Eom, Ashill,

Arbaugh and Stapleton (2012) corroborated the relationship between the achievement of the learning objectives and the stability of the technological infrastructure of e-learning systems.

An unstable system may be the cause of many conflicts in e-learning activities. If the system stops being accessible to users for some period of time or doesn't offer adequate performance in interactions between tutors and students, discontent and lack of motivation of the participants in the training activity may occur.

In addition to providing the technological infrastructure of an e-learning system, with the necessary measures in terms of sizing and fail tolerance (on servers, lines of communication, and software services), solutions against potential malicious attacks on system availability must be set up.

The attacks on the availability of the system can happen, making it impossible or making the connection between origin and destination fail, where it might occur the destruction of files or lines, either on flooding information channel of communication in order to produce a collapse and therefore the non-availability of the system (Nicholova & Nickolov, 2007). The most common flood attack is called Denial of Service (DoS), which consists on physically exhausting the server resources, or the bandwidth of network that gives access to it, thus limiting the system response to the users requests.

There are different approaches to defend against DoS attacks, depending on whether it is preventing the attack, combating the attack during its execution, or after occurring the attack. Defence strategies go through the redefinition of the topology of the network, installing firewalls with advanced package filtering rules, use of routers and switches that have functions to control traffic on the network or implement access control lists as well as the implementation of load balancing systems and flow control (Zargar, Joshi, & Tipper, 2013).

System Integrity

Virtual training environments that support online learning processes in which activities are developed either fully or partially, may be a source of conflict if they are victims of attacks on their integrity. Let's see what the main integrity vulnerabilities of e-learning platforms, as well as the measures that can be taken in this point.

Cross-Site Scripting

Also known as XSS, it's a security vulnerability that affects web applications including virtual training environments. By sending a malicious code, usually operated by a script that runs in a browser, it suggests those who receive it that it came from a reliable source. Once executed, the malicious code can access cookies, session IDs of users in the e-learning environment, and other sensitive information retained in browsers, being able to modify the content of the HTML page displayed (OWASP, 2014a).

The interactivity of current virtual training environments allows continuous exchange of information between the user and the system, which favours the manipulation of this type of vulnerability by users with intention of attacking the system.

The vulnerabilities of cross-site scripting can be a potentially dangerous security problem for a system of online training, which should be primarily addressed by ensuring the code of the Web application. Hydara, Sultan, Zulzalil and Admodisastro (2015), after analysing the state of the art in research on XSS, designate a series of techniques to preserve the security of a system against XSS attacks:

- Static analysis. Deep revision of the code of an application with the idea of finding security flaws.
- Dynamic analysis. Examination of application behaviour at runtime.
- Secure programming. Monitoring a set of rules for the development of an application to get a code that is not vulnerable to these attacks.
- Modelling. Using computer modelling techniques to analyse the behaviour of the system in relation to different inputs (abstraction, model checking, simulation, etc.).

If the system uses some of this techniques it´s possible avoid this vulnerabilities in e-learning environment.

Cross-Site Request Forgery

In the field of e-learning, XSRF type attack occurs when a website, email or malicious program makes the browser think that it is an authenticated user performing an unwanted action in such environment (OWASP, 2015). For example, the attacker can make the user administrator of an e-learning environment run, unconsciously, certain critical operation (such as deleting users, activities, etc.), masking the operation through a link on a forum or modifying the URL associated with an image.

Most of the virtual training environments handle the concept of session identifier, so those requests to the Server are authenticated and are not executed if this identifier is not provided, or the provided ID is different from the corresponding to the logged on user. The problem can occur if the necessary precautions are not taken in the management and the delivery of the session identifiers, as they can be used by the attacker to complete the accessing for XSRF. This effect can be mitigated by encrypting the identification information session between the source and destination.

Other methods to prevent XSRF attacks include HTTP headers in communications between the authenticated user and the server. There are several variations such as: Refer Header, Custom Header, and Origin Header. It is also possible to incorporate the use of a captcha that has to be resolved before sending the request to the server (Barth, Jackson, Mitchell, 2008), although this method can be very time consuming for users who continually need to perform operations, under an administrative role.

SQL Code Injection

The current virtual training environments, like any web application, support a database server where all system configurations are stored, courses, activities, users, etc. Normally, in a virtual training environment there is a continuous exchange of information between database server and web server, as part of the process of the requests received from the application clients (users).

SQL code injection attack is defined to run an unexpected SQL statement from a workstation connected to the system. This type of attack can cause the insertion, update or deletion of sensitive data in e-learning environment, or perform administrative operations, such as shutting down the database or restoring its contents with unwanted information (Randive, Khatke, & Reddi, 2014).

If we consider that the database in a virtual training environment stores information of the system, training processes, and personal data of users, the attacks of SQL injection may cause conflicts of violation of confidentiality, identity loss, modification or restriction of the level of the user access to the system, as well as provoke an interference in the normal operation causing integrity system failures among others.

To prevent conflicts arising from SQL injection vulnerabilities in an e-learning system the following defences may be used (OWASP, 2014b):

- Implement prepared statements, to isolate the SQL statement defining the parameters run by the server at runtime, thereby separating code and data.
- Use stored procedures to keep all codes that can be executed in the database itself.
- Using the technique Escaping All User Supplied Input, to ensure that database does not confuse the developer code with the potential attacker code.

Today most applications of e-learning environment are based on the database, so this is the backbone for most of the applications and her security is the major issue.

Confidentiality

From the point of view of students, personal data protection and anonymity are considered key aspects that may also be the source of conflicts and which should be protected in training activities in e-learning mode. In this sense, it is also considered a priority that students can control the visibility of potentially confidential information, such as training history and user profile on system (May, Fessakis, Dimitra-copoulou, & George, 2012).

This claim of confidentiality of users in e-learning environments can conflict with strict instructional design in which tutors or coordinators of training need to have detailed information on the monitoring of the participants (connection time intervals working in the system, etc.).

An attack on privacy in an e-learning system can be a first step to perpetrate other types of attacks such as availability or integrity. Confidentiality attacks tend to be based on espionage the communications exchanged by specific participants, or traffic in general between an origin and a destination, with the intention of analysing observed data and decrypt it (Nicholova & Nickolov, 2007).

Privacy in a virtual training environment is a source of conflict that requires the implementation of technologies to protect the users' identity, using an anonymous communication system and establishing highly secure cryptographic protocols to prevent access to private information that is exchanged in e-learning environment. In this case, the goal is not to avoid traffic observation, but preventing its access by the attacker.

Authentication

Online access to private services of e-learning systems requires identity authentication of users by entering credentials. Identity in virtual training environments can be a source of conflict mainly in two ways. On the one hand, an attacker can try to appropriate other users' credentials in order to obtain their personal information, or to perform unwanted actions on the system. Spoofing of authenticated users can be given by session hijacking attacks (Costinela-Luminiţa & Nicoleta-Magdalena, 2012), which consist of an ID theft of an authenticated user session, without knowing access credentials of that user.

In another sense, the impersonation in an e-learning system can be done in a conscious and fraudulent manner. While conducting activities or tasks that are part of courses or other training activities in e-learning mode, a user can use an authentication from another and make certain tasks on his behalf. Certain activities such as conducting examinations require further certification of presence of the person during the performance of the activity, and thus avoid invasion.

Virtual learning environments should offer mechanisms that allow eliminating or mitigating the appearance of such conflicts and thus aim at a series of models that allow the increasing of reliability of the user validation:

- Improvements in authentication process:
  - Ensure the strength of passwords and use advanced cryptographic protocols and strategies for the improvement of safety as the password salting (Clair et al., 2006).
  - Add a captcha in the login page to prevent attacks (Arakeylan, 2013).
  - Using smart cards as a second safety factor for user authentication (Sun, 2000).
- Delegate user identification in external directory services such as LDAP, Shibboleth, CAS, IMAP, etc.
- Encrypt all communications between users and e-learning system using SSL on the whole website and enable regeneration systems session IDs.
- Ensure the physical presence of users of an e-learning environment through the implementation of biometric systems (Gonzalez, Anido, Alba & García, 2008). Examples of these applications are real time recognition of: iris; face; fingerprints; palm prints or voice.

All of these techniques have proposed solutions and contrameasures to overcome the attacks in e-learning environment.

CONCLUSION

Computer systems and technological infrastructures that accommodate educational activities developed in e-learning modality can be the source of numerous conflicts affecting the normal development of the training process.

System stability is a fundamental premise to ensure the absence of conflict in e-learning environments. This stability can be altered by abnormal or unexpected system operation, which may be originated in structural failure or software, or can be caused intentionally by people or entities with opposing interests to the attacked institution.

Different types of instability can lead to various conflicts in the field of e-learning. The problems of system availability, as DoS, can cause conflicts of poor image, lack of confidence of users participating in school, and stress produced by the inability or difficulty to perform in a timely manner the activities proposed. On the other hand, XSS or XSRF vulnerabilities or SQL injection attacking the integrity of the system may cause conflicts distorting completely the information received by the participant in an online training and may lead to mistakes, misunderstandings or dropouts. Users of e-learning systems, who are victims of attacks like identity theft, or access to confidential information, will lose their motivation to the training activity and their confidence in the system.

These obstacles to normal development of training in e-learning environments may also cause conflicts on the side of the educational institution, as the loss of the users' confidence is clearly detrimental to its image as a provider of educational services, and get a weak position when compared to other institutions. Other companies or organizations might take advantage of confidential information to their own benefit.

Also depending on the technological complexity of the system, the detection and the stabilization of an e-learning environment that was a victim of an attack of availability, integrity or intrusion, may have a high cost to the institution. We have also seen that the false authentication of users may cause conflicts when it comes to persuade possible participants in a certain training online activity.

Therefore, providers of e-learning activities institutions must establish the appropriate measures and security mechanisms to prevent and deal with potential instability and vulnerability of their systems and ensure the integrity and privacy of information exchanged in the training processes. Ensuring system security and preventing these conflicts are not an easy task. There are several solutions that range from a careful design of the system infrastructure and network, a deep revision of the application code and databases to comply with the latest safety requirements, encryption of all communications exchanged in the course of e-learning activities and the use of biometrics in the authentication process.

REFERENCES

Arakeylan, V. A. (2013). Vulnerable Security Problems in Learning Management System (LMS) Moodle. *Mathematical Problems of Computer Science*, *39*, 129–134.

Barth, A., Jackson, C., & Mitchell, J. C. (2008). Robust Defenses for Cross-site Request Forgery. In *Proceedings of the 15th ACM Conference on Computer and Communications Security* (pp. 75–88). New York, NY: ACM. doi:10.1145/1455770.1455782

Clair, L., Johansen, L., Enck, W., Pirretti, M., Traynor, P., McDaniel, P., & Jaeger, T. (2006). Password Exhaustion: Predicting the End of Password Usefulness. In *Information Systems Security* (pp. 37-55). Heidelberg, Germany: Springer. Retrieved July 17, 2015, from http://www.enck.org/pubs/iciss06a.pdf

Clark, R. C., & Mayer, R. E. (Eds.). (2011). *E-Learning and the Science of Instruction – Proven Guidelines for consumers and designers of multimedia learning* (3rd ed.). John Wiley & Sons. Inc. doi:10.1002/9781118255971

Costinela-Luminiţa, C., & Nicoleta-Magdalena, C. (2012). E-learning Security Vulnerabilities. *Procedia: Social and Behavioral Sciences*, *46*, 2297–2301. doi:10.1016/j.sbspro.2012.05.474

De Barros, P. M. (2011). *Incidência e impacto do cyberbullying nos alunos do terceiro ciclo do ensino básico público português*. University of Granada. Retrieved July 18, 2015, from http://0-hera.ugr.es.adrastea.ugr.es/tesisugr/20058068.pdf

Eom, S., Ashill, N. J., Arbaugh, J. B., & Stapleton, J. L. (2012). The role of information technology in e-learning systems success. *Human Systems Management*, *31*, 147–163.

Fundación Telefónica. (2014). *La Sociedad de la Información en España 2013*. Barcelona: Ariel.

García-Peñalvo, F. J., & Seoane Pardo, A. M. (2015). Una revisión actualizada del concepto de eLearning. Décimo Aniversario. *Education in the Knowledge Society*, *16*(1), 119. doi:10.14201/eks2015161119144

González, E., Anido, L., Alba, J. L., & García, C. (2008). Is My Student at the Other Side? Applying Biometric Web Authentication to E-Learning Environments. In *Eighth IEEE International Conference on Advanced Learning Technologies, 2008. ICALT '08* (pp. 551-553). Retrieved July 16, 2015, from http://www.researchgate.net/profile/Jose_Luis_Alba-Castro/publication/221423359_Is_My_Student_at_the_Other_Side_Applying_Biometric_Web_Authentication_to_E-Learning_Environments/links/0912f4ffc67056eb8d000000.pdf

Hydara, I., Sultan, A. B., Zulzalil, H., & Admodisastro, N. (2015). Current state of research on cross-site scripting (XSS) – A systematic literature review. *Information and Software Technology*, *58*, 170–186. doi:10.1016/j.infsof.2014.07.010

May, M., Fessakis, G., Dimitracopoulou, A., & George, S. (2012). A Study on User's Perception in E-learning Security and Privacy Issues. In *2012 IEEE 12th International Conference on Advanced Learning Technologies (ICALT)* (pp. 88-89). DOI: doi:10.1109/ICALT.2012.145

Nicholova, M., & Nickolov, E. (2007). Threat model for user security in e-learning systems. *International Journal Information Technologies and Knowledge*, *1*, 341–347.

Nordin, N., Embi, M., & Yunus, M. M. (2010). Mobile Learning Framework for Lifelong Learning. Social and Behavioral Sciences, 7, 130-138. doi:10.1016/j.sbspro.2010.10.019

OWASP. (2014a). *Cross-site Scripting (XSS)*. Retrieved July 16, 2015, from https://www.owasp.org/index.php/XSS

OWASP. (2014b). *SQL Injection Prevention Cheat Sheet*. Recovered from https://www.owasp.org/index.php/SQL_Injection_Prevention_Cheat_Sheet

OWASP. (2015). *Cross-Site Request Forgery (CSRF)*. Recovered from https://www.owasp.org/index.php/Cross-Site_Request_Forgery_(CSRF)

Raaij, E. M., & Schepers, J. J. L. (2006). *The Acceptance and Use of a Virtual Learning Environment in China*. Retrieved July 8, 2015, from http://www.sciencedirect.com/science/article/pii/S0360131506001382

Randive, P. U., Khatke, M. B., & Reddi, M. B. (2014). An Approach for Prevention of SQL Injection Attacks on Database: A Review. *International Journal of Innovative Research in Advanced Engineering*, *1*(3), 38–41.

Romero, J. J., Moreno, A., & Sola, T. (2012). Estudio de necesidades de formación de los profesores andaluces en el ámbito de la autoría de materiales educativos digitales en ambientes virtuales de aprendizaje. *Journal for Educators, Teachers and Trainers*, *3*(1), 92–108.

Sangrà, A., Vlachopoulos, D., & Cabrera, N. (2012). Building an inclusive definition of e-learning: An approach to the conceptual framework. *The International Review of Research in Open and Distributed Learning*, *13*(2), 145–159.

Stone, D. E., & Zheng, G. (2014). Learning Management Systems in a Changing Environment. In V. Wang (Ed.), *Handbook of Research on Education and Technology in a Changing Society*. IGI Global. Retrieved July 16, 2015, from http://www.researchgate.net/publication/267625754_Learning_Management_Systems_in_a_Changing_Environment

Sun, H. M. (2000). An efficient remote use authentication scheme using smart cards. *IEEE Transactions on Consumer Electronics*, *46*(4), 958–961. doi:10.1109/30.920446

Trujillo, J. M., Cáceres, M. P., Hinojo, F. J., & Aznar, I. (2011). Aprendizaje cooperativo en entornos virtuales: El proyecto Redes Educativas y Organizativas Interuniversitarias. *Educar*, *47*(1), 95–119.

Trujillo, J. M., Hinojo, F. J., & Aznar, I. (2011). Propuestas de trabajo innovadoras y colaborativas e-learning 2.0 como demanda de la sociedad del conocimiento. *Estudios Sobre Educación, 20*, 141-159.

Zargar, S. T., Joshi, J., & Tipper, D. (2013). A Survey of Defense Mechanisms Against Distributed Denial of Service (DDoS) Flooding Attacks. *IEEE Communications Surveys and Tutorials*, *15*(4), 2046–2069. doi:10.1109/SURV.2013.031413.00127

KEY TERMS AND DEFINITIONS

Authentication: Is the act of confirming the truth of an attribute of a single piece of data claimed true by an entity.

Confidentially: Is data that are classified, where limited persons are authorized to use.

Conflicts: Are incompatibility or interference in events or activities.

Cross-Site Request Forgery: Or XSRF is a type of malicious exploit of a website where unauthorized commands are transmitted from a user that the website trusts.

Cross-Site Scripting: Is a type of computer security vulnerability typically found in web applications.

Denial of Service: Is an attack to make a machine or network resource unavailable to is intended users, where the services of a host connected to Internet are suspended or interrupted.

Security: Is the degree of resistance or protection to attacks from the Internet.

SQL Code Injection: Is a code injection technique used to attack data-driven applications.

Vulnerabilities: Is a weakness, which allows an attacker to reduce a system's information assurance.

Compilation of References

Aarts, E., & Grotenhuis, F. (2011). Ambient Intelligence 2. 0. *Towards Synergetic Prosperity*, *3*, 3–11. doi:10.3233/AIS-2011-0090

Aarts, E., & Wichert, R. (2009). Ambient intelligence. In *Technology Guide* (pp. 244–249). Springer Berlin Heidelberg. doi:10.1007/978-3-540-88546-7_47

Abbas, S., & Sawamura, H. (2012). Argument mining based on a structured database and its usage in an intelligent tutoring environment. *Knowledge and Information Systems*, *30*(1), 213–246. doi:10.1007/s10115-010-0371-3

Abras, C., Maloney-Krichmar, D., & Preece, J. (2004). User-centered design. In Encyclopedia of Human-Computer Interaction. Thousand Oaks, CA: Sage Publications.

Ahmad, S., Battle, A., Malkani, Z., & Kamvar, S. (2011). The Jabberwocky Programming Environment for Structured Social Computing. In *Proceedings of the 24th Annual ACM Symposium on User Interface Software and Technology* (pp. 53–64). Retrieved from http://dl.acm.org/citation.cfm?id=2047203

Akyildiz, I. F., & Vuran, M. C. (2010). *Wireless sensor networks* (Vol. 4). John Wiley & Sons. doi:10.1002/9780470515181

Alami, R., Robert, F., Ingrand, F., & Suzuki, S. (1995). Multi-robot cooperation through incremental plan-merging. In *IEEE International Conference on Robotics and Automation* (ICRA), (pp. 2573–2579).

Alam, S., Shafi, K., Abbass, H. A., & Barlow, M. (2009). An ensemble approach for conflict detection in Free Flight by data mining. *Transportation Research*, *17*(Part C), 298–317. doi:10.1016/j.trc.2008.12.002

Alejo, D., Cobano, J. A., Heredia, G., & Heredia, G. (2013). Particle Swarm Optimization for collision-free 4D trajectory planning in Unmanned Aerial Vehicles. *International Conference on Unmanned Aircraft Systems (ICUAS)*. doi:10.1109/ICUAS.2013.6564702

Almeida, T. (2001). *Lei de defesa do Consumidor Anotada*. Lisboa: Instituto do Consumidor. (In Portuguese)

Alphandéry, P., & Fortier, A. (2001). Can a Territorial Policy be Based on Science Alone? The System for Creating the Natura 2000 Network in France. *Sociologia Ruralis*, *41*(3), 311–328. doi:10.1111/1467-9523.00185

Alterman, A. (2003). A piece of yourself: Ethical issues in biometric identification. *Ethics and Information Technology*, *5*(3), 139–150. doi:10.1023/B:ETIN.0000006918.22060.1f

Alzaghoul, A. F. (2012). The implication of the learning theories on implementing e-learning courses. *The Research Bulletin of Jordan*, *2*(2), 27–30.

Amason, A. C. (1996). Distinguishing the Effects of Functional and Dysfunctional Conflict on Strategic Decision Making: Resolving a Paradox for Top Management Groups. *Academy of Management Journal*, *39*(1), 123–148. doi:10.2307/256633

Amason, A. C., & Sapienza, H. J. (1997). The Effects of Top Management Team Size and Interaction Norms on Cognitive and Affective Conflict. *Journal of Management*, *23*(4), 495–516. doi:10.1177/014920639702300401

Amgoud, L., & Maudet, N. (2002). Strategical considerations for argumentative agents (preliminary report). In *9th International Workshop on Non-Monotonic Reasoning* (LNAI), (pp. 399–407). Springer.

Amgoud, L. (2003). A formal framework for handling conflicting desires. In *7th European Conference on Symbolic and Quantitative Approaches to Reasoning with Uncertainty, ECSQARU-03*, (LNAI) (vol. 2711, pp. 552–563). Springer. doi:10.1007/978-3-540-45062-7_45

Amgoud, L., & Hameurlain, N. (2006). A formal model for designing dialogue strategies. In *5th International Joint Conference on Autonomous Agents and Multiagent Systems, AAMAS-06*. ACM Press. doi:10.1145/1160633.1160706

Amgoud, L., & Kaci, S. (2004). On the generation of bipolar goals in argumentation-based negotiation. In *Argumentation in Multi-Agent Systems: State of the art survey* (LNAI), (Vol. 3366, pp. 192–207). Springer.

Amgoud, L., & Kaci, S. (2005). On the study of negotiation strategies. In *AAMAS 2005 Workshop on Agent Communication*. ACM Press.

Andersson, I., Petersson, M., & Jarsjö, J. (2012). Impact of the European Water Framework Directive on local-level water management: Case study Oxunda Catchment, Sweden. *Land Use Policy*, *29*(1), 73–82. doi:10.1016/j.landusepol.2011.05.006

Andrade, F., Carneiro, D., & Novais, P. (2010). A Inteligência Artificial na Resolução de Conflitos em Linha. *Scientia Iuridica*, *59*(321), 137–164.

Andrew, J. S. (2001). Examining the Claims of Environmental ADR Evidence from Waste Management Conflicts in Ontario and Massachusetts. *Journal of Planning Education and Research*, *21*(2), 166–183. doi:10.1177/0739456X0102100205

Annunziato, M., & Pierucci, P. (2003). The emergence of social learning in artificial societies. In *Applications of evolutionary computing* (pp. 467–478). Springer Berlin Heidelberg. doi:10.1007/3-540-36605-9_43

Arakeylan, V. A. (2013). Vulnerable Security Problems in Learning Management System (LMS) Moodle. *Mathematical Problems of Computer Science*, *39*, 129–134.

Argente, E., Botti, V., Carrascosa, C., Giret, A., Julian, V., & Rebollo, M. (2011). An abstract architecture for virtual organizations: The THOMAS approach. *Knowledge and Information Systems*, *29*(2), 379–403. doi:10.1007/s10115-010-0349-1

Armbrust, M., Fox, A., Griffith, R., Joseph, A. D., Katz, R., Konwinski, A., & Zaharia, M. et al. (2010). A view of cloud computing. *Communications of the ACM*, *53*(4), 50–58. doi:10.1145/1721654.1721672

Arnavas, D. P. (2004). *Alternative Dispute Resolution for Government Contracts*. Riverwoods: CCH Incorporated.

Aronov, B., de Berg, M., van der Stappen, A. F., Svestka, P., & Vleugels, J. (1999). Motion planning for multiple robots. *Discrete & Computational Geometry*, *22*(4), 505–525. doi:10.1007/PL00009476

Atkinson, K. (2005). *What Should We Do? Computational Representation of Persuasive Argument in Practical Reasoning*. (PhD thesis). Liverpool University.

Atkinson, K., & Bench-Capon, T. (2007). Practical reasoning as presumptive argumentation using action based alternating transition systems. *Artificial Intelligence*, *171*(10-15), 855–874. doi:10.1016/j.artint.2007.04.009

Aylett, R., & Barnes, D. (1998). A multi-robot architecture for planetary rovers. In *5th ESA Workshop on Advanced Space Technologies for Robotics and Automation*.

Azhar, M. Q., Parsons, S., & Sklar, E. (2013). An Argumentation-based Dialogue System for Human-Robot Collaboration (Demonstration). In *12th International Conference on Autonomous Agents and Multiagent Systems* (AA-MAS), (pp. 1353–1354).

Bai, C., & Zhang, X. (2011). Aircraft Landing Scheduling in the Small Aircraft Transportation System. *IEEE International Conference on Computational and Information Sciences*. doi:10.1109/ICCIS.2011.65

Barki, H., & Hartwick, J. (2004). Conceptualizing the construct of interpersonal conflict. *The International Journal of Conflict Management*, *15*(3), 216–244. doi:10.1108/eb022913

Baron, R. A. (1990). Conflict in Organizations. In K. R. Murphy & F. E. Saal (Eds.), *Psychology in Organizations: Integrating Science and Practice*. Hillsdale, NJ: Lawrence Erlbaum and Associates.

Barraquand, J., & Latombe, J.-C. (1991). Robot motion planning: A distributed representation approach. *The International Journal of Robotics Research*, *10*(6), 628–649. doi:10.1177/027836499101000604

Barr, S., & Prillwitz, J. (2012). Green travelers? Exploring the spatial context of sustainable mobility styles. *Applied Geography (Sevenoaks, England)*, *32*(2), 798–809. doi:10.1016/j.apgeog.2011.08.002

Barth, A., Jackson, C., & Mitchell, J. C. (2008). Robust Defenses for Cross-site Request Forgery. In *Proceedings of the 15th ACM Conference on Computer and Communications Security* (pp. 75–88). New York, NY: ACM. doi:10.1145/1455770.1455782

Basu, S., Pollack, R., & Roy, M.-F. (2000). Computing Roadmaps of Semi-algebraic Sets on a Variety. *Journal of the American Mathematical Society*, *13*(01), 55–82. doi:10.1090/S0894-0347-99-00311-2

Battistich, V., Schaps, E., & Wilson, N. (2004). Effects of an elementary school intervention on students' "connectedness" to school and social adjustment during middle school. *The Journal of Primary Prevention*, *24*(3), 243–262. doi:10.1023/B:JOPP.0000018048.38517.cd

Baxter, J., & Galbraith, C. A. (Eds.). (2010). *People and nature in conflict: can we reconcile hen harrier conservation and game management?* Edinburgh, UK: Academic Press.

Beals, A. R., & Siegel, B. J. (1966). *Divisiveness and social conflict: an athropological approach*. Stanford, CA: Stanford University Press.

Beam, C., & Segev, A. (1997). Automated negotiations: A survey of the state of the art. *Wirtschaftsinformatik*, *39*(3), 263–268.

Bean, M., Fisher, L., & Eng, M. (2007). Assessment in Environmental and Public Policy Conflict Resolution: Emerging Theory, Patterns of Practice, and a Conceptual Framework. *Conflict Resolution Quarterly*, *24*(4), 447–468. doi:10.1002/crq.184

Beeco, J. A., & Brown, G. (2013). Integrating space, spatial tools and spatial analysis into the human dimensions of parks and outdoor recreation. *Applied Geography (Sevenoaks, England)*, *38*, 76–85. doi:10.1016/j.apgeog.2012.11.013

Bellucci, E., Lodder, A., & Zeleznikow, J. (2004). Integrating artificial intelligence, argumentation and game theory to develop an online dispute resolution environment. In *Proceedings of the 16th IEEE International Conference on Tools with Artificial Intelligence*. Washington, DC: IEEE Computer Society. doi:10.1109/ICTAI.2004.75

Bench-Capon, T. J. (1998). Specification and implementation of Toulmin dialogue game. In *International Conferences on Legal Knowledge and Information Systems*. IOS Press.

Bench-Capon, T., & Dunne, P. (2007). Argumentation in artificial intelligence. *Artificial Intelligence*, *171*(10-15), 619–938. doi:10.1016/j.artint.2007.05.001

Bennewitz, M., Burgard, W., & Thrun, S. (2001). Optimizing schedules for prioritized path planning of multi-robot systems. In *IEEE International Conference on Robotics and Automation* (ICRA), (pp. 271–276). doi:10.1109/ROBOT.2001.932565

Bennewitz, M., Burgard, W., & Thrun, S. (2002). Finding and optimizing solvable priority schemes for decoupled path planning techniques for teams of mobile robots. *Robotics and Autonomous Systems*, *41*(2), 89–99. doi:10.1016/S0921-8890(02)00256-7

Bënohr, I. (2012). Alternative dispute resolution for consumers in the EU. In C. Christopher Hodges, I. Benöhr, & N. Creutzfeldt-Banda (Eds.), *Consumer ADR in Europe*. Oxford, UK: Bloomsbury Publishing.

Bercht, M. (2001). *Em direção a agentes pedagógicos com dimensões afetivas. Tese de Doutorado (Doutorado em Ciência da Computação)*. Porto Alegre: Universidade Federal do Rio Grande do Sul.

Bertot, J. C., Jaeger, P. T., & Hansen, D. (2012). The Impact of Polices on Government Social Media Usage: Issues, Challenges, and Recommendations. *Government Information Quarterly*, *29*(1), 30–40. doi:10.1016/j.giq.2011.04.004

Besnard, P., & Hunter, A. (2008). *The elements of argumentation*. The MIT Press. doi:10.7551/mitpress/9780262026437.001.0001

Bies, R. J., Shapiro, D. L., & Cummings, L. L. (1988). Casual Accounts and Managing Organizational Conflict. *Communication Research*, *15*(4), 381–399. doi:10.1177/009365088015004003

Billingham, R. E., & Sack, A. R. (1987). Conflict Tactics and The Level of Emotional Commitment Among Unmarried. *Human Relations*, *40*(1), 59–74. doi:10.1177/001872678704000105

Binding, K. (1913). *Grundriß des deutschen Strafrechts. Allgemeiner Teil* (8th ed.). Leipzig, Germany: Meiner.

Binetti, G., Naso, D., & Turchiano, B. (2013). Decentralized task allocation for surveillance systems with critical tasks. *Robotics and Autonomous Systems*, *61*(12), 1653–1664. doi:10.1016/j.robot.2013.06.007

Binmore, K., Rubinstein, A., & Wolinsky, A. (1986). The Nash bargaining solution in economic modelling. *The Rand Journal of Economics*, *17*(2), 176–188. doi:10.2307/2555382

Bisno, H. (1988). *Managing Conflict*. Newbury Park, CA: Sage.

Blake, R., & Mouton, J. (1964). *The Managerial Grid*. Houston, TX: Gulf Publishing.

Blake, S., Browne, J., & Sime, S. (2014). *A Practical Approach to Alternative Dispute Resolution*. Oxford, UK: Oxford University Press.

Boella, G., Van Der Torre, L., & Verhagen, H. (2006). Introduction to normative multiagent systems. *Computational & Mathematical Organization Theory*, *12*(2), 71–79. doi:10.1007/s10588-006-9537-7

Bonson, E., Torres, L., Royo, S., & Flores, F. (2012). Local e-Government 2.0. Social Media and Corporate Transparency in Municipalities. *Government Information Quarterly*, *29*(2), 123–132. doi:10.1016/j.giq.2011.10.001

Botelho, S. S. C., & Alami, R. (1999). *M+:* A scheme for multi-robot cooperation through negotiated task allocation and achievement. In *International Conference on Robotics and Automation* (ICRA), (vol. 2, pp. 1234–1239). doi:10.1109/ROBOT.1999.772530

Botelho, S. S. C., & Alami, R. (2000). Robots that cooperatively enhance their plans. In *5th International Symposium on Distributed Autonomous Robotic Systems* (DARS).

Botetzagias, I., & Karamichas, J. (2009). Grassroots mobilisations against waste disposal sites in Greece. *Environmental Politics*, *18*(6), 939–959. doi:10.1080/09644010903345702

Boulding, E. (1962). *Conflict and Defense*. New York: Harper and Row.

Boulding, K. E. (1963). *Conflict and defense*. New York, NY: Harper & Row.

Bouton, M. E. (2009). Behaviourism, thoughts, and actions. *British Journal of Psychology*, *100*(S1), 181–183. doi:10.1348/000712609X415140 PMID:19351440

Brabham, D. C. (2008a). Crowdsourcing as a model for problem solving an introduction and cases. *Convergence (London)*, *14*(1), 75–90. doi:10.1177/1354856507084420

Brabham, D. C. (2008b). Moving the crowd at iStockphoto: The composition of the crowd and motivations for participation in a crowdsourcing application. *First Monday*, *13*(6), 1–22. doi:10.5210/fm.v13i6.2159

Braithwaite, J. (2002). *Restorative justice and responsive regulation*. Oxford, UK: Oxford University Press.

Braithwaite, J. (2003). Principles of Restorative Justice. In A. Hirsch, J. Roberts, A. Bottoms, K. Roach, & M. Schiff (Eds.), *Restorative Justice and Criminal Justice. Competing or Reconcilable Paradigms?* (pp. 1–20). Oxford, UK: Hart Publishing.

Brans, J. P., Vincke, P., & Mareschal, B. (1986). How to select and how to rank projects: The PROMETHEE method. *European Journal of Operational Research*, *24*(2), 228–238. doi:10.1016/0377-2217(86)90044-5

Brennan, R., Baines, P., & Garneau, P. (2008). *Contemporary strategic marketing*. Palgrave Macmillan.

Browder, G. (2000). An analysis of the negotiations for the 1995 mekong agreement. *International Negotiation*, *5*(2), 237–261. doi:10.1163/15718060020848758

Brown, G., & Brabyn, L. (2012). An analysis of the relationships between multiple values and physical landscapes at a regional scale using public participation GIS and landscape character classification. *Landscape and Urban Planning*, *107*(3), 317–331. doi:10.1016/j.landurbplan.2012.06.007

Brown, G., & Kyttä, M. (2014). Key issues and research priorities for public participation GIS (PPGIS): A synthesis based on empirical research. *Applied Geography (Sevenoaks, England)*, *46*, 122–136. doi:10.1016/j.apgeog.2013.11.004

Brown, R., & Gaertner, S. (Eds.). (2003). *Blackwell Handbook of Social Psychology: Intergroup Processes*. Oxford, UK: Blackwell publishing. doi:10.1002/9780470693421

Buckley, S. (1989) Fast motion planning for multiple moving robots. In *IEEE International Conference on Robotics and Automation* (ICRA), (pp. 322–326). doi:10.1109/ROBOT.1989.100008

Buffett, S., & Spencer, B. (2007). A bayesian classifier for learning opponents' preferences in multi-object automated negotiation. *Electronic Commerce Research and Applications*, *6*(3), 274–284. doi:10.1016/j.elerap.2006.06.008

Bui, H., Venkatesh, S., & Kieronska, D. (1999). Learning Other Agents' Preferences in Multi-Agent Negotiation Using the Bayesian Classifier. *International Journal of Cooperative Information Systems*, *8*(4), 275–293. doi:10.1142/S0218843099000149

Buratti, C., Conti, A., Dardari, D., & Verdone, R. (2009). An overview on wireless sensor networks technology and evolution. *Sensors (Basel, Switzerland)*, *9*(9), 6869–6896. doi:10.3390/s90906869 PMID:22423202

Burton, J. W. (1998). Conflict Resolution: The Human Dimension. *The International Journal for Peace Studies*. Retrieved from http://www.gmu.edu/programs/icar/ijps/vol3_1/burton.htm

Burton, J. W. (1998). Conflict Resolution: The Human Dimension. *International Journal of Peace Studies*, *3*(1), 4.

Buss, H. (2009). *Measuring and Reducing the Cost of Conflict at Work in UNHCR: The Business Case of Conflict Management*. Institut universitaire Kurt Bösch.

Butler, S. J., Boccaccio, L., Gregoryc, R. D., Vorisekd, P., & Norrisa, K. (2010). Quantifying the impact of land-use change to European farmland bird populations. *Agriculture, Ecosystems & Environment*, *137*(3-4), 348–357. doi:10.1016/j.agee.2010.03.005

Caloud, P., Choi, W., Latombe, J.-C., Pape, C. L., & Yim, M. (1990). Indoor automation with many mobile robots. In *International Workshop on Intelligent Robotics and Systems* (IROS).

Canavese, D., Siquiera Ortega, N. R., & Queiros, M. (2014). The assessment of local sustainability using fuzzy logic: An expert opinion system to evaluate environmental sanitation in the Algarve region, Portugal. *Ecological Indicators*, *36*, 711–718. doi:10.1016/j.ecolind.2013.09.030

Canny, J. F. (1991). Computing roadmaps of general semi-algebraic sets. *Applied Algebra, Algebraic Algorithms and Error–Correcting Codes. Lecture Notes in Computer Science*, *539*, 94–107. doi:10.1007/3-540-54522-0_99

Cap, M., Novak, P., Kleiner, A., Selecky, M., & Pechoucek, M. (2015). *Prioritized Planning Algorithms for Trajectory Coordination of Multiple Mobile Robots. IEEE Transactions on Automation Science and Engineering*.

Capobianco, M., Chesñevar, C. I., & Simari, G. R. (2005). Argumentation and the dynamics of warranted beliefs in changing environments. *Autonomous Agents and Multi-Agent Systems*, *11*(2), 127–151. doi:10.1007/s10458-005-1354-8

Caragliu, A., Del Bo, C., & Nijkamp, P. (2011). Smart cities in Europe. *Journal of Urban Technology*, *18*(2), 65–82. doi:10.1080/10630732.2011.601117

Carbonneau, R., Kersten, G. E., & Vahidov, R. (2008). Predicting opponent's moves in electronic negotiations using neural networks. *Expert Systems with Applications*, *34*(2), 1266–1273. doi:10.1016/j.eswa.2006.12.027

Carbonneau, R., Kersten, G., & Vahidov, R. (2011). Pairwise issue modeling for negotiation counteroffer prediction using neural networks. *Decision Support Systems*, *50*(2), 449–459. doi:10.1016/j.dss.2010.11.002

Carneiro, D., Novais, P., & Neves, J. (2014). Information Retrieval. In D. Carneiro, P. Novais & J. Neves (Eds.), Conflict Resolution and its Context (pp. 141-162). Cham: Springer.

Carneiro, D., Novais, P., Andrade, F., Zeleznikow, J., & Neves, J. (2009). The Legal Precedent in Online Dispute Resolution. In G. Governatori (Ed.), Legal Knowledge and Information Systems (pp. 47-52). Amsterdam: IOS Press.

Carneiro, D., Novais, P., Andrade, F., Zeleznikow, J., & Neves, J. (2012). *Context-aware Environments for Online Dispute Resolution*. Paper presented at GDN 2012 - The 12th international annual meeting of the Group Decision and Negotiation Conference, Recife, Brazil.

Carneiro, D., Gomes, M., Novais, P., & Neves, J. (2011). Developing Dynamic Conflict Resolution Models Based on the Interpretation of Personal Conflict Styles. In L. Antunes & H. S. Pinto (Eds.), *EPIA* (Vol. 7026, pp. 44–58). Springer. doi:10.1007/978-3-642-24769-9_4

Carneiro, D., Novais, P., Andrade, F., Zeleznikow, J., & Neves, J. (2013). Using case-based reasoning and principled negotiation to provide decision support for dispute resolution. *Knowledge and Information Systems*, *36*(3), 789–826. doi:10.1007/s10115-012-0563-0

Carneiro, D., Novais, P., & Neves, J. (2013). Using genetic algorithms to create solutions for conflict resolution. *Neurocomputing*, *109*, 16–26. doi:10.1016/j.neucom.2012.03.024

Carnevale, P. J., & Pruitt, D. G. (1992). Negotiation and Mediation. *Annual Review of Psychology, 43*(1), 531–582. doi:10.1146/annurev.ps.43.020192.002531

Cartwright, D., & Atkinson, K. (2009). Using Computational Argumentation to Support E-participation. *IEEE Intelligent Systems, 24*(5), 42–52. doi:10.1109/MIS.2009.104

Casbeer, D. W., & Holsapple, R. W. (2011). Column generation for a UAV assignment problem with precedence constraints. *International Journal of Robust and Nonlinear Control, 21*(12), 1421–1433. doi:10.1002/rnc.1722

Castells, M. (2005). A sociedade em rede. In G. Cardoso & C. Conceição (Eds.), *A sociedade em rede em Portugal*. Porto: Campo das Letras.

Castro, C. S. (2005). *Direito da Informática, Privacidade e Dados Pessoais*. Coimbra: Almedina. (in Portuguese)

Chaimowicz, L., Sugar, T., Kumar, V., & Campos, M. (2001). An architecture for tightly couple multi-robot cooperation. In *IEEE International Conference on Robotics and Automation* (ICRA), (pp. 2992–2997).

Chang, S. L., Yang, F. T., Wu, W. P., Cho, Y. A., & Chen, S. W. (2011). Nighttime pedestrian detection using thermal imaging based on HOG feature. In *International Conference on System Science and Engineering* (pp. 694-698). Macao: IEEE. doi:10.1109/ICSSE.2011.5961992

Cheng, J., & Zhang, G. (2013). Multi-objective Differential Evolution: A Recent Survey. *Soft Computing with Applications, 1*(1). doi:10.4156/sca.vol1.issue1.1

Chen, J., & Sun, D. (2012). Coalition-based approach to task allocation of multiple robots with resource constraints. *IEEE Transactions on Automation Science and Engineering, 9*(3), 516–528. doi:10.1109/TASE.2012.2201470

Chen, M. (2006). Understanding the Benefits and Detriments of Conflict on Team Creativity Process. *Creativity and Innovation Management, 15*(1), 105–116. doi:10.1111/j.1467-8691.2006.00373.x

Chesñevar, C., Maguitman, A., & Simari, G. (2007). Recommender Systems based on Argumentation. in Emerging Artificial Intelligence Applications in Computer Engineering. IOS Press.

Chesñevar, C., Maguitman, A., Estevez, E., Osman, N., & Sierra, C. (2013) E2 participation: electronically empowering citizens for social innovation through agreement technologies. In *Proceeding of 14th Annual International Conference on Digital Government Research DG.O 2013*. ACM Press. doi:10.1145/2479724.2479772

Chesñevar, C., Maguitman, A., Estévez, E., & Brena, R. (2012). Integrating Argumentation Technologies and Context-Based Search for Intelligent Processing of Citizens' Opinion in Social Media. In *Proceedings of 6th International Conference on Theory and Practice of Electronic Governance, ICEGOV '12*, (pp. 171-174). ACM Press. doi:10.1145/2463728.2463762

Chesñevar, C., Maguitman, A., & González, M. (2014). Empowering citizens through opinion mining from twitter-based arguments. In *Proceedings of 6th International Conference on Theory and Practice of Electronic Governance, ICEGOV '12*, (pp. 275-278). ACM Press. doi:10.1145/2691195.2691282

Che, Y., Yang, K., Jin, Y., Zhang, W., Shang, Z., & Tai, J. (2013). Residents' concerns and attitudes toward a municipal solid waste landfill: Integrating a questionnaire survey and GIS techniques. *Environmental Monitoring and Assessment, 185*(12), 10001–11001. doi:10.1007/s10661-013-3308-y PMID:23793647

Chiddarwar, S. S., & Babu, N. R. (2011). Conflict Free Coordinated Path Planning for Multiple Robots Using a Dynamic Path Modification Sequence. *Robotics and Autonomous Systems, 59*(7–8), 508–518. doi:10.1016/j.robot.2011.03.006

Chinchilla, R. (2011). Ethical and Social consequences of Biometric Technologies. *Journal of Industrial Technology, 27*(1).

Chklovski, T. (2003). Learner: A System for Acquiring Commonsense Knowledge by Analogy. In *Proceedings of the 2nd ACM International Conference on Knowledge Capture* (pp. 4–12). Retrieved from http://dl.acm.org/citation.cfm?id=945650

Choi, N., Song, I. Y., & Han, H. (2006). A survey on ontology mapping. *SIGMOD Record*, *35*(3), 34–41. doi:10.1145/1168092.1168097

Chopra, A. K., & Singh, M. P. (2013). *Multiagent Systems: A Modern Approach to Distributed Artificial Intelligence. In Agent Communication* (pp. 101–141). The MIT Press.

Christie, N. (1977). Conflicts as property. *The British Journal of Criminology*, *17*(1), 1–15.

Chua, E. G., & Gundykunst, W. B. (1987). Conflict Resolution Styles in Low and High-Context Cultures. *Communication Research Reports*, *4*(1), 32–37.

Clair, L., Johansen, L., Enck, W., Pirretti, M., Traynor, P., McDaniel, P., & Jaeger, T. (2006). Password Exhaustion: Predicting the End of Password Usefulness. In *Information Systems Security* (pp. 37-55). Heidelberg, Germany: Springer. Retrieved July 17, 2015, from http://www.enck.org/pubs/iciss06a.pdf

Clark, C., Rock, S., & Latombe, J.-C. (2003). Motion planning for multiple robot systems using dynamic networks. In *IEEE International Conference on Robotics and Automation* (ICRA), (pp. 4222–4227).

Clark, R. C., & Mayer, R. E. (Eds.). (2011). *E-Learning and the Science of Instruction – Proven Guidelines for consumers and designers of multimedia learning* (3rd ed.). John Wiley & Sons. Inc. doi:10.1002/9781118255971

Clegg, S. (1990). *Modern Organizations: Organization Studies in the Postmodern World*. London: Sage Publications Ltd.

Cobano, J. A., Conde, R., Alejo, D., & Ollero, A. (2011). Conflict detection and resolution algorithm for en-route conflicts in dense non-segregated aerial traffic. *1st Int. Conf. on Application and Theory of Automation in Command and Control Systems (ATACCS 2011)*.

Cocea, M., & Weibelzahl, S. (2007). Eliciting motivation knowledge from log files towards motivation diagnosis for Adaptive Systems. *User Modeling 2007* (LNCS). Springer Berlin / Heidelberg.

Coehoorn, R., & Jennings, N. (2004). Learning on opponent's preferences to make effective multi-issue negotiation trade-offs. In *The 6th International Conference on Electronic Commerce (ICEC'04)*, (pp. 59–68).

Coelho, J. P., Moura Oliveira, P. B., Boaventura Cunha, J., & Vrancic, D. (2006). On-Line Control using the Particle Swarm Optimisation Algorithm. *The 6th Asian Control Conference*.

Cogoy, M., & Steininger, K. W. (2007). *Transforming Environmental and Natural Resource Use Conflicts. In The Economics of Global Environmental Change: International Cooperation for Sustainability*. Edward Elgar Publishing.

Coleman, P. T. (2003). Characteristics of Protracted, Intractable Conflict: Toward the Development of a Metaframework-I. *Peace and Conflict*, *9*(1), 1–37. doi:10.1207/S15327949PAC0901_01

Conde, R., Alejo, D., Cobano, J. A., Viguria, A., & Ollero, A. (2012). Conflict Detection and Resolution Method for Cooperating Unmanned Aerial Vehicles. *Journal of Intelligent & Robotic Systems*, *65*(1-4), 495–505. doi:10.1007/s10846-011-9564-6

Cooper, S., & Taleb-Bendiab, A. (1998). CONCENSUS: Multi-party negotiation support for conflict resolution in concurrent engineering design. *Journal of Intelligent Manufacturing*, *9*(2), 155–159. doi:10.1023/A:1008820029707

Corne, D., & Knowles, J. (2007). Techniques for Highly Multiobjective Optimisation: Some Nondominated Points are Better than Others. Academic Press.

Cortés, P. (2010). *Online Dispute Resolution for Consumers in the European Union*. Oxon, UK: Routledge.

Coser, L. A. (1956). *The Functions of Social Conflict*. Academic Press.

Coser, L. A. (1956). *The Functions of Social Conflict*. New York: Macmillan.

Coser, L. A. (1967). *Continuities in the study of Social Conflict*. New York: Free Press.

Costa, D. G., Guedes, L. A., Vasques, F., & Portugal, P. (2013). Adaptive monitoring relevance in camera networks for critical surveillance applications. *International Journal of Distributed Sensor Networks*, *2013*, 836721. doi:10.1155/2013/836721

Costinela-Luminiţa, C., & Nicoleta-Magdalena, C. (2012). E-learning Security Vulnerabilities. *Procedia: Social and Behavioral Sciences*, *46*, 2297–2301. doi:10.1016/j.sbspro.2012.05.474

Criado, N., Argente, E., & Botti, V. (2013). THOMAS: An Agent Platform For Supporting Normative Multi-Agent Systems. *Journal of Logic and Computation.*, *23*(2), 309–333. doi:10.1093/logcom/exr025

Cui, R., Gao, B., & Guo, J. (2012). Pareto-optimal coordination of multiple robots with safety guarantees. *Autonomous Robots*, *32*(3), 189–205. doi:10.1007/s10514-011-9265-9

Daft, R. (2012). *Organization theory and design*. Cengage Learning.

Daly, K., & Proietti-Scifoni, G. (2010). Reparation and restoration. In M. Tonry (Ed.), *Oxford Handbook of Crime and Criminal Justice* (pp. 207–253). New York: Oxford University Press.

Daniels, S. E., & Walker, G. B. (2001). *Working Through Environmental Conflict: The Collaborative Learning Approach*. Praeger.

Davidsson, P., & Johansson, S. (2006). On the potential of norm-governed behavior in different categories of artificial societies. *Computational & Mathematical Organization Theory*, *12*(2-3), 169–180. doi:10.1007/s10588-006-9542-x

Dawson, R., & Bynghall, S. (2015). *Crowdsourcing landscape*. Retrieved from http://rossdawson.com/frameworks/crowdsourcing-landscape-version-2/

De Barros, P. M. (2011). *Incidência e impacto do cyberbullying nos alunos do terceiro ciclo do ensino básico público português*. University of Granada. Retrieved July 18, 2015, from http://0-hera.ugr.es.adrastea.ugr.es/tesisugr/20058068.pdf

De Dreu, C. K. W. (2006). When Too Much and Too Llittle Hurts: Evidence For a Curvilinear Relationship Between Task Conflict and Innovation in Teams. *Journal of Management*, *32*(1), 83–107. doi:10.1177/0149206305277795

de Dreu, C. K. W. (2008). The virtue and vice of workplace conflict : Food for (pessimistic) thought. *Journal of Organizational Behavior*, *29*(1), 5–18. doi:10.1002/job.474

De Dreu, C. K. W., & Gelfand, M. J. (2008). *The Psychology of Conflict and Conflict Management in Organizations*. Oxford, UK: Taylor & Francis.

De Dreu, C. K. W., & Van de Vliert, E. (Eds.). (1997). *Using Conflict in Organizations*. London: Sage.

De Dreu, C. K. W., & Weingart, L. R. (2003). Task Versus Relationship Conflict, Team Member Satisfaction, and Team Effectiveness: A Meta-Analysis. *The Journal of Applied Psychology*, *88*, 741–749. doi:10.1037/0021-9010.88.4.741 PMID:12940412

De la Prieta, F., Rodríguez, S., Bajo, J., & Corchado, J. M. (2013). A multiagent system for resource distribution into a Cloud Computing environment. In *Advances on Practical Applications of Agents and Multi-Agent Systems* (pp. 37–48). Springer Berlin Heidelberg. doi:10.1007/978-3-642-38073-0_4

De Vries, B. R., Leenes, R., & Zeleznikow, J. (2005) Fundamentals of providing negotiation support online: the need for developing BATNAs. In *Proceedings of the Second International ODR Workshop*. Wolf Legal Publishers.

De Vries, B. R., Leenes, R., & Zeleznikow, J. (2005). Fundamentals of providing negotiation support online: The need for developing BATNAs. In *Proceedings of the Second International ODR Workshop*, (pp.59–67). Tilburg: Wolf Legal Publishers.

Dear, M. (1992). Understanding and Overcoming the NIMBY Syndrome. *Journal of the American Planning Association*, *58*(3), 288–300. doi:10.1080/01944369208975808

Deb, K., & Jain, H. (2012). Handling many-objective problems using an improved NSGA-II procedure. In *IEEE Congress on Evolutionary Computation (CEC)*. doi:10.1109/CEC.2012.6256519

Deb, K., Pratap, A., Agarwal, S., & Meyarivan, T. (2002). A Fast and Elitist Multiobjective Genetic Algorithm: NSGA–II. *IEEE Transactions on Evolutionary Computation*, *6*(2), 182–197. doi:10.1109/4235.996017

Deutsch, M. (2008). Cooperation and Conflict: A Personal Perspective on the History of the Social Psychological Study of Conflict Resolution. In International Handbook of Organizational Teamwork and Cooperative Working (pp. 9–43). John Wiley & Sons Ltd. http://doi.org/ doi:<ALIGNMENT.qj></ALIGNMENT>10.1002/9780470696712.ch2

Deutsch, M. (1949). A Theory of Cooperation and Competition. *Human Relations*, *2*(2), 129–152. doi:10.1177/001872674900200204

Deutsch, M. (1973). Conflicts: Productive and Destructuve. In F. E. Jandt (Ed.), *Conflict Resolution Through Communication* (p. 156). New York: Harper & Row.

Deutsch, M. (1973). *The resolution of conflict: Constructive and destructive processes*. New Haven, CT: Yale University Press.

Deutsch, M., & Coleman, P. (Eds.). (2000). *The Handbook of Conflict Resolution: Theory and practice*. San Francisco, CA: Jossey Bass.

Di Paola, D., Naso, D., Milella, A., Cicirelli, G., & Distante, A. (2010). Multi-sensor surveillance of indoor environments by an autonomous mobile robot. *International Journal of Intelligent Systems Technologies and Applications*, *8*(1–4), 18–35. doi:10.1504/IJISTA.2010.030187

Di Paola, D., Naso, D., Turchiano, B., Cicirelli, G., & Distante, A. (2009). Matrix-based discrete event control for surveillance mobile robotics. *Journal of Intelligent & Robotic Systems*, *56*(5), 513–541. doi:10.1007/s10846-009-9326-x

Dias, M. B. (2004). *TraderBots: A New Paradigm for Robust and Efficient Multirobot Coordination in Dynamic Environments*. (PhD thesis). Robotics Institute, Carnegie Mellon University.

Diehk, P. F., & Gleditsch, N. P. (Eds.). (2001). *Environmental Conflict*. Oxford, UK: Westview.

DiMaio, A. (2009). *Government 2.0: A Gartner Definition*. Retrieved February 28, 2014, from http://blogs.gartner.com/andrea_dimaio/2009/11/13/government-2-0-a-gartner-definition/

Dimech, M., Darmanin, M., Smith, P., Kaiser, M., & Schembri, P. (2009). Fishers' perception of a 35-year old exclusive Fisheries Management Zone. *Biological Conservation*, *142*(11), 2691–2702. doi:10.1016/j.biocon.2009.06.019

Doan, A., Ramakrishnan, R., & Halevy, A. Y. (2011). Crowdsourcing systems on the world-wide web. *Communications of the ACM*, *54*(4), 86–96. doi:10.1145/1924421.1924442

Dollár, P., Wojek, C., Schiele, B., & Perona, P. (2012). Pedestrian detection: An evaluation of the state of the art. *IEEE Transactions on Pattern Analysis and Machine Intelligence*, *34*(4), 743–761. doi:10.1109/TPAMI.2011.155 PMID:21808091

Donohue, W., & Colt, R. (1992). *Managing Interpersonal Conflict*. Newbury Park, CA: Sage. doi:10.4135/9781483325873

Dougui, N., Delahaye, D., Puechmorel, S., & Mongeau, M. (2013). A light-propagation model for aircraft trajectory planning. *Journal of Global Optimization*, *56*(3), 873–895. doi:10.1007/s10898-012-9896-1

Downes, S. (2005, October). E-learning 2.0. *eLearn*.

Dung, P. M. (1995). On the acceptability of arguments and its fundamental role in nonmonotonic reasoning, logic programming, and n-person games. *Artificial Intelligence*, *77*(2), 321–357. doi:10.1016/0004-3702(94)00041-X

Durand, N., Alliot, J. M., & Noailles, J. (1996). Automatic aircraft conflict resolution using genetic algorithms. In *Proceedings of the 1996 ACM symposium on Applied Computing*, (pp. 289-298).

Ebner, M. (2007). E-learning 2.0 = e-learning 1.0 + web 2.0? *Availability, Reliability and Security, International Conference on*.

EC. (2010). *Environment: Italy faces Court for failing to implement EU law on waste*. Author.

EC. (2014). *Environment: European Commission takes Slovenia to Court for pollution problems from waste disposal*. Author.

Eisen, J. (1998). Are We Ready for Mediation in Cyberspace? *Brigham Young University Law Review*, *1998*, 1305–1358.

Elwood, S., Goodchild, M. F., & Sui, D. (2013). Prospects for VGI research and the emerging fourth paradigm. In *Crowdsourcing Geographic Knowledge* (pp. 361–375). Springer. doi:10.1007/978-94-007-4587-2_20

Emami, H., & Derakhshan, F. (2014). Multi-Agent Based Solution for Free Flight Conflict Detection and Resolution using Particle Swarm Optimization Algorithm. *U.P.B. Sci. Bull., Series C, 76*(3), 49-64.

Enzweiler, M., & Gavrila, D. M. (2009). Monocular pedestrian detection: Survey and experiments. *IEEE Transactions on Pattern Analysis and Machine Intelligence*, *31*(12), 2179–2195. doi:10.1109/TPAMI.2008.260 PMID:19834140

Eom, S., Ashill, N. J., Arbaugh, J. B., & Stapleton, J. L. (2012). The role of information technology in e-learning systems success. *Human Systems Management*, *31*, 147–163.

Epp, C., Lippold, M., & Mandryk, R. L. (2011). Identifying emotional states using keystroke dynamics. In *Proceedings of the SIGCHI Conference on Human Factors in Computing Systems*, (pp. 715–724). ACM. DOI doi:10.1145/1978942.1979046

Erdmann, M., & Lozano-Perez, T. (1986). On multiple moving objects. In *IEEE International Conference on Robotics and Automation* (ICRA), (pp. 1419–1424).

Erdmann, M., & Lozano-Perez, T. (1987). On multiple moving objects. *Algorithmica*, *2*(1-4), 477–521. doi:10.1007/BF01840371

Erétéo, G., Gandon, F. L., Corby, O., & Buffa, M. (2009). *Semantic Social Network Analysis*. Presented at the Web Science. Retrieved from http://hal.inria.fr/inria-00378174

Esparcia, S., & Argente, E. (2011). *Defining Virtual Organizations Following a Formal Approach. In Agents and Artificial Intelligence 2011*. Revised Selected Papers.

European Union. (2005). *Multi-criteria analysis*. Retrieved from http://ec.europa.eu/europeaid/evaluation/methodology/tools/too_cri_whe_en.htm#03

Faber, L. G., Maurits, N. M., & Lorist, M. M. (2012). Mental fatigue affects visual selective attention. *PLoS ONE*, *7*(10), e48073. doi:10.1371/journal.pone.0048073 PMID:23118927

Faratin, P., Sierra, C., & Jennings, N. (1998). Negotiation Decision Functions for Autonomous Agents. *International Journal of Robotics and Autonomous Systems, 24*(3-4), 159–182. doi:10.1016/S0921-8890(98)00029-3

Faratin, P., Sierra, C., & Jennings, N. (2002). Using Similarity Criteria to Make Issue Trade-Offs in Automated Negotiations. *Artificial Intelligence, 142*(2), 205–237. doi:10.1016/S0004-3702(02)00290-4

Faridani, S., Hartmann, B., & Ipeirotis, P. G. (2011). What's the right price? pricing tasks for finishing on time. In *Proceedings of AAAI Workshop on Human Computation*. Retrieved from http://www.aaai.org/ocs/index.php/WS/AAAIW11/paper/download/3994/4269

Fatima, S. S., Wooldridge, M. J., & Jennings, N. R. (2004). An agenda-based framework for multi-issue negotiation. *Artificial Intelligence, 152*(1), 1–45. doi:10.1016/S0004-3702(03)00115-2

Ferber, J. (1999). *Multi-agent systems: an introduction to distributed artificial intelligence* (Vol. 1). Reading: Addison-Wesley.

Ferber, J., Gutknecht, O., & Michel, F. (2004). From agents to organizations: an organizational view of multi-agent systems. In *Agent-Oriented Software Engineering IV* (pp. 214–230). Springer Berlin Heidelberg. doi:10.1007/978-3-540-24620-6_15

Fernández-Caballero, A., Castillo, J. C., Serrano-Cuerda, J., & Maldonado-Bascón, S. (2011). Real-time human segmentation in infrared videos. *Expert Systems with Applications, 38*(3), 2577–2584. doi:10.1016/j.eswa.2010.08.047

Ferrati, M., & Pallottino, L. (2013). A time expanded network based algorithm for safe and efficient distributed multi-agent coordination. In *IEEE Conference on Decision and Control*, (pp. 2805–2810). doi:10.1109/CDC.2013.6760308

Ferrera, E., Castaño, A. R., Capitán, J., Marrón, P. J., & Ollero, A. (2014). Multi-robot Operation System with Conflict Resolution. In *ROBOT2013: First Iberian Robotics Conference Advances in Intelligent Systems and Computing*, (vol. 252, pp. 407–419).

Fink, C. F. (1968). Some Conceptual Difficulties in the Theory of Social Conflict. *The Journal of Conflict Resolution, 12*(4), 412–460. doi:10.1177/002200276801200402

Finkelstein, A., Harman, M., Mansouri, S. A., Ren, J., & Zhang, Y. (2008). Fairness Analysis. In *Requirements Assignments,16th IEEE International Requirements Engineering Conference*, (pp. 115-124). Doi:10.1109/RE.2008.61

Fink, J., Hsieh, M. A., & Kumar, V. (2008). Multi-Robot Manipulation via Caging in Environments with Obstacles. In *IEEE International Conference on Robotics and Automation* (ICRA), (pp. 1471–1476). doi:10.1109/ROBOT.2008.4543409

Fisher, B., & Thomas, B. (1996). *Real Dream Teams*. Delray Beach, FL: St. Louis Press.

Fisher, R., Ury, W. L., & Patton, B. (1991). *Getting to Yes: Negotiating Agreement without Giving In*. New York, NY: Penguin Books.

Foley, T. (2007). Environmental Conflict Resolution: Relational and Environmental Attentiveness as Measures of Success. *Conflict Resolution Quarterly, 24*(4), 485–504. doi:10.1002/crq.186

Follett, M. P. (1925). Constructive Conflict. In H. C. Metcalf (Ed.), *Scientific Foundations of Business Administration*. Baltimore, MD: Williams and Wilkins.

Foster, I., Kesselman, C., & Tuecke, S. (2001). The anatomy of the grid: Enabling scalable virtual organizations. *International Journal of High Performance Computing Applications, 15*(3), 200–222. doi:10.1177/109434200101500302

Fox, J., & Parsons, S. (1998). Arguing about beliefs and actions. In *Applications of Uncertainty Formalisms* (Vol. 1455, pp. 266–302). Springer. doi:10.1007/3-540-49426-X_13

Freire, H. F., Moura Oliveira, P. B., Solteiro Pires, E. J., & Bessa, M. (2014). Many-Objective PSO PID Controller Tuning. In *Proceedings of the 11th Portuguese Conference on Automatic Control Lecture Notes in Electrical Engineering*. Springer. doi:10.1007/978-3-319-10380-8_18

Frey, M. (2002). *Alternative Methods of Dispute Resolution*. Cengage Learning.

Friedman, G. (1996). Alternative Dispute Resolution and Emerging Online Technologies: Challenges and Opportunities. *Hastings Communications and Entertainment Law Journal*, *19*, 695–718.

Fundación Telefónica. (2014). *La Sociedad de la Información en España 2013*. Barcelona: Ariel.

Furlong, G. T. (2006). The conflict resolution toolbox: models and maps for analyzing diagnosing and resolving conflict. New Delhi: Wiley India (P) Ltd.

Gaio Jûnior, A. P. (2008). *Direito Processual Civil*. Belo Horizonte: Del Rey.

Galain Palermo, P., & Garreaud, A. (2012). Truth Commissions and the Reconstruction of the Past in the Post-Dictatorial Southern Cone: Concerning the Limitations for Understanding Evil. In K. Ambos, L. Coutinho, M. Palma, & P. Mendes (Eds.), Eichmann in Jerusalem – 50 Years After: An Interdisciplinary Approach (pp. 181-198). Berlin: Duncker & Humblot.

Galain Palermo, P. (2009). *La reparación del daño como equivalente funcional de la pena*. Montevideo: Universidad Católica del Uruguay.

Galain Palermo, P. (2015). *Justicia de Transición? Mecanismos políticos y jurídicos para la elaboración del pasado*. Valencia: Tirant lo Blanch.

Galanter, M. (1993). *Direito em abundância:a a actividade legislativa no Atlântico Norte. Revista Critica de Ciências Sociais, n.º 36*. Coimbra: Centro de Estudos Sociais. (In Portuguese)

Galitsky, B., & McKenna, E. (2009). *Sentiment Extraction from Consumer Reviews for Providing Product Recommendations*. US Patent Application US 2009/0282019 A1

Galitsky, B., & de la Rosa, J. L. (2011). Concept-based learning of human behavior for customer relationship management. *Information Sciences*, *181*(10), 2016–2035. doi:10.1016/j.ins.2010.08.027

García, A., & Simari, G. (2004). Defeasible Logic Programming: An Argumentative Approach. *Theory and Practice of Logic Programming*, *4*(1-2), 95–138. doi:10.1017/S1471068403001674

García-Peñalvo, F. J., & Seoane Pardo, A. M. (2015). Una revisión actualizada del concepto de eLearning. Décimo Aniversario. *Education in the Knowledge Society*, *16*(1), 119. doi:10.14201/eks2015161119144

Garfinkel, H. (1967). *Studies in Ethnomethodology*. Englewood Cliffs, NJ: Prentice Hall.

Gavrielides, T. (2011). Restorative Practices: From the early societies to the 1970s. *Internet Journal of Criminology*, *2011*, 1–20.

Gavrilidis, A. A., Grădinaru, S. R., Iojă, I. C., Cârstea, E. M., & Pătru-Stupariu, I. (2015). Land use and land cover dynamics in the periurban area of an industrialized East-European city. An overview of the last 100 years. *Carpathian Journal of Earth and Environmental Sciences*, *10*(4), 29–38.

Gayle, R., Sud, A., Lin, M. C., & Manocha, D. (2007). Reactive deformation roadmaps: motion planning of multiple robots in dynamic environments. In *International Conference on Intelligent Robots and Systems* (IROS), (pp. 3777–3783). doi:10.1109/IROS.2007.4399287

Gelfond, M., & Lifschitz, V. (1988). The stable model semantics for logic programming. In R. Kowalski, & K. Bowen (Eds.), *Logic Programming – Proceedings of the Fifth International Conference and Symposium,* (pp. 1070-1080). Academic Press.

Georgakopoulos, D., Hornick, M., & Sheth, A. (1995). An overview of workflow management: From process modeling to workflow automation infrastructure. *Distributed and Parallel Databases, 3*(2), 119–153. doi:10.1007/BF01277643

Gerkey, B. P., & Mataric, M. J. (2002). Sold! Auction methods for multi-robot control. *IEEE Transactions on Robotics and Automation. Special Issue on Multi-Robot Systems, 18*(5), 758–768.

Ge, S. S., & Cui, Y. J. (1997). Dynamic motion planning for mobile robots using potential field method. *Autonomous Robots, 13*(3), 207–222. doi:10.1023/A:1020564024509

Getzels, J. W., & Guba, E. (1954). Role, Role Confict, and Effectiveness: An Empirical Study. *American Sociological Review, 19*(2), 164–175. doi:10.2307/2088398

Gibson, J. L., Ivancevish, J. M., & Donnelly, J. H. Jr. (1991). *Organizations: Behavior Structure Processes.* Homewood, Illinois: Irwin.

Giordano, V., Zhang, J. B., Naso, D., & Lewis, F. L. (2008). Integrated supervisory and operational control of a warehouse with a matrix-based approach. *IEEE Transactions on Automation Science and Engineering, 5*(1), 53–70. doi:10.1109/TASE.2007.891472

Gissi, E., Siciliano, G., & Reho, M. (2011). *Biomass production and land use management in the Italian context: regulations, conflicts, and impacts* Paper presented at the 51st Congress of the European Regional Science Association, Barcelona, Spain.

Given, B. K. (1998). Psychological and neurobiological support for learning-style instruction: Why it works. *National Forum of Teacher Education Journal, 8.*

Goldberg, D. E. (1989). *Genetic Algorithms in Search, Optimization and Machine Learning.* Boston, MA: Addison-Wesley Longman Publishing Co., Inc.

Goldberg, E. D. (1989). *Genetic Algorithms in Search.* Optimization and Machine Learning, Adison Wesley P.C.

Golden, B., Raghavan, S., & Wasil, E. (2008). *The Vehicle Routing Problem: Latest Advances and New Challenges* (Vol. 43). Springer. doi:10.1007/978-0-387-77778-8

Goldman, R. M. (1966). A Theory of Conflict Processes and Organizational Offices. *The Journal of Conflict Resolution, 10*(3), 328–343. doi:10.1177/002200276601000305

Goleman, D. (1995). *Emotional Intelligence.* Bantam Books.

Goleman, D. (1997). *Working with Emotional Intelligence.* New York, NY: Bantam.

Golfarelli, M., Maio, D., & Rizzi, S. (1997). *A task-swap negotiation protocol based on the contract net paradigm.* Technical Report 005-97, Research Center for Informatics and Telecommunication Systems (CSITE), University of Bologna.

Gomes, M., Oliveira, T., Carneiro, D., Novais, P., & Neves, J. (2014). Studying the Effects of Stress on Negotiation Behavior. *Cybernetics and Systems, 45*(3), 279–291. doi:10.1080/01969722.2014.894858

Gomes, M., Oliveira, T., Silva, F., Carneiro, D., & Novais, P. (2014). Establishing the Relationship between Personality Traits and Stress in an Intelligent Environment. In *Modern Advances in Applied Intelligence* (pp. 378–387). Springer International Publishing. doi:10.1007/978-3-319-07467-2_40

González, E., Anido, L., Alba, J. L., & García, C. (2008). Is My Student at the Other Side? Applying Biometric Web Authentication to E-Learning Environments. In *Eighth IEEE International Conference on Advanced Learning Technologies, 2008. ICALT '08* (pp. 551-553). Retrieved July 16, 2015, from http://www.researchgate.net/profile/Jose_Luis_Alba-Castro/publication/221423359_Is_My_Student_at_the_Other_Side_Applying_Biometric_Web_Authentication_to_E-Learning_Environments/links/0912f4ffc67056eb8d000000.pdf

González, M. P., Chesñevar, C., & Brena, R. (2015). Modeling User's Sentiment in User Segmentations: An Argumentation Approach for User Centered Design. *Lecture Notes in Computer Science Series*, *9172*, 595–606. doi:10.1007/978-3-319-20612-7_56

Goodchild, M. F., & Glennon, J. A. (2010). Crowdsourcing geographic information for disaster response: A research frontier. *International Journal of Digital Earth*, *3*(3), 231–241. doi:10.1080/17538941003759255

Goodman, J. W. (2003). *The pros and cons of online dispute resolution: an assessment of cyber-mediation websites.* Retrieved from http://scholarship.law.duke.edu/cgi/viewcontent.cgi?article=1073&context=dltr

Goodman, J. (2003). The pros and cons of online dispute resolution: An assessment of cyber-mediation websites. *Duke Law and Technology Review*, *2*(1), 1–16.

Goroshko, O. I. & Samoilenko S. A. (2011). Twitter as a Conversation through e-learning Context. *Revista de Informatica Sociala*, (15).

Goubet, E., Katz, J., & Porikli, F. (2006). Pedestrian tracking using thermal infrared imaging. *SPIE Conference on Infrared Technology and Applications*, *6206*, 797-808.

Gouveia, L. M., & Gaio, S. (Eds.). (2004). Sociedade da Informação: balanço e implicações. Porto: Edições Universidade Fernando Pessoa. (In Portuguese)

Gouveia, M. F. (2014). *Curso de Resolução Alternativa de Litígios*. Coimbra: Almedina.

Grădinaru, S. R., Iojă, C. I., Onose, D. A., Gavrilidis, A. A., Pătru-Stupariu, I., Kienast, F., & Hersperger, A. M. (2015). Land abandonment as a precursor of built-up development at the sprawling periphery of former socialist cities. *Ecological Indicators*, *57*, 305–313. doi:10.1016/j.ecolind.2015.05.009

Granger, G., Durand, N., & Alliot, J. M. (2001). *Optimal Resolution of En Route Conflicts*. 4th ATM R&D Seminar, Santa Fe, NM.

Greenberg, J., & Baron, R. A. (1993). *Behavior in Organizations: Understanding and Managing the Human Side of Work* (4th ed.). Boston, MA: Allyn and Bacon.

Grodzinska-Jurczak, M., & Cent, J. (2011). Expansion of Nature Conservation Areas: Problems with Natura 2000 Implementation in Poland? *Environmental Management*, *47*(1), 11–27. doi:10.1007/s00267-010-9583-2 PMID:21107836

Grosse, K., González, M. P., Chesñevar, C., & Maguitman, A. G. (2015). Integrating argumentation and sentiment analysis for mining opinions from Twitter. *AI Communications*, *28*(3), 387–401. doi:10.3233/AIC-140627

Gruber, T. (2008). Collective knowledge systems: Where the social web meets the semantic web. *Web Semantics: Science, Services, and Agents on the World Wide Web*, *6*(1), 4–13. doi:10.1016/j.websem.2007.11.011

Guerra, A. (2004). A privacidade no local de trabalho – as novas tecnologias e o controlo dos trabalhadores através de sistemas automatizados; uma abordagem ao Código do Trabalho. Almedina, Coimbra. (in Portuguese)

Guerrero, J., & Oliver, G. (2012). Multi-robot coalition formation in real-time scenarios. *Robotics and Autonomous Systems*, *60*(10), 1295–1307. doi:10.1016/j.robot.2012.06.004

Guo, L., & Lease, M. (2011). Personalizing Local Search with Twitter (2011). In *Proceedings of theWorkshop on Enriching Information Retrieval. 34th International ACM SIGIR Conference on Research and Development in Information Retrieval, SIGIR 2011*. ACM Press.

Guo, Y., & Parker, E. (2002). A Distributed and Optimal Motion Planning Approach for Multiple Mobile Robots. In *IEEE International Conference on Robotics and Automation* (ICRA), (pp. 2612–2619).

Guttman, R. H., Moukas, A. G., & Maes, P. (1998). Agent-mediated electronic commerce: A survey. *The Knowledge Engineering Review*, *13*(2), 147–159. doi:10.1017/S0269888998002082

Hafeez, A., Kandil, N. H., Al-Omar, B., Landolsi, T., & Al-Ali, A. R. (2014). Smart Home Area Networks Protocols within the Smart Grid Context. *Journal of Communication*, *9*(9).

Hague, J. (1974). *Communication and Organizational Control*. New York: Wiley.

Halley, D. J., & Rosell, F. (2002). The beaver's reconquest of Eurasia: Status, population development and management of a conservation success. *Mammal Review*, *32*(3), 153–178. doi:10.1046/j.1365-2907.2002.00106.x

Hall, J. (1969). *Conflict Management Survey*. Conroe, TX: Teleometrics.

Hamblin, C. L. (1970). *Fallacies*. Methuen Co. Ltd.

Hamre, B. K., Pianta, R. C., & Bear, G. (Eds.). (2006). Student-Teacher Relationships. In Children's needs III: Development, prevention, and intervention, (pp. 59-71). Washington, DC: National Association of School Psychologists.

Hang, L. (2001). Online Dispute Resolution Systems: The Future of Cyberspace Law. *Santa Clara Law Review*, *41*, 837–866.

Harris, C. G. (2011). Dirty Deeds Done Dirt Cheap: A Darker Side to Crowdsourcing. In *IEEE International Conference on Privacy, Security, Risk and Trust* (pp. 1314–1317). Retrieved from http://ieeexplore.ieee.org/xpls/abs_all.jsp?arnumber=6113302

Hartley, R. E. (2002). *Alternative Dispute Resolution in Civil Justice Systems*. Georgia: LFB Scholarly Publishing LLC.

Hassemer, W. (1988). Variationen der positiven Generalprävention. In B. Schünemann et al. (Ed.), *Positive Generalprävention Kritische Analysen im deutsch-englischen Dialog, Upsala Symposium 1996* (pp. 29-50). Heidelberg, Germany: Müller.

Hassemer, W. (1981). *Einführung in die Grundlagen des Strafrechts*. Munich, Germany: Beck.

Hassemer, W. (2002). Darf der strafende Staat Verurteilte bessern wollen? Resozialisiergun im Rahmen positiver Generalprävention. In C. Prittwitz et al. (Eds.), *Festschrift für Klaus Lürsenn* (pp. 221–240). Baden-Baden: Nomos.

Haykin, S. (2009). *Neural Networks and Learning Machines* (3rd ed.). New York: Prentice Hall.

Hedelin, B., & Lindh, M. (2008). Implementing the EU Water Framework Directive – Prospects for Sustainable Water Planning in Sweden. *European Environment*, *18*(6), 327–344. doi:10.1002/eet.489

Heman, R., & Raybould, A. (2014). Expert opinion vs. empirical evidence. *GM Crops and Food: Biotechnology in Agriculture and the Food Chain*, *5*(1), 8–10. doi:10.4161/gmcr.28331 PMID:24637724

Henle, K., Alard, D., Clitherow, J., Cobb, P., Firbank, L., Kull, T., & Young, J. et al. (2008). Identifying and managing the conflicts between agriculture and biodiversity conservation in Europe–A review. *Agriculture, Ecosystems & Environment*, *124*(1-2), 60–71. doi:10.1016/j.agee.2007.09.005

Heras, S., Atkinson, K., Botti, V., Grasso, F., Julian, V., & McBurney, P. (2010). How argumentation can enhance dialogues in social networks. In *Frontiers in Artificial Intelligence and Applications. Proceedings of COMMA*.

Hert, P., Gutwirth, S., Moscibroda, A., Wright, D., & Gonzale-Fuster, G. (2009). Legal Safeguards for Privacy and Data Protection in Ambient Intelligence. *Personal and Ubiquitous Computing, 13*(6), 435–444. doi:10.1007/s00779-008-0211-6

Hewitt, C. (1991). Open information systems semantics for distributed artificial intelligence. *Artificial Intelligence, 47*(1-3), 79–106. doi:10.1016/0004-3702(91)90051-K

Hillier, F. S., & Lieberman, G. J. (2009). *Introduction to Operations Research* (9th ed.). McGraw-Hill.

Hindriks, K. V., & Tykhonov, D. (2008). Opponent modelling in automated multi-issue negotiation using Bayesian learning. In *The 7th International Joint Conference on Autonomous Agents and Multiagent Systems (AAMAS'08).*

Hirata, Y., Kume, Y., Wang, Z., & Kosuge, K. (2003). Decentralized control of multiple mobile manipulators based on virtual 3-D caster motion for handling an object in cooperation with a human. In *IEEE International Conference on Robotics and Automation* (ICRA), (vol. 1, pp. 938–943). doi:10.1109/ROBOT.2003.1241713

Hirsch, H. (1969). Zur Abrenzung Von Strafrecht und Zivilrecht. In P. Bockelmann, A. Kaufmann, & U. Klug (Eds.), *Festschrift für Karl Engish zum 70. Geburtstag* (pp. 304–327). Frankfurt: Klostermann.

Hirsch, H. (1990). Wiedergutmachung des Schadens im Rahmen des materiellen Strafrechts. *ZStW, 102*(3), 534–562. doi:10.1515/zstw.1990.102.3.534

Hiziroglu, A. (2013). Soft Computing Applications in Customer Segmentation: State-of-Art Review and Critique. *Expert Systems with Applications, 40*(16), 6491–6507. doi:10.1016/j.eswa.2013.05.052

Hocker, J. L., & Wilmot, W. W. (1991). *Interpersonal Conflict* (3rd ed.). Dubuque, IA: Brown.

Holland J. H., (1975). *Adaptation in Natural and Artificial Systems*. MIT Press.

Hollands, R. G. (2008). Will the real smart city please stand up? Intelligent, progressive or entrepreneurial? *City, 12*(3), 303–320. doi:10.1080/13604810802479126

Holt, J. L., & DeVore, C. J. (2005). Culture, gender, organizational role, and styles of conflict resolution: A meta-analysis. *International Journal of Intercultural Relations, 29*(2), 165–196. doi:10.1016/j.ijintrel.2005.06.002

Horling, B., & Lesser, V. (2008). Using quantitative models to search for appropriate organizational designs. *Autonomous Agents and Multi-Agent Systems, 16*(2), 95–149. doi:10.1007/s10458-007-9020-y

Horvitz, E., Jacobs, A., & Hovel, D. (1999). Attention-sensitive alerting. In *Proceedings of the Fifteenth Conference on Uncertainty in Artificial Intelligence*, (pp. 305–313). Morgan Kaufmann Publishers Inc.

Howe, J. (2006). The rise of crowdsourcing. *Wired Magazine, 14*(6), 1–4.

Howe, J. (2008). *Crowdsourcing: Why the Power of the Crowd is Driving the Future of Business*. Century.

Hübner, J. F., Sichman, J. S., & Boissier, O. (2002). A model for the structural, functional, and deontic specification of organizations in multiagent systems. *Advances in Artificial Intelligence*.

Hulstijn, J., & van der Torre, L. (2004). Combining goal generation and planning in an argumentation framework. In *10th International Workshop on Non-Monotonic Reasoning* (LNAI). Springer-Verlag.

Hu, Q., Pan, F., Pan, X., Zhang, D., Li, Q., & Pan, Z. (2014). Spatial analysis of climate change in Inner Mongolia during 1961-2012, China. *Applied Geography (Sevenoaks, England)*.

Huxley, E. (1939). *Red strangers*. London: Chatto and Windus.

Hwang, K., & Yang, C. (2009). Automated Inattention and Fatigue Detection System in Distance Education for Elementary School Students. *Journal of Educational Technology & Society*, *12*, 22–35.

Hydara, I., Sultan, A. B., Zulzalil, H., & Admodisastro, N. (2015). Current state of research on cross-site scripting (XSS) – A systematic literature review. *Information and Software Technology*, *58*, 170–186. doi:10.1016/j.infsof.2014.07.010

Infante, E. (1998). On the interpersonal conflict definition: Cluster analysis application to the semantic study. *Revista de Psicología Social*, *13*(3), 485–493. doi:10.1174/021347498760349733

In, Y., & Serrano, R. (2003). Agenda restrictions in multi-issue bargaining (II): Unrestricted agendas. *Economics Letters*, *79*(3), 325–331. doi:10.1016/S0165-1765(02)00321-X

Ioja, I. C. (2013). Metode de cercetare şi evaluare a stării mediului. Bucureşti: Ed. Etnografică.

Iojă, I. C., Niţă, M., Vânău, G., Onose, D., Gavrilidis, A., & Hossu, C. A. (2015). Environmental Conflicts Management, in Romanian (Managementul conflictelor de mediu). Bucharest: University of Bucharest.

Iojă, I. C., Niţă, M. R., Vânău, G. O., Onose, D. A., & Gavrilidis, A. A. (2014). Using multi-criteria analysis in identifying spatial land-use conflicts in the Bucharest Metropolitan Area. *Ecological Indicators*, *42*, 112–121. doi:10.1016/j.ecolind.2013.09.029

Ioja, I. C., Rozylowicz, L., Pătroescu, M., Niţă, M. R., & Vânau, G. O. (2011). Dog walkers' vs. other visitors' perceptions: The importance of planning sustainable urban parks in Bucharest, romania. *Landscape and Urban Planning*, *103*(1), 74–82. doi:10.1016/j.landurbplan.2011.06.002

Ipeirotis, P. G., Provost, F., & Wang, J. (2010). Quality management on amazon mechanical turk. In *Proceedings of the ACM SIGKDD Workshop on Human Computation* (pp. 64–67). Retrieved from http://dl.acm.org/citation.cfm?id=1837906

Ishibuhi, H., Tsukamoto, N., & Nojima, Y. (2008). Evolutionary many-objective optimization: A short review. *IEEE Congress on Evolutionary Computation. IEEE World Congress on Computational Intelligence*.

Isto, P., & Saha, M. (2006). A slicing connection strategy for constructing PRMs in high-dimensional cspaces. In *International Conference on Robotics and Automation* (ICRA), (pp. 1249–1254). doi:10.1109/ROBOT.2006.1641880

Ito, T., Klein, M., & Hattori, H. (2008). A multi-issue negotiation protocol among agents with nonlinear utility functions. *Multiagent and Grid Systems*, *4*(1), 67–83.

Jackson, A. L. R. (2011). Renewable energy vs. biodiversity: Policy conflicts and the future of nature conservation. *Global Environmental Change*, *21*(4), 1195–1208. doi:10.1016/j.gloenvcha.2011.07.001

Jain, B. A., & Solomon, J. S. (2000). The effect of task complexity and conflict handling styles on computer-supported negotiations. *Information & Management*, *37*(4), 161–168. doi:10.1016/S0378-7206(99)00049-X

Janssen, J. A. E. B., Krol, M. S., Schielen, R. M. J., Hoekstra, A. Y., & de Kok, J. L. (2010). Assessment of uncertainties in expert knowledge, illustrated in fuzzy rule-based models. *Ecological Modelling*, *221*(9), 1245–1251. doi:10.1016/j.ecolmodel.2010.01.011

Jehn, K. A. (1994). Enhancing effectivenes: An investigation of advantages and disadvantages of value-based intragroup conflict. *The International Journal of Conflict Management*, *5*(3), 223–238. doi:10.1108/eb022744

Jehn, K. A. (1995). A Multimethod Examination of the Benefits and Detriments of Intragroup Conflict. *Administrative Science Quarterly*, *40*(2), 256–282. doi:10.2307/2393638

Jehn, K. A. (1997). A qualitative analysis of conflict types and dimensions in organizational groups. *Administrative Science Quarterly*, *42*(3), 530–557. doi:10.2307/2393737

Jehn, K. A., & Mannix, E. A. (2001). The dynamic nature of conflict: A longitudinal study of intragroup conflict and group performance. *Academy of Management Journal*, *44*(2), 238–251. doi:10.2307/3069453

Jehn, K. A., Northcraft, G., & Neale, M. A. (1999). Why difference makes a difference: A field study of diversity, conflict and performance in work group. *Administrative Science Quarterly*, *44*(4), 741–763. doi:10.2307/2667054

Jennings, N. R., Faratin, P., Lomuscio, A. R., Parsons, S., Wooldridge, M. J., & Sierra, C. (2001). Automated negotiation: Prospects, methods and challenges. *Group Decision and Negotiation*, *10*(2), 199–215. doi:10.1023/A:1008746126376

Jensen, C., & Scacchi, W. (2004). *Collaboration, Leadership, Control, and Conflict Negotiation in the Netbeans.org Community.* Paper presented at the 4th workshop on Open Source Software Engineering, Edinburgh, UK. doi:10.1049/ic:20040264

Johnson, R., & Scicchitano, M. (2012). Don't call me NIMBY: Public attitudes toward solid waste facilities. *Environment and Behavior*, *44*(3), 410–426. doi:10.1177/0013916511435354

Johnstone, G., & Ness, D. (2007). The meaning of restorative justice. In G. Johnstone & D. Ness (Eds.), *Handbook of Restorative Justice* (pp. 5–23). Devon: Willan Publishing.

Jones, A. H., & Moura Oliveira, P. B. (1995). Genetic Auto-Tuning of PID Controllers. In *Proceedings of the First IEE Conference on Genetic Algorithms in Engineering Systems: Innovations and Applications* (GALESIA'95). doi:10.1049/cp:19951039

Jones, A. H., & Moura Oliveira, P. B. (1996). Auto-Tuning of PI Smith Predictor Controllers using Genetic Algorithms. *Control'96:UKACC International Conference on Control*. doi:10.1049/cp:19960595

Jones, R. E., & Deckro, R. F. (1993). The Social Psychology of Project Management Conflict. *European Journal of Operational Research*, *64*(2), 216–228. doi:10.1016/0377-2217(93)90178-P

Jonker, C. M., Robu, V., & Treur, J. (2007). An agent architecture for multi-attribute negotiation using incomplete preference information. *Autonomous Agents and Multi-Agent Systems*, *15*(2), 221–252. doi:10.1007/s10458-006-9009-y

Jonker, C. M., & Treur, J. (2001). An Agent Architecture for Multi-Attribute Negotiation. In *The 17th International Joint Conference on Artificial Intelligence (IJCAI'01)*.

Jordan, J. V. (1990). *Courage in Connection: Conflict, Compassion, and Creativity.* Retrieved from Kabanoff, B. (1987). Predictive Validity of the MODE Conflict Instrument. *The Journal of Applied Psychology*, *72*, 160–163.

Jurin, R., Roush, D., & Danter, J. (2010). *Managing Conflicts. In Environmental Communication. Skills and Principles for Natural Resource Managers, Scientists, and Engineers*. New York: Springer - Verlag.

Kaidi, R., Lazaar, M., & Ettaouil, M. (2014). Neural Network Apply to predict aircraft trajectory for conflict resolution. In *International Conference on Intelligent Systems: Theories and Applications* (SITA). doi:10.1109/SITA.2014.6847309

Kakas, A., Kowalski, R., & Toni, F. (1998). The role of abduction in logic programming. In D. Gabbay, C. Hogger, & I. Robinson (Eds.), *Handbook of Logic in Artificial Intelligence and Logic Programming* (Vol. 5, pp. 235–324). Oxford, UK: Oxford University Press.

Kakas, A., Maudet, N., & Moraitis, P. (2005). Modular Representation of Agent Interaction Rules through Argumentation. *Autonomous Agents and Multi-Agent Systems*, *11*(2), 189–206. doi:10.1007/s10458-005-2176-4

Kala, R., Shukla, A., & Tiwari, R. (2010). Dynamic Environment Robot Path Planning Using Hierarchical Evolutionary Algorithms. *Cybernetics and Systems: An International Journal*, *41*(6), 435–454. doi:10.1080/01969722.2010.500800

Katsch, E. (1996). Dispute Resolution in Cyberspace. *Connecticut Law Review*, *28*, 953–980.

Katsch, E., & Rifkin, J. (2001). *Online Dispute Resolution, Resolving Conflicts in Cyberspace*. San Francisco, CA: Jossey-Bass Wiley Company.

Katzenback, J. R., & Smith, D. K. (1994, March-April). The Discipline of Teams. *Harvard Business Review*.

Kaufmann-Kohler, G., & Schultz, T. (2004). *Online Dispute Resolution: Challenges for Contemporary Justice*. The Hague: Kluwer Law International.

Kavraki, L. E., Svestka, P., Latombe, J. C., & Overmars, M. (1996). Probabilistic roadmaps for path planning in high dimensional configuration spaces. *IEEE Transactions on Robotics and Automation*, *12*(4), 566–580. doi:10.1109/70.508439

Kawauchi, Y., Inaba, M., & Fukuda, T. (1993). A Principle of Distributed Decision Making of Cellular Robotic System (CEBOT). In *International Conference on Robotics and Automation* (ICRA), (vol. 3, pp. 833–838). doi:10.1109/ROBOT.1993.292248

Keeney, R. L., & Raiffa, H. (1993). *Decisions with Multiple Objectives: Preferences and Value Tradeoffs*. Cambridge University Press. doi:10.1017/CBO9781139174084

Kennedy, J., & Eberhart, R. C. (1995). Particle swarm optimization. *Proc. IEEE Int. Conf. on Neural Networks, 4*, 1942–1948. doi:10.1109/ICNN.1995.488968

Kerner, H. (1983). *Diversion statt Strafe? Probleme und Gefahren einer neuen Strategie strafrechtlicher Sozialkontrolle*. Heidelberg: Kriminalistik Verlag.

Khan, F. A. (2010). Identifying and Incorporating Affective States and Learning Styles in Web-based Learning Management Systems. *Interaction Design and Architecture(s) Journal, 9-10*, 85-103.

Kiener, J., & von Stryk, O. (2010). Towards cooperation of heterogeneous, autonomous robots: A case study of humanoid and wheeled robots. *Robotics and Autonomous Systems*, *58*(7), 21–929. doi:10.1016/j.robot.2010.03.013

Kilmann, R. H., & Thomas, K. W. (1977). Developing a Forced-Choice Measure of Conflict-Handling Behavior: The MODE Instrument. *Educational and Psychological Measurement*, *37*(2), 309–325. doi:10.1177/001316447703700204

Kirby, R., Broz, F., Forlizzi, J., Michalowski, M. P., Mundell, A., Rosenthal, … Wang, J. (2005). Designing Robots for Long-Term Social Interaction. In *IEEE/RSJ International Conference on Intelligent Robots and Systems* (IROS), (pp. 2199–2204).

Kitano, H., & Tadokoro, S. (2001). RoboCup Rescue: A Grand Challenge for Multiagent and Intelligent Systems. *AI Magazine*, *22*(1), 39–52.

Kittur, A., Chi, E. H., & Suh, B. (2008). Crowdsourcing user studies with Mechanical Turk. In *Proceedings of the SIGCHI Conference on Human Factors in Computing Systems* (pp. 453–456). Retrieved from http://dl.acm.org/citation.cfm?id=1357127

Kittur, A., Khamkar, S., André, P., & Kraut, R. (2012). CrowdWeaver: visually managing complex crowd work. In *Proceedings of the ACM 2012 Conference on Computer Supported Cooperative Work* (pp. 1033–1036). Retrieved from http://dl.acm.org/citation.cfm?id=2145357

Kittur, A., Smus, B., Khamkar, S., & Kraut, R. E. (2011). Crowdforge: Crowdsourcing Complex Work. In *Proceedings of the 24th Annual ACM Symposium on User Interface Software and Technology* (pp. 43–52). Retrieved from http://dl.acm.org/citation.cfm?id=2047202

Klaming, L., Van Veenen, J., & Leenes, R. 2004. I want the opposite of what you want: Summary of a study on the reduction of fixed-pie perceptions in online negotiations. In M. Poblet (Ed.), *Expanding the horizons of ODR – Proceedings of the 5th international workshop on Online Dispute Resolution* (pp. 84-94). Academic Press.

Klausner, M. (2007). High Performance Work Teams. In A. Farazmand (Ed.), *Strategic Public Personnel Administration* (Vol. 2, pp. 301–318). Westport, CT: Proeger.

Klausner, M., & Groves, M. A. (1994). Organizational Conflict. In A. Farazmand (Ed.), *Handbook of Bureaucracy* (pp. 355–372). New York, NY: CRC Press.

Klein, M., & Iandoli, L. (2008). *Supporting collaborative deliberation using a large-scale argumentation system:* The MIT Collaboratorium. Technical Report 4691-08, MIT Sloan.

Klein, M., Faratin, P., Sayama, H., & Bar-Yam, Y. (2003). Negotiating Complex Contracts. *Group Decision and Negotiation*, *12*(2), 111–125. doi:10.1023/A:1023068821218

Klem, A. M., & Connell, J. P. (2004). Relationships matter: Linking teacher support to student engagement and achievement. *The Journal of School Health*, *74*(7), 262–273. doi:10.1111/j.1746-1561.2004.tb08283.x PMID:15493703

Kloskowski, J. (2011). Human–wildlife conflicts at pond fisheries in eastern Poland: Perceptions and management of wildlife damage. *European Journal of Wildlife Research*, *57*(2), 295–304. doi:10.1007/s10344-010-0426-5

Knust, N. (2013). *Entwicklung eines pluralistischen Rechtsmodells am Beispiel des ruandischen Völkermordes*. Berlin: Duncker & Humblot.

Kochan, T., Cummings, L. C., & Huber, G. (1976). Operationalizin the Concepts of Goals and Goal Incompatibility in Organizational Behavior Research. *Human Relations*, *29*(6), 527–544. doi:10.1177/001872677602900603

Kolb, D. M., & Putnam, L. L. (1992). The multiple faces of conflict in organizations. *Journal of Organizational Behavior*, *13*(3), 311–324. doi:10.1002/job.4030130313

Kolb, D., & Bartunek, J. M. (Eds.). (1992). *Hidden Conflict in Organizations: Uncovering Behind-the-Scenes Disputes*. Newbury Park, CA: Sage. doi:10.4135/9781483325897

Kornhauser, D., Miller, G., & Spirakis, P. (1984). Coordinating pebble motion on graphs, the diameter of permutation groups, and applications. In *Foundations of Computer Science (FOCS)* (pp. 241–250). Los Alamitos, CA: IEEE Computer Society Press. doi:10.1109/SFCS.1984.715921

Kort, B., & Reilly, R. (2001). *Analytical Models of Emotions, Learning and Relationships: Towards an Affect-sensitive Cognitive Machine*. MIT Media Lab Tech Report No 548.

Kosuge, K., & Oosumi, T. (1996). Decentralized Control of Multiple Robots Handling an Object. In: *International Conference on Intelligent Robots and Systems* (IROS), (pp. 318–323). doi:10.1109/IROS.1996.570694

Kraus, S. (1997). Negotiation and cooperation in multi-agent environments. *Artificial Intelligence*, *94*(1-2), 79–97. doi:10.1016/S0004-3702(97)00025-8

Kraus, S., Sycara, K., & Evenchik, A. (1998). Reaching agreements through argumentation: A logical model and implementation. *Artificial Intelligence Journal*, *104*(1-2), 1–69. doi:10.1016/S0004-3702(98)00078-2

Kraybill, R. (2011). *Style Matters*. Academic Press.

Krieger, M. J. B., & Billeter, J. B. (2000). The call of duty: Self-organised task allocation in a population of up to twelve mobile robots. *Robotics and Autonomous Systems*, *30*(1–2), 65–84. doi:10.1016/S0921-8890(99)00065-2

Krontiris, A., & Bekris, K. E. (2011). Using Minimal Communication to Improve Decentralized Conflict Resolution for Non-holonomic Vehicles. In *IEEE/RSJ International Conference on Intelligent Robots and Systems*, (pp. 3235–3240).

Kubo, R., & Ohnishi, K. (2006). An Extraction Method of Environmental Surface Profile Using Planar End-Effectors. In *IEEE International Workshop on Advanced Motion Control*, (pp. 368–373). doi:10.1109/AMC.2006.1631686

Kubo, R., & Ohnishi, K. (2006b). Hybrid Control for Multiple Robots in Grasping and Manipulation. In *IEEE International Power Electronics and Motion Control Conference*, (pp. 367–372). doi:10.1109/EPEPEMC.2006.283187

Kuffner, J. J., & Lavalle, S. M. (2000). RRT-Connect: An efficient approach to single-query path planning. In *International Conference on Robotics and Automation* (ICRA), (pp. 995–1001). doi:10.1109/ROBOT.2000.844730

Kulkarni, A. P., Can, M., & Hartmann, B. (2011). Turkomatic: Automatic Recursive Task and Workflow Design for Mechanical Turk. In *Proceedings of the 2011 Annual Conference on Extended Abstracts on Human Factors in Computing Systems* (pp. 2053–2058). Retrieved from http://dl.acm.org/citation.cfm?id=1979865

Kume, Y., Hirata, Y., Wang, Z., & Kosuge, K. (2002). Decentralized control of multiple mobile manipulators handling a single object in coordination. In *IEEE/RSJ International Conference on Intelligent Robots and Systems* (IROS), (vol. 3, pp. 2758–2763). doi:10.1109/IRDS.2002.1041687

Kurdek, L. A. (1994). Conflict Resolution Styles in Gay, Lesbian, Heterosexual Nonparent, and Heterosexual Parent Couples. *Journal of Marriage and the Family*, *56*(3), 705–722. doi:10.2307/352880

LaValle, S. M. (2006). *Planning Algorithms*. Cambridge, UK: Cambridge University Press. doi:10.1017/CBO9780511546877

Lai, G., Sycara, K., & Li, C. (2008). A decentralized model for automated multi-attribute negotiations with incomplete information and general utility functions. *Multiagent and Grid Systems*, *4*(1), 45–65.

Lalwani, S., Singhal, S., Kumar, R., & Gupta, N. (2013). A comprehensive survey: Applications of multi-objective particle swarm optimization (MOPSO) algorithm. *Transactions on Combinatorics*, *2*(1), 39-101.

Landemore, H. (2014). Inclusive Constitution-Making: The Icelandic Experiment. *Journal of Political Philosophy*. Retrieved from http://onlinelibrary.wiley.com/doi/10.1111/jopp.12032/full

Landes, W. M., & Posner, R. A. (1976). Legal precedent: A theoretical and empirical analysis. *The Journal of Law & Economics*, *19*(2), 249–307. doi:10.1086/466868

Lane, F. S. III. (2003). *The naked employee – how technology is compromising workplace privacy*. AMACOM.

Latruffe, L., & Davidova, S. (2007). Common Agricultural Policy direct payments and distributional conflicts over rented land within corporate farms in the New Member States. *Land Use Policy*, *24*(2), 451–457. doi:10.1016/j.landusepol.2006.06.003

LaValle, S. M., & Hutchinson, S. A. (1998). Optimal Motion Planning for Multiple Robots Having Independent Goals. *IEEE Transactions on Robotics and Automation*, *14*(6), 912–925. doi:10.1109/70.736775

Lawrence, P. (1997). *Workflow handbook 1997*. John Wiley & Sons, Inc. Retrieved from http://dl.acm.org/citation.cfm?id=272945

Lawrence, P. R., & Lorsch, J. W. (1967). Differentiation and Integration in Complex Organizations. *Administrative Science Quarterly*, *12*(1), 1–47. doi:10.2307/2391211

Lawrence, P. R., & Lorsch, J. W. (1967). New Management job: The Integrator. *Harvard Business Review*, (November - December), 142–151.

Leake, D. B. (1994). Case-based reasoning. *The Knowledge Engineering Review*, *9*(01), 61–64. doi:10.1017/S0269888900006585

Lefait, G., & Kechadi, T. (2010). *Customer Segmentation Architecture Based on Clustering Techniques.* Digital Society, 2010. ICDS '10. Fourth International Conference on Digital Society. doi:10.1109/ICDS.2010.47

Leroy, S., Laumond, J. P., & Simeon, T. (1999). Multiple path coordination for mobile robots: A geometric algorithm. In *International Joint Conference on Artificial Intelligence* (IJCAI), (pp. 1118–1123).

Leung, M., Liu, A. M. M., & Ng, S. T. (2005). Is There a Relationship Between Construction Conflicts and Participants' Satisfaction? *Engineering, Construction, and Architectural Management*, *12*(2), 149–167. doi:10.1108/09699980510584494

Levine, S. S., & Kurzban, R. (2006). Explaining Clustering in Social Networks: Towards an Evolutionary Theory of Cascading Benefits. *Managerial and Decision Economics*, *27*(2-3), 173–187. doi:10.1002/mde.1291

Lewicki, R. J. (1983). Lying and Deception: A Behavioral Model. In M. H. Bazerman & R. J. Lewicki (Eds.), *Negotiating in Organizations*. Beverly Hills, CA: Sage.

Lewicki, R., Gray, B., & Elliott, M. (2003). *Making Sense of Intractable Environmental Conflicts. Concepts And Cases* (2nd ed.). Island Press.

Lian, K. Y., Hsiao, S. J., & Sung, W. T. (2013). Intelligent multi-sensor control system based on innovative technology integration via ZigBee and Wi-Fi networks. *Journal of Network and Computer Applications*, *36*(2), 756–767. doi:10.1016/j.jnca.2012.12.012

Licklider, J. C. R. (1960). Man-computer symbiosis. *IRE Transactions on Human Factors in Electronics*, (1), 4–11.

Lide, C. (1996). ADR and Cyberspace: The Role of Alternative Dispute Resolution in Online Commerce, Intellectual Property and Defamation. *Ohio State Journal on Dispute Resolution*, *12*, 192–222.

Lidskog, R., & Olausson, U. (2013). To spray or not to spray: The discursive construction of contested environmental issues in the news media. *Discourse. Context and Media*, *2*(3), 123–130. doi:10.1016/j.dcm.2013.06.001

Liefferink, D., Wiering, M., & Uitenboogaart, Y. (2011). The EU Water Framework Directive: A multi-dimensional analysis of implementation and domestic impact. *Land Use Policy*, *28*(4), 712–722. doi:10.1016/j.landusepol.2010.12.006

Li, J., Gong, W., Li, W., & Liu, X. (2010). Robust pedestrian detection in thermal infrared imagery using the wavelet transform. *Infrared Physics & Technology*, *53*(4), 267–273. doi:10.1016/j.infrared.2010.03.005

Lindell, L., Mellin, M., Musil, P., Przybysz, J., & Zimmerman, H. (1995). Status and population development of breeding Cormorants Phalacrocorax carbo sinensis of the central European flyway. *Ardea*, *83*(1), 81–92.

Liszt, F. (1912). *Lehrbuch des Deutschen Strafrechts*. Berlin: Walter de Gruyter.

Little, G., Chilton, L. B., Goldman, M., & Miller, R. C. (2010). Turkit: Human Computation Algorithms on Mechanical Turk. In *Proceedings of the 23rd Annual ACM Symposium on User Interface Software and Technology* (pp. 57–66). Retrieved from http://dl.acm.org/citation.cfm?id=1866040

Liu, B. (2010). Sentiment Analysis: A Multifaceted Problem. *IEEE Intelligent Systems*, *25*(3), 76–80.

Liu, J., Cai, B., Wang, Y., & Wang, J. (2013). A lane level positioning-based cooperative vehicle conflict resolution algorithm for unsignalized intersection collisions. *Computers & Electrical Engineering*, *39*(5), 1381–1398. doi:10.1016/j.compeleceng.2013.04.011

Liu, L., & Shell, D. A. (2011). Assessing optimal assignment under uncertainty: An interval-based algorithm. *The International Journal of Robotics Research*, *30*(7), 936–953. doi:10.1177/0278364911404579

Liu, L., & Shell, D. A. (2012). Large-scale multi-robot task allocation via dynamic partitioning and distribution. *Autonomous Robots*, *33*(3), 291–307. doi:10.1007/s10514-012-9303-2

Liu, Y., Osvalder, A., & Karlsson, M. (2010). Considering the Importance of User Profiles in Interface Design. In R. Matrai (Ed.), *User Interfaces*. InTech. doi:10.5772/8903

Liu, Y., Seet, B. C., & Al-Anbuky, A. (2013). An ontology-based context model for Wireless Sensor Network (WSN) management in the internet of things. *Journal of Sensor and Actuator Networks*, *2*(4), 653–674. doi:10.3390/jsan2040653

Li, Y., Gupta, K., & Payandeh, S. (2005). Motion planning of multiple agents in virtual environments using coordination graphs. In *IEEE International Conference on Robotics and Automation* (ICRA), (pp. 378–383).

Lodder, A. R., & Zeleznikow, J. (2005). Preface. *Artificial Intelligence and Law*, *13*(2), 189–192. doi:10.1007/s10506-006-9010-4

Lodder, A., & Zeleznikow, J. (2010). *Enhanced Dispute Resolution through the use of Information Technology*. Cambridge, UK: Cambridge University Press. doi:10.1017/CBO9780511777554

Lomuscio, A., Wooldridge, M., & Jennings, N. (2003). A Classification Scheme for Negotiation in Electronic Commerce. *Group Decision and Negotiation*, *12*(1), 31–56. doi:10.1023/A:1022232410606

Lopes, D., & Patrão, A. (2014). *Lei da Mediação Comentada*. Coimbra: Almedina.

Lopes, F., Wooldridge, M., & Novais, A. Q. (2008). Negotiation among autonomous computational agents: Principles, analysis and challenges. *Artificial Intelligence Review*, *29*(1), 1–44. doi:10.1007/s10462-009-9107-8

Lopez de Mantaras, R. (2001). Case-Based Reasoning. In Machine Learning and Its Applications (LNCS), (Vol. 2049, pp. 127-145). Springer. doi:10.1007/3-540-44673-7_6

Lorenzetti, C., & Maguitman, A. (2009). A Semi-supervised Incremental Algorithm to Automatically Formulate Topical Queries. *Information Science*, *179*(12), 1881–1892. doi:10.1016/j.ins.2009.01.029

Lovelace, K., Shapiro, D. L., & Weingart, L. R. (2001). Maximizing Crossfunctional New Product Teams' Innovativeness and Constraint Ahderence: A Conflict Information Exchanges Perspective. *Academy of Management Journal*, *44*, 779–783. doi:10.2307/3069415

Lowndes, V., Pratchett, L., & Stoker, G. (2001a). Trends in public participation: Part 1 - local government perspectives. *Public Administration*, *79*(1), 205–222. doi:10.1111/1467-9299.00253

Lowndes, V., Pratchett, L., & Stoker, G. (2001b). Trends in public participation: Part 2 - citizens' perspectives. *Public Administration*, *79*(2), 445–455. doi:10.1111/1467-9299.00264

Lucas, B. D., & Kanade, T. (1981). An iterative image registration technique with an application to stereo vision. In *Proceedings of the 1981 DARPA Image Understanding Workshop* (pp. 121-130). Palo Alto, CA: DARPA.

Lucas, P. (2004). Quality checking of medical guidelines through logical abduction. In F. Coenen, A. Preece, & A. Mackintosh (Eds.), *Research and Developments in Intelligent Systems XX* (pp. 309–321). London: Springer. doi:10.1007/978-0-85729-412-8_23

Luck, M., & McBurney, P. (2008). Computing as Interaction: Agent and Agreement Technologies. In *Proc. IEEE Conference on Distributed Human-Machine Systems*.

LUCRA. (2011). *Land Use Conflict Risk Assessment*. Australia: New South Wales Government.

Ludwig, S. A. (2008a). Agent-Based Assistant for e-Negotiations. *Work (Reading, Mass.)*, 514–524.

Ludwig, S. A. (2008b). Agent-based assistant for e-negotiations. In *Proceedings of the 17th international conference on Foundations of intelligent systems* (pp. 514–524). Berlin: Springer-Verlag. doi:10.1007/978-3-540-68123-6_56

Luhmann, N. (2005). *Soziologische Aufklärung 6. Die Soziologie und der Mensch* (2nd ed.). Wiesbaden: Verlag für Sozialwissenschaften.

Lumelsky, V. J., & Harinarayan, K. R. (1997). Decentralized motion planning for multiple mobile robots: The cocktail party model. *Journal of Autonomous Robots*, *4*(1), 121–135. doi:10.1023/A:1008815304810

Lumerman, P., Psathakis, J., & Ortiz, M. (2011). *Climate Change Impacts on Socio - environmental Conflicts: Diagnosis and Challenges of the Argentinean Situation*. Brussels: Initiative for Peacebuilding.

Luna, E. (2003). Punishment Theory, Holism, and the Procedural Conception of Restorative Justice. *Utah Law Review*, (1), 205–302.

Luo, S., Xia, H., Yoshida, T., & Wang, Z. (2009). Toward collective intelligence of online communities: A primitive conceptual model. *Journal of Systems Science and Systems Engineering*, *18*(2), 203–221. doi:10.1007/s11518-009-5095-0

Luz, N., Poblet, M., Silva, N., & Novais, P. (2015). Defining Human-Machine Micro-Task Workflows for Constitution Making. Lecture Notes in Business Information Processing, 218. doi:10.1007/978-3-319-19515-5_26

Luz, N., Silva, N., Maio, P., & Novais, P. (2012). *Ontology Alignment through Argumentation*. Presented at the AAAI Spring Symposium - Wisdom of the Crowd, Palo Alto, CA.

Luz, N. (2015). *Ontology-based Representation and Generation of Workflows for Micro-Task Human-Machine Computation*. Universidade do Minho.

Ma, H., Zhou, D., Liu, C., Lyu, M. R., & King, I. (2011). Recommender systems with social regularization. In *Proceedings of the fourth ACM international conference on Web search and data mining* (pp. 287–296). Retrieved from http://dl.acm.org/citation.cfm?id=1935877

Maantay, J., & Ziegler, J. (2006). *GIS for the Urban Environment*. Redlands, CA: ESRI Press.

Machado, J., Abelha, A., Novais, P., Neves, J., & Neves, J. (2010). Quality of service in healthcare units. *International Journal of Computer Aided Engineering and Technology*, *2*(4), 436–449. doi:10.1504/IJCAET.2010.035396

Madden, F., & McQuinn, B. (2014). Conservation's blind spot: The case for conflict transformation in wildlife conservation. *Biological Conservation*, *178*, 97–106. doi:10.1016/j.biocon.2014.07.015

Maguitman, A., Leake, D., & Reichherzer, T. (2005). Suggesting novel but related topics: towards context-based support for knowledge model extension, In *Proceedings of the 2005 International Conference on Intelligent User Interfaces* (pp. 207-214). ACM Press. doi:10.1145/1040830.1040876

Maguitman, A., Leake, D., Reichherzer, T., & Menczer, F. (2004). Dynamic Extraction of Topic Descriptors and Discriminators: Towards Automatic Context-Based Topic Search. In *Proceedings of 2004 ACM CIKM International Conference on Information and Knowledge Management*, (pp. 463-472). ACM Press. doi:10.1145/1031171.1031260

Maier, H. R., Kapelan, Z., Kasprzyk, J., Kollat, J., Matott, L. S., Cunha, M. C., & Reed, P. M. et al. (2014). Evolutionary algorithms and other metaheuristics in water resources: Current status, research challenges and future directions. *Environmental Modelling & Software*, *62*, 271–299. doi:10.1016/j.envsoft.2014.09.013

Maio, P., & Silva, N. (2011). A Three-Layer Argumentation Framework. In *First International Workshop on the Theory and Applications of Formal Argumentation (TAFA) at IJCAI*.

Malaek, M. B., & Alaeddini, A. (2009). Conflict Resolution Maneuvers Based on Genetic Algorithm Modified Webs. *IEEE Aerospace Conference*. doi:10.1109/AERO.2009.4839430

March, J. G., & Simon, H. A. (1958). *Organizations*. New York: Wiley.

March, J., & Simon, H. A. (1958). *Organizations*. New York, NY: Wiley.

Marder, N. S. (2005). Cyberjuries: The Next New Thing? *Information & Communications Technology Law, 14*(2), 165–198. doi:10.1080/13600830500042756

Marek, J. (1966). Conflict, a battle of strategies. In J. Lawrence (Ed.), *Organizational research and the social science* (p. 64). London: Tavistock.

Margarita, R. S., & Coello, C. A. C. (2006). Multi-objective particle swarm optimizers: A survey of the state-of-the-art. *International Journal of Computational Intelligence Research, 2*(3).

Marshall, T. (1996). The evolution of restorative justice in Britain. *European Journal on Criminal Policy and Research, 4*(4), 21–43. doi:10.1007/BF02736712

Martí Màrmol, J. L. (2002). *Perspectivas del Derecho en la Negociación de Conflictos*. UOC.

Maser, C., & Pollio, C. A. (2012). *Resolving environmental conflicts*. CRC Press.

Mas, I., & Kitts, C. A. (2012). Object manipulation using cooperative mobile multi-robot systems. In *World Congress on Engineering and Computer Science*, (vol. 1, pp. 324–329).

Mason, S., & Rychard, S. (2005). *Conflict Analysis Tools*. Bern: Academic Press.

Mason, S., & Spillman, K. (2002). *Environmental Conflicts and Regional Conflict Management* (Vol. 2). Welfare Economics and Sustainable Development.

Mason, W., & Watts, D. J. (2010). Financial incentives and the performance of crowds. *ACM SigKDD Explorations Newsletter, 11*(2), 100–108. doi:10.1145/1809400.1809422

Mataric, M. J., Nilsson, M., & Simsarin, K. T. (1995). Cooperative multi-robot box-pushing. In *IEEE/RSJ International Conference on Intelligent Robots and Systems* (IROS), (vol. 3, pp. 556–561).

Mate, M. (2011). *Tratado de la injusticia*. Madrid: Anthropos.

Matos, N., Sierra, C., & Jennings, N. (1998). Determining Successful Negotiation Strategies: An Evolutionary Approach. In *The 3rd International Conference on Multi Agent Systems (ICMAS '98)*. Washington, DC: IEEE Computer Society. doi:10.1109/ICMAS.1998.699048

Matwin, S., Szpakowicz, S., Koperczak, Z., Kersten, G. E., & Michalowski, G. (1989). NEGOPLAN: An Expert System Shell for Negotiation Support. *IEEE Expert, 4*(4), 50–62. doi:10.1109/64.43285

May, M., Fessakis, G., Dimitracopoulou, A., & George, S. (2012). A Study on User's Perception in E-learning Security and Privacy Issues. In *2012 IEEE 12th International Conference on Advanced Learning Technologies (ICALT)* (pp. 88-89). Doi:10.1109/ICALT.2012.145

Mayer, B. (2000). *The dynamics of conflict resolution: A practitioners guide*. Wiley.

Mayer, R. E., & Moreno, R. (1998). A split-attention effect in multimedia learning: Evidence for dual processing systems in working memory. *Journal of Educational Psychology*, *90*(2), 312–320. doi:10.1037/0022-0663.90.2.312

McBurney, P., & Parsons, S. (2002). Dialogue games in multi-agent systems. Informal Logic. *Special Issue on Applications of Argumentation in Computer Science*, *22*(3), 257–274.

McCold, P. (1996). Restorative justice and the role of community. In B. Galaway & J. Hudson (Eds.), *Restorative Justice: International Perspectives* (pp. 85–101). New York: Criminal Justice Press.

McDermott, E. P., & Berkeley, A. E. (1996). *Alternative Dispute Resolution in the Workplace: Concepts and Techniques for Human Resource Executives and Their Counsel*. Greenwood Publishing Group.

Medina, F. J., Munduate, L., Dorado, M., & Guerra, J. M. (2005). Types of Intragroup Conflict and Affective Reactions. *Journal of Managerial Psychology*, *20*(3/4), 219–230. doi:10.1108/02683940510589019

Melamed, J. (2002). *Divorce Mediation and the Internet*. Retrieved May, 30, 2015, from http://www.mediate.com/articles/melamed9.cfm

Melé, P. (2012). Pour une géographie des conflits urbains de proximité en Amérique Latine. *Géocarrefour, 87*(1).

Mellinger, D., Shomin, M., Michael, N., & Kumar, V. (2013) Cooperative Grasping and Transport Using Multiple Quadrotors. In *International Symposium on Distributed Autonomous Robotic Systems* (DARS), (pp. 545–558). doi:10.1007/978-3-642-32723-0_39

Mendes, R., Kennedy, J., & Neves, J. (2004). The fully informed particle swarm: Simpler, maybe better. *IEEE Transactions on Evolutionary Computation*, *8*(3), 204–210. doi:10.1109/TEVC.2004.826074

Mentzas, G., Halaris, C., & Kavadias, S. (2001). Modelling business processes with workflow systems: An evaluation of alternative approaches. *International Journal of Information Management*, *21*(2), 123–135. doi:10.1016/S0268-4012(01)00005-6

Michael, N., Zavlanos, M. M., Kumar, V., & Pappas, G. J. (2008). Distributed multi-robot task assignment and formation control. In *International Conference on Robotics and Automation* (ICRA), (pp. 128–133). doi:10.1109/ROBOT.2008.4543197

Michelman, P. (1998). Precision Object Manipulation with a Multifingered Robot Hand. *IEEE Transactions on Robotics and Automation*, *14*(1), 105–113. doi:10.1109/70.660851

Mitton, N., Papavassiliou, S., Puliafito, A., & Trivedi, K. S. (2012). Combining Cloud and sensors in a smart city environment. *EURASIP Journal on Wireless Communications and Networking*, (1): 1–10.

Modgil, S., Toni, F., Bex, F., Bratko, I., Chesñevar, C., Dvorak, W., . . . Woltran, S. (2012). The Added Value of Argumentation. In Agreement Technology Handbook. Academic Press.

Montemayor, G., & Wen, J. T. (2005). Decentralized Collaborative Load Transport by Multiple Robots. In *IEEE International Conference on Robotics and Automation* (ICRA), (pp. 372–377). doi:10.1109/ROBOT.2005.1570147

Moore, C. W. (1986). *The Mediation Process: Practical Strategies for Resolving Conflict*. Wiley.

Moravec, J. W. (2008). A new paradigm of knowledge production in higher education. *On the Horizon*, *16*(3), 123–136. doi:10.1108/10748120810901422

Mordini, E., & Ashton, H. (2012). *The Transparent Body: Medical Information, Physical Privacy and Respect for Body Integrity. In Second Generation Biometrics: The Ethical, Legal and Social Context* (Vol. 11). The International Library of Ethics, Law and Technology. doi:10.1007/978-94-007-3892-8

Mordini, E., & Petrini, C. (2007). Ethical and Social implications of biometric identification technology. *Annali dell'Istituto Superiore di Sanita*, *43*(1), 5–11. PMID:17536148

Moreira, T. C. (2010). *A Privacidade dos Trabalhadores e as Novas Tecnologias de Informação e Comunicação: contributo para um estudo dos limites do poder de controlo electrónico do empregador.* Coimbra: Almedina. (in Portuguese)

Morgan-Davis, C., & Waterhouse, T. (2010). Future of the hills of Scotland: Stakeholders' preferences for policy priorities. *Land Use Policy*, *27*(2), 387–398. doi:10.1016/j.landusepol.2009.05.002

Morrill, C. (1995). *The Executive Way: Conflict Management in Corporations.* Chicago: The University of Chicago Press.

Moura Oliveira, P. B. & Jones, A. H. (1997). Evolutionary Approaches to the Design of Cascade Controllers. *5as Jornadas Hispano-Lusas de Ingeniería Eléctrica, 3*, pp. 1745-1752.

Moura Oliveira, P. B. (2001). Design of Discrete Non-linear Two-degrees-of-freedom PID Controllers using Genetic Algorithms. In *Fifth International Conference on Artificial Neural Networks and Genetic Algorithms*, (pp. 320-323). Springer Computer Science. doi:10.1007/978-3-7091-6230-9_79

Moura Oliveira, P. B. (2005). Modern Heuristics Review for PID Control Systems Optimization: a Teaching Experiment. *IEEE-International Conference on Control and Automation* (ICCA2005), (pp. 828-833). doi:10.1109/ICCA.2005.1528237

Moura Oliveira, P. B., & Jones, A. H. (2000). Co-Evolutionary Design of PID Control Structures. In *Proceedings of the IFAC Workshop on Digital Control: Past, Present and Future of PID Control- PID'00*. Pergamon.

Moura Oliveira, P. B., Boaventura, J., Solteiro Pires, E. J., & Vrancic, D. (2009). Multi-objective Particle Swarm Optimization Design of PID Controllers. *Workshop on Soft Computing Models in Industrial Applications (SOCO'09), Part II* (LNCS), (vol. 5518, pp. 1222-1230). Springer-Verlag.

Moura Oliveira, P. B., Boaventura Cunha, J., & Coelho, J. P. (2002). Design of PID Controllers using the Particle Swarm Algorithm. *23rd IASTED International Conference in Modelling, Identification and Control (MIC 2002)*, (pp. 263-268).

Moura Oliveira, P. B., & Jones, A. H. (1997). Robust Co-evolutionary Design of SISO Smith Predictor for PID Controllers. *2nd IEE Conference on Genetic Algorithms in Engineering Systems: Innovations and Applications*. doi:10.1049/cp:19971231

Munawar, K., & Uchiyama, M. (1999). Experimental verification of distributed event-based control of multiple unifunctional manipulators. In *IEEE International Conference on Robotics and Automation* (ICRA), (pp. 1213–1218). doi:10.1109/ROBOT.1999.772527

Mutlu, B. (2011). Designing embodied cues for dialog with robots. *AI Magazine*, *32*(4), 17–30.

Nair, N. (2008). Towards understanding the role of emotions in conflict: A review and future directions. *The International Journal of Conflict Management*, *19*(4), 359–381. doi:10.1108/10444060810909301

Nandalal, K. D. W., & Simonovic, S. P. (2003). Conflict Resolution Support System: A Software for the Resolution of Conflicts in Water Resource Management. University of Western Ontario.

Nash, H. A. (2009). The Revised Directive on Waste: Resolving Legislative Tensions in Waste Management? *Journal of Environmental Law*, *21*(1), 139–149. doi:10.1093/jel/eqp001

Nash, J. F. (1950). The bargaining problem. *Econometrica*, *18*(2), 155–162. doi:10.2307/1907266

Naso, D., Surico, M., & Turchiano, B. (2007). Reactive scheduling of a distributed network for the supply of perishable products. *IEEE Transactions on Automation Science and Engineering*, *4*(3), 407–423. doi:10.1109/TASE.2006.884672

Naso, D., & Turchiano, B. (2005). Multicriteria meta-heuristics for AGV dispatching control based on computational intelligence. *IEEE Transactions on Systems, Man, and Cybernetics. Part B, Cybernetics*, *35*(2), 208–226. doi:10.1109/TSMCB.2004.842249 PMID:15828651

Navarro, M., Bhatnagar, D., & Liang, Y. (2011, October). An integrated network and data management system for heterogeneous WSNs. In *Mobile Adhoc and Sensor Systems (MASS), 2011 IEEE 8th International Conference on* (pp. 819-824). IEEE. doi:10.1109/MASS.2011.94

Navarro, E., Fernández-Caballero, A., & Martínez-Tomás, R. (2014). Intelligent multisensory systems in support of information society. *International Journal of Systems Science*, *45*(4), 711–713. doi:10.1080/00207721.2014.844916

Neumann, M. A., Chin, M. H., & Kitts, C. A. (2014). Object Manipulation through Explicit Force Control Using Co-operative Mobile Multi-Robot Systems. In *World Congress on Engineering and Computer Science* (WCECS), (vol. 1, pp. 364–369).

Neves, J., Guimarães, T., Gomes, S., Vicente, H., Santos, M., Neves, J., . . . Novais, P. (2015). Logic Programming and Artificial Neural Networks in Breast Cancer Detection. In I. Rojas, G. Joya, & A. Catala (Eds.), Advances in Computational Intelligence – Part II (LNCS), (vol. 9095, pp. 211–224). Cham, Switzerland: Springer International Publishing. doi:10.1007/978-3-319-19222-2_18

Neves, J., Machado, J., Analide, C., Abelha, A., & Brito, L. (2007). The halt condition in genetic programming. In J. Neves, M. F. Santos, & J. Machado (Eds.), *Progress in Artificial Intelligence: 13th Portuguese Conference on Artificial Intelligence, EPIA 2007, Workshops: GAIW, AIASTS, ALEA, AMITA, BAOSW, BI, CMBSB, IROBOT, MASTA, STCS, and TEMA, Guimarães, Portugal, December 3-7, 2007, Proceedings* (LNAI), (Vol. 4874, pp. 160-169). Berlin, Germany: Springer. doi:10.1007/978-3-540-77002-2_14

Neves, J. (1984). A logic interpreter to handle time and negation in logic databases. In R. L. Muller, & J. J. Pottmyer (Eds.), *Proceedings of the Annual Conference of the ACM on the Fifth Generation Challenge* (pp. 50-54). New York, NY: Association for Computing Machinery.

Nicholova, M., & Nickolov, E. (2007). Threat model for user security in e-learning systems. *International Journal Information Technologies and Knowledge*, *1*, 341–347.

Niță, M. R. (2012). *Dinamica rezidențialului în Zona Metropolitană a Municipiului București și proiecția ei în starea mediului*. București: Ed. Universității din București.

Niță, M. R., Ioja, I. C., Rozylowicz, L., Onose, D. A., & Tudor, A. C. (2014). Land use consequences of the evolution of cemeteries in the Bucharest Metropolitan Area. *Journal of Environmental Planning and Management, 57*(7), 1066-1082. Doi: 10.1080/09640568.2013.815607

Nordin, N., Embi, M., & Yunus, M. M. (2010). Mobile Learning Framework for Lifelong Learning. Social and Behavioral Sciences, 7, 130-138. doi:10.1016/j.sbspro.2010.10.019

Notini, J. (2005). *Effective alternatives analysis in mediation: "BATNA/WATNA" analysis demystified*. Retrieved March 13, 2015, from http://www.mediate.com/articles/notini1.cfm

Noy, N. F. (2004). Semantic integration: A survey of ontology-based approaches. *SIGMOD Record*, *33*(4), 65–70. doi:10.1145/1041410.1041421

Nunneri, C., & Hofmann, J. (2005). A participatory approach for Integrated River Basin Management in the Elbe catchment. *Estuarine, Coastal and Shelf Science*, *62*(3), 521–537. doi:10.1016/j.ecss.2004.09.015

O'Connor, S. (1998). Collected, Tagged, & Archived: The Burgeoning Use of Biometrics in Personal Identification. *Bender's Immigr. Bull. 1245.*

O'Donnell, P. A., & Lozano-Perez, T. (1989). Deadlock-free and collision-free coordination of two robot manipulators. In *IEEE International Conference on Robotics and Automation* (ICRA), (pp. 484–489).

O'Malley, R., Jones, E., & Glavin, M. (2010). Detection of pedestrians in far-infrared automotive night vision using region-growing and clothing distortion compensation. *Infrared Physics & Technology, 53*(6), 439–449. doi:10.1016/j.infrared.2010.09.006

O'Reilly, T. (2010). Government as a Platform. *Innovations, 6*(1), 13–40. doi:10.1162/INOV_a_00056

O'Rourke, E. (2014). The reintroduction of the white-tailed sea eagle to Ireland: People and wildlife. *Land Use Policy, 38*, 129–137. doi:10.1016/j.landusepol.2013.10.020

Oliver, J. R. (1996). On Artificial Agents for Negotiation in Electronic Commerce. In *The 29 Hawaii International Conference on System Sciences (HICSS'96)*. Washington, DC: IEEE Computer Society. doi:10.1109/HICSS.1996.495355

Olmeda, D., de la Escalera, A., & Armingol, J. M. (2011). Far infrared pedestrian detection and tracking for night driving. *Robotica, 29*(4), 495–505. doi:10.1017/S0263574710000299

Onose, D. A., Ioja, I. C., Vânău, G. O., Niţă, M. R., Ciocănea, C. M., & Mirea, D. A. (2013). Spatial and temporal dynamics of residential areas affected by the industrial function in a post-communist city. Case study Bucharest. *Real Corp 2013 Planning Times*, 821-830.

Onose, D. A., Niţă, M. R., Ciocănea, C. M., Pătroescu, M., Vânău, G. O., & Bodescu, F. (2015). Identifying critical areas of exposure to environmental conflicts using expert opinion and multi-criteria analysis. *Carpathian Journal of Earth and Environmental Sciences, 10*(4), 15–28.

Osborne, M. J., & Rubinstein, A. (1999). *A Course in Game Theory*. MIT Press.

Osman, N., Sierra, C., McNeill, F., Pane, J., & Debenham, J. (2013). Trust and Matching Algorithms for Selecting Suitable Agents. *ACM Transactions on Intelligent Systems and Technology, 5*(1), 16–16. doi:10.1145/2542182.2542198

Ossowski, S. (2013). *Agreement Technologies. In Law, Governance and Technology Series* (Vol. 8). Springer.

Ossowski, S. (Ed.). (2013). *Handbook of Agreement Technologies (vol. 8)*. New York: Springer Verlag.

OWASP. (2014a). *Cross-site Scripting (XSS)*. Retrieved July 16, 2015, from https://www.owasp.org/index.php/XSS

OWASP. (2014b). *SQL Injection Prevention Cheat Sheet*. Recovered from https://www.owasp.org/index.php/SQL_Injection_Prevention_Cheat_Sheet

OWASP. (2015). *Cross-Site Request Forgery (CSRF)*. Recovered from https://www.owasp.org/index.php/Cross-Site_Request_Forgery_(CSRF)

Owens, S., & Cowell, R. (2011). *Land and Limits: interpreting sustainability in the planning process*. New York: Routledge.

Owusu, G., Oteng-Ababio, M., & Afutu-Kotey, R. L. (2012). Conflicts and governance of landfills in a developing country city, Accra. *Landscape and Urban Planning, 104*(1), 105–113. doi:10.1016/j.landurbplan.2011.10.005

Paavola, J. (2003). *Environmental justice and governnce: theory and lessons from the implementation of the European Union's Habitat Directive*. CSERGE Working Paper EDM, 03-05.

Palmer, S., Cooper, C., & Thomas, K. (2003). *Creating a Balance: Managing Stress*. London: British Library.

Panagiotis, G., Tsianos, N., Lekkas, Z., Mourlas, C., & Samaras, G. (2008). Capturing Essential Intrinsic User Behaviour Values for the Design of Comprehensive Web-based Personalized Environments. *Computers in Human Behavior*, *24*(4), 1434–1451. doi:10.1016/j.chb.2007.07.010

Paolacci, G., Chandler, J., & Ipeirotis, P. (2010). Running experiments on amazon mechanical turk. *Judgment and Decision Making*, *5*(5), 411–419.

Papazoglou, M. P., & Georgakopoulos, D. (2003). Service-oriented computing. *Communications of the ACM*, *46*(10), 25–28.

Parsons, S., Rodriguez-Aguilar, J. A., & Klein, M. (2011). Auctions and bidding: A guide for computer scientists. *ACM Computing Surveys*, *43*(2), 10. doi:10.1145/1883612.1883617

Parsons, S., Sierra, C., & Jennings, N. R. (1998). Agents that reason and negotiate by arguing. *Journal of Logic and Computation*, *8*(3), 261–292. doi:10.1093/logcom/8.3.261

Parsons, T. (1951). *The Social System*. Glencoe, IL: The Free Press.

Passino, K. M. (2002). Biomimicry of bacterial foraging for distributed optimization and control. *IEEE Control Systems Magazine*, *22*(3), 52–67. doi:10.1109/MCS.2002.1004010

Peasgood, M., Clark, C., & McPhee, J. (2008). A Complete and scalable strategy for coordinating multiple robots within roadmaps. *IEEE Transactions on Robotics*, *24*(2), 283–292. doi:10.1109/TRO.2008.918056

Pedroso, J. (2006). A justiça em Portugal entre a(s) crise(s) e a(s) oportunidade(s) – Contributo para a construção de um novo paradigma de política pública de justiça. In Scientia Iuridica, Tomo LV – n.º 306 – abril/junho de 2006. (In Portuguese)

Peng, J., & Akella, S. (2005). Coordinating multiple robots with kinodynamic constraints along specified paths. *The International Journal of Robotics Research*, *24*(4), 295–310. doi:10.1177/0278364905051974

Pereira, L. M., & Anh, H. T. (2009). Evolution prospection. In K. Nakamatsu (Ed.), *New Advances in Intelligent Decision Technologies: Results of the First KES International Symposium IDT 2009 (Studies in Computational Intelligence)* (Vol. 199, pp. 51-64). Berlin, Germany: Springer. doi:10.1007/978-3-642-00909-9_6

Pereira, G. A. S., Campos, M. F. M., & Kumar, V. (2004). Decentralized Algorithms for Multi-Robot Manipulation via Caging. *The International Journal of Robotics Research*, *23*(7–8), 783–795. doi:10.1177/0278364904045477

Perrow, C. (1986). *Complex Organizations*. New York, NY: Random House.

Picard, R. W. (2000). *Affective Computing*. The MIT Press.

Pimenta, A., Carneiro, D., Novais, P., & Neves, J. (2013). Monitoring mental fatigue through the analysis of keyboard and mouse interaction patterns.LNAI, 8073, 222–231. Doi:10.1007/978-3-642-40846-5_23

Pinyol, I., & Sabater-Mir, J. (2013). Computational trust and reputation models for open multi-agent systems: A review. *Artificial Intelligence Review, Springer Netherlands.*, *40*(1), 1–25. doi:10.1007/s10462-011-9277-z

Pires, E. J. S., Moura Oliveira, P. B., & Machado, J. A. T. (2005). *Multi objective MaxiMin Sorting Scheme,* (Vol. 3410). Notes in Comp. Science.

Poblet, M. (2011). *Mobile Technologies for Conflict Management: Online Dispute Resolution, Governance, Participation* (Vol. 2). Springer Science & Business Media. Retrieved from https://www.google.com/books?hl=pt-PT&lr=&id=RDwp2TrEaKQC&oi=fnd&pg=PR5&dq=introduction+to+mobile+technologies,+conflict+management,+and+odr&ots=m8yvuJ8Kph&sig=PCPszF7-W44V0mkqFUSbsRL1XRE

Poblet, M., García-Cuesta, E., & Casanovas, P. (2014). Crowdsourcing Tools for Disaster Management: A Review of Platforms and Methods. In *AI Approaches to the Complexity of Legal Systems* (pp. 261–274). Springer. Retrieved from http://link.springer.com/chapter/10.1007/978-3-662-45960-7_19

Poblet, M., & Casanovas, P. (2007). Emotions in ODR. *International Review of Law Computers & Technology*, *21*(2), 145–156. doi:10.1080/13600860701492146

Pohl, A. J., & Lamont, G. B. (2008). Multi-objective UAV mission planning using evolutionary computation. In *Winter Simulation Conference*, (pp. 1268–1279). doi:10.1109/WSC.2008.4736199

Pondy, L. (1964). Organizational Conflict: Concepts and Models. In H. J. Leavitt, L. Pondy, & M. Boje (Eds.), *Readings in Managerial Psychology* (p. 513). Chicago: Chicago University Press.

Pondy, L. (1967). Reflections on Organizational Conflict. *Journal of Organizational Behavior*, *13*(3), 257–261. doi:10.1002/job.4030130305

Pondy, L. R. (1967). *Organizational Conflict: Concepts and Models* (Vol. 2). Sage Publications, Inc.

Popper, K. R. (1966). The Open Society and Its Enemies: The Spell of Plato (vol. 1; 5th ed.). London: Routledge & Kegan Paul.

Porter, J. (2008). *Designing for the Social Web*. Peachpit Press.

Prensky, M. (2001). Digital natives, digital immigrants.On the Horizon, 9(5).

Pruitt, D. G. (1981). *Negotiation Behavior*. Academic Press.

Pruitt, D. G. (1983). Strategic Choice in Negotiation. *The American Behavioral Scientist*, *27*(2), 167–194. doi:10.1177/000276483027002005

Pruitt, D. G., & Carnevale, P. J. (1993). *Negotiation and Social Conflict*. Buckingham, UK: Open University Press.

Pruitt, D. G., & Rubin, J. Z. (1986). *Social Conflict: Escalation, Stalemate, Settlement*. New York, NY: Random House.

Purwin, O., D'Andrea, R., & Lee, J. W. (2008). Theory and implementation of path planning by negotiation for decentralized agents. *Robotics and Autonomous Systems*, *56*(5), 422–436. doi:10.1016/j.robot.2007.09.020

Putnam, L. L., & Wilson, C. E. (1982). Communicative Strategies in Organizational Conflicts: Reliability and Validity of a Measurement Scale. In M. Burgoon (Ed.), *Communication Yearbook 6* (pp. 629–652). Beverly Hills, CA: Sage.

Quinn, A. J., & Bederson, B. B. (2011). Human Computation: A Survey and Taxonomy of a Growing Field. In *Proceedings of the SIGCHI Conference on Human Factors in Computing Systems* (pp. 1403–1412). New York, NY: ACM. http://doi.org/ doi:10.1145/1978942.1979148

Raaij, E. M., & Schepers, J. J. L. (2006). *The Acceptance and Use of a Virtual Learning Environment in China*. Retrieved July 8, 2015, from http://www.sciencedirect.com/science/article/pii/S0360131506001382

Rahim, M. A. (1983). A Measure of Styles of Handling Interpersonal Conflict. *Academy of Management Journal*, *26*(2), 368–376. doi:10.2307/255985 PMID:10263067

Rahim, M. A. (1983). *Rahim Organizational Conflict Inventories*. Palo Alto, Calif.: Consulting Psychologists Press.

Rahim, M. A. (1986). *Managing Conflict in Organizations*. New York, NY: Praeger.

Rahim, M. A., & Bonoma, T. V. (1979). Managing Organizational Conflict: A Model for Diagnosis and Intervention. *Psychological Reports*, *44*(3c), 1323–1344. doi:10.2466/pr0.1979.44.3c.1323

Rahwan, I. (2006). *Argumentation in multi-agent systems*. Autonomous Agents and Multiagent Systems. *Guest Editorial, 11*(2), 115–125.

Rahwan, I., & Amgoud, L. (2006). An argumentation-based approach for practical reasoning. In *5th International Joint Conference on Autonomous Agents and Multiagent Systems, AAMAS-06*. ACM Press. doi:10.1145/1160633.1160696

Rahwan, I., & Larson, K. (2008). Mechanism design for abstract argumentation. In *Proceedings of the 7th international joint conference on Autonomous agents and multiagent systems* (vol. 2, pp. 1031–1038). ACM Press.

Rahwan, I., & Larson, K. (2009). *Argumentation and Game Theory*. Argumentation in Artificial Intelligence.

Rahwan, I., Ramchurn, S. D., Jennings, N. R., Mcburney, P., Parsons, S., & Sonenberg, L. (2003). Argumentation-based negotiation. *The Knowledge Engineering Review, 18*(04), 343–375. doi:10.1017/S0269888904000098

Rahwan, I., & Simari, G. (Eds.). (2009). *Argumentation in Artificial Intelligence*. Springer.

Raiffa, H. (1982). *The art and science of negotiation: how to resolve conflicts and get the best out of bargaining*. Cambridge, MA: The Belknap Press of Harvard University Press.

Raiffa, H. (1982). *The Art and Science of Negotiation: How to Resolve Conflicts and Get the Best Out of Bargaining*. Cambridge, MA: Belknap Press.

Ramzan, M., Khan, Q. M., Iqbal, M. A., Aasem, M., Jaffar, A., Anwar, S., & Alam, M. et al. (2012). A genetic algorithms based approach for conflicts resolution in requirement. *International Journal of the Physical Sciences, 6*(4), 828–836.

Randive, P. U., Khatke, M. B., & Reddi, M. B. (2014). An Approach for Prevention of SQL Injection Attacks on Database: A Review. *International Journal of Innovative Research in Advanced Engineering, 1*(3), 38–41.

Rands, M., Levinger, G., & Mellinger, G. D. (1981). Patterns of Conflict Resolution and Marital Satisfaction. *Journal of Family Issues, 2*, 297–321.

Rashedi, E., Nezamabadi-pour, H., & Saryazdi, S. (2009). GSA: A Gravitational Search Algorithm. *Information Sciences, 179*(13), 2232–2248. doi:10.1016/j.ins.2009.03.004

Rebera, A. P., & Mordini, E. (2013). Age Factors in Biometric Processing. In The Institution of Engineering and Technology. Stevenage.

Rebollo, M., Carrascosa, C., & Palomares, A. (2014). Follow the leader in a consensus network as a solution to manage a smart grid: the Balearic Islands case. In *Proceedings of the 2014 international conference on Autonomous agents and multi-agent systems* (AAMAS '14). International Foundation for Autonomous Agents and Multiagent Systems.

Reed, C., & Walton, D. (2005). Towards a formal and implemented model of argumentation schemes in agent communication. *Autonomous Agents and Multi-Agent Systems, 11*(2), 173–188. doi:10.1007/s10458-005-1729-x

Reggio, F. (2010). *Giustizia dialogica. Luci e ombre della Restorative Justice*. Milan: Franco Angeli.

Rego, H., Moreira, T., Morales, E., & Garcia, F. J. (2010). Metadata and Knowledge Management drivenWeb-based Learning Information System towardsWeb/e-learning 3.0.[iJET]. *International Journal of Emerging Technologies in Learning, 5*(2), 36–44.

Reichers, A. E. (1986). Conflict and Organizational Commitments. *The Journal of Applied Psychology, 71*(3), 7. doi:10.1037/0021-9010.71.3.508

Reiter, R. (1980). A logic for default reasoning. *Artificial Intelligence, 13*(1-2), 81–132. doi:10.1016/0004-3702(80)90014-4

Richardson, W. (2005). The educator's guide to the read/write web. *Educational Leadership, 63*(4), 24.

Robbins, S. P. (1974). *Managing Organizational Conflict: A Nontraditional Approach*. Englewood Cliffs, NJ: Prentice-Hall.

Robbins, S. P., & Judge, T. (2007). *Organizational Behavior*. Pearson/Prentice Hall.

Rodrigues, M., Fdez-Riverola, F., & Novais, P. (2011). Moodle and Affective Computing –Knowing Who's on the Other Side. *ECEL-2011 – 10th European Conference on Elearning*. University of Brighton.

Rodrigues, M., Fdez-Riverola, F., & Novais, P. (2012). An approach to assessing stress in e-learning students. *ECEL-2012 – 11th European Conference on E-Learning*. Retrieved from http://repositorium.sdum.uminho.pt/handle/1822/23894

Rodrigues, M., Gonçalves, S., Carneiro, D., Novais, P., & Fdez-Riverola, F. (2013). Keystrokes and Clicks: Measuring Stress on E-learning Students. In *Management Intelligent Systems, Second International Symposium*. Springer.

Rodriguez, M. D., & Shah, M. (2007). Detecting and segmenting humans in crowded scenes. In *Proceedings of the 15th International Conference on Multimedia* (pp. 353-356). Augsburg: ACM. doi:10.1145/1291233.1291310

Romero, J. J., Moreno, A., & Sola, T. (2012). Estudio de necesidades de formación de los profesores andaluces en el ámbito de la autoría de materiales educativos digitales en ambientes virtuales de aprendizaje. *Journal for Educators, Teachers and Trainers, 3*(1), 92–108.

Roscia, M., Longo, M., & Lazaroiu, G. C. (2013, October). Smart city by multi-agent systems. In *Renewable Energy Research and Applications (ICRERA), 2013 International Conference on* (pp. 371-376). IEEE. doi:10.1109/ICRERA.2013.6749783

Ross, R., & DeWine, S. (1982). Interpersonal Conflict: Measurement and Validation. Louisville, KY: Academic Press.

Ross, L. (1977). The Intuitive Psycologist and His Shortcomings: Distortions in the Attribution Process. In L. Berkowitz (Ed.), *Advances in Experimental and Social Psycology*. New York, NY: Academic Press.

Roth, B., & Rotolo, A. (2007). Strategic argumentation: a game theoretical investigation. In *Proceedings of the Eleventh International Conference on Artificial Intelligence and Law*. ACM Press.

Rowlands, I. H. (2005). The European directive on renewable electricity: Conflicts and compromises. *Energy Policy, 33*(8), 965–974. doi:10.1016/j.enpol.2003.10.019

Roxin, C. (1973). *Kriminalpolitik und Strafrechtssystem*. Berlin, New York: De Gruyter. doi:10.1515/9783110903577

Roxin, C. (1992). Zur Wiedergutmachung als einer "dritten Spur" im Sanktionensystem. In G. Arzt et al. (Eds.), *Festschrift für Jürgen Baumann zum 70 Geburtstag 22. Juni 1992* (pp. 243–254). Bielefeld: Gieseking Verlag.

Rubin, B. D. (Ed.). (1978). *The variable nature of news media influence*. New Brunswick.

Rubinstein, A. (1982). Perfect equilibrium in a bargaining model. *Econometrica, 50*(1), 155–162. doi:10.2307/1912531

Rule, C., & Nagarajan, C. (2011). Crowdsourcing Dispute Resolution over Mobile Devices. In *Mobile Technologies for Conflict Management* (pp. 93–106). Springer. doi:10.1007/978-94-007-1384-0_8

Ryan, M. R. K. (2007). Graph decomposition for efficient multi-robot path planning. In *International Joint Conference on Artificial Intelligence* (IJCAI), (pp. 2003–2008).

Saaty, T. (2001). *Decision Making with Dependence and Feedback: The Analytic Network Process: the Organization and Prioritization of Complexity*. Pittsburgh, PA: RWS Publications.

Sabater, J., & Sierra, C. (2005). Review on computational trust and reputation models. *Artificial Intelligence Review, 24*(1), 33–60. doi:10.1007/s10462-004-0041-5

Saha, M., & Isto, P. (2006). Multi-robot motion planning by incremental coordination. In *IEEE/RSJ International Conference on Intelligent Robots and Systems* (IROS), (pp. 5960–5963).

Saint, P. M., Flavell, R. J., & Fox, P. F. (2009). *NIMBY Wars. The Politics of Land Use*. Hingham, MA: Saint University Press.

Sanchez-Anguix, V., Julian, V., Botti, V., & García-Fornes, A. (2013). Tasks for agent-based negotiation teams: Analysis, review, and challenges. *Engineering Applications of Artificial Intelligence*, *26*(10), 2480–2494. doi:10.1016/j.engappai.2013.07.006

Sanchez, G., & Latombe, J. C. (2002). Using a PRM planner to compare centralized and decoupled planning for multi-robot systems. In *International Conference on Robotics and Automation* (ICRA), (Vol. 2, pp. 2112–2119). doi:10.1109/ROBOT.2002.1014852

Sangrà, A., Vlachopoulos, D., & Cabrera, N. (2012). Building an inclusive definition of e-learning: An approach to the conceptual framework. *The International Review of Research in Open and Distributed Learning*, *13*(2), 145–159.

Santana, G. (2007). *La justicia restaurativa y la mediación penal*. Madrid: Iustel.

Sarasua, C., Simperl, E., & Noy, N. F. (2012). CrowdMap: Crowdsourcing Ontology Alignment with Microtasks. In *The Semantic Web – ISWC 2012* (pp. 525–541). Springer. Retrieved from http://link.springer.com/chapter/10.1007/978-3-642-35176-1_33

Savelsbergh, M. W. P., & Sol, M. (1995). The general pickup and delivery problem. *Transportation Science*, *29*(1), 17–29. doi:10.1287/trsc.29.1.17

Schaffers, H., Komninos, N., Pallot, M., Trousse, B., Nilsson, M., & Oliveira, A. (2011). Smart Cities and the Future Internet: Towards Cooperation Frameworks for Open Innovation. *Future Internet Assembly*, *6656*, 431–446. doi:10.1007/978-3-642-20898-0_31

Schmidt, A., Ivanova, A., & Schafer, M. (2013). Media attention for climate change around the world: A comparative analysis of newspaper in 27 countries. *Global Environmental Change*, *23*(5), 1233–1248. doi:10.1016/j.gloenvcha.2013.07.020

Schmidtz, D., & Willott, E. (Eds.). (2002). *Natural enemies: An anatomy of environmental conflict*. New York: Oxford University Press.

Schmitz, A. (2010). "Drive-Thru" Arbitration in the Digital Age: Empowering Consumers Through Regulated ODR. *Baylor Law Review*, *62*, 178.

Schneider, J., Groza, T., & Passant, A. (2013). A review of argumentation for the Social Semantic Web. *Semantic Web*, *4*(2), 159–218.

Schöch, H. (1988). Strafrecht im demokratischen Rechtsstat. Yur konkreten Utopie der Wiedergutmachung im Strafverfahren. In A. Kaufmann et al. (Eds.), *Festschrift für Maihofer zum 70. Geburtstag* (pp. 461–479). Frankfurt: Kostermann.

Schöch, H. (1992). Verwarnung statt Strafe. In G. Arzt et al. (Eds.), *Festschrift für Jürgen Baumann zum 70 Geburtstag 22. Juni 1992* (pp. 255–268). Bielefeld: Gieseking Verlag.

Schwartz, W. R., Kembhavi, A., Harwood, D., & Davis, L. S. (2009). Human detection using partial least squares analysis. In *Proceedings of the IEEE 12th International Conference on Computer Vision* (pp. 24-31). Kyoto: IEEE. doi:10.1109/ICCV.2009.5459205

Segaran, T. (2007). *Programming Collective Intelligence: Building Smart Web 2.0 Applications*. O'Reilly Media.

Sheather, S. J., & Jones, M. C. (1991). A reliable data-based bandwidth selection method for kernel density estimation. *Journal of the Royal Statistical Society. Series B. Methodological*, 683–690.

Sherif, M. (1966). *In Common Predicament: Social Psychology of Intergroup Conflict and Cooperation*. Boston: Houghton Mifflin.

Sherman, L. (1993). Defiance, Deterrence and Irrelevance: A Theory of the Criminal Sanction. *Journal of Research in Crime and Delinquency*, *30*(4), 445–473. doi:10.1177/0022427893030004006

Sherman, L., & Strang, H. (2007). *Restorative justice: the evidence*. The Smith Institute.

Sherman, L., & Strang, H. (2010). Restorative Justice as a Psychological Treatment: Healing Victims and Reintegrating Offenders. In G. Towl & D. Crichton (Eds.), *Handbook of Forensic Psychology*. Amsterdam: Elsevier.

Sherman, L., Strang, H., & Newbury-Birch, D. (2008). *Restorative justice*. Youth Justice Board.

Shockley-Zalabak, P. (1988). Assessing the Hall conflict Management Survey. *Management Communication Quarterly*, *1*(3), 302–320. doi:10.1177/0893318988001003003

Sidaway, R. (2005). *Resolving environmental disputes: from conflict to consensus*. London: Earthscan.

Sierra, C., Botti, V., & Ossowski, S. (2011). *Agreement Computing*. KI-Kunstliche Intelligenz.

Sierra, C., Botti, V., & Ossowski, S. (2011). Agreement computing. *KI-Künstliche Intelligenz*, *25*(1), 57–61. doi:10.1007/s13218-010-0070-y

Silva, S. T. (2010). *Um Novo Direito Administrativo?* Coimbra: Imprensa da Universidade de Coimbra. doi:10.14195/978-989-26-0208-0

Simari, G. R., Garcia, A. J., & Capobianco, M. (2004). Actions, planning and defeasible reasoning. In *10th International Workshop on Non-Monotonic Reasoning* (LNAI), (pp. 377–384). Springer.

Siméon, T., Leroy, S., & Laumond, J.-P. (2002). Path coordination for multiple mobile robots: A resolution complete algorithm. *IEEE Transactions on Robotics and Automation*, *18*(1), 42–49. doi:10.1109/70.988973

Simmons, R., Apfelbaum, D., Fox, D., Goldman, R. P., Haigh, K. Z., Musliner, D. J., … Thrun, S. (2000b). Coordinated deployment of multiple heterogeneous robots. In *International Conference on Intelligent Robotics and Systems* (IROS), (*vol. 3*, pp. 2254–2260).

Simmons, R., Apfelbaum, D., Burgard, W., Fox, D., Thrun, S., & Younes, H. (2000). Coordination for multi-robot exploration and mapping. In *National Conference on Artificial Intelligence*.

Simons, T. L., & Peterson, R. S. (2000). Task Conflict and Relationship Conflict in Top Management Teams: The Pivotal Role of Intragroup Trust. *The Journal of Applied Psychology*, *85*(1), 102–111. doi:10.1037/0021-9010.85.1.102 PMID:10740960

Singh, P., Lin, T., Mueller, E. T., Lim, G., Perkins, T., & Zhu, W. L. (2002). Open Mind Common Sense: Knowledge Acquisition from the General Public. In *On the Move to Meaningful Internet Systems 2002: CoopIS, DOA, and ODBASE* (pp. 1223–1237). Springer. Retrieved from http://link.springer.com/chapter/10.1007/3-540-36124-3_77

Skinner, E. A., & Belmont, M. J. (1993). Motivation in the classroom: Reciprocal effects of teacher behavior and student engagement across the school year. *Journal of Educational Psychology*, *85*(4), 571–581. doi:10.1037/0022-0663.85.4.571

Smith, L. H., & Renzulli, J. S. (1984). Learning style preferences: A practical approach for classroom teachers. *Theory into Practice*, *23*(1), 44–50. doi:10.1080/00405848409543088

Smith, S. L., & Bullo, F. (2009). Monotonic target assignment for robotic networks. *IEEE Transactions on Automatic Control, 54*(9), 2042–2057. doi:10.1109/TAC.2009.2026926

Socklingam, S., & Doswell, A. (1999). Conflict in BPR. *Knowledge and Process Management, 6*(3), 146–153. doi:10.1002/(SICI)1099-1441(199909)6:3<146::AID-KPM63>3.0.CO;2-3

Solovey, K., & Halperin, D. (2014). k-color multi-robot motion planning. *The International Journal of Robotics Research, 33*(1), 82–97. doi:10.1177/0278364913506268

Song, P., & Kumar, V. (2002). A potential field based approach to multi-robot manipulation. In *IEEE International Conference on Robotics and Automation* (ICRA), (vol. 2, pp. 1217–1222). doi:10.1109/ROBOT.2002.1014709

Staiger, I. (2010). Restorative Justice and Victims of Terrorism. In R. Letschert, I. Staiger, & A. Pemberton (Eds.), *Assisting Victims of Terrorism: Towards a European Standard of Justice* (pp. 267–337). London: Springer.

Steenbergen, W. (2005). Rationalizing dispute resolution: From best alternative to the most likely one. In *Proceedings of the 5th international workshop on Online Dispute Resolution*. Retrieved April 18, 2015, from http://cli.vu/pubdirectory/250/manuscript.pdf

Steenbergen, W. (2005). Rationalizing Dispute Resolution: from best alternative to the most likely one. In *Proceedings of 3rd ODR Workshop.*

Steffek, J. (2009). Discursive legitimation in environmental governance: Discourse and Expertise in Forest and Environmental Governance. *Forest Policy and Economics, 11*(5-6), 313–318. doi:10.1016/j.forpol.2009.04.003

Steibel, F., & Estevez, E. (2012). Designing argumentative metrics for online consultation portals in Brazil. In *Proceedings of the 13th Annual International Conference on Digital Government Research DG.O 2012* (pp. 272-273). ACM Press. doi:10.1145/2307729.2307781

Stoll-Kleemann, S. (2001). Opposition to the Designation of Protected Areas in Germany. *Journal of Environmental Planning and Management, 44*(1), 109–128. doi:10.1080/09640560123606

Stone, D. E., & Zheng, G. (2014). Learning Management Systems in a Changing Environment. In V. Wang (Ed.), *Handbook of Research on Education and Technology in a Changing Society*. IGI Global. Retrieved July 16, 2015, from http://www.researchgate.net/publication/267625754_Learning_Management_Systems_in_a_Changing_Environment

Storn, R., & Price, K. (1997). Differential Evolution: A Simple and Efficient Adaptive Scheme for Global Optimization Over Continuous Spaces. *Journal of Global Optimization, 11*(4), 341–349. doi:10.1023/A:1008202821328

Strang, H. (2001). *Restorative Justice Programs in Australia: A report to the Criminology Council*. Retrieved May, 30, 2015, from http://www.criminologyresearchcouncil.gov.au/reports/strang/

Streng, F. (1991). *Strafrechtliche Sanktionen. Grundlagen und Anwendung*. Stuttgart: Kohlhammer.

Such, J. M., Espinosa, A., Garcia-Fornes, A., & Botti, V. (2011). Partial identities as a foundation for Trust and Reputation. *Engineering Applications of Artificial Intelligence, 24*(7), 1128–1136. doi:10.1016/j.engappai.2011.06.008

Sugar, T., Desai, J., Ostrowski, J., & Kumar, V. (2001). Coordination of multiple mobile manipulators. In *IEEE International Conference on Robotics and Automation* (ICRA), (pp. 3284–3289).

Sui, D., & Goodchild, M. (2011). The convergence of GIS and social media: Challenges for GIScience. *International Journal of Geographical Information Science, 25*(11), 1737–1748. doi:10.1080/13658816.2011.604636

Sui, D., Goodchild, M., & Elwood, S. (2013). Volunteered geographic information, the exaflood, and the growing digital divide. In *Crowdsourcing geographic knowledge* (pp. 1–12). Springer. doi:10.1007/978-94-007-4587-2_1

Sun, H. M. (2000). An efficient remote use authentication scheme using smart cards. *IEEE Transactions on Consumer Electronics*, *46*(4), 958–961. doi:10.1109/30.920446

Sun, S. G., & Park, H. (2001). Segmentation of forward-looking infrared image using fuzzy thresholding and edge detection. *Optical Engineering (Redondo Beach, Calif.)*, *40*(11), 2638–2645. doi:10.1117/1.1409563

Surowiecki, J. (2004). *The Wisdom of Crowds: Why the Many Are Smarter Than the Few and How Collective Wisdom Shapes Business, Economies, Societies and Nations*. New York: Doubleday.

Susskind, L., & Cruikshank, J. (1987). *Breaking the Impasse: Consensual Approaches To Resolving Public*. New York: Basic Books.

Svestka, P., & Overmars, M. H. (1998). Coordinated path planning for multiple robots. *Robotics and Autonomous Systems*, *23*(3), 125–152. doi:10.1016/S0921-8890(97)00033-X

Sycara, K. (1989). Multi-agent compromise via negotiation. *Distributed Artificial Intelligence*, *2*(1), 119–139.

Sycara, K. P. (1989). *Multiagent compromise via negotiation*. In Distributed. *Artificial Intelligence*, *2*, 119–137.

Sycara, K. P. (1990). Negotiation Planning. *An AI Approach*, *46*(1), 216–234.

Sycara, K. P. (1991). Problem restructuring in negotiation. *Management Science*, *37*(10), 1248–1268. doi:10.1287/mnsc.37.10.1248

Talia, D. (2012). Clouds meet agents: Toward intelligent cloud services. *IEEE Internet Computing*, *16*(2), 78–81. doi:10.1109/MIC.2012.28

Tang, Y., Cai, K., McBurney, P., Sklar, E., & Parsons, S. (2011). Using argumentation to reason about trust and belief. *Journal of Logic and Computation*, *22*(5), 979–1018.

Tapscott, D. (1998). *Growing Up Digital. The Rise of the Net Generation*. New York: McGraw Hill. Retrieved from http://www.growingupdigital.com/index.html

Tella, J. L., Forero, M. G., Hiraldo, F., & Donazar, J. A. (1998). Conflicts Between Lesser Kestrel Conservation and European Agricultural Policies as Identified by Habitat Use Analyses. *Conservation Biology*, *12*(3), 593–604. doi:10.1046/j.1523-1739.1998.96288.x

Thomas, K. W. (1976). Conflict and Conflict Management. In M. D. Dunnette (Ed.), *Handbook of Industrial and Organizational Psychology*. Chicago: Rand-McNally.

Thomas, K. W. (1984). Dynamics of Escalation/De-Escalation. In J. Veiga & J. Yanouzas (Eds.), *The Dynamics of Organization Theory* (pp. 283–300). St. Paul, MN: West.

Thomas, K. W. (1992). Conflict and Negotiation Processes in Organizations. In M. D. Dunnette (Ed.), *Handbook of Industrial and Organizational Psychology* (2nd ed.; pp. 889–935). Palo Alto, CA: Consulting Psychologists Press.

Thomas, K. W., & Kilmann, R. H. (1974). *The Thomas-Kilmann Conflict Mode Instrument*. Tuxedo, NY: Xicom.

Thompson, J. D. (1967). *Organizations in Action*. New York, NY: McGraw-Hill.

Tjosvold, D. (2006). Defining conflict and making choices about its management. *The International Journal of Conflict Management*, *17*(2), 87–95. doi:10.1108/10444060610736585

Tolbert, P., & Hall, R. (2009). *Organizations: Structures, Processes and Outcomes*. Upper Saddle River, NJ: Pearson.

Torre, A., Melot, R., Magsi, H., Bossuet, L., Cadoret, A., Caron, A., & Kolokouris, O. et al. (2014). Identifying and measuring land-use and proximity conflicts: Methods and identification. *SpringerPlus*, *3*(1), 85. doi:10.1186/2193-1801-3-85 PMID:24600543

Torroni, P., & Toni, F. (2011). Bottom up argumentation. In *Proceedings of First Intl. Workshop on Theoretical and Formal Argumentation (TAFA). IJCAI 2011* (LNCS), (pp. 249-262). Springer Verlag.

Toth, P., & Vigo, D. (2001). *The Vehicle Routing Problem*. Philadelphia, PA: Society for Industrial and Applied Mathematics.

Toulmin, S. (1959). *The uses of argument*. Cambridge, UK: Cambridge University Press.

Trice, H., & Beyer, J. M. (1993). *The Culture of Work Organizations*. Englewood Cliffs, NJ: Prentice Hall.

Trujillo, J. M., Hinojo, F. J., & Aznar, I. (2011). Propuestas de trabajo innovadoras y colaborativas e-learning 2.0 como demanda de la sociedad del conocimiento. *Estudios Sobre Educación, 20*, 141-159.

Trujillo, J. M., Cáceres, M. P., Hinojo, F. J., & Aznar, I. (2011). Aprendizaje cooperativo en entornos virtuales: El proyecto Redes Educativas y Organizativas Interuniversitarias. *Educar, 47*(1), 95–119.

Tudor, A. C., Iojă, C. I., Hersperger, A. M., & Patru-Stupariu, I. (2013). Is the residential land use incompatible with cemeteries location? Assessing the attitudes of urban residents. *Carpathian Journal of Earth and Environmental Sciences, 8*(2), 153–162.

Tudor, A. C., Ioja, C. I., Rozylowicz, L., Patru-Stupariu, I., & Hersperger, A. M. (2015). Similarities and differences in the assessment of land-use associations by local people and experts. *Land Use Policy, 49*, 341–351. doi:10.1016/j.landusepol.2015.07.001

Tudor, C. A., Iojă, C. I., Patru-Stupariu, I., Nita, M. R., & Hersperger, A. M. (2014). How successful is the resolution of land-use conflicts? A comparison of cases from Switzerland and Romania. *Applied Geography (Sevenoaks, England), 47*, 125–136. doi:10.1016/j.apgeog.2013.12.008

Turner, M. E., & Pratkanis, A. (1994). Social Identity Maintenance Prescriptions for Preventing Groupthink: Reducing Identity Protection and Enhancing Intellectual Conflict. *The International Journal of Conflict Management, 5*(3), 254–270. doi:10.1108/eb022746

U.S. Department of Education. (2009). *Evaluation of Evidence-Based Practices in Online Learning: A Meta-Analysis and Review of Online Learning Studies*. Retrieved from http://www.ed.gov/rschstat/eval/tech/evidence-based-practices/finalreport.pdf

Umbreit, M., Coates, R., & Vos, B. (2004). Restorative justice versus community justice: Clarifying a muddle or generating confusion? *Contemporary Justice Review, 7*(1), 81–89. doi:10.1080/1028258042000212030

UN General Assembly. (2014). *Report of the Open Working Group of the General Assembly on Sustainable Development Goals*. Retrieved December 16, 2015, from http://www.un.org/ga/search/view_doc.asp? symbol=A/68/970&Lang=E

UNEP. (2015a). *Environmental Cooperation for Peacebuilding*. UNEP.

UNEP. (2015b). *United Nations Environment Programme*. UNEP.

Uyarra, E., & Gee, S. (2013). Transforming urban waste into sustainable material and energy usage: The case of Greater Manchester (UK). *Journal of Cleaner Production, 50*, 101–110. doi:10.1016/j.jclepro.2012.11.046

Vaandering, D. (2011). A faithful compass: Rethinking the term restorative justice to find clarity. *Contemporary Justice Review, 14*(3), 307–328. doi:10.1080/10282580.2011.589668

Van de Vliert, E., & Kabanoff, B. (1990). Toward Theory-Based Measures of Conflict Management. *Academy of Management Journal, 33*(1), 199–209. doi:10.2307/256359

Van de Vliert, E., & Prein, H. C. M. (1989). The Difference in the Meaning of Forcing in the Conflict Management of Actors and Observers. In M. A. Rahim (Ed.), *Managing conflict: An interdisciplinary approach* (pp. 51–63). New York, NY: Praeger.

van den Berg, J., Snoeyink, J., Lin, M., & Manocha, D. (2009). Centralized Path Planning for Multiple Robots: Optimal Decoupling into Sequential Plans. In Robotics: Science and Systems (RSS).

van den Berg, J., & Overmars, M. (2005). Prioritized motion planning for multiple robots. In *International Conference on Intelligent Robots and Systems* (IROS), (pp. 430–435).

Van Den Herik, J., & Dimov, D. (2012). Towards Crowdsourced Online Dispute Resolution. *J. Int'l Com. L. & Tech., 7*, 99.

Van Der Aalst, W. M., Ter Hofstede, A. H., & Weske, M. (2003). Business process management: A survey. In *Business process management* (pp. 1–12). Springer. doi:10.1007/3-540-44895-0_1

Van Gramberg, B. (2006). *Managing Workplace Conflict: Alternative Dispute Resolution in Australia*. Sydney: Federation Press.

Vanaret, C., Gianazza, D., Durand, N., & Gotteland, J. B. (2012). *Benchmarking conflict resolution algorithms*. ICRAT 2012, 5th International Conference on Research in Air Transportation, Berkeley, CA.

Vasconcelos, W. W., Kollingbaum, M. J., & Norman, T. J. (2009). Normative conflict resolution in multi-agent systems. *Autonomous Agents and Multi-Agent Systems, 19*(2), 124–152. doi:10.1007/s10458-008-9070-9

Velagapudi, P., Sycara, K. P., & Scerri, P. (2010). Decentralized prioritized planning in large multirobot teams. In *International Conference on Intelligent Robots and Systems* (IROS), (pp. 4603–4609). doi:10.1109/IROS.2010.5649438

Verma, V. K. (1998). Conflict Management. In *The Project Management Institute Project Management Handbook*. Jeffery Pinto.

Vicente, H., Couto, C., Machado, J., Abelha, A., & Neves, J. (2012). Prediction of Water Quality Parameters in a Reservoir using Artificial Neural Networks. *International Journal of Design & Nature and Ecodynamics, 7*(3), 309–318. doi:10.2495/DNE-V7-N3-309-318

Vicente, H., Dias, S., Fernandes, A., Abelha, A., Machado, J., & Neves, J. (2012). Prediction of the Quality of Public Water Supply using Artificial Neural Networks. *Journal of Water Supply: Research & Technology - Aqua, 61*(7), 446–459. doi:10.2166/aqua.2012.014

Vicente, H., Roseiro, J., Arteiro, J., Neves, J., & Caldeira, A. T. (2013). Prediction of bioactive compound activity against wood contaminant fungi using artificial neural networks. *Canadian Journal of Forest Research, 43*(11), 985–992. doi:10.1139/cjfr-2013-0142

Von Ahn, L. (2009). Human Computation. In 46th ACM IEEE Design Automation Conference (pp. 418–419). Retrieved from http://ieeexplore.ieee.org/xpls/abs_all.jsp?arnumber=5227025

von der Dunk, A., Grêt-Regamey, A., Dalang, T., & Hersperger, A. (2011). Defining a typology of peri-urban land-use conflicts –A case study from Switzerland. *Landscape and Urban Planning, 101*(2), 149–156. doi:10.1016/j.landurbplan.2011.02.007

Wagner, G., Kang, M., & Choset, H. (2012). Probabilistic path planning for multiple robots with subdimensional expansion. In *International Conference on Robotics and Automation* (ICRA), (pp. 2886–2892). doi:10.1109/ICRA.2012.6225297

Wallenius, J., Dyer, J. S., Fishburn, P., Steuer, R., Zionts, S., & Deb, K. (2008). Multiple Criteria Decision Making, Multiattribute Utility Theory: Recent Accomplishments and What Lies Ahead. *Management Science, 54*(7), 1336–1349. doi:10.1287/mnsc.1070.0838

Walton, D. (1996). *Argumentation Schemes for Presumptive Reasoning*. Routledge Publishers.

Walton, D., & Krabbe, E. C. W. (1995). *Commitment in Dialogue: Basic Concepts of Interpersonal Reasoning*. State University of New York Press.

Walton, R. E. (1966). A theory of conflict in lateral organizational relationships. In J. Lawrence (Ed.), *Operational research and the social sciences* (p. 411). London: Tavistock.

Wang, Z., Nakano, E., & Matsukawa, T. (1994). Cooperating Multiple Behavior-Based Robots for Object Manipulation. In *International Conference on Intelligent Robots and Systems* (IROS), (vol. 3, pp. 1524–1531). doi:10.1007/978-4-431-68275-2_33

Wang, J. T., Chen, D. B., Chen, H. Y., & Yan, J. Y. (2012). On pedestrian detection and tracking in infrared videos. *Pattern Recognition Letters, 33*(6), 775–785. doi:10.1016/j.patrec.2011.12.011

Wan, J., & Liu, L. (2013). Distributed Bayesian inference for consistent labeling of tracked objects in nonoverlapping camera networks. *International Journal of Distributed Sensor Networks, 2013*, 613246. doi:10.1155/2013/613246

Wasserman, S., & Faust, K. (1994). *Social Network Analysis: Methods and Applications*. Cambridge University Press. doi:10.1017/CBO9780511815478

Watkin, L. (2012). *Environmental conflict and decision-making: the case of hydroelectric power*. Academic Press.

Weber, R. H. (2010). Internet of Things–New security and privacy challenges. *Computer Law & Security Report, 26*(1), 23–30. doi:10.1016/j.clsr.2009.11.008

Weimin, X., & Wenhong, X. (2007). *E-Learning Assistant System Based on Virtual Human Interaction Technology, ICCS 2007* (LNCS). Springer Berlin / Heidelberg.

Wells, T. (1980). *Keeping Your Cool Under Fire: Communicating Non-defensively*. New York, NY: McGraw-Hill.

Wen, J., & Kreutz-Delgado, K. (1992). Motion and force control of multiple robotic manipulators. *Automatica, 28*(4), 729–743. doi:10.1016/0005-1098(92)90033-C

West, M. A., & Anderson, N. R. (1996). Innovation in top management teams. *The Journal of Applied Psychology, 81*(6), 680–693. doi:10.1037/0021-9010.81.6.680

Wheeler, S. (2011). *E-learning 3.0: Learning through the eXtended Smart Web*. In National IT Training Conference.

Whitfield, D. P., Ruddock, M., & Bullman, R. (2008). Expert opinion as a tool for quantifying bird tolerance to human disturbance. *Biological Conservation, 141*(11), 2708–2717. doi:10.1016/j.biocon.2008.08.007

Wilde, Z., & Gaibrois, L. (2003). *O que é a Mediação*. Coimbra Editora. (In Portuguese)

Willett, W., Heer, J., & Agrawala, M. (2012). Strategies for crowdsourcing social data analysis. In *Proceedings of the 2012 ACM Annual conference on Human Factors in Computing Systems* (pp. 227–236). Retrieved from http://dl.acm.org/citation.cfm?id=2207709

Williamson, R., Purcell, S., Sterne, A., Hotopof, M., Farmer, A., & Sham, P. (2005). The relationship of fatigue to mental and physical health in a community sample. *Social Psychiatry and Psychiatric Epidemiology, 2*(2), 126–135. doi:10.1007/s00127-005-0858-5 PMID:15685404

Willmott, S., Vreeswijk, G., Chesñevar, C., South, M., McGinnis, J., Modgil, S., & Simari, G. et al. (2006). Towards an argument interchange format for Multi-Agent Systems. In *3rd International Workshop on Argumentation in Multi-Agent Systems, ArgMAS-06*. ACM Press.

Wilson, J. A., & Jerrell, S. L. (1981). Conflict: Malignant, Beneficial, or Benign. *New Directions for Higher Education, 1981*(3), 105–123. doi:10.1002/he.36919813510

Wodak, R., de Cillia, R., Reisigl, M., & Liebhart, K. (1999). *The discursive construction of national identity*. Edinburgh, UK: Edinburgh University Press.

Wolsink, M. (2004). Policy Beliefs in Spatial Decisions: Contrasting Core Beliefs Concerning Space-making for Waste Infrastructure. *Urban Studies (Edinburgh, Scotland), 41*(13), 2669–2690. doi:10.1080/0042098042000294619

Wolsink, M. (2010). Contested environmental policy infrastructure: Socio-political acceptance of renewable energy, water, and waste facilities. *Environmental Impact Assessment Review, 30*(5), 302–311. doi:10.1016/j.eiar.2010.01.001

Wrbka, S. (2014). *European Consumer Access to Justice Revisited*. Cambridge, UK: Cambridge University Press. doi:10.1017/CBO9781139680431

Wright, M. (1991). *Justice for Victims and Offenders. A restorative Response to Crime* (2nd ed.). Winchester: Waterside Press.

Wright, M., & Zernova, M. (2007). Alternative visions of restorative justice. In G. Johnstone & D. Ness (Eds.), *Handbook of Restorative Justice* (pp. 91–108). Devon: Willan Publishing.

Xue, J. Z., Xiang, M. G., Inseok, H., & Kai, Q. C. (2013). A hybrid distributed-centralized conflict resolution approach for multi-aircraft based on cooperative co-evolutionary. *Science China, 56*. DOI: 10.1007/s11432-013-4836-3

Yampolskiy, R. V., & Govindaraju, V. (2008). Behavioural biometrics: A survey and classification. *International Journal of Biometrics, 1*(1), 81–113. doi:10.1504/IJBM.2008.018665

Yang, X. S., & Deb, S. (2009). Cuckoo Search via Lévy flights. In *NaBIC World Congress on Nature & Biologically Inspired Computing*.

Yang, C. M., Li, J. J., & Chiang, H. C. (2011). Stakeholders' perspective on the sustainable utilization of marine protected areas in Green Islanf, Taiwan. *Ocean and Coastal Management, 54*(10), 771–780. doi:10.1016/j.ocecoaman.2011.08.006

Yang, X. S. (2008). Firefly algorithm. In X.-S. Yang (Ed.), *Nature-inspired metaheuristic algorithms* (pp. 79–90). Wiley Online Library.

Yiu, T. W., & Construction, C. U. (2005). *A behavioral analysis of construction dispute negotiation*. City University of Hong Kong. Retrieved from http://books.google.pt/books?id=pm7VNwAACAAJ

Yoshikawa, T., & Zheng, X. (1990). Coordinated Dynamic Hybrid Position/Force Control for Multiple robot Manipulators Handling One Constrained Object. In *IEEE International Conference on Robotics and Automation* (ICRA), (vol. 2, pp. 1178–1183). doi:10.1109/ROBOT.1990.126156

Young, J., Watt, A., Nowicki, P., Alard, D., Clitherow, J., Henle, K., & Richards, C. et al. (2005). Towards sustainable land use: Identifying and managing the conflicts between human activities and biodiversity conservation in Europe. *Biodiversity and Conservation, 14*(7), 1641–1661. doi:10.1007/s10531-004-0536-z

Yuen, M.-C., King, I., & Leung, K.-S. (2011). A Survey of Crowdsourcing Systems. In *IEEE International Conference on Privacy*. Boston, MA: Security, Risk and Trust. doi:10.1109/PASSAT/SocialCom.2011.203

Yun, S., & Kim, H.-G. (2009). *Modeling User Interactions in Online Social Networks*. Presented at the Asian Workshop of Social Web and Interoperability, Shanghai, China. Retrieved from http://www.slideshare.net/Channy/modeling-user-interactions-in-online-social-networks

Yu, W., Peng, J., Zhang, X., & Lin, K.-c. (2014). A Cooperative Path Planning Algorithm for a Multiple Mobile Robot System in a Dynamic Environment. *International Journal of Advanced Robotic Systems*, *11*, 136.

Zambonelli, F., Jennings, N. R., & Wooldridge, M. (2001). Organisational rules as an abstraction for the analysis and design of multi-agent systems. *International Journal of Software Engineering and Knowledge Engineering*, *11*(03), 303–328. doi:10.1142/S0218194001000505

Zargar, S. T., Joshi, J., & Tipper, D. (2013). A Survey of Defense Mechanisms Against Distributed Denial of Service (DDoS) Flooding Attacks. *IEEE Communications Surveys and Tutorials*, *15*(4), 2046–2069. doi:10.1109/SURV.2013.031413.00127

Zato, C., De Paz, J. F., de Luis, A., Bajo, J., & Corchado, J. M. (2012). Model for assigning roles automatically in egovernment virtual organizations. *Expert Systems with Applications*, *39*(12), 10389–10401. doi:10.1016/j.eswa.2012.01.185

Zehr, H. (2004). *El Pequeño Libro de la Justicia Restaurativa*. Good Books.

Zeleznikow, J., & Bellucci, E. (2012). Legal Fairness in Alternative Dispute Resolution Processes – Implications for Research and Teaching. *Australasian Dispute Resolution Journal*, *23*, 265–273.

Zeng, D., & Sycara, K. (1998). Bayesian learning in negotiation. *International Journal of Human-Computer Studies*, *48*(1), 125–141. doi:10.1006/ijhc.1997.0164

Zhao, S. Z., & Suganthan, P. N. (2011). Two-lbests based multi-objective particle swarm optimizer. *Engineering Optimization*, *43*(1), 1–17. doi:10.1080/03052151003686716

Zitzler, E., Laumanns, M., & Thiele, L. (2001). *SPEA2: Improving the Strength Pareto Evolutionary Algorithm*. Technical Report 103, Computer Engineering and Networks Laboratory (TIK), Swiss Federal Institute of Technology (ETH) Zurich.

Zlot, R., & Stentz, A. (2005). Complex Task Allocation for Multiple Robots. In *International Conference on Robotics and Automation* (ICRA), (pp. 1515–1522).

Zlot, R., Stentz, A., Dias, M. B., & Thayer, S. (2002). Multi-robot exploration controlled by a market economy. In *International Conference on Robotics and Automation* (ICRA), (pp. 3016–3023). doi:10.1109/ROBOT.2002.1013690

Zribi, M., & Ahmed, S. (1991). Predictive adaptive control of multiple robots in cooperation motion. In *IEEE Conference on Decision and Control*, (pp. 2416–2421). doi:10.1109/CDC.1991.261787

Zuckerman, A. (1999). *Civil Justice in Crisis*. Oxford University Press.

Zuindeau, B. (Ed.). (2010). *Conflits environnementaux et territoires*. Presses Universitaires du Septentrion.

About the Contributors

Paulo Novais is an Associate Professor with Habilitation of Computer Science at the Department of Informatics, in the School of Engineering of the University of Minho (Portugal) and a researcher at the ALGORITMI Centre in which he is the coordinator of the research group Intelligent Systems Lab, and the coordinator of the research line in "Ambient intelligence for well-being and Health Applications". From the same university he received a PhD in Computer Science in 2003 and his Habilitation in Computer Science in 2011. He started his career developing scientific research in the field of Intelligent Systems/Artificial Intelligence (AI), namely in Knowledge Representation and Reasoning, Machine Learning and Multi-Agent Systems. His interest, in the last years, was absorbed by the different, yet closely related, concepts of Ambient Intelligence, Ambient Assisted Living, Intelligent Environments, AI and Law, Conflict Resolution and the incorporation of AI methods and techniques in these fields. His main research aim is to make systems a little more smart, intelligent and also reliable. He has led and participated in several research projects sponsored by Portuguese and European public and private Institutions and has supervised several PhD and MSc students. He is the co-author of over 230 book chapters, journal papers, conference and workshop papers and books. He is the president of APPIA (the Portuguese Association for Artificial Intelligence) for 2016/2017 and member of the executive committee of the IBERAMIA (IberoAmerican Society of Artificial Intelligence). During the last years he has served as an expert/reviewer of several institutions such as EU Commission and FCT (Portuguese agency that supports science, technology and innovation).

Davide Carneiro is an Invited Professor at the Department of Informatics of the University of Minho and at the Polytechnic Institute of Porto. He is also a researcher at the Algoritmi center, in the Department of Informatics, University of Minho, Braga, Portugal. He holds a PhD from a joint Doctoral Programme in Computer Science of three top Portuguese Universities. He develops scientific research in the field of Artificial Intelligence, with applications in Human-Computer Interaction and Context-aware Computing. His main interest lies in acquiring information in a non-intrusive way, from the human's interaction with the computer, namely to assess stress and mental fatigue. He has participated in several research projects in the fields of Ambient Intelligence and Online Dispute Resolution. He is the co-author of several publications in his field of interest, including one book and over fifty book chapters, journal papers and conference and workshop papers. In 2008 he was awarded the TLeIA08 - a National Award for Artificial Intelligence projects attributed by the Portuguese Artificial Intelligence Association and in 2009 he has been awarded an Academic Merit Scholarship by the Portuguese Government.

* * *

Carlos Carrascosa was born in Valencia (Spain) and received the M.S. degree in Computer Science from the Universidad Politécnica de Valencia (UPV) in 1995. He obtained his Ph.D. in the Departamento de Sistemas Informáticos y Computación at UPV and is currently a lecturer involved in teaching several AI-related subjects at the UPV. His research interests include MAS, social emotions, consensus in MAS, Intelligent Virtual Environments, learning, serious games, information retrieval, and real-time systems.

José Carlos Castillo holds a Ms.C. degree in Advanced Computer Technologies (2008) and a Ph.D. degree in Computer Science (2012) from the University of Castilla-La Mancha, Spain. From 2006 to 2012 he worked at the natural and artificial Interaction Systems (n&aIS) group at the Albacete Research Institute of Informatics, Spain focusing on computer vision techiques for the detection of human activities and frameworks for intelligent monitoring and activity interpretation. From October, 2012 to September 2013 he worked as a post-doctoral researcher at the institute for Systems and Robotics (ISR), Instituto Superior Técnico (IST) of the Tecnical University of Lisbon (UTL), where he is focused on networked robot systems, robotics and computer vision and intelligent control systems. From September 2013 up to now he is working as a post-doctoral fellow at the RoboticsLab of the Universidad Carlos III de Madrid, where he is teaching and researching on social robotics and computer visión techniques for Human-Robot Interaction.

Pablo Chamoso is a PhD student on Computer Engineering in the University of Salamanca. His interest is in multi-agent systems, distributed artificial intelligence, wireless sensor networks, cloud computing and smart cities.

Carlos Chesñevar is independent researcher from the National Council of Scientific and Technical Research (CONICET), Argentina, and vice-director of the Research Institute for Computer Science and Engineering of the Universidad Nacional del Sur (ICIC-UNS, Bahía Blanca, Argentina). He has carried out posdoctoral activities at the University of Lleida (Spain) as researcher in Artificial Intelligence from 2003 to 2007. He has led several scientific projects related to argumentation and technological applications, supported by different funding agencies (DAAD Germany, CONICET Argentina, Microsoft Research Latinamerica, etc.). He has been also representing Argentina as an expert in argumentation within an ESF-funded COST Action on Agreement Technologies. He has participated as PC member in most major AI conferences (IJCAI, AAMAS, ECSQARU, etc.) and has published more than 25 journal articles, 7 book chapters and more than 100 papers in international and national conferences in his research area. He has carried out research stances in different universities (Imperial College, London, UK ; University Leipzig, Leipzig, Germany; Washington University, USA, among others). He has supervised several PhD and MSc Theses in Computer Science, particularly related to argumentation in Artificial Intelligence and its applications. Carlos Chesñevar has also been a member of the ICEGOV Programme Committee for the conferences in 2013 and 2014.

Juan Manuel Corchado (born May 15, 1971 in Salamanca, Spain) is a Spanish computer scientist, professor, researcher and author. He is Vice President for Research and Technology Transfer since December 2013 and Full Professor with Chair at the University of Salamanca. Hc is the Director of the Science Park of the University of Salamanca and Director of the Doctoral School of the University. He has been twice elected Dean at School of Science of the University of Salamanca. In addition to a PhD in Computer Sciences from the University of Salamanca, he holds a PhD in Artificial Intelligence from the University of the West of Scotland. Corchado is the Director of the BISITE (Bioinformatic, Intelligent Systems and Educational Technology) Research Group, which he created in 2.000, President of the IEEE Systems, Man and Cybernetics Spanish Chapter, Academic Director of the Institute of Digital Art and Animation of the University of Salamanca. He also oversees the Master's programs in Digital Animation, Security, Mobile Technology, Community Management and Management for TIC enterprises at the University of Salamanca. Corchado is also editor and Editor-in-Chief of Specialized Journals like ADCAIJ (Advances in Distributed Computing and Artificial Intelligence Journal) and IJDCA (International Journal of Digital Contents and Applications).

Dalila Alves Durães is a teacher with a graduation in Electronics, Robotics and Computer Science at the Department of Mathematics and Experimental Sciences in the Caldas das Taipas Higher School, Guimarães, Portugal, where she has coordinated, since 2009, the Section of Computer Science and she is also director of the Professional Course of Multimedia. She is a researcher at the Intelligent Systems Lab in Minho University, Braga, Portugal (http://islab.di.uminho.pt). She received her degree in Electronics and Computer Science Engineer at Lusíada University in 1995, and in 2004 she finished her MSc in Industrial Electronics Engineering in the area of Automation and Robotics at Minho University, Portugal. In 2012, she completed her PHD in Education Science in the area of Curriculum, Teaching and Educational Institutions at Granada University, Spain. She started her career developing scientific research in the field of microstructures in silicon, particularly bulk-micromachining. Collaborative learning, e-learning environment, and how technology can enhance learning absorbed her interest in the last years. Her main research aims is attentiveness and engagement in learning activities using technology. She is co-author of over 15 chapters, journal paper, conference and workshop papers and books. She also has been guiding student internships in companies since 2004, project managerlab of "LabMultimedia" since 2009, and team of project lab "Automation and Robotics".

Elsa Estevez is a senior academic program officer at the United Nations University Operating Unit on Policy-Driven Electronic Governance in Guimaraes, Portugal. Her research interests include electronic participation, electronic governance for sustainable development, electronic governance education, smart cities for sustainable development, and the government chief information officer function. Estevez received a PhD in computer science from the National University of the South, Argentina.

Florentino Fdez-Riverola, Ph.D. from the University of Vigo, Spain. He was born in Langen-Hessen (Germany). He was Director of the CITI research centre (http://www.citi.uvigo.es/) and currently he is Associate Professor in the Computer Science Department of the University of Vigo. Being the lead researcher of the SING group (http://sing.ei.uvigo.es/), he is joint author of several books and book chapters, as well as the author of numerous articles published by well-known houses such as the Springer-Verlag, Ios Press, Kluwer, etc.

Antonio Fernández-Caballero received his M.S. degree in Computer Science from the School of Computer Science at the Technical University of Madrid, Spain, and he received his Ph.D. degree from the Department of Artificial Intelligence of the National University for Distance Education, Spain. He is Full Professor at the University of Castilla-LaMancha, Albacete, Spain. He is the head of the "natural and artificial Interaction Systems" team, belonging to the Laboratory on User Inteaction and Software Engineering research laboratory at the Computer Science Research Institute at Albacete (i3A) since

2001. Among his research interests are computer vision, pattern recognition, human-machine interaction, mobile robotics and multi-agent systems. He has authored more than 300 scientific contributions. He is Topic Editor-in-Chief of the International Journal of Advanced Robotic Systems for Vision Systems and Specialty Chief Editor for Vision Systems Theory, Tools and Applications in the journal Frontiers in Robotics and AI. He is Associate Editor of Pattern Recognition Letters, and Member of the Editorial Boards of Journal of Physical Agents, The Scientific World Journal, ISRN Signal Processing and Applied Sciences. He is Guest Editor of a number of special issues of leading international journals.

Pedro Miguel Freitas has a PHD in Law (Criminal Sciences). He is a Professor at the University of Minho, School of Law, Portugal. His current research interests encompass Criminal Law, Criminal Procedure, Cybercrime, Terrorism and Restorative Justice. He has authored several academic articles and presented papers at numerous international and national scientific events. He is a member of the Secure Platform for Accredited Cybercrime Experts of Europe (Europol), the Lusophone Observatory of Human Rights, the Latinamerican Observatorium for Research on Crime Policy and Criminal Law Reform, the European Group on Sentencing and Penal Decision-Making, the Human Rights Centre for Interdisciplinary Research, the Centre of Studies in European Union Law and one of the Founding Members of the Lusophone Institute of Criminal Justice. He is the Director of a training program for victim-offender mediators at the Portuguese Institute of Psychology (Portugal).

Marco Vieira Gomes is a researcher at Intelligent Systems Lab at Department of Informatics at the University of Minho. His primary research interests focus on Ambient Intelligence (AmI), Behavioral Analysis and Conflict topics. Currently, he is pursuing the following main lines of research, despite being naturally different, share some core ideas that bind them: the use of non-invasive and non-intrusive approaches; the use of techniques from Artificial Intelligence/Intelligent Systems; the training of the appropriate models with data collected from behavioral studies. Moreover, he is also a Ph.D. candidate at the University of Minho, where he furthers research on Intelligent Environments to Support Decision-Making Processes. He also holds a Master's of Science degree in Informatics (Theme: Behavioural and Context Analysis in an ODR Environment) and a bachelor's degree in Computer Science and Mathematics both from University of Minho.

Sérgio Gonçalves is a Researcher Informatics Department of the University of Vigo, Ourense. He is currently enrolled in a Doctoral Program in Informatics Engineering ate the same university. He develops scientific research in the field of Artificial Intelligence, namely Knowledge Representation and Machine Learning applied to the e-learning field and Intelligent Environments. He is the co-author of several publications in this field of interest.

Maria Paula Gozalez is assistant researcher at CONICET (National Council of Scientific and Technical Research, Argentina) and member of the Artificial Intelligence Research and Development Laboratory (LIDIA Lab) at the Department of Computer Science and Engineering of the Universidad Nacional del Sur in Bahia Blanca, Argentina. Her research interests cover the areas of Usability Engineering, Computer Supported Collaborative Work (CSCW), Recommender Systems and Argumentative Systems.

José Javier Romero Díaz de la Guardia, Bachelor in Computer Sciences and international PhD in Educational Sciences from the University of Granada. Researcher in different areas of educational technology as virtual learning environments, digital educational resources and e-learning design. He has coordinated several projects to implement ICT in schools, and participated in numerous educational and teaching innovation programs. With extensive professional experience as a coach in teachers training activities, computer science teacher in vocational education, information technologies consultant and system integrator. Currently works as a lecturer in the Department of Educational Innovation and ICT at the International University of La Rioja.

Saleem Gul has several years of field experience in projects spread across countries such as USA, Canada, Guyana, and Pakistan. In addition, he is a British Council Certified Corporate Trainer and has been conducting the Project Management Institute's (PMI) Project Management Professional (PMP) exam preparation training for the last 9 year. During the time this training has been running over 3500 individuals have been trained; these trainings have been conducted in Pakistan and UK. He holds a PhD in the Management of Complex Projects from the University of Southampton, UK. His research interests include: conflict and negotiations, complexity theory, modelling and simulation, qualitative techniques, and research philosophy. Presently, Dr. Gul is an Assistant Professor at the Institute of Management Sciences, Peshawar Pakistan.

Stella Heras (Ph.D.) is a postdoc researcher at GTI-IA Research Group of the Universitat Politècnica de Valencia, Spain. She holds a M.Sc. in Computer Science from the same university and an Executive Master in Project Management from the Universitat de València, Spain. Her research interests are centred on the area of argumentation theory, persuasive technologies and social recommendation. Currently, she leads the research project "Social Recommendation Persuasive Techniques", founded by the Spanish Ministry of Education, Culture and Sports under the Program for R&D Valorisation and Joint Resources VLC/CAMPUS. Also, she collaborates with international and national research communities as program and organisation committee of several conferences and workshops.

Cristian Ioja is Head of Department Regional Geography and Environment, Professor in the Faculty of Geography at the University of Bucharest and Senior Researcher in Centre for Environmental Research. Cristian Ioja earned his M.S. in Sustainable Management of Water Resources and his PhD in Geography at the University of Bucharest. In 2015 obtain the Habilitation in Environmental Sciences. He is the president of the Society for Urban Ecology – South Eastern Europe Chapter. The research activities are focused on environmental assessment of different land-uses in urban areas, understanding the relation between built-up and green infrastructure, socio-economic drivers and promotion of urban sustainable planning. His current researches are linked by environmental conflict assessment in natural and human ecosystems, consequences of urbanization on ecosystems services supply, green infrastructure assessments and Natura 2000 sites planning. More of his research results are transferred at administrative level in Urban Master Plans, Environmental Actions Plans and protected areas management plans, in order to improve the decision makings process and natural ecosystems management. Cristian Iojă was principal investigator of 9 national research grants funded by Romanian National Research Foundation or other public institutions. He has published 9 books and more papers related with environmental planning, urban green infrastructure, land-use changes and biodiversity conservation in Biological Conservation, Ecological Indicators, Applied Geography, Urban Forestry and Urban Greening, Landscape and Urban Planning and other international journals.

Vicente Julian holds a position of Associate Professor of Computer Science at the Universitat Politècnica de València (UPV) where he has taught since 1996. Vicente Julian is member of the GTI-IA research group, and Deputy Director of the Official Master in Artificial Intelligence, Pattern Recognition and Digital Imaging at the UPV. Four international projects, two international excellence networks, twenty one Spanish projects and four technology transfer projects have covered the research on Artificial Intelligence. He has more than 50 works published in journals with outstanding positions in the list of the Journal Citation Reports, or published in conference proceedings that have a system of external peer review and dissemination of knowledge comparable to journals indexed in relevant positions.

Michael Klausner earned his BA in Sociology with a minor in Psychology from Herbert Lehman College in the Bronx (CUNY). He earned his MA and Ph.D. from the University of Illinois, Urbana-Champaign. He has published in the areas of Organizational Socialization, Organizational Conflict, Sociological Theory and the Effects of Social Media on Cognition. He has taught courses on: Sociological theory, Deviance, Socialization, Small Groups, Organizational Behavior and Social Problems as well as the Introduction to Sociology. Currently he is conducting research on the determinants of successful innovations using "SPD Smart Glass" as a case study. In addition, he is researching the effects of Smart Phones and the Social Media on cognition and interpersonal relationships. The psychology of learning and teaching is another area of his interests.

María T. López received her degree in Physics from the University of Valencia, Spain, in 1991, and received her Ph.D. from the Department of Artificial Intelligence of the National University for Distance Education, Spain, in 2004. Since 1991, she is an Associate Professor with the Department of Computing Systems at the University of Castilla-La Mancha, Spain. Her research interests are in Image Processing and Computer Vision. María T. López is member of the IAPR.

Francisco Javier Hinojo Lucena, Diploma in Physical Education, Bachelor in Psychology and PhD in Educational Sciences from the University of Granada. It has more than one hundred scientific publications in the national and international level. He has worked as a lecturer at the University of Costa Rica and the Superior School of Education of the Polytechnic Institute of Portalegre, Guarda and Odivelas (Portugal) as well as the University of Bologna (Italy), among others. He has been granted with several academic awards and scholarships in the higher education area, from the Ministry of Education, Foreign Office in Spain, and the University of Granada. He also has participated in different research and educational innovation projects, in research lines as professional training and lifelong learning. Currently he works as professor in the Department of Didactics and School Organization of the University of Granada.

Nuno Luz is a Computer Science PhD student in a joint doctoral programme between the Portuguese Universities of Minho, Aveiro and Porto. He received a BSc and an MSc in Computer Engineering from the School of Engineering – Polytechnic of Porto (ISEP) in 2008 and 2010. In 2008, he joined the Knowledge Engineering and Decision Support Research Center (GECAD) as a research fellow for the ToursPlan (Tours Planning Support System) project, which lasted until 2010.

Ana Gabriela Maguitman is an Independent Researcher at the National Council for Science and Technology (CONICET) of Argentina and an Adjunct Professor at the Department of Computer Science and Engineering of the Universidad Nacional del Sur (Argentina). She earned a PhD in Computer

Science from Indiana University (USA). She is a member of the Editorial Board of the Expert Systems with Applications journal and an Academic Editor of the PeerJ Computer Science Journal. She has been a Program Committee member of several scientific events such as CONTEXT, MRC, IBERAMIA, IJCAI, ACM Hypertext, FLAIRS, INTERACT, CLEI and CMC. She has published in various journals, including Information Processing and Management, Information Science, Journal of the Association for Information Science and Technology, and Knowledge-Based Systems, among others.

Tomás Sola Martínez, Professor and researcher at Granada University, Professor University in Didactics and School Organization. As Coordinator of the PhD Program: Curriculum, Teaching and Educational Institutions has directed more than 70 internationally doctoral theses in Portugal, Colombia, Mexico, Costa Rica and Ecuador. All the research and the teachers contributions are being published in books, papers, communications and articles that, in some way, cast a reflection and a constructive proposal for educational improvement of the global society and the knowledge that this 21st century demands as imperative priority. Special education, organization of institutions and training are the key to their work. It has the following awards: Trophy in Honour of Excellence Educational, Title and Medal of Doctor Honoris Cause Title and Medal of Master in Educational Management granted by the Latin American Council for Educational Quality Honour 2011.

Ester Martinez-Martin is an Assistant Professor at Jaume-I University (Spain) and member of the Robotic Intelligence Laboratory. She holds a B.Sc. in Computer Engineering (2004) and a Ph.D. in Computer Engineering (2011), both from Jaume-I University. Her education is completed with postgraduate certificates in different topics such as computer design, programming languages and web design. She has been involved in robotics research, being part of several national and international projects (e.g. FP7 Eyeshots (Heterogeneous 3D Perception across Visual Fragments), and FP7 GRASP (Emergence of cognitive grasping through emulation, introspection and surprise)). Her research background has been extended by participating in several relevant international conferences and schools, as well as with research stays at University of Genoa and SungKyunKwan University. She is author and co-author of relevant scientific publications – including the book Robust motion detection in real-life scenarios (Springer 2012), "Computer Vision Methods for Robot Tasks: Motion Detection, Depth Estimation and Tracking" (AICom), "A Panoramic vision system for human- robot interaction" (HRI 2010), "Safety for human-robot interaction in dynamic environments" (ISAM 2009) – and editor of one book: "Swarm Robotics" (In-Tech). She has been the Organization Chair of the 12th International UJI Robotics School on Perceptual Robotics for Humanoids (2012), and has collaborated in some conference committees and outreach activities.

Teresa Coelho Moreira has a PhD in Labour Law, summa cum Laude and she is Professor in University of Minho, School of Law, Portugal of 1st, 2nd and 3rd cycle degree courses (graduation, master and PhD in Law). The Course areas include Labour Law, European Labour Law, Privacy and Data Protection and Equality and Non Discrimination in the Employment Relationship. She is also lecturer at National and International Seminars, Academic Conferences, and Congresses. She participates also as a lecture in postgraduate studies in Labour Law and Privay and Data Protection in different national and international Universities. She is author of various publications, national and international in books and articles, in Labour Law, European Labour Law, Privacy and Data Protection and Equality and Nondiscrimination, having participated in several international projects. She co-organizes the National

Portuguese Congress of Labour Law since 2006 and she is vice-director of the Human Rights Centre for Interdisciplinary Research, member of the Board of the Portuguese National Association of Labour Law, member of the Scientific Committee of the Labour Law Review, Minerva– Revista de Estudos Laborais, member of the Scientific Committee of the Review with peer review, Scientia Iuridica, member of the Editorial Office of the Questões Laborais, periodical with peer review, reviewer of the Review Questões Laborais, member of the Law Studies Association and member of the Honorary Committee of the Association of Young Labour Law Scholars.

José Neves is Full Professor of Computer Science at Minho University, Portugal, since 1983. Jose Neves is the Deputy Director of the Division for Artificial Intelligence (AI). He received his PhD in Computer Science from Heriot Watt University, Scotland, in 1983. His current research interests relate to the areas of knowledge representation and reasoning, evolutionary intelligence, machine learning, soft computing, aiming to construct dynamic virtual worlds of complex symbolic entities that compete against one another in which fitness is judged by one criterion alone, intelligence, here measured in terms of a process of quantification of the quality of their knowledge, leading to the development of new procedures and other metaheuristics and their application in complex tasks of optimization and model inference in distinct areas, namely in the healthcare arena (e.g., machine learning in an intensive care unit environment).

Paulo Moura Oliveira received the Electrical Engineering degree in 1991, from the UTAD University, Portugal, MSc in Industrial Control Systems in 1994 and PhD in Control Engineering in 1998, both from Salford University, Manchester, UK. He is an Associated Professor with Habilitation at the Engineering Department of UTAD University and a researcher at the INESC TEC institute. Currently, he is the director of the PhD Course in Electrical and Computers Engineering in UTAD. His research interests are focused on the fields of control engineering, intelligent control, PID control, control education, evolutionary and natural inspired algorithms for single and multiple objective optimization problem solving. He is author in more than 100 peer-reviewed scientific publications.

Pablo Galain Palermo is a Post-Doc Marie Curie Fellow and holds a European Doctorate in Law. He carries out research in the areas of criminal law, criminal procedural law, and international criminal law. He wrote his doctoral thesis on "Reparation as the functional equivalent of punishment." Additional research priorities include restorative justice, the goal of punishment, alternative methods of conflict resolution in Latin America, and case disposition alternatives in Germany and Portugal. He is also working on selected aspects of international criminal law and the political-legal problems surrounding the implementation of the Rome Statute in Uruguay. Pablo Galain Palermo's current research focuses are on transitional justice and coming to terms with the past (Vergangenheitsbewältigung), victim reparation according to the jurisprudence of the Inter-American Court of Human Rights, and the disappearance of persons within the framework of state terrorism. He is also the Director of the Latinamerican Observatorium for Research on Crime Policy and Criminal Law Reform.

Javier Bajo Perez received a PhD. in Computer Science and Artificial Intelligence from the University of Salamanca in 2007. At present he is Associate Professor at the Polytechnic University of Madrid (Spain). He is post-graduate secretariat of the Department of Artificial Intelligence and Coordinator of the Research Master in Artificial Intelligence at the Polytechnic University of Madrid. Previously, from 2003 to 2012, he was associate professor and CEO of the Data Center at the Pontifical University of Salamanca. He obtained an Information Technology degree (MSc) at the University of Valladolid (Spain) in 2001 and a Engineering in Computer Sciences degree (MSc) at the Pontifical University of Salamanca in 2003. He has been member of the organising and scientific committee of several international symposiums such as NATO-ASI, DCAI, CAEPIA, IWANN, IDEAL, HAIS, PAAMS, etc. and co-author of more than 200 papers published in recognized journal, workshops and symposiums, most of them related to intelligent systems and ambient intelligence, paying special attention to decision support systems, context aware and information fusion (please see the DBLP records http://www.informatik. uni-trier.de/~ley/pers/hd/b/Bajo:Javier.html for more information).

Eduardo Solteiro Pires received the degree in Electrical Engineering at the University of Coimbra, in 1993. He pursued post graduate studies and obtained, in 1999, an MSc degree in Electrical and Computer Engineering at the University of Oporto. In 2006, he graduated with a PhD degree at UTAD University. Since 2006 he works as an Assistant Professor at the Engineering Department of UTAD University. His main research interests are in evolutionary computation, multi-objective problems, fractional calculus, and diffusion of innovation.

Angel P. del Pobil is a professor at Jaume I University (Spain), where he was the founding director of the UJI Robotic Intelligence Laboratory. He has been Co-Chair of two Technical Committees of the IEEE Robotics and Automation Society and is a member of the Governing Board of the Intelligent Autonomous Systems (IAS) Society (2012-present) and EURON (European Robotics Research Network of Excellence, 2001-2009). He has over 250 publications, including 13 books, the last three published recently by Springer. Prof. del Pobil was co-organizer of some 50 workshops and tutorials including: five at ICRA (1996, 2000, 2010-2012), ten at IROS (2000, 2004-2013), three at RSS (2008-2010, 2012), ECAI'04, ICAR'05 and ACM/IEEE HRI 2010. He was Program Co-Chair of the 11th International Conference on Industrial and Engineering Applications of Artificial Intelligence, and General Chair of the 13th International Conference on Adaptive Behaviour (SAB 2014) and of five editions of the International Conference on Artificial Intelligence and Soft Computing (2004-2008). He is Associate Editor for ICRA (2009-2015) and IROS (2007-2012) and has served on the program committees of over 130 international conferences, such as IJCAI, ICPR, ICRA, IROS, EUROS, IAS, ICAR, CIRA, etc. The UJI Robotic Intelligence Lab has organized 12 consecutive editions of IURS, the International UJI Robotics School. He has been General Chair for IURS 2005 on Robotics and Neuroscience, IURS 2006 on Humanoid Robots, IURS 2009 on Visuomotor Coordination, IURS 2012 on Perceptual Robotics and the 2015 IEEE-RAS Summer School on Experimental Methodology, Performance Evaluation and Benchmarking in Robotics. He has been involved in robotics research for the last 29 years. Professor del Pobil has been invited speaker of 63 tutorials, plenary talks, and seminars in 14 countries. He serves as associate or guest editor for 12 journals, and as expert for research evaluation at the European Commission, the US National Science Foundation and the Spain Ministry of Science. He has supervised 16 Ph.D. Thesis, including winner and finalists of the Georges Giralt EURON PhD Award and the Robotdalen Scientific Award Honorary Mention. He has been Principal Investigator of 30 research projects. Del Pobil is an active member of the IEEE Robotics and Automation Society and a lifetime member of the Association of the Advancement of Artificial Intelligence (AAAI).

Marta Poblet, Associate Professor Marta Poblet is Vice-Chancellor's Principal Research Fellow at RMIT University's Graduate School of Business and Law. She is one of the co-founders of the Institute of Law and Technology at the Autonomous University of Barcelona and past researcher at ICREA (Catalonia). She holds a PhD in law (Stanford University 2002) and a Master in International Legal Studies (Stanford University 2000). Her research interests cover different areas of law and technology, including mobile technologies, open data, crowdsourcing, conflict management and crisis mapping. She has published more than 40 scientific articles on these topics in international journals and books.

Fernando De la Prieta, PhD on Computer Engineer from the University of Salamanca. As a researcher his interest is in multi-agent systems, virtual organizations, distributed artificial intelligence, cloud computing and technology-enhanced learning. He has published articles in international journals and prestigious international conferences, and has participated in different research projects both at European and national level. Additionally he has participated in the organization and program committee of several international conferences and journals.

Victor Sanchez-Anguix was born in Valencia, Spain, in 1985. I received a BSc in Computer Science at Universitat Politècnica de València. Later, I obtained a MSc in Artificial Intelligence and Pattern Recognition by Universitat Politècnica de València. In February 2013 I defended my PhD. thesis in Artificial Intelligence at Universitat Politècnica de València. I was awarded with a Magna Cum Laude award and an award for being one of the the top 10% theses presented during 2013 at Universitat Politècnica de València. Currently, I am a lecturer at University of Coventry. My work dwells between multi-agent systems, data mining, recommender systems, machine learning, artificial intelligence, and automated negotiation.

Juan Serrano-Cuerda received his Master in Computer Science from the University of Castilla-La Mancha, Spain in 2007. He holds a PhD on robust human detection based on colour and infrared video fusion in the n&aIS (natural and artificial Interaction Systems) research group at the Albacete Research Institute of Informatics (2012). His main research interests are computer vision and image processing.

Henrique Vicente was born in S. Martinho do Porto, Portugal and went to the University of Lisbon, where he studied Chemistry and obtained his degrees in 1988. He joined the University of Évora in 1989 and received his PhD in Chemistry in 2005. He is now Auxiliary Professor at the Department of Chemistry at the University of Évora. He is a researcher at the Évora Chemistry Center and his current interests include Water Quality Control, Lakes and Reservoirs Management, Data Mining, Knowledge Discovery from Databases, Knowledge Representation and Reasoning Systems, Evolutionary Intelligence and Intelligent Information Systems.

John Zeleznikow has conducted research and taught in Australian, US, French, Dutch, Israeli, Belgian, German, UK and Polish universities for forty years. He is the author of 3 research monographs, 75 refereed journal articles and over 200 refereed conference articles. John has also won over $A 7 million in competitive research grants. He has successfully supervised 15 PhD students (including one who is a professor at Harvard Medical School) and 6 postdoctoral fellows and over 50 honours students. On November 16 2005, he and a former PhD student Dr. Emilia Bellucci won their heat of ABC television's New Inventors program for software that assists divorcing couples to negotiate their disputes. Over the past twenty years, Professor Zeleznikow has focused on how Artificial Intelligence can be used to enhance decision-making. Specific examples have been created in the domains of law, negotiation and sport. His research findings have been utilised by law and mediation firms, Victoria Legal aid, Relationships Australia Queensland, Victorian Institute of Sport, Australian Institute of Sport and Relationships Australia Victoria.

Index

A

B

C

Information Resources Management Association

Become an IRMA Member

Members of the **Information Resources Management Association (IRMA)** understand the importance of community within their field of study. The Information Resources Management Association is an ideal venue through which professionals, students, and academicians can convene and share the latest industry innovations and scholarly research that is changing the field of information science and technology. Become a member today and enjoy the benefits of membership as well as the opportunity to collaborate and network with fellow experts in the field.

IRMA Membership Benefits:

- **One FREE Journal Subscription**

- **30% Off Additional Journal Subscriptions**

- **20% Off Book Purchases**

- Updates on the latest events and research on Information Resources Management through the IRMA-L listserv.

- Updates on new open access and downloadable content added to Research IRM.

- A copy of the Information Technology Management Newsletter twice a year.

- A certificate of membership.

IRMA Membership $195

Scan code to visit irma-international.org and begin by selecting your free journal subscription.

Membership is good for one full year.

Lightning Source UK Ltd.
Milton Keynes UK
UKHW030829270422
402039UK00002B/26

9 781522 502456